PENGUIN BOOKS

THE EQUITY SHARING BOOK

Elaine St. James and Diana Bull bring over thirty years' experience in the field of real estate to their equity sharing program. Since 1986 they have completed over three hundred equity-share arrangements based on the techniques outlined in this book. They are cofounders of the National Institute of Equity Sharing (NIES) which, among other things, offers training programs to real estate agents, accountants, attorneys, escrow officers, and lenders. The National Institute of Equity Sharing is located at 133 East De La Guerra, Suite 184, Santa Barbara, CA., 93101.

Diana Bull and Elaine St. James

THE EQUITY SHARING BOOK

HOW TO BUY A HOME EVEN IF YOU CAN'T AFFORD THE DOWN PAYMENT

■ ■ ■

PENGUIN

PENGUIN BOOKS
Published by the Penguin Group
Viking Penguin, a division of Penguin Books USA Inc.,
40 West 23rd Street, New York, New York 10010, U.S.A.
Penguin Books Ltd, 27 Wrights Lane,
London W8 5TZ, England
Penguin Books Australia Ltd, Ringwood,
Victoria, Australia
Penguin Books Canada Ltd, 2801 John Street,
Markham, Ontario, Canada L3R 1B4
Penguin Books (N.A.) Ltd, 182–190 Wairau Road,
Auckland 10, New Zealand

Penguin Books Ltd, Registered Offices:
Harmondsworth, Middlesex, England

First published in Penguin Books 1990

1 3 5 7 9 10 8 6 4 2

Grateful acknowledgment is made for permission to use
the following material:
Tables from *Payment Tables for Conventional and FHA Loans,* Publication no. 491,
Rev., Copyright 1981, 1983 by Financial Publishing Company, Boston, MA.
Definitions reprinted from the *Real Estate Dictionary,* Publication no. 510,
Fourth Edition, Copyright 1986 by Financial Publishing Company, Boston, MA.

LIBRARY OF CONGRESS CATALOGING IN PUBLICATION DATA
Bull, Diana.
The Equity sharing book: how to buy a home even if you can't afford
the down payment/Diana Bull and Elaine St. James.
p. cm.
ISBN 0 14 01.2658 9
1. Mortgage loans, Equity sharing. I. St. James, Elaine. II. Title.
HG2040.45.B85 1990
332.7'22—dc20 89–28028

Printed in the United States of America
Set in Meridien
Designed by Victoria Hartman

Foreword

America appears to be at a housing crossroads. Either we solve the housing affordability problem by helping to fulfill the "American dream" of home ownership, or we become ensnared in the European/Japanese nightmare where 50 percent or more of all income is utilized for housing. This crisis will dominate the discussion on housing during the 1990s and into the twenty-first century. It is the core of the housing affordability crisis in America.

Equity sharing is an effective, workable solution for those attempting to live in high-cost areas in the United States. It is also a convenient mechanism for parents to help children to afford a home in the future. Equity sharing also benefits non-resident owners looking to maximize their investment while reducing or eliminating the management, maintenance, and upkeep responsibilities of owning investment property.

I recommend that anyone interested in this topic read *The Equity Sharing Book*. It is an excellent practical guide to equity sharing.

Norman D. Flynn
1990 President
National Association of Realtors

Acknowledgments

The authors wish to thank Jo Wideman and Monica Metz for their contribution to the form and content of this book. We appreciate the support and encouragement of Judy Babcock, Tami Weiss, Linda Erickson, and Amy Carver. Special thanks go to Betty Carroll, a dedicated real estate professional who has spent years helping the concept of equity sharing evolve, and to Wolcott Gibbs, Jr., for his invaluable assistance in the completion of this work.

Contents

2 · HOW IT WORKS 22

3 · PROJECTIONS: WHERE DO YOU GO FROM HERE? 40

4 · UNDERSTANDING THE TAX PICTURE 59

Introduction

If you're one of the millions of Americans who are ready to give up on the prospect of ever owning your own home, don't give up just yet! You *can* own your own home, and in this book we're going to show you exactly how you can do it.

We know it can be done because we've helped hundreds of people achieve home ownership—people just like you, who have good jobs, good credit, some cash in the bank, and who thought they had it made—until they tried to buy a home. Then they found out that the cash they'd diligently been saving wasn't enough for the 20 percent down payment most lenders require today. Or they found they couldn't qualify for the loan. They, and you, are not alone.

HOME OWNERSHIP AND THE AMERICAN DREAM

There are 43,000,000 Americans in the first-time home buyers' age group of twenty-five to thirty-five. In a recent survey of this group conducted by the National Association of Realtors, 87 percent of the respondents listed owning a home as the most important element in fulfilling the "American dream." Home ownership is valued more than a happy marriage, an interesting job, high pay, or even having a lot of money. Yet 43 percent of the survey respondents said they were unable to buy a home because the price was too high for them to qualify for the loan; 82 percent said they didn't have enough cash for the down payment. When you look at the cost of housing today, it's not hard to figure out why. Consider these facts:

• The national median cost of a starter home is $89,100. It takes an income of $36,000 to buy that home, but the national median income is $32,100. In many areas of the country, only 15 percent of the households could afford the 1989 median-priced single-family home, and most of the 15 percent were already homeowners!

• In ten major metropolitan areas—which contain over 45,000,000 people—the median selling price for a house is over $145,000. To buy a home in one of these areas, you'd need over $35,000 in the bank and an income of over $50,000 a year.

• In more than eighty cities across the United States, the average cost of a home is currently above the $124,875 limit set by the Federal Housing Authority (FHA). This means that FHA financing, which first-time home buyers have traditionally relied on to get them into home ownership, is no longer a viable option for buyers in these areas.

What it boils down to is that in most parts of the country incomes have not kept pace with increased housing costs and, as a result, millions of people like you have literally been priced out of the housing market.

It is mind-boggling to realize that there are people with $25,000 in the bank and an annual income of $50,000 who simply cannot afford to buy a home. But it's true.

Fortunately, there is an answer to this problem. It's called equity sharing, and that's what this book is all about. Equity sharing is the safe, easy way for you and millions of other Americans to get off the rental treadmill and start to share in the benefits of home ownership.

WHAT IS EQUITY SHARING?

In its simplest terms, equity sharing is the way at least two parties—an *owner-occupant* and *non-resident owner*—pool their funds to buy a property.

There are many ways equity sharing can work, most of which are completely described in this book. In the usual equity-sharing purchase, a non-resident owner—we'll tell you how to find one later—puts up a portion of the down payment but will not live in the house. The owner-occupant—who has a good job, a good credit history, and some cash in the bank—also puts up part of the down payment, will live in the home, take care of maintenance and upkeep, and make most or all of the monthly mortgage, tax, and insurance payments. Both parties are listed on the deed and on the mortgage. The percentages of ownership are usually based on the percentage of the down payment each has contributed. (We'll show you a number of different ways percentages of ownership can be negotiated.)

Both occupant and non-resident get to share in the tax benefits. When the property is sold or refinanced, the down payment contribution is returned to each party, and the profit or increased equity is shared between the occupant and the non-resident, according to their percentages of ownership.

HALF A LOAF IS BETTER THAN NONE

It goes without saying that in the best of all possible worlds home buyers wouldn't have to share their equity. But when you look at what it takes to buy a home today, and when you realize that the only choice for many people is to share the equity or continue to rent, it's easy to see that half a loaf or even a quarter of a loaf is better than none. And it's a partial loaf for only a little while. The long-term goal of all our shared-equity arrangements is for the owner-occupants to eventually own a home on their own. We'll show you exactly how that's done.

The principle of equity sharing has been around for some time, but in the past it's been used almost exclusively by parents who were helping their children buy a first home. Now, however, the latest refinements in equity sharing make the typical parent-child arrangement a much sounder business strategy for the parents, and allow both parties to take advantage of the tax benefits that are often overlooked in "family" housing purchases.

In addition, the unique advantages of equity sharing, which we'll outline in detail for you in the next chapter, make it a win-win arrangement for unrelated non-resident owners and owner-occupants. The benefits of equity sharing are available to all house-hunters, as well as to investors who want to realize the great potential in real estate ownership without taking on the burdens of management, maintenance, and upkeep of the property.

WHAT YOU'LL FIND IN THIS BOOK

In *The Equity Sharing Book* we'll explain how it all works. Specifically, this equity share guide will:

- Give you fact-filled case histories of various equity-share arrangements, some of which will reflect your own situation, so you can figure out how to make best use of the funds you have available, and how you can expect to benefit.

• Spell out for you the advantages and the drawbacks of equity sharing from both the owner-occupant's and the non-resident owner's viewpoints. You'll have the information you need to decide whether this kind of investment will make sense for you.

• Discuss the pitfalls you should be aware of and show you step-by-step how to avoid them.

• Explain, in plain language, the current tax law as it relates to equity sharing. You'll learn how to avoid arrangements that could cost you valuable tax benefits.

• Tell you specifically why you should avoid *partnerships* in your equity-share purchase.

• Teach you how to use our easy-to-follow worksheets. We'll go through all the numbers involved in an equity-share purchase, including evaluating the initial purchase, working out the tax savings for both the occupant and the non-resident, and calculating projections based on different rates of appreciation you can expect in your area.

• Outline how owner-occupants can use U.S. Tax Code Section 1034 to postpone paying tax on their gains indefinitely. And show how non-resident owners can use Section 1031 tax-deferred exchanges to defer the tax on their gains in order to maximize profits when the property is sold.

• Give you some options to consider when it's time to move on. Should you refinance and sell? Or refinance and hold? Or refinance, hold, and buy another property?

• Provide a point-by-point explanation of our comprehensive equity-share agreement, covering all the issues that should be addressed in order to protect both the owner-occupant and the non-resident owner. Most accountants agree that an equity-share agreement should be signed prior to the purchase of the property so that the participants can take advantage of the tax savings available to them.

• Show you how to put it all together: how to get started, how to work with a real estate agent, how to find the property, how to find a non-resident owner, how to find a lender, how to put your equity-share team together.

• Answer, in straightforward terms, the most commonly asked questions about equity sharing.

• Give you a complete glossary of the technical terms you'll come across when you start getting into real estate, with a concise, nontechnical explanation of what each term means. (Words and terms included in the Glossary are printed in **boldface type** the first time they appear in the text.)

• Provide you with blank copies of all our worksheets, which you can use to evaluate on paper any equity-share purchase you might be considering.

• And provide you with one of the most comprehensive equity-sharing agreements available, which you can adapt to your own circumstances.

ABOUT THE AUTHORS

Diana Bull and Elaine St. James have had extensive experience in real estate, both as investors and as owners, particularly in putting together equity-share arrangements not only for themselves but for other owner-occupants and non-resident owners.

Diana has been a licensed real estate agent since 1972 and a licensed broker since 1974, and has owned and managed three real estate brokerage firms. Diana is currently the owner of a real estate firm that specializes in equity-share purchases for both owner-occupants and non-resident owners.

Since 1984, Diana has been a consultant for Educational Video on Mortgage Finance for the National Association of Realtors. She was president of the Santa Barbara Board of Realtors in 1982 and was chosen Realtor of the Year in 1985. She was listed in *Who's Who of American Women* in 1984.

Elaine St. James bought her first property in 1977 and has continued to buy condominiums and single-family homes, as well as apartment buildings, for her own portfolio. She acquired her real estate license and has completed major rehabilitations of over a dozen single-family homes and apartment buildings in both New England and California.

Elaine has had extensive hands-on experience in preparing properties to maximize their resale value. She recently completed a series of tax-deferred exchanges on her own holdings and, in addition to the rental properties she owns, has purchased over a dozen equity-shared houses and condominiums.

She has written reviews for Book-of-the-Month Club in the areas of real estate and finance, and has published articles on real estate in consumer magazines.

Elaine and Diana are founders, along with their colleagues Betty Carroll and Monica Metz, of the National Institute of Equity Sharing (NIES), an organization that trains real estate agents and brokers in the art of structuring equity-share purchases for both owner-occupants and non-resident owners. NIES also serves as a referral network to match occupants and non-resident owners across the country with real estate agents who have completed its equity-sharing seminars.

HOW TO GET THE MOST OUT OF THIS BOOK

If this book is your first exposure to real estate, you may find the numbers and the calculations confusing at first—possibly even overwhelming. Don't despair. They're not as complicated as they may first appear. As often happens when learning something new, you may find that a concept doesn't become clear until you've read the explanation through two or three times.

To develop a clear understanding of what the equity-sharing process all means, you should plan to read the book through from start to finish and don't worry if there are details that aren't clear to you at first. Then go back and re-read the book, this time with pencil and calculator in hand, and actually work through the numbers on the worksheets we've completed for you. Once you feel comfortable with the calculations, photocopy as many copies of the blank worksheets as you might need, and use them to work through the figures on a property you're considering.

And don't be like some of the young couples we've worked with, who don't want to take the first step until they totally and completely understand every last detail in the process. And who, consequently, are still renting! Accept the fact that you may never totally and completely understand all the details. Elaine St. James is living proof that you don't have to know everything about real estate before you can get started buying it. Here is her story:

> My Dad had been urging me for years to start "building an estate." So, after much prodding from him, I finally had enough money set aside to start investing. Early in January of 1977 I sat down with Anne, a good friend of mine who was an experienced real estate agent, and told her I wanted to start buying investment properties.
>
> Anne went over all the numbers with me, and we even went out and looked at a couple of properties, although there was nothing on the market right then that suited my needs.

> She called me a couple of weeks later and told me she had something she thought I might be interested in. It was about eight o'clock on a Friday night, and the listing would be on the multiple listing computer the next morning; it required a $5,000 investment, and if I wanted it I'd have to act fast. I drove by the property that night, liked what I saw, and decided to go for it. I met with Anne early the next morning to write up the offer, and we closed a month or so later.
>
> I went right home after the closing and called my Dad back in Kansas. "Hey, Dad—I just bought my first investment property."
>
> "That's great, honey. What interest rate are you paying?"
>
> "Interest rate?" I didn't know!
>
> "Well, how many points did you have to pay?"
>
> "Points?" I didn't even know what a point was, let alone how many I'd paid.
>
> Now mind you, I'm sure that Anne went over all those things with me when we first sat down, but I hadn't really understood them, and they must have gone in one ear and out the other. I'm certain that in the history of real estate few people have purchased a property knowing less about what they were doing than I did. All I knew was that real estate was where I wanted to put my money, and I still feel that way today.
>
> As it turned out, I sold that property a little over a year later and came out of the closing with $25,000 in my pocket. Since then, I've closed on dozens of properties, and I've learned a couple of things about buying real estate, but I'm sure glad I didn't let little things like points and interest rates get in the way of starting my investment program.

Buying your first property—or even your second or third—is serious business, and we're not suggesting for a moment that you jump in with your eyes closed. What we *are* saying is, don't let the fear of the unknown keep you from enjoying the benefits of owning and living in your own home or from buying an investment property.

Admittedly, purchasing a property using the techniques of equity sharing makes the process slightly more complex than buying on your own. But, if you do your homework, the process will be only slightly more complex. By the time you finish reading this book in the way we've suggested, you'll know everything you need to know to structure a sound equity-share arrangement.

We know from our own experience and from the experiences of the hundreds of owner-occupants and non-resident owners we've worked with that the rewards of owning your own home will be well worth the time and effort you put into understanding how it all works.

WHO SHOULD READ THIS BOOK

While this book is written primarily for the owner-occupant, there are at least two other parties in the equity-share arrangement who will benefit from reading and understanding this book, namely, the non-resident owner and the real estate agent. An owner who's had some experience in purchasing investment property will already have an understanding of the numbers and the terminology involved in the purchase of real estate. And any landlord who has dealt first-hand with the headaches of rental-property management will immediately see that a share of the equity is a reasonable price to pay for having management-free, vacancy-free, no-negative-cash-flow property. Chapters 3, 4, and 5 will be of particular interest to the non-resident owner.

Equity sharing is also a valuable tool for real estate agents. We receive dozens of calls each month from agents around the country who have heard about our equity-sharing program. The information contained in this book will make it easier for real estate agents anywhere to help their clients structure sound equity-share arrangements and to help clients they might otherwise have turned away to buy their own home.

THE WAVE OF THE FUTURE

We believe equity sharing will be the method of choice in purchasing residential real estate for home buyers and investors in the years to come. For increasing numbers of first-time buyers it may be the *only* way to get a foot in the door of the housing market. The information provided in this book will give you the facts you need to decide whether equity sharing is right for you, and it will help you put together a sound and workable equity-share arrangement.

You *can* own your own home. Read on, and find out how.

THE EQUITY SHARING BOOK

1

Why Equity Sharing?

Let's take a brief look (we'll get into more details in the next chapter) at how a home would be purchased with equity sharing, so you can see the advantages for both the owner-occupant and the non-resident owner.

Jim and Linda Burtt are a young couple in their early thirties. A two-bedroom, two-bath starter home in their area costs $150,000. The normal 20 percent down payment on this house would be $30,000, and they could expect to pay an additional $4,500 for **closing costs**. (You can figure that closing costs—loan **points**, attorney or **escrow** fees, recording costs, etc.—run about 3 percent of the purchase price.) The Burtts would have a $120,000 mortgage; at an 8 percent variable interest rate, their principal and interest payment would be $880.53 a month. Add to that approximately $200 a month for taxes and insurance, and they would have a total principal, interest, taxes, and insurance (**PITI**) payment of $1,081.

The Burtts have close to $20,000 in savings and a combined monthly income of $3,500, and they just barely meet the minimum monthly income required by the lender to qualify for the loan. (We'll show you later in this chapter how to calculate the amount of loan you can qualify for.) In fact, they are so close to the limit that many lenders would approve the loan only if their application were backed by someone with a stronger financial statement.

If the Burtts were able to get 90 percent financing, so their down payment was only $15,000, they *might* be able to buy this property on their own—except that the resulting $135,000 mortgage would mean a monthly PITI payment of $1,190, which most lenders would consider too much of a stretch for them.

So in order to purchase this property on their own, the Burtts need an additional $15,000, which they simply do not have. The only way they can buy this home is with an equity-share arrangement—for example, one in which they put up 50 percent of the $30,000 down payment and pay half of the closing costs. A non-resident owner would put up the other half of the down payment and the other half of the closing costs. Three to five years down the road, the property could either be refinanced (we'll show you how this works in Chapter 3) or sold, and the increased **equity** would be shared between the Burtts and the non-resident, according to their percentages of ownership.

It's obvious why the Burtts would want to enter into an equity-share arrangement: the only way they can get into the housing market is to be willing to share the appreciation of the property with someone else in exchange for the additional money they need to make the down payment and to qualify for the loan. They realize that half a loaf is better than none.

But why would someone want to be involved in an equity-share arrangement as a non-resident owner? There are several reasons. One is that equity sharing allows a non-resident to purchase a property that is relatively free from management hassles. The Burtts will have approximately $20,000 of their own money in the property—they'll have an "equity position" in it— and, unlike tenants, will be highly motivated to take good care of the property and do whatever they can to enhance its value and thus maximize their investment in it. With the Burtts living in the house, the non-resident owner won't have to deal with costly and troublesome vacancies, management, upkeep, and the other worries that come with having tenant-occupied property.

Second, if the non-resident were to purchase this $150,000 property on the same terms on his own, he would need an additional $15,000 to make up the other half of the down payment. (This is assuming he could even get 80 percent financing, which is becoming harder and harder for non-resident owners to do. Many lenders now want a 30 percent down payment on non-owner-occupied property.) In addition, he'd need another $3,000 to $4,000 to cover the balance of the closing costs. Then he'd have to go to the expense, time, and trouble of finding a tenant to live in the property.

The expected rent on this property would be approximately $800 per month. Remember, the monthly PITI runs just under $1,100, which means the non-resident would have about $300 in out-of-pocket expenses each month.

Before the 1986 tax law changes, these costs could be deducted by the non-resident owner and, therefore, provided valuable tax savings. But since the new tax law limits the amount of loss non-resident owners can write off, it often doesn't make sense for them to bear the burden of these monthly expenses. In many cases, the average landlord can't afford the negative cash flow generated by rental properties today. Consequently, many buyers are willing to give additional ownership to an owner-occupant who can handle the total monthly payment, thereby avoiding negative cash flow.

Many owners are tired of dealing with tenant problems and are willing to give up a portion of the property's **appreciation** in order to get a trouble-free investment that doesn't cost several hundred dollars a month to carry.

Finally, many lenders today are unable, because of new underwriting guidelines, to loan money to an owner who already possesses more than four rental properties. Often the only way a non-resident buyer can get a loan on a residential property is by teaming up with an owner-occupant to get an owner-occupied loan, with a lower interest rate and lower down-payment requirements. Equity sharing makes investment in residential real estate not only affordable but possible in today's market.

So, the owner-occupant gets:
Home ownership
Tax benefits
Help with loan approval
Lower down payment
Share in the appreciation
Help with repairs and maintenance

The non-resident owner gets:
A relatively trouble-free investment
Tax benefits
No vacancies
Help with repairs and maintenance
Lower down payment
Reduced or no negative cash flow

EQUITY SHARING: AN IDEA WHOSE TIME IS NOW

By being willing to share in the future appreciation of the property, the owner-occupant and the non-resident owner can both have a piece of the real estate pie. It is truly a win-win situation. Considering the realities of the housing and real estate investment market today, there has never been a better time for occupants and non-residents to pool their resources and their funds to purchase real estate. Equity sharing makes it possible for both parties to maximize the benefits and minimize the difficulties of owning residential real estate.

THE DRAWBACKS OF EQUITY SHARING

From time to time we come across people who say, "Equity sharing? No way. You won't find me getting locked into a long-term investment with someone I don't know. And besides, I don't want to have to share my equity with anyone."

This statement pretty well sums up the three perceived drawbacks of equity sharing: One, you have to *share* the equity. Two, you have to be involved on a long-term basis—three to five years. And three, equity sharing means buying a property with another person, and, human nature being what it is, this can cause problems you wouldn't have if you purchased the property on your own.

Let's address each of these issues in turn. First, for the owner-occupants, it's not a question of "giving up" equity—it's actually an opportunity to earn a portion of the equity they wouldn't otherwise have been able to earn. For the non-resident owner, the equity question is a trade-off—a virtually trouble-free, vacancy-free, no-negative-cash-flow property in exchange for a portion of the equity. So, sharing the equity needn't be considered a drawback. Instead, it can be thought of as an opportunity for both parties.

Second, as for the time period, you should understand that real estate is a long-term investment. While it's true that there are buyers who make what seem like quick and easy profits in real estate, these represent the exceptions rather than the rule, and the quick turnaround is not the type of investment we are talking about here.

The third concern, getting locked into an investment with someone else, is valid whether you know the other parties well or not, and we'll be addressing it throughout the book. As we proceed, we're going to show you how to select an equity-share co-purchaser, how to hold the property, and how to structure your equity-share agreement to maximize the benefits and minimize the pitfalls of locking into a long-term business relationship with someone else.

In the meantime, you need to understand that any investment carries with it a certain risk factor, and real estate is no exception. Unlike throwing away money at a roulette wheel or commodity trading, real estate investing is a *calculated* risk, and, if you follow common-sense, time-tested procedures, you'll be stacking the deck in your favor.

Equity sharing is relatively new; there has never before been the tremendous need for it that there is now. And, as with anything new, a lot of people who haven't done their homework will be jumping on the bandwagon. We've no doubt that there will be problems as a result. But in our opinion, and in the opinion of the hundreds of owner-occupants and non-resident owners, the potential rewards of a properly structured equity-share purchase far outweigh the risks.

It's obviously foolish to lock yourself into an investment with someone you don't know, or with whom you're not compatible, or whose credit report or references you haven't checked out, or without getting the professional advice of your attorney and/or accountant. But if you approach an equity-share arrangement with caution and follow the procedures we're going to outline in this book, your risk will be greatly reduced and you'll have the opportunity—one you might not otherwise have had—of owning your own home.

SOME TERMS YOU NEED TO KNOW

Before we go any further, there are a few real estate terms you need to understand fully. If you were buying your home on your own, you wouldn't need to have more than a passing acquaintance with terms like **escrow**, **leverage**, and **depreciation**. Indeed, there are millions of people who have owned their homes for years who don't know much about their mortgage other than what payment they have to make on it every month.

But there's more to equity sharing than owning your own home, at least in the early years. It is also an investment, and the better you understand the terminology involved, from both the owner-occupant's and the non-resident owner's point of view, the better position you'll be in to take proper advantage of your equity-share arrangement.

For most real estate terms, the glossary at the back of this book should provide adequate definitions. But a few terms are so basic—and so often misused—that we've provided the following expanded explanations of them.

Leverage

Leverage is a word people use a lot when they talk about real estate and, on the face of it, it seems a fairly simple concept. But leverage is a deceptive term because people think of it in relation to construction or physics, but not to economics. So they *think* they understand it, but in fact they don't.

We were surprised recently, after discussing leverage with a friend who is a highly regarded and successful professional in his field, to find that even though he was saying "yes, yes," when it came right down to it he really didn't understand how leverage works. We find this is true of many people. We took a quick survey one afternoon to see how many people could define leverage. Not one person we queried was able to come up with a satisfactory definition of leverage. So don't feel bad if you can't, either. But here is your chance to get a clear understanding of this very important real estate concept.

Leverage in real estate can be defined as using a small amount of money to control a large property investment. This is exactly what you do when, for example, you purchase a $100,000 home with 10 percent (or $10,000) down and a mortgage of 90 percent (or $90,000). Let's compare an investment like real estate, where typically you utilize leverage, with another type of investment, such as a Certificate of Deposit (CD), where you don't normally use leverage.

Now is the time to get out your calculator (an ordinary four-function machine will do nicely) and run the numbers with us on this example:

Let's say you have $50,000 to invest; you plan to put $25,000 into a three-year CD that's paying 8 percent, and you plan to put the other $25,000 into a piece of real estate in a market that is appreciating at 8 percent. (In this example we'll assume the buyer has used the $25,000 as a 20 percent down payment on a $125,000 property.) How would these two investments compare at the end of three years?

Take a few moments to study Table 1-A. Compare the value of the CD after three years—$31,492—with the value of the real estate after sales costs and paying off the mortgage—$46,441. As you can see, the $25,000 CD has an 8.6 percent annual rate of return, while the same amount invested in real estate produced a 28.6 percent annual return. The reason is that with the CD you are multiplying the *$25,000* times 8 percent, while with the real estate you are multiplying *$125,000* times 8 percent—and that is leverage. With the CD, you control $25,000 with $25,000; with the real estate, you control, thanks to the mortgage, $125,000 with $25,000.

Keep in mind that the figures in Table 1-A do not take the tax picture into consideration. The gain on the CD would be taxable at whatever your tax rate is (see the 1988 Tax Rate Schedules in the Appendix for an *estimate* of what your tax would be, based on your income and your filing status), so your after-tax return could be even less than 8 percent. With the real estate investment, on the other hand, you not only reduce your yearly income-tax bill by deducting the interest on the mortgage, but you can also **roll over** your gain almost indefinitely without paying tax on it. Both these factors will increase your return on the real estate even more. We'll show you exactly how this works in Chapter 4.

Furthermore, with the CD, you can't expect much more than an 8 to 9 percent rate of return. But in many areas of the country real estate will produce anywhere from 8 percent to 15 percent appreciation—or even more.

Take some time right now to see what would happen to the numbers in Table 1-A if you were to experience a 12 percent to 15 percent rate

TABLE 1-A

Three-year comparison of $25,000 in an 8% Certificate of Deposit with $25,000 in real estate that is averaging 8% per year appreciation.

CD @ 8%	*Real Estate @ 8%*
$25,000	$125,000
× 1.08	× 1.08
$27,000 Year 1	$135,000
× 1.08	× 1.08
$29,160 Year 2	$145,800
× 1.08	× 1.08
$31,492 Year 3	$157,464
	$157,464
	− 11,022 Less 7% Sales Costs
	$146,441
	− 100,000 Less Mortgage
$31,492	$ 46,441
− 25,000 Less Initial Investment	− 25,000 Less Initial Investment
$ 6,492 Gain	$ 21,441 Gain
$6,492 ÷ $25,000 = 26% return, divided by 3 years = 8.6% annual return	$21,441 ÷ $25,000 = 86% return, divided by 3 years = 28.6% annual return

of appreciation on that $125,000 property in the same time period. The results are truly amazing. And leverage is what gives real estate such a tremendous advantage over almost any other type of investment. In fact, there *is* no other investment that offers returns of up to 50 percent and more with the minimal risk found in a wise real estate purchase.

Depreciation

Depreciation as it relates to real estate is really quite simple. People often confuse it with deterioration of the property or with a reduction in the property's value (as in the opposite of *appreciation*), but depreciation is actually a tax bookkeeping term that applies to investment property.

As you know, the tax law allows homeowners to deduct from their income the interest they pay on their mortgage each year. Non-resident owners can deduct the interest, too, but since that deduction is offset by the rental income from the property, Uncle Sam devised depreciation as an additional **writeoff** for non-resident owners.

A simplified depreciation calculation for a $100,000 house on a small lot might look something like this:

1. $100,000 Purchase Price
2. *-20,000* Less the value of the land
3. $ 80,000 Amount that can be depreciated
4. Divide $80,000 by 27.5 years to get
5. $2,909 The annual depreciation writeoff.

You start with the purchase price of the property (1), then you deduct the value of the land (2) because the tax law allows only the improvements on the land, i.e., the house, to be depreciated. Then you divide the resulting amount (3) by 27.5, which is the number of years over which the current tax law says a residential income property can be depreciated (4). (When the property is sold, by the way, the new owner sets up a new depreciation schedule.) This gives you the annual depreciation writeoff (5) that a buyer could take. If he is in a top bracket, say 43 percent with combined state and federal rates, this $2,909 depreciation writeoff could save $1,250 a year in taxes ($2,909 x .43) on income up to $100,000. (We'll talk more about this in Chapter 4.)

It is important that you correctly assess the value of the land. If the property were a house on five acres, obviously the land-to-value ratio would be much greater than the 20 percent we've used here in our example of a house on a small lot. The land-to-value ratio of a condominium, however, might be only 10 percent. In many communities the tax assessment on file in the Tax Assessor's Office will give the land-to-value ratio. A tax adviser should be consulted when setting up a depreciation schedule.

Depreciation doesn't affect the owner-occupant since you can't take depreciation on your primary residence. However, as we'll see in Chapter 3, it might affect you later on in your investment program. It's important to understand how depreciation works and how it can affect the tax picture.

Escrow

If you live in a state where, by law or by custom, attorneys handle the closing on the purchase or sale of a property, you may find the term *escrow* confusing. But it simply refers to the process of closing which, rather than being handled by an attorney, is handled by an escrow officer who records the appropriate documents and transfers the funds in the transaction. In states where attorneys are involved, the final stage of the purchase transaction is referred to as the *closing*. In escrow states it is referred to as the *close of escrow*.

A WORD ABOUT MORTGAGES

Pay attention now. If you're not familiar with real estate loans, then you should plan to read this next section several times, or until you understand it thoroughly.

One of the most confusing aspects of real estate to someone who has never purchased property before is the mortgage loan. Time and again we've watched clients' eyes glaze over when the subject of loans comes up. Some people are quite simply intimidated by the numbers. But if they can open their minds long enough to let just a few real estate number concepts sink in, they find the arithmetic itself is really quite simple.

Another factor that still affects people is the bad reputation that mortgages got, justifiably, during the Depression. Many people lost everything when their banks foreclosed on their mortgages when the payments could not be met. We've all heard those horror stories, and perhaps some of us have even been affected by them. But one thing to remember is that prior to the 1930s mortgages were usually interest only loans rather than **amortized** loans as they are today. What this means is that back then, if a bank loaned you $25,000 at 5 percent for 10 years, you had to make an interest payment each month for the use of the money, and then at the end of the 10 years you still had to pay back the $25,000 itself.

After the Depression, the weakness of this system was obvious, and it became common practice for lenders to **amortize** loans. This means that each monthly payment includes interest *and* part of the principal, rather than interest only. With the standard fixed-rate and variable-rate loans of today, therefore, by the time you make the last payment (if you've kept the property for the full 25- or 30-year term of the loan), you will have completely paid off the mortgage.

It's important to keep in mind that in the early years of a loan, only a small amount of the principal is amortized, or paid off, with each payment. Not until the later years of the loan does a significant portion of the monthly payment go toward paying off the original loan amount. Most lenders will supply you with a computer printout that will show you exactly how much of your monthly payment is interest and how much goes to pay off the principal. We'll talk more about this when we discuss the tax picture in Chapter 4, because it will be important to you to know what portion of your monthly payment is interest (which is tax deductible) and what portion reduces the principal loan amount.

HOW TO CALCULATE THE AMOUNT OF REAL ESTATE LOAN YOU CAN QUALIFY FOR

If you don't already know the amount of loan you can qualify for, you can figure, as a rough estimate, that most lenders today require that your monthly principal, interest, tax, and insurance payment (PITI) be no more than 28 percent to 33 percent of your gross monthly income. Generally speaking, the lower your other debt, such as car payments, the higher the loan-payment-to-income ratio you'll be allowed.

Let's say your gross monthly income is $2,500; 33 percent of that is $825, which would be the maximum monthly PITI payment you'd be allowed to carry. When you deduct the monthly charge for property taxes and insurance—let's say it's $150 a month—that leaves $675 for the principal and interest portion of the payment. If you have a financial calculator, or access to one through a broker, you can easily figure out the size of mortgage you could carry with this monthly payment. Otherwise, you can use the Amortization Tables in the Appendix in *reverse* to get a quick idea. (These tables cover what are currently the most typical interest rates, from 7 to 13 percent, and are included here for quick and easy reference as we go through the examples. Complete Amortization Tables, with interest rates from 6 to 20 percent, are available in most bookstores.)

Let's assume for the moment that you can get a 30-year variable-rate loan at 8 percent. Go to the 8 percent page in the tables and run your finger down the 30-year column until you come close to $675, then read the mortgage amount from the left-hand column. Now you know you can qualify for a loan of *approximately* $90,000. When you go to apply for a mortgage, which we'll talk about in Chapter 6, the loan officer or your real estate agent can show you the amount you can carry and what the monthly payment would be at various interest rates.

In an equity-share purchase, most lenders want the owner-occupants to be able to qualify for the loan on the basis of their own income, rather than relying heavily on the non-resident owner's income. However, if your income does fall a little short, a strong financial statement from the non-resident can often make the difference in getting the loan approved.

TYPES OF LOANS

From the 1930s to the late 1970s, the 30-year fixed-rate loan was the standard mortgage that most people took out when they bought their homes. But with the spiralling interest rates of the late 70s and early 80s, the banks no longer wanted to lock into a fixed rate for 30 years, so the variable-rate loan, with the rate tied to an index or to the **Treasury-bill** rate, was instituted. In the last ten years, literally hundreds of types of loans have been introduced into the market, and for the first-time borrower it can appear confusing. Don't let yourself be intimidated by the variety of mortgages available. For our purposes in equity sharing, there are three basic types of loans you should be familiar with:

Fixed-Rate Loans, where the rate of interest remains the same over the life of the loan.

Variable-Rate Loans, where the rate of interest can increase or decrease each year, depending on changes in the **prime lending rate** or some other national or regional index.

Negative Amortization Loans, variable-rate loans for which the interest rate can change each year but for which the payment can increase only by a small percentage (usually 7 to 8 percent) of the previous year's monthly payments.

Generally speaking, the interest rate on a fixed-rate loan is 2.5 to 3 percentage points higher than the starting rate of a variable-rate or a negative-amortization loan. A higher income is needed to qualify for the fixed-rate loan, and its monthly payment will be higher for the first few years.

In parts of the country where property values are appreciating, we feel it makes sense for first-time home buyers to use a variable-rate loan with its lower starting rate. This is especially valid in an equity-share purchase where, as we'll see later, the loan will usually be kept in place only three to five years. Not only does the lower starting rate keep the monthly payment lower during the first few years of ownership, but it also makes it easier for loan applicants with lower incomes to get loan approval, since they don't have to be able to qualify for the higher monthly payment of a fixed-rate loan.

For example, the monthly payment on a $100,000 loan at 8 percent interest for 30 years is $733.77, while at 10 percent it is $877.58—an increase of $143.81 per month. All other things being equal, and assuming an applicant had the income *potential* to handle the probable increase in the annual payment on a variable-rate loan, a lender might be more inclined to approve a loan on which the monthly payment was $144 *less* for the first year. After all, lenders are in business to make money, and they aren't going to make money if the people they loan money to can't meet the monthly payment. The lower the monthly payment, the easier it will be for the borrower to make it—and loans are approved on that basis.

(Throughout this book, where we could conveniently do so to simplify the examples, we have rounded the numbers to the nearest whole number. However, when you start working with lenders and amortization tables, you'll find the loan payment will always show the exact dollars and cents. Therefore, many of our examples are shown this way, too. We figure you might as well start getting used to it!)

We recommend that you stay with variable rates that have an annual cap of 2 percent or less. This means that a starting rate of 7 percent could not increase to more than 9 percent at the beginning of the second year, or 11 percent at the beginning of the third. We also recommend that you have a lifetime cap of not more than 5 percent, which means that with the 7 percent starting rate, the interest rate could not go higher than 12 percent over the life of the loan.

Should You Have a Variable- or Fixed-Rate Loan?

On a national average, mortgages are held for only seven years. And so it is surprising to learn from a 1988 survey conducted by the National Association of Realtors that 49 percent of all mortgages are still fixed-rate loans.

It's certainly comforting to know what your monthly payment is going to be from year to year, and if you knew that you'd be remaining in a home for ten or fifteen years or longer, a fixed-rate loan might make sense. But take a look now at Table 1-B, which compares fixed- and variable-rate loans having a normal beginning rate difference of 3 percent. You'll see that even if the variable-rate loan increases each year to the maximum of its annual cap (in this case, 2 percent), at the end of the third year you would still be ahead by $2,605 with the variable-rate. If the rate doesn't go to the maximum increase each year, you're even further ahead with the variable-rate.

Even at the end of the fifth year, assuming a maximum 2 percent rate increase for three years out of five, you would have paid a total of only $1,101 more on the variable-rate loan. Averaged over the five-year period this means only $18 more a month. Again, if the rate does not go to the maximum 2 percent annual increase for those three years, you're ahead with the variable-rate loan.

If you assume, from the fifth year to the tenth year, a five-year period of high interest rates at the maximum rate of 13 percent—a scenario most economists see as unlikely—the total payments for the variable-rate loan over the entire ten-year period would be $123,636, or $9,356 more than the fixed-rate's payments. This difference averages out to only $78 more a month over the ten years. But if you assume a more likely—and very conservative—scenario, like the one we've shown in Table 1-B, then you're still ahead by $1,550 after ten years with the variable-rate loan.

Another factor in favor of variable-rate loans is that they are almost always **assumable**. Conventional fixed-rate loans are almost never assumable. The advantage of an assumable loan is that if you have to sell your home in a slow market, when interest rates are high, it may be easier for a buyer to qualify for your lower-rate assumable loan than to get approved for a higher fixed-rate loan. This advantage could make

TABLE 1-B

Comparison of total annual principal and interest payments over a ten-year period for a variable-rate loan of $100,000, with a start rate of 8%, with a fixed-rate loan of $100,000 at 11%. Numbers have been rounded to nearest dollar.

	Variable-Rate Loan	*Fixed-Rate Loan*	*Increase/Decrease over Variable-Rate Loan*
Year 1	$ 8,805 at 8%	$ 11,428	
Year 2	$ 10,531 at 10%	$ 11,428	
Year 3	$ 12,343 at 12%	$ 11,428	
	$ 31,679	$ 34,284	+$2,605
Year 4	$ 14,219 at 14%	$ 11,428	
Year 5	$ 12,343 at 12%	$ 11,428	
	$ 58,241	$ 57,140	−$1,101
Year 6	$ 12,343 at 12 %	$ 11,428	
Year 7	$ 11,428 at 11%	$ 11,428	
Year 8	$ 10,531 at 10%	$ 11,428	
Year 9	$ 9,656 at 9%	$ 11,428	
Year 10	$ 10,531 at 10%	$ 11,428	
	$112,730	$114,280	+$1,550

your property more marketable than if you had a non-assumable fixed-rate loan. Also, unlike many fixed-rate loans, an assumable loan can be paid off at any time without penalty.

For some people, the security of knowing what the payments will be each year would be worth the additional amount they might have to pay. But it's our belief, based on our experience with loan applicants, that most people who chose fixed-rate loans have never worked through the numbers.

So that's what we suggest you do. In fact, why don't you do it right now: get some paper and a pencil and turn to the Amortization Tables in the Appendix. Spend a few minutes figuring out what your monthly payment would be on a fixed-rate loan for a property you are considering, then figure out the monthly payment for a variable-rate loan on the same amount. If you don't know what the fixed or variable rates are in your area at the moment, call a mortgage broker or the loan department of a local bank and ask them. Loan officers will be happy to give you that information over the phone.

When you've calculated the annual payment for the first year at the current fixed and variable rates for the amount of loan you are considering, figure out what the monthly payment would be for the second year on the variable-rate loan if the rate increased by the maximum 2 percent and what the payment would be if the rate increased by only 1 percent. Work up a couple of charts like the one in Table 1-B for five or ten years, then total the amounts. Spend some time figuring out what your monthly payment would be if your *loan amount* were slightly higher, or lower. (Don't forget to include an estimate for taxes and insurance. If you don't know the tax rate, call your local property tax assessor's office and find out; then get a quote for the insurance coverage from an insurance agent.) What monthly PITI payment are you comfortable with? Would your income and/or your budget support a 2 percent increase in the interest rate next year?

And remember there are many different types of variable-rate loans available, with various annual and lifetime caps. When it comes time to shop for a loan, you'll want to be sure you understand what you're getting. If the annual cap were 3 percent, the numbers in Table 1-B for the variable-rate loan would obviously be quite different.

Once you really know, from running the numbers, what effect the annual and lifetime caps would have on your monthly payment—the worst-case scenario—you'll feel much more comfortable with a variable-rate loan.

In the meantime, read the next section on **negative-amortization loans**, and then come back to your payment table and run the numbers using that type of loan. There is nothing like calculating the numbers to dispel the aura of mystery that so many people associate with the word *mortgage*. After you've spent some time working out the financial variables, you'll be far less intimidated by mortgages in general and variable-rate mortgages in particular.

Negative-Amortization Loans

It's unfortunate that the name for this real estate loan has such a *negative* connotation, because for many situations a negative-amortization loan is very advantageous. There's no question that, unlike a rose, this loan by any other name would seem much sweeter. "Delayed amortization" might provide no more understanding of the nature of this loan than "negative amortization" does, but the name wouldn't be as much of a turn-off to the uninitiated loan applicant. (Before reading on, you might want to turn back to page 10 and review our explanation of amortization.)

A negative-amortization loan, commonly called a "negative-am loan," is a variable-rate mortgage in which the annual interest rate can increase by, say, 2 percent, but the monthly payment can increase by only 7.5 percent of the *previous monthly payment.*

For example, on our $100,000 mortgage, the monthly payment at 8 percent interest is $733.77 for the first year. At the end of that year the loan balance is $99,165. On a standard variable-rate loan, if the interest rate went up 2 percentage points to 10 percent, the new monthly payment starting with the second year would be $875.11. On a negative-am loan, where the actual payment can increase by no more than 7.5 percent of the previous payment, the new monthly payment at the start of the second year would be increased by $55.03, to $788.80 ($733.77 x 7.5 percent = $55.03)—even though the 2 percent increase in the interest rate had brought the monthly amount owed to $877.58.

In this example, the difference between the actual interest-rate increase (to $875.11) and the 7.5 percent *payment* increase (to $788.80) is $86.31 a month. This amount times 12 months is $1,035.72, which is the amount of "negative amortization" that is added to the total loan amount. You would be paying interest not only on the balance of $99,165, but also on this additional amount. Over three or four years, assuming interest rates were going up steadily, you could be adding $3,000 to $4,000 in deferred interest (or negative amortization) to the loan amount.

But if the lower payments make it possible for you to get loan approval when you can't otherwise, and if you are in a rapidly appreciating market where the value of property is increasing by considerably more than the amount of the deferred interest, a negative-am loan might be well worth your while. As long as you know what the downside can be and have calculated what your worst-case "deferred interest" would add up to, and as long as you know you will have the funds to cover it, the negative-am loan is a viable vehicle to get you into your first property. It is also important to note that you can pay down the negative amount at any time; so that if you were expecting a substantial increase in salary in a year or two, you could plan to use your increased income to pay the loan payment as though it were a standard variable-rate loan.

Easy-Qualifier Loans

Another loan you should be familiar with is the 25 percent down easy qualifier. This type of loan is not available everywhere, but it is becoming more and more popular, especially with self-employed people.

One of the advantages of being self-employed is that the IRS allows you to take business deductions against your income. This becomes a disadvantage, however, when you go to apply for a loan and your tax return shows a minimal net income. With an easy-qualifier loan you can be qualified on the basis of gross income rather than net income.

Basically, an easy-qualifier loan works like this: as long as you and the non-resident owner have 25 percent of the down payment and have an excellent credit record, the lender will accept your statement of income without the time-consuming process of employment and/or tax-return verification. The theory is that people with excellent credit who have 25 percent of their own cash in a property are good credit risks. The advantages to both the lender and the applicant are the speed and ease with which a loan can be approved.

The income stated on the loan application must be realistic, of course: an application showing a meter maid earning $125,000 a year would raise eyebrows, and the lender always reserves the right to verify anything that looks suspicious. But for self-employed people and for non-resident owners with complicated financial statements, easy qualifiers are often a simpler way to get a mortgage.

GO FOR IT

Several years ago, a young couple, Bill and Jane Miller, came into our office. They were in their early thirties, they'd been married about five years and had two children, a boy of four and a baby girl of eighteen months. Bill had a very good job, with fine long-term prospects, working for a pharmaceuticals company, and Jane worked part-time as a licensed vocational nurse. They had a respectable combined income of about $49,000 a year, plus bonuses from time to time from Bill's profit-sharing plan through his employer. They had an excellent rental situation—a small two-bedroom house in a nice neighborhood, for which they paid only $700 a month in rent. This was about $400 under fair market rent, but because the Millers were very responsible tenants, always paid the rent on time, and had made many improvements to the property, it was worth the absentee landlord's while to keep the rent low. With the help of the reduced rent, plus Bill's bonuses, the Millers had been able to set aside close to $12,000.

They were desperate to own their own home. Even though their rent was low, it was still $700 wasted every month. Because they had no writeoffs, they were paying far more than they should have been on their income taxes. And every year they saw the price of a starter home getting further and further beyond their reach.

They came to us to find out what they could do to own their own home.

So we showed them. We sat down with them and went over their whole financial situation. We outlined how, with the cash they had available, they could get into an equity-share position on a $178,000 two-bedroom, two-bath condominium in an excellent location. We knew a condo wasn't their ultimate dream house, but we showed them how this would be a temporary situation—perhaps for two or three years—that would enable them to at least get their foot in the home-ownership door. Eventually, the Millers would be able to trade up into their own home, with full ownership—which, as we've already said, is always the ultimate goal for the owner-occupant in an equity-share purchase.

Bill, who is a very bright guy and very good at what he does, simply didn't understand the numbers. He was uneasy with the thought of leaving his comfortable $700-a-month rental and signing on for a much larger monthly mortgage payment. We met with him and Jane several times, and he called us regularly over a period of a couple of weeks with questions and objections he had come up with—all his "what if"s: What if he lost his job? What if the housing market turned bad? What if the economy went into a recession? What if interest rates went up?

We referred him to several accountants, one of whom he met with. We also suggested he run the numbers and the equity-share concept by his attorney. Both the accountant and the attorney agreed that this purchase would be a good forward step for the Millers.

But somehow, Bill just couldn't make himself take the plunge. He was scared. He remained concerned about the increase in the monthly payments, from $700 to $1,300, even though the lender had personally assured Bill that his income would qualify for the variable-rate loan and the potential payment increases. The accountant also showed Bill how, thanks to the interest writeoff, his out-of-pocket expenses after taxes would be several hundred dollars *less* than the increase in monthly payment. (We'll show you how this works in Chapter 4.)

Finally, after several weeks of agonizing deliberation, Bill made up his mind: he decided to wait.

Jane was heartbroken. And we were very sorry that we hadn't been able to make Bill see that if he didn't get started soon, it would only get more and more difficult—if not impossible—for them to own their own home.

All of Bill's "what if"s were legitimate concerns, ones that anybody who buys a home should have. But each question could be dealt with. If he lost his job—an unlikely prospect for him—he could probably get another in the same or a similar industry. (If he lost his job and he were renting, he'd still have to make his rent payment each month.) But yes, if he lost his job and couldn't get another one, it's possible that he'd have to sell the property. That's a risk one takes. If the housing market went bad or the economy went into a recession, the same thing could happen. And there have been doomsayers from day one who have been predicting that the next big crash is just around the corner; it *could* happen. It is a risk—but a *calculated* one, and the chances are far greater that the Millers would make money on this purchase than that they would lose it.

We ran into Bill and Jane recently. The were still renting their cute little house, though the landlord had increased their rent to $950 a month. Bill had continued to get an annual bonus, so their savings would have been close to $15,000, except that they'd decided to buy a new car; now they had only $9,700 in savings. The condo they originally looked at is now selling for close to $250,000. Had they purchased it back then, they would now have a net equity of close to $25,000—more than double their original investment. (We'll show you how these numbers break out in Chapter 3.)

But what's even more discouraging is that for Bill and Jane to buy that home today it would take, including closing costs, close to $15,000 down—50 percent more than it did two years ago; and their monthly payment, rather than starting at roughly $1,350 as it would have then, would today be more than $1,700. Even if they now had the $15,000 down payment, their income hasn't increased enough to enable them to qualify for the new monthly payment, and of course they don't even have the $15,000 for the down payment, because they spent over $8,000 on their new car—which lost several thousand dollars in value the day they drove it off the lot.

Our hearts go out to them. Will they ever be able to own their own home? Maybe. Maybe they'll inherit some money. Maybe Bill will make a gigantic leap forward in terms of his career. Maybe housing prices will fall. Anything is possible. But if only they'd been able to grit their teeth and take the leap.

What we want you to understand is that every first-time buyer is scared. Very few get through the close of the sale without suffering "buyer's remorse." If you've done your homework (which we'll show you how to do), if you've gotten competent advice (which we'll show you how to do), and if you've found the right property in the right area and structured an advantageous equity-share agreement (which we'll show you how to do)—you'll still be scared but, we hope, will go ahead anyway. We know from the people who've done it—and for whom equity sharing and home ownership are working—that the rewards of being in your own home are well worth the fear of the unknown and the anxiety and sleepless nights that many first-time buyers go through before they finally get into their own home.

First-Time Non-resident Owners Get Cold Feet, Too

First-time buyers are not the only ones who suffer from the fear of the unknown. Would-be non-resident owners are often just as bad, and sometimes worse. Worse because they've presumably purchased their own homes and should be familiar with the process.

As it turned out, the non-resident we had lined up to back Bill and Jane Miller was a young divorced woman in her late thirties, who came to us because she'd recently received an insurance settlement of $40,000. Sue Parsons already owned her own home and had two teenage daughters she was supporting with the income from her own business, which was doing quite well. An equity-share position in the condo that Bill and Jane were considering would have required $31,000 of the cash she had available. This would have left her a comfortable cushion of $9,000.

When Bill and Jane decided not to buy, however, Sue had second thoughts herself. Even though she owned her own home, she "was never very good with numbers." Aside from the equity she had in her home, her $40,000 settlement was the first "real" money she'd ever had—and she was afraid of losing it. She had friends and well-meaning family who cautioned her against doing anything too rash. So Sue kept her $40,000 safe in an 8 percent money market fund, which in the past two and a half years has earned her roughly $8,500. Had she put $31,000 into real estate with the Millers, she now would have had a net equity of $68,000, which she could tax-defer into other real estate. Even were she to have "cashed in" and paid the tax on the gain (not an option we recommend—we'll see why in Chapter 4), she would still have nearly doubled her original investment.

Sue feels secure with her $48,500, and we haven't had the heart to tell her what that amount could have been in just thirty months.

In the next chapter we'll show you case histories of both owner-occupants and non-resident owners who had the same doubts that the Millers and Sue had, but who took the risk and who now, thanks to equity sharing, own their own homes.

·2·

How It Works

Now let's get into specifics. To do that, we'll look at the details of actual case histories taken from our files. In order to show you the broad range of possibilities, we'll be looking at four different percentage-of-ownership splits:

25% Occupant/75% Non-resident
50% Occupant/50% Non-resident
70% Occupant/30% Non-resident
40% Occupant (with only 25% invested)/60% Non-resident

A WORD ABOUT OUR WORKSHEETS

In each case history outlined in this chapter, we will give you a brief sketch of the participants and provide completed worksheets so you can see how the numbers break out.

The Equity-Share Worksheet that we use throughout this chapter provides a place for you to keep track of basic information about a prospective purchase, including the price, the down payment, the cash supplied by each owner, the percentages of ownership, the amount to be financed, and the total monthly PITI to be paid by the owner-occupant.

In Chapter 3 we'll explain how to use our Projections Worksheet and show you how to evaluate your options when it comes time to sell or refinance.

In Chapter 4 we'll show you how you can use the Rent Calculation Worksheet to establish the documentation required for tax purposes by the IRS.

Start Using the Worksheets

This is a "working" chapter, and, as we've said before, the best way for you to become familiar with how equity sharing can work for you is to run the numbers yourself. As we proceed, take some time to go over each of the completed worksheets contained in these chapters. Then, using the blank worksheets supplied in the Appendix, fill in the figures that apply to your own situation. It's not that the numbers themselves are difficult, merely that the concepts they illustrate are often new to people or are ones that most people don't regularly encounter in their lives. As in any learning situation, repetition is a powerful tool. Work through the numbers until you're comfortable with them. After you've completed a couple of worksheets, you'll begin to see how simple real estate numbers really are.

DON'T BE PUT OFF BY OUR HOUSING COSTS

The housing costs shown in these case histories reflect the high cost of homes in California, one of the most expensive housing areas in the country. If you live in an area where property values are appreciating but the cost of a starter home is only half or even a third of the costs shown here, be grateful! Equity sharing will still work for you. Once you understand the basics, the principles of equity sharing can be used in almost any market where incomes have not kept pace with housing costs.

EQUITY SHARING IS NOT "NOTHING DOWN"

People often think of equity sharing as an arrangement in which the non-resident owner puts up the money needed to buy the property and the occupant moves in and makes all the payments. In the early 1980s, many equity-sharing purchases were actually structured this way. However, there are two potential problems with such a setup.

First, if a percentage of ownership is given to an owner-occupant who hasn't put up any of his own money, the IRS could determine that a "gift" was made of part of the property, and the transaction could be subject to a gift tax. In certain family arrangements this may be acceptable, but in an equity-share purchase, where the parties do not know each other, a no-money-down deal has a second drawback, since it may put the non-resident in a vulnerable position. The occupant, having nothing to lose, could simply walk away from the property if things get tough. Someone who has money in the property is much less likely to walk away from it.

For these reasons we require all of our owner-occupants to have at least 25 percent of the down payment (5 percent of the purchase price) before we will consider them as equity-share candidates. Many lenders are requiring this as well, for the same reason: borrowers who have some of their own cash in the property are unlikely to default on the loan.

COUNSELING WITH OUR CLIENTS

Before we take our clients out to look at properties, we spend a considerable amount of time with them in order to determine exactly what their needs are. This process, which we call counseling, is an integral part of structuring our equity-share purchases.

We need to know how much cash our clients have available for the down payment, and the source of that cash (except in special circumstances, lenders will not allow borrowed funds to be used for the down payment). We also explore other possible sources of cash that our clients might not have considered. One person had $5,000 worth of paintings she was willing to sell to add to her down payment funds; another sold an antique car.

We work very closely with qualified loan officers, who run credit checks to make certain that clients have good credit records, or help them correct questionable ones. The loan officer also verifies clients' incomes and calculates their monthly expenses. Once we have a handle on these items, we have a much better idea of the amount of mortgage they can qualify for and what price range we should be researching for them.

NOW TO THE CASE HISTORIES

Case History #1: 25% Occupant/ 75% Non-resident.

Tom and Margaret Kennedy are a young couple in their early thirties. Tom is a deep-sea diver and earns $24,000 a year; Margaret is a manager of a local bank and earns $22,000 a year. They had been married six years and were living in a one-bedroom apartment, when the landlord increased their rent to $1,050 a month. This was under fair-market rent, but the landlord was willing to keep the rent below market because the Kennedys had been such excellent tenants.

Still, the Kennedys knew they could do better and wanted very much to get into their own home. After investigating the local market, they found they'd have to pay close to $200,000 for a home they'd be willing to give up their wonderful apartment for.

A Savings Plan Helped—But Not Enough

The Kennedys started a savings plan when they were first married and had maintained it consistently since then. As a result, they were able to save almost $12,000. Margaret knew from her experience in the bank that their income would qualify them for a mortgage of approximately $155,000. This meant that on a $200,000 property they'd need $40,000 for the 20 percent down payment and another $6,000 for closing costs.

For the Kennedys, coming up with the $40,000 for the down payment, plus closing costs, was close to impossible. Their next-best course of action would have required enough cash for a 10 percent down payment, so they could go for 90 percent financing. But 10 percent down, plus closing costs, would still require $26,000—twice the amount of cash they had. Even if they'd had $26,000, their combined income wouldn't have been sufficient to enable them to qualify for the $180,000 loan.

The Kennedys were very discouraged. They had $12,000 in cash and a combined income that would qualify them for a $155,000 mortgage, and they were unable to buy a home. But they weren't willing to give up yet. A friend of theirs had heard about our equity-share seminars and suggested they call for an appointment, which they did.

After counseling with the Kennedys, we could see that, with only $12,000 in savings and no possible source of additional cash, the only way they could get into the $200,000 property they wanted would be through an equity-share purchase in which they would have 25 percent ownership. We spent a lot of time going over the numbers with them, including the projections we discuss in the next chapter. The Kennedys wanted their own home; for them a quarter of a slice was a lot better than nothing at all. They decided to go for it.

After running the appropriate credit checks and income verifications, we began to look for the property. The Kennedys soon found a two-bedroom, one-and-a-half bath condo that they liked very much. The purchase price was $195,000.

As you can see from their worksheet, a 20 percent down payment left a mortgage of $156,000, which they already knew was in their ballpark. They could contribute 25 percent of the down payment, or $9,750, plus 25 percent of the closing costs, or $1,462, for a total contribution of $11,212. Because their condo would rent for $1,400 a month, their percentage of ownership was based on the percentage of the down payment they contributed.

Note that their total monthly expenses would be roughly $300 more than they had been paying for rent. (However, as we'll learn in Chapter 4, when they calculate what they'll save in income taxes now that they can write off mortgage interest, their monthly housing costs with home ownership are only slightly more than their cost to rent.) In any case, the Kennedys wanted this condominium unit; it suited their needs and they could get into it with only 25 percent of the down payment. Now all they needed was a non-resident owner willing to supply 75 percent of the down payment and closing costs, or approximately $34,000.

A Good Match Is Important

We had already alerted one of our non-resident owner clients, Bea Hammer, that we had a well-qualified couple who needed help with the down payment in order to get into their "starter" home. We went over the numbers with Bea, who was very interested in an equity-share arrangement. A meeting was arranged with the Kennedys and Bea so both parties would have a chance to get acquainted and determine if their goals were compatible.

Bea Hammer is a single woman in her mid-forties who had owned several rental properties and was tired of the management headaches. She was more than willing to share a portion of the future appreciation of an investment property in return for a trouble-free, no-negative-cash-flow investment.

Bea recognized immediately that the Kennedys would be a very compatible match for her. She appreciated the fact that they were flexible in their time-frame goals: based on the outcome of several different projection scenarios (which we'll go through in Chapter 3), they would be willing to move out of the property in two to three years if the current level of appreciation continued and they could build up sufficient equity; or they would be willing to stay in it for several years longer, if necessary.

The Kennedys felt that even if they did have to wait four or five years to maximize their equity build-up, at the very least they would be able

FIGURE 2-A

EQUITY SHARE WORKSHEET

Owner-Occupant: *Tom and Margaret Kennedy*

Non-resident Owner: *Bea Hammer*

Property Address: ______

PURCHASE PRICE		$ 195,000
Less Down Payment at 20 % Down		– 39,000
AMOUNT TO BE FINANCED		$ 156,000
Total Down Payment Required:	$ 39,000	
Less Cash from Owner-Occupant:	– 9,750	
Amount Needed from Non-resident Owner:	$ 29,250	
Closing Costs (Estimate 3% of Purchase Price) Paid According to % of Ownership	$ 5,850	
Owner-Occupant:	$ 1,462	
Non-resident Owner:	$ 4,387	

PERCENTAGE OF OWNERSHIP:

25 % Owner-Occupant 75 % Non-resident Owner

LOAN INFORMATION

____ Years FIXED at ____ %

30 Years VARIABLE at 7½ %

2 % Annual Cap 5 % Lifetime Cap

____ % Annual Payment Cap if Negative Am Loan

Monthly PRINICPAL & INTEREST (From Amortization Table)	$ 1,091
Monthly Property TAX (Tax divided by 12 months)	$ 162
Monthly INSURANCE Payment (Premium divided by 12 months)	$ 30
Monthly PITI (Principal, Interest, Tax, Insurance)	$ 1,283
If Condo, add monthly Association Dues	$ 80
TOTAL MONTHLY EXPENSE PAID BY OWNER-OCCUPANT	$ 1,363

to enjoy the tax benefits of property ownership during that time. Besides, they would be in a position to continue saving money to add to the down payment on their next home, not to mention the fact that they would now have the satisfaction of living in a home that belonged to them.

We set up escrow, drew up their shared equity agreement, and in less than two months the Kennedys were in their own home—and loving it! And Bea Hammer, for only $34,000, has a trouble-free investment in an appreciating asset, with tax benefits and no negative cash flow.

This is an excellent example of the type of situation we see all the time. We know that, though the numbers may be different, the circumstances are the same for millions of would-be first-time home buyers and non-resident owners around the country: young couples with a substantial joint income, who can qualify for the loan but simply don't have the cash for even half of the down payment, can team up with purchasers who have the additional funds needed to buy the property and who are willing to give up a portion of the appreciation for a no-hassle, no-negative investment.

Equity sharing provides a safe, easy, workable solution for first-time home buyers with limited cash and makes it possible for them to get into the housing market.

Case History #2: 50% Occupant/50% Non-resident.

Jack Haley is a 27-year-old single man who earns close to $50,000 a year from his own business, which he started right out of college. The business has done very well, and he was able to set aside close to $30,000, which he wanted to put into real estate. He liked his $750-a-month apartment well enough, but realized that he was getting no tax benefit from renting and also no equity build-up.

When Jack first came to see us, he had already found a condominium he wanted to buy, with three bedrooms, two and a half baths, a pool, and a clubhouse. He had talked to several lenders and knew that he could qualify for a mortgage of $150,000. Because he is self-employed, Jack is a good candidate for an easy-qualifier loan (see page 16).

The price of the condo Jack wanted was $200,000. If he went for an easy-qualifier loan to cover the 25 percent down payment, he would need a total of $50,000 down, plus another $6,000 to cover closing costs. (The numbers are similar to those of the Kennedys' home in Case History #1, but the circumstances are quite different.)

As you can see from Jack's worksheet, he needed another $28,000 to purchase this property. Because of his self-employed status, Jack also needed a non-resident owner who looked good on paper to help him get loan approval.

If Jack purchased this property, his monthly housing payment (PITI) would be close to double what he was paying in rent. But he was willing and able to pay that amount, and felt the trade-off in tax benefits and the satisfaction of home ownership were worth the extra cost.

Jack actually had several options. He could have borrowed against his business for the additional amount, and, in fact, he had an open line of credit on which to draw. But he'd planned to use those funds for expanding his company and decided to keep the expansion option open.

He could have obtained the additional cash he needed from his father. But he felt very strongly that he wanted to buy the property without asking his family for the money.

A third option would have been to take a one-third ownership with a non-resident who could provide the remaining two-thirds of the down payment. This would have required only $16,500 for Jack's portion of the down payment and $1,980 for his portion of the closing costs, or a total of $18,480. But Jack felt that to make it worth his while to give up his comfortable, inexpensive apartment while doubling his monthly housing expense, he really wanted to have a 50 percent position.

After counseling with us and going over all the possibilities, he finally decided on the plan he felt would work best for him.

We had non-resident owner clients, the Schifflers, who had just relocated to our area and were starting a new consulting business. They owned their own home and had a number of rental properties and substantial cash. They wanted to continue investing in real estate, but they had neither the time nor the energy to deal with the management and maintenance headaches that come with rental property.

We suggested that Jack and the Schifflers pool their cash and go for 50/50 ownership, with a 25 percent down easy qualifier-loan. This would mean they'd need a total of $56,000 for the down payment and closing costs, to which they would each contribute on a 50/50 basis.

After dealing with a series of tenant problems in their other properties, the Schifflers were delighted at the prospect of sharing ownership with someone as responsible and conscientious as Jack. With Jack's excellent

FIGURE 2-B

EQUITY SHARE WORKSHEET

Owner-Occupant: Jack Haley

Non-resident Owner: The Schifflers

Property Address: ______

PURCHASE PRICE $ 200,000

Less Down Payment at 25 % Down − 50,000

AMOUNT TO BE FINANCED $ 150,000

Total Down Payment Required: $ 50,000

Less Cash from Owner-Occupant: − 25,000

Amount Needed from Non-resident Owner: $ 25,000

Closing Costs (Estimate 3% of Purchase Price) Paid According to % of Ownership $ 6,000

Owner-Occupant: $ 3,000

Non-resident Owner: $ 3,000

PERCENTAGE OF OWNERSHIP:

50 % Owner-Occupant 50 % Non-resident Owner

LOAN INFORMATION

____ Years FIXED at ____ %

30 Years VARIABLE at 7 5/8 %

2 % Annual Cap 5 % Lifetime Cap

____ % Annual Payment Cap if Negative Am Loan

Monthly PRINICPAL & INTEREST (From Amortization Table) $ 1,062

Monthly Property TAX (Tax divided by 12 months) $ 162

Monthly INSURANCE Payment (Premium divided by 12 months) $ 30

Monthly PITI (Principal, Interest, Tax, Insurance) $ 1,254

If Condo, add monthly Association Dues $ 130

TOTAL MONTHLY EXPENSE PAID BY OWNER-OCCUPANT $ 1,384

references, and with $28,000 of his own money in the property, the Schifflers felt certain this equity-share arrangement would make a trouble-free arrangement for them.

Some time after Jack and the Schifflers closed on this property, Jack came into a totally unexpected windfall of $40,000. The Schifflers offered to let him buy them out, since we had assured them there were other equity-share purchases they could get into. However, Jack was very comfortable with their arrangement and decided to leave things as they were. Jack has since used his additional cash to back two other owner-occupants in equity share purchases, taking the maximum advantage of leverage.

Case History #3: 70% Occupant/30% Non-resident.

Charles and Marie Driscoll were a young couple in their mid-thirties who came to us because they were getting divorced and wanted us to list their home, which they had bought for $150,000 two years previously. They each wanted to take their share of equity and buy another property, but they weren't certain they would have sufficient cash after the sale to do this.

We determined that their home would sell for approximately $189,000. Their mortgage on it was $125,000, which would leave them each with about $25,000 cash after the sale. In order to defer the tax on their gain, they each needed to buy a replacement residence valued at $90,000 or more. (We'll discuss tax deferral in Chapter 4.)

Charles' income of $42,000 a year was enough so he could qualify for 90 percent financing on a $159,000 condo and get into it with 100 percent ownership.

Marie's $29,000-a-year income limited her to a $100,000 mortgage. After an extensive search, we found a one-bedroom, one-bath condo in a nice area, two blocks from her office, for $129,000. As her worksheet shows, with a 25-percent-down easy-qualifier loan, her $25,000 cash from their joint ownership would give her 70 percent ownership in this property. She needed only 30 percent of the down payment from a non-resident owner.

From the non-resident's point of view, Marie already had a proven track record of owning and caring for her own home. This was an excellent opportunity for a non-resident with roughly $10,000 cash to get into a 30 percent ownership position in a trouble-free, vacancy-free property with an experienced home owner.

Laura Taylor, the non-resident we teamed Marie up with, is a young

FIGURE 2-C

EQUITY SHARE WORKSHEET

Owner-Occupant: Marie Driscoll

Non-resident Owner: Laura Taylor

Property Address: ______

PURCHASE PRICE $ 129,000

Less Down Payment at 25 % Down − 32,250

AMOUNT TO BE FINANCED $ 96,750

Total Down Payment Required: $ 32,250

Less Cash from Owner-Occupant: − 22,575

Amount Needed from Non-resident Owner: $ 9,675

Closing Costs (Estimate 3% of Purchase Price) Paid According to % of Ownership $ 3,870

Owner-Occupant: $ 2,709

Non-resident Owner: $ 1,161

PERCENTAGE OF OWNERSHIP:

70 % Owner-Occupant   30 % Non-resident Owner

LOAN INFORMATION

____ Years FIXED at ____ %

30 Years VARIABLE at 7 7/8 %

2 % Annual Cap   5 % Lifetime Cap

7½ % Annual Payment Cap if Negative Am Loan

Monthly PRINICPAL & INTEREST (From Amortization Table) $ 702

Monthly Property TAX (Tax divided by 12 months) $ 108

Monthly INSURANCE Payment (Premium divided by 12 months) $ 20

Monthly PITI (Principal, Interest, Tax, Insurance) $ 830

If Condo, add monthly Association Dues $ 75

TOTAL MONTHLY EXPENSE PAID BY OWNER-OCCUPANT $ 905

woman just two years out of college. She received, as a graduation present from her parents, $12,000 in cash, which she has kept in a CD. Because her plans for her immediate future are unsettled, and because she has an ideal and very inexpensive living arrangement with her former college roommates, she doesn't want to get into her own home just yet. However, she sees what's happening with real estate prices and feels that a real estate purchase would be the best way to maximize the cash she has available.

Co-owning with Marie at this point would be ideal for her because it would put her money to work until she decides where her career plans will take her. Perhaps in a couple of years she'll be in a position to buy Marie out and move into this property herself.

Marie knows she doesn't want to stay in this unit forever. She and her ex-husband had owned a spacious two-bedroom, two-bath unit, and this smaller condo cramps her style. But considering that she hadn't been sure she'd be able to buy any property with only half the equity from her former home, Marie is delighted to be able to maintain both home ownership and her tax benefits. She has a place of her own and is building equity so she can buy a larger property as soon as the market and her projected income increases will allow her to.

Marie is an example of another type of potential home buyer who can benefit from equity sharing. According to Census Bureau statistics, over a million couples divorce each year. The median age for divorced males is 32.4; for females, 30. Several hundred thousand of these young people have equity from their joint home ownership. But with increased real estate prices, half of that equity often isn't sufficient to get them into another property on their own. Once again, equity sharing meets a tremendous need and provides a win-win situation for everyone involved.

Case History #4: Occupant with Only 25% of the Down Payment Gets 40% Ownership with "Sweat Equity"/Non-resident with 75% of the Down Payment Gets 60% Ownership.

Edward and Ellen Brown had lived for many years in the Midwest, where they owned their own home. They are in their mid-forties and have two teenage children. Two years ago, Ed got an offer to come to California to run an exciting new business. They jumped at the chance. They were amazed and very disappointed, however, to find that the equity they had in their house wasn't enough to get them into a home in our high-priced community. They had no choice but to rent.

Ellen refused to give up her dream of owning their own home. When she saw an ad for one of our equity sharing seminars, she dragged Ed along. Ellen knew that Ed's business required him to keep a carpenter and an electrician on staff full-time. Her idea was to find a "fixer-upper" into which she and Ed could put a portion of the cash from the sale of their previous home, plus their design talents, and contribute the use of the carpenter and electrician to maximize their percentage of ownership.

Ed and Ellen had about $25,000 in cash, and their income qualified them for a $275,000 loan. We found them a property which had been listed for $395,000 and needed a lot of fixing, on which we negotiated a $330,000 purchase price. The house is in an area where surrounding homes are in the $450,000 range, so with the right improvements there's a lot of appreciation potential.

As you can see from their worksheet, Ed and Ellen put up 25 percent of the down payment and 40 percent of the closing costs, for a total of $24,585. We brought in three non-resident owners who contributed a total of $67,815. The loan amount was $247,500, and the non-residents agreed to give the Browns a 40 percent ownership position in consideration of the improvements they would make to the property (their **sweat equity**).

The Browns want to make this house their permanent home. They're planning to upgrade the value of the house significantly, so that within a few years they'll be able to refinance and buy out the non-residents. The non-residents plan to pull out their original cash investment plus their profits when the property is refinanced and purchase another property in an equity-share arrangement.

The non-resident owners, three professional women who have known each other for many years and have been involved in previous equity-share purchases, are excited about the good buy they've been able to get on this property. That, combined with the improvements the Browns will add to it, will give them an extra edge to their investment dollars. Any one of the three non-residents could have put up the cash on her own. But because they've had such good experiences working together in shared equity purchases, they decided to spread their risk and split the benefits of equity sharing.

The Browns spent many hours with the non-residents before they closed on the property, going over each of the items they planned to

FIGURE 2-D

EQUITY SHARE WORKSHEET

Owner-Occupant: Edward and Ellen Brown

Non-resident Owner: Ericson / Williams / Parenty

Property Address: ______

PURCHASE PRICE		$ 330,000
Less Down Payment at 25 % Down		– 82,500
AMOUNT TO BE FINANCED		$ 247,500
Total Down Payment Required:	$ 82,500	
Less Cash from Owner-Occupant:	– 20,625	
Amount Needed from Non-resident Owner:	$ 61,875	
Closing Costs (Estimate 3% of Purchase Price) Paid According to % of Ownership	$ 9,900	
Owner-Occupant:	$ 3,960	
Non-resident Owner:	$ 5,940	

PERCENTAGE OF OWNERSHIP:
40 % Owner-Occupant 60 % Non-resident Owner

LOAN INFORMATION

____ Years FIXED at ____ %
30 Years VARIABLE at 7¾ %
2 % Annual Cap 5 % Lifetime Cap
____ % Annual Payment Cap if Negative Am Loan

Monthly PRINICPAL & INTEREST (From Amortization Table)	$ 1,773
Monthly Property TAX (Tax divided by 12 months)	$ 275
Monthly INSURANCE Payment (Premium divided by 12 months)	$ 60
Monthly PITI (Principal, Interest, Tax, Insurance)	$ 2,108
If Condo, add monthly Association Dues	$ Ø
TOTAL MONTHLY EXPENSE PAID BY OWNER-OCCUPANT	$ 2,108

upgrade and change. Each party's projected improvements and future capital contributions were specifically detailed in their shared-equity agreement.

The Browns will also be contributing cash with many of the improvements they will be making. The parties agreed that the Browns would be responsible for the first $2,000 on each of the major improvements, and that any additional funds required would then be contributed by the parties based on their percentages of ownership. Once again, equity sharing has provided a means for a family to purchase a home they otherwise would not have been able to buy.

HOW TO DETERMINE PERCENTAGE OF OWNERSHIP

As you've seen from the case histories we've discussed here, all the percentages of ownership (with the exception of the Browns') were based on the percentage of the down payment and closing costs supplied by each party. In the case of the Browns, even though they supplied only 25 percent of the down payment funds, the non-resident owners agreed to give them an additional 15 percent ownership, for a total of 40 percent, because of all the work, time, and expertise the Browns would be contributing to increase the value of the property. This additional 15 percent ownership was negotiated between the parties.

Several other methods can be used to determine the percentage of ownership, depending on your local market. Often the owner-occupants may receive an additional portion of ownership to compensate for the fact that their monthly payment is considerably more than what the non-resident would be able to get if the property were rented. In such a case the percentage negotiated would depend on the local rental market.

For example, let's look at one way the percentage of ownership might be structured if the owner-occupants and the non-resident owners each contribute 50 percent of the down payment (or $28,000 each) on a property that would rent for only $1,000 a month, but for which the monthly expenses were $1,400. The ownership is adjusted by calculating the total amount the occupant contributes to the non-resident's portion of the shortfall during the time they own the property together. In this case, if they owned the home for three years, the occupant would have paid $7,200 of the non-resident's portion of the shortfall ($1,400 – $1,000 = $400 a month shortfall x 50% ownership = $200 a month x 36 months = $7,200). Therefore, the owner-occupant's total contribution would be $35,200 (which is 56% of the total contributions), as compared to $28,000 (or 44%) from the non-resident owner. The percentages of ownership would be adjusted to correspond to the contribution percentages: 56 percent for the occupant and 44 percent for the non-resident.

A method that accountants like to use is to credit 100 percent of the shortfall to the owner-occupants and then "discount" the shortfall to the present value. To show how this works, let's look at an example we call "Monica's Condo" (You'll need a financial calculator to help you determine present value.):

Monica and her non-resident owner purchased a condo for $215,000. They each contributed $21,500, or 50 percent of the $43,000 down payment. The condo had previously rented for $1,000 a month. The total monthly expenses were $1,610, and both parties agreed to a two-year holding period. This meant that over the two years Monica would be contributing $14,640 (24 months x $610) on behalf of the non-resident.

Monica's $14,640 contribution has a present value of $12,551 at 8 percent. In other words, if $12,551 were put in the bank today at 8 percent, it would grow to $14,640 over two years. Accordingly, Monica's non-resident owner gave her credit for $34,051 (her $21,500 down payment and $12,551 for the shortfall) which, divided by both parties' total contribution of $55,551, equals 61 percent ownership. To keep it simple, Monica and her non-resident agreed to a 60 percent ownership for Monica and a 40 percent ownership for the non-resident.

Another method favored by accountants is to consider the total after-tax consequences an owner would have if he owned the property 100 percent as a rental. Many accountants use this method as a starting point before adding the value of reduced management, maintenance, and upkeep that an owner-occupant contributes. With this method the accountant would calculate the rental property's performance based on actual rent, rent increases expected over the holding period, actual expenses, anticipated expense increases, and depreciation; the accountant then determines the actual out-of-pocket expenses based on the non-resident owner's tax circumstances. The total after-tax negative cash flow over the holding period is then discounted to present value and credited to the owner-occupant. See Appendix for a breakdown of this method.

No matter which method or combination of methods you use to determine percentage of ownership, the important considerations are to keep it simple, don't be greedy, and make it a win-win situation for all parties.

EQUITY SHARING OFFERS MANY POSSIBILITIES

The techniques of equity sharing can be used to meet the needs of millions of home buyers across the nation. With a little imagination and a strong determination to own their own home, people have been able to make equity sharing work for them in many other ways:

• We recently closed escrow on a purchase in which the non-resident owner had very little cash but did have a substantial cash flow from a trust fund. The owner-occupant supplied the cash for the down payment but, because of his recent divorce, a major portion of his monthly income was being paid to his ex-wife for a three-year payout.

We structured the purchase so that the non-resident would make the monthly payments for a period of three years. The non-resident's cash contribution over that time would match the occupant's down payment. After three years, the parties plan to refinance (or sell the property) and share the equity on a 50/50 basis.

• There are many parts of the country where developers have overbuilt and now have an inventory of properties they cannot sell. Equity sharing is an excellent way for them to move their inventory without taking huge losses, while at the same time helping buyers get into home ownership.

• Equity sharing is not just for the lower end of the housing market. We recently placed a couple in a $700,000 house using equity sharing. They had moved here from a very comfortable $250,000 five-bedroom, five-bath home on two acres in the Midwest. They had an opportunity to relocate to our area, with excellent income prospects, but the equity in their previous home, though considerable for their area, wasn't sufficient to enable them to live here in the style to which they'd become accustomed. Their income qualified them for a $525,000 mortgage, and we structured a 50/50 equity share arrangement, with each party putting in $100,000 to cover the 25 percent down on an easy-qualifier loan, plus the closing costs.

• Another exciting high-end property for which we recently structured an equity-sharing arrangement was a $1,100,000 oceanfront home in a neighborhood of homes costing $2,000,000 and more. A contractor and his wife had just sold their $500,000 home, with a profit of $250,000. We combined them with a non-resident owner who matched their cash down. The contractor's cash was put into the property as the down payment, and the investor's cash went into a fund for the improvements that the contractor planned to make to the house. They each plan to pocket close to half a million dollars from the sale once the improvements are made.

• We have been working closely with both city and county government offices to help arrange equity-share purchases for their employees who are required to live in the city or county but who, because of the high cost of housing, cannot afford to do so. Equity sharing makes it possible for police, firefighters, and other government employees to own their own homes in the areas they serve.

• We've also worked with local college and university systems in setting up equity share purchases to keep their administrators and teachers in the university area.

• A recent study conducted by the *Harvard Business Review* found that businesses in high-cost housing regions are spending billions of dollars to finance employee mortgages, relocate workers around the country, and subsidize incomes to help meet housing costs. Equity sharing provides a means for corporations to assist in the relocation and housing of their employees, while at the same time sharing the benefits of the continued increases in housing costs.

If you've read this chapter carefully, and worked out the numbers on the worksheets as we suggested, you will have a good understanding of some of the different ways equity sharing can work for you.

Now let's go on to Chapter 3, where we'll show you how to calculate your equity, based on various rates of appreciation you might expect to experience in your area. Then we'll discuss the options you have once you've made your initial equity share purchase.

·3·

Projections: Where Do You Go From Here?

Now we come to the fun part! This is where you'll learn to do projections on the property you're considering, so you can see what the possibilities might be once you've put your money to work in real estate. We developed the Projections Worksheet so you can see how much your property would be worth at different rates of appreciation over different time periods. We're going to take you step by step through the worksheet so you can learn to use this method to evaluate all the different properties you might be considering and any percentage of ownership you might negotiate.

Obviously, there is more than one way to estimate future value, and you may have come across other useful formulas for evaluating real estate investments. We like this method because it's simple and straightforward, and we find that people new to real estate calculations can relate to it easily. If you have another process that works for you, by all means use it. The important thing is that you have a reliable system that will help you calculate the cash you'll have available when you either refinance or sell the property.

First we will take you, section by section, through the blank worksheet to explain the purpose of each part and to show you how the calculations are made. Then, using the numbers from Case History #1 in Chapter 2, we'll walk you through Tom and Margaret Kennedy's Projections Worksheet. We will consider various appreciation rates the Kennedys might expect to experience over the next three to five years, and then discuss the options they might have, depending on their income and what happens in their local real estate market.

KNOW YOUR OWN MARKET

To help you with your own projections, it will be important for you to have an idea of the average rate of appreciation that's taken place in the area where you're considering buying. Keep in mind that housing markets tend to be local and reflect local conditions, such as new construction, the job market, growth restrictions, and other factors specific to an area.

If you've been dreaming and scheming of owning your own home, you probably already have a good idea of what's been happening to housing costs in your town. If you don't know, one of the best ways to find out is by contacting a local real estate agent—or contact several, and ask them at what rates property has been appreciating. Or get in touch with the Board of Realtors and ask to see the statistics from their multiple listing system.

You can also get this information from a local banker or loan officer, an accountant, or possibly an attorney who specializes in real estate transactions. (We'll talk more in Chapter 6 about setting up your team of professionals to help you with your equity-share purchase.) Read the real estate section of your local paper and talk to friends and acquaintances who've been selling or buying real estate to get a feel for what has been happening to property values in your area.

You should also begin developing a sense for what might happen to affect property values in the future. For example, you may find that home prices have remained fairly stable over the past few years, but now there's talk about a large company moving into the area, bringing in a lot of new employees. This could be good news: a basic economic factor affecting housing costs is supply and demand, and if you anticipate an influx of new workers, you know they'll have to find places to live. If the supply of housing is limited, an influx of buyers could cause a big jump in local housing costs.

On the other hand, if one of the major industries in your area is shutting down, and people will be leaving to find employment elsewhere, that could have an adverse effect on the price of housing. Learn to keep your eyes and ears open, and talk to anyone who can help you get a feel for your market.

In many parts of the country, property values have appreciated at an average annual rate of 15 percent over the past several years. These areas are, of course, excellent for equity-sharing arrangements. But we're going to show you how, thanks to leverage, equity sharing is still an excellent way to maximize the cash you have available and to get started owning your own home even in places where appreciation rates are only 8 percent.

UNDERSTANDING THE IMPORTANCE OF REFINANCING

There are basically two ways the owner-occupant can buy out the non-resident owners—through refinancing or through selling the property. As you'll see, one function of the Projections Worksheet is to help you calculate how much cash you would have available if you either refinanced or sold the property three to five or more years down the road or as soon as the equity build-up would allow. Before we get into the specifics of how that calculation works, we want you to understand why refinancing is such an important option in an equity-share purchase and, in many cases, a necessary one.

Remember that equity sharing is a means to an end, and while it is possible that you will be staying in the same house, it's almost certain that you won't be holding on to the same mortgage. So you need to keep an open mind about refinancing.

Most home buyers tend to approach financing their home as something they do once or twice in their lifetime, or only when they sell their house to buy another one. And until the last ten years or so, before the housing market changed so dramatically, having a fixed-rate mortgage which you held on to for years and years often made good sense—especially if you had a low fixed-rate and interest rates were rising.

But as we know, the market *has* changed: not only are interest rates much more volatile today than they have been in the past forty years, but now, as we discussed in Chapter 1, there are variable-rate mortgages that move up and down with market rates. So it often happens that a homeowner is locked into a 10 percent fixed-rate mortgage when variable-rate loans are at 7 percent. If it seemed to you that the economy was going to remain fairly steady for the next few years, it might make sense to refinance that 10 percent fixed-rate loan and get a 7 percent variable-rate mortgage, especially if you knew you were going to be selling the property in a couple of years anyway. Remember, from our discussion of fixed-rate versus variable-rate loans, how in many instances you're ahead of the game with a variable-rate.

We'll show you in detail the different ways refinancing can work as we go through the Projections Worksheet. Just bear in mind that you need to be able to compare the option of refinancing with the option of selling, and that's one thing the Projections Worksheet will help you to do.

When you first purchased the property, you'll recall that your lender was willing to loan you 80 percent of its value. On a refinance, most lenders will finance only 75 percent of the appraised value. This is referred to as the **loan-to-value (LTV) ratio**.

We want to share the refinancing experiences of a friend of ours to give you an idea of how refinancing can work for you.

A REFINANCE JUNKIE

In 1981 our friend Susan Camara moved with her three young sons to southern California. She had some cash from a recent divorce settlement and wanted to buy a home. She found a property she liked for $170,000, but the only mortgage she could get on it was an 18.5 percent fixed-rate with a five-year **balloon payment**, which meant that the entire mortgage would have to be paid off in five years.

The thought of locking into a fixed rate of 18.5 percent was terrifying enough, but the idea of having to come up with the money to pay off the entire mortgage in just five years was almost more than she could bear. Fortunately for Susan, her father was involved in the real estate industry and assured her that interest rates would be back down in a couple of years. He urged her to go ahead and buy, with the idea of refinancing when rates came down. It was only after he promised to buy the property from her if she were unable to refinance that she took the leap and bought the house.

Sure enough, in 1983, fixed-rates were down to 12.5 percent, and she refinanced the property with a 30-year loan, lowered her monthly payment, and took out some cash to refurbish the house with new carpets, drapes, and a new coat of paint.

Four years later, in 1987, she refinanced a second time, lowering her interest rate to an 8.5 percent variable. Again she took out some cash, this time to become an equity share investor.

This year, now that her variable-rate loan is up to 10.8 percent, she plans to refinance yet again, this time with an 8 percent variable-rate loan. She wants to pull out $37,500 and purchase two more equity-share properties. For the first time she'll be increasing her monthly payment, but her income is sufficient to carry it. She still has 36 percent equity in her home and all the cash she has pulled out has been tax-free.

Table 3-A shows a breakdown of Susan's refinancing numbers. Take a few moments to study the breakdown so you can see how Susan was able to continue to lower her monthly payment—except for the 1989 refinance—while at the same time maximizing the equity she has in the property.

Unless you're in an area of exceptionally high appreciation, you probably won't be refinancing as frequently as Susan has, but we want you to be aware of how refinancing can work and be prepared to take advantage of this option if the opportunity is there.

TABLE 3-A

Breakdown of refinancing numbers for Susan Camara from 1981 through 1989

	Purchase	*First Refinance*	*Second Refinance*	*Third Refinance*
Property Value	$170,000	$240,000	$320,000	$389,000
New Loan	136,000	166,000	205,000	250,000
Interest Rate	18.5% F	12.5% F	8.5% V	8% V
LTV Ratio	80%	69%	64%	64%
Less Old Loan		136,000	166,000	205,000
Gross Proceeds		30,000	39,000	45,000
Refinance Costs		5,000±	6,000±	7,500±
Net Proceeds		25,000	33,000	37,500
Monthly Payment	2,105	1,772	1,576	1,834
Year	1981	1983	1987	1989

(F = Fixed-rate; V = Variable-rate)

IMPORTANT CAVEAT

You'll notice that Susan's refinancing funds were used to enhance the value of her property (the new carpet and paint) or to purchase new appreciating assets (real estate). She never spent her refinance funds on consumer goods that lose their value as soon as the sale is rung up.

Once you put your assets to work in real estate, you will be amazed at how quickly your equity can start to build up. If you've never had access to a large sum of money before, it can be quite a heady experience to refinance and suddenly find you've got $20,000 in the bank, tax free. We want you to realize that the temptation to start spending it can be great. Just think of all the things you've been wanting to have—a new car, a new boat, possibly a trip to the Caribbean. You name it, the list is endless. But one thing you absolutely cannot do is allow yourself to use that money for anything other than real estate. The equity you're building in your shared-equity property will one day become your dream house. Once you start spending it, it'll be gone before you know it.

ONWARD AND UPWARD

Let's take a look now at the Projections Worksheet in Figure 3-A. You see that it has four sections:

Section A provides, for easy reference, a recap of the basic information about the property—including the price, the amount of the loan, and the down payment and percentage of ownership of both the owner-occupant and the non-resident owner.

Section B provides space for calculating four different rates of appreciation over various time periods, so you can see, for example, what would happen if that big company does move into town. Or what might happen if it moves out. You can also compare the difference between, say, 8 percent and 12 percent appreciation in your housing market, to see what effect a four-percentage-point increase would have on the value of your property.

The amounts in Section B are compounded yearly, so that if you were assuming an appreciation rate of 8 percent on a $200,000 purchase price, the figure in the left-hand column for Year 1 would be $216,000 ($200,000 x 1.08%); for Year 2, the figure would be $233,280 ($216,000 x 1.08); the figure for Year 3 would be $251,942 ($233,280 x 1.08), and so on. Of course, these figures are estimates, and the market price you use for refinancing (or for sales, if you were to sell the property) would be rounded up or down to the closest market price. So, $251,942 might become $250,000, or possibly $252,000, or maybe even $249,000.

We want to emphasize that the appreciation rates you'll be using at the tops of the columns in Section B are *average* rates over a long term—some years the appreciation will be higher than, say, 8 percent and some years lower. Maybe there will be a year or two when the value of the property in your area doesn't change at all. Real estate markets tend to be cyclical, and you'll need to develop a sense of where you are in the cycle in order for the averages to have any real validity.

Once you've got a feel for your market and for where you are in the cycle, you'll most likely need to use only one to two rates of appreciation to get an accurate projection of how the property's value might grow.

The rates in our Best Guess column are just that —our best guess as

FIGURE 3-A

EQUITY-SHARE PROJECTIONS WORKSHEET

A. PURCHASE INFORMATION:

(O.O.) ______	(N.O.) ______
O.O. Contribution $______	% Ownership ______
N.O. Contribution $______	% Ownership ______
Purchase Price $______	Loan Amount $______

B. VALUE OF PROPERTY OVER TEN-YEAR PERIOD AT FOUR RATES OF APPRECIATION

	___ %	___ %	___ %	Best Guess	
Year 1	______	______	______	______	___ %
Year 2	______	______	______	______	___ %
Year 3	______	______	______	______	___ %
Year 4	______	______	______	______	___ %
Year 5	______	______	______	______	___ %
Year 6	______	______	______		
Year 7	______	______	______		
Year 8	______	______	______		
Year 9	______	______	______		
Year 10	______	______	______		

C. OPTION #1: REFINANCE		D. OPTION #2: SELL	
1. Market Value	$______	18. Sales Price	$______
2. Times ___% LTV	× ___ %*	19. Less Sale Cost	× .93***
3. New Loan	$______	20. Gross Profit	$______
4. Less Old Loan	$ – ______	21. Less Old Loan	$ – ______
5. Gross Profit	$______	22. Net Profit	$______
6. Less Refi. Costs	$ – ______ **		
7. Net Profit	$______		
8. Less O.O. Contr.	$ – ______	23. Less O.O. Contr.	$ – ______
9. Less N.O. Contr.	$ – ______	24. Less N.O. Contr.	$ – ______
10. Net Cash Out	$______	25. Net Cash Out	$______
11. Times O.O.%	× ___ %	26. Times O.O.%	× ___ %
12. O.O. Cash Out	$______	27. O.O. Cash Out	$______
13. #10 × N.O.%	× ___ %	28. #26 × N.O.%	× ___ %
14. N.O. Cash Out	$______	29. N.O. Cash Out	$______
15. #8 + #12 = O.O. Total Cash Out	$______	30. #24 + #28 = O.O Total Cash Out	$______
16. #9 + #14 = N.O. Total Cash Out	$______	31. #25 + #30 = N.O. Total Cash Out	$______
17. New PITI	$______	32. New PITI	$______

*Figure 75% **Figure 2% of Sales Price ***Figure 7% of Sales Price

to what annual property values will do over the next few years, based on what we know to be happening in the local market. For example, the rate of appreciation for our area in 1988 was 19.5 percent. Because this area is in great demand *and* we have city and county no-growth plans and water moratoriums in effect that will limit the supply of housing for the foreseeable future, local economists and housing gurus are predicting the rate for our housing market will continue at around 15 to 20 percent for the next couple of years. But we know those rates can't go on indefinitely, so, if we were buying a property today, for our Best Guess we might use 20 percent for Years 1 and 2, then figure Years 3 and 4 would drop back to 15 percent and 12 percent, and Year 5 would possibly be 10 percent. On the other hand, if we knew that our market was going into a slump, those numbers would be much lower. Because the Best Guess appreciation rates will differ from year to year, we've left spaces for you to note the percentage of each annual estimated rate.

You'll notice that our Best Guess column goes only through the fifth year; this is basically a short-term forecast since it's difficult to "best guess" housing costs beyond four or five years with any real accuracy.

In the end, our Best Guess may or may not have any relation to what actually happens in the market, but it is a useful exercise and a challenge to see how good we are at predicting our housing market. We suggest you get into practice by using the Best Guess column, too. As you can see, the Best Guess rates mentioned above average a little over 16 percent (25 + 20 + 15 + 12 + 10 = 82 divided by 5 years = 16.4%). So in this case, the Best Guess rates over the five-year period average out about the same as what we *know* our rates have been over the long haul. But since timing is a very important factor in real estate, if you felt strongly that, based on local conditions, the appreciation rate was going to be high for the next couple of years, your plans for the holding period might be quite different than if you felt you were entering into a slower market-growth rate. Having a feel for how your market might react over the next few years will enable you to take much more effective advantage of the market cycles. When you come to the shared equity agreement, which we discuss in Chapter 5, you'll have a better idea of how to structure the holding period.

Section C shows you how to calculate the funds you will have available if you refinance.

To many people, refinancing seems almost like magic. One day all your assets are locked into your property—and the next day you've got cash in the bank. Let's go step by step through the refinancing process so you can see how it works.

Let's say you've done the appreciation calculations for Section B, and you want to figure out how much cash both the owner-occupant and the non-resident owner could get out by refinancing at one of the projected property values.

Take the "Property Value" figure you want to work with from Section B and plug it into Section C, Market Value (1). Multiply the Market Value by 75 percent (2) to get the New Loan amount (3). (Remember, most lenders today will refinance at only 75 percent loan-to-value ratio (LTV)—so the new loan can be no more than 75 percent of the value of the property.) Then deduct the Original Loan (4), since you have to pay off an existing loan when you take out the new one. That gives you the Gross Profit (5). Next, deduct the costs of refinancing (6)—usually about 2 percent of the sales price—to get the Net Profit (7). Now you deduct both the owner-occupant's down payment (not including closing costs) (8) and the non-resident owner's down payment (not including closing costs) (9), to get the total Net Cash (10) that you'll be sharing, based on your percentage of ownership. (Closing costs are considered a "cost of doing business" and are not calculated in the payback.)

The Net **Cash Out** (10) is multiplied by the occupant's percentage of ownership (11) to give you the owner-occupant's Cash Out (12) and then by the non-resident's percentage (13) to give you the Non-resident Owner's Cash Out (14). Each of those amounts (12) and (14) is added to each cash contribution—(8) and (9), respectively—to arrive at the total amount of cash each party will have when the proceeds are distributed, (15) for the occupant and (16) for the non-resident.

Finally, you'll want to calculate the monthly payment on the new loan (17). When we get into the actual numbers in the next part of this chapter you'll see that it's important to be able to determine how your monthly payment will be affected by refinancing. Often, by lowering your interest rate you can increase the mortgage amount, as our friend Susan did, while reducing your monthly payment.

Section D will enable you to determine what the consequences would be if you sold the property, so you can compare selling the property with refinancing it.

From the projected Sales Price (18) you deduct the Costs of the Sale (19). You can usually estimate that the real estate agent's fee will be about 6%, and add another 1% for closing costs and attorney or escrow fees; multiply the sales price by .93% (100% − 7%) to get the Gross Profit (20).

From this you deduct the original loan amount (21) to get the Net Profit (22). From this point on, the calculations are the same as in Section C: from the Net Profit you deduct the original down payment contribution of both the owner-occupant (23) and the non-resident owner (24) to get the Net Cash Out (25); then you add the cash out and the original contribution of each party to get the total cash available to each party.

If you sell the property in order to use the proceeds to purchase another property, you'll want to estimate what the replacement property would cost and calculate what the new monthly payment would be (32).

The Reality of the Market Versus Your Projections

The Projections Worksheet is designed to be used as a planning tool. The numbers are rough calculations and are used only to give you some idea of the options you would have under different appreciation scenarios. When you see how various appreciation rates would affect the value of the property, and when you learn to gauge where you are in your market cycle, you'll get a better feel for how you need to plan in order to maximize your ownership position. Will you be able to refinance or sell in three years, or should you plan for a longer holding period? Will the cash out from refinancing be sufficient to buy out the non-resident, or will you need to sell the property to do that? Will your salary increases be big enough to handle the increased PITI payments if you refinance? If you sell will the proceeds be enough to buy another property?

Also, keep in mind that figures such as Gross Profit and Cash Out do not include any of the principal reduction or tax savings. These numbers would, in some cases, greatly enhance your return, but for the estimating purposes of the Worksheet and to keep these calculations as simple as possible, they are not included here.

LET'S LOOK AT THE KENNEDYS' PROJECTIONS

When you study the Kennedys' Projections Worksheet, Figure 3-B, for a few minutes, you begin to see the tremendous number of options they have, once they've started to build up equity in their own home.

As you can see, we ran the numbers at 8 percent, 12 percent, 15 percent and at our variable "Best Guess." Notice that, at an average of 8 percent appreciation, they would have to hold the property for six years before it was in the $300,000 range, while at 12 percent they'd have to hold it for four years to be at $305,000. And at 15 percent, they'd have to hold the property for only three years to be at $298,000. At our "Best Guess" the property would take only two years to reach $298,000 (seems incredible, yet we've seen it happen!), but remember, you don't have to experience such high appreciation rates to benefit from equity sharing, as long as you know your options and are willing to be patient.

NOW LET'S LOOK AT THE POSSIBILITIES

Here are some of the options the Kennedys will have in three to five years with the property they purchased, depending on the market and their income at that time:

1. Refinance and partially buy out the non-resident owner, to gain 50 percent ownership.
2. Refinance and buy out the non-resident, to gain 100 percent ownership.
3. Refinance, stay in the first property, and purchase another equity share property as non-resident owners.
4. Refinance, keep the first property as an equity share arrangement, put in a new owner-occupant, and equity share another property as 25 to 50 percent owner-occupants.
5. Sell and buy a larger property as 25 percent owner.
6. Sell and buy a larger property as 50 percent owner.
7. Sell and buy in a less expensive area as 100 percent owner.

Let's look at each of these options in detail:

1. Refinance and buy out the non-resident to gain 50 percent ownership.

In the event that the rate of appreciation were to continue at 15 percent for three years, the property would have a market value of roughly $298,000. The cash proceeds after paying off the mortgage and the costs of refinancing are $61,540 (7). The total cash available after refinancing would be $15,385 (15) for the Kennedys and $46,155 (16) for Bea Hammer. Note that we've used $156,000 for the old loan

FIGURE 3-B

EQUITY-SHARE PROJECTIONS WORKSHEET

A. PURCHASE INFORMATION:

(O.O.) Kennedys — (N.O.) Hammer

O.O. Contribution $ 9,750 — % Ownership 25%

N.O. Contribution $ 29,250 — % Ownership 75%

Purchase Price $ 195,000 — Loan Amount $ 156,000

B. VALUE OF PROPERTY OVER TEN-YEAR PERIOD AT FOUR RATES OF APPRECIATION

	8 %	12 %	15 %	Best Guess	
Year 1	210,000	218,000	225,000	243,000	25 %
Year 2	227,500	244,000	258,000	298,000	20 %
Year 3	245,500	273,000	298,000	335,000	15 %
Year 4	265,000	305,000	340,000	370,000	10 %
Year 5	286,500	345,000	390,000	400,000	8 %
Year 6	310,000	385,000	450,000		
Year 7	334,000	430,000	519,000		
Year 8	360,000	482,000	595,000		
Year 9	389,000	540,000	685,000		
Year 10	420,000	605,000	875,000		

C. OPTION #1: REFINANCE

1. Market Value $ 298,000
2. Times 75 % LTV × 75 %*
3. New Loan $ 223,500
4. Less Old Loan $– 156,000±
5. Gross Profit $ 67,500
6. Less Refi. Costs $– 5,960**
7. Net Profit $ 61,540
8. Less O.O. Contr. $– 9,750
9. Less N.O. Contr. $– 29,250
10. Net Cash Out $ 22,540
11. Times O.O.% × 25 %
12. O.O. Cash Out $ 5,635
13. #10 × N.O.% × 75 %
14. N.O. Cash Out $ 16,905
15. #8 + #12 = O.O. Total Cash Out $ 15,385
16. #9 + #14 = N.O. Total Cash Out $ 46,155
17. New PITI $ 1,832

D. OPTION #2: SELL

18. Sales Price $ 298,000
19. Less Sale Cost × .93***
20. Gross Profit $ 277,140
21. Less Old Loan $– 156,000±
22. Net Profit $ 121,140
23. Less O.O. Contr. $– 9,750
24. Less N.O. Contr. $– 29,250
25. Net Cash Out $ 82,140
26. Times O.O.% × 25 %
27. O.O. Cash Out $ 20,535
28. #26 × N.O.% × 75 %
29. N.O. Cash Out $ 61,605
30. #24 + #28 = O.O Total Cash Out $ 30,285
31. #25 + #30 = N.O. Total Cash Out $ 90,855
32. New PITI $ 2,405

*Figure 75% **Figure 2% of Sales Price ***Figure 7% of Sales Price

amount (4), but remember that there will have been some principal paydown each year, so the actual payoff amount would be less than the original loan. In the case of a negative am loan, however, the payoff amount could be more than the original loan amount.

The equity in the property after refinancing is $74,500 ($298,000 less the new loan of $223,500 = $74,500). If the Kennedys wanted to acquire an additional 25 percent ownership to bring them up to a 50 percent position, they could pay Bea Hammer 25 percent of the net equity, or $18,625. The Kennedys' cash out after refinancing is $15,385 (15), so they would need to come up with approximately $3,300 from their savings. Then, with the parties in a 50/50 position, any appreciation from this point on would be shared equally.

Not only could refinancing at this point put the Kennedys in a 50 percent ownership position, but this could be an excellent way for the non-resident to go. She would get back her original investment of $29,250, plus her share of the proceeds from refinancing, which is $16,905, plus the $18,625 from the Kennedys for the 25 percent share she would be selling to them. The total cash to her would be $64,780, and she would then have a 50 percent equity position in an appreciating asset in which her original costs plus profits had been paid. She could either use the cash for whatever she wanted and pay taxes on her gain or, as we'll see in the next chapter, defer the tax on her gain into another property. (As we already know, however, if she's a wise purchaser, she'll continue to keep her investment fund growing in an appreciating asset—real estate.)

DON'T FORGET THE NEW MORTGAGE PAYMENT

Before we go any further, let's take a moment to see how the Kennedys' monthly payments would be affected by the new mortgage. Remember, their original loan was $156,000, and their starting PITI payment at 7.5 percent was $1,283. We are now at a point three to five years down the road. If the interest rate has increased by the maximum allowable 2 percent each year (remember, there's a 2 percent annual cap and a 5 percent lifetime cap on their variable-rate loan), after the end of the second year the PITI payment, at 11.5 percent, will be approximately $1,737. ($1,544.87 Principal and Interest, plus $192 Taxes and Insurance.)

It is possible that the starting rate on their new loan of $223,500 would be lower than the final rate on their old one—say 8 percent, which would make their new PITI payment $1,832, or only $95 more a month than their most recent payment. They would thus have increased their loan amount by $77,500 and increased their monthly payment by less than $100. Obviously, their ability to do this would depend on the level of interest rates at the time they refinanced and whether or not their (we hope) increased salary would enable them to meet the new monthly payments.

2. Refinance and buy out the non-resident owner to gain 100 percent ownership.

Using the same $298,000 market value, if we deduct the original loan of $156,000, we see that the equity is $142,000. When we deduct the Kennedy's original down payment contribution of $9,750 and Bea's original contribution of $29,250 we have a profit of $103,000. The Kennedys' 25 percent of that is $25,750; Bea's 75 percent is $77,250. So, to buy Bea out, the Kennedys need $106,500 (Bea's $29,250 contribution plus her profit of $77,250.)

If the Kennedys were to refinance at a 75 percent LTV, they would end up with $61,540 cash out (Line 7 on their Projections Worksheet.) This means they'd need an additional $44,960 in cash (106,500 – $61,540.)

However, since they are buying Bea out, the transaction could be considered a new purchase, and they could be able to get an 80 percent LTV loan. The numbers would look like this:

1.	Market Value	$298.000
2.	Times 80% LTV	×.80
3.	New Loan	$238,400
4.	Less Old Loan	–156,000
5.	Gross Profit	82,400
6.	Less Refi costs	–5,960
7.	Net Profit	$ 76,440

In this case, they would need only $30,060 in additional cash ($106,500–$76,440) for the buyout. We could assume that in the intervening three years they would have saved a portion of this—say $15,000—through their savings plan. This means they'd need only $15,060 more from another source, such as an inheritance or a bonus.

This would probably be a major stretch for most people, but in fact this exact scenario happened with one of our owner-occupants, who got a large commission check from a sales project he was working on and was thus able to buy out his non-resident owner. Without this infusion of cash, he would probably have had to wait a couple more years before he could buy the non-resident out completely.

3. Refinance, stay in the first property, and purchase another equity share property as a non-resident.

In addition to owning their own home, the Kennedys have the goal of starting to build a real estate portfolio. To do this they could stay in the first property, take the $15,385 cash from refinancing it and, perhaps with matching funds from what they had saved in the meantime, get into a 30 to 50 percent ownership position as non-resident owners in another equity-shared property. The strategy would work something like this: let's say the new property the Kennedys are considering has a price of $300,000; a 20 percent down payment would require $60,000. The Kennedys have $15,385 from refinancing, which is a little more than 25 percent of a $60,000 down payment. (Remember, they'd need to have funds to cover a portion of the closing costs on the new property, too.) Whatever additional cash they could add to that from their savings would increase their percentage of ownership accordingly. Or, if that were all the cash they wanted to put in at that point, we could, as we frequently do, place them with two or three other non-resident owners and an owner-occupant.

In another three years or so, the Kennedys might be able to refinance both properties and use those funds to completely buy out the non-resident in their first property. At the same time, they could retain their interest in the second property and, possibly with additional money from their continued savings, either increase their percentage of ownership in the second property or purchase a 25 percent position in a third property.

Take some time right now with your calculator and a worksheet to see how the numbers for these scenarios would break out. Obviously, any of these options would require a good appreciation rate or a longer holding time, plus additional funds, either from a savings plan (which we know the Kennedys are capable of maintaining), or from continued salary increases for both of them, or both.

But with proper planning and an understanding of the options, the Kennedys could realistically achieve any of these goals.

4. Refinance, keep the first property as non-resident owner with Bea Hammer, and purchase another equity shared property as an owner-occupant.

This option is similar in terms of the numbers to option 3, but it gives the Kennedys the chance to move into a property larger than the two-bedroom, one-and-a-half-bath condominium they started with. That first condo would then be rented out and, since it's unlikely that the rent would completely cover the Kennedys' monthly payment on the refinanced loan, they would, based on the terms of their agreement with Bea Hammer, need to find money to pay for the additional amount of that monthly payment. There's a reasonable chance that their incomes would have increased enough so they could take care of the additional expense and also cover the new payment on the new, larger property. Note that the first property would no longer be considered, for tax purposes, an equity share as defined by the Internal Revenue Code (IRC) Section 280(A)(d)(3) but, rather, a rental property, and Bea Hammer and the Kennedys would be considered investors.

Also, the Kennedys would be responsible for the tenant management and upkeep of the first property. Assuming that Bea Hammer wanted to stay in the first property, she would probably agree to such an arrangement. In fact, with the funds she receives from the refinancing of the first property, she would be a most likely candidate to back the Kennedys in their new larger home.

5. Sell and buy a larger property as 30 percent owner-occupants.

As you start talking to real estate purchasers, one comment you'll hear over and over again is that the biggest mistake they've made in their investment program was to sell a property—any property. If an owner wants to get some cash out of a property, in most instances it is far better to refinance and keep the property than to sell. By refinancing, not only do you get most of the cash you need and also get to keep the property, but, as we've said before, you don't have to pay taxes on the cash from the refinance. But if you sell the property, you lose a valuable leveraged asset, and both parties may incur a tax liability. As we'll see in the next chapter, though, the tax consequences of selling can be deferred to a later time.

At some point in your investment plan there may be no other way to accomplish your goals except by selling. Let's compare, for example, the total cash out for the Kennedys ($15,385) if they refinance at $298,000, with their cash out ($30,285) if they sell at the same price. As you see, it's almost twice as much. Let's say the Kennedys had had a child or two in the years since they bought their first condo. Now, three to four years later, their two-bedroom unit is just too small for their growing family. They might decide to take their cash out from the sale and purchase a $350,000 house as 30 percent owners. The numbers would look like this:

$350,000	Purchase Price
×.20	Down
$70,000	Down Payment
+$10,500	Closing Costs
$80,500	Cash Required
×.30	Ownership
$24,150	Cash needed for 30% ownership

$280,000 new mortgage

The PITI payment on the new loan at 8 percent would be $2,405 monthly (33). ($2,055 Principal and Interest, plus $350 Taxes and Insurance.)

With the $30,285 from the sale of the condo, they could purchase their new house and have money left over for refurbishing. Or, for less than $350,000, they could possibly get into a larger house that would be a fixer-upper and use their savings for refurbishing it, to increase the value of the property while also increasing their ownership position by 10 or 15 percent through sweat equity, as the Jacksons did in Case History #4.

6. Sell and buy a larger property as 50 percent owners.

The circumstances here might be similar to option 5, except that by adding their savings to the cash out they could be able to get into a 50 percent or better ownership position in the larger property. The numbers might look like this:

$350,000	Purchase Price
×.20	Down
$70,000	Down Payment
+$10,500	Closing Costs
$80,500	Total Needed to Purchase
×.50	Ownership
$40,250	Cash needed from the Kennedys
−$30,285	Cash out from the Sale
$9,965	Additional Needed from Savings for 50% Ownership

7. *Sell and buy in a less expensive area as 100 percent owners.*

It could be that the Kennedys like their first home well enough but, because of a job change, the location has become inconvenient for them. Selling their first unit would enable them to own 100 percent of a home in a more convenient but perhaps not so expensive area. The numbers might look like this, with a 90 percent LTV:

$225,000	Purchase Price
×.10	Down
$22,500	Down Payment
+$6,000	Closing Costs
$28,500	Needed to Buy
−$30,285	From Sale of First Condo
$1,785	To go into Savings or for refurbishing

This option would depend on the Kennedys' ability at that time to qualify for 90 percent financing, which their salary increases in the intervening years would most likely enable them to do. This scenario has in fact happened to a number of our owner-occupants who were transferred or who took jobs in other, less expensive areas of the country. One was able to pull his equity out of his two-bedroom, one-and-a-half-bath condo and combine it with his savings to use as a down payment on a larger three-bedroom, two-bath house on an acre of land in the Northwest. The purchase price was $90,000, and when the down payment was subtracted he was left with a $67,500 mortgage.

In this case, he took a salary cut, but the reduced payment on his new mortgage, which is half of his previous mortgage, and the fact that he owns his new home on his own make it well worth his while.

All the options we've discussed here apply to any of the case histories discussed in Chapter 2, and, for that matter, to almost any equity-share arrangement you might be considering. And the variations and expansions on these options are practically endless. We hope you're starting to see that the possibilities, once you get started in equity sharing, are limited only by your imagination.

Every now and then we come across a client who has the ability to immediately grasp the full implications of the options we've discussed here. But for most of us, it takes time to develop a comfortable working understanding of these ideas. You may have to go through this chapter several times with calculator in hand and work out the numbers before you really feel comfortable with the possibilities. If that's what it takes, do it. Make as many copies of the worksheets as you need, and plug in the numbers for your own housing costs on a property in your area. Run through a dozen different appreciation rates and time periods. Also, just for fun, take a few moments to see what the Kennedys' total cash out would be if they'd had a 50 percent ownership position. How much more cash would they have needed going in? How much more cash would they have had when they refinanced at $298,000? If they sold at $298,000? Then do the same calculations for your own prospective purchase. We promise that the more you work with the numbers, the more fun they'll become.

Before long you'll find you won't even need the worksheets—you'll develop a feel for what differently priced homes would cost at different rates of appreciation for different time periods.

Here's another interesting projection for you to work through: if you continue to rent, what will it cost to buy a home in your area in three years? In five years? How much will you need for a 20 percent down payment in three years? In five years? You can see that if you purchase a home now with equity sharing you'll be in a much stronger position in two to three years, and much closer to 100 percent ownership of your own home, than if you wait.

In the next chapter we'll take a look at how Uncle Sam will help you own your own home.

·4·

Understanding the Tax Picture

In this chapter we'll be exploring the tax ramifications of real estate in general and equity sharing in particular. These are not complicated concepts, but if you aren't used to thinking in terms of the tax picture, you will want to pay close attention. Most investors already have a good idea of how their taxes are affected by their real estate holdings, but it's surprising how many homeowners do not. If you're a potential owner-occupant who is new to real estate, it will be to your benefit to develop a clear understanding not only of how your tax bill is reduced by home ownership, but how the non-resident owner's tax picture is affected as well.

We will be discussing three aspects of the tax picture. First, we'll look at how real estate ownership affects the annual tax return of both the owner-occupant and the non-resident owner. We'll talk about some terms you need to know and the records you'll need to keep to enable you to maximize your tax savings.

Second, we're going to discuss Section 280(A)(d)(3), the segment of the Tax Code that relates to equity sharing (commonly, and hereafter, referred to simply as *280A*). We'll show you how to use the Rent Calculation Worksheet to set up the documentation you'll need to meet the requirements of the Code.

Third, we'll see how IRC Section 1034 and IRC Section 1031 make it possible for the occupant and the non-resident to defer the tax on their gains when their property is sold.

HOW THE PROPERTY SHOULD BE HELD TO MAXIMIZE BENEFITS

Before we get into the tax picture itself, we want to talk about how the property should be held in order to maximize the benefits of equity sharing.

For our purposes in equity sharing, there are basically three forms of ownership that we need to consider: **Partnership, joint tenancy,** and **tenancy in common.** In most of our equity-sharing arrangements, ownership is structured as tenants-in-common. However, this is an area where it is especially important for you to get professional legal advice for your own circumstances.

Partnership

We frequently hear about equity-share purchases that are structured as partnerships, but we *strongly* advise against this arrangement. In the first place, in such a setup the property is owned by the partnership itself and the resident partner must pay rent to the partnership for the use of the property; consequently, he loses one of the major tax benefits of home ownership, interest deductibility—which, as we'll see in a bit, can be significant.

Secondly, this form of ownership requires the additional time and, if you use an accountant, the added expense of filing a K-1 tax return with the IRS each year. Third, each partner is liable for the acts of the others, within the scope of the partnership. So a partnership arrangement puts you in a vulnerable situation should your partner encounter serious financial difficulties.

But one of the most compelling reasons for avoiding partnerships in an equity-share purchase is that, as of this writing, most accountants agree that participants in an equity-share arrangement that is structured as a partnership cannot roll over their gain into a tax-deferred exchange when the property is sold. Therefore, the tax on any gain from a real estate partnership has to be paid within the same tax period.

Let's go back for a moment to the "sell" projections for the Kennedys in the last chapter. Since they are in a 43 percent tax bracket (federal and state combined), if they had to pay tax on their roughly $20,000 profit when they sold the property, the cash they'd have available for reinvestment would be reduced by close to $9,000 ($20,000 × .43). That's a lot of money to pay to Uncle Sam if they don't have to, and it would drastically reduce their options.

The ability to defer your gain to a later time gives you a tremendous advantage in your investment program. Unless your legal or tax adviser recommends a partnership for your particular circumstances, you should avoid this form of ownership for equity-share arrangements. In fact, we recommend that you delete the word *partnership* from your real estate vocabulary for the time being.

Joint Tenancy

As joint tenants, two or more persons have undivided shares with the right of survivorship: if one joint tenant dies, his or her interest passes to the surviving joint tenant(s) under the law. Unless you're in a 50 percent ownership position with a friend or family member whom you wish to inherit your percentage of ownership in the event of your death, we don't recommend joint-tenancy ownership.

Tenancy in Common

Our equity-share purchases are structured as tenancies in common for a number of reasons. First, tenants-in-common may hold unequal interests in a property: one party could own 25 percent, while the other owned 75 percent. As we've already seen, unequal ownership is a frequent occurrence in equity-share purchases.

Second, tenants-in-common can hold their interests in different manners: Mr. and Mrs. Owner-Occupant can hold them as community property (if you live in a community property state) or as joint tenants; Mr. Non-resident, as an unmarried man; Ms. Non-resident, as a single woman; Mrs. Newlywed Non-resident, as her sole and separate property; . . . and all of them, as tenants-in-common.

Third, in tenancy in common there are no "partner" liabilities. So, your ownership position can be better protected.

Fourth, as tenants-in-common both the occupant and the non-resident can take advantage of the tax-writeoff benefits of owning real estate: interest and property-tax deductions for the occupant and depreciation for the non-resident, based on their percentage of ownership (or, in the case of the occupant, greater than the percentage of ownership, as we'll see). We'll show you exactly how this works later in this chapter.

Fifth, and very important, all parties under tenancy-in-common ownership can defer the tax on their gain on the property when it is sold.

YOUR HOME, SWEET HOME, WILL SAVE YOU TAXES

Your home—whether you own it on your own or in an equity-share arrangement—will probably be one of the best tax shelters you'll ever have. Not only is the federal government willing to subsidize your mortgage payments in the form of tax writeoffs for the interest payments, but it'll also let you keep all of the profit when you sell, provided you purchase another home that costs at least as much as the one you sell.

To take the maximum advantage of the tax savings, it's important that you understand the difference between the principal and the interest on your mortgage payment, and that you understand **basis,** both of which we'll discuss in this chapter.

Uncle Sam's Subsidy: Understanding Principal Versus Interest

Remember in Chapter 1 we pointed out that the portion of the principal that gets paid off in the early years of your mortgage payments is minuscule. It's discouraging in one sense: here you are making these huge monthly payments, and only a small portion goes toward paying off the loan amount you owe. But, as we're about to see, it is good news in terms of tax savings.

Table 4-A below shows the breakdown over the years between payment of the principal, which is not deductible, and the interest, which *is,* on a $100,000 loan at 10 percent for 30 years. If you have a variable-rate mortgage, it is impossible to predict precisely what the payment will be from year to year, but this table will give you a general idea of the small amount that actually goes toward the principal in the early years. You will receive a statement from your lender at the end of each year showing the amount of your total annual mortgage payment that's deductible interest and the amount that has gone toward paying down the principal. This form should be kept in your tax file to verify the interest deduction you claim when you file your return.

As you can see from this example, in the first year $9,974.96 of the monthly principal and interest payment, or 95 percent, would be deductible as interest. Even in the fifteenth year (in the unlikely event that the mortgage is kept in place that long) close to 80 percent of the monthly mortgage payment is deductible.

TABLE 4-A

Breakdown of the principal and interest portions of the annual mortgage payment of a $100,000 loan at 10% for 30 years

Year	*Annual Payments*	*Principal*	*Interest*
1	$10,530.84	$ 555.88	$9,974.96
2	10,530.84	614.10	9,916.74
3	10,530.84	678.39	9,852.45
4	10,530.84	749.44	9,781.40
5	10,530.84	827.91	9,702.93
10	10,530.84	1,362.16	9,168.68
15	10,530.84	2,241.18	8,289.66
20	10,530.84	3,687.44	6,843.40
25	10,530.84	6,066.94	4,463.90
30	10,530.84	9,982.00	548.84

Home Ownership and the 1040 Long Form: Tax Savings for the Owner-Occupant

To show you what this deduction means to you in actual tax dollars saved, let's take a closer look at how being able to deduct your mortgage interest would affect your tax return.

If your taxable income is less than $50,000 and you've never owned a home before, you've probably had no deductions to itemize and you've probably been filling out Form 1040A, the "short form," when you've filed your tax returns. Once you own your own home, you'll be filing Form 1040, the "long form," to take advantage of the itemized deductions you can claim.

As we've already seen, the mortgage interest deduction alone on a $100,000 loan at 10 percent for 30 years is close to $10,000. That's twice the standard $5,000 deduction you get as a married couple filing jointly on the short form. And with the long form other expenses that you couldn't include on the short form become tax-saving writeoffs. These may include medical expenses, state and local income taxes, personal property taxes, automobile license fees, interest expenses, charitable contributions, casualty or theft losses, moving expenses, and job-related and other miscellaneous expenses.

So the mortgage interest deduction you can take—even if it is only a portion of an equity share purchase—is just the beginning of the tax benefits that come with owning your own home.

Let's compare the short-form tax return Tom and Margaret Kennedy filed before they bought their home (Figure 4-B. Form 1040A) with the long form they used the year they bought it (Figure 4-C. Form 1040, including Schedule A—Itemized Deductions). To simplify this exercise we're going to assume they owned the property as 100 percent owners for the entire year. (Later in this chapter we'll show you how to calculate your tax writeoff on your equity-sharing ownership.)

Remember, the Kennedys have a combined income of $46,000. They had $250 of taxable dividends for an adjusted gross income of $46,250.

Take a few moments to study the two tax returns. Using the short form, after the Kennedys take their standard deduction of $5,000 plus their personal exemption of $3,900, their taxable income is $37,350. The tax due on this amount is $6,640. (See "Married filing jointly" in the Tax Table in the Appendix.)

Now look at the long form (Figure 4-C. Form 1040, including Schedule A—Itemized Deductions). As property owners, in addition to their interest deduction of $11,957, the Kennedys also get to deduct another $6,652 in itemized deductions, which are shown on their Schedule A, including almost $2,000 in property taxes and $3,900 in **loan origination fees** (points), in addition to other expenses, for a total of $18,609 in itemized deductions. This brings their taxable income down to $23,741 and their tax bill down to $3,559, for a savings of $3,081 in taxes over what they would have paid, using the short form.

Because they were able to itemize deductions, their tax bill was less than half of what they would have had to pay had they not been able to itemize. (Note that the deduction for points on the loan is a one-time occurrence, but now that they've begun itemizing, they'll find many other expenses they'll be able to deduct throughout the years.)

We want to emphasize that we've included these sample tax returns for purposes of illustration only. Even as you read this, the tax laws are changing and the forms we've shown here may also be changing in whole or in part. The consensus among financial forecasters, however, is that while tax rates and other aspects of the tax law may be changing, the interest deduction for homeowners will probably not change in the foreseeable future. For that reason, we want you to understand in principle what the interest deduction means in terms of dollars in your pocket at the end of the tax year.

We hope that after reviewing these examples, you can begin to see the incredible difference home ownership can make to your income tax bill. And the figures we've shown here don't even include the

Form **1040A** | Department of the Treasury—Internal Revenue Service
U.S. Individual Income Tax Return (0) **1988**

OMB No. 1545-0085

Step 1 Label

Use IRS label. Otherwise, please print or type.

LABEL HERE

Your first name and initial (if joint return, also give spouse's name and initial) — Last name: *Tom and Margaret Kennedy*

Present home address (number, street, and apt. no.). (If you have a P.O. Box, see page 13 of the instructions.)

City, town or post office, state, and ZIP code

Your social security no.

Spouse's social security no.

For Privacy Act and Paperwork Reduction Act Notice, see page 3.

Presidential Election Campaign Fund

Do you want $1 to go to this fund? ☐ Yes ☐ No

If joint return, does your spouse want $1 to go to this fund? ☐ Yes ☐ No

Note: *Checking "Yes" will not change your tax or reduce your refund.*

Step 2 Check your filing status (Check only one)

1 ☐ Single (See if you can use Form 1040EZ.)

2 ☑ Married filing joint return (even if only one had income)

3 ☐ Married filing separate return. Enter spouse's social security number above and spouse's full name here.

4 ☐ Head of household (with qualifying person). (See page 15.) If the qualifying person is your child but not your dependent, enter this child's name here.

5 ☐ Qualifying widow(er) with dependent child (year spouse died ▶ 19____). (See page 16.)

Step 3 Figure your exemptions (See page 16 of instructions.)

6a ☑ **Yourself** If someone (such as your parent) can claim you as a dependent on his or her tax return, do not check box 6a. But be sure to check the box on line 15b on page 2.

6b ☑ **Spouse**

No. of boxes checked on 6a and 6b: 2

c Dependents: 1. Name (first, initial, and last name)	2. Check if under age 5	3. If age 5 or older, dependent's social security number	4. Relationship	5. No. of months lived in your home in 1988

No. of your children on 6c who:
- lived with you
- didn't live with you due to divorce or separation (see page 19)

No. of other dependents listed on 6c

If more than 7 dependents, see page 19.

Attach Copy B of Form(s) W-2 here.

d If your child didn't live with you but is claimed as your dependent under a pre-1985 agreement, check here ▶ ☐

e Total number of exemptions claimed.

Add numbers entered on lines above: 2

Step 4 Figure your total income

Attach check or money order here.

7	Wages, salaries, tips, etc. This should be shown in Box 10 of your W-2 form(s). (Attach Form(s) W-2.)	7	46,000
8a	**Taxable** interest income (see page 22). (If over $400, also complete and attach Schedule 1, Part II.)	8a	
b	**Tax-exempt** interest income (see page 23). (DO NOT include on line 8a.)	8b	
9	Dividends. (If over $400, also complete and attach Schedule 1, Part III.)	9	250
10	Unemployment compensation (insurance) from Form(s) 1099-G.	10	
11	Add lines 7, 8a, 9, and 10. Enter the total. This is your **total income.**	▶ 11	46,250

Step 5 Figure your adjusted gross income

12a	Your IRA deduction from applicable worksheet. Rules for IRAs begin on page 24.	12a	
b	Spouse's IRA deduction from applicable worksheet. Rules for IRAs begin on page 24.	12b	
c	Add lines 12a and 12b. Enter the total. These are your **total adjustments.**	12c	
13	Subtract line 12c from line 11. Enter the result. This is your **adjusted gross income.** (If this line is less than $18,576 and a child lived with you, see "Earned Income Credit" (line 23b) on page 34 of instructions.)	▶ 13	46,250

Form **1040A** (1988)

1988 **Form 1040A** Page 2

Step 6
Figure your standard deduction, exemption amount, and taxable income

14	Enter the amount from line 13.	14	46,250
15a	Check if: ☐ **You** were 65 or older ☐ Blind / ☐ **Spouse** was 65 or older ☐ Blind — **Enter number of boxes checked** ▶ 15a ☐		
b	If someone (such as your parent) can claim you as a dependent, check here . . . ▶15b ☐		
c	If you are married filing separately and your spouse files Form 1040 and itemizes deductions, see page 28 and check here . . . ▶15c ☐		
16	**Standard deduction.** See pages 28–29 for the amount to enter.	16	5,000
17	Subtract line 16 from line 14. Enter the result. (If line 16 is more than line 14, enter -0-.)	17	41,250
18	Multiply $1,950 by the total number of exemptions claimed on line 6e.	18	3,900
19	Subtract line 18 from line 17. Enter the result. (If line 18 is more than line 17, enter -0-.) This is your **taxable income.**	▶ 19	37,350

If You Want IRS To Figure Your Tax, See Page 29 of the Instructions.

Step 7
Figure your tax, credits, and payments (including advance EIC payments)

Caution: If you are under age 14 and have more than $1,000 of investment income, check here . . . ▶ ☐
Also see page 30 to see if you have to use Form 8615 to figure your tax.

20	Find the tax on the amount on line 19. Check if from: ☑ Tax Table (pages 37–42) or ☐ Form 8615	20	6,640
21	Credit for child and dependent care expenses. Complete and attach Schedule 1, Part I.	21	
22	Subtract line 21 from line 20. Enter the result. (If line 21 is more than line 20, enter -0-.) This is your **total tax.**	▶ 22	6,640
23a	Total Federal income tax withheld—from Box 9 of your W-2 form(s). (If any is from Form(s) 1099, check here ▶ ☐ .) 23a 9,200		
b	Earned income credit, from the worksheet on page 35 of the instructions. Also see page 34. 23b		
24	Add lines 23a and 23b. Enter the total. These are your **total payments.**	▶ 24	9,200

Step 8
Figure your refund or amount you owe

25	If line 24 is more than line 22, subtract line 22 from line 24. Enter the result. This is the **amount of your refund.**	25	2,560
26	If line 22 is more than line 24, subtract line 24 from line 22. Enter the result. This is the **amount you owe.** Attach check or money order for full amount payable to "Internal Revenue Service." Write your social security number, daytime phone number, and "1988 Form 1040A" on it.	26	

Step 9
Sign your return

Under penalties of perjury, I declare that I have examined this return and accompanying schedules and statements, and to the best of my knowledge and belief, they are true, correct, and complete. Declaration of preparer (other than the taxpayer) is based on all information of which the preparer has any knowledge.

Your signature X	Date	Your occupation
Spouse's signature (if joint return, both must sign) X	Date	Spouse's occupation

Paid preparer's use only

Preparer's signature X	Date	Preparer's social security no.
Firm's name (or yours if self-employed)		Employer identification no.
Address and ZIP code		Check if self-employed ☐

1988 **Schedule 1 (Form 1040A)** OMB No. 1545-0085

Name(s) as shown on Form 1040A. (Do not complete if shown on other side.) Your social security number

Part II **Interest income** (see page 22 of the instructions)

Complete this part and attach Schedule 1 to Form 1040A if you received over $400 in taxable interest. Even if you are not required to complete this part, you must report all interest on Form 1040A.

Note: *If you received a Form 1099-INT or Form 1099-OID from a brokerage firm, enter the firm's name and the total interest shown on that form.*

1 List name of payer	Amount
Paine Webber	$ 250
	$
	$
	$
	$
	$
	$
	$
	$
	$
	$
	$
	$
	$
	$
	$
	$
	$
	$

2 Add amounts on line 1. Enter the total here and on Form 1040A, line 8a. 2 250

Part III **Dividend income** (see page 23 of the instructions)

Complete this part and attach Schedule 1 to Form 1040A if you received over $400 in dividends. Even if you are not required to complete this part, you must report all taxable dividends on Form 1040A.

Note: *If you received a Form 1099-DIV from a brokerage firm, enter the firm's name and the total dividends shown on that form.*

1 List name of payer	Amount
	$
	$
	$
	$
	$
	$
	$
	$
	$
	$
	$
	$
	$
	$
	$
	$
	$
	$
	$

2 Add amounts on line 1. Enter the total here and on Form 1040A, line 9. 2

☆ U.S. GOVERNMENT PRINTING OFFICE: 1988-0-205-136 E.I. No.: 94-2249262

Form **1040** Department of the Treasury—Internal Revenue Service
U.S. Individual Income Tax Return **1988** (0)

For the year Jan.–Dec. 31, 1988, or other tax year beginning , 1988, ending , 19 OMB No. 1545-0074

Label

Use IRS label. Otherwise, please print or type.

LABEL HERE

Your first name and initial (if joint return, also give spouse's name and initial) Last name
TOM AND MARGARET KENNEDY

Present home address (number, street, and apt. no. or rural route). (If a P.O. Box, see page 6 of Instructions.)

City, town or post office, state, and ZIP code

Your social security number

Spouse's social security number

For Privacy Act and Paperwork Reduction Act Notice, see Instructions.

Presidential Election Campaign

Do you want $1 to go to this fund? Yes No
If joint return, does your spouse want $1 to go to this fund? Yes No
Note: *Checking "Yes" will not change your tax or reduce your refund.*

Filing Status

Check only one box.

1 [ ] Single
2 [ ] Married filing joint return (even if only one had income)
3 [X] Married filing separate return. Enter spouse's social security no. above and full name here.
4 [ ] Head of household (with qualifying person). (See page 7 of Instructions.) If the qualifying person is your child but not your dependent, enter child's name here.
5 [ ] Qualifying widow(er) with dependent child (year spouse died ▶ 19). (See page 7 of Instructions.)

Exemptions

(See Instructions on page 8.)

6a [✓] Yourself If someone (such as your parent) can claim you as a dependent, do not check box 6a. But be sure to check the box on line 33b on page 2.
b [✓] Spouse

No. of boxes checked on 6a and 6b: 2

c **Dependents:**

(1) Name (first, initial, and last name)	(2) Check if under age 5	(3) If age 5 or older, dependent's social security number	(4) Relationship	(5) No. of months lived in your home in 1988

If more than 6 dependents, see Instructions on page 8.

No. of your children on 6c who:
● lived with you
● didn't live with you due to divorce or separation
No. of other dependents listed on 6c

d If your child didn't live with you but is claimed as your dependent under a pre-1985 agreement, check here ▶ [ ]
e Total number of exemptions claimed

Add numbers entered on lines above ▶ 2

Income

Please attach Copy B of your Forms W-2, W-2G, and W-2P here.

If you do not have a W-2, see page 6 of Instructions.

Please attach check or money order here.

Line	Description		Amount
7	Wages, salaries, tips, etc. *(attach Form(s) W-2)*	7	46,250
8a	**Taxable** interest income *(also attach Schedule B if over $400)*	8a	
b	**Tax-exempt** interest income (see page 11). DON'T include on line 8a — 8b		
9	Dividend income *(also attach Schedule B if over $400)*	9	250
10	Taxable refunds of state and local income taxes, if any, from worksheet on page 11 of Instructions	10	
11	Alimony received	11	
12	Business income or (loss) *(attach Schedule C)*	12	
13	Capital gain or (loss) *(attach Schedule D)*	13	
14	Capital gain distributions not reported on line 13 (see page 11)	14	
15	Other gains or (losses) *(attach Form 4797)*	15	
16a	Total IRA distributions — 16a; 16b Taxable amount (see page 11)	16b	
17a	Total pensions and annuities — 17a; 17b Taxable amount (see page 12)	17b	
18	Rents, royalties, partnerships, estates, trusts, etc. *(attach Schedule E)*	18	
19	Farm income or (loss) *(attach Schedule F)*	19	
20	Unemployment compensation (insurance) (see page 13)	20	
21a	Social security benefits (see page 13) — 21a		
b	Taxable amount, if any, from the worksheet on page 13	21b	
22	Other income (list type and amount—see page 13)	22	
23	Add the amounts shown in the far right column for lines 7 through 22. This is your **total income** ▶	23	46,250

Adjustments to Income

(See Instructions on page 13.)

Line	Description		Amount
24	Reimbursed employee business expenses from Form 2106, line 13	24	
25a	Your IRA deduction, from applicable worksheet on page 14 or 15	25a	
b	Spouse's IRA deduction, from applicable worksheet on page 14 or 15	25b	
26	Self-employed health insurance deduction, from worksheet on page 15	26	
27	Keogh retirement plan and self-employed SEP deduction	27	
28	Penalty on early withdrawal of savings	28	
29	Alimony paid (recipient's last name and social security no.)	29	
30	Add lines 24 through 29. These are your **total adjustments** ▶	30	

Adjusted Gross Income

Line	Description		Amount
31	Subtract line 30 from line 23. This is your **adjusted gross income.** *If this line is less than $18,576 and a child lived with you, see "Earned Income Credit" (line 56) on page 19 of the Instructions. If you want IRS to figure your tax, see page 16 of the Instructions* ▶	31	46,250

Form 1040 (1988) Page 2

Section	Line	Description	Box	Amount
Tax Computation	32	Amount from line 31 (adjusted gross income)	32	46,250
	33a	Check if: ☐ **You** were 65 or older ☐ Blind; ☐ **Spouse** was 65 or older ☐ Blind. Add the number of boxes checked and enter the total here ▶	33a	
	b	If someone (such as your parent) can claim you as a dependent, check here ▶	33b ☐	
	c	If you are married filing a separate return and your spouse itemizes deductions, or you are a dual-status alien, see page 16 and check here ▶	33c ☐	
	34	Enter the **larger** of: • Your **standard deduction** (from page 17 of the Instructions), **OR** • Your **itemized deductions** (from Schedule A, line 26). If you itemize, attach Schedule A and check here ▶ ☐	34	18,609
	35	Subtract line 34 from line 32. Enter the result here	35	27,641
	36	Multiply $1,950 by the total number of exemptions claimed on line 6e	36	3,900
	37	**Taxable income.** Subtract line 36 from line 35. Enter the result (if less than zero, enter zero)	37	23,741
		Caution: If under age 14 and you have more than $1,000 of investment income, check here ▶ ☐ and see page 17 to see if you have to use Form 8615 to figure your tax.		
	38	Enter tax. Check if from: ☐ Tax Table, ☐ Tax Rate Schedules, or ☐ Form 8615	38	3,559
	39	Additional taxes (see page 17). Check if from: ☐ Form 4970 ☐ Form 4972	39	
	40	Add lines 38 and 39. Enter the total ▶	40	3,559
Credits (See Instructions on page 18.)	41	Credit for child and dependent care expenses *(attach Form 2441)*	41	
	42	Credit for the elderly or the disabled *(attach Schedule R)*	42	
	43	Foreign tax credit *(attach Form 1116)*	43	
	44	General business credit. Check if from: ☐ Form 3800 or ☐ Form (specify)	44	
	45	Credit for prior year minimum tax *(attach Form 8801)*	45	
	46	Add lines 41 through 45. Enter the total	46	
	47	Subtract line 46 from line 40. Enter the result (if less than zero, enter zero) ▶	47	3,559
Other Taxes (Including Advance EIC Payments)	48	Self-employment tax *(attach Schedule SE)*	48	
	49	Alternative minimum tax *(attach Form 6251)*	49	
	50	Recapture taxes (see page 18). Check if from: ☐ Form 4255 ☐ Form 8611	50	
	51	Social security tax on tip income not reported to employer *(attach Form 4137)*	51	
	52	Tax on an IRA or a qualified retirement plan *(attach Form 5329)*	52	
	53	Add lines 47 through 52. This is your **total tax** ▶	53	3,559
Payments Attach Forms W-2, W-2G, and W-2P to front.	54	Federal income tax withheld (If any is from Form(s) 1099, check ▶ ☐)	54	9,200
	55	1988 estimated tax payments and amount applied from 1987 return	55	
	56	Earned income credit (see page 19)	56	
	57	Amount paid with Form 4868 (extension request)	57	
	58	Excess social security tax and RRTA tax withheld (see page 20)	58	
	59	Credit for Federal tax on fuels *(attach Form 4136)*	59	
	60	Regulated investment company credit *(attach Form 2439)*	60	
	61	Add lines 54 through 60. These are your **total payments** ▶	61	9,200
Refund or Amount You Owe	62	If line 61 is larger than line 53, enter amount **OVERPAID** ▶	62	
	63	Amount of line 62 to be **REFUNDED TO YOU** ▶	63	5,641
	64	Amount of line 62 to be applied to your 1989 estimated tax ▶	64	Ø
	65	If line 53 is larger than line 61, enter **AMOUNT YOU OWE.** Attach check or money order for full amount payable to "Internal Revenue Service." Write your social security number, daytime phone number, and "1988 Form 1040" on it	65	
		Check ▶ ☐ if Form 2210 (2210F) is attached. See page 21. **Penalty:** $		

Please Sign Here

Under penalties of perjury, I declare that I have examined this return and accompanying schedules and statements, and to the best of my knowledge and belief, they are true, correct, and complete. Declaration of preparer (other than taxpayer) is based on all information of which preparer has any knowledge.

Your signature	Date	Your occupation
Spouse's signature (if joint return, BOTH must sign)	Date	Spouse's occupation

Paid Preparer's Use Only

Preparer's signature	Date	Check if self-employed ☐	Preparer's social security no.
Firm's name (or yours if self-employed) and address		E.I. No.	
		ZIP code	

SCHEDULES A&B (Form 1040)
Department of the Treasury Internal Revenue Service (0)

Schedule A—Itemized Deductions

(Schedule B is on back)

▶ **Attach to Form 1040.** ▶ **See Instructions for Schedules A and B (Form 1040).**

OMB No. 1545-0074
1988
Attachment Sequence No. **07**

Name(s) as shown on Form 1040 | Your social security number

Section	Line	Description	Box	Amount	Line	Total
Medical and Dental Expenses	1a	Prescription medicines and drugs, insulin, doctors, dentists, nurses, hospitals, medical insurance premiums you paid, etc.	1a			
(Do not include expenses reimbursed or paid by others.)	b	Other (list—include hearing aids, dentures, eyeglasses, transportation and lodging, etc.) ▶	1b			
(See Instructions on page 23.)	2	Add lines 1a and 1b, and enter the total here	2			
	3	Multiply the amount on Form 1040, line 32, by 7.5% (.075)	3			
	4	Subtract line 3 from line 2. If zero or less, enter -0-. **Total** medical and dental ▶			4	Ø
Taxes You Paid	5	State and local income taxes	5	240		
	6	Real estate taxes	6	1,944		
(See Instructions on page 23.)	7	Other taxes (list—include personal property taxes) ▶	7			
	8	Add the amounts on lines 5 through 7. Enter the total here. **Total** taxes ▶			8	2,184
Interest You Paid		**Note:** *New rules apply to the home mortgage interest deduction. See Instructions.*				
	9a	Deductible home mortgage interest you paid to financial institutions (report deductible points on line 10)	9a	11,957		
(See Instructions on page 24.)	b	Deductible home mortgage interest you paid to individuals (show that person's name and address) ▶	9b			
	10	Deductible points. (See Instructions for special rules.)	10	3,900		
	11	Deductible investment interest (see page 24)	11			
	12a	Personal interest you paid (see page 24) [12a]				
	b	Multiply the amount on line 12a by 40% (.40). Enter the result	12b			
	13	Add the amounts on lines 9a through 11, and 12b. Enter the total here. **Total** interest ▶			13	15,857
Gifts to Charity	14	Contributions by cash or check. (If you gave $3,000 or more to any one organization, show to whom you gave and how much you gave.) ▶	14	568		
(See Instructions on page 25.)	15	Other than cash or check. (You must attach Form 8283 if over $500.)	15			
	16	Carryover from prior year	16			
	17	Add the amounts on lines 14 through 16. Enter the total here. **Total** contributions ▶			17	568
Casualty and Theft Losses	18	Casualty or theft loss(es) (attach Form 4684). (See page 25 of the Instructions.) ▶			18	Ø
Moving Expenses	19	Moving expenses (attach Form 3903 or 3903F). (See page 26 of the Instructions.) ▶			19	Ø
Job Expenses and Most Other Miscellaneous Deductions	20	Unreimbursed employee expenses—job travel, union dues, job education, etc. (You MUST attach Form 2106 in some cases. See Instructions.) ▶	20			
(See page 26 for expenses to deduct here.)	21	Other expenses (investment, tax preparation, safe deposit box, etc.). List type and amount ▶	21			
	22	Add the amounts on lines 20 and 21. Enter the total.	22			
	23	Multiply the amount on Form 1040, line 32, by 2% (.02). Enter the result here	23			
	24	Subtract line 23 from line 22. Enter the result (if zero or less, enter zero) ▶			24	Ø
Other Miscellaneous Deductions	25	Other (from list on page 26 of Instructions). Enter type and amount ▶			25	Ø
Total Itemized Deductions	26	Add the amounts on lines 4, 8, 13, 17, 18, 19, 24, and 25. Enter the total here. Then enter on Form 1040, line 34, the LARGER of this total or your standard deduction from page 17 of the Instructions ▶			26	18,609

For Paperwork Reduction Act Notice, see Form 1040 Instructions.

Schedule A (Form 1040) 1988

Schedules A&B (Form 1040) 1988 — OMB No. 1545-0074 — Page 2

Name(s) as shown on Form 1040. (Do not enter name and social security number if shown on other side.) — Your social security number

Schedule B—Interest and Dividend Income

Attachment Sequence No. 08

Part I Interest Income

(See Instructions on pages 10 and 26.)

If you received more than $400 in taxable interest income, you must complete Part I and Part III and list ALL interest received. You must report all interest on Form 1040, even if you are not required to complete Part I and Part III. If you received, as a nominee, interest that actually belongs to another person, or you received or paid accrued interest on securities transferred between interest payment dates, see page 27.

Interest Income		Amount
1 Interest income from seller-financed mortgages. (See Instructions and list name of payer.) ▶	1	
2 Other interest income (list name of payer) ▶	2	
3 Add the amounts on lines 1 and 2. Enter the total here and on Form 1040, line 8a. ▶	3	

Note: If you received a Form 1099–INT or Form 1099–OID from a brokerage firm, list the firm's name as the payer and enter the total interest shown on that form.

Part II Dividend Income

(See Instructions on pages 11 and 27.)

If you received more than $400 in gross dividends and/or other distributions on stock, complete Part II and Part III. You must report all taxable dividends on Form 1040, even if you are not required to complete Part II and Part III. If you received, as a nominee, dividends that actually belong to another person, see page 27.

Dividend Income			Amount
4 Dividend income (list name of payer—include on this line capital gain distributions, nontaxable distributions, etc.) ▶ Paine Webber		4	250
5 Add the amounts on line 4. Enter the total here		5	
6 Capital gain distributions. Enter here and on line 13, Schedule D.*	6		
7 Nontaxable distributions. (See Schedule D Instructions for adjustment to basis.)	7		
8 Add the amounts on lines 6 and 7. Enter the total here		8	
9 Subtract line 8 from line 5. Enter the result here and on Form 1040, line 9 ▶		9	250

Note: If you received a Form 1099-DIV from a brokerage firm, list the firm's name as the payer and enter the total dividends shown on that form.

**If you received capital gain distributions but do not need Schedule D to report any other gains or losses, enter your capital gain distributions on Form 1040, line 14.*

Part III Foreign Accounts and Foreign Trusts

(See Instructions on page 27.)

If you received more than $400 of interest or dividends, OR if you had a foreign account or were a grantor of, or a transferor to, a foreign trust, you must answer both questions in Part III.

	Yes	No
10 At any time during the tax year, did you have an interest in or a signature or other authority over a financial account in a foreign country (such as a bank account, securities account, or other financial account)? (See page 27 of the Instructions for exceptions and filing requirements for Form TD F 90-22.1.)		
If "Yes," enter the name of the foreign country ▶		
11 Were you the grantor of, or transferor to, a foreign trust which existed during the current tax year, whether or not you have any beneficial interest in it? If "Yes," you may have to file Form 3520, 3520-A, or 926		

For Paperwork Reduction Act Notice, see Form 1040 Instructions. — **Schedule B (Form 1040) 1988**

savings in state taxes—which, in California, can save you up to another 9 percent. (If you don't know what your state tax rate is you can contact your state's taxing authority.)

Tax Savings for the Non-resident Owner

As you know from our discussion of depreciation in Chapter 1, Bea Hammer, the Kennedys' non-resident owner, can depreciate the property over 27.5 years. Assuming the building is 85 percent of the value of the property, the amount that can be depreciated is $165,750 ($195,000 × .85). (We're using 85 percent for the value of the building, but remember that a tax adviser should be consulted when setting up a depreciation schedule.) Since Bea Hammer is a 75 percent owner, most accountants agree she would be able to take 75 percent of the depreciation, so that the amount she can depreciate is $124,312 ($165,750 × .75). This gives her an annual depreciation of $4,520 ($124,312 divided by 27.5 years). In her current federal and state tax bracket of 43 percent, this can, depending on her income, save her $1,944 a year in taxes ($4,520 × .43).

The calculation for the depreciation writeoff for Bea Hammer's 75 percent ownership looks something like this:

$195,000	Condo purchase price
– $29,250	Less the value of the land
$165,750	Amount that can be depreciated
×.75	Times Bea's percentage of ownership
$124,312	Amount Bea can depreciate
	Divided by 27.5 years equals:
$4,520	Annual depreciation writeoff
×.43	Times total federal and state tax rate
$1,944	Estimated annual tax savings, depending on income

It has always been true that one should not invest in real estate solely for its tax benefits, and that truth has been reinforced since the new IRS regulations reduced the tax writeoff for investors. Prior to the 1986 Tax Law, any amount of loss (including depreciation) could be written off against ordinary income.

Now an investor can deduct only $25,000 of rental losses (including depreciation) against up to $100,000 of other income. An investor who earns from $100,000 up to $150,000 gets only 50 cents of tax benefit for every dollar of tax loss. On incomes over $150,000, there is now no immediate tax benefit from real estate losses. (However, a loss can be carried forward and "runs with the property," so that when the property is sold, the loss can be written off against any gain.)

To qualify for these tax benefits, investors must "actively participate" in the management of their property. Though the law is vague on this point, it means that while investors don't have to fix leaky roofs themselves, they should be involved in approval of the tenants, in setting rents, and in approving capital expenditures. Non-resident owners in an equity-share arrangement structured the way we outline are automatically so involved.

Also, you should know that depreciation is only a temporary writeoff. When the property is sold the depreciation taken during the period of ownership is added back, or "recaptured," and thereby increases the taxable gain on the property.

It is vital that you keep in mind that the tax laws are constantly changing. For this reason, and because you may have special circumstances that should be taken into account, you should consult a tax adviser before you make any investment that will affect your tax picture.

Record-keeping and Keeping Track of Your Basis

Once you own your own home there is another term you'll need to add to your real estate vocabulary: Basis.

Basis is, quite simply, the home's value for tax purposes. It is the figure that you'll compare to the amount you get when you sell your home, so you can determine what your taxable gain is. It's important to keep track of your basis as you move from one property to another.

The record-keeping for your basis starts with what you pay for the property, plus certain components of the closing costs, some of which are considered expenses that you can deduct from your income, and some of which are part of the cost of acquiring the house and are therefore included in the basis. If you have an accountant prepare your tax returns, he will be able to determine from your closing statement which amounts will add to your basis and which are deductions.

If you complete your own return, you should know that, as a general rule, points, prepaid interest, and prepaid taxes are deductible items and don't add to the basis. In an equity-share purchase, the owner-occupants usually pay the prepaid property taxes and interest and a portion of the points and, therefore, most accountants agree, get to deduct them in the year they are paid, though this is not specifically spelled out in the tax law. The non-resident owners may also deduct the points they pay, but they are written off over the life of the loan.

Other closing costs are usually not deductible and are added to the purchase price to increase the basis. These may include attorney fees, escrow fees, recording fees, transfer taxes, property inspection fees, title insurance premiums, and many other fees connected with the purchase of the property. Be sure to keep copies of your closing statements so you or your accountant can accurately determine your basis.

You'll also want to have copies of your property tax bill, along with bills for any other taxes you pay, as well as copies of the annual mortgage statement provided by your lender showing how much interest you've paid for the year. Since it is your basis that is used to calculate your gain when you sell the property, we'll talk more specifically about basis calculations when we get to our discussion of tax-deferred exchanges later in this chapter.

Improvements and Repairs

For tax purposes any work you do on the house is divided between what are considered *repairs* and what are considered *improvements* that increase the value of the property. Repairs are non-deductible expenses for the owner-occupants; non-resident owners, however, can write off repairs to the extent they pay for them. The cost for improvements is non-deductible to either party, but those costs add to your basis and ultimately will save on your tax bill. Fixing a leak in the roof or replacing a broken doorknob would be considered repairs; a room addition, kitchen or bath renovation, landscaping, or a patio construction would be considered improvements.

Remember the Browns, in Case History #4, who planned to make major improvements to their property to increase its value? After a predetermined amount was contributed to the renovation, additional costs were shared by the owner-occupants and the non-resident owners according to their percentages of ownership. Neither party was able to deduct these expenses, but they are added to each one's basis and will eventually reduce their taxable gains.

You should plan to keep copies of all receipts for items that would qualify as improvements. Set up an "improvements" file and keep it updated annually during the time you own the property, so that when it comes time to sell, you'll have the documentation you need to adjust your basis accordingly.

THE TAX CODE AND EQUITY SHARING

Now let's talk about the portion of the Internal Revenue Code that relates specifically to equity sharing. Section 280A was established by Congress to make sure that fair rent was charged in an equity-share arrangement, especially between family members. The IRS doesn't want parents who buy a home for their children to charge them a ridiculously low rent, then claim as tax deductions not only the depreciation but also the huge losses that would result from the low rent.

Section 280A is vague and provides no definitive guidelines on equity sharing. There have been no court cases, few rulings, and no specific regulations that deal with equity sharing. As time goes on and equity sharing becomes more and more popular, specific guidelines will no doubt be established in the Tax Code. In the meantime, Section 280A is all there is.

Prior to starting our equity-sharing program, therefore, we met with dozens of accountants, attorneys, and tax advisers (including a former IRS agent) who had had experience with equity sharing. The methods we use in structuring our equity-sharing purchases are based on the advice of these professionals and their understanding of the tax law.

Section 280A is reprinted below for your information. You might want to read it through. As you'll see in the next chapter, we include the text of 280A as part of our shared-equity agreement to make certain all parties have read it and, to the extent possible, understand it.

CODE 280A(d)(3)

(3)Rental to Family member, etc., for use as principal residence.—

(A) In general.—A taxpayer shall not be treated as using a dwelling unit for personal purposes by reason of a rental arrangement for any period if for such period such dwelling unit is rented, at a fair rental, to any person for use as such person's principal residence.

(B) Special rules for rental to person having interest in unit.—

(i) Rental must be pursuant to shared equity financing agreement.—Subparagraph (A) shall apply to a rental to a person who has an interest in the dwelling unit only if such rental is pursuant to a shared equity financing agreement.

(ii) Determination of fair rental. In the case of a rental pursuant to a shared equity financing agreement, fair rental shall be determined as of the time the agreement is entered into and by taking into account the occupant's qualified ownership interest.

(C) Shared Equity Financing Agreement.—For the purpose of this paragraph, the term "shared equity financing agreement" means an agreement under which

(i) 2 or more persons acquire qualified ownership interests in a dwelling unit, and

(ii) the person (or persons) holding one (1) or more of such interests

(I) is entitled to occupy the dwelling unit for use as a personal residence, and

(II) is required to pay rent to one (1) or more other persons holding qualified ownership interests in the dwelling unit.

(D) Qualified Ownership Interest.—For the purposes of this paragraph, the term "qualified ownership interest" means an undivided interest for more than 50 years in the entire dwelling unit and appurtenant land being acquired in the transaction to which the shared equity financing agreement relates.

There are two things to note concerning Section 280A. First, in order to be assured of getting the appropriate tax benefits, your equity-share purchase must be "pursuant to a shared equity financing agreement." Don't worry about the term "financing"—the agreement has nothing to do with financing. (This is a perfect example of the confusing terminology found in the Tax Code.) In the next chapter, we're going to show you how to put your shared-equity agreement together.

Second, you'll note that the owner-occupant is required to pay rent to the non-resident owner for use of the portion of the property that the non-resident owns. This does not mean that an additional rent is paid to the non-resident over and above the monthly payment the occupant is responsible for. Rather, what happens is that a portion of the mortgage payment is paid as rent to the non-resident. The non-resident then makes his payment to the lender, based on his percentage of ownership.

Keep in mind that the biggest tax advantage for the owner-occupant is the interest deduction. Also—though it is not specifically stated in the tax law—most accountants agree that if the occupant pays the property taxes he can deduct them. However, an owner-occupant cannot deduct his insurance expense nor, if the property is a condo, the monthly association dues.

The only tax benefit to the non-resident owner is the depreciation for his percentage of ownership. (And, if the property is a condo, the non-resident does get to write off his percentage of the monthly association dues against the rent.) Since the owner-occupant is the only one who gets tax benefits from the monthly payment, we want to structure that payment so that he gets the maximum tax benefit possible within the law.

In an equity-share arrangement, any amount of the monthly payment that is paid as rent cannot be deducted as interest by the owner-occupant on his tax return. Therefore, to maximize the owner-occupant's tax writeoff, we want, within reason, to keep this rent payment as low as possible.

Because we know an owner-occupant will make his payments on time and will be taking good care of the property, we can justify a reduction in the rent. Landlords do this all the time to keep good tenants. What we have to avoid is the type of ridiculously low rent that Section 280A is intended to prevent. Our advisers agree that a rent 10 percent below the market rate is fair for a responsible occupant.

To see how this works, let's look at Jack Haley's equity-share arrangement with the Schifflers. The fair market rent on Jack's property is $900 a month. With his good-tenant discount, we could reasonably say that $810 would be a fair rent ($900 less 10 percent). Because the Schifflers own 50 percent of the property, the rent Jack would pay them would be half of that, or $405 a month ($810 × .50).

Jack's monthly mortgage payment is $1,062. When we deduct the $405 rent from Jack's monthly payment of $1,062, that leaves approximately $657 as his interest writeoff. (Bear in mind that a portion of his monthly payment goes toward the principal, but to keep this example as simple as possible, we've not shown it here.) This writeoff gives Jack an annual interest deduction of approximately $7,884 ($657 × 12 months). In his 33 percent tax bracket, this deduction could save him close to $2,602 a year in taxes ($7,884 × .33). Without the good-tenant rent reduction, his interest writeoff would be only $7,344 ($1,062 − $450 = $612 × 12 months), and his tax savings would be $2,424. By being able to take advantage of the rent reduction for a responsible occupant, Jack adds another $540 to his writeoff, which means roughly another $178 in tax savings ($540 × .33).

Also, you can see that even though Jack is a 50 percent owner, he actually gets to write off a disproportionate amount—62 percent—of the interest payment on his Schedule A ($657 divided by $1062). But his total writeoff is actually higher than 62 percent.

Remember from our discussion of the 1040 long form that interest is only one of the tax deductions Jack gets to take now that he's a homeowner. In addition to 62 percent of the interest writeoff, he also gets to deduct 100 percent of the property taxes he pays, plus, if applicable, any of the other Schedule A expenses we discussed earlier. If we assume a minimum of $5,000 in additional Schedule A writeoffs—not counting the one-time loan origination fee (points)—the total of the deductions Jack can take as an owner-occupant is approximately $14,000. In his tax bracket this could mean a savings of $4,620 in taxes for the year ($14,000 × .33).

Thus, home ownership actually saves him $385 a month in taxes the first year ($4,620 divided by 12 months). Even though his total payment, including taxes, insurance, and condo association fees, is $1,422 a month, after taxes it drops to $1,037 a month ($1,422 − $385). What this boils down to is that Jack is paying only $137 a month more to own his own home than it would cost him to rent, and he has 50 percent ownership in a highly leveraged, appreciating asset.

RENT CALCULATION WORKSHEET

Now we want to show you how the monthly payment is structured. In order to satisfy the rent requirement of the tax code, all our equity-share arrangements are set up so that the fair market rent is established before the close of escrow, and the rent the owner-occupant will pay for the non-resident owner's portion of the property, including the good-tenant discount, is written into the shared equity agreement.

Documentation is set up so that the parties can verify that the rent was actually paid and that their equity-share arrangement complies with the requirements of 280A. To simplify this documentation process, we devised the Rent Calculation Worksheet shown in Figure 4-D, Rent Calculation Worksheet—For Single Family Home. The documentation process works like this:

At the first of each month when the mortgage payment and rent are due, the owner-occupant writes two checks. One, Check A, is made payable to the non-resident owner to cover the agreed-upon rent for the non-resident's portion of the property. The second, Check B, is made payable to the lender and consists of the principal and interest payment, less the rent check (A). Both these checks are sent to the non-resident, who in turn deposits the rent check and makes out his own check (Check C) payable to the lender in the same amount as the rent. The non-resident then sends both checks to the lender.

What this monthly exercise does is establish what accountants call an "audit trail," sometimes referred to as a "paper trail." The purpose of the audit trail is to be able to show, in the event of an audit, that the parties have consistently, on a month-to-month basis, adhered to the terms of their Shared Equity Financing Agreement.

Note that when you establish the rent a landlord would charge to a responsible tenant, it's a good idea to support your calculations with ads from the local newspaper showing that comparable units are in fact renting for approximately that amount. By doing so you could show, in the event of a tax audit, that your rent schedule was reasonable. If you fail to establish that the rent is reasonable, the IRS could disallow the entire equity-share arrangement, which could mean loss of tax benefits to both parties.

Figure 4-E shows a completed Rent Calculation Worksheet. For this example we're using Jack Haley's numbers as though they were for a single-family home. In the next section we'll show how the numbers work for a condominium.

Rent Calculation Worksheet—For Condominium

In many parts of the country, condominiums are very popular with first-time buyers because they provide newer construction with more amenities for less than the cost of a single-family home. For this reason

FIGURE 4-D

RENT CALCULATION WORKSHEET—FOR SINGLE FAMILY HOME

Owner-Occupant(s) (O.O.) ________________ % Ownership ____

Non-resident Owner(s) (N.O.) ________________ % Ownership ____

________________ % Ownership ____

Property Address: ________________

Principal & Interest (Paid by O.O.) $________

Fair Market Rent: $________

Less Good-Tenant Discount $–________

RENT: $________

Times N.O. % Ownership: × ________ %

RENT PAID TO N.O.: $________

CHECKS WRITTEN BY OWNER-OCCUPANT, SENT TO NON-RESIDENT OWNER:

A. RENT (Payable to Non-resident Owner) Check A $________

B. PRINCIPAL & INTEREST PAYMENT, LESS RENT(Check A) (Payable to Lender) Check B $________

TOTAL PAID BY OWNER-OCCUPANT: $________

CHECK WRITTEN BY NON-RESIDENT OWNER FROM RENT RECEIVED, SENT TO LENDER:

C. MORTGAGE PAYMENT in the amount of the RENT (Check A) (Payable to Lender) Check C $________

TOTAL PAID BY NON-RESIDENT OWNER (Check C) $________

LESS TOTAL RENT RECEIVED BY NON-RESIDENT OWNER (Check A) $–________

0

FIGURE 4-E

RENT CALCULATION WORKSHEET—FOR SINGLE FAMILY HOME

Owner-Occupant(s) (O.O.) Jack Haley % Ownership 50

Non-resident Owner(s) (N.O.) The Schifflers % Ownership 50

% Ownership ____

Property Address: ____

Principal & Interest (Paid by O.O.) $ 1,062

Fair Market Rent: $ 900

Less Good-Tenant Discount $– 90

RENT: $ 810

Times N.O. % Ownership: × 50 %

RENT PAID TO N.O.: $ 405

CHECKS WRITTEN BY OWNER-OCCUPANT, SENT TO NON-RESIDENT OWNER:

A. RENT (Payable to Non-resident Owner) Check A $ 405

B. PRINCIPAL & INTEREST PAYMENT, LESS RENT(Check A) (Payable to Lender) Check B $ 657

TOTAL PAID BY OWNER-OCCUPANT: $ 1,062

CHECK WRITTEN BY NON-RESIDENT OWNER FROM RENT RECEIVED, SENT TO LENDER:

C. MORTGAGE PAYMENT in the amount of the RENT (Check A) (Payable to Lender) Check C $ 405

TOTAL PAID BY NON-RESIDENT OWNER (Check C) $ 405

LESS TOTAL RENT RECEIVED BY NON-RESIDENT OWNER (Check A) $– 405

0

we have developed the Rent Calculation Worksheet—For Condominium, Figure 4-F.

The Documentation process for a condominium works like this:

At the first of each month, when the mortgage payment and rent are due, the owner-occupant, who will be making the monthly payments, writes three checks. One, Check A, is made payable to the non-resident owner to cover the rent on the non-resident's portion of the property. The second, Check B, is made payable to the condo association, for the owner-occupant's portion of the monthly fee. The third, Check C, payable to the lender, is the mortgage payment, plus 100 percent of the condo dues, less the rent (Check A) and less the owner-occupant's percentage of the condo dues (Check B). The total of checks A, B, and C should equal the total paid by the owner-occupant.

These checks are sent to the non-resident owner, who deposits the rent check and writes two checks, D and E. Check D is made payable to the condo association, based on the non-resident's percentage of ownership. The second, Check E, is made payable to the lender in the same amount as the rent received, less the non-resident's percentage of the condo dues. The non-resident then forwards both of the mortgage checks to the lender and both condo association dues checks to the condo association.

Figure 4-G shows the filled-in Rent Calculation Worksheet for the condominium Jack Haley purchased with the Schifflers. You'll find blank Rent Calculation Worksheets for both single-family homes and condominiums in the Appendix.

The monthly exercise outlined on the Rent Calculation Worksheet accomplishes a number of things:

1. It provides a system whereby the non-resident owner knows that the monthly principal and interest payment is being made in a timely manner.
2. It provides documentation for the IRS that the rent has been paid each month to the non-resident owner for the non-resident's portion of the property.
3. It establishes the amount of principal and interest payment that is made by the owner-occupant each month, the interest portion of which is deductible on his tax return.
4. The rental income received by the non-resident owner is offset

FIGURE 4-F

RENT CALCULATION WORKSHEET—FOR CONDOMINIUM

Owner-Occupant(s) (O.O.) ____________________ % Ownership ____

Non-resident Owner(s) (N.O.) ____________________ % Ownership ____

____________________ % Ownership ____

Property Address: ____________________

Principal & Interest (Paid by O.O.) $__________

Condo Association Dues (Paid by O.O.) $__________

TOTAL PAID BY O.O.: $__________

Fair Market Rent: $__________

Less Good-Tenant Discount $–__________

RENT: $__________

Times N.O. % Ownership: ×__________%

RENT PAID TO N.O.: $__________

CHECKS WRITTEN BY OWNER-OCCUPANT, SENT TO NON-RESIDENT OWNER:

A. RENT (Payable to Non-resident Owner) Check A $__________

B. O.O. % OF CONDO DUES (Payable to Assoc.) Check B $__________

C. PRINCIPAL & INTEREST PAYMENT PLUS 100% OF CONDO DUES, LESS RENT (Check A) and LESS O.O. % of CONDO DUES (Check B) (Payable to Lender) Check C $__________

TOTAL PAID BY OWNER-OCCUPANT $__________

CHECKS WRITTEN BY NON-RESIDENT OWNER FROM RENT RECEIVED:

D. N.O. % OF CONDO DUES (Payable to Assoc.) Check D $__________

E. Check payable to Lender in the Amount of the RENT (Check A), less N.O. % of Condo Dues (Check D) Check E $__________

TOTAL RENT PAID BY NON-RESIDENT OWNER (Check D + E) $__________

LESS TOTAL RENT RECEIVED BY NON-RESIDENT OWNER (Check A) $–__________

0

FIGURE 4-G

RENT CALCULATION WORKSHEET—FOR CONDOMINIUM

Owner-Occupant(s) (O.O.) Jack Haley % Ownership 50

Non-resident Owner(s) (N.O.) The Schifflers % Ownership 50

______________ % Ownership ____

Property Address: ______________

Principal & Interest (Paid by O.O.) $ 1,062

Condo Association Dues (Paid by O.O.) $ 130

TOTAL PAID BY O.O.: $ 1,192

Fair Market Rent: $ 900

Less Good-Tenant Discount $– 90

RENT: $ 810

Times N.O. % Ownership: × 50 %

RENT PAID TO N.O.: $ 405

CHECKS WRITTEN BY OWNER-OCCUPANT, SENT TO NON-RESIDENT OWNER:

A. RENT (Payable to Non-resident Owner) Check A $ 405

B. O.O. % OF CONDO DUES (Payable to Assoc.) Check B $ 65

C. PRINCIPAL & INTEREST PAYMENT PLUS 100% OF CONDO DUES, LESS RENT (Check A) and LESS O.O. % of CONDO DUES (Check B) (Payable to Lender) Check C $ 722

TOTAL PAID BY OWNER-OCCUPANT $ 1,192

CHECKS WRITTEN BY NON-RESIDENT OWNER FROM RENT RECEIVED:

D. N.O. % OF CONDO DUES (Payable to Assoc.) Check D $ 65

E. Check payable to Lender in the Amount of the RENT (Check A), less N.O. % of Condo Dues (Check D) Check E $ 340

TOTAL RENT PAID BY NON-RESIDENT OWNER (Check D + E) $ 405

LESS TOTAL RENT RECEIVED BY NON-RESIDENT OWNER (Check A) $– 405

0

by the checks he writes to the lender and to the condo association and makes it possible for the non-resident to completely expense, or "zero out," the rental income so there will be no tax on this income.

5. The check the non-resident writes to the condo association for his portion of the association dues is the non-resident's documentation of this writeoff.

Once you've gone through the appropriate worksheet a couple of times, it should be quite clear how this bookkeeping process works.

Some lenders set up the monthly payment on the loan so that it includes not only the principal and interest but also the property tax and, in some cases, the homeowner's insurance. The lender thus collects the appropriate amount on a monthly basis and then makes the quarterly or semi-annual tax and insurance payments for you. Your monthly payment coupon book will give a breakdown of your payment, showing how much goes toward these expenses. If this is the case with the lender you choose, then you'll need to keep this procedure in mind when using the Rent Calculation Worksheet. Simply make sure these amounts are included in the check the owner-occupant pays to the lender, in addition to the owner-occupant's portion of the mortgage payment.

A third item from the text of 280A that might have piqued your interest is the clause in the last paragraph that says " 'qualified ownership interest' means an undivided interest for more than 50 years . . ." This relates to the holding period for the equity-share purchase. We'll discuss this in the next chapter, on the shared equity agreement, when we talk about holding periods and *termination events*.

TAX-DEFERRED EXCHANGES

For the Owner-occupant: IRC Section 1034. Rollover of Gain on Sale of Principal Residence.

Section 1034 is the part of the Tax Code that makes it possible for homeowners to defer the tax on their gain when they sell their home. It's one of the most valuable tax benefits that homeowners enjoy.

You're not required to file any forms with the IRS when you purchase your home or when you make those improvements that add to the basis. But when it comes time to sell, as we've already seen, improvement costs will adjust your basis upwards. Your adjusted basis is what you paid for the house plus the improvements. Your profit on the sale is the difference between the adjusted basis and the amount you net from the sale after all sales costs—commissions, escrow fees, etc.—are deducted.

When it comes time to calculate the profit from the sale of your home, you'll be glad you kept that file with the receipts showing what the improvements to the property cost. This is where those costs get added to your basis and thus reduce your tax bill.

It is quite easy for homeowners to defer the tax on their gain; all they have to do is buy a new home that costs at least as much as what they sell the old one for and complete Tax Form 2119, to be filed with their tax return. Note: You have to purchase your new home within two years of selling the old one. You should be aware that the IRS is completely inflexible about this time period. If you don't complete the purchase within the two years from the sale, you forfeit the rollover privilege and must pay the tax on your gain.

Let's look at how a tax rollover would work for Jack Haley. (To start with, we'll assume Jack owns the property 100 percent; then we'll show you how it will work with his actual shared-equity ownership.)

You'll recall that he purchased his condo for $200,000. He had $565 in non-deductible closing costs which were added to the basis, plus $1,200 in landscaping improvements he made to the property during the time he owned it. This gives him a total adjusted basis of $201,765.

If he sells the property in three years for a net amount, after closing costs, of $295,000, his gain will be $93,235 ($295,000 − $201,765). As long as he purchases his new home for $295,000 or more within two years of the closing, the tax on that gain is deferred. Let's say the cost of his new home is $325,000, plus $700 in non-deductible closing costs and $6,500 for the new deck he adds to the house, for a total of $332,200. Instead of reporting the gain from the first home as income, he reduces the basis of his new home by the amount of the gain, so the new basis is $238,965 ($322,200 − $93,235).

So the calculation for Jack's basis would look like this:

$200,000	Purchase Price
+565	Non-deductible Closing Costs
+1,200	Improvements
$201,765	Basis
$295,000	Net Sales Price
-201,765	Less Basis
$93,235	Gain (Deferred)
$325,000	Replacement Property
+700	Non-deductible Closing Costs
+6,500	Improvements
$332,200	New Purchase Price
−93,235	Less Deferred Gain
$238,965	New Basis

When he sells the second house for, let's say, $400,000, the gain, as far as the IRS is concerned, would be the combination of the $93,235 gain from the first house and the $67,800 from the second house, or $161,035.

Now, remembering that Jack is a 50 percent owner in his equity-shared property, his gain on the $295,000 net sale would be 50 percent of the $93,235, or $46,618. If he purchased the second home as a 100 percent owner, the purchase price on his second home could be $147,500 or more (one half of the $295,000 net selling price, since he owned only half of the property) without incurring a tax. If he paid less than $147,500 for his new home—let's say $130,000—he would be taxed on the difference of $17,500 at his then-current tax rate of, we'll assume, 28 percent. So, under the current tax law in a 28 percent bracket, he could owe $4,900 in tax ($17,500 × .28), assuming he had no capital losses to offset that gain.

There is currently no limit on the number of times or the amount a homeowner can rollover from one house to the next. But the basis is affected each time you buy and sell, and that's why it is important for you and your accountant to keep track of it.

Under the current tax law, you can keep *buying up* (buying for at least what you sold your previous house for) and keep deferring the tax. However, there may eventually come a time when you're ready to buy a smaller house that you can own free and clear, using the equity you've built up from appreciation and from your tax savings. At present the IRS will allow homeowners a one-time exclusion of up to $125,000 in gain if they are at least fifty-five years old and if they have lived in the house for at least three of the last five years prior to the sale.

For the Non-resident Owner: IRC Section 1031. Exchange of Property Held for Productive Use or Investment.

The non-resident owner has the same option of deferring the tax on his gain from the sale of investment property, though the rules are different and much more stringent. To qualify for a tax-deferred exchange, the property the non-resident purchases must be "like kind," which essentially means exchanging property held for investment purposes for another investment property. For example, if your non-resident owner wanted to take the funds from the sale of your equity-shared property, he could either buy another single-family rental residence, or he could buy a duplex, or even a commercial building that he would hold for investment. The closing on the sale must be simultaneous with the closing of the new purchase. If the closings were not simultaneous, the transaction would be considered a delayed exchange. To qualify for a delayed exchange, the non-resident owner must "identify" the replacement property within 45 days of the closing of the first property, and the closing of the replacement property must be completed within 180 days of the closing of the first property or within 180 days of the due date for the filing of the tax return for the taxable year in which the transfer occurs.

Also, it is vital to the integrity of the exchange that the non-resident owner not touch the funds from the sale. Rather, the funds should be transferred from the closing to an escrow agent or an attorney who can act as an accommodator. A Section 1031 tax-deferred exchange is not difficult but, as far as the IRS is concerned, the *form* of the exchange is critical. This means all the *t*s have to be crossed and all the *i*s have to be dotted. Therefore, before attempting a Section 1031 tax-deferred exchange, a non-resident owner should get competent advice from a qualified exchange broker or should have the exchange handled by an attorney or an escrow officer qualified in such exchanges.

The full texts of Section 1034 and Section 1031 of the Tax Code appear in the Appendix, for your information.

Before you start the next chapter, go make a big pot of coffee, flip back to the beginning of this chapter, and read it again. Make sure you've got a calculator, a pencil, and a straight-backed chair. The concepts in this chapter are not difficult, but if they are new to you, a second or third reading may be necessary before they all start to make sense.

Now that you understand the tax picture, it is time to start putting together your shared-equity agreement.

·5·

The Shared-Equity Financing Agreement

The Shared-Equity Financing Agreement is one of the most important elements of your equity-share purchase. This Agreement should cover, in writing, all the terms you have agreed to with your equity-share purchaser and should spell out all the obligations, restrictions, and requirements that apply to both parties.

Also, as you know from reading Section 280A in Chapter 4, the IRS requires that the rental must be pursuant to a Shared-Equity Financing Agreement.

As any attorney will tell you, a contract is only as good as the intentions of the parties entering into it. That is why it is vital that you know as much as possible about your co-purchaser. And the best contract is the one that collects dust on the shelf because neither party ever has to look at it once it is signed. In the event of a problem, both parties should be able to look to the contract rather than the courts for a solution. For this reason, your contract should be as comprehensive as possible.

The 32-clause Shared-Equity Financing Agreement we have developed is the most complete, detailed, and researched such contract available today. It has been thoroughly examined and analyzed by dozens of attorneys, accountants, and tax advisers representing both owner-occupants and non-resident owners. We encourage you to use it in your equity-share purchase, adapting it to your own needs as necessary.

In the following pages the Agreement is reprinted in its entirety on the right side of the page. Our explanatory comments, where required, appear on the left side of the page, opposite the clauses of the contract to which they refer. (In the Appendix we're also including a blank Agreement for you to adapt for your own use.)

In the next chapter we'll talk about how to go about finding the right non-resident owner and provide a checklist of questions you should go over with your non-resident owner before you actually sign the Agreement.

Once again, we urge you to get legal advice for your own circumstances. Also, because regulations vary from state to state, we urge you to seek your own legal counsel for information about state disclosure requirements, if any, that may affect your equity-share transactions. In fact, you'll see in Clause 32 that we require all our purchasers to seek the advice of their own independent counsel.

RECITALS. In order to take advantage of the tax benefits, all shared-equity purchases must be pursuant to IRC Section 280A, and we therefore include that section of the Code as part of the Agreement.

A. As we discussed in Chapter 4, the majority of our shared-equity purchases are structured for tenancy in common. However, joint tenancy could be used if each party wants the other to inherit his or her interest in the event of death. This contingency usually applies in a family equity-share arrangement.

1. Acquisition of the Property.

(c). The "Initial Cash Contribution" is the down payment. The percentages of ownership are usually, though not always, based on the percentage of the down payment supplied by each party. Make sure the contributions of the parties are accurately shown here. The Initial Cash Contribution is the *priority return* (the first obligation that must be paid off) to each party when the property is either sold or refinanced.

SHARED-EQUITY FINANCING AGREEMENT

THIS AGREEMENT is made and entered into this ________ day of ____________, 19___, by and between ("Owner-Occupants"), and ("Non-resident Owners"), as tenants-in-common.

RECITALS

This Agreement is entered into on the basis of the following facts, understandings, and intentions of the parties and is pursuant to IRC Section 280A (Attachment A).

A. Non-resident Owners and Owner-Occupants intend to acquire, as tenants-in-common, that certain real property (the "Property") located and described as:
in the city of:

B. Owner-Occupants intend, upon acquisition of the Property, to occupy the Property as a residence.

C. The parties enter into this Agreement in order to set forth their respective rights and obligations.

D. No promises or representations have been made as to what the value of the Property may be in the future.

In consideration of the mutual covenants and agreements contained herein and other valuable consideration, the parties agree as follows:

1. Acquisition of the Property.

(a) The purchase price of the Property is $______________, in accordance with the terms of the agreement entered into with the seller of the Property.

(b) The parties shall obtain a loan (the "Mortgage Loan") in the amount of $_________________. The Mortgage Loan will be held by ____.

(c) The balance of the purchase price shall be paid in cash (the "Initial Cash Contributions"). The Cash Contributions shall be paid by the parties hereto into escrow for the purchase of the Property on or before the date of said purchase (the "Closing Date") as follows:

______________________ dollars ($_________________)
by the Owner-Occupants

______________________ dollars ($_________________)
by the Non-resident Owners

(d). Closing costs are separate from the "Initial Cash Contribution." They are usually contributed according to the percentages of ownership, i.e., a 50 percent owner would pay 50 percent of the closing costs. If they are not allocated according to ownership, be certain to indicate here how they are to be divided and what the payback, if any, should be.

2. Ownership percentages. The agreed-upon percentages of ownership are specified on the deed and are recorded as shown in the Agreement.

3. Maintenance. This is a fill-in-the-blank item. We usually agree that after the owner-occupant has paid the first $200 in maintenance costs in any one calendar year, any amount above that $200 is shared by the parties, based on their percentages of ownership. An older property may require a higher amount than a newer property. The actual dollar amount is negotiable between the parties.

(d) Closing costs shall be paid in accordance with each party's Ownership Percentage; except that association dues, if any, interest, and property tax prorations will be paid by Owner-Occupants. A copy of the Escrow Closing Statement will be attached to this Agreement (Attachment B).

(e) It is agreed that any accounting for federal and/or state income tax purposes generated by payment of closing costs for acquisition of the Property, including loan fees, shall be claimed by Owner-Occupants and Non-resident Owners in accordance with the percentages in which they furnish such funds.

2. Ownership percentages.

Non-resident Owners and Owner-Occupants shall own undivided interests in the Property, as tenants-in-common. The percentages of ownership for Non-resident Owners and Owner-Occupants (the "Ownership Percentages") are:

______________________ (%) to ______________________
______________________ (%) to ______________________

3. Maintenance of the Property.

(a) Owner-Occupants shall, at their sole cost and expense, maintain the Property and every part thereof in good and sanitary condition and repair. Owner-Occupants shall repair any and all damage to or in the Property occurring while the Property is held in co-tenancy hereunder, whether or not such damage is covered by insurance. It is agreed that the cost of repairs which do not arise as a result of any failure by Owner-Occupants to maintain the Property pursuant to the provisions hereof, including but not limited to repairs to appliances, heating and air conditioning equipment, plumbing and electrical systems, shall be shared by the parties in accordance with their Ownership Percentages, after Owner-Occupants have paid the first $__________ of such costs in any one calendar year. Repairs which result from or become necessary as a result of Owner-Occupants' failure to maintain the Property and every part thereof as provided herein shall be performed at Owner-Occupants' sole cost and expense. Owner-Occupants shall be responsible for the full cost of repairs of any damages to the property resulting from the lack of care, negligence, or any wilful act by Owner-Occupants. At the termination of this Agreement, the Owner-Occupants shall restore the Property to its present condition, normal wear and tear excepted.

(b) Owner-Occupants shall pay for all water, gas, heat, light, power, telephone service, and all other services and utilities supplied

4. Improvements and Alterations.

(a). This is also a fill-in-the-blank clause and is negotiable between the parties. We usually say that anything under $200 shall not require the non-resident owners' consent. This enables the owner-occupant to change a doorknob, paint a room, add some landscaping, or make other minor alterations. Any changes over $200 (or the negotiated dollar amount) would have to be agreed to by the non-resident and paid for according to the percentages of ownership.

(b). This paragraph spells out improvements to be made by the owner-occupant upon acquisition of the property. We usually secure two or more bids by licensed contractors and document all details of the projected work as an addendum to the Agreement. This precaution is very important when sweat equity is part of a fixer-upper property.

to the Property during the time the Property is held in co-tenancy hereunder.

4. Improvements and Alterations.

(a) Owner-Occupants shall not make or cause to be made any alterations, additions, or improvements on or to the Property or any part thereof without the prior written consent of the Non-resident Owners, except that any alteration, addition, or improvement costing less than $____________ shall not require Non-resident Owners' written consent or contribution, provided that it would not detract from the value or appearance of the Property and provided further that said expenditure, alteration, addition, or improvement shall not be reimbursed upon sale or refinance. Nothing in this Paragraph shall impair Owner-Occupants' obligation to maintain and repair the Property as previously set forth. Should Non-resident Owners consent, in writing, to any alteration, addition, or improvement costing more than $____________, the parties will agree at that time, in writing, as to the division of cost and return due each party upon sale or refinance of the Property.

(b) If improvements or alterations are deemed necessary by the parties upon acquisition of the Property, Owner-Occupants shall contribute to the Property those certain improvements as set forth in Addendum A, attached to this document. The value of said improvements shall be determined by securing bids from Licensed Contractors. These improvements shall be completed within (_________) months of the Closing Date, and the entire cost of supplies, materials, and labor shall be borne by the Owner-Occupants. Upon Sale or other Termination Event, Owner-Occupants shall be entitled to be paid an amount equal to the value established in Addendum A, after all other obligations set forth under Termination Events have been satisfied, and prior to distribution of any profits. The adjustment described in this Paragraph shall not alter the original Ownership Percentages as described in Paragraph 3 for purposes of distribution of any additional amounts as specified under Termination Events of this Agreement.

5. Liens.

The parties hereto shall not permit liens or encumbrances of any kind to be placed against the Property including, but not limited to, taxes, judgments, construction work, repair or restoration, or materials furnished. In the event of a violation of this Paragraph by either party, a default may be declared pursuant to Paragraph 14(b)(ii) and Paragraph 20, and the amount of the lien shall be deducted from the proceeds due to the defaulting party as a result of a sale, refinance, or

6. Transactions Requiring Consent of Both Parties. We record a "Memorandum of Shared-Equity Financing Agreement" with the County Recorder's Office on all our shared-equity purchases. This memorandum is a simple document stating that the parties hold the property, identified by its legal description and parcel number, subject to the terms of a Shared-Equity Financing Agreement. This puts any potential lender on notice in the event one party tries to borrow against his or her share of his ownership. Your attorney or escrow officer can draft this memorandum. All the parties should sign it and it should be recorded.

8. Waiver of Right to Partition. Partition is one of the legal remedies that can be used to resolve disputes in real property ownership. When there is no contract between the parties that spells out their agreement, the parties can sue to partition the property in order to allocate ownership under the provision recorded in the deed.

condemnation of the Property or as a result of any other disposition of the Property.

6. Transactions Requiring Consent of Both Parties.

After acquisition of the Property, the prior written consent of all parties shall be required before any of the following actions may be taken:

(a) The sale, transfer, exchange, lease, or other disposition of all or any portion of or any interest in the Property, except as made pursuant to Paragraphs 14, 16, and 17;

(b) Any modification, amendment, alteration, or extension of the terms of any existing financing on the Property;

(c) Acquisition of any new financing for the Property, or the placing of any further encumbrance on the Property, except financing specifically agreed upon at the time the parties acquire the Property;

(d) Modification of insurance required by the terms of this Agreement; provided, however, that Owner-Occupants may, at Owner-Occupants' sole cost and expense, increase coverage without prior approval of Non-resident Owners.

7. Use of Property.

(a) Owner-Occupants shall use the Property as their primary residence and for no other purpose unless such purpose is agreed upon in writing by all parties hereto.

(b) Owner-Occupants shall not do or permit anything to be done in or about the Property, nor bring or keep anything thereon, which will increase the existing insurance rate or otherwise adversely affect any policy of fire or other insurance on the Property or any part thereof, or use or allow the Property to be used in any way that may conflict with any law, statute, ordinance, or government regulation now in force or which may be enacted. Owner-Occupants shall not cause, maintain, or permit any nuisance or waste to be committed in, or about the Property. Owner-Occupants shall not use the Property for any commercial or business purpose whatsoever except for a home office.

8. Waiver of Right to Partition.

The parties further acknowledge that their relationship as co-owners is not a partnership, and no party shall have any liability for debts or obligations of the other party. Each of the parties acknowledges that it would be prejudicial to the interests of the parties if any party

In an equity-share purchase, however, there are other considerations besides ownership, such as additional contributions or payments made by one party in the event of a default, that could affect the ultimate ownership. Therefore, rather than partition the property, we want the court to be able to look to the contract for the rights and remedies of the parties.

9. Insurance. Most insurance companies will name all the owners on one policy. However, if an insurance company will name only the owner-occupant for fire and contents, the non-resident owner still needs liability coverage.

In order for the non-resident to get this coverage from an insurance carrier, the owner-occupant will need to provide the non-resident with a copy of the homeowner's policy on the new property, listing the non-resident as an "additional insured." The non-resident owner should send the owner-occupant's policy to his carrier so that the negotiable liability coverage listed in this clause (usually $500,000) can be extended to the non-resident owner.

With a copy of this policy, the non-resident can then obtain the liability coverage from his homeowner's insurance carrier and, in turn, provide a copy of the insurance coverage information to the owner-occupant.

were to file an action for partition of the Property. Accordingly, each of the parties hereby waives any and all right which he or she may otherwise have to seek a partition of the Property by court action, without the prior written consent of all the other parties.

9. Insurance.

(a) The Owner-Occupants shall maintain on the Property at all times fire and casualty insurance with extended coverage endorsements upon all buildings and improvements located on the Property to not less than one hundred percent of the full replacement cost thereof not covered by policies held by other entities such as but not limited to a Homeowners' Association. Such insurance policy shall contain a provision by which its coverage is automatically increased on an annual basis to cover increases in the value of the Property. The right and authority to adjust and settle any loss with the insurer shall be exercisable only by all parties acting jointly. Subject to the requirements of the lender, the insurance proceeds, with the exception of temporary living expenses, received shall be used to pay for restoration and reconstruction of the Property to be commenced as soon as possible after receipt of the proceeds from the insurance, and Owner-Occupants shall use due diligence to repair or reconstruct the Property within a reasonable period of time. Nothing contained in this Paragraph shall be construed to grant to Non-resident Owners any interest in insurance maintained by Owner-Occupants on personal property owned by Owner-Occupants.

(b) At all times while the Property is held in co-tenancy hereunder, there shall be maintained by each party comprehensive public liability insurance covering the Property, insuring against the risks of bodily injury, property damage, and personal injury liability with respect to the Property, with policy limits of not less than $500,000 per occurrence.

(c) Owner-Occupants shall indemnify, defend, and hold the Non-resident Owners harmless from any and all claims, costs, including, without limitation, attorneys' fees, causes of action or liability for any injury or damage to any person or property whatsoever, occurring on or about the Property, or any part thereof, arising out of the intentional or negligent act or omission of any kind by the Owner-Occupants.

(d) If the Property is a condominium, at all times there shall (f). Since this Agreement binds the heirs in the event of death, the non-resident owner might want to consider taking out a life insurance policy on the owner-occupant in the amount of the mortgage, naming the non-resident as beneficiary.

10. Loan Interest Payments and Operating Expenses. This clause outlines the documentation required to comply with IRC Section 280A. Prompt payment is necessary to protect the credit of all parties.

be maintained, at the sole cost of the Owner-Occupants, a condominium insurance policy covering the contents and insuring (to not less than the full replacement cost) against loss of/or damage to the appliances, fixtures, improvements, and other appurtenances which are co-owned by the parties pursuant to the Agreement to the extent not covered by Homeowners' Association dues and/or policy.

(e) Owner-Occupants shall be responsible for compliance with the terms of the insurance policies required hereunder and shall deliver copies of the policies to Non-resident Owners. All such insurance documents shall name Owner-Occupants and Non-resident Owners as joint insureds. Unless Non-resident Owners object in writing within thirty days of receipt of the policy, the insurance shall be deemed in compliance with the terms of this Agreement. No such policy shall be cancelled or subject to reduction of coverage, or other modifications. The Owner-Occupants shall furnish renewals or binders to the Non-resident Owners, or the Non-resident Owners may order such insurance and charge the costs thereof to the Owner-Occupants, which amount shall be payable by the Owner-Occupants upon demand.

(f) If the Non-resident Owners elect to place a Term Life Insurance Policy upon the life of one of the Owner-Occupants for an amount equal to the Mortgage Loan, the Owner-Occupants will co-operate in the acquisition of said policy. The Non-resident Owners shall bear the entire monthly premium of said policy, and shall be named as sole Beneficiary.

10. Loan Interest Payments and Operating Expenses.

(a) Owner-Occupants shall, personally or through a designated collection agency, from the funds jointly contributed by the parties, make timely payments of the Mortgage Loan installments, real property taxes, insurance, fees to Homeowners or Condominium Associations (if any), and other costs of ownership and operation for the Property.

(b) Non-resident Owners shall be obligated to contribute funds only to the extent of the amount of the rent received by Non-resident Owners for their Ownership Percentage in the Property pursuant to Paragraph 11 below.

(c) Owner-Occupants shall be obligated to contribute funds as follows:

(i) Pay rent as defined in compliance with IRC Section 280A and set forth in Paragraph 11 below.

11. Fair Market Rental. As we explained in Chapter 4, it's necessary to determine the fair market rent the property would bring and then make the appropriate adjustments, based on the percentages of ownership. You can use the Rent Calculation Worksheet in the Appendix to establish the proportion to be paid to the non-resident owner. Remember, the lower the rent, the more disproportionate a writeoff the owner-occupant can take. Don't forget to document your file with rental ads on comparable properties. Failure to do so could cause the IRS to disallow the entire shared-equity agreement.

(ii) Pay any additional amounts necessary to meet the total expenses set forth in this Paragraph including, but not limited to, the Mortgage Loan payments, any increases in the Mortgage Loan payments, late payment penalties, real property taxes and tax assessments, insurance, and Homeowner or Condominium fees (if any). Owner-Occupants understand that the payments may increase or decrease in amounts due to fluctuations in interest rate, taxes or insurance.

(d) Special assessments by Condominium or Homeowners' Associations for capital improvements shall be shared by the parties in accordance with their Ownership Percentages.

(e) Owner-Occupants and Non-resident Owners shall each report for tax purposes those items pertaining to that party and the payments made by that party. For tax purposes, no relationship other than that of tenants-in-common is created or implied hereby. Owner-Occupants and Non-resident Owners shall not be liable for the debts or obligations of the other except as herein provided.

11. Fair Market Rental.

(a) Pursuant to Internal Revenue Code Section 280A, Owner-Occupants shall make payments to Non-resident Owners for Owner-Occupants' use and occupancy of Non-resident Owners' interest in the Property. The parties hereby agree that the fair market rental for the entirety of the Property is ______________ dollars per month. Subject to the provisions of Paragraph 11(b), Owner-Occupants shall pay to Non-resident Owners on the __________ day of each month throughout the term hereof the amount of ______________ dollars as rent for Owner-Occupants' use, occupancy, and enjoyment of Non-resident Owners' _________ Percent Ownership Percentage in the Property (the "Rent").

(b) The Rent will be reviewed annually on the anniversary of the Closing Date. If Owner-Occupants and Non-resident Owners cannot agree upon fair market rent, they shall, at their joint expense, employ a professional Property Manager to conduct a rental survey. If agreement still cannot be reached, each party shall employ a professional Property Manager. Each party shall pay for the Property Manager which that party selected. Non-resident Owners shall have the right to inspect the Property prior to the rental survey and shall provide to the Property Managers a list of those matters, if any, with respect to which Owner-Occupants have not satisfied their obligation of repair and maintenance. In such event, the Property Managers shall determine the fair

13. Additional Contributions. Let's say it becomes necessary to replace the roof; it has to be done and both parties agree to it. But it may happen at a time when one or the other party doesn't have the cash available. Rather than take out a personal loan, one of the parties can choose to have his portion of the expense, plus interest, deducted from his share of the eventual profits or from the cash from refinancing. This assumes that the other party has the necessary funds available and is willing to provide them for this purpose. This clause prepares both parties for such an event and also sets a reasonable interest rate to be charged. (If you don't already know, find out what the usury laws are in your state.)

In the event the owner-occupant cannot make the monthly payments market rent of the Property as if all such matters had been properly repaired or maintained. The average of the findings of the three rental surveys shall then be deemed to be fair market rent. The parties agree to cooperate in expediting the foregoing procedure to determine the fair market rental within Forty-Five days after failure to agree upon fair market rental.

12. Occupancy and Entry by Non-resident Owners.

Except as otherwise provided, Owner-Occupants shall have exclusive rights to occupancy and possession of the Property and Non-resident Owners shall have no such rights. While the Property is held in co-tenancy hereunder, Non-resident Owners may enter the Property only in the following cases:

(a) Once every ________ months to inspect the Property;

(b) In case of emergency;

(c) To cure defaults by Owner-Occupants of their obligations under this Agreement;

(d) Pursuant to court order; or

(e) In the event Owner-Occupants abandon or surrender the Property;

(f) Upon invitation or permission of the Owner-Occupants;

(g) Under the circumstances specified elsewhere in this Agreement.

Wherever reasonable and practicable, the Non-resident Owners shall give the Owner-Occupants twenty-four hours prior notice of intention to enter or inspect the property. Any such entry or inspection shall be between the hours of 9:00 A.M. and 5:00 P.M. unless otherwise agreed.

13. Additional Contributions.

(a) Should additional contributions be deemed desirable and/or necessary, Owner-Occupants and Non-resident Owners are responsible for making all contributions promptly and fully. To the extent that either Owner-Occupants or Non-resident Owners shall furnish funds for any authorized purpose in excess of their Ownership Percentages of such costs, the party supplying the funds shall receive reimbursement for the amount of those costs plus ________ percent interest per annum, compounded annually.

(b) If any party has not received full reimbursement for additional contributions prior to a Termination Event or Refinancing, the remaining amount due shall be deducted from the pro-rata repay-

and the non-resident owner advances the payment, it would be considered an "additional contribution" and falls under this Paragraph.

14. Termination Events and Procedures. This section covers all or most of the termination events you are likely to encounter in an equity-share purchase. Basically, what it does is give either party the opportunity to get out of the property after a specified period of time and allows the property to be either refinanced or sold should it become desirable or necessary to do so.

There is always the possibility, however, that unforeseen circumstances will force one party or the other to terminate the Agreement prematurely. This is one of the major risks of equity sharing: if one party is forced to terminate at a time when the real estate market is down, it could create a loss. However, if you have been diligent in the selection of your equity-share partner and thoroughly understand each other's goals, you should be able to work together to minimize or eliminate the losses that might be caused by any termination event.

Obviously, this is a crucial aspect of the Agreement. As we have said before, it is very important that your time-frame goals be compatible so that once you agree on how long you plan to hold the property, and each makes plans accordingly, you can work within that schedule.

(a). The time period in this fill-in-the-blank section is usually set by the owner-occupants as a statement of how long they plan on living in the property before they have to think of moving again. (In brokers' jargon, 14(a) is sometimes referred to as the "no-call" provision, and the time specified as the no-call period.)

Of course there may be market considerations that could change the length of the time period. Rapid appreciation in the first few years of ownership might make it possible to refinance sooner than expected, or a recession might mean you would want to refinance before interest rates go up. The important thing here is to give all parties a time frame within which to operate, but do understand that in order to maximize the return on your investment all parties must be reasonable.

You may recall that IRC Section 280A speaks of "an undivided inment of the Initial Cash Contribution of the non-contributing party(ies) and, if necessary, from any additional share of the proceeds due the non-contributing party(ies) as described in Paragraph 14(g).

(c) The adjustments described in this Paragraph shall not alter the Ownership Percentages as described in Paragraph 2 for purposes of distribution of any additional amounts as specified in Paragraph 14(g).

14. Termination Events and Procedures.

(a) The Property will not be sold within the first ________ months after Closing Date unless agreed in writing by Owner-Occupants and Non-resident Owners.

terest for more than fifty years.'' This provision was included to protect homeowners from a developer trying to force them out of a property before they were ready to sell. That situation seldom occurs anymore, but in order to adhere to the intent of the Code we don't set a definite termination date in the Agreement. Instead, we spell out both parties' options and set forth procedures for termination.

(b) The parties agree to sell or exchange the Property and to liquidate the co-ownership upon the occurrence of any of the following (the "Termination Events"):

(i) The vacating or abandonment of the Property by the Owner-Occupants. Should Owner-Occupants abandon or vacate said Property for a continuous period of fourteen days except for holiday vacations, Non-resident Owners shall have the exclusive right to terminate Owner-Occupants' tenancy and to lease said Property. All rental payments received by Non-resident Owners shall be used for Property expenses, including but not limited to, mortgage payments, insurance, taxes, and maintenance.

(ii) Any party's breach of any covenant, obligation, or provision contained in this Agreement, including obligations to make payments required by this Agreement whereby the breach remains unremedied for the period set forth in Paragraph 20, below. Notice to Terminate must be duly noticed in writing. All provisions of Paragraph 20 shall apply.

(iii) The Non-resident Owners' election to terminate this Agreement if Owner-Occupants fail to make any payment as and when required by this Agreement within fifteen calendar days from the date on which such payment was to be made. Notice to Terminate shall be duly noticed in writing. Time is of the essence.

(iv) The making by the Owner-Occupants of any general assignment for the benefit of creditors; the filing against Owner-Occupants of a petition to have them or any one of them adjudged bankrupt, or a petition for reorganization or arrangement under any law relating to bankruptcy, unless, in the case of a petition filed against them, such petition shall be dismissed within sixty days after its filing; the appointment of a trustee or a receiver to take possession of substantially all of their assets, or of Owner-Occupants' interest in this Agreement or the Property, where such seizure shall not be discharged or released within thirty days.

(v) Occurrence of the events specified above in Paragraph

(f). This is an important clause that should remain in the agreement to protect both parties.

(g). Specifies the order in which various financial obligations must be cleared when the equity-share arrangement is terminated. Note that the Initial Cash Contributions come first, adjusted for any additional contributions either may have made. After these two requisites and after adjustment for any improvements that have added to the property's value, then the profits are to be shared according to the percentages of ownership.

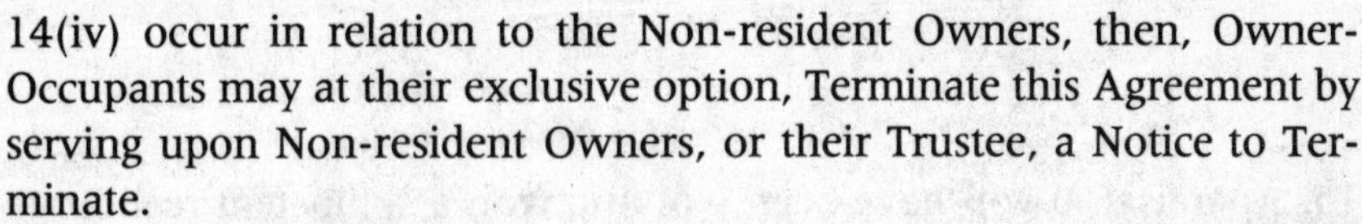

14(iv) occur in relation to the Non-resident Owners, then, Owner-Occupants may at their exclusive option, Terminate this Agreement by serving upon Non-resident Owners, or their Trustee, a Notice to Terminate.

(vi) After ______________ (__________) years from Closing Date, Owner-Occupants or Non-resident Owners may deliver to the other a written Notice to Terminate.

(c) In the event the Non-resident Owners elect to effect a Section 1031 Exchange of their Ownership Percentage in the Property, at no additional expense to the Owner-Occupants, Owner-Occupants agree to co-operate in said exchange for the benefit of the Non-resident Owners.

(d) Upon the occurrence of a Termination Event, the parties shall cause the Property to be sold or exchanged as soon as practicable thereafter, and in any event within one hundred twenty days of the occurrence of such Termination Event. Until the close of escrow for the sale or exchange of the Property, each party shall remain fully liable for all costs, expenses, and rent as set forth in this Agreement.

(e) Unless unanimously agreed otherwise, the parties shall grant an Exclusive Right to Sell listing on the Property to __________ or assignee for a period of not less than one hundred twenty days. Said Broker/s shall cause the Property to be listed in the ______________ Multiple Listing Service and exercise due diligence in marketing the Property.

(f) Each of the parties pledges its interest to the other as security for the obligations set forth herein, including all expenses, costs, and attorneys' fees expended in enforcing this Agreement.

(g) The proceeds from the sale, refinance, condemnation, or other disposition of the Property, after deduction of the then existing Mortgage Loan balance and the closing costs according to Ownership Percentages, shall be distributed as follows: First, to repayment of each party's Initial Cash Contribution, as described in Paragraph 1(c); second, adjusted for any additional contributions, as specified in Paragraph 13; third, adjusted for any improvements per value established in Addendum A, in accordance with Paragraph 4(b); and fourth, the balance to the parties in accordance with their respective Ownership Percentages. In the event of breach or default of any covenant or condition of this Agreement, the non-breaching or non-defaulting parties shall have first priority upon the proceeds of sale to the full extent of their Initial Cash Contribution, all sale closing costs, and any additional contri-

15. Appraisal. If you have been working with a competent real estate agent who is familiar with the market values in your area, it will be fairly simple to establish the market price for your property. If not, one way to establish the price is through a professional appraisal, though it is a good idea to keep in mind that in a rapidly appreciating market, a professional appraisal is often lower than the market price. If the parties cannot agree on a value, three appraisals are averaged.

16. Owner-Occupants' Option to Purchase. Because the property is the owner-occupants' primary residence, they are given the first option to buy out the non-residents, if they so desire, after the "no-call" time period has elapsed. Their option is forefeited, however, if they do not remedy a default that the non-resident owners have properly notified them of, according to the provisions of Clause 20.

butions, before any return of funds to the breaching or defaulting parties.

15. Appraisal.

Upon notice of termination, the parties shall have thirty days to agree on the listing price or the fair market value of the Property. If the parties are unable to reach agreement, the fair market value (the "Appraisal Value") of the Property shall be determined by certified appraisal to be made by an independent fee appraiser, selected by the mutual agreement of the Owner-Occupants and the Non-resident Owners. If the parties are still unable to reach agreement, the fair market value of the Property shall be determined by certified appraisal to be made by two independent fee appraisers, one to be selected and paid for by the Owner-Occupants and the other to be selected and paid for by the Non-resident Owners. Non-resident Owners shall have the right to inspect the Property prior to the appraisal and shall provide the appraisers with a list of those matters, if any, with respect to which Owner-Occupants have not satisfied their obligation of repair and maintenance. In such event, the appraisers shall determine the Appraisal Value of the Property as if all such matters had been properly repaired or maintained. The Appraisal Value of the Property shall be deemed to be the average of the three appraisal values determined by the appraisers. The parties agree to cooperate in expediting the foregoing procedure to the end that the Appraisal Value be determined within forty-five days after a Termination Event.

16. Owner-Occupants' Option to Purchase.

Within fifteen days after agreement on a price or receipt from the appraisers of the Appraisal Value, Owner-Occupants shall have the first right and option (the "Owner-Occupants' Option") to elect to purchase the Non-resident Owners' interest in the Property. The Purchase Price shall be paid to the Non-resident Owners in cash, unless otherwise agreed to in the written agreement and duly executed by all parties hereto. This option shall be exercised in writing on a bona-fide offer-to-purchase form. All provisions of Paragraph 14(g) shall apply. However, if Owner-Occupants do not remedy a default pursuant to Paragraph 20, then their first option to purchase the Non-resident Owners' interest shall be automatically forfeited without notice or other action on Non-resident Owners' part.

17. Non-resident Owners' Option to Purchase. If the owner-occupants elect not to exercise their option to buy out the non-resident, the non-resident has the option to buy out the owner-occupants.

If there is more than one non-resident owner, a clause should be included indicating which non-resident owner has first right to purchase the property if the owner-occupants do not elect to exercise this option. Usually, the non-resident owner with the larger percentage of ownership wants the next option after the owner-occupant. In one case, two non-resident owners agreed that the non-resident wishing to move into the property as a principal residence could have first option after the owner-occupants.

19. Default by Owner-Occupants. This paragraph terminates the owner-occupants' right to occupy the property if they default on their payments. Our attorneys have cited the California Civil Code for this question; make certain your Agreement cites the appropriate laws for your state.

17. Non-resident Owners' Option to Purchase.

In the event Owner-Occupants

(i) Do not exercise the Owner-Occupants' Option by written notice to Non-resident Owners of such exercise within fifteen days after determination of the Appraisal Value;

(ii) Do not close the purchase of Non-resident Owners' interest within ninety days after the Termination Event; then Non-resident Owners may purchase Owner-Occupants' interest in the property on the same terms as specified in Paragraph 16, less the cost of Owner-Occupants' unfulfilled repair and maintenance obligations, if any. Non-resident Owners' option to purchase shall be exercised in writing on a bona-fide offer-to-purchase form. All provisions of Paragraph 14(g) shall apply.

18. Exercise of Option to Purchase.

Exercise of option to purchase, whether by Owner-Occupants or Non-resident Owners, shall be evidenced by written agreement which shall call for a closing at a title or escrow company selected by the purchaser, located within the same county as the Property, not less than thirty days nor more than ninety days from the date of said Termination Event, and cash deposit shall be made into such escrow, within 10 working days thereafter, in an amount of not less than ______________________ ($______________). The premium for a policy of title insurance, recording, escrow, and other closing costs shall be borne by the parties per their Ownership Percentages as reflected in this Agreement. Sole possession shall be given to the Buyer concurrent with the closing of escrow.

19. Default by Owner-Occupants.

In the event of default in payments by the Owner-Occupants on the encumbrances as herein before described, Owner-Occupants' RIGHT TO OCCUPY SAID PROPERTY MAY BE TERMINATED BY NON-RESIDENT OWNERS ON WRITTEN NOTICE TO OWNER-OCCUPANTS EVEN THOUGH OWNER-OCCUPANTS MAY HAVE SOME EQUITABLE INTEREST IN THE PROPERTY. Further, in the event of any default by Owner-Occupants of any of the terms and conditions of this Agreement, Non-resident Owners may terminate the lease provided for in this Agreement, take possession of the Property, and recover damages pursuant to California Civil Code 1951.2 in addition to all other remedies available to Non-resident Owners at law or in equity.

20. Notice of Default. The procedure to follow in case of default by either party is critical. Be sure you understand its provisions.

20. Notice of Default.

In the event of any default by either party, the other party shall give a written notice specifying the nature of the default, after which the defaulting party shall have fifteen days from receipt of said notice to remedy said default. If said default is not remedied in fifteen days:

(a) And the default is by the Owner-Occupants, Non-resident Owners may pay the cost of remedying said default and charge said cost to Owner-Occupants as Additional Contributions pursuant to Paragraph 13.

(b) Or if the default is by the Non-resident Owners, Owner-Occupants may pay the cost of remedying said default and charge said cost to Non-resident Owners as Additional Contributions pursuant to Paragraph 13.

21. Purchase of Defaulting Party's Interest.

In the event that a default by either party is not remedied pursuant to Paragraph 20, then the defaulting party hereby gives the non-defaulting party the right to purchase the defaulting party's interest in the Property exercisable on the terms and conditions set forth in Paragraphs 15, 16, 17, and 18, above.

22. Distribution of Cash from Refinancing or Insurance.

In the event the Property is refinanced, or in the event of receipt of any casualty insurance proceeds or condemnation award with respect to the Property, any cash arising therefrom not used to reconstruct or replace the Property shall be applied and distributed to the parties pursuant to Paragraph 14(g). Non-resident Owners agree to assign Non-resident Owners' interest in any monies paid by the insurance company for Owner-Occupants' personal property to Owner-Occupants.

23. Eminent Domain.

If all or any part of the Property shall be taken or appropriated by any public or quasi-public authority under the power of Eminent Domain (a "Taking"), any award resulting from such Taking shall be distributed to the parties in accordance with Paragraph 14(g).

24. Indemnification.

Owner-Occupants shall hold Non-resident Owners harm-

less from, and defend and indemnify Non-resident Owners against, any and all claims, costs, including, without limitation, attorneys' fees, causes of action, or liability for any injury or damage to any person or property in, on, or about the Property when such injury or damage shall be caused in part or in whole by the intentional or negligent act or omission of Owner-Occupants, Owner-Occupants' agents, employees, or invitees. Non-resident Owners shall hold Owner-Occupants harmless from, and defend and indemnify Owner-Occupants against, any and all claims, costs, including, without limitation, attorneys' fees, causes of action, or liability for any injury or damage to any person or property in, on, or about the Property when such injury or damage shall be caused in part or in whole by the intentional or negligent act or omission of Non-resident Owners, Non-resident Owners' agents, employees, or invitees.

25. Notices.

Any notice or other communication required or desired to be served, given, or delivered hereunder shall be in writing and shall be deemed to have been duly served, given, or delivered upon personal delivery or upon deposit (within the continental United States) in the United States mail, registered, or certified, with proper postage or other charges prepaid and addressed to the party to be notified as follows:

To Non-resident Owners: ______________________________

____

____

To Owner-Occupants: ______________________________

____

____

or in the manner prescribed herein to such other address or addresses of which any party may notify the other party in writing.

26. Successors and Assigns.

Owner-Occupants and Non-resident Owners may not assign, transfer, sell, mortgage, pledge, hypothecate, or encumber the Property or Agreement or any interest therein. Owner-Occupants shall not permit any person other than Owner-Occupants' immediate family to occupy or use the Property or any portion thereof without the prior written consent of Non-resident Owners. The Owner-Occupants must also occupy the Property as a principal residence. Subject to the fore-

31. Miscellaneous. Our Agreement specifies that any questions arising under it shall be settled according to the state laws of California. Your attorney can make sure that the Agreement is adapted to the laws of your state.

going restrictions, this Agreement shall inure to the benefit of and bind the heirs, executors, administrators, successors, and assigns of the respective parties hereto.

27. Entire Agreement.

This Agreement contains the entire agreement of the parties with respect to the matters covered herein, and no other agreement, statement, or promise made by any party which is not contained herein shall be binding or valid. This Agreement may be modified or amended only by a written instrument duly executed by all parties hereto.

28. Attorneys' Fees.

If any party should bring legal action to construe or enforce any of the terms or conditions of this Agreement, the prevailing party in that action shall be entitled to recover reasonable attorneys' fees from the non-prevailing party, together with all costs, expenses, and reasonable attorneys' fees incurred in enforcing any judgment entered therein or in an appeal therefrom.

29. Severability.

The provisions of this Agreement are intended to be severable. If any term or provision of this Agreement is illegal or invalid for any reason whatsoever, such illegality or invalidity shall not affect the validity of the remainder of this Agreement.

30. Time is of the essence in this Agreement.

31. Miscellaneous.

This Agreement shall be governed by the laws of the State of California, and any question arising hereunder shall be construed or determined according to such law. Headings at the beginning of each numbered paragraph of this Agreement are solely for the convenience of the parties and are not a part of this Agreement. The singular or plural shall each be deemed to include the others whenever the context so requires. The waiver of any party or the breach by the other of any term, covenant, or condition herein contained shall not be deemed to be a waiver of any subsequent breach of the same or any other term, covenant, or condition herein contained.

32. Further Assurances.

The parties covenant and agree to take such further actions and to execute, acknowledge, and deliver such additional documents

Arbitration. We have never used an arbitration clause in our Shared-Equity Financing Agreement. However, arbitration is something you may have heard about as a method for resolving disagreements. In the event of a dispute between the parties, arbitration could be a simple and relatively inexpensive way to settle the issue. On the other hand, your arbitrator could be an inexperienced businessperson or an attorney who has no knowledge of equity sharing. And if arbitration is specified in the Agreement it would be mandatory and binding, without right of appeal, so you would want to be certain that you understand the arbitration laws in your state.

Here is a suggested Arbitration Clause:

Should any controversy arise regarding this Agreement or regarding the parties' ownership interests in the property, the controversy shall be settled by arbitration through the American Arbitration Association, using its Commercial Arbitration Rules. The arbitrator may award to the prevailing party, and against the non-prevailing party, reasonable sums for attorney fees and other arbitration expenses.

including, without limitation, loan documents, escrow instructions, and other instruments as may be reasonably required to implement the terms and conditions of this Agreement.

IN WITNESS HEREOF, this Agreement is entered into on the date first above written. All parties have been advised to seek tax and legal counsel of their own separate choosing as to the terms and conditions herein and fully understand and agree to this Agreement prior to signing this document.

Non-resident Owners

Dated:____________________, 19____ By:________________

Dated:____________________, 19____ By:________________

Owner-Occupants

Dated:____________________, 19____ By:________________

Dated:____________________, 19____ By:________________

·6·

Putting It All Together

OK. Now you know what equity sharing is. You know a number of different ways an equity-share arrangement can be structured. You know how to project what will happen to the value of your property under different appreciation scenarios. You know what the tax benefits of home ownership are. You know how to draw up an equity-share agreement that will protect you under a wide variety of circumstances. So where do you go from here?

GET A PROFESSIONAL TO HELP YOU

The best advice we can give you in this regard is find a competent real estate agent who's familiar with equity sharing and who is willing and able to help you use equity sharing to get into home ownership.*

It is *possible* to put together an equity-share arrangement without a real estate agent, but having a good agent will make it so much *easier*. In many parts of the country purchasing a home has become a complicated and confusing procedure, simply because of all the paperwork brought about by consumer protection laws. One can lose interest in ever owning a home by just looking at the stack of forms that are

*You'll often see the terms "real estate agent," "broker," and "Realtor" used interchangeably. A "real estate agent" can be either a "sales agent" or a "broker." Both are licensed by the state to practice real estate. This means they have completed a course of study covering the principles and practices of real estate and have passed a state-sponsored license exam which, in most states, can be kept current by continuing education in the field of real estate. In some states, a real estate broker has been a licensed real estate agent or salesperson for at least two years or has a related four-year college degree and has passed a more advanced broker's license exam. All brokers are sales agents but not all agents are brokers. Brokers usually, though not always, have their own brokerage offices and have licensed agents working for them on an independent contractual basis. A Realtor is either an agent or a broker who belongs to the local Board of Realtors and consequently to the National Association of Realtors. This is a self-governing body of agents and brokers that sets ethical standards for the real estate industry and that also serves as a lobbying force in Washington to protect the interests of the housing industry on a state and national basis.

required by various local, state, and federal entities before the property can change hands.

A competent real estate agent can help you complete these forms and greatly simplify this sometimes forbidding process. Also, buying your first home can be unnerving. There are so many unknowns and, being only human, we are often afraid of the unknown. It seems like such a big step: it's all the money you've got in the world; you're looking at monthly payments that appear staggering; you're bombarded with terms you've never heard of; and you feel as if you're signing your life away. At two o'clock in the morning, the idea of staying in your rental property seems like a much more sensible plan. We'll talk more about this condition in a bit, but a competent agent recognizes these symptoms of "buyer's remorse" and can help guide you through the psychological ups and downs of buying your own home.

Also, unless you have a lot of experience negotiating on your own behalf, you'll be in a much stronger position when it comes time to make the offer if you have an experienced negotiator working for you.

Having said this, we have to add that finding a competent agent may be the most difficult step you encounter in an equity-share purchase.

Like a Good Man, a Good Agent Is Hard to Find

As licensed agents we can tell you from our own experience—and the experiences of our clients—that some real estate agents are just plain lazy. For many agents, equity sharing is something new, and it is, in fact, more complicated than a conventional purchase. Because of this, some agents don't want to take the time and trouble to learn how to put an equity-share purchase together. Instead, they'll tell prospective buyers that equity sharing doesn't work, or that it's not safe, or that it's too complicated and creates too many problems.

We are among the most active real estate agents in our area because we've made a practice of structuring home ownership for clients whom other brokers have turned away. Our owner-occupants and non-resident owners alike are delighted with their equity-share arrangements. Equity sharing does work. Yet we regularly have clients who tell us that before they found us they had agent after agent tell them, "Sorry, you just don't have enough money to buy a home right now. Come back next year." Or, "You can't afford a house here. You'll have to move to the next town up the road and commute an hour or two to your job." One agent actually told prospective clients that equity sharing was against the law. These clients, by the way, are now 50 percent owners in a beautiful home within ten minutes of their place of work, and they're ecstatic to be owning their own home.

How to Pick the First Member of Your Team

The truth is that in the real estate business, as in any other business, 20 percent of the people do 80 percent of the work. Your job is to find one among that 20 percent. How do you do it?

One way for you to find such an agent is to talk to everyone you know who has purchased a home. Start making a list of names of real estate agents that people recommend.

If you don't know anyone who's purchased a home with equity sharing, you might call escrow officers in your area to see if any of them are currently handling equity-share purchases. If they are, get the names of the agents who are representing those purchases. If you live in an area where real estate closings are handled by attorneys, call attorneys who specialize in real estate. (You'll eventually need an attorney on your team to help you finalize your shared-equity agreement. We'll talk more about this below.)

Also, start keeping your eye on the ads in the real estate section of your local newspaper. Often agents who specialize in certain aspects of real estate, such as equity sharing or tax-deferred exchanges, advertise their specialty.

Another source to call might be your local Board of Realtors to see if it has the names of real estate agents who are involved in equity sharing.

If none of these calls turns up an agent who knows equity sharing, then go back to the first step and get the names of as many highly recommended realtors as you can. You're looking for an agent who is experienced, competent, patient, and excellent on follow-through; someone who is a real go-getter and who is willing to hold your hand every step of the way if necessary.

Keep in mind that the real estate business, by its very nature, lends itself to part-time work, or to people who work on just one or two deals a year. For equity sharing—in fact for any purchase—you'll want to avoid a part-time agent and, for the most part, you'll want to steer clear of inexperienced agents.

The ideal person to help you put together your equity-share arrangement is someone who has been in the real estate business full time for at least three or four years and who is active on a day-to-day basis with the local real estate market. This will be someone who knows a good buy when one comes up and who knows the market well enough to steer you clear of overpriced properties. (You'll need to know the market yourself, and we'll talk about this later.) A good agent will be someone who has had experience negotiating a fair purchase price and who knows how to hold a deal together when the seller gets nervous, when the seller's agent leaves town for the week, and when you get scared and are ready to back out of the whole thing.

The real estate agent you use should be familiar with and preferably have experience in tax-deferred exchanges, not only for the benefit of your non-resident owner but, as we saw in the last chapter, for your own benefit if you decide to keep your first property as an investment and need to defer the tax on it. Don't ever, ever, ever let a real estate agent, or an accountant, or an attorney tell you a tax-deferred exchange is too much trouble so just go ahead and pay the tax. There is never any reason to pay more tax than you have to. People who tell you differently simply don't know what they're talking about. Your agent/attorney/accountant should be talking you *into* tax-deferred exchanges. As we explained in Chapter 4, the form of a tax-deferred exchange must be followed exactly, but for someone who is familiar with the process, nothing could be simpler. If you come across anyone who tells you otherwise, you should start looking immediately for their replacement on your team. We speak from experience: failure to follow this advice could cost you thousands of dollars.

In addition to following the ads, you might consider running a small ad of your own in the real estate section of your local paper. Wording like, "home-buyer looking for real estate agent experienced in handling equity sharing and tax-deferred exchanges," should get some responses. You'll want to screen them carefully, with some questions along the lines of those we list in the next section.

Also, be prepared for some agents who will try to talk you out of equity sharing, or who will try to convince you they know all about equity sharing when in fact they don't. The last half-dozen questions on the list should help you weed those out. It may turn out that you can purchase 100 percent of a property on your own, and if so that's great—we regularly work with clients who come to us for help in structuring an equity-share purchase, and we find after qualifying them that they are able to get into 100 percent ownership. But you want to be sure you have an agent who knows how to arrange an equity-share purchase if it turns out that that's the only way you can get into home ownership.

Some Things You'll Want to Know Before You Decide on a Real Estate Agent

We've developed the following list of questions which you can use as a guide when trying to find an agent to work with. You'll want to ask all potential agents:

How long have they been licensed?

What type of license do they hold?

Do they work at real estate full time?

What price range do they deal with? (In large cities where there's a wide range of home prices, it's difficult to be an expert in every price range. Look for an agent who works regularly in and is thoroughly familiar with the price range you can afford.)

Do they work regularly with first-time buyers? (Some agents specialize in higher-priced properties and consequently are used to dealing with buyers who've been through the home buying process many times before. They often forget that home buying can be an intimidating process the first time around.)

Can they give you the names of satisfied clients you can call for references? (Get those references and check them out.)

What do they do when they have a client who can qualify for the loan but who doesn't have enough cash for the down payment?

Are they familiar with equity sharing? If so, how many equity-share purchases have they put together in the past year? Have they represented the buyer or the seller? You want one who has represented the buyer. (Get those references and check them out.)

How do they structure an equity-share arrangement? Are both owners on the deed? Are both owners on the loan? What holding time do they feel works for their market—three years? Five years?

Do they require that part of the down payment come from the owner-occupant? (As we've said before, "nothing down" arrangements are seldom advantageous for either party.)

How do they negotiate the percentage of ownership?

Will they help you work out some projections for an equity-share purchase, based on the rate of appreciation in your market?

Do they understand the tax consequences of equity sharing? Have they handled tax-deferred exchanges? If not, can they recommend an accountant, an escrow officer, or an attorney who does?

Do they have a shared-equity financing agreement? If so, find out how extensive it is. At what point in the buying process is the agreement signed? It must be prior to the closing to meet the requirements of Tax Code 280A.

If they are not familiar with equity sharing, are they at least open to the idea and willing to help you? If you are unable to find an agent who is experienced in this specialty, at the very least you'll want to find one who is receptive to the possibilities and willing to learn. Following the steps we've outlined in this book, and especially using the outline of our shared-equity financing agreement, an experienced agent should be able to guide you in setting up a sound shared-equity arrangement.

Finding the Rest of Your Team

Once you've found a real estate agent you can work with, putting together the rest of your team will be relatively easy. To begin with, a good agent whose knowledge and expertise you trust will probably be able to refer you to other qualified professionals. You'll need:

An attorney.
An accountant.
An escrow agent (or attorney) to handle the closing.

A mortgage broker or loan officer.
An insurance agent.

Attorneys and Accountants

You'll want to have an attorney review your shared-equity financing agreement to make sure it addresses your particular circumstances. If you live in an area where closings are handled by attorneys, you'll probably use the same attorney for the closing, too. If you are working with a good real estate agent, he or she is going to have a list of several attorneys and accountants who know and/or specialize in real estate transactions.

You'll want to get references from a prospective attorney, which you should check thoroughly. You'll also want an attorney or accountant whom you are considering to answer the same kinds of questions we listed above. You'll want both your attorney and your accountant to specialize in real estate. Ideally, they should own investment property themselves so they are personally and professionally familiar with the benefits and the pitfalls of owning real estate. If you are unable to find an attorney who has worked with equity sharing before, at the very least you'll want one who is receptive to the idea. This will be someone who is willing to discuss your situation with you to make certain that the shared-equity financing agreement you draw up will adequately protect you.

Also, both these members of your team should be experienced in tax-deferred exchanges. It would be a good idea for you to get the names of clients for whom they have completed exchanges and check these references carefully.

The Escrow Officer

If your closing is handled by an escrow officer, you'll want one who has an excellent reputation for following escrow instructions and for acting as a "referee" for both the buyer and the seller and, again, one experienced in tax-deferred exchanges. Your escrow officer will act as an impartial agent for both the buyer and the seller in preparing all the papers relating to the transaction, getting everything properly signed, delivered, and recorded, and then accounting to the parties for the funds involved. Since the escrow instructions are complicated in an equity-share arrangement—considerations include percentages of ownership, how ownership is to be held, separate accountings for incoming funds, tax-deferred funds to be held—the operative qualification is "an excellent reputation for following escrow instructions." The best reference would probably come from your real estate agent, who has presumably had experience working with a competent escrow officer.

Mortgage Broker

Mark Twain once said that when the end of the world came, he wanted to be in New England because everything happens fifteen years later there. We feel pretty much the same way about banks: many of them are still fifteen years behind the rest of the business world. They're often inflexible, they're usually run by very conservative people who aren't always fully aware of what's happening outside their walls, and they're not always what you'd call receptive to new ideas, particularly ones they didn't think of first.

If you were to walk in off the street and attempt to get a loan for a property that was being purchased in an equity-share arrangement or, in banking language, by "non-related co-borrowers," most loan officers wouldn't know how to deal with it and probably wouldn't be willing or able to help you much. If they did agree to arrange a loan for your equity-share purchase, they'd most likely demand a higher non-owner-occupied rate.

In most areas of the country, one of the best ways for you to obtain a loan for equity sharing is to contact a mortgage broker who works either independently for a wide variety of different lenders, including some banks, within your area or for a mortgage company that does business with a wide variety of lenders.

If you are working with a real estate agent, he or she will no doubt be able to refer you to a competent, experienced loan broker. If you're on your own, check the Yellow Pages and start calling. In either case you'll want answers to many of the questions we listed above. This is a very important step and must not be overlooked. In many states the licensing and regulation of loan brokers (as opposed to loan officers in a bank, which operates under the aegis of federal banking regulations) leaves much to be desired. There are many good ones, but you must screen them carefully.

A loan broker who has handled equity-share purchases will no doubt have a list of lenders who will loan to non-related co-borrowers at lower owner-occupied rates. Otherwise, you'll have to start interviewing until you find a loan broker who is willing to search for lenders who are receptive to equity sharing. A good mortgage broker who does a lot of business (and therefore has a lot of clout) and who understands the concept and the importance of equity sharing not only in terms of widening the market for home buyers but for non-resident owners as well, should have no trouble convincing banks and other lenders of the viability of this type of purchase.

When we started out, we were fortunate enough to be able to work with an excellent mortgage broker who saw the need for equity-sharing lenders and was willing to blaze trails in terms of convincing lenders to loan to non-related co-borrowers. Now she has a corner on the market in our area because she has become known for her willingness to educate lenders. Lenders love her because she is constantly bringing them new, qualified loan applicants who would otherwise have been turned away.

After you've found your mortgage broker or loan officer, you'll want to set up an appointment to meet and determine your loan qualifications. The first thing the loan broker should do is run a complete credit check on you to make certain that you have good credit. The report we use is a combination of TRW and Trans Union and Statewide and is one of the most comprehensive credit reports available. This report costs approximately $50, but it is a vital step in the process and well worth the expense. A spotless record with no late payments ever will make your loan application a much simpler procedure. If your credit report shows some late notices and you have a legitimate excuse, a good loan broker can help you present to the lender a loan application package that will have a good chance of being approved.

And by the way, once you get a loan you'll want to be certain to always make your monthly payments on time. Lenders will overlook a late Sears payment or two, but they are not so lenient when it comes to mortgage payments. Even one late mortgage payment could make it very difficult for you to get another loan. Maintaining a spotless credit record is an important step in your equity sharing program.

If you've completed the exercises in this book, you'll already have a good idea of the amount of loan you can qualify for. In any case, your loan officer should be able to go over that process with you, answer any questions you may have about different types of loans, and even help you compare the payments on different loan amounts or on different types of loans. Or you can use the Loan Program Comparison Worksheet in Figure 6-A for this purpose.

This pre-qualification makes it possible for you to lock in a favorable rate so that when you open escrow you'll know what your mortgage

FIGURE 6-A

Prepared for: ____________________ Prepared by: ____________________

Property Address: ____________________ Loan Amount: ____________________

____

Date: ____________________ LTV: ____________________

LOAN PROGRAM COMPARISONS

1. Loan type					
2. Initial interest rate					
3. Term (25, 30 years)					
4. Lender fees, points					
5. Prepayment penalty					
6. Co-borrowers allowed?					
7. Max. yearly Negative Am					
8. Assumable?					
9. Which index is used?					
10. When is margin set?					
11. How often do interest rate adjustments occur?					
12. How often do payment adjustments occur?					
13. Interest rate caps					
14. What period covered by caps?					
15. Against what interest rate is cap increased?					
16. Are there payment increase caps?					
17. How much? How long?					
18. Do interest and payment caps apply to up and down interest moves?					
19. Does index look to most recent change or the average?					
20. Initial payment					

interest rate will be. Once you have had your credit standing verified and you've been qualified for a loan amount, you'll be in a much stronger position when it comes time to make an offer on a property. A wise seller, in a position to choose among several offers, will be much more inclined to accept an offer from a pre-qualified buyer than from a buyer whose credit position is unknown.

Any non-resident owner you work with should go through exactly the same credit and loan verification procedure. A competent mortgage broker knows that lenders who will loan to non-related co-borrowers are looking for both borrowers to be financially solid. People sometimes have the idea that teaming one financially weak party with one who is stronger will be acceptable to a lender, but that is usually not the case. You will want to avoid any weak links at all costs, and a good mortgage broker can help you do this.

Insurance Agent

An insurance agent should be relatively easy to find. You may want an independent agent who represents a wide variety of insurance carriers so you can get the most competitive rates. You may already have a helpful agent who handles your auto and life insurance. If so, discuss your prospective home purchase to see if you can get competitive rates.

Also, you'll need to make certain your agent understands that your home insurance policy must list both you and your non-resident owner as co-owners and co-insureds, as we said in Chapter 5. Most companies will do this with no difficulty. If, for any reason, yours won't, shop around or get recommendations from your realtor for one who will.

GET TO KNOW YOUR HOUSING MARKET

If you haven't already done so, it's time to begin looking at properties. One of the best ways to become familiar with the market is to start going to open houses, with or without your real estate agent. It is often through these open houses, which are usually held on Saturdays and Sundays, that new listings are introduced to the market. Open houses are open to the buying public as well as to real estate agents and are usually listed in the real estate section of your newspaper. In some areas the Board of Realtors provides a list of the open houses each week.

Spend as much time as you can looking at open houses or condos in your price range. In addition, you'll want to spend time with your real estate agent seeing homes that never had an open house or whose open house you missed. Keep a record of the houses that sell so you can get a feel for how close to their asking prices houses are actually selling. In a slow-moving market you may be able to get an offer accepted at 10 percent or even 20 percent below the asking price. In a fast-moving market you may have to come much closer to the asking price to get your offer accepted.

Once you find a house you like, talk to people in the neighborhood. Find out what they like and don't like about the area. Are there major changes projected, such as new roads or school closings or new commercial developments, that might adversely affect the value of the property? Do they know of any problems with the house? Some states now require a full disclosure from the seller about any existing or potential problems, but where such disclosure is not required, it's often a matter of "buyer beware." Once you've had your offer accepted, you'll no doubt have a thorough inspection of the property by a competent home-inspection service or licensed contractor. But it won't hurt to do whatever legwork you can ahead of time so you're at least aware of any potential problems.

And don't forget to work the numbers. Take your pocket mortgage-amortization book and your calculator along. Figure out what the probable monthly payment will be on each property you are considering. If you're lucky, your final decision won't be made solely on the basis of the numbers—there are intangibles, such as the particular ambiance of a house, that may be more important than the bottom line. But you should at least know what the bottom line is.

And while you're at it, think about the houses that particularly appeal to you—the ones you're ready to make an offer on the minute you pull up to the curb, or as soon as you step in the front door. Generally speaking, these houses, which are said to have "curb appeal," are the ones that sell the fastest and get the best prices. Try to analyze what makes them so desirable. Usually you'll find they are impeccably maintained both inside and out, and all the normal day-to-day clutter has been removed. There may be fresh flowers or potted plants ingeniously placed throughout the house. Maybe there's a fire in the fireplace or delicious smells of home baking coming from the kitchen. The overall feeling is inviting, and you're certain you could step right in and be at home. Remember the feelings this type of home imparts because you'll want to create the same type of atmosphere when it comes time to put your property on the market.

Notice that we're not saying this is necessarily the type of home you should buy. In fact, if you have imagination and can look past the clutter of a similar home that doesn't "show" as well, you may be able to get that home for a better price and create your own ambiance once you own it.

Just remember to use your property search as a time not only to learn the market so you can get the best buy, but also to learn what you need to do to get the best price when it comes time for you to sell.

FINDING A NON-RESIDENT OWNER

Once you've been qualified for a loan and have become familiar with the market, it's time to start looking for a non-resident owner. If you're working with an agent, he or she may have a source of investor money to connect you with. If not, it's time for you to start asking. Do you have parents or brothers or sisters or any other relatives who would be able to back you? How about business contacts? Perhaps your employer? Anyone you know who has owned a home for a number of years in a good real estate market is a potential non-resident owner. If they have a loan with a high variable or fixed interest rate this might be a good time for them to refinance and take out some cash to invest in your equity-share purchase. They could lower their monthly payment and take advantage of leverage to maximize the return on their equity dollars, while at the same time reducing their tax bill with the increased deductible interest on their own home and the depreciation of the equity-shared property.

If you don't know anyone in that position, you might try running a want ad in the investment section of your newspaper: "Well-qualified home buyer looking for non-resident co-owner interested in low-risk, highly-leveraged, management-free owner-occupied property."

Another source for your non-resident owner might be among owners of rental property who are tired of maintenance and tenant management and who would be willing to give up a share of the future appreciation in a property they now own in exchange for some immediate cash (your down payment) and a trouble-free occupant. Try an ad such as: "Rental property owners: tired of tenant headaches? Need some additional cash for your equity? I'm a qualified home buyer looking for an equity share position in a good area. I'll make your monthly payments and give you cash for a portion of your equity and a share in the future appreciation." Rental property is also an excellent source for "sweat-equity" ownership. An equity-share arrangement in a tenant-occupied property that has deteriorated but can, with a little fixing, be turned into a "curb appeal" property that will benefit both you and the current owner.

Other potential equity-share purchasers are empty-nesters who are looking to move to a smaller, less expensive home. They might be willing to put a portion of their excess cash into a well-managed appreciating asset as a means of maximizing the growth of their capital. Or they might be willing to sell a portion of their larger home to you as an equity-share purchaser and use the cash you pay as a down payment to buy their smaller home.

Attorneys and accountants are often good sources for money; sometimes, believe it or not, bankers are, too. If you have a good relationship with an officer of your bank (and if you haven't, develop one) who is familiar with your banking history, he might be more than happy to connect you with other clients who are financially solid and looking for a good investment.

Once you've narrowed the list down to a couple of the most likely co-owners, you'll want to meet with them to discuss the possibilities and see if you like each other. You'll want to know if they've been involved in equity sharing before and, if so, do they have specific references you can check. They'll want to check yours, too, of course. This is one of the most valuable services an experienced equity-share real estate agent can provide—working as a matchmaker for both parties. We regularly have several dozen owner-occupants and non-resident owners we're working with at any one time. Once we've gone through our counseling sessions, which we do with non-resident owners as well, and once every client has been pre-qualified, we know enough about them to effect a good match.

Even with a matchmaker doing the legwork, you'll want to know as much as possible about your co-owner before you make an offer on a property. By the time you're ready to make an offer on a property, you will presumably have had an initial meeting with your potential co-owner and will have a specific property in mind which the co-owner has seen and approved. If you find a property before you've made a definite decision about a non-resident owner, make your offer contingent upon finding a non-resident owner within so many days.

Following are some points you should think about and/or discuss with your non-resident owner:

Do you basically like each other?

You won't be living together and in the normal course of events, after the closing takes place, you probably won't even see each other more than once or twice a year. But you need to have mutual trust in each other and a willingness to work together on any problem that might arise.

Do you both like the property?

Obviously, there are certain considerations here that are going to be more important to the owner-occupants than to the non-resident owner. Since the owner-occupants are going to be living in it we usually encourage them to select the property and then make sure the non-resident likes it, too. Even though he is not going to live in the property, the non-resident owner needs to be certain that the location is good and that the potential for resale is such that it will maximize the investment.

Do you both agree on how the property should look when it comes time to sell?

One of the key factors in the success of an equity-share arrangement is the marketability of the property when it's put up for sale. It is important that the non-resident owner be assured ahead of time that the owner-occupant has the ability to show the property to its best advantage or at the very least the willingness to learn how to do this.

One way to ascertain this ahead of time is for the non-resident owner to visit the prospective owner-occupants in their current residence to literally check out their living habits and estimate their ability to show the property to its best advantage. Slovenly housekeepers are not going to make good equity-share owner-occupants. Any thoughts or opinions the parties have in this regard should be discussed ahead of time and written into the agreement. Since most of our owner-occupants are first-time buyers, they are usually happy to defer to the experience of a co-owner who knows how a property should be shown to maximize the sale price.

How will you handle alterations and improvements?

It is important to go through the property together ahead of time to see what needs to be changed in order to maximize the value when it's time to sell.

The owner-occupants might like to make some changes that would enhance their own comfort or enjoyment but that won't necessarily enhance the value of the property. The co-owner might have no objections to such changes being made, but may not want to share the cost. As much as possible these things should be decided ahead of time.

For example, let's say all the windows need new coverings—drapes or mini-blinds or shutters. After checking around you find that for $1,500 you can get adequate mini-blinds that would look good, be functional, and add to the value of the property. But let's say the owner-occupant wants "plantation shutters" that cost $3,000. The co-owner would probably be happy to go along with half of the cost of the mini-blinds (assuming 50/50 ownership) but any expense over that amount would be borne by the owner-occupant.

What about pets?

Generally speaking, non-resident owners prefer not to have pets because of the added wear and tear on the property. At the same time, though, an owner-occupant has more incentive than a tenant would to make sure there is no damage to the property by pets. Whatever the decision, it should be clearly spelled out in the equity-share agreement.

Are your plans for the time you wish to hold the property compatible?

Most of the shared-equity purchases we arrange are set up so that all parties must unanimously agree not to sell the property before an agreed-upon time, usually two to five years from the date of purchase. As you know from Chapter 5, owner-occupants usually have the option of establishing how long they want to be in the property before the parties can decide to sell or refinance. This gives the owner-occupants the security of not being forced to move out of their home before the agreed-upon time and also complies with the fifty-year rule set out in 280A. After the specified period of time, either party can give the other party a ninety-day notice of desire to sell. If you're in an area that has slow to moderate appreciation, you may have to hold the property for a longer period of time to get the maximum benefit from the appreciation.

But if the owner-occupant is looking at the property as someplace to live in forever and the non-resident owner would like to be out of it in two years, your time-frame goals may not be compatible. Of course, as we saw in Chapter 3, if the appreciation potential is good, it is possible that in two to three years the property could be refinanced, and the owner-occupant could take a portion of the increased equity and buy out the non-resident. It is important that each of you understand the other's goals and that you put your understanding in writing in your agreement.

What plans do the parties have for when it comes time to either sell or refinance?

Is it possible that you would both want to maintain your interest in the property and purchase another property either together or separately? If so, how will the first property be managed? This should be decided ahead of time. Assuming the parties are compatible, equity sharing can be an excellent long-term investment program. We have heard equity sharing described as "buying a home with a stranger," but if you do equity sharing right, you'll know more about your co-purchaser than you know about most of your family and many of your friends. Getting to know your co-owner is one of the best ways to insure the success of your equity-share purchase.

Once you've had your offer accepted, you can proceed with the loan application and start drawing up your shared equity agreement, which you'll want to sign prior to the closing.

The process we've described here—from putting your team together to getting an accepted offer—can take anywhere from a few days to several months. We frequently see people moving into our area who've taken a few days off from their jobs to scout the territory. Perhaps they are being transferred and have only a short time to get familiar with the market, put their team together, get qualified, meet their potential co-owner, find a property they like, and get an offer accepted. Preferably, however, the process will require a couple of months. Whenever possible it's best to take enough time to become thoroughly familiar with the market and with your co-owner so there are no surprises later on. Just don't wait so long that the market moves beyond your reach.

Once you've got an accepted offer, be prepared for two things.

The first is writer's cramp. In California a home buyer signs anywhere from fifteen to eighteen single-spaced legal-sized forms from the time the offer is made through the closing. In other states the paperwork may not be as onerous, but having to read and sign even half a dozen legal documents can be overwhelming. In escrow states your real estate agent and your escrow officer will help you through this process. In attorney states, your attorney will accompany you to the closing. In either case, don't feel rushed. Take your time and make certain that each form you sign accurately represents your position. If you have questions, ask them. If the numbers aren't clear to you, work them through. As much as you can, enjoy the process and learn from it—and take notes to keep in your file for the next time you buy.

The second thing to be prepared for, and one that is sometimes exacerbated by the first, is buyer's remorse. Every now and then we come across clients who don't seem to be affected by this temporary malady, but they're rare. It may take anywhere from a couple of hours to a week for the euphoria of finally buying your own home to be replaced by gut-wrenching doubts, woeful misgivings, and late-night floor-pacing when you're certain you've done absolutely the wrong thing. You may wake up in a cold sweat thinking, "My God, what have I done? I can't afford this house! How will I ever make the monthly payments? What if the roof leaks? Or the foundation sinks? Did I pay too much? What if I lose my job? How could I have let that agent/banker/accountant/attorney talk me into this crazy scheme?"

At odd moments of the day you may find yourself in a state of complete catatonia, followed by periods of extreme agitation. Having sweaty palms or tremors probably won't incapacitate you, but co-workers may worry about your blank stares and vague mutterings. These or any number of other symptoms may occur and can last from a few minutes to several weeks. Don't worry. These are perfectly natural human reactions. Soon you'll be congratulating yourself for being so smart and for putting the whole thing together. After you've made a couple of monthly payments you'll have to pinch yourself from time to time to make sure it's not just a dream. Of course, it is a dream—the American Dream—and now you're part of it. It's time to enjoy it.

WHAT TO DO AFTER YOU SAY YOU DO

You've closed on the property. The moving van (or your friend's borrowed truck) has just pulled out of the driveway, and you're all unpacked and settled in. Where do you go from here? What can you do at this point to get the most from your equity-share investment? The most important step is to immediately set up an ongoing plan to keep the property well maintained and in good shape. This shouldn't be difficult. If the house was in top condition when you bought it, keep it that way; improve it if you can. At the very least, you'll want to establish a habit of keeping up with repairs and maintenance.

If you've never owned your own home before, you've probably not had to worry too much about upkeep—either the landlord took care of things or you got by with as little maintenance as possible. But now that you have an investment in your home it's important to stay on top of the little problems that always seem to need attention around a house and that can cause a property to lose value rapidly if not corrected. Details like broken door handles, torn screens, worn steps, loose window casings, cracked window panes, chipped tiled, clogged gutters, leaky faucets, blocked drains. The list seems endless, but if you set up a year-round maintenance schedule, it'll be much easier to keep up with the things that need to be done. Remember that an equity-share arrangement is different from owning your home completely. Now you have a responsibility not only to yourself but to your co-owner to keep the property in "marketable" condition. An ongoing maintenance program will be reflected in the overall look and feel of a property and will help you to get top dollar when it comes time to sell.

You will have discussed with your co-owner ahead of time a plan for determining which expenses you will be sharing and which ones you will be solely responsible for. As you know from the shared-equity agreement, most of our equity-share arrangements are structured so that the owner-occupant takes care of the routine maintenance and upkeep of the property up to an agreed-upon amount and the major repairs (of a roof, for example) and replacements (of, let's say, appliances) are shared between the parties, based on their percentages of ownership.

If you purchased a fixer-upper with the idea of adding sweat equity to your ownership position, it will be doubly important for you to keep track of receipts and replacement costs, not only in terms of your equity, but also to keep track of your basis, as we explained in Chapter 4.

Some non-resident owners will want to take a total hands-off position and, assuming you've done your homework and worked things out as much as possible ahead of time, it may not be necessary to be in touch with your co-owner except, at the very minimum, to establish the rent for the coming year.

Other non-resident owners, particularly those willing to be involved in a fixer-upper arrangement, may want to take a more active part in the changes you'll be making to the property, especially if, like the Browns in our Case History #4, the changes to the property are major.

HOME, SWEET HOME: HOW TO SHOW IT TO BEST ADVANTAGE

Some people we know inhabit homes that look on a day-to-day basis just the way they do when they're put on the market to sell; they're showcases.

But if you're like most of us, your daily schedule and your lifestyle are simply too hectic for you to keep your home in tip-top "show" condition all the time. When it comes time to sell, you may need to make some changes in your routine so that your house is always ready to be shown to prospective buyers.

Here's where good real estate agents can be worth their weight in gold. A top agent is used to "marketing" properties for sale and will know what you'll need to do to your home to make it show well. Constructive ideas from your agent, plus the tips you picked up when you were first looking at properties and noticed which ones were especially appealing to you, will work for starters. If you need more help—after all, it will probably be several years since you've actively shopped for properties—then study pictures in home magazines and try to get a feel for what makes the homes they show so inviting. You'll notice an absence of clutter and a strategic placement of plants or flowers. You'll also notice color coordination that's pleasing to the eye. Color has a strong psychological effect on people and should be kept in mind when you establish your decorating theme.

Take a cold, critical look at your home to see what horizontal surfaces can be cleared of "stuff." Probably all of them! Tabletops, kitchen and bath counters, desks, mantle pieces, credenzas, night stands. Remove stacks of magazines and newspapers. Clear off the coffee table and in place of all the everyday jumble put a single bowl of fresh flowers. Store that comfortable but worn-out overstuffed chair or that beat-up table you made in college in the garage.

If you have a favorite painting on the wall that might be jarring or controversial, replace it with something more conventional. We once listed a property for sale that was owned by an artist and his wife. The house showed well in every respect except for the somewhat morbid paintings that hung throughout it. When we took the listing we strongly suggested the paintings be removed, but the owners balked at the idea. After the house had been listed for a month in a fast-moving seller's market, with not a single offer, we told the sellers that if they wanted to sell they'd *have* to take down the paintings. Reluctantly they did, replaced them with far less expensive but more conventional prints, and the property sold almost immediately.

Never overestimate the ability of the average buyer to look beyond the clutter. Most people see only what is there and simply don't have the knack of seeing the possibilities. Also, clutter is confusing to the mind. A cleared, neat, and well-balanced space will make it easier for buyers to put themselves and their possessions into the "picture," which is exactly what you want them to do.

If you have pets, you may want to consider boarding them, at least during the first few weeks the property is on the market and actively being shown. There are few things more distracting to a potential buyer than an overly friendly dog salivating all over him the moment he walks through the door—except for an unfriendly one lunging for his throat. We once had clients who refused even to get out of the car when they heard the growls and snarls of Rover pulling at his leash in the side yard.

Be accommodating when people want to see the property. Remember that buyers, like you, often have hectic schedules. The only time they may be able to see a property is after work or on weekends—the time when you'd least like to have it shown.

When a buyer comes to look, be out of the house if possible, even if it means walking around the block or going next door to visit a neighbor. Put yourself in the buyer's position. It's much easier to make a decision on a house if you're free to browse through it at your leisure and aren't being made uncomfortable by over-anxious sellers.

We once found ourselves in the position of having to make a quick decision on the purchase of a new house. We had been looking all week and finally by Friday evening had narrowed the choice down to two houses. We had to fly out early the next morning and wanted to see both places before we made the final choice. The broker called both sellers to arrange appointments for that evening. One seller didn't want to be bothered on a Friday night; the other was in the middle of a small dinner party but said, "Sure, come on over." By the time we got there the guests had been moved out to the back lawn. We had a chance to wander through the house again and make our final decision. It was an easy choice: we bought the house we could see.

KEEP UP WITH THE MARKET

Now that you own your own home, it doesn't mean you can sit back and forget what's happening in real estate. You've put your eggs in a basket, and now you have to watch that basket very carefully.

Stay in touch with your real estate agent to find out what's happening with the market. Keep your eye on the real estate section of the newspaper. From time to time drop in on open houses in homes that are comparable to yours to see what's happening with prices (all the while picking up tips on what shows well and what doesn't). If this sounds like work, it really isn't. You can make a fun project out of it, especially if you find yourself in a rapidly appreciating market. Keeping tabs on the market will help you gauge when it's time to either sell or refinance. It might not be so much fun if you find the market stagnating or, worse, losing value. If you find this happening, don't panic. In fact, expect it to happen; even the hottest markets go through slow or declining periods.

If you've kept in touch with your real estate agent and the housing prices in your area, you'll know whether you're experiencing a temporary blip in the market or if there are major changes locally (or even nationally, like higher interest rates) that are causing a standstill or a setback.

If the cause is national, there's probably little you can do about it except sit tight. If the cause is local or regional, such as what happened in recent years in Denver and Dallas because of the drop in oil prices, you may have to decide whether you should hang in or bail out and move elsewhere—if possible, to a better market. This could be a tough decision, but it's not out of the question. Many people in these areas cut their losses and moved to better markets where they more than made up for the slow market they'd been in. Many of those who stayed and sat tight will be rewarded for their patience when those markets take off again soon, as many housing forecasters are predicting they will.

KEEP YOUR SAVINGS PLAN GOING

Now that you own your home it's more important than ever to keep up your savings plan. In the first place, owning a home is often more expensive than you think it will be. No matter how well you've budgeted for maintenance and upkeep, there will always be unexpected expenses you'll have to deal with. In fact, you should count on the unexpected and set aside a contingency fund to cover it.

Secondly, the more savings you're able to set aside for your dream home, the better position you'll be in when you come to sell or refinance. Reread the options we discussed in Chapter 3 and work out your own projections based on how much you'll be able to save over the next few years.

Sit down and work out a budget. Home economy experts agree that having a planned budget is one of the surest and easiest ways to set money aside. Make payments to your savings plan each month just as you make your other monthly payments. There are many excellent books available to help you tailor a budget to your own circumstances. Find or develop a method that works for you and stick to it.

We read recently about a young Vietnamese couple who came to this country with no money, no job prospects, no friends, and no family to help them. But they had lots of determination and the dream of owning their own home. Within a few years they had purchased a home and had it simply but elegantly furnished. Everyone wondered how they had done it. Here's how: they didn't own a TV or a radio. They never ate out or went to the movies. They bought their clothes second-hand. They didn't own a car—they biked to their jobs. They had cleverly salvaged and refinished what little furniture they had. (Though we tend to forget it, this is how many of our parents and grandparents bought their first homes.)

These days, not everyone would be willing to make the sacrifices this couple made to own their own home, but it shows that if you want something bad enough, almost anything is within your reach. If you want to own your own home, you can. We've done the hard part—showing you how to do it. Now the easy part—going out and doing it—is up to you!

·7·

Questions and Answers

After working with hundreds of equity-share owner-occupants and non-resident owners, we have assembled a list of the questions people most frequently ask about equity sharing.

Is equity sharing something new?

No. Equity-sharing techniques have been used for many years to help first-time buyers get into the housing market. Traditionally, parents have helped their children buy their first home. Now, with the refinements in our shared-equity agreement, not only parents and family members but also unrelated owner-occupants and non-resident co-owners can take advantage of the many benefits equity sharing offers.

To date, thousands of homes have been purchased across the country using equity-share methods. Consequently, more and more banks, attorneys, escrow officers, and real estate brokers are familiar with this type of purchase. Even the Federal Housing Authority (FHA) has approved loans for equity-share purchases.

Wouldn't owner-occupants be better off buying the house on their own?

Yes, absolutely, if they have the cash needed for the down payment and the closing costs and if they can qualify for the loan on their own. With the high cost of housing today, many people simply do not have the necessary funds, which is why equity sharing is becoming more and more popular. With equity sharing you can have the benefits of home ownership, including the tax advantages, even if you don't have all the cash required for the down payment.

Would owner-occupants be better off to wait until they have enough money so they can afford to buy the property on their own?

Possibly, if the owner-occupants are expecting a substantial amount of cash in the near future, say from an inheritance or from a large bonus. But if property values continue to appreciate, the amount they will need to put down will increase as well. In the meantime, the owner-occupants will lose out on the tax benefits of owning real estate as well as the joys of being in their own home.

Why would non-resident owners want to provide part of the down payment for people they don't know?

If the owner-occupants have a good credit rating, secure jobs, and a history of taking good care of the properties they've rented, there are many prospective co-owners who would be willing to share the appreciation of a property for a management-free, vacancy-free, no-negative-cash-flow property. As additional security for non-resident owners in the event of default, the owner-occupants pledge their interest in the property to fulfill the terms and conditions of the shared-equity agreement.

How much of the down payment should come from the owner-occupants?

At the very minimum, the owner-occupants should contribute 25 percent of the down payment (5 percent of the purchase price, on a 20 percent down payment). This will give them a minimum of 25 percent ownership. Most non-resident owners want the owner-occupants to have their own money in the property. Owner-occupants with a vested interest will be much more likely to take good care of the property and to live up to the terms of the shared-equity agreement. In addition, most lenders require that 5 percent of the funds come from the owner-occupant in order for the buyers to qualify for more favorable owner-occupied rates and terms.

Does the owner-occupant have title to the property?

Yes. Both the non-resident owner and the owner-occupant must apply for a loan and be approved by the lender. They are both listed on the loan and on the deed based on their percentages of ownership, and the deed is recorded at the time of closing.

Why should the property be held as a tenancy in common rather than as a partnership?

Most accountants agree that under the current tax law property held in partnership cannot qualify for the tax-deferred exchange provisions of the tax code for owner-occupants or non-resident owners. Therefore, any profits from the property are taxed at the time the property is sold. Tenancy-in-common ownership allows tax on profits to be deferred to a later time and gives equal rights to all parties.

How do owner-occupants qualify for a shared-equity purchase?

Owner-occupants need to qualify for the loan just as though they were purchasing the property on their own, but they'll have the additional strength of the non-resident owner's financial statement. First, they should meet with a loan officer or a mortgage broker to determine what loan amount they can afford. A credit report will be obtained to show that they have good credit and a history of paying their bills on time. The non-resident owner goes through the same process. Each party will complete a mortgage loan application. After the property is located and the Offer to Purchase has been accepted, the property will be appraised and will have to meet the lender's requirements, i.e., size, construction, building codes. Then the loan applications, credit reports, and appraisal will be submitted to the lender for final approval.

How much should owner-occupants plan to pay each month?

Most lenders require that the owner-occupants' monthly income be about three times the amount of their total monthly housing expenses, excluding utilities. The ratio of monthly payment to income varies from 28 percent to 33 percent, depending on the other debts (such as car payments, charge accounts, and other consumer loans) the loan applicants may have. The owner-occupants' monthly payment, including principal, interest, taxes, and insurance, is usually higher than the rent payment for a comparable property. But after the tax savings of home ownership is calculated the PITI payment will often be very close to the rent charge for a similar home.

What happens if the owner-occupants are unable to make the payments?

Just as if they had purchased the property on their own, they could lose their interest in the property if payments are not made on time. However, before lenders approve a loan they will make all the necessary credit, employment, and bank verifications to determine that the owner-occupants can reasonably afford the payments. If they default on the loan payments, the property might have to be sold, as described under "termination events" in the shared equity agreement discussed in Chapter 5.

How are repairs and maintenance of the property handled?

Normal maintenance and minor repairs are taken care of by the owner-occupant. The shared-equity agreement provides that any repairs over an agreed-upon amount, for example $100, will be shared between the owner-occupant and the non-resident owner, based on their percentages of ownership.

How are improvements to the property paid for?

The shared-equity agreement provides that any alterations or improvements must be agreed on by both parties. Any improvements over an agreed-upon amount, for example $200, will be shared by all parties based on their percentages of ownership.

What happens if the owner-occupant and the non-resident owner don't get along?

If there is a major disagreement, it could force a termination event, as outlined in the equity-share agreement, Paragraph 14. However, if they have screened each other carefully ahead of time, and if their goals for the property are agreed on beforehand, there should be little cause for major disagreements. There is always a risk, as with any type of investment. But if the parties enter into the agreement with good faith, compatible goals, and a willingness to communicate and deal with problems equitably, there should be few, if any, problems.

Is there tax due on the money received when the property is refinanced?

No. That is one of the attractions of refinancing: an owner-occupant can pull cash out of a property by refinancing and incur no tax consequences. For the non-resident owner, a recent change in the tax law requires that the funds taken from the refinancing of an investment property be reinvested in another investment property in order for the investor to get the interest deduction for the increase in the mortgage on the refinanced property. Investors should consult a tax adviser on this matter.

Do non-resident owners get interest on the money they put up?

No. The return to the non-resident owners is in the appreciation of the property, just as if they were purchasing it on their own.

What happens in the event of a breach of contract by the non-resident owner?

Because an equity-share purchase is structured so that the owner-occupant is responsible for the monthly payment and occupies the property, there is very little opportunity for the non-resident owner to breach the contract. However, in the event the non-resident owner *did* breach the contract, the owner-occupant's recourse is outlined in our Shared-Equity Financing Agreement, specifically in Paragraph 14, Termination Events and Procedures, and Paragraph 20, Notice of Default. As long as the owner-occupant continues to meet the payment obligation under the Agreement, and as long as he has possession of the property, he runs very little risk of loss from default by the non-resident owner.

What happens in the event of a breach of contract by the owner-occupant?

Because the owner-occupant occupies the property and because the owner-occupant is, in most cases, required to meet the monthly payment obligations of the purchase, the party at greater risk in an equity-share arrangement is the non-resident owner. The biggest risk is that the owner-occupant might default on the loan. But the owner-occupant has contributed at least 25 percent of the down payment, so the chances of default are far less than, say, of a tenant defaulting on a lease. Still, it *could* happen. Paragraph 14, Termination Events and Procedures, Paragraph 19, Default by Owner-Occupant, Paragraph 20, Notice of Default, and Paragraph 21, Purchase of Defaulting Party's Interest, all address this issue. Basically, what happens is that a breach of the Shared-Equity Agreement is dealt with by a court order under contract law. The court would look to the contract for the intent of the parties. That's why it is extremely important for you to use a comprehensive contract that addresses all possible contingencies.

The time it takes for the court order to resolve the issue can vary from county to county and from state to state. Unlike the tenant in a lease, the owner-occupant in a shared-equity arrangement has equity in the property; that equity is contractually committed as security for any costs incurred in enforcing the Agreement. Thus, any expenses the non-resident owner may incur because of an owner-occupant's breach—such as payment of the monthly expenses—would be recovered by the non-resident from the owner-occupant's share of the equity.

As any landlord who's been through an eviction process knows, it can take, depending on your location, up to a year to evict a tenant from a rental property. During that time, the landlord is making payments on the mortgage, taxes, etc. After the tenant is out, there's little or no chance that he can be forced to make restitution to the landlord for the losses incurred. So, even though there is some risk to the non-resident owner if the owner-occupant should default, the possible losses are far less than those a landlord almost certainly faces when evicting a tenant.

Further, our Agreement states (Paragraph 19) that in the event of a default by the owner-occupant, his right to occupy the property shall terminate despite his equity interest in the property. The non-resident owner can then terminate the Agreement and take possession of the property, pursuant to the appropriate civil code in your state. It is important that you know what that code is and that it be cited in your Shared-Equity Financing Agreement.

How are Shared Equity Mortgages different from equity sharing?

In a shared equity mortgage, rather than contributing to the down payment and becoming part owner of the property, a non-resident investor carries a second mortgage against the property at a nominal rate, say 6 percent per year. Depending on the amount of the second, the investor gets to share in anywhere from 40 percent to 60 percent of the future appreciation of the property. Shared equity mortgages are usually structured for a minimum five-year holding period. The owner-occupant has to qualify for the mortgage payment, including the payment on the second mortgage, on his own and is the sole owner of the property and is solely responsible for the mortgage. The benefit for the owner-occupant is that he gets the entire interest write-off.

The drawback, in addition to the locked-in and usually longer holding period, is that the owner-occupant has to make the additional monthly payment on the second mortgage. The drawback for the investor is that he cannot use Tax Code Section 1031 to defer his gain when the property sells. However, many investors prefer to invest in mortgages, and shared equity mortgages are a good vehicle for them.

Glossary

Adjustable Mortgage Loans (AMLs): Mortgage loans under which the interest rate is periodically adjusted to more closely coincide with current rates. The amounts and times of adjustment are agreed to at the inception of the loan. Also called: Adjustable Rate Loans, Adjustable Rate Mortgages (ARMs), Flexible Rate Loans, Variable Rate Loans.

Alterations: Changes in the interior or exterior of a building that do not change its exterior dimensions.

Amortization: Payment of a debt in installments of principal and interest, rather than interest-only payments.

Amortize: To reduce a debt by regular payments of both principal and interest, as opposed to interest-only payments.

Annual Percentage Rate (APR): The actual annual rate of interest for a loan over its projected life, as opposed to its starting interest rate or nominal rate before compounding. For example: 6 percent add-on interest would be much more than 6 percent simple interest. The APR is disclosed as a requirement of federal truth-in-lending statutes.

Appreciation: The increase in value of a property beyond that brought about by an increase in the general cost of living. Commonly but incorrectly used to describe an increase in value through inflation.

Arbitration Clause: A clause in a lease calling for the decision of a third party (arbiter) regarding disputes over future rents based on negotiation. Also used in construction contracts, disputes between brokers, etc.

Arrears: (1) Payment made after it is due is in arrears. (2) Interest is said to be paid *in arrears* since it is paid to the date of payment rather than in advance, as is rent. Example: A rental payment made July 1 pays the rent to August 1. An interest payment made July 1 pays the interest to July 1.

Asking Price: The price at which a seller is offering property for sale. The eventual selling price may be lower after negotiation with a buyer.

Assess: To fix a value; to appraise. Most commonly used in connection with taxes.

Assessed Value: Value placed upon a property by the tax assessor for property tax purposes.

Assessment: (1) The estimation of value of property for tax purposes. (2) A levy against property in addition to general taxes. Usually for improvements such as streets, sewers, etc.

Assign: To transfer property or an interest in property.

Assignee: One who receives an assignment. (Pl.—assigns.)

Assignment: Transfer to another party of any property, real or personal, or of any rights or estates in said property. Common assignments are of leases, mortgages, deeds of trust, but the general term encompasses all transfers of title.

Assignor: One who makes an assignment.

Assumable: (See Assumption of Mortgage).

Assumption Fee: Lender's charge for paperwork involved in processing records for a new buyer assuming an existing loan.

Assumption of Mortgage: Agreement by a buyer to assume the liability under an existing note secured by a mortgage or deed of trust. The lender usually must approve the new debtor in order to release the existing debtor (usually the seller) from liability.

Balloon Note: A note calling for periodic payments which are insufficient to fully amortize the face amount of the note prior to maturity but that requires that a principal sum known as a "balloon payment" be paid at maturity.

Balloon Payment: The principal sum due when a balloon note matures.

Basis Point: A finance term meaning a yield of 1/100th of 1 percent annually.

Blanket Mortgage: (1) A mortgage covering more than one property of the mortgagor, such as a mortgage covering all the lots of a builder in a subdivision. (2) A mortgage covering all real property of the mortgagor, both present and future. When used in this meaning, it is also called a "general mortgage."

Bona Fide Purchaser: A purchaser in good faith, for valuable consideration, without notice or knowledge of adverse claims of others. Sometimes abbreviated to B.F.P.

Breach of Contract: Failure to perform a contract, in whole or part, without legal excuse.

Broker, Real Estate: One who is licensed by the state to carry on the business of dealing in real estate. A broker may receive a commission for his or her part in bringing together a buyer and seller, landlord and tenant, or parties to an exchange.

Brokerage: The act of bringing together principals (buyer-seller; landlord-tenant; etc.) for a fee or commission, rather than acting as a principal.

Broom Clean: A term used to describe the condition of a building delivered to a buyer or tenant. As the term indicates, the floors are swept and free of debris.

Buydown: A payment to a lender from a seller, buyer, third party, or some combination of these, causing the lender to reduce the interest rate during the early years (usually the first one to five years) of the loan.

Buyer's Market: A market condition favoring the buyer. In real estate, when there are more homes for sale than there are interested buyers.

Capital Gain: Gain realized from the sale of capital assets. Generally, the difference between cost and selling price, less certain deductible expenses. Used mainly for income tax purposes.

Cash Flow: In investment property, the cash an investor is left with each month after paying his operating expenses and debt service (the loan) out of the income generated by the property.

Cash Out: To take the entire amount of the equity in cash when the property is sold rather than retain some interest in the property.

Cash Sale: A sale for full payment in cash, as opposed to a credit sale. A payment by check is considered cash. May be qualified, as "cash to new loan," "cash to existing loan," etc.

Caveat Emptor: "Let the buyer beware." Legal maxim stating that the buyer takes the risk regarding quality or condition of an item purchased, unless it is protected by warranty or there is misrepresentation. Recent consumer protection laws have placed more responsibility for disclosure on sellers and brokers.

CC&Rs (Covenants, Conditions, and Restrictions): A term used in some areas referring to the restrictive limitations which may be placed on property. In other areas, simply called restrictions.

Certificate of Title: In areas where attorneys examine abstracts or chains of title, a written opinion executed by the examining attorney stating that title is vested as stated in the abstract.

Closing: (1) in real estate sales, the final procedure in which documents are executed and/or recorded and the sale (or loan) is completed. (2) A selling term meaning the point at which the client or customer is asked to agree to the sale or purchase and sign the contract. (3) The final call in a metes and bounds legal description which "closes" the boundaries of the property.

Closing Costs: Expenses incidental to a sale of real estate, such as loan fees, title fees, appraisal fees, etc.

Closing Statement: The statement which lists the financial settlement between buyer and seller and also the costs each must pay. Separate statements for buyer and seller are sometimes prepared.

Commission: An amount paid to an agent (real estate broker) as compensation for his services. In a property sale, this amount is generally paid by the seller as a percentage of the sale price.

Community Property: Property owned in common by a husband and wife that was not acquired as separate property. A classification of property peculiar to certain states.

Comparables: Properties used as comparisons to determine the value of a specific property.

Compound Amount of an Invested Sum: The total amount at the end of a given period, including the reinvestment of all interest plus the original amounts invested.

Compound Interest: Interest paid on accumulated interest as well as on the principal of a loan.

Condominium: A structure of two or more units, the interior spaces of which are individually owned; the balance of the property (both land and building) is owned in common by the owners of the individual units. The size of each unit is measured from the interior surfaces (exclusive of paint or other finishes) of the exterior walls, floors, and ceiling. The balance of the property is called the common area.

Consideration: Anything which is, legally, of value, and induces one to enter into a contract.

Contingency: Commonly, the dependence upon a stated event which must occur before a contract is binding. For example: the sale of a house, contingent upon the buyer obtaining financing.

Contract: An agreement between two or more persons or entities which creates or modifies a legal relationship. Generally based upon offer and acceptance.

Contract of Sale: In some areas of the country, synonymous with land and contract. In other areas, synonymous with purchase agreement.

Conventional Loan: A mortgage or deed of trust not obtained under a government insured program (such as FHA or VA).

Cotenancy: A general term covering both joint tenancy and tenancy in common.

Counselor (Counsellor): (1) A lawyer. (2) One designated as a real estate counselor by the American Society of Real Estate Counselors. The designation indicates an extremely high standard of knowledge and experience on the part of the conferee.

Counteroffer: An offer (instead of acceptance) in response to an offer. For example: A offers to buy B's house for X dollars. B, in response, offers to sell to A at a higher price. B's offer to A is a counteroffer.

Creative Financing: A general term which encompasses any method of financing property other than traditional real estate lending.

Credit: (1) The financial worthiness of a borrower. The history of whether this borrower has met financial obligations on time in the past. (2) An accounting term designating money received or receivable, as opposed to a debit, which is money paid or payable.

Credit Report: A report on the past ability of a loan applicant to pay installment payments. Several national and local companies make such reports.

Deed: Actually, any one of many conveyancing or financing instruments, but generally a conveyancing instrument, given to pass fee title to property upon sale.

Deed of Trust: An instrument used in many states in place of a mortgage. Property is transferred to a trustee by the borrower (trustor) in favor of the lender (beneficiary) and recovered upon payment in full.

Default: An omission or failure to perform a legal duty.

Deferred Maintenance: Repairs necessary to put a property in good condition. A concern of a purchaser. An owner may have an account for such maintenance.

Department of Real Estate: That department of the state government responsible for the licensing and regulation of persons engaged in the real estate business. The person heading the department is usually called the real estate commissioner. Other names for the department are the Division of Real Estate and the Real Estate Commission.

Deposit: Money given by a buyer with an offer to purchase in order to show good faith. Also called *earnest money*.

Depreciable Life: A tax term meaning the number of years used to determine depreciation of an asset (generally a building). The time used is determined by the local IRS office under general guidelines.

Depreciation: (1) Decrease in value to real property improvements caused by deterioration or obsolescence. (2) A loss in value as an accounting procedure to use as a deduction for income tax purposes.

Deterioration: A gradual wearing away of a structure through use or exposure to the elements, rather than a sudden destruction. Also called physical depreciation.

Disbursements: Payments made during the course of an escrow or at closing.

Down Payment: Cash paid by a buyer toward the purchase price of a property as opposed to that portion of the purchase price that is financed.

Eminent Domain: A governmental right to acquire private property for public use by condemnation, and the payment of just compensation.

Encumbrance, Incumbrance: A claim, lien, charge, or liability attached to and binding real property. Any right to, or interest in, land which may exist in one other than the owner, but which will not prevent the transfer of fee title.

Equity: The market value of real property, less the amount of existing liens.

Equity Build-Up: An increase in the difference between a property's value and the amount of any liens against that property. Can be brought about by appreciation of the property and/or by reduction of the principal on a mortgage or deed of trust by the mortgagor.

Equity Loan: A loan to a property owner that is secured by that property (sometimes in the form of a second mortgage), and the amount of which is based on the owner's equity in the property.

Escrow: Delivery of a deed by a grantor to a third party for delivery to the grantee upon the happening of a contingent event. Modernly, in some states, all instruments necessary to the sale (including funds) are delivered to a third (neutral) party, with instructions as to their use.

Escrow Instructions: Instructions signed by both buyer and seller which enable an escrow agent to carry out the procedures necessary to transfer real property, a business, or other assignable interest.

Escrow Officer: An escrow agent. In some states, one who has, through experience and education, gained a certain degree of expertise in escrow matters.

Exchange: Under Internal Revenue Code Section 1031, a transfer of real property which has certain tax advantages over a sale. Definite procedures must be followed in order to qualify the transfer as an exchange.

Fair Market Value: Projected price that probably would be negotiated between a willing seller and a willing buyer within a reasonable amount of time for a given property. Usually arrived at by comparable sales in the area.

Fannie Mae: (See: FNMA).

Fee Simple: An estate under which the owner is entitled to unrestricted powers to dispose of the property, and which can be left by will or inherited. Commonly, a synonym for ownership.

FHA (Federal Housing Administration): A federal agency which insures first mortgages, enabling lenders to loan a very high percentage of the sale price.

FHLMC (Freddie Mac): Federal Home Loan Mortgage Corporation. A federal agency purchasing first mortgages, both conventional and federally insured, from members of the Federal Reserve System and the Federal Home Loan Bank System.

First Mortgage: A mortgage having priority over all other voluntary liens against certain property. In the event of a sale or foreclosure of the property, the first mortgage is paid off first. An exception might be a federal or state tax lien.

Fixed-Rate Mortgage: A mortgage having a rate of interest that remains the same for the life of the mortgage.

Flexible-Rate Mortgage: (See: Adjustable Mortgage Loans).

Floating Rate: (See: Variable Interest Rate).

FNMA (Fannie Mae): A private corporation dealing in the purchase of first mortgages, at discounts.

Foreclosure: A proceeding in or out of court, to extinguish all rights, title, and interest, of the owner(s) of property in order to sell the property to satisfy a lien against it.

Free and Clear: Real property against which there are no liens, especially voluntary liens (mortgages).

Full Disclosure: In real estate, revelation of all the known facts which may affect the decision of a buyer or tenant. A broker must disclose known defects in the property for sale or lease. A builder must give to a potential buyer the facts of his new development (are there adequate school facilities? sewer facilities? is there an airport nearby? etc.). A broker cannot charge a commission to both a buyer and seller unless both know and agree.

GNMA (Ginnie Mae): Government National Mortgage Association. A federal association, working with FHA, which offers special assistance in obtaining mortgages and purchases mortgages in a secondary capacity.

Graduated Payment Mortgage: A mortgage or deed of trust calling for increasingly higher payments over the term of the loan. This allows the buyer low beginning payments which later increase as (theoretically) the buyer's earnings increase.

Grant Deed: One of the many types of deeds used to transfer real property. Contains warranties against prior conveyances or encumbrances. When title insurance is purchased, warranties in a deed are of little practical significance.

Grantee: One to whom a grant is made. Generally, the buyer.

Grantor: One who grants property or property rights.

Homeowners' Association: (1) An association of people who own homes in a given area, formed for the purpose of improving or maintaining the quality of the area. (2) An association formed by a builder of condominiums or planned developments and required by statute in some states. The builder's participation as well as the duties of the association are controlled by statute.

Hypothecate: To mortgage or pledge without delivery of the security to the lender.

Income Property: Property which produces income, usually in the form of rent.

Incumbrance: (See: Encumbrance).

Independent Appraisal: An appraisal by one who has no interest in the property and nothing to gain from a high or low appraisal.

Indexing: Altering mortgage term, payment, or rate according to inflation and/or a suitable mortgage-rate index.

Installment Note: A note calling for payment of both principal and interest in specified amounts or specified minimum amounts, at specific intervals.

Installment Sale: A tax term used to describe a sale that is usually accomplished by use of a land contract. If the seller receives less than 30 percent of the sale price in the year of the sale (not including interest), the tax on the profit (gain) from the sale may be paid over the installment period, provided the 30 percent rule is followed each year.

Institutional Lenders: Banks, savings and loan associations, and other businesses that make loans to the public in the ordinary course of business, as opposed to individuals or companies that make loans to employees.

Insured Mortgage: A mortgage insured against loss to the mortgagee in the event of default and a failure of the mortgaged property to satisfy the balance owing plus costs of foreclosure. May be insured by FHA, VA, or by independent mortgage insurance companies.

Interest: Money charged for the use of money (principal).

Interest Rate Cap: The maximum interest rate increase on an Adjustable Mortage Loan. For example: the interest rate on a 12 percent loan with a 5 percent interest rate cap could not exceed 17 percent over the life of the loan.

Investment Property: Generally, any property purchased for the primary purpose of making a profit, either from rental income or from resale.

Investment Yield: The gain from an investment in real property from both income and resale. Expressed as a percentage of the amount invested.

Involuntary Lien: A lien, such as a tax lien, judgment lien, etc., which attaches to property without the consent of the owner, as opposed to a mortgage lien, to which the owner agrees.

Joint Tenancy: An undivided interest in property, taken by two or more joint tenants. The interests must be equal, accruing under the same conveyance, and beginning at the same time. Upon the death of a joint tenant, the interest passes to the surviving joint tenants rather than to the heirs of the deceased.

Landlord: An owner of leased real estate.

Lender: Any person or entity advancing funds which are to be repaid. A general term encompassing all mortgagees and beneficiaries under deeds of trust.

Leverage: The use of financing to allow a small amount of cash to purchase a large property investment.

Liability: A general term encompassing all types of debts and obligations.

Lien: A form of encumbrance that makes the property security for payment of a debt.

Like Kind Property: A tax term used in exchanges. An investment property may be exchanged for like kind property and the tax on the profit from the sale (capital gain) postponed. The term does not refer to the physical similarity of the properties but to the purpose and intent (investment) of the taxpayer.

Line of Credit: An amount of money a borrower may obtain from a bank without a special credit check. The money is generally for business purposes, and the amount would not include the borrower's own home loan and other personal secured loans.

Listing: An agreement between an owner of real property and a real estate agent, whereby the agent agrees to secure a buyer or tenant for specific property at a certain price and under certain terms in return for a fee or commission.

Loan: A lending of a principal sum of money to one who promises to repay said sum, plus interest.

Loan Constant: The yearly percentage of interest which remains the same over the life of an amortized loan, based on the monthly payment in relation to the principal. For example: A $1,000 loan at 9 percent interest for twenty years can be amortized at $9 per month. The constant interest rate is figured by finding one year's payments ($9 × 12 months = $108) and expressing this amount as a percentage of the principal (10.8 percent of $1000).

Loan Origination Fee: A one-time set-up fee charged by the lender.

Loan Package: The file of all items necessary for the lender to decide to give or not give a loan. These items would include information on the prospective borrower (loan application, credit report, financial statement, employment letters, etc.) and information on the property (appraisal, survey, etc.). There may be a charge for "packaging" the loan.

Loan Policy: A title insurance policy insuring a mortgagee or beneficiary under a deed of trust against loss caused by invalid title in the borrower or loss of priority of the mortgage or deed of trust.

Loan-to-Value (LTV) Ratio: The ratio, expressed as a percentage, of the amount of a loan to the value or selling price of the real property. Usually, the higher the percentage, the greater the interest charged. Maximum percentages for banks, savings and loans, or government-insured loans, are set by statute.

Maintenance: The ongoing process of keeping a property in condition to efficiently serve its intended purpose.

Maintenance Fee: As applied to condominiums and planned developments, the amount charged each unit owner to maintain the common area. Usually a monthly fee paid as part of the budget.

Market Value: As applied to a property, the highest price a willing buyer would pay and a willing seller accept, both being fully informed, and the property exposed for a reasonable period of time. The market value may be different from the price a property can actually be sold for at a given time (market price).

Marketability: Salability. The probability of selling a property at a specific time, price, and on specific terms.

Market-Value Approach: Appraisal of a property by comparing the prices of similar properties (comparables) recently sold. The degree of similarity of the properties and circumstances of the sales are the important characteristics to consider.

Mortgage: (1) To pledge as security, real property for the payment of a debt. The borrower (mortgagor) retains possession and use of the property. (2) The instrument by which real estate is pledged as security for the repayment of a loan.

Mortgage Banker: A company providing mortgage financing with its own funds rather than simply bringing together lender and borrower, as does a mortgage broker. Although the mortgage banker uses its own funds, these funds are generally borrowed and the financing is either short-term or, if long-term, the mortgages are sold to investors (often insurance companies) within a short time.

Mortgage Broker: One who, for a fee, brings together a borrower and a lender and handles the necessary applications for the borrower to obtain a loan against real property by giving a mortgage or deed of trust as security. Also called a loan broker.

Mortgage Company: A privately owned company authorized usually by the state, to service real estate loans.

Mortgage Insurance: Insurance written by an independent mortgage insurance company (referred to as an MIC) protecting the mortgage lender against loss incurred by a mortgage default, thus enabling the lender to lend a higher percentage of the sale price. The Federal Government writes this form of insurance through the FHA and the VA.

Mortgagee: The party lending money and receiving a mortgage. Some states treat the mortgagee as the "legal" owner, entitled to rents from the property. Other states treat the mortgagee as a secured creditor, the mortgagor being the owner. The latter is the more modern and accepted view.

Mortgagor: A party who borrows money and gives a mortgage.

Multiple Listing: A listing, usually an exclusive right to sell, submitted to all members of an association, so that each may have an opportunity to sell a property.

NAR (National Association of Realtors): An association of people engaged in the real estate business. Organized in 1908, it currently lists over half a million members. With headquarters in Chicago, it is dedicated to the betterment of the real estate industry through education, legislation, and high ethical standards for its members.

NAREB (National Association of Real Estate Boards): A national trade association whose members include not only real estate brokers, but appraisers, property managers, and other affiliated groups.

Negative Amortization: A condition created when loan payments are structured to be less than the interest due, and therefore the principal of the loan increases with each payment by the amount of the interest not paid.

Negative Cash Flow: When the monthly income from an investment property is less than that property's expenses. The owner must come up with cash each month to meet these expenses.

Net After Taxes: The net income from property after income tax is paid.

Net Before Taxes: Net income from a property before payment of income tax, but after payment of property taxes.

Net Profit: Remaining profit on an investment property after deduction of all expenses from income for a given period. Generally classified as either net before taxes or net after taxes.

Non-Recourse Loan: A loan not allowing for a deficiency judgment. The lender's only recourse in the event of default is the security (property), and the borrower is not personally liable.

Note: An unilateral agreement containing an express and absolute promise of the signer to pay to a named person, or order, or bearer, a definite sum of money at a specified date or on demand. Usually provides for interest and, concerning real property, is secured by a mortgage or trust deed.

Notice of Default: A notice filed to show that the borrower under a mortgage or deed of trust is in default (behind on the payments).

Open House: A house that is open without appointment to prospective buyers (or tenants) for inspection during certain hours and days of the week.

Open Listing: A written authorization to a real estate agent by a property owner stating that a commission will be paid to the agent upon presentation of an offer which meets a specified price and terms. However, the agent has no exclusive right to sell and must bring in his offer before any other offer is presented or accepted.

Origination Fee: A fee charged by a lender for making a real estate loan. Usually a percentage of the amount loaned, such as 1 percent.

Owner-Occupied: Describing a property, one that is inhabited by its owner.

Paper: A mortgage, deed of trust, or land contract, which is given instead of cash. A seller receives "paper" when he receives a mortgage, deed of trust, or land contract as part of the purchase price.

Partnership: As defined by the Uniform Partnership Act, "an association of two or more persons to carry on as co-owners, a business for profit." The business must be lawful and the partners must agree to share in the profit or loss (but not necessarily equally).

Payment Cap: A ceiling placed on the amount of the monthly payment under an Adjustable Mortgage Loan, regardless of increases in the interest rate.

Payoff: The payment in full of an existing loan or other lien.

Per Annun: Yearly; annually.

Physical Depreciation: (See: Deterioriation).

PI (Principal and Interest): Term describing monthly payments on real property that include only the principal and interest on a mortgage loan and not property taxes and hazard insurance.

PITI (Principal, Interest, Taxes and Insurance): A term encompassing the four major portions of a usual monthly payment on real property: principal, interest, taxes, and insurance.

Points: (See: Loan Origination Fee). One point is one percent of the loan.

Power of Attorney: An authority by which one person (principal) enables another (attorney in fact) to act for him. (1) General power of attorney—authorizes sale, mortgaging, etc., of all property of the principal. Invalid in some jurisdictions. (2) Special power-of-attorney—specifies property, buyers, price, and terms. How specific it must be varies in each state.

Preliminary Title Report: A report showing the condition of title before a sale or loan transaction. After completion of the transaction, a title insurance policy is issued.

Prepaid Interest: Interest paid before becoming due.

Prepaid Items: Those expenses of property which are paid in advance and usually prorated upon sale, such as taxes, insurance, rent, etc.

Prepayment Penalty: A penalty under a note, mortgage, or deed of trust, imposed if and when the loan is paid off before it is due.

Prime Lending Rate: The most favorable interest rates charged by a commercial bank of short-term loans (not mortgages).

Principal: (1) The person who gives authority to an agent or attorney (see: Attorney in Fact). (2) Amount of a debt, not including interest. (3) The face of a note, mortgage, etc.

Private Mortgage Insurance: Insurance against a loss by a lender in the event of default by a borrower (mortgagor). The insurance is similar to insurance by a governmental agency such as FHA, except that it is issued by a private insurance company. The premium is paid by the borrower and is included in the mortgage payment.

Property Tax: Generally, a tax levied on both real and personal property, based on the value of the property.

Prorate: To divide in proportionate shares, such as taxes, insurance, rent, or other items which buyer and seller share as of the time of closing, or other agreed upon time.

Purchase Money Mortgage: A mortgage given from buyer to seller to secure all or a portion of the purchase price of a property.

Rate Index: An index used to adjust the interest rate of an adjustable mortgage loan, for example: the change in U.S. Treasury securities (T-Bills) with a one-year maturity. The weekly average yield on said securities, adjusted to a constant maturity of one year, which is the result of weekly sales, may be obtained weekly from the Federal Reserve Statistical Release H.15 (519). This change in interest rates is the "index" for the change in the specific Adjustable Mortgage Loan.

Real Estate Board: A board composed of regular members (real estate brokers and salespersons) and affiliate members (lenders, title companies, etc.) for the purpose of furthering the real estate business in a given area.

Real Estate License: A state license granted to one as a broker or salesperson after he has passed an examination. Some states have educational requirements that must be met before one can take the examination.

Realtor: A designation given to a real estate broker who is a member of a board associated with the National Association of Real Estate Boards.

Refinancing: The renewing of an existing loan with the same lender or a new lender.

Regulation Z: Federal Reserve regulation issued under the Truth-in-Lending Law which requires that a credit purchaser be advised in writing of all costs connected with the credit portion of the purchase.

Rehabilitation: Synonymous with reconditioning, except when used in connection with urban renewal, at which time it encompasses all types of changes, including structural and even street changes.

Remodeling: Improving a structure by changing its plan, characteristics, or function, as opposed to reconditioning.

RESPA (Real Estate Settlement Procedures Act): A federal statute effective June 20, 1975, requiring disclosure of certain costs in the sale of residential (one- to four-family) improved property which is to be financed by a federally insured lender.

Right of Survivorship: The right of a survivor of a deceased person to the property of said deceased. A distinguishing characteristic of a joint tenancy relationship.

Roll Over: Tax jargon which means to transfer the equity, including the taxable portion of an increase in the value of a property, to a new property without immediate tax consequences. Usually used in reference to an Internal Revenue Code Section 1031 tax deferred exchange.

Sales Contract: Another name for a sales agreement, purchase agreement, etc. Not to be confused with a land contract, which is a conditional sales contract.

SAM: (See: Shared Appreciation Mortgage).

Savings and Loan Association: Originally an association chartered to hold savings and make real estate loans. Federally insured and regulated. Active in long-term financing rather than construction loans. Recent changes in federal controls have enabled these associations to offer checking accounts, consumer loans, and other services traditionally offered by banks.

Second Mortgage: A mortgage which ranks after a first mortgage in priority and would be second in line to be paid off in the event of a sale of the property. Properties may have two, three, or more mortgages, deeds of trust, or land contracts, as liens at the same time. Legal priority would determine whether they are called a first, second, third, etc., lien.

Secondary Financing: A loan secured by a mortgage or trust deed, which lien is junior (secondary) to another mortgage or trust deed.

Secondary Mortgage Market: The buying and selling of first mortgages or trust deeds by banks, insurance companies, government agencies, and other mortgagees. This provides lenders with additional supplies of money for new loans. The mortgages may be sold at full value (par) or above, but are usually sold at a discount. The secondary mortgage market should not be confused with a second mortgage.

Settlement Statement: A statement prepared by broker, escrow agent, or lender, giving a complete breakdown of costs involved in a real estate sale. A separate statement is prepared for the seller and buyer.

Shared Equity Mortgage: A financing arrangement under which the lender offers a lower interest rate in return for a percentage of the appreciation (profit) when the property is sold.

Simple Interest: Interest computed on principal alone, as opposed to compound interest.

Single-Family House: A general term originally used to distinguish a house designed for use by one family from an apartment house. More recently, used to distinguish a house with no common area from a planned development or condominium.

"Subject To" Clause: A clause in a deed stating that the grantee takes title "subject to" an existing mortgage. The original mortgagor is alone responsible for any deficiency should there be foreclosure of the mortgage. Differs from an "assumption" clause, whereby the grantee "assumes" and agrees to pay the existing mortgage.

Sweat Equity: Ownership in a property earned by physically doing the work to improve that property rather than paying cash for it.

Tax Base: The assessed valuation of real property, which is multiplied by the tax rate to determine the amount of tax due.

Tax Lien: (1) A lien for nonpayment of property taxes. Attaches only to the property upon which the taxes are unpaid. (2) A federal income tax lien. May attach to all property of the one owing the taxes.

Tax Rate: Traditionally, the ratio of dollars of tax per hundred or per thousand dollars of valuation. Modernly, has become to be expressed as a percentage of valuation.

Tax Shelter: A general term used to include any property which gives the owner certain income tax advantages, such as deductions for property taxes, maintenance, mortgage interest, insurance, and especially depreciation.

Tenancy in Common: An undivided ownership in real estate by two or more persons. The interests need not be equal, and, in the event of the death of one of the owners, no right of survivorship in the other owners exists.

"Time is of the Essence": Clause used in contracts to bind one party to performance at or by a specified time in order to bind the other party to performance.

Title: Evidence that the owner of land is in lawful possession thereof; an instrument evidencing such ownership.

Title Insurance: Insurance against loss resulting from defects of title to a specifically described parcel of real property. Defects may run to the fee (chain of title) or to encumbrances.

Title Search: A review of all recorded documents affecting a specific piece of property to determine the present condition of title.

Transfer Tax: State tax on the transfer of real property. Based on purchase price or money changing hands. Check statutes for each state. Also called documentary transfer tax.

Treasury Bills: Interest-bearing U.S. government obligations sold weekly. The change in interest rates paid on these obligations is frequently used as the Rate Index of Adjustable Mortgage Loans.

Undivided Interest: A partial interest by two or more people in the same property, the respective shares of which may be equal or unequal.

Unencumbered: Free of liens and other encumbrances. Free and clear.

Valuable Consideration: A legal term meaning any consideration sufficient to support a contract. The word "valuable" does not mean *of great value* but merely *having value.*

Variable Interest Rate: An interest rate that fluctuates as the prevailing rate moves up or down. In mortgages there are usually maximums as to the frequency and amount of fluctuation. Also called "flexible interest rate."

Voluntary Lien: A lien placed against real property by the voluntary act of the owner. Most commonly, a mortgage or deed of trust.

Warranty Deed: A deed used in many states to convey fee title to real property. Until the widespread use of title insurance, warranties by the grantor were very important to the grantee. When title insurance is purchased, warranties become less important as a practical means of recovery by the grantee for defective title.

Without Recourse: A finance term. A mortgage or deed of trust securing a note without recourse allows the lender to look only to the security (property) for repayment in the event of default and not to the borrower personally.

Writeoff: An expense that is deducted (written off) from one's annual gross income, thereby reducing the amount of one's taxable income.

Yield: Ratio of income from an investment to the total cost of the investment over a given period of time.

Appendixes

7% MONTHLY PAYMENT
NECESSARY TO AMORTIZE A LOAN

TERM / AMOUNT	1 YEAR	2 YEARS	3 YEARS	4 YEARS	5 YEARS	7 YEARS	8 YEARS	10 YEARS	12 YEARS
$ 25	2.17	1.12	.78	.60	.50	.38	.35	.30	.26
50	4.33	2.24	1.55	1.20	1.00	.76	.69	.59	.52
75	6.49	3.36	2.32	1.80	1.49	1.14	1.03	.88	.78
100	8.66	4.48	3.09	2.40	1.99	1.51	1.37	1.17	1.03
200	17.31	8.96	6.18	4.79	3.97	3.02	2.73	2.33	2.06
300	25.96	13.44	9.27	7.19	5.95	4.53	4.10	3.49	3.09
400	34.62	17.91	12.36	9.58	7.93	6.04	5.46	4.65	4.12
500	43.27	22.39	15.44	11.98	9.91	7.55	6.82	5.81	5.15
600	51.92	26.87	18.53	14.37	11.89	9.06	8.19	6.97	6.18
700	60.57	31.35	21.62	16.77	13.87	10.57	9.55	8.13	7.20
800	69.23	35.82	24.71	19.16	15.85	12.08	10.91	9.29	8.23
900	77.88	40.30	27.79	21.56	17.83	13.59	12.28	10.45	9.26
1000	86.53	44.78	30.88	23.95	19.81	15.10	13.64	11.62	10.29
2000	173.06	89.55	61.76	47.90	39.61	30.19	27.27	23.23	20.57
3000	259.59	134.32	92.64	71.84	59.41	45.28	40.91	34.84	30.86
4000	346.11	179.10	123.51	95.79	79.21	60.38	54.54	46.45	41.14
5000	432.64	223.87	154.39	119.74	99.01	75.47	68.17	58.06	51.42
6000	519.17	268.64	185.27	143.68	118.81	90.56	81.81	69.67	61.71
7000	605.69	313.41	216.14	167.63	138.61	105.65	95.44	81.28	71.99
8000	692.22	358.19	247.02	191.57	158.41	120.75	109.07	92.89	82.28
9000	778.75	402.96	277.90	215.52	178.22	135.84	122.71	104.50	92.56
10000	865.27	447.73	308.78	239.47	198.02	150.93	136.34	116.11	102.84
15000	1297.91	671.59	463.16	359.20	297.02	226.40	204.51	174.17	154.26
20000	1730.54	895.46	617.55	478.93	396.03	301.86	272.68	232.22	205.68
25000	2163.17	1119.32	771.93	598.66	495.03	377.32	340.85	290.28	257.10
30000	2595.81	1343.18	926.32	718.39	594.04	452.79	409.02	348.33	308.52
35000	3028.44	1567.05	1080.70	838.12	693.05	528.25	477.19	406.38	359.94
36000	3114.97	1611.82	1111.58	862.07	712.85	543.34	490.82	418.00	370.22
37000	3201.49	1656.59	1142.46	886.02	732.65	558.43	504.45	429.61	380.51
38000	3288.02	1701.36	1173.33	909.96	752.45	573.53	518.09	441.22	390.79
39000	3374.55	1746.14	1204.21	933.91	772.25	588.62	531.72	452.83	401.07
40000	3461.07	1790.91	1235.09	957.85	792.05	603.71	545.35	464.44	411.36
41000	3547.60	1835.68	1265.97	981.80	811.85	618.80	558.99	476.05	421.64
42000	3634.13	1880.45	1296.84	1005.75	831.66	633.90	572.62	487.66	431.93
43000	3720.66	1925.23	1327.72	1029.69	851.46	648.99	586.25	499.27	442.21
44000	3807.18	1970.00	1358.60	1053.64	871.26	664.08	599.89	510.88	452.49
45000	3893.71	2014.77	1389.47	1077.59	891.06	679.18	613.52	522.49	462.78
46000	3980.24	2059.54	1420.35	1101.53	910.86	694.27	627.16	534.10	473.06
47000	4066.76	2104.32	1451.23	1125.48	930.66	709.36	640.79	545.71	483.34
48000	4153.29	2149.09	1482.11	1149.42	950.46	724.45	654.42	557.33	493.63
49000	4239.82	2193.86	1512.98	1173.37	970.26	739.55	668.06	568.94	503.91
50000	4326.34	2238.63	1543.86	1197.32	990.06	754.64	681.69	580.55	514.20
51000	4412.87	2283.41	1574.74	1221.26	1009.87	769.73	695.32	592.16	524.48
52000	4499.40	2328.18	1605.61	1245.21	1029.67	784.82	708.96	603.77	534.76
53000	4585.92	2372.95	1636.49	1269.16	1049.47	799.92	722.59	615.38	545.05
54000	4672.45	2417.72	1667.37	1293.10	1069.27	815.01	736.23	626.99	555.33
55000	4758.98	2462.50	1698.25	1317.05	1089.07	830.10	749.86	638.60	565.61
56000	4845.50	2507.27	1729.12	1340.99	1108.87	845.20	763.49	650.21	575.90
57000	4932.03	2552.04	1760.00	1364.94	1128.67	860.29	777.13	661.82	586.18
58000	5018.56	2596.81	1790.88	1388.89	1148.47	875.38	790.76	673.43	596.47
59000	5105.08	2641.59	1821.75	1412.83	1168.28	890.47	804.39	685.05	606.75
60000	5191.61	2686.36	1852.63	1436.78	1188.08	905.57	818.03	696.66	617.03
61000	5278.14	2731.13	1883.51	1460.73	1207.88	920.66	831.66	708.27	627.32
62000	5364.66	2775.90	1914.39	1484.67	1227.68	935.75	845.30	719.88	637.60
63000	5451.19	2820.68	1945.26	1508.62	1247.48	950.84	858.93	731.49	647.89
64000	5537.72	2865.45	1976.14	1532.56	1267.28	965.94	872.56	743.10	658.17
65000	5624.24	2910.22	2007.02	1556.51	1287.08	981.03	886.20	754.71	668.45
66000	5710.77	2955.00	2037.89	1580.46	1306.88	996.12	899.83	766.32	678.74
67000	5797.30	2999.77	2068.77	1604.40	1326.69	1011.21	913.46	777.93	689.02
68000	5883.82	3044.54	2099.65	1628.35	1346.49	1026.31	927.10	789.54	699.30
69000	5970.35	3089.31	2130.52	1652.30	1366.29	1041.40	940.73	801.15	709.59
70000	6056.88	3134.09	2161.40	1676.24	1386.09	1056.49	954.37	812.76	719.87
75000	6489.51	3357.95	2315.79	1795.97	1485.09	1131.96	1022.53	870.82	771.29
80000	6922.14	3581.81	2470.17	1915.70	1584.10	1207.42	1090.70	928.87	822.71
100000	8652.68	4477.26	3087.71	2394.63	1980.12	1509.27	1363.38	1161.09	1028.39

MONTHLY PAYMENT 7%
NECESSARY TO AMORTIZE A LOAN

TERM / AMOUNT	15 YEARS	18 YEARS	20 YEARS	25 YEARS	28 YEARS	29 YEARS	30 YEARS	35 YEARS	40 YEARS
$ 25	.23	.21	.20	.18	.17	.17	.17	.16	.16
50	.45	.41	.39	.36	.34	.34	.34	.32	.32
75	.68	.62	.59	.54	.51	.51	.50	.48	.47
100	.90	.82	.78	.71	.68	.68	.67	.64	.63
200	1.80	1.64	1.56	1.42	1.36	1.35	1.34	1.28	1.25
300	2.70	2.45	2.33	2.13	2.04	2.02	2.00	1.92	1.87
400	3.60	3.27	3.11	2.83	2.72	2.69	2.67	2.56	2.49
500	4.50	4.08	3.88	3.54	3.40	3.37	3.33	3.20	3.11
600	5.40	4.90	4.66	4.25	4.08	4.04	4.00	3.84	3.73
700	6.30	5.71	5.43	4.95	4.76	4.71	4.66	4.48	4.36
800	7.20	6.53	6.21	5.66	5.44	5.38	5.33	5.12	4.98
900	8.09	7.34	6.98	6.37	6.12	6.05	5.99	5.75	5.60
1000	8.99	8.16	7.76	7.07	6.80	6.73	6.66	6.39	6.22
2000	17.98	16.32	15.51	14.14	13.60	13.45	13.31	12.78	12.43
3000	26.97	24.47	23.26	21.21	20.39	20.17	19.96	19.17	18.65
4000	35.96	32.63	31.02	28.28	27.19	26.89	26.62	25.56	24.86
5000	44.95	40.78	38.77	35.34	33.99	33.61	33.27	31.95	31.08
6000	53.93	48.94	46.52	42.41	40.78	40.33	39.92	38.34	37.29
7000	62.92	57.09	54.28	49.48	47.58	47.05	46.58	44.72	43.51
8000	71.91	65.25	62.03	56.55	54.37	53.78	53.23	51.11	49.72
9000	80.90	73.40	69.78	63.62	61.17	60.50	59.88	57.50	55.93
10000	89.89	81.56	77.53	70.68	67.97	67.22	66.54	63.89	62.15
15000	134.83	122.33	116.30	106.02	101.95	100.82	99.80	95.83	93.22
20000	179.77	163.11	155.06	141.36	135.93	134.43	133.07	127.78	124.29
25000	224.71	203.88	193.83	176.70	169.91	168.04	166.33	159.72	155.36
30000	269.65	244.66	232.59	212.04	203.89	201.64	199.60	191.66	186.43
35000	314.59	285.43	271.36	247.38	237.87	235.25	232.86	223.60	217.51
36000	323.58	293.59	279.11	254.45	244.66	241.97	239.51	229.99	223.72
37000	332.57	301.74	286.87	261.51	251.46	248.69	246.17	236.38	229.93
38000	341.56	309.90	294.62	268.58	258.26	255.41	252.82	242.77	236.15
39000	350.55	318.05	302.37	275.65	265.05	262.14	259.47	249.16	242.36
40000	359.54	326.21	310.12	282.72	271.85	268.86	266.13	255.55	248.58
41000	368.52	334.36	317.88	289.78	278.64	275.58	272.78	261.94	254.79
42000	377.51	342.52	325.63	296.85	285.44	282.30	279.43	268.32	261.01
43000	386.50	350.67	333.38	303.92	292.24	289.02	286.09	274.71	267.22
44000	395.49	358.83	341.14	310.99	299.03	295.74	292.74	281.10	273.43
45000	404.48	366.98	348.89	318.06	305.83	302.46	299.39	287.49	279.65
46000	413.47	375.14	356.64	325.12	312.62	309.18	306.04	293.88	285.86
47000	422.45	383.29	364.40	332.19	319.42	315.91	312.70	300.27	292.08
48000	431.44	391.45	372.15	339.26	326.22	322.63	319.35	306.66	298.29
49000	440.43	399.60	379.90	346.33	333.01	329.35	326.00	313.04	304.51
50000	449.42	407.76	387.65	353.39	339.81	336.07	332.66	319.43	310.72
51000	458.41	415.91	395.41	360.46	346.61	342.79	339.31	325.82	316.93
52000	467.40	424.07	403.16	367.53	353.40	349.51	345.96	332.21	323.15
53000	476.38	432.22	410.91	374.60	360.20	356.23	352.62	338.60	329.36
54000	485.37	440.38	418.67	381.67	366.99	362.96	359.27	344.99	335.58
55000	494.36	448.53	426.42	388.73	373.79	369.68	365.92	351.38	341.79
56000	503.35	456.69	434.17	395.80	380.59	376.40	372.57	357.76	348.01
57000	512.34	464.84	441.93	402.87	387.38	383.12	379.23	364.15	354.22
58000	521.33	473.00	449.68	409.94	394.18	389.84	385.88	370.54	360.44
59000	530.31	481.15	457.43	417.00	400.97	396.56	392.53	376.93	366.65
60000	539.30	489.31	465.18	424.07	407.77	403.28	399.19	383.32	372.86
61000	548.29	497.46	472.94	431.14	414.57	410.00	405.84	389.71	379.08
62000	557.28	505.62	480.69	438.21	421.36	416.73	412.49	396.10	385.29
63000	566.27	513.77	488.44	445.28	428.16	423.45	419.15	402.48	391.51
64000	575.26	521.93	496.20	452.34	434.95	430.17	425.80	408.87	397.72
65000	584.24	530.08	503.95	459.41	441.75	436.89	432.45	415.26	403.94
66000	593.23	538.24	511.70	466.48	448.55	443.61	439.10	421.65	410.15
67000	602.22	546.39	519.46	473.55	455.34	450.33	445.76	428.04	416.36
68000	611.21	554.55	527.21	480.61	462.14	457.05	452.41	434.43	422.58
69000	620.20	562.70	534.96	487.68	468.93	463.77	459.06	440.82	428.79
70000	629.18	570.86	542.71	494.75	475.73	470.50	465.72	447.20	435.01
75000	674.13	611.63	581.48	530.09	509.71	504.10	498.98	479.15	466.08
80000	719.07	652.41	620.24	565.43	543.69	537.71	532.25	511.09	497.15
100000	898.83	815.51	775.30	706.78	679.61	672.14	665.31	638.86	621.44

7⅛% MONTHLY PAYMENT

NECESSARY TO AMORTIZE A LOAN

TERM / AMOUNT	1 YEAR	2 YEARS	3 YEARS	4 YEARS	5 YEARS	7 YEARS	8 YEARS	10 YEARS	12 YEARS
$ 25	2.17	1.13	.78	.61	.50	.38	.35	.30	.26
50	4.33	2.25	1.55	1.21	1.00	.76	.69	.59	.52
75	6.50	3.37	2.33	1.81	1.49	1.14	1.03	.88	.78
100	8.66	4.49	3.10	2.41	1.99	1.52	1.37	1.17	1.04
200	17.32	8.97	6.19	4.81	3.98	3.04	2.74	2.34	2.08
300	25.98	13.45	9.29	7.21	5.96	4.55	4.11	3.51	3.11
400	34.64	17.94	12.38	9.61	7.95	6.07	5.48	4.68	4.15
500	43.30	22.42	15.47	12.01	9.94	7.58	6.85	5.84	5.18
600	51.96	26.90	18.57	14.41	11.92	9.10	8.22	7.01	6.22
700	60.61	31.39	21.66	16.81	13.91	10.61	9.59	8.18	7.25
800	69.27	35.87	24.75	19.21	15.89	12.13	10.96	9.35	8.29
900	77.93	40.35	27.85	21.61	17.88	13.64	12.33	10.51	9.32
1000	86.59	44.83	30.94	24.01	19.87	15.16	13.70	11.68	10.36
2000	173.17	89.66	61.87	48.01	39.73	30.31	27.40	23.36	20.71
3000	259.76	134.49	92.81	72.02	59.59	45.47	41.09	35.03	31.06
4000	346.34	179.32	123.74	96.02	79.45	60.62	54.79	46.71	41.41
5000	432.93	224.15	154.68	120.03	99.31	75.77	68.49	58.38	51.76
6000	519.51	268.98	185.61	144.03	119.17	90.93	82.18	70.06	62.11
7000	606.10	313.81	216.54	168.03	139.03	106.08	95.88	81.73	72.46
8000	692.68	358.64	247.48	192.04	158.89	121.24	109.57	93.41	82.81
9000	779.26	403.47	278.41	216.04	178.75	136.39	123.27	105.08	93.16
10000	865.85	448.30	309.35	240.05	198.61	151.54	136.97	116.76	103.51
15000	1298.77	672.44	464.02	360.07	297.91	227.31	205.45	175.14	155.26
20000	1731.69	896.59	618.69	480.09	397.21	303.08	273.93	233.51	207.02
25000	2164.61	1120.74	773.36	600.11	496.51	378.85	342.41	291.89	258.77
30000	2597.54	1344.88	928.03	720.13	595.81	454.62	410.89	350.27	310.52
35000	3030.46	1569.03	1082.70	840.15	695.11	530.39	479.37	408.64	362.27
36000	3117.04	1613.86	1113.64	864.16	714.97	545.54	493.06	420.32	372.63
37000	3203.63	1658.69	1144.57	888.16	734.83	560.70	506.76	431.99	382.98
38000	3290.21	1703.52	1175.51	912.17	754.69	575.85	520.45	443.67	393.33
39000	3376.80	1748.35	1206.44	936.17	774.55	591.01	534.15	455.34	403.68
40000	3463.38	1793.18	1237.38	960.18	794.41	606.16	547.85	467.02	414.03
41000	3549.96	1838.00	1268.31	984.18	814.27	621.31	561.54	478.70	424.38
42000	3636.55	1882.83	1299.24	1008.18	834.13	636.47	575.24	490.37	434.73
43000	3723.13	1927.66	1330.18	1032.19	853.99	651.62	588.93	502.05	445.08
44000	3809.72	1972.49	1361.11	1056.19	873.85	666.77	602.63	513.72	455.43
45000	3896.30	2017.32	1392.05	1080.20	893.72	681.93	616.33	525.40	465.78
46000	3982.89	2062.15	1422.98	1104.20	913.58	697.08	630.02	537.07	476.13
47000	4069.47	2106.98	1453.92	1128.21	933.44	712.24	643.72	548.75	486.48
48000	4156.06	2151.81	1484.85	1152.21	953.30	727.39	657.41	560.42	496.83
49000	4242.64	2196.64	1515.78	1176.21	973.16	742.54	671.11	572.10	507.18
50000	4329.22	2241.47	1546.72	1200.22	993.02	757.70	684.81	583.77	517.53
51000	4415.81	2286.30	1577.65	1224.22	1012.88	772.85	698.50	595.45	527.88
52000	4502.39	2331.13	1608.59	1248.23	1032.74	788.01	712.20	607.12	538.23
53000	4588.98	2375.96	1639.52	1272.23	1052.60	803.16	725.89	618.80	548.58
54000	4675.56	2420.79	1670.46	1296.24	1072.46	818.31	739.59	630.48	558.94
55000	4762.15	2465.61	1701.39	1320.24	1092.32	833.47	753.29	642.15	569.29
56000	4848.73	2510.44	1732.32	1344.24	1112.18	848.62	766.98	653.83	579.64
57000	4935.31	2555.27	1763.26	1368.25	1132.04	863.77	780.68	665.50	589.99
58000	5021.90	2600.10	1794.19	1392.25	1151.90	878.93	794.37	677.18	600.34
59000	5108.48	2644.93	1825.13	1416.26	1171.76	894.08	808.07	688.85	610.69
60000	5195.07	2689.76	1856.06	1440.26	1191.62	909.24	821.77	700.53	621.04
61000	5281.65	2734.59	1887.00	1464.27	1211.48	924.39	835.46	712.20	631.39
62000	5368.24	2779.42	1917.93	1488.27	1231.34	939.54	849.16	723.88	641.74
63000	5454.82	2824.25	1948.86	1512.27	1251.20	954.70	862.85	735.55	652.09
64000	5541.41	2869.08	1979.80	1536.28	1271.06	969.85	876.55	747.23	662.44
65000	5627.99	2913.91	2010.73	1560.28	1290.92	985.01	890.25	758.90	672.79
66000	5714.57	2958.74	2041.67	1584.29	1310.78	1000.16	903.94	770.58	683.14
67000	5801.16	3003.57	2072.60	1608.29	1330.64	1015.31	917.64	782.26	693.49
68000	5887.74	3048.40	2103.54	1632.30	1350.50	1030.47	931.33	793.93	703.84
69000	5974.33	3093.22	2134.47	1656.30	1370.36	1045.62	945.03	805.61	714.19
70000	6060.91	3138.05	2165.40	1680.30	1390.22	1060.78	958.73	817.28	724.54
75000	6493.83	3362.20	2320.08	1800.33	1489.52	1136.54	1027.21	875.66	776.30
80000	6926.76	3586.35	2474.75	1920.35	1588.82	1212.31	1095.69	934.03	828.05
100000	8658.44	4482.93	3093.43	2400.43	1986.03	1515.39	1369.61	1167.54	1035.06

MONTHLY PAYMENT 7⅛%

NECESSARY TO AMORTIZE A LOAN

TERM / AMOUNT	15 YEARS	18 YEARS	20 YEARS	25 YEARS	28 YEARS	29 YEARS	30 YEARS	35 YEARS	40 YEARS
$ 25	.23	.21	.20	.18	.18	.18	.17	.17	.16
50	.46	.42	.40	.36	.35	.35	.34	.33	.32
75	.68	.62	.59	.54	.52	.52	.51	.49	.48
100	.91	.83	.79	.72	.69	.69	.68	.65	.64
200	1.82	1.65	1.57	1.43	1.38	1.37	1.35	1.30	1.27
300	2.72	2.47	2.35	2.15	2.07	2.05	2.03	1.95	1.90
400	3.63	3.30	3.14	2.86	2.76	2.73	2.70	2.60	2.53
500	4.53	4.12	3.92	3.58	3.44	3.41	3.37	3.24	3.16
600	5.44	4.94	4.70	4.29	4.13	4.09	4.05	3.89	3.79
700	6.35	5.76	5.48	5.01	4.82	4.77	4.72	4.54	4.42
800	7.25	6.59	6.27	5.72	5.51	5.45	5.39	5.19	5.05
900	8.16	7.41	7.05	6.44	6.20	6.13	6.07	5.83	5.68
1000	9.06	8.23	7.83	7.15	6.88	6.81	6.74	6.48	6.31
2000	18.12	16.46	15.66	14.30	13.76	13.61	13.48	12.96	12.62
3000	27.18	24.69	23.49	21.45	20.64	20.42	20.22	19.43	18.92
4000	36.24	32.92	31.32	28.60	27.52	27.22	26.95	25.91	25.23
5000	45.30	41.15	39.15	35.74	34.40	34.03	33.69	32.39	31.53
6000	54.35	49.37	46.97	42.89	41.28	40.83	40.43	38.86	37.84
7000	63.41	57.60	54.80	50.04	48.16	47.64	47.17	45.34	44.14
8000	72.47	65.83	62.63	57.19	55.03	54.44	53.90	51.82	50.45
9000	81.53	74.06	70.46	64.33	61.91	61.25	60.64	58.29	56.75
10000	90.59	82.29	78.29	71.48	68.79	68.05	67.38	64.77	63.06
15000	135.88	123.43	117.43	107.22	103.18	102.07	101.06	97.15	94.58
20000	181.17	164.57	156.57	142.96	137.58	136.10	134.75	129.53	126.11
25000	226.46	205.71	195.71	178.70	171.97	170.12	168.43	161.92	157.64
30000	271.75	246.85	234.85	214.44	206.36	204.14	202.12	194.30	189.16
35000	317.05	287.99	273.99	250.18	240.76	238.17	235.81	226.68	220.69
36000	326.10	296.22	281.82	257.32	247.64	244.97	242.54	233.16	227.00
37000	335.16	304.45	289.65	264.47	254.51	251.78	249.28	239.63	233.30
38000	344.22	312.68	297.48	271.62	261.39	258.58	256.02	246.11	239.61
39000	353.28	320.91	305.30	278.77	268.27	265.39	262.76	252.58	245.91
40000	362.34	329.13	313.13	285.91	275.15	272.19	269.49	259.06	252.22
41000	371.40	337.36	320.96	293.06	282.03	279.00	276.23	265.54	258.52
42000	380.45	345.59	328.79	300.21	288.91	285.80	282.97	272.01	264.83
43000	389.51	353.82	336.62	307.36	295.79	292.61	289.70	278.49	271.13
44000	398.57	362.05	344.45	314.51	302.66	299.41	296.44	284.97	277.44
45000	407.63	370.27	352.27	321.65	309.54	306.21	303.18	291.44	283.74
46000	416.69	378.50	360.10	328.80	316.42	313.02	309.92	297.92	290.05
47000	425.75	386.73	367.93	335.95	323.30	319.82	316.65	304.40	296.35
48000	434.80	394.96	375.76	343.10	330.18	326.63	323.39	310.87	302.66
49000	443.86	403.19	383.59	350.24	337.06	333.43	330.13	317.35	308.97
50000	452.92	411.42	391.41	357.39	343.94	340.24	336.86	323.83	315.27
51000	461.98	419.64	399.24	364.54	350.81	347.04	343.60	330.30	321.58
52000	471.04	427.87	407.07	371.69	357.69	353.85	350.34	336.78	327.88
53000	480.10	436.10	414.90	378.83	364.57	360.65	357.08	343.25	334.19
54000	489.15	444.33	422.73	385.98	371.45	367.46	363.81	349.73	340.49
55000	498.21	452.56	430.56	393.13	378.33	374.26	370.55	356.21	346.80
56000	507.27	460.78	438.38	400.28	385.21	381.07	377.29	362.68	353.10
57000	516.33	469.01	446.21	407.43	392.09	387.87	384.02	369.16	359.41
58000	525.39	477.24	454.04	414.57	398.97	394.68	390.76	375.64	365.71
59000	534.45	485.47	461.87	421.72	405.84	401.48	397.50	382.11	372.02
60000	543.50	493.70	469.70	428.87	412.72	408.28	404.24	388.59	378.32
61000	552.56	501.93	477.53	436.02	419.60	415.09	410.97	395.07	384.63
62000	561.62	510.15	485.35	443.16	426.48	421.89	417.71	401.54	390.93
63000	570.68	518.38	493.18	450.31	433.36	428.70	424.45	408.02	397.24
64000	579.74	526.61	501.01	457.46	440.24	435.50	431.18	414.50	403.55
65000	588.80	534.84	508.84	464.61	447.12	442.31	437.92	420.97	409.85
66000	597.85	543.07	516.67	471.76	453.99	449.11	444.66	427.45	416.16
67000	606.91	551.29	524.49	478.90	460.87	455.92	451.40	433.92	422.46
68000	615.97	559.52	532.32	486.05	467.75	462.72	458.13	440.40	428.77
69000	625.03	567.75	540.15	493.20	474.63	469.53	464.87	446.88	435.07
70000	634.09	575.98	547.98	500.35	481.51	476.33	471.61	453.35	441.38
75000	679.38	617.12	587.12	536.08	515.90	510.35	505.29	485.74	472.90
80000	724.67	658.26	626.26	571.82	550.29	544.38	538.98	518.12	504.43
100000	905.84	822.83	782.82	714.78	687.87	680.47	673.72	647.65	630.54

7¼% MONTHLY PAYMENT

NECESSARY TO AMORTIZE A LOAN

TERM / AMOUNT	1 YEAR	2 YEARS	3 YEARS	4 YEARS	5 YEARS	7 YEARS	8 YEARS	10 YEARS	12 YEARS
$ 25	2.17	1.13	.78	.61	.50	.39	.35	.30	.27
50	4.34	2.25	1.55	1.21	1.00	.77	.69	.59	.53
75	6.50	3.37	2.33	1.81	1.50	1.15	1.04	.89	.79
100	8.67	4.49	3.10	2.41	2.00	1.53	1.38	1.18	1.05
200	17.33	8.98	6.20	4.82	3.99	3.05	2.76	2.35	2.09
300	26.00	13.47	9.30	7.22	5.98	4.57	4.13	3.53	3.13
400	34.66	17.96	12.40	9.63	7.97	6.09	5.51	4.70	4.17
500	43.33	22.45	15.50	12.04	9.96	7.61	6.88	5.88	5.21
600	51.99	26.94	18.60	14.44	11.96	9.13	8.26	7.05	6.26
700	60.65	31.43	21.70	16.85	13.95	10.66	9.64	8.22	7.30
800	69.32	35.91	24.80	19.25	15.94	12.18	11.01	9.40	8.34
900	77.98	40.40	27.90	21.66	17.93	13.70	12.39	10.57	9.38
1000	86.65	44.89	31.00	24.07	19.92	15.22	13.76	11.75	10.42
2000	173.29	89.78	61.99	48.13	39.84	30.44	27.52	23.49	20.84
3000	259.93	134.66	92.98	72.19	59.76	45.65	41.28	35.23	31.26
4000	346.57	179.55	123.97	96.25	79.68	60.87	55.04	46.97	41.68
5000	433.22	224.44	154.96	120.32	99.60	76.08	68.80	58.71	52.09
6000	519.86	269.32	185.95	144.38	119.52	91.30	82.56	70.45	62.51
7000	606.50	314.21	216.95	168.44	139.44	106.51	96.31	82.19	72.93
8000	693.14	359.09	247.94	192.50	159.36	121.73	110.07	93.93	83.35
9000	779.78	403.98	278.93	216.57	179.28	136.94	123.83	105.67	93.76
10000	866.43	448.87	309.92	240.63	199.20	152.16	137.59	117.41	104.18
15000	1299.64	673.30	464.88	360.94	298.80	228.23	206.38	176.11	156.27
20000	1732.85	897.73	619.84	481.25	398.39	304.31	275.17	234.81	208.36
25000	2166.06	1122.16	774.79	601.57	497.99	380.38	343.97	293.51	260.44
30000	2599.27	1346.59	929.75	721.88	597.59	456.46	412.76	352.21	312.53
35000	3032.48	1571.02	1084.71	842.19	697.18	532.54	481.55	410.91	364.62
36000	3119.12	1615.90	1115.70	866.25	717.10	547.75	495.31	422.65	375.04
37000	3205.76	1660.79	1146.69	890.31	737.02	562.97	509.07	434.39	385.45
38000	3292.40	1705.67	1177.68	914.38	756.94	578.18	522.83	446.13	395.87
39000	3379.04	1750.56	1208.67	938.44	776.86	593.40	536.58	457.87	406.29
40000	3465.69	1795.45	1239.67	962.50	796.78	608.61	550.34	469.61	416.71
41000	3552.33	1840.33	1270.66	986.56	816.70	623.83	564.10	481.35	427.12
42000	3638.97	1885.22	1301.65	1010.63	836.62	639.04	577.86	493.09	437.54
43000	3725.61	1930.10	1332.64	1034.69	856.54	654.26	591.62	504.83	447.96
44000	3812.25	1974.99	1363.63	1058.75	876.46	669.47	605.38	516.57	458.38
45000	3898.90	2019.88	1394.62	1082.81	896.38	684.69	619.14	528.31	468.80
46000	3985.54	2064.76	1425.62	1106.88	916.30	699.90	632.89	540.05	479.21
47000	4072.18	2109.65	1456.61	1130.94	936.21	715.12	646.65	551.79	489.63
48000	4158.82	2154.53	1487.60	1155.00	956.13	730.33	660.41	563.53	500.05
49000	4245.46	2199.42	1518.59	1179.06	976.05	745.55	674.17	575.27	510.47
50000	4332.11	2244.31	1549.58	1203.13	995.97	760.76	687.93	587.01	520.88
51000	4418.75	2289.19	1580.57	1227.19	1015.89	775.98	701.69	598.75	531.30
52000	4505.39	2334.08	1611.56	1251.25	1035.81	791.19	715.44	610.49	541.72
53000	4592.03	2378.96	1642.56	1275.31	1055.73	806.41	729.20	622.23	552.14
54000	4678.68	2423.85	1673.55	1299.37	1075.65	821.62	742.96	633.97	562.55
55000	4765.32	2468.74	1704.54	1323.44	1095.57	836.84	756.72	645.71	572.97
56000	4851.96	2513.62	1735.53	1347.50	1115.49	852.06	770.48	657.45	583.39
57000	4938.60	2558.51	1766.52	1371.56	1135.41	867.27	784.24	669.19	593.81
58000	5025.24	2603.39	1797.51	1395.62	1155.33	882.49	798.00	680.93	604.22
59000	5111.89	2648.28	1828.51	1419.69	1175.25	897.70	811.75	692.67	614.64
60000	5198.53	2693.17	1859.50	1443.75	1195.17	912.92	825.51	704.41	625.06
61000	5285.17	2738.05	1890.49	1467.81	1215.09	928.13	839.27	716.15	635.48
62000	5371.81	2782.94	1921.48	1491.87	1235.01	943.35	853.03	727.89	645.89
63000	5458.45	2827.82	1952.47	1515.94	1254.92	958.56	866.79	739.63	656.31
64000	5545.10	2872.71	1983.46	1540.00	1274.84	973.78	880.55	751.37	666.73
65000	5631.74	2917.60	2014.45	1564.06	1294.76	988.99	894.30	763.11	677.15
66000	5718.38	2962.48	2045.45	1588.12	1314.68	1004.21	908.06	774.85	687.56
67000	5805.02	3007.37	2076.44	1612.19	1334.60	1019.42	921.82	786.59	697.98
68000	5891.66	3052.25	2107.43	1636.25	1354.52	1034.64	935.58	798.33	708.40
69000	5978.31	3097.14	2138.42	1660.31	1374.44	1049.85	949.34	810.07	718.82
70000	6064.95	3142.03	2169.41	1684.37	1394.36	1065.07	963.10	821.81	729.23
75000	6498.16	3366.46	2324.37	1804.69	1493.96	1141.14	1031.89	880.51	781.32
80000	6931.37	3590.89	2479.33	1925.00	1593.55	1217.22	1100.68	939.21	833.41
100000	8664.21	4488.61	3099.16	2406.25	1991.94	1521.52	1375.85	1174.02	1041.76

MONTHLY PAYMENT 7¼%

NECESSARY TO AMORTIZE A LOAN

TERM / AMOUNT	15 YEARS	18 YEARS	20 YEARS	25 YEARS	28 YEARS	29 YEARS	30 YEARS	35 YEARS	40 YEARS
$ 25	.23	.21	.20	.19	.18	.18	.18	.17	.16
50	.46	.42	.40	.37	.35	.35	.35	.33	.32
75	.69	.63	.60	.55	.53	.52	.52	.50	.48
100	.92	.84	.80	.73	.70	.69	.69	.66	.64
200	1.83	1.67	1.59	1.45	1.40	1.38	1.37	1.32	1.28
300	2.74	2.50	2.38	2.17	2.09	2.07	2.05	1.97	1.92
400	3.66	3.33	3.17	2.90	2.79	2.76	2.73	2.63	2.56
500	4.57	4.16	3.96	3.62	3.49	3.45	3.42	3.29	3.20
600	5.48	4.99	4.75	4.34	4.18	4.14	4.10	3.94	3.84
700	6.40	5.82	5.54	5.06	4.88	4.83	4.78	4.60	4.48
800	7.31	6.65	6.33	5.79	5.57	5.52	5.46	5.26	5.12
900	8.22	7.48	7.12	6.51	6.27	6.20	6.14	5.91	5.76
1000	9.13	8.31	7.91	7.23	6.97	6.89	6.83	6.57	6.40
2000	18.26	16.61	15.81	14.46	13.93	13.78	13.65	13.13	12.80
3000	27.39	24.91	23.72	21.69	20.89	20.67	20.47	19.70	19.20
4000	36.52	33.21	31.62	28.92	27.85	27.56	27.29	26.26	25.59
5000	45.65	41.51	39.52	36.15	34.81	34.45	34.11	32.83	31.99
6000	54.78	49.82	47.43	43.37	41.77	41.34	40.94	39.39	38.39
7000	63.91	58.12	55.33	50.60	48.74	48.22	47.76	45.96	44.78
8000	73.03	66.42	63.24	57.83	55.70	55.11	54.58	52.52	51.18
9000	82.16	74.72	71.14	65.06	62.66	62.00	61.40	59.09	57.58
10000	91.29	83.02	79.04	72.29	69.62	68.89	68.22	65.65	63.97
15000	136.93	124.53	118.56	108.43	104.43	103.33	102.33	98.48	95.96
20000	182.58	166.04	158.08	144.57	139.24	137.77	136.44	131.30	127.94
25000	228.22	207.55	197.60	180.71	174.04	172.22	170.55	164.12	159.92
30000	273.86	249.06	237.12	216.85	208.85	206.66	204.66	196.95	191.91
35000	319.51	290.57	276.64	252.99	243.66	241.10	238.77	229.77	223.89
36000	328.64	298.87	284.54	260.22	250.62	247.99	245.59	236.33	230.29
37000	337.76	307.17	292.44	267.44	257.58	254.88	252.41	242.90	236.68
38000	346.89	315.47	300.35	274.67	264.54	261.77	259.23	249.46	243.08
39000	356.02	323.77	308.25	281.90	271.51	268.65	266.05	256.03	249.48
40000	365.15	332.07	316.16	289.13	278.47	275.54	272.88	262.59	255.87
41000	374.28	340.38	324.06	296.36	285.43	282.43	279.70	269.16	262.27
42000	383.41	348.68	331.96	303.58	292.39	289.32	286.52	275.72	268.67
43000	392.54	356.98	339.87	310.81	299.35	296.21	293.34	282.29	275.06
44000	401.66	365.28	347.77	318.04	306.31	303.10	300.16	288.85	281.46
45000	410.79	373.58	355.67	325.27	313.28	309.98	306.98	295.42	287.86
46000	419.92	381.88	363.58	332.50	320.24	316.87	313.81	301.98	294.25
47000	429.05	390.19	371.48	339.72	327.20	323.76	320.63	308.54	300.65
48000	438.18	398.49	379.39	346.95	334.16	330.65	327.45	315.11	307.05
49000	447.31	406.79	387.29	354.18	341.12	337.54	334.27	321.67	313.44
50000	456.44	415.09	395.19	361.41	348.08	344.43	341.09	328.24	319.84
51000	465.57	423.39	403.10	368.64	355.05	351.32	347.91	334.80	326.24
52000	474.69	431.69	411.00	375.86	362.01	358.20	354.74	341.37	332.63
53000	483.82	440.00	418.90	383.09	368.97	365.09	361.56	347.93	339.03
54000	492.95	448.30	426.81	390.32	375.93	371.98	368.38	354.50	345.43
55000	502.08	456.60	434.71	397.55	382.89	378.87	375.20	361.06	351.82
56000	511.21	464.90	442.62	404.78	389.85	385.76	382.02	367.63	358.22
57000	520.34	473.20	450.52	412.00	396.81	392.65	388.85	374.19	364.62
58000	529.47	481.50	458.42	419.23	403.78	399.53	395.67	380.76	371.01
59000	538.59	489.81	466.33	426.46	410.74	406.42	402.49	387.32	377.41
60000	547.72	498.11	474.23	433.69	417.70	413.31	409.31	393.89	383.81
61000	556.85	506.41	482.13	440.92	424.66	420.20	416.13	400.45	390.20
62000	565.98	514.71	490.04	448.15	431.62	427.09	422.95	407.01	396.60
63000	575.11	523.01	497.94	455.37	438.58	433.98	429.78	413.58	403.00
64000	584.24	531.32	505.85	462.60	445.55	440.86	436.60	420.14	409.40
65000	593.37	539.62	513.75	469.83	452.51	447.75	443.42	426.71	415.79
66000	602.49	547.92	521.65	477.06	459.47	454.64	450.24	433.27	422.19
67000	611.62	556.22	529.56	484.29	466.43	461.53	457.06	439.84	428.59
68000	620.75	564.52	537.46	491.51	473.39	468.42	463.88	446.40	434.98
69000	629.88	572.82	545.36	498.74	480.35	475.31	470.71	452.97	441.38
70000	639.01	581.13	553.27	505.97	487.31	482.20	477.53	459.53	447.78
75000	684.65	622.63	592.79	542.11	522.12	516.64	511.64	492.36	479.76
80000	730.30	664.14	632.31	578.25	556.93	551.08	545.75	525.18	511.74
100000	912.87	830.18	790.38	722.81	696.16	688.85	682.18	656.47	639.68

7⅜% MONTHLY PAYMENT

NECESSARY TO AMORTIZE A LOAN

TERM / AMOUNT	1 YEAR	2 YEARS	3 YEARS	4 YEARS	5 YEARS	7 YEARS	8 YEARS	10 YEARS	12 YEARS
$ 25	2.17	1.13	.78	.61	.50	.39	.35	.30	.27
50	4.34	2.25	1.56	1.21	1.00	.77	.70	.60	.53
75	6.51	3.38	2.33	1.81	1.50	1.15	1.04	.89	.79
100	8.67	4.50	3.11	2.42	2.00	1.53	1.39	1.19	1.05
200	17.34	8.99	6.21	4.83	4.00	3.06	2.77	2.37	2.10
300	26.01	13.49	9.32	7.24	6.00	4.59	4.15	3.55	3.15
400	34.68	17.98	12.42	9.65	8.00	6.12	5.53	4.73	4.20
500	43.35	22.48	15.53	12.07	9.99	7.64	6.92	5.91	5.25
600	52.02	26.97	18.63	14.48	11.99	9.17	8.30	7.09	6.30
700	60.69	31.46	21.74	16.89	13.99	10.70	9.68	8.27	7.34
800	69.36	35.96	24.84	19.30	15.99	12.23	11.06	9.45	8.39
900	78.03	40.45	27.95	21.71	17.99	13.75	12.44	10.63	9.44
1000	86.70	44.95	31.05	24.13	19.98	15.28	13.83	11.81	10.49
2000	173.40	89.89	62.10	48.25	39.96	30.56	27.65	23.62	20.97
3000	260.10	134.83	93.15	72.37	59.94	45.83	41.47	35.42	31.46
4000	346.80	179.78	124.20	96.49	79.92	61.11	55.29	47.23	41.94
5000	433.50	224.72	155.25	120.61	99.90	76.39	69.11	59.03	52.43
6000	520.20	269.66	186.30	144.73	119.88	91.66	82.93	70.84	62.91
7000	606.90	314.60	217.35	168.85	139.86	106.94	96.75	82.64	73.40
8000	693.60	359.55	248.40	192.97	159.83	122.22	110.57	94.45	83.88
9000	780.30	404.49	279.44	217.09	179.81	137.49	124.39	106.25	94.37
10000	867.00	449.43	310.49	241.21	199.79	152.77	138.22	118.06	104.85
15000	1300.50	674.15	465.74	361.81	299.68	229.15	207.32	177.08	157.28
20000	1734.00	898.86	620.98	482.42	399.58	305.54	276.43	236.11	209.70
25000	2167.50	1123.57	776.23	603.02	499.47	381.92	345.53	295.13	262.12
30000	2601.00	1348.29	931.47	723.62	599.36	458.30	414.64	354.16	314.55
35000	3034.50	1573.00	1086.71	844.23	699.26	534.69	483.74	413.18	366.97
36000	3121.19	1617.94	1117.76	868.35	719.23	549.96	497.56	424.99	377.46
37000	3207.89	1662.89	1148.81	892.47	739.21	565.24	511.39	436.79	387.94
38000	3294.59	1707.83	1179.86	916.59	759.19	580.52	525.21	448.60	398.43
39000	3381.29	1752.77	1210.91	940.71	779.17	595.79	539.03	460.40	408.91
40000	3467.99	1797.72	1241.96	964.83	799.15	611.07	552.85	472.21	419.40
41000	3554.69	1842.66	1273.01	988.95	819.13	626.35	566.67	484.01	429.88
42000	3641.39	1887.60	1304.06	1013.07	839.11	641.62	580.49	495.82	440.37
43000	3728.09	1932.54	1335.11	1037.19	859.08	656.90	594.31	507.62	450.85
44000	3814.79	1977.49	1366.15	1061.31	879.06	672.18	608.13	519.43	461.34
45000	3901.49	2022.43	1397.20	1085.43	899.04	687.45	621.95	531.23	471.82
46000	3988.19	2067.37	1428.25	1109.55	919.02	702.73	635.77	543.04	482.31
47000	4074.89	2112.32	1459.30	1133.67	939.00	718.01	649.60	554.84	492.79
48000	4161.59	2157.26	1490.35	1157.79	958.98	733.28	663.42	566.65	503.27
49000	4248.29	2202.20	1521.40	1181.91	978.96	748.56	677.24	578.45	513.76
50000	4334.99	2247.14	1552.45	1206.04	998.94	763.84	691.06	590.26	524.24
51000	4421.69	2292.09	1583.50	1230.16	1018.91	779.11	704.88	602.06	534.73
52000	4508.39	2337.03	1614.54	1254.28	1038.89	794.39	718.70	613.87	545.21
53000	4595.09	2381.97	1645.59	1278.40	1058.87	809.67	732.52	625.67	555.70
54000	4681.79	2426.91	1676.64	1302.52	1078.85	824.94	746.34	637.48	566.18
55000	4768.49	2471.86	1707.69	1326.64	1098.83	840.22	760.16	649.28	576.67
56000	4855.19	2516.80	1738.74	1350.76	1118.81	855.50	773.99	661.09	587.15
57000	4941.89	2561.74	1769.79	1374.88	1138.79	870.77	787.81	672.89	597.64
58000	5028.59	2606.69	1800.84	1399.00	1158.76	886.05	801.63	684.70	608.12
59000	5115.29	2651.63	1831.89	1423.12	1178.74	901.33	815.45	696.50	618.61
60000	5201.99	2696.57	1862.94	1447.24	1198.72	916.60	829.27	708.31	629.09
61000	5288.69	2741.51	1893.98	1471.36	1218.70	931.88	843.09	720.11	639.58
62000	5375.39	2786.46	1925.03	1495.48	1238.68	947.16	856.91	731.92	650.06
63000	5462.09	2831.40	1956.08	1519.60	1258.66	962.43	870.73	743.72	660.55
64000	5548.79	2876.34	1987.13	1543.72	1278.64	977.71	884.55	755.53	671.03
65000	5635.49	2921.29	2018.18	1567.84	1298.61	992.99	898.38	767.33	681.52
66000	5722.19	2966.23	2049.23	1591.97	1318.59	1008.26	912.20	779.14	692.00
67000	5808.89	3011.17	2080.28	1616.09	1338.57	1023.54	926.02	790.94	702.49
68000	5895.59	3056.11	2111.33	1640.21	1358.55	1038.82	939.84	802.75	712.97
69000	5982.29	3101.06	2142.38	1664.33	1378.53	1054.09	953.66	814.55	723.46
70000	6068.99	3146.00	2173.42	1688.45	1398.51	1069.37	967.48	826.36	733.94
75000	6502.48	3370.71	2328.67	1809.05	1498.40	1145.75	1036.59	885.38	786.36
80000	6935.98	3595.43	2483.91	1929.65	1598.29	1222.14	1105.69	944.41	838.79
100000	8669.98	4494.28	3104.89	2412.07	1997.87	1527.67	1382.11	1180.51	1048.48

MONTHLY PAYMENT 7⅜%
NECESSARY TO AMORTIZE A LOAN

TERM / AMOUNT	15 YEARS	18 YEARS	20 YEARS	25 YEARS	28 YEARS	29 YEARS	30 YEARS	35 YEARS	40 YEARS
$ 25	.23	.21	.20	.19	.18	.18	.18	.17	.17
50	.46	.42	.40	.37	.36	.35	.35	.34	.33
75	.69	.63	.60	.55	.53	.53	.52	.50	.49
100	.92	.84	.80	.74	.71	.70	.70	.67	.65
200	1.84	1.68	1.60	1.47	1.41	1.40	1.39	1.34	1.30
300	2.76	2.52	2.40	2.20	2.12	2.10	2.08	2.00	1.95
400	3.68	3.36	3.20	2.93	2.82	2.79	2.77	2.67	2.60
500	4.60	4.19	3.99	3.66	3.53	3.49	3.46	3.33	3.25
600	5.52	5.03	4.79	4.39	4.23	4.19	4.15	4.00	3.90
700	6.44	5.87	5.59	5.12	4.94	4.89	4.84	4.66	4.55
800	7.36	6.71	6.39	5.85	5.64	5.58	5.53	5.33	5.20
900	8.28	7.54	7.19	6.58	6.35	6.28	6.22	5.99	5.84
1000	9.20	8.38	7.98	7.31	7.05	6.98	6.91	6.66	6.49
2000	18.40	16.76	15.96	14.62	14.09	13.95	13.82	13.31	12.98
3000	27.60	25.13	23.94	21.93	21.14	20.92	20.73	19.97	19.47
4000	36.80	33.51	31.92	29.24	28.18	27.90	27.63	26.62	25.96
5000	46.00	41.88	39.90	36.55	35.23	34.87	34.54	33.27	32.45
6000	55.20	50.26	47.88	43.86	42.27	41.84	41.45	39.93	38.94
7000	64.40	58.63	55.86	51.17	49.32	48.81	48.35	46.58	45.42
8000	73.60	67.01	63.84	58.48	56.36	55.79	55.26	53.23	51.91
9000	82.80	75.39	71.82	65.78	63.41	62.76	62.17	59.89	58.40
10000	92.00	83.76	79.80	73.09	70.45	69.73	69.07	66.54	64.89
15000	137.99	125.64	119.70	109.64	105.68	104.59	103.61	99.81	97.33
20000	183.99	167.52	159.60	146.18	140.90	139.46	138.14	133.07	129.78
25000	229.99	209.39	199.50	182.72	176.13	174.32	172.67	166.34	162.22
30000	275.98	251.27	239.40	219.27	211.35	209.18	207.21	199.61	194.66
35000	321.98	293.15	279.29	255.81	246.58	244.05	241.74	232.87	227.10
36000	331.18	301.53	287.27	263.12	253.62	251.02	248.65	239.53	233.59
37000	340.38	309.90	295.25	270.43	260.67	257.99	255.55	246.18	240.08
38000	349.58	318.28	303.23	277.74	267.71	264.96	262.46	252.83	246.57
39000	358.78	326.65	311.21	285.05	274.76	271.94	269.37	259.49	253.06
40000	367.97	335.03	319.19	292.36	281.80	278.91	276.28	266.14	259.55
41000	377.17	343.40	327.17	299.67	288.85	285.88	283.18	272.79	266.03
42000	386.37	351.78	335.15	306.97	295.89	292.85	290.09	279.45	272.52
43000	395.57	360.15	343.13	314.28	302.94	299.83	297.00	286.10	279.01
44000	404.77	368.53	351.11	321.59	309.98	306.80	303.90	292.75	285.50
45000	413.97	376.91	359.09	328.90	317.03	313.77	310.81	299.41	291.99
46000	423.17	385.28	367.07	336.21	324.07	320.75	317.72	306.06	298.48
47000	432.37	393.66	375.05	343.52	331.12	327.72	324.62	312.71	304.97
48000	441.57	402.03	383.03	350.83	338.16	334.69	331.53	319.37	311.45
49000	450.77	410.41	391.01	358.14	345.21	341.66	338.44	326.02	317.94
50000	459.97	418.78	398.99	365.44	352.25	348.64	345.34	332.67	324.43
51000	469.17	427.16	406.97	372.75	359.30	355.61	352.25	339.33	330.92
52000	478.37	435.53	414.95	380.06	366.34	362.58	359.16	345.98	337.41
53000	487.56	443.91	422.93	387.37	373.39	369.55	366.06	352.63	343.90
54000	496.76	452.29	430.91	394.68	380.43	376.53	372.97	359.29	350.39
55000	505.96	460.66	438.89	401.99	387.48	383.50	379.88	365.94	356.87
56000	515.16	469.04	446.87	409.30	394.52	390.47	386.78	372.59	363.36
57000	524.36	477.41	454.85	416.61	401.57	397.44	393.69	379.25	369.85
58000	533.56	485.79	462.83	423.92	408.61	404.42	400.60	385.90	376.34
59000	542.76	494.16	470.81	431.22	415.66	411.39	407.50	392.55	382.83
60000	551.96	502.54	478.79	438.53	422.70	418.36	414.41	399.21	389.32
61000	561.16	510.91	486.76	445.84	429.75	425.33	421.32	405.86	395.80
62000	570.36	519.29	494.74	453.15	436.79	432.31	428.22	412.51	402.29
63000	579.56	527.67	502.72	460.46	443.84	439.28	435.13	419.17	408.78
64000	588.76	536.04	510.70	467.77	450.88	446.25	442.04	425.82	415.27
65000	597.96	544.42	518.68	475.08	457.92	453.22	448.94	432.47	421.76
66000	607.15	552.79	526.66	482.39	464.97	460.20	455.85	439.13	428.25
67000	616.35	561.17	534.64	489.69	472.01	467.17	462.76	445.78	434.74
68000	625.55	569.54	542.62	497.00	479.06	474.14	469.66	452.43	441.22
69000	634.75	577.92	550.60	504.31	486.10	481.12	476.57	459.09	447.71
70000	643.95	586.29	558.58	511.62	493.15	488.09	483.48	465.74	454.20
75000	689.95	628.17	598.48	548.16	528.37	522.95	518.01	499.01	486.64
80000	735.94	670.05	638.38	584.71	563.60	557.81	552.55	532.27	519.09
100000	919.93	837.56	797.97	730.88	704.50	697.27	690.68	665.34	648.86

7½% MONTHLY PAYMENT
NECESSARY TO AMORTIZE A LOAN

TERM / AMOUNT	1 YEAR	2 YEARS	3 YEARS	4 YEARS	5 YEARS	7 YEARS	8 YEARS	10 YEARS	12 YEARS
$ 25	2.17	1.13	.78	.61	.51	.39	.35	.30	.27
50	4.34	2.25	1.56	1.21	1.01	.77	.70	.60	.53
75	6.51	3.38	2.34	1.82	1.51	1.16	1.05	.90	.80
100	8.68	4.50	3.12	2.42	2.01	1.54	1.39	1.19	1.06
200	17.36	9.00	6.23	4.84	4.01	3.07	2.78	2.38	2.12
300	26.03	13.50	9.34	7.26	6.02	4.61	4.17	3.57	3.17
400	34.71	18.00	12.45	9.68	8.02	6.14	5.56	4.75	4.23
500	43.38	22.50	15.56	12.09	10.02	7.67	6.95	5.94	5.28
600	52.06	27.00	18.67	14.51	12.03	9.21	8.34	7.13	6.34
700	60.74	31.50	21.78	16.93	14.03	10.74	9.72	8.31	7.39
800	69.41	36.00	24.89	19.35	16.04	12.28	11.11	9.50	8.45
900	78.09	40.50	28.00	21.77	18.04	13.81	12.50	10.69	9.50
1000	86.76	45.00	31.11	24.18	20.04	15.34	13.89	11.88	10.56
2000	173.52	90.00	62.22	48.36	40.08	30.68	27.77	23.75	21.11
3000	260.28	135.00	93.32	72.54	60.12	46.02	41.66	35.62	31.66
4000	347.03	180.00	124.43	96.72	80.16	61.36	55.54	47.49	42.21
5000	433.79	225.00	155.54	120.90	100.19	76.70	69.42	59.36	52.77
6000	520.55	270.00	186.64	145.08	120.23	92.03	83.31	71.23	63.32
7000	607.31	315.00	217.75	169.26	140.27	107.37	97.19	83.10	73.87
8000	694.06	360.00	248.85	193.44	160.31	122.71	111.08	94.97	84.42
9000	780.82	405.00	279.96	217.62	180.35	138.05	124.96	106.84	94.98
10000	867.58	450.00	311.07	241.79	200.38	153.39	138.84	118.71	105.53
15000	1301.37	675.00	466.60	362.69	300.57	230.08	208.26	178.06	158.29
20000	1735.15	900.00	622.13	483.58	400.76	306.77	277.68	237.41	211.05
25000	2168.94	1124.99	777.66	604.48	500.95	383.46	347.10	296.76	263.81
30000	2602.73	1349.99	933.19	725.37	601.14	460.15	416.52	356.11	316.57
35000	3036.51	1574.99	1088.72	846.27	701.33	536.84	485.94	415.46	369.33
36000	3123.27	1619.99	1119.83	870.45	721.37	552.18	499.82	427.33	379.89
37000	3210.03	1664.99	1150.94	894.62	741.41	567.52	513.71	439.20	390.44
38000	3296.79	1709.99	1182.04	918.80	761.45	582.86	527.59	451.07	400.99
39000	3383.54	1754.99	1213.15	942.98	781.48	598.20	541.48	462.94	411.54
40000	3470.30	1799.99	1244.25	967.16	801.52	613.54	555.36	474.81	422.10
41000	3557.06	1844.99	1275.36	991.34	821.56	628.87	569.24	486.68	432.65
42000	3643.82	1889.99	1306.47	1015.52	841.60	644.21	583.13	498.55	443.20
43000	3730.57	1934.99	1337.57	1039.70	861.64	659.55	597.01	510.42	453.75
44000	3817.33	1979.99	1368.68	1063.88	881.67	674.89	610.90	522.29	464.30
45000	3904.09	2024.99	1399.78	1088.06	901.71	690.23	624.78	534.16	474.86
46000	3990.85	2069.99	1430.89	1112.23	921.75	705.57	638.66	546.03	485.41
47000	4077.60	2114.99	1462.00	1136.41	941.79	720.90	652.55	557.90	495.96
48000	4164.36	2159.99	1493.10	1160.59	961.83	736.24	666.43	569.77	506.51
49000	4251.12	2204.99	1524.21	1184.77	981.86	751.58	680.31	581.64	517.07
50000	4337.88	2249.98	1555.32	1208.95	1001.90	766.92	694.20	593.51	527.62
51000	4424.63	2294.98	1586.42	1233.13	1021.94	782.26	708.08	605.38	538.17
52000	4511.39	2339.98	1617.53	1257.31	1041.98	797.60	721.97	617.25	548.72
53000	4598.15	2384.98	1648.63	1281.49	1062.02	812.93	735.85	629.12	559.27
54000	4684.91	2429.98	1679.74	1305.67	1082.05	828.27	749.73	640.99	569.83
55000	4771.66	2474.98	1710.85	1329.84	1102.09	843.61	763.62	652.86	580.38
56000	4858.42	2519.98	1741.95	1354.02	1122.13	858.95	777.50	664.73	590.93
57000	4945.18	2564.98	1773.06	1378.20	1142.17	874.29	791.39	676.61	601.48
58000	5031.94	2609.98	1804.17	1402.38	1162.21	889.62	805.27	688.48	612.04
59000	5118.69	2654.98	1835.27	1426.56	1182.24	904.96	819.15	700.35	622.59
60000	5205.45	2699.98	1866.38	1450.74	1202.28	920.30	833.04	712.22	633.14
61000	5292.21	2744.98	1897.48	1474.92	1222.32	935.64	846.92	724.09	643.69
62000	5378.96	2789.98	1928.59	1499.10	1242.36	950.98	860.80	735.96	654.25
63000	5465.72	2834.98	1959.70	1523.28	1262.40	966.32	874.69	747.83	664.80
64000	5552.48	2879.98	1990.80	1547.45	1282.43	981.65	888.57	759.70	675.35
65000	5639.24	2924.98	2021.91	1571.63	1302.47	996.99	902.46	771.57	685.90
66000	5725.99	2969.98	2053.02	1595.81	1322.51	1012.33	916.34	783.44	696.45
67000	5812.75	3014.98	2084.12	1619.99	1342.55	1027.67	930.22	795.31	707.01
68000	5899.51	3059.98	2115.23	1644.17	1362.59	1043.01	944.11	807.18	717.56
69000	5986.27	3104.98	2146.33	1668.35	1382.62	1058.35	957.99	819.05	728.11
70000	6073.02	3149.98	2177.44	1692.53	1402.66	1073.68	971.88	830.92	738.66
75000	6506.81	3374.97	2332.97	1813.42	1502.85	1150.38	1041.30	890.27	791.42
80000	6940.60	3599.97	2488.50	1934.32	1603.04	1227.07	1110.71	949.62	844.19
100000	8675.75	4499.96	3110.63	2417.90	2003.80	1533.83	1388.39	1187.02	1055.23

MONTHLY PAYMENT 7½%
NECESSARY TO AMORTIZE A LOAN

TERM / AMOUNT	15 YEARS	18 YEARS	20 YEARS	25 YEARS	28 YEARS	29 YEARS	30 YEARS	35 YEARS	40 YEARS
$ 25	.24	.22	.21	.19	.18	.18	.18	.17	.17
50	.47	.43	.41	.37	.36	.36	.35	.34	.33
75	.70	.64	.61	.56	.54	.53	.53	.51	.50
100	.93	.85	.81	.74	.72	.71	.70	.68	.66
200	1.86	1.69	1.62	1.48	1.43	1.42	1.40	1.35	1.32
300	2.79	2.54	2.42	2.22	2.14	2.12	2.10	2.03	1.98
400	3.71	3.38	3.23	2.96	2.86	2.83	2.80	2.70	2.64
500	4.64	4.23	4.03	3.70	3.57	3.53	3.50	3.38	3.30
600	5.57	5.07	4.84	4.44	4.28	4.24	4.20	4.05	3.95
700	6.49	5.92	5.64	5.18	5.00	4.95	4.90	4.72	4.61
800	7.42	6.76	6.45	5.92	5.71	5.65	5.60	5.40	5.27
900	8.35	7.61	7.26	6.66	6.42	6.36	6.30	6.07	5.93
1000	9.28	8.45	8.06	7.39	7.13	7.06	7.00	6.75	6.59
2000	18.55	16.90	16.12	14.78	14.26	14.12	13.99	13.49	13.17
3000	27.82	25.35	24.17	22.17	21.39	21.18	20.98	20.23	19.75
4000	37.09	33.80	32.23	29.56	28.52	28.23	27.97	26.97	26.33
5000	46.36	42.25	40.28	36.95	35.65	35.29	34.97	33.72	32.91
6000	55.63	50.70	48.34	44.34	42.78	42.35	41.96	40.46	39.49
7000	64.90	59.15	56.40	51.73	49.91	49.41	48.95	47.20	46.07
8000	74.17	67.60	64.45	59.12	57.03	56.46	55.94	53.94	52.65
9000	83.44	76.05	72.51	66.51	64.16	63.52	62.93	60.69	59.23
10000	92.71	84.50	80.56	73.90	71.29	70.58	69.93	67.43	65.81
15000	139.06	126.75	120.84	110.85	106.94	105.86	104.89	101.14	98.72
20000	185.41	169.00	161.12	147.80	142.58	141.15	139.85	134.85	131.62
25000	231.76	211.25	201.40	184.75	178.22	176.44	174.81	168.57	164.52
30000	278.11	253.50	241.68	221.70	213.87	211.72	209.77	202.28	197.43
35000	324.46	295.75	281.96	258.65	249.51	247.01	244.73	235.99	230.33
36000	333.73	304.20	290.02	266.04	256.64	254.06	251.72	242.73	236.91
37000	343.00	312.65	298.07	273.43	263.77	261.12	258.71	249.47	243.49
38000	352.27	321.09	306.13	280.82	270.89	268.18	265.71	256.22	250.07
39000	361.54	329.54	314.19	288.21	278.02	275.24	272.70	262.96	256.65
40000	370.81	337.99	322.24	295.60	285.15	282.29	279.69	269.70	263.23
41000	380.08	346.44	330.30	302.99	292.28	289.35	286.68	276.44	269.81
42000	389.35	354.89	338.35	310.38	299.41	296.41	293.68	283.19	276.39
43000	398.62	363.34	346.41	317.77	306.54	303.46	300.67	289.93	282.98
44000	407.89	371.79	354.47	325.16	313.67	310.52	307.66	296.67	289.56
45000	417.16	380.24	362.52	332.55	320.80	317.58	314.65	303.41	296.14
46000	426.43	388.69	370.58	339.94	327.92	324.64	321.64	310.16	302.72
47000	435.70	397.14	378.63	347.33	335.05	331.69	328.64	316.90	309.30
48000	444.97	405.59	386.69	354.72	342.18	338.75	335.63	323.64	315.88
49000	454.24	414.04	394.75	362.11	349.31	345.81	342.62	330.38	322.46
50000	463.51	422.49	402.80	369.50	356.44	352.87	349.61	337.13	329.04
51000	472.78	430.94	410.86	376.89	363.57	359.92	356.60	343.87	335.62
52000	482.05	439.39	418.91	384.28	370.70	366.98	363.60	350.61	342.20
53000	491.32	447.84	426.97	391.67	377.82	374.04	370.59	357.35	348.78
54000	500.59	456.29	435.03	399.06	384.95	381.09	377.58	364.10	355.36
55000	509.86	464.74	443.08	406.45	392.08	388.15	384.57	370.84	361.94
56000	519.13	473.19	451.14	413.84	399.21	395.21	391.57	377.58	368.52
57000	528.40	481.64	459.19	421.23	406.34	402.27	398.56	384.32	375.11
58000	537.67	490.09	467.25	428.62	413.47	409.32	405.55	391.07	381.69
59000	546.94	498.54	475.30	436.01	420.60	416.38	412.54	397.81	388.27
60000	556.21	506.99	483.36	443.40	427.73	423.44	419.53	404.55	394.85
61000	565.48	515.44	491.42	450.79	434.85	430.49	426.53	411.29	401.43
62000	574.75	523.89	499.47	458.18	441.98	437.55	433.52	418.04	408.01
63000	584.02	532.34	507.53	465.57	449.11	444.61	440.51	424.78	414.59
64000	593.29	540.79	515.58	472.96	456.24	451.67	447.50	431.52	421.17
65000	602.56	549.24	523.64	480.35	463.37	458.72	454.49	438.26	427.75
66000	611.83	557.69	531.70	487.74	470.50	465.78	461.49	445.01	434.33
67000	621.10	566.14	539.75	495.13	477.63	472.84	468.48	451.75	440.91
68000	630.37	574.59	547.81	502.52	484.75	479.89	475.47	458.49	447.49
69000	639.64	583.04	555.86	509.91	491.88	486.95	482.46	465.23	454.07
70000	648.91	591.49	563.92	517.30	499.01	494.01	489.46	471.97	460.65
75000	695.26	633.73	604.20	554.25	534.66	529.30	524.42	505.69	493.56
80000	741.61	675.98	644.48	591.20	570.30	564.58	559.38	539.40	526.46
100000	927.02	844.98	805.60	739.00	712.87	705.73	699.22	674.25	658.08

7⅝% MONTHLY PAYMENT

NECESSARY TO AMORTIZE A LOAN

TERM / AMOUNT	1 YEAR	2 YEARS	3 YEARS	4 YEARS	5 YEARS	7 YEARS	8 YEARS	10 YEARS	12 YEARS
$ 25	2.18	1.13	.78	.61	.51	.39	.35	.30	.27
50	4.35	2.26	1.56	1.22	1.01	.78	.70	.60	.54
75	6.52	3.38	2.34	1.82	1.51	1.16	1.05	.90	.80
100	8.69	4.51	3.12	2.43	2.01	1.55	1.40	1.20	1.07
200	17.37	9.02	6.24	4.85	4.02	3.09	2.79	2.39	2.13
300	26.05	13.52	9.35	7.28	6.03	4.63	4.19	3.59	3.19
400	34.73	18.03	12.47	9.70	8.04	6.17	5.58	4.78	4.25
500	43.41	22.53	15.59	12.12	10.05	7.71	6.98	5.97	5.31
600	52.09	27.04	18.70	14.55	12.06	9.25	8.37	7.17	6.38
700	60.78	31.54	21.82	16.97	14.07	10.79	9.77	8.36	7.44
800	69.46	36.05	24.94	19.39	16.08	12.33	11.16	9.55	8.50
900	78.14	40.56	28.05	21.82	18.09	13.87	12.56	10.75	9.56
1000	86.82	45.06	31.17	24.24	20.10	15.41	13.95	11.94	10.62
2000	173.64	90.12	62.33	48.48	40.20	30.81	27.90	23.88	21.24
3000	260.45	135.17	93.50	72.72	60.30	46.21	41.85	35.81	31.86
4000	347.27	180.23	124.66	96.95	80.39	61.61	55.79	47.75	42.48
5000	434.08	225.29	155.82	121.19	100.49	77.01	69.74	59.68	53.10
6000	520.90	270.34	186.99	145.43	120.59	92.41	83.69	71.62	63.72
7000	607.71	315.40	218.15	169.67	140.69	107.81	97.63	83.55	74.34
8000	694.53	360.46	249.31	193.90	160.78	123.21	111.58	95.49	84.96
9000	781.34	405.51	280.48	218.14	180.88	138.61	125.53	107.42	95.58
10000	868.16	450.57	311.64	242.38	200.98	154.01	139.47	119.36	106.20
15000	1302.23	675.85	467.46	363.56	301.47	231.01	209.21	179.04	159.30
20000	1736.31	901.13	623.28	484.75	401.95	308.01	278.94	238.72	212.40
25000	2170.38	1126.42	779.10	605.94	502.44	385.01	348.68	298.39	265.50
30000	2604.46	1351.70	934.91	727.12	602.93	462.01	418.41	358.07	318.60
35000	3038.53	1576.98	1090.73	848.31	703.41	539.01	488.14	417.75	371.70
36000	3125.35	1622.04	1121.90	872.55	723.51	554.41	502.09	429.68	382.32
37000	3212.17	1667.09	1153.06	896.78	743.61	569.81	516.04	441.62	392.94
38000	3298.98	1712.15	1184.22	921.02	763.71	585.21	529.98	453.55	403.56
39000	3385.80	1757.21	1215.39	945.26	783.80	600.61	543.93	465.49	414.18
40000	3472.61	1802.26	1246.55	969.50	803.90	616.01	557.88	477.43	424.80
41000	3559.43	1847.32	1277.72	993.73	824.00	631.41	571.82	489.36	435.42
42000	3646.24	1892.38	1308.88	1017.97	844.10	646.81	585.77	501.30	446.04
43000	3733.06	1937.43	1340.04	1042.21	864.19	662.21	599.72	513.23	456.66
44000	3819.87	1982.49	1371.21	1066.45	884.29	677.61	613.67	525.17	467.28
45000	3906.69	2027.55	1402.37	1090.68	904.39	693.01	627.61	537.10	477.90
46000	3993.50	2072.60	1433.53	1114.92	924.49	708.41	641.56	549.04	488.52
47000	4080.32	2117.66	1464.70	1139.16	944.58	723.81	655.51	560.97	499.14
48000	4167.13	2162.71	1495.86	1163.39	964.68	739.21	669.45	572.91	509.76
49000	4253.95	2207.77	1527.02	1187.63	984.78	754.61	683.40	584.85	520.38
50000	4340.76	2252.83	1558.19	1211.87	1004.88	770.01	697.35	596.78	531.00
51000	4427.58	2297.88	1589.35	1236.11	1024.97	785.41	711.29	608.72	541.62
52000	4514.39	2342.94	1620.52	1260.34	1045.07	800.81	725.24	620.65	552.24
53000	4601.21	2388.00	1651.68	1284.58	1065.17	816.21	739.19	632.59	562.86
54000	4688.02	2433.05	1682.84	1308.82	1085.26	831.61	753.13	644.52	573.48
55000	4774.84	2478.11	1714.01	1333.06	1105.36	847.01	767.08	656.46	584.10
56000	4861.65	2523.17	1745.17	1357.29	1125.46	862.41	781.03	668.39	594.72
57000	4948.47	2568.22	1776.33	1381.53	1145.56	877.81	794.97	680.33	605.34
58000	5035.28	2613.28	1807.50	1405.77	1165.65	893.21	808.92	692.27	615.96
59000	5122.10	2658.34	1838.66	1430.00	1185.75	908.61	822.87	704.20	626.58
60000	5208.91	2703.39	1869.82	1454.24	1205.85	924.01	836.81	716.14	637.20
61000	5295.73	2748.45	1900.99	1478.48	1225.95	939.41	850.76	728.07	647.82
62000	5382.54	2793.51	1932.15	1502.72	1246.04	954.81	864.71	740.01	658.44
63000	5469.36	2838.56	1963.32	1526.95	1266.14	970.21	878.65	751.94	669.06
64000	5556.17	2883.62	1994.48	1551.19	1286.24	985.61	892.60	763.88	679.68
65000	5642.99	2928.67	2025.64	1575.43	1306.34	1001.01	906.55	775.81	690.30
66000	5729.80	2973.73	2056.81	1599.67	1326.43	1016.41	920.50	787.75	700.92
67000	5816.62	3018.79	2087.97	1623.90	1346.53	1031.81	934.44	799.68	711.54
68000	5903.43	3063.84	2119.13	1648.14	1366.63	1047.21	948.39	811.62	722.16
69000	5990.25	3108.90	2150.30	1672.38	1386.73	1062.61	962.34	823.56	732.78
70000	6077.06	3153.96	2181.46	1696.61	1406.82	1078.01	976.28	835.49	743.40
75000	6511.14	3379.24	2337.28	1817.80	1507.31	1155.01	1046.02	895.17	796.50
80000	6945.22	3604.52	2493.10	1938.99	1607.80	1232.01	1115.75	954.85	849.60
100000	8681.52	4505.65	3116.37	2423.73	2009.75	1540.01	1394.69	1193.56	1062.00

MONTHLY PAYMENT 7⅝%
NECESSARY TO AMORTIZE A LOAN

TERM / AMOUNT	15 YEARS	18 YEARS	20 YEARS	25 YEARS	28 YEARS	29 YEARS	30 YEARS	35 YEARS	40 YEARS
$ 25	.24	.22	.21	.19	.19	.18	.18	.18	.17
50	.47	.43	.41	.38	.37	.36	.36	.35	.34
75	.71	.64	.61	.57	.55	.54	.54	.52	.51
100	.94	.86	.82	.75	.73	.72	.71	.69	.67
200	1.87	1.71	1.63	1.50	1.45	1.43	1.42	1.37	1.34
300	2.81	2.56	2.44	2.25	2.17	2.15	2.13	2.05	2.01
400	3.74	3.41	3.26	2.99	2.89	2.86	2.84	2.74	2.67
500	4.68	4.27	4.07	3.74	3.61	3.58	3.54	3.42	3.34
600	5.61	5.12	4.88	4.49	4.33	4.29	4.25	4.10	4.01
700	6.54	5.97	5.70	5.23	5.05	5.00	4.96	4.79	4.68
800	7.48	6.82	6.51	5.98	5.78	5.72	5.67	5.47	5.34
900	8.41	7.68	7.32	6.73	6.50	6.43	6.38	6.15	6.01
1000	9.35	8.53	8.14	7.48	7.22	7.15	7.08	6.84	6.68
2000	18.69	17.05	16.27	14.95	14.43	14.29	14.16	13.67	13.35
3000	28.03	25.58	24.40	22.42	21.64	21.43	21.24	20.50	20.02
4000	37.37	34.10	32.54	29.89	28.86	28.57	28.32	27.33	26.70
5000	46.71	42.63	40.67	37.36	36.07	35.72	35.39	34.16	33.37
6000	56.05	51.15	48.80	44.83	43.28	42.86	42.47	41.00	40.04
7000	65.39	59.67	56.93	52.30	50.49	50.00	49.55	47.83	46.72
8000	74.74	68.20	65.07	59.78	57.71	57.14	56.63	54.66	53.39
9000	84.08	76.72	73.20	67.25	64.92	64.28	63.71	61.49	60.06
10000	93.42	85.25	81.33	74.72	72.13	71.43	70.78	68.32	66.74
15000	140.12	127.87	121.99	112.08	108.20	107.14	106.17	102.48	100.10
20000	186.83	170.49	162.66	149.43	144.26	142.85	141.56	136.64	133.47
25000	233.54	213.11	203.32	186.79	180.33	178.56	176.95	170.80	166.84
30000	280.24	255.73	243.98	224.15	216.39	214.27	212.34	204.96	200.20
35000	326.95	298.35	284.64	261.50	252.45	249.98	247.73	239.12	233.57
36000	336.29	306.88	292.78	268.98	259.67	257.12	254.81	245.95	240.24
37000	345.63	315.40	300.91	276.45	266.88	264.27	261.89	252.79	246.92
38000	354.97	323.93	309.04	283.92	274.09	271.41	268.97	259.62	253.59
39000	364.32	332.45	317.17	291.39	281.31	278.55	276.04	266.45	260.26
40000	373.66	340.97	325.31	298.86	288.52	285.69	283.12	273.28	266.94
41000	383.00	349.50	333.44	306.33	295.73	292.83	290.20	280.11	273.61
42000	392.34	358.02	341.57	313.80	302.94	299.98	297.28	286.94	280.28
43000	401.68	366.55	349.70	321.28	310.16	307.12	304.36	293.78	286.96
44000	411.02	375.07	357.84	328.75	317.37	314.26	311.43	300.61	293.63
45000	420.36	383.60	365.97	336.22	324.58	321.40	318.51	307.44	300.30
46000	429.70	392.12	374.10	343.69	331.79	328.55	325.59	314.27	306.98
47000	439.05	400.64	382.23	351.16	339.01	335.69	332.67	321.10	313.65
48000	448.39	409.17	390.37	358.63	346.22	342.83	339.75	327.94	320.32
49000	457.73	417.69	398.50	366.10	353.43	349.97	346.82	334.77	327.00
50000	467.07	426.22	406.63	373.58	360.65	357.11	353.90	341.60	333.67
51000	476.41	434.74	414.76	381.05	367.86	364.26	360.98	348.43	340.34
52000	485.75	443.26	422.90	388.52	375.07	371.40	368.06	355.26	347.02
53000	495.09	451.79	431.03	395.99	382.28	378.54	375.14	362.10	353.69
54000	504.44	460.31	439.16	403.46	389.50	385.68	382.21	368.93	360.36
55000	513.78	468.84	447.29	410.93	396.71	392.83	389.29	375.76	367.03
56000	523.12	477.36	455.43	418.40	403.92	399.97	396.37	382.59	373.71
57000	532.46	485.89	463.56	425.88	411.14	407.11	403.45	389.42	380.38
58000	541.80	494.41	471.69	433.35	418.35	414.25	410.53	396.26	387.05
59000	551.14	502.93	479.82	440.82	425.56	421.39	417.60	403.09	393.73
60000	560.48	511.46	487.96	448.29	432.77	428.54	424.68	409.92	400.40
61000	569.82	519.98	496.09	455.76	439.99	435.68	431.76	416.75	407.07
62000	579.17	528.51	504.22	463.23	447.20	442.82	438.84	423.58	413.75
63000	588.51	537.03	512.35	470.70	454.41	449.96	445.92	430.41	420.42
64000	597.85	545.56	520.49	478.18	461.63	457.10	452.99	437.25	427.09
65000	607.19	554.08	528.62	485.65	468.84	464.25	460.07	444.08	433.77
66000	616.53	562.60	536.75	493.12	476.05	471.39	467.15	450.91	440.44
67000	625.87	571.13	544.89	500.59	483.26	478.53	474.23	457.74	447.11
68000	635.21	579.65	553.02	508.06	490.48	485.67	481.30	464.57	453.79
69000	644.55	588.18	561.15	515.53	497.69	492.82	488.38	471.41	460.46
70000	653.90	596.70	569.28	523.00	504.90	499.96	495.46	478.24	467.13
75000	700.60	639.32	609.95	560.36	540.97	535.67	530.85	512.40	500.50
80000	747.31	681.94	650.61	597.72	577.03	571.38	566.24	546.56	533.87
100000	934.13	852.43	813.26	747.15	721.29	714.22	707.80	683.19	667.33

7¾% MONTHLY PAYMENT

NECESSARY TO AMORTIZE A LOAN

TERM / AMOUNT	1 YEAR	2 YEARS	3 YEARS	4 YEARS	5 YEARS	7 YEARS	8 YEARS	10 YEARS	12 YEARS
$ 25	2.18	1.13	.79	.61	.51	.39	.36	.31	.27
50	4.35	2.26	1.57	1.22	1.01	.78	.71	.61	.54
75	6.52	3.39	2.35	1.83	1.52	1.16	1.06	.91	.81
100	8.69	4.52	3.13	2.43	2.02	1.55	1.41	1.21	1.07
200	17.38	9.03	6.25	4.86	4.04	3.10	2.81	2.41	2.14
300	26.07	13.54	9.37	7.29	6.05	4.64	4.21	3.61	3.21
400	34.75	18.05	12.49	9.72	8.07	6.19	5.61	4.81	4.28
500	43.44	22.56	15.62	12.15	10.08	7.74	7.01	6.01	5.35
600	52.13	27.07	18.74	14.58	12.10	9.28	8.41	7.21	6.42
700	60.82	31.58	21.86	17.01	14.11	10.83	9.81	8.41	7.49
800	69.50	36.10	24.98	19.44	16.13	12.37	11.21	9.61	8.56
900	78.19	40.61	28.10	21.87	18.15	13.92	12.61	10.81	9.62
1000	86.88	45.12	31.23	24.30	20.16	15.47	14.01	12.01	10.69
2000	173.75	90.23	62.45	48.60	40.32	30.93	28.02	24.01	21.38
3000	260.62	135.35	93.67	72.89	60.48	46.39	42.03	36.01	32.07
4000	347.50	180.46	124.89	97.19	80.63	61.85	56.04	48.01	42.76
5000	434.37	225.57	156.11	121.48	100.79	77.31	70.05	60.01	53.44
6000	521.24	270.69	187.33	145.78	120.95	92.78	84.06	72.01	64.13
7000	608.12	315.80	218.55	170.08	141.10	108.24	98.07	84.01	74.82
8000	694.99	360.91	249.77	194.37	161.26	123.70	112.08	96.01	85.51
9000	781.86	406.03	281.00	218.67	181.42	139.16	126.09	108.01	96.20
10000	868.73	451.14	312.22	242.96	201.57	154.62	140.10	120.02	106.88
15000	1303.10	676.71	468.32	364.44	302.36	231.93	210.15	180.02	160.32
20000	1737.46	902.27	624.43	485.92	403.14	309.24	280.20	240.03	213.76
25000	2171.83	1127.84	780.53	607.40	503.93	386.55	350.25	300.03	267.20
30000	2606.19	1353.41	936.64	728.88	604.71	463.86	420.30	360.04	320.64
35000	3040.56	1578.97	1092.75	850.36	705.50	541.17	490.35	420.04	374.08
36000	3127.43	1624.09	1123.97	874.65	725.66	556.64	504.36	432.04	384.77
37000	3214.30	1669.20	1155.19	898.95	745.81	572.10	518.37	444.04	395.46
38000	3301.17	1714.31	1186.41	923.24	765.97	587.56	532.38	456.05	406.15
39000	3388.05	1759.43	1217.63	947.54	786.13	603.02	546.39	468.05	416.83
40000	3474.92	1804.54	1248.85	971.83	806.28	618.48	560.40	480.05	427.52
41000	3561.79	1849.65	1280.07	996.13	826.44	633.95	574.41	492.05	438.21
42000	3648.67	1894.77	1311.29	1020.43	846.60	649.41	588.42	504.05	448.90
43000	3735.54	1939.88	1342.52	1044.72	866.75	664.87	602.43	516.05	459.59
44000	3822.41	1984.99	1373.74	1069.02	886.91	680.33	616.44	528.05	470.27
45000	3909.28	2030.11	1404.96	1093.31	907.07	695.79	630.45	540.05	480.96
46000	3996.16	2075.22	1436.18	1117.61	927.23	711.25	644.46	552.05	491.65
47000	4083.03	2120.33	1467.40	1141.90	947.38	726.72	658.47	564.05	502.34
48000	4169.90	2165.45	1498.62	1166.20	967.54	742.18	672.48	576.06	513.03
49000	4256.78	2210.56	1529.84	1190.50	987.70	757.64	686.49	588.06	523.71
50000	4343.65	2255.67	1561.06	1214.79	1007.85	773.10	700.50	600.06	534.40
51000	4430.52	2300.79	1592.28	1239.09	1028.01	788.56	714.51	612.06	545.09
52000	4517.39	2345.90	1623.51	1263.38	1048.17	804.03	728.52	624.06	555.78
53000	4604.27	2391.01	1654.73	1287.68	1068.32	819.49	742.53	636.06	566.46
54000	4691.14	2436.13	1685.95	1311.98	1088.48	834.95	756.54	648.06	577.15
55000	4778.01	2481.24	1717.17	1336.27	1108.64	850.41	770.55	660.06	587.84
56000	4864.89	2526.35	1748.39	1360.57	1128.79	865.87	784.56	672.06	598.53
57000	4951.76	2571.47	1779.61	1384.86	1148.95	881.34	798.57	684.07	609.22
58000	5038.63	2616.58	1810.83	1409.16	1169.11	896.80	812.58	696.07	619.90
59000	5125.50	2661.69	1842.05	1433.45	1189.27	912.26	826.59	708.07	630.59
60000	5212.38	2706.81	1873.27	1457.75	1209.42	927.72	840.60	720.07	641.28
61000	5299.25	2751.92	1904.50	1482.05	1229.58	943.18	854.61	732.07	651.97
62000	5386.12	2797.03	1935.72	1506.34	1249.74	958.65	868.62	744.07	662.66
63000	5473.00	2842.15	1966.94	1530.64	1269.89	974.11	882.63	756.07	673.34
64000	5559.87	2887.26	1998.16	1554.93	1290.05	989.57	896.64	768.07	684.03
65000	5646.74	2932.37	2029.38	1579.23	1310.21	1005.03	910.65	780.07	694.72
66000	5733.62	2977.49	2060.60	1603.52	1330.36	1020.49	924.66	792.08	705.41
67000	5820.49	3022.60	2091.82	1627.82	1350.52	1035.96	938.67	804.08	716.10
68000	5907.36	3067.71	2123.04	1652.12	1370.68	1051.42	952.68	816.08	726.78
69000	5994.23	3112.83	2154.27	1676.41	1390.84	1066.88	966.69	828.08	737.47
70000	6081.11	3157.94	2185.49	1700.71	1410.99	1082.34	980.70	840.08	748.16
75000	6515.47	3383.51	2341.59	1822.19	1511.78	1159.65	1050.75	900.08	801.60
80000	6949.84	3609.07	2497.70	1943.66	1612.56	1236.96	1120.80	960.09	855.04
100000	8687.29	4511.34	3122.12	2429.58	2015.70	1546.20	1401.00	1200.11	1068.80

MONTHLY PAYMENT $7\frac{3}{4}\%$

NECESSARY TO AMORTIZE A LOAN

TERM / AMOUNT	15 YEARS	18 YEARS	20 YEARS	25 YEARS	28 YEARS	29 YEARS	30 YEARS	35 YEARS	40 YEARS
$ 25	.24	.22	.21	.19	.19	.19	.18	.18	.17
50	.48	.43	.42	.38	.37	.37	.36	.35	.34
75	.71	.65	.62	.57	.55	.55	.54	.52	.51
100	.95	.86	.83	.76	.73	.73	.72	.70	.68
200	1.89	1.72	1.65	1.52	1.46	1.45	1.44	1.39	1.36
300	2.83	2.58	2.47	2.27	2.19	2.17	2.15	2.08	2.03
400	3.77	3.44	3.29	3.03	2.92	2.90	2.87	2.77	2.71
500	4.71	4.30	4.11	3.78	3.65	3.62	3.59	3.47	3.39
600	5.65	5.16	4.93	4.54	4.38	4.34	4.30	4.16	4.06
700	6.59	6.02	5.75	5.29	5.11	5.06	5.02	4.85	4.74
800	7.54	6.88	6.57	6.05	5.84	5.79	5.74	5.54	5.42
900	8.48	7.74	7.39	6.80	6.57	6.51	6.45	6.23	6.09
1000	9.42	8.60	8.21	7.56	7.30	7.23	7.17	6.93	6.77
2000	18.83	17.20	16.42	15.11	14.60	14.46	14.33	13.85	13.54
3000	28.24	25.80	24.63	22.66	21.90	21.69	21.50	20.77	20.30
4000	37.66	34.40	32.84	30.22	29.19	28.92	28.66	27.69	27.07
5000	47.07	43.00	41.05	37.77	36.49	36.14	35.83	34.61	33.84
6000	56.48	51.60	49.26	45.32	43.79	43.37	42.99	41.54	40.60
7000	65.89	60.20	57.47	52.88	51.09	50.60	50.15	48.46	47.37
8000	75.31	68.80	65.68	60.43	58.38	57.83	57.32	55.38	54.13
9000	84.72	77.40	73.89	67.98	65.68	65.05	64.48	62.30	60.90
10000	94.13	86.00	82.10	75.54	72.98	72.28	71.65	69.22	67.67
15000	141.20	128.99	123.15	113.30	109.47	108.42	107.47	103.83	101.50
20000	188.26	171.99	164.19	151.07	145.95	144.56	143.29	138.44	135.33
25000	235.32	214.98	205.24	188.84	182.44	180.69	179.11	173.05	169.16
30000	282.39	257.98	246.29	226.60	218.93	216.83	214.93	207.66	202.99
35000	329.45	300.97	287.34	264.37	255.41	252.97	250.75	242.27	236.82
36000	338.86	309.57	295.55	271.92	262.71	260.20	257.91	249.19	243.59
37000	348.28	318.17	303.76	279.48	270.01	267.42	265.08	256.11	250.35
38000	357.69	326.77	311.97	287.03	277.30	274.65	272.24	263.03	257.12
39000	367.10	335.37	320.17	294.58	284.60	281.88	279.41	269.95	263.89
40000	376.52	343.97	328.38	302.14	291.90	289.11	286.57	276.88	270.65
41000	385.93	352.57	336.59	309.69	299.20	296.33	293.73	283.80	277.42
42000	395.34	361.16	344.80	317.24	306.49	303.56	300.90	290.72	284.19
43000	404.75	369.76	353.01	324.80	313.79	310.79	308.06	297.64	290.95
44000	414.17	378.36	361.22	332.35	321.09	318.02	315.23	304.56	297.72
45000	423.58	386.96	369.43	339.90	328.39	325.25	322.39	311.48	304.48
46000	432.99	395.56	377.64	347.46	335.68	332.47	329.55	318.41	311.25
47000	442.40	404.16	385.85	355.01	342.98	339.70	336.72	325.33	318.02
48000	451.82	412.76	394.06	362.56	350.28	346.93	343.88	332.25	324.78
49000	461.23	421.36	402.27	370.12	357.58	354.16	351.05	339.17	331.55
50000	470.64	429.96	410.48	377.67	364.87	361.38	358.21	346.09	338.31
51000	480.06	438.56	418.69	385.22	372.17	368.61	365.38	353.01	345.08
52000	489.47	447.16	426.90	392.78	379.47	375.84	372.54	359.94	351.85
53000	498.88	455.75	435.11	400.33	386.77	383.07	379.70	366.86	358.61
54000	508.29	464.35	443.32	407.88	394.06	390.29	386.87	373.78	365.38
55000	517.71	472.95	451.53	415.44	401.36	397.52	394.03	380.70	372.15
56000	527.12	481.55	459.74	422.99	408.66	404.75	401.20	387.62	378.91
57000	536.53	490.15	467.95	430.54	415.95	411.98	408.36	394.55	385.68
58000	545.94	498.75	476.16	438.10	423.25	419.20	415.52	401.47	392.44
59000	555.36	507.35	484.36	445.65	430.55	426.43	422.69	408.39	399.21
60000	564.77	515.95	492.57	453.20	437.85	433.66	429.85	415.31	405.98
61000	574.18	524.55	500.78	460.76	445.14	440.89	437.02	422.23	412.74
62000	583.60	533.15	508.99	468.31	452.44	448.11	444.18	429.15	419.51
63000	593.01	541.74	517.20	475.86	459.74	455.34	451.34	436.08	426.28
64000	602.42	550.34	525.41	483.42	467.04	462.57	458.51	443.00	433.04
65000	611.83	558.94	533.62	490.97	474.33	469.80	465.67	449.92	439.81
66000	621.25	567.54	541.83	498.52	481.63	477.02	472.84	456.84	446.57
67000	630.66	576.14	550.04	506.08	488.93	484.25	480.00	463.76	453.34
68000	640.07	584.74	558.25	513.63	496.23	491.48	487.17	470.68	460.11
69000	649.49	593.34	566.46	521.18	503.52	498.71	494.33	477.61	466.87
70000	658.90	601.94	574.67	528.74	510.82	505.93	501.49	484.53	473.64
75000	705.96	644.93	615.72	566.50	547.31	542.07	537.31	519.14	507.47
80000	753.03	687.93	656.76	604.27	583.79	578.21	573.13	553.75	541.30
100000	941.28	859.91	820.95	755.33	729.74	722.76	716.42	692.18	676.62

7⅞% MONTHLY PAYMENT
NECESSARY TO AMORTIZE A LOAN

TERM / AMOUNT	1 YEAR	2 YEARS	3 YEARS	4 YEARS	5 YEARS	7 YEARS	8 YEARS	10 YEARS	12 YEARS
$ 25	2.18	1.13	.79	.61	.51	.39	.36	.31	.27
50	4.35	2.26	1.57	1.22	1.02	.78	.71	.61	.54
75	6.52	3.39	2.35	1.83	1.52	1.17	1.06	.91	.81
100	8.70	4.52	3.13	2.44	2.03	1.56	1.41	1.21	1.08
200	17.39	9.04	6.26	4.88	4.05	3.11	2.82	2.42	2.16
300	26.08	13.56	9.39	7.31	6.07	4.66	4.23	3.63	3.23
400	34.78	18.07	12.52	9.75	8.09	6.21	5.63	4.83	4.31
500	43.47	22.59	15.64	12.18	10.11	7.77	7.04	6.04	5.38
600	52.16	27.11	18.77	14.62	12.13	9.32	8.45	7.25	6.46
700	60.86	31.62	21.90	17.05	14.16	10.87	9.86	8.45	7.53
800	69.55	36.14	25.03	19.49	16.18	12.42	11.26	9.66	8.61
900	78.24	40.66	28.16	21.92	18.20	13.98	12.67	10.87	9.69
1000	86.94	45.18	31.28	24.36	20.22	15.53	14.08	12.07	10.76
2000	173.87	90.35	62.56	48.71	40.44	31.05	28.15	24.14	21.52
3000	260.80	135.52	93.84	73.07	60.65	46.58	42.22	36.21	32.27
4000	347.73	180.69	125.12	97.42	80.87	62.10	56.30	48.27	43.03
5000	434.66	225.86	156.40	121.78	101.09	77.63	70.37	60.34	53.79
6000	521.59	271.03	187.68	146.13	121.30	93.15	84.44	72.41	64.54
7000	608.52	316.20	218.96	170.49	141.52	108.67	98.52	84.47	75.30
8000	695.45	361.37	250.23	194.84	161.74	124.20	112.59	96.54	86.05
9000	782.38	406.54	281.51	219.19	181.95	139.72	126.66	108.61	96.81
10000	869.31	451.71	312.79	243.55	202.17	155.25	140.74	120.67	107.57
15000	1303.96	677.56	469.19	365.32	303.25	232.87	211.10	181.01	161.35
20000	1738.62	903.41	625.58	487.09	404.34	310.49	281.47	241.34	215.13
25000	2173.27	1129.26	781.97	608.86	505.42	388.11	351.84	301.68	268.91
30000	2607.92	1355.11	938.37	730.63	606.50	465.73	422.20	362.01	322.69
35000	3042.58	1580.97	1094.76	852.41	707.59	543.35	492.57	422.34	376.47
36000	3129.51	1626.14	1126.04	876.76	727.80	558.87	506.64	434.41	387.22
37000	3216.44	1671.31	1157.32	901.11	748.02	574.39	520.71	446.48	397.98
38000	3303.37	1716.48	1188.60	925.47	768.24	589.92	534.79	458.54	408.74
39000	3390.30	1761.65	1219.88	949.82	788.45	605.44	548.86	470.61	419.49
40000	3477.23	1806.82	1251.15	974.18	808.67	620.97	562.93	482.68	430.25
41000	3564.16	1851.99	1282.43	998.53	828.89	636.49	577.01	494.74	441.01
42000	3651.09	1897.16	1313.71	1022.89	849.10	652.01	591.08	506.81	451.76
43000	3738.02	1942.33	1344.99	1047.24	869.32	667.54	605.15	518.88	462.52
44000	3824.95	1987.50	1376.27	1071.59	889.54	683.06	619.23	530.94	473.27
45000	3911.88	2032.67	1407.55	1095.95	909.75	698.59	633.30	543.01	484.03
46000	3998.81	2077.84	1438.83	1120.30	929.97	714.11	647.37	555.08	494.79
47000	4085.75	2123.01	1470.11	1144.66	950.19	729.63	661.45	567.15	505.54
48000	4172.68	2168.18	1501.38	1169.01	970.40	745.16	675.52	579.21	516.30
49000	4259.61	2213.35	1532.66	1193.37	990.62	760.68	689.59	591.28	527.05
50000	4346.54	2258.52	1563.94	1217.72	1010.84	776.21	703.67	603.35	537.81
51000	4433.47	2303.69	1595.22	1242.07	1031.05	791.73	717.74	615.41	548.57
52000	4520.40	2348.86	1626.50	1266.43	1051.27	807.25	731.81	627.48	559.32
53000	4607.33	2394.03	1657.78	1290.78	1071.49	822.78	745.89	639.55	570.08
54000	4694.26	2439.20	1689.06	1315.14	1091.70	838.30	759.96	651.61	580.83
55000	4781.19	2484.37	1720.34	1339.49	1111.92	853.83	774.03	663.68	591.59
56000	4868.12	2529.54	1751.61	1363.85	1132.14	869.35	788.11	675.75	602.35
57000	4955.05	2574.71	1782.89	1388.20	1152.35	884.87	802.18	687.81	613.10
58000	5041.98	2619.88	1814.17	1412.55	1172.57	900.40	816.25	699.88	623.86
59000	5128.91	2665.05	1845.45	1436.91	1192.79	915.92	830.33	711.95	634.62
60000	5215.84	2710.22	1876.73	1461.26	1213.00	931.45	844.40	724.01	645.37
61000	5302.77	2755.39	1908.01	1485.62	1233.22	946.97	858.47	736.08	656.13
62000	5389.70	2800.56	1939.29	1509.97	1253.44	962.49	872.55	748.15	666.88
63000	5476.64	2845.73	1970.57	1534.33	1273.65	978.02	886.62	760.21	677.64
64000	5563.57	2890.90	2001.84	1558.68	1293.87	993.54	900.69	772.28	688.40
65000	5650.50	2936.07	2033.12	1583.03	1314.09	1009.07	914.76	784.35	699.15
66000	5737.43	2981.24	2064.40	1607.39	1334.30	1024.59	928.84	796.41	709.91
67000	5824.36	3026.42	2095.68	1631.74	1354.52	1040.11	942.91	808.48	720.66
68000	5911.29	3071.59	2126.96	1656.10	1374.74	1055.64	956.98	820.55	731.42
69000	5998.22	3116.76	2158.24	1680.45	1394.95	1071.16	971.06	832.61	742.18
70000	6085.15	3161.93	2189.52	1704.81	1415.17	1086.69	985.13	844.68	752.93
75000	6519.80	3387.78	2345.91	1826.58	1516.25	1164.31	1055.50	905.02	806.71
80000	6954.46	3613.63	2502.30	1948.35	1617.33	1241.93	1125.86	965.35	860.49
100000	8693.07	4517.04	3127.88	2435.43	2021.67	1552.41	1407.33	1206.69	1075.62

MONTHLY PAYMENT 7⅞%

NECESSARY TO AMORTIZE A LOAN

TERM / AMOUNT	15 YEARS	18 YEARS	20 YEARS	25 YEARS	28 YEARS	29 YEARS	30 YEARS	35 YEARS	40 YEARS
$ 25	.24	.22	.21	.20	.19	.19	.19	.18	.18
50	.48	.44	.42	.39	.37	.37	.37	.36	.35
75	.72	.66	.63	.58	.56	.55	.55	.53	.52
100	.95	.87	.83	.77	.74	.74	.73	.71	.69
200	1.90	1.74	1.66	1.53	1.48	1.47	1.46	1.41	1.38
300	2.85	2.61	2.49	2.30	2.22	2.20	2.18	2.11	2.06
400	3.80	3.47	3.32	3.06	2.96	2.93	2.91	2.81	2.75
500	4.75	4.34	4.15	3.82	3.70	3.66	3.63	3.51	3.43
600	5.70	5.21	4.98	4.59	4.43	4.39	4.36	4.21	4.12
700	6.64	6.08	5.81	5.35	5.17	5.12	5.08	4.91	4.81
800	7.59	6.94	6.63	6.11	5.91	5.86	5.81	5.61	5.49
900	8.54	7.81	7.46	6.88	6.65	6.59	6.53	6.32	6.18
1000	9.49	8.68	8.29	7.64	7.39	7.32	7.26	7.02	6.86
2000	18.97	17.35	16.58	15.28	14.77	14.63	14.51	14.03	13.72
3000	28.46	26.03	24.87	22.91	22.15	21.94	21.76	21.04	20.58
4000	37.94	34.70	33.15	30.55	29.53	29.26	29.01	28.05	27.44
5000	47.43	43.38	41.44	38.18	36.92	36.57	36.26	35.06	34.30
6000	56.91	52.05	49.73	45.82	44.30	43.88	43.51	42.08	41.16
7000	66.40	60.72	58.01	53.45	51.68	51.20	50.76	49.09	48.02
8000	75.88	69.40	66.30	61.09	59.06	58.51	58.01	56.10	54.88
9000	85.37	78.07	74.59	68.72	66.45	65.82	65.26	63.11	61.74
10000	94.85	86.75	82.87	76.36	73.83	73.14	72.51	70.12	68.60
15000	142.27	130.12	124.31	114.54	110.74	109.70	108.77	105.18	102.90
20000	189.69	173.49	165.74	152.72	147.65	146.27	145.02	140.24	137.19
25000	237.12	216.86	207.17	190.89	184.56	182.84	181.27	175.30	171.49
30000	284.54	260.23	248.61	229.07	221.47	219.40	217.53	210.36	205.79
35000	331.96	303.60	290.04	267.25	258.38	255.97	253.78	245.42	240.09
36000	341.45	312.28	298.33	274.88	265.77	263.28	261.03	252.44	246.95
37000	350.93	320.95	306.62	282.52	273.15	270.60	268.28	259.45	253.81
38000	360.42	329.62	314.90	290.16	280.53	277.91	275.53	266.46	260.67
39000	369.90	338.30	323.19	297.79	287.91	285.22	282.78	273.47	267.52
40000	379.38	346.97	331.48	305.43	295.30	292.54	290.03	280.48	274.38
41000	388.87	355.65	339.76	313.06	302.68	299.85	297.28	287.50	281.24
42000	398.35	364.32	348.05	320.70	310.06	307.16	304.53	294.51	288.10
43000	407.84	372.99	356.34	328.33	317.44	314.48	311.78	301.52	294.96
44000	417.32	381.67	364.62	335.97	324.83	321.79	319.04	308.53	301.82
45000	426.81	390.34	372.91	343.60	332.21	329.10	326.29	315.54	308.68
46000	436.29	399.02	381.20	351.24	339.59	336.42	333.54	322.56	315.54
47000	445.78	407.69	389.48	358.88	346.97	343.73	340.79	329.57	322.40
48000	455.26	416.37	397.77	366.51	354.35	351.04	348.04	336.58	329.26
49000	464.75	425.04	406.06	374.15	361.74	358.36	355.29	343.59	336.12
50000	474.23	433.71	414.34	381.78	369.12	365.67	362.54	350.60	342.98
51000	483.71	442.39	422.63	389.42	376.50	372.98	369.79	357.62	349.84
52000	493.20	451.06	430.92	397.05	383.88	380.30	377.04	364.63	356.70
53000	502.68	459.74	439.20	404.69	391.27	387.61	384.29	371.64	363.56
54000	512.17	468.41	447.49	412.32	398.65	394.92	391.54	378.65	370.42
55000	521.65	477.08	455.78	419.96	406.03	402.24	398.79	385.66	377.28
56000	531.14	485.76	464.06	427.60	413.41	409.55	406.04	392.68	384.14
57000	540.62	494.43	472.35	435.23	420.80	416.86	413.29	399.69	391.00
58000	550.11	503.11	480.64	442.87	428.18	424.18	420.55	406.70	397.86
59000	559.59	511.78	488.92	450.50	435.56	431.49	427.80	413.71	404.71
60000	569.07	520.46	497.21	458.14	442.94	438.80	435.05	420.72	411.57
61000	578.56	529.13	505.50	465.77	450.32	446.12	442.30	427.74	418.43
62000	588.04	537.80	513.79	473.41	457.71	453.43	449.55	434.75	425.29
63000	597.53	546.48	522.07	481.04	465.09	460.74	456.80	441.76	432.15
64000	607.01	555.15	530.36	488.68	472.47	468.06	464.05	448.77	439.01
65000	616.50	563.83	538.65	496.32	479.85	475.37	471.30	455.78	445.87
66000	625.98	572.50	546.93	503.95	487.24	482.68	478.55	462.80	452.73
67000	635.47	581.17	555.22	511.59	494.62	490.00	485.80	469.81	459.59
68000	644.95	589.85	563.51	519.22	502.00	497.31	493.05	476.82	466.45
69000	654.44	598.52	571.79	526.86	509.38	504.62	500.30	483.83	473.31
70000	663.92	607.20	580.08	534.49	516.76	511.94	507.55	490.84	480.17
75000	711.34	650.57	621.51	572.67	553.68	548.50	543.81	525.90	514.47
80000	758.76	693.94	662.95	610.85	590.59	585.07	580.06	560.96	548.76
100000	948.45	867.42	828.68	763.56	738.23	731.34	725.07	701.20	685.95

8% MONTHLY PAYMENT

NECESSARY TO AMORTIZE A LOAN

TERM / AMOUNT	1 YEAR	2 YEARS	3 YEARS	4 YEARS	5 YEARS	7 YEARS	8 YEARS	10 YEARS	12 YEARS
$ 25	2.18	1.14	.79	.62	.51	.39	.36	.31	.28
50	4.35	2.27	1.57	1.23	1.02	.78	.71	.61	.55
75	6.53	3.40	2.36	1.84	1.53	1.17	1.07	.91	.82
100	8.70	4.53	3.14	2.45	2.03	1.56	1.42	1.22	1.09
200	17.40	9.05	6.27	4.89	4.06	3.12	2.83	2.43	2.17
300	26.10	13.57	9.41	7.33	6.09	4.68	4.25	3.64	3.25
400	34.80	18.10	12.54	9.77	8.12	6.24	5.66	4.86	4.33
500	43.50	22.62	15.67	12.21	10.14	7.80	7.07	6.07	5.42
600	52.20	27.14	18.81	14.65	12.17	9.36	8.49	7.28	6.50
700	60.90	31.66	21.94	17.09	14.20	10.92	9.90	8.50	7.58
800	69.60	36.19	25.07	19.54	16.23	12.47	11.31	9.71	8.66
900	78.29	40.71	28.21	21.98	18.25	14.03	12.73	10.92	9.75
1000	86.99	45.23	31.34	24.42	20.28	15.59	14.14	12.14	10.83
2000	173.98	90.46	62.68	48.83	40.56	31.18	28.28	24.27	21.65
3000	260.97	135.69	94.01	73.24	60.83	46.76	42.42	36.40	32.48
4000	347.96	180.91	125.35	97.66	81.11	62.35	56.55	48.54	43.30
5000	434.95	226.14	156.69	122.07	101.39	77.94	70.69	60.67	54.13
6000	521.94	271.37	188.02	146.48	121.66	93.52	84.83	72.80	64.95
7000	608.92	316.60	219.36	170.90	141.94	109.11	98.96	84.93	75.78
8000	695.91	361.82	250.70	195.31	162.22	124.69	113.10	97.07	86.60
9000	782.90	407.05	282.03	219.72	182.49	140.28	127.24	109.20	97.43
10000	869.89	452.28	313.37	244.13	202.77	155.87	141.37	121.33	108.25
15000	1304.83	678.41	470.05	366.20	304.15	233.80	212.06	182.00	162.37
20000	1739.77	904.55	626.73	488.26	405.53	311.73	282.74	242.66	216.50
25000	2174.72	1130.69	783.41	610.33	506.91	389.66	353.42	303.32	270.62
30000	2609.66	1356.82	940.10	732.39	608.30	467.59	424.11	363.99	324.74
35000	3044.60	1582.96	1096.78	854.46	709.68	545.52	494.79	424.65	378.86
36000	3131.59	1628.19	1128.11	878.87	729.96	561.11	508.93	436.78	389.69
37000	3218.58	1673.41	1159.45	903.28	750.23	576.69	523.06	448.92	400.51
38000	3305.57	1718.64	1190.79	927.70	770.51	592.28	537.20	461.05	411.34
39000	3392.55	1763.87	1222.12	952.11	790.78	607.87	551.34	473.18	422.16
40000	3479.54	1809.10	1253.46	976.52	811.06	623.45	565.47	485.32	432.99
41000	3566.53	1854.32	1284.80	1000.93	831.34	639.04	579.61	497.45	443.81
42000	3653.52	1899.55	1316.13	1025.35	851.61	654.63	593.75	509.58	454.64
43000	3740.51	1944.78	1347.47	1049.76	871.89	670.21	607.88	521.71	465.46
44000	3827.50	1990.01	1378.81	1074.17	892.17	685.80	622.02	533.85	476.28
45000	3914.48	2035.23	1410.14	1098.59	912.44	701.38	636.16	545.98	487.11
46000	4001.47	2080.46	1441.48	1123.00	932.72	716.97	650.29	558.11	497.93
47000	4088.46	2125.69	1472.81	1147.41	953.00	732.56	664.43	570.24	508.76
48000	4175.45	2170.91	1504.15	1171.83	973.27	748.14	678.57	582.38	519.58
49000	4262.44	2216.14	1535.49	1196.24	993.55	763.73	692.70	594.51	530.41
50000	4349.43	2261.37	1566.82	1220.65	1013.82	779.32	706.84	606.64	541.23
51000	4436.41	2306.60	1598.16	1245.06	1034.10	794.90	720.98	618.78	552.06
52000	4523.40	2351.82	1629.50	1269.48	1054.38	810.49	735.11	630.91	562.88
53000	4610.39	2397.05	1660.83	1293.89	1074.65	826.07	749.25	643.04	573.70
54000	4697.38	2442.28	1692.17	1318.30	1094.93	841.66	763.39	655.17	584.53
55000	4784.37	2487.51	1723.51	1342.72	1115.21	857.25	777.52	667.31	595.35
56000	4871.36	2532.73	1754.84	1367.13	1135.48	872.83	791.66	679.44	606.18
57000	4958.35	2577.96	1786.18	1391.54	1155.76	888.42	805.80	691.57	617.00
58000	5045.33	2623.19	1817.51	1415.95	1176.04	904.01	819.93	703.71	627.83
59000	5132.32	2668.42	1848.85	1440.37	1196.31	919.59	834.07	715.84	638.65
60000	5219.31	2713.64	1880.19	1464.78	1216.59	935.18	848.21	727.97	649.48
61000	5306.30	2758.87	1911.52	1489.19	1236.87	950.76	862.34	740.10	660.30
62000	5393.29	2804.10	1942.86	1513.61	1257.14	966.35	876.48	752.24	671.13
63000	5480.28	2849.32	1974.20	1538.02	1277.42	981.94	890.62	764.37	681.95
64000	5567.26	2894.55	2005.53	1562.43	1297.69	997.52	904.75	776.50	692.77
65000	5654.25	2939.78	2036.87	1586.84	1317.97	1013.11	918.89	788.63	703.60
66000	5741.24	2985.01	2068.21	1611.26	1338.25	1028.70	933.03	800.77	714.42
67000	5828.23	3030.23	2099.54	1635.67	1358.52	1044.28	947.16	812.90	725.25
68000	5915.22	3075.46	2130.88	1660.08	1378.80	1059.87	961.30	825.03	736.07
69000	6002.21	3120.69	2162.21	1684.50	1399.08	1075.45	975.44	837.17	746.90
70000	6089.20	3165.92	2193.55	1708.91	1419.35	1091.04	989.57	849.30	757.72
75000	6524.14	3392.05	2350.23	1830.97	1520.73	1168.97	1060.26	909.96	811.84
80000	6959.08	3618.19	2506.91	1953.04	1622.12	1246.90	1130.94	970.63	865.97
100000	8698.85	4522.73	3133.64	2441.30	2027.64	1558.63	1413.67	1213.28	1082.46

MONTHLY PAYMENT 8%
NECESSARY TO AMORTIZE A LOAN

TERM / AMOUNT	15 YEARS	18 YEARS	20 YEARS	25 YEARS	28 YEARS	29 YEARS	30 YEARS	35 YEARS	40 YEARS
$ 25	.24	.22	.21	.20	.19	.19	.19	.18	.18
50	.48	.44	.42	.39	.38	.37	.37	.36	.35
75	.72	.66	.63	.58	.57	.56	.56	.54	.53
100	.96	.88	.84	.78	.75	.74	.74	.72	.70
200	1.92	1.75	1.68	1.55	1.50	1.48	1.47	1.43	1.40
300	2.87	2.63	2.51	2.32	2.25	2.22	2.21	2.14	2.09
400	3.83	3.50	3.35	3.09	2.99	2.96	2.94	2.85	2.79
500	4.78	4.38	4.19	3.86	3.74	3.70	3.67	3.56	3.48
600	5.74	5.25	5.02	4.64	4.49	4.44	4.41	4.27	4.18
700	6.69	6.13	5.86	5.41	5.23	5.18	5.14	4.98	4.87
800	7.65	7.00	6.70	6.18	5.98	5.92	5.88	5.69	5.57
900	8.61	7.88	7.53	6.95	6.73	6.66	6.61	6.40	6.26
1000	9.56	8.75	8.37	7.72	7.47	7.40	7.34	7.11	6.96
2000	19.12	17.50	16.73	15.44	14.94	14.80	14.68	14.21	13.91
3000	28.67	26.25	25.10	23.16	22.41	22.20	22.02	21.31	20.86
4000	38.23	35.00	33.46	30.88	29.88	29.60	29.36	28.42	27.82
5000	47.79	43.75	41.83	38.60	37.34	37.00	36.69	35.52	34.77
6000	57.34	52.50	50.19	46.31	44.81	44.40	44.03	42.62	41.72
7000	66.90	61.25	58.56	54.03	52.28	51.80	51.37	49.72	48.68
8000	76.46	70.00	66.92	61.75	59.75	59.20	58.71	56.83	55.63
9000	86.01	78.75	75.28	69.47	67.21	66.60	66.04	63.93	62.58
10000	95.57	87.50	83.65	77.19	74.68	74.00	73.38	71.03	69.54
15000	143.35	131.25	125.47	115.78	112.02	111.00	110.07	106.54	104.30
20000	191.14	175.00	167.29	154.37	149.36	147.99	146.76	142.06	139.07
25000	238.92	218.75	209.12	192.96	186.69	184.99	183.45	177.57	173.83
30000	286.70	262.49	250.94	231.55	224.03	221.99	220.13	213.08	208.60
35000	334.48	306.24	292.76	270.14	261.37	258.99	256.82	248.60	243.36
36000	344.04	314.99	301.12	277.86	268.84	266.39	264.16	255.70	250.32
37000	353.60	323.74	309.49	285.58	276.31	273.78	271.50	262.80	257.27
38000	363.15	332.49	317.85	293.30	283.77	281.18	278.84	269.90	264.22
39000	372.71	341.24	326.22	301.01	291.24	288.58	286.17	277.01	271.18
40000	382.27	349.99	334.58	308.73	298.71	295.98	293.51	284.11	278.13
41000	391.82	358.74	342.95	316.45	306.18	303.38	300.85	291.21	285.08
42000	401.38	367.49	351.31	324.17	313.64	310.78	308.19	298.31	292.04
43000	410.94	376.24	359.67	331.89	321.11	318.18	315.52	305.42	298.99
44000	420.49	384.99	368.04	339.60	328.58	325.58	322.86	312.52	305.94
45000	430.05	393.74	376.40	347.32	336.05	332.98	330.20	319.62	312.90
46000	439.60	402.49	384.77	355.04	343.51	340.38	337.54	326.73	319.85
47000	449.16	411.24	393.13	362.76	350.98	347.78	344.87	333.83	326.80
48000	458.72	419.99	401.50	370.48	358.45	355.18	352.21	340.93	333.75
49000	468.27	428.74	409.86	378.19	365.92	362.58	359.55	348.03	340.71
50000	477.83	437.49	418.23	385.91	373.38	369.98	366.89	355.14	347.66
51000	487.39	446.24	426.59	393.63	380.85	377.38	374.22	362.24	354.61
52000	496.94	454.99	434.95	401.35	388.32	384.78	381.56	369.34	361.57
53000	506.50	463.74	443.32	409.07	395.79	392.18	388.90	376.44	368.52
54000	516.06	472.48	451.68	416.79	403.25	399.58	396.24	383.55	375.47
55000	525.61	481.23	460.05	424.50	410.72	406.98	403.58	390.65	382.43
56000	535.17	489.98	468.41	432.22	418.19	414.37	410.91	397.75	389.38
57000	544.73	498.73	476.78	439.94	425.66	421.77	418.25	404.85	396.33
58000	554.28	507.48	485.14	447.66	433.13	429.17	425.59	411.96	403.29
59000	563.84	516.23	493.50	455.38	440.59	436.57	432.93	419.06	410.24
60000	573.40	524.98	501.87	463.09	448.06	443.97	440.26	426.16	417.19
61000	582.95	533.73	510.23	470.81	455.53	451.37	447.60	433.26	424.15
62000	592.51	542.48	518.60	478.53	463.00	458.77	454.94	440.37	431.10
63000	602.07	551.23	526.96	486.25	470.46	466.17	462.28	447.47	438.05
64000	611.62	559.98	535.33	493.97	477.93	473.57	469.61	454.57	445.00
65000	621.18	568.73	543.69	501.69	485.40	480.97	476.95	461.67	451.96
66000	630.74	577.48	552.06	509.40	492.87	488.37	484.29	468.78	458.91
67000	640.29	586.23	560.42	517.12	500.33	495.77	491.63	475.88	465.86
68000	649.85	594.98	568.78	524.84	507.80	503.17	498.96	482.98	472.82
69000	659.40	603.73	577.15	532.56	515.27	510.57	506.30	490.09	479.77
70000	668.96	612.48	585.51	540.28	522.74	517.97	513.64	497.19	486.72
75000	716.74	656.23	627.34	578.87	560.07	554.96	550.33	532.70	521.49
80000	764.53	699.98	669.16	617.46	597.41	591.96	587.02	568.21	556.25
100000	955.66	874.97	836.45	771.82	746.76	739.95	733.77	710.27	695.32

8⅛% MONTHLY PAYMENT

NECESSARY TO AMORTIZE A LOAN

TERM / AMOUNT	1 YEAR	2 YEARS	3 YEARS	4 YEARS	5 YEARS	7 YEARS	8 YEARS	10 YEARS	12 YEARS
$ 25	2.18	1.14	.79	.62	.51	.40	.36	.31	.28
50	4.36	2.27	1.57	1.23	1.02	.79	.72	.61	.55
75	6.53	3.40	2.36	1.84	1.53	1.18	1.07	.92	.82
100	8.71	4.53	3.14	2.45	2.04	1.57	1.43	1.22	1.09
200	17.41	9.06	6.28	4.90	4.07	3.13	2.85	2.44	2.18
300	26.12	13.59	9.42	7.35	6.11	4.70	4.27	3.66	3.27
400	34.82	18.12	12.56	9.79	8.14	6.26	5.69	4.88	4.36
500	43.53	22.65	15.70	12.24	10.17	7.83	7.11	6.10	5.45
600	52.23	27.18	18.84	14.69	12.21	9.39	8.53	7.32	6.54
700	60.94	31.70	21.98	17.14	14.24	10.96	9.95	8.54	7.63
800	69.64	36.23	25.12	19.58	16.27	12.52	11.37	9.76	8.72
900	78.35	40.76	28.26	22.03	18.31	14.09	12.79	10.98	9.81
1000	87.05	45.29	31.40	24.48	20.34	15.65	14.21	12.20	10.90
2000	174.10	90.57	62.79	48.95	40.68	31.30	28.41	24.40	21.79
3000	261.14	135.86	94.19	73.42	61.01	46.95	42.61	36.60	32.68
4000	348.19	181.14	125.58	97.89	81.35	62.60	56.81	48.80	43.58
5000	435.24	226.43	156.98	122.36	101.69	78.25	71.01	61.00	54.47
6000	522.28	271.71	188.37	146.83	122.02	93.90	85.21	73.20	65.36
7000	609.33	317.00	219.76	171.31	142.36	109.54	99.41	85.40	76.26
8000	696.37	362.28	251.16	195.78	162.70	125.19	113.61	97.60	87.15
9000	783.42	407.56	282.55	220.25	183.03	140.84	127.81	109.80	98.04
10000	870.47	452.85	313.95	244.72	203.37	156.49	142.01	121.99	108.94
15000	1305.70	679.27	470.92	367.08	305.05	234.73	213.01	182.99	163.40
20000	1740.93	905.69	627.89	489.44	406.73	312.98	284.01	243.98	217.87
25000	2176.16	1132.11	784.86	611.80	508.41	391.22	355.01	304.98	272.33
30000	2611.39	1358.53	941.83	734.15	610.09	469.46	426.01	365.97	326.80
35000	3046.62	1584.96	1098.80	856.51	711.77	547.70	497.02	426.97	381.27
36000	3133.67	1630.24	1130.19	880.98	732.11	563.35	511.22	439.17	392.16
37000	3220.72	1675.52	1161.59	905.46	752.45	579.00	525.42	451.36	403.05
38000	3307.76	1720.81	1192.98	929.93	772.78	594.65	539.62	463.56	413.95
39000	3394.81	1766.09	1224.37	954.40	793.12	610.30	553.82	475.76	424.84
40000	3481.85	1811.38	1255.77	978.87	813.46	625.95	568.02	487.96	435.73
41000	3568.90	1856.66	1287.16	1003.34	833.79	641.60	582.22	500.16	446.63
42000	3655.95	1901.95	1318.56	1027.81	854.13	657.24	596.42	512.36	457.52
43000	3742.99	1947.23	1349.95	1052.29	874.46	672.89	610.62	524.56	468.41
44000	3830.04	1992.52	1381.34	1076.76	894.80	688.54	624.82	536.76	479.31
45000	3917.09	2037.80	1412.74	1101.23	915.14	704.19	639.02	548.96	490.20
46000	4004.13	2083.08	1444.13	1125.70	935.47	719.84	653.22	561.15	501.09
47000	4091.18	2128.37	1475.53	1150.17	955.81	735.49	667.42	573.35	511.98
48000	4178.22	2173.65	1506.92	1174.64	976.15	751.14	681.62	585.55	522.88
49000	4265.27	2218.94	1538.31	1199.12	996.48	766.78	695.82	597.75	533.77
50000	4352.32	2264.22	1569.71	1223.59	1016.82	782.43	710.02	609.95	544.66
51000	4439.36	2309.51	1601.10	1248.06	1037.15	798.08	724.22	622.15	555.56
52000	4526.41	2354.79	1632.50	1272.53	1057.49	813.73	738.42	634.35	566.45
53000	4613.46	2400.07	1663.89	1297.00	1077.83	829.38	752.62	646.55	577.34
54000	4700.50	2445.36	1695.28	1321.47	1098.16	845.03	766.82	658.75	588.24
55000	4787.55	2490.64	1726.68	1345.95	1118.50	860.68	781.02	670.95	599.13
56000	4874.59	2535.93	1758.07	1370.42	1138.84	876.32	795.22	683.14	610.02
57000	4961.64	2581.21	1789.47	1394.89	1159.17	891.97	809.42	695.34	620.92
58000	5048.69	2626.50	1820.86	1419.36	1179.51	907.62	823.62	707.54	631.81
59000	5135.73	2671.78	1852.25	1443.83	1199.84	923.27	837.82	719.74	642.70
60000	5222.78	2717.06	1883.65	1468.30	1220.18	938.92	852.02	731.94	653.60
61000	5309.83	2762.35	1915.04	1492.78	1240.52	954.57	866.22	744.14	664.49
62000	5396.87	2807.63	1946.44	1517.25	1260.85	970.22	880.42	756.34	675.38
63000	5483.92	2852.92	1977.83	1541.72	1281.19	985.86	894.62	768.54	686.28
64000	5570.96	2898.20	2009.22	1566.19	1301.53	1001.51	908.82	780.74	697.17
65000	5658.01	2943.49	2040.62	1590.66	1321.86	1017.16	923.02	792.93	708.06
66000	5745.06	2988.77	2072.01	1615.13	1342.20	1032.81	937.22	805.13	718.96
67000	5832.10	3034.05	2103.41	1639.60	1362.54	1048.46	951.42	817.33	729.85
68000	5919.15	3079.34	2134.80	1664.08	1382.87	1064.11	965.63	829.53	740.74
69000	6006.20	3124.62	2166.20	1688.55	1403.21	1079.76	979.83	841.73	751.63
70000	6093.24	3169.91	2197.59	1713.02	1423.54	1095.40	994.03	853.93	762.53
75000	6528.47	3396.33	2354.56	1835.38	1525.23	1173.65	1065.03	914.92	816.99
80000	6963.70	3622.75	2511.53	1957.74	1626.91	1251.89	1136.03	975.92	871.46
100000	8704.63	4528.44	3139.41	2447.17	2033.63	1564.86	1420.03	1219.90	1089.32

MONTHLY PAYMENT 8⅛%

NECESSARY TO AMORTIZE A LOAN

TERM / AMOUNT	15 YEARS	18 YEARS	20 YEARS	25 YEARS	28 YEARS	29 YEARS	30 YEARS	35 YEARS	40 YEARS
$ 25	.25	.23	.22	.20	.19	.19	.19	.18	.18
50	.49	.45	.43	.40	.38	.38	.38	.36	.36
75	.73	.67	.64	.59	.57	.57	.56	.54	.53
100	.97	.89	.85	.79	.76	.75	.75	.72	.71
200	1.93	1.77	1.69	1.57	1.52	1.50	1.49	1.44	1.41
300	2.89	2.65	2.54	2.35	2.27	2.25	2.23	2.16	2.12
400	3.86	3.54	3.38	3.13	3.03	3.00	2.97	2.88	2.82
500	4.82	4.42	4.23	3.91	3.78	3.75	3.72	3.60	3.53
600	5.78	5.30	5.07	4.69	4.54	4.50	4.46	4.32	4.23
700	6.75	6.18	5.91	5.47	5.29	5.25	5.20	5.04	4.94
800	7.71	7.07	6.76	6.25	6.05	5.99	5.94	5.76	5.64
900	8.67	7.95	7.60	7.03	6.80	6.74	6.69	6.48	6.35
1000	9.63	8.83	8.45	7.81	7.56	7.49	7.43	7.20	7.05
2000	19.26	17.66	16.89	15.61	15.11	14.98	14.85	14.39	14.10
3000	28.89	26.48	25.33	23.41	22.66	22.46	22.28	21.59	21.15
4000	38.52	35.31	33.77	31.21	30.22	29.95	29.70	28.78	28.19
5000	48.15	44.13	42.22	39.01	37.77	37.43	37.13	35.97	35.24
6000	57.78	52.96	50.66	46.81	45.32	44.92	44.55	43.17	42.29
7000	67.41	61.78	59.10	54.61	52.88	52.41	51.98	50.36	49.33
8000	77.04	70.61	67.54	62.41	60.43	59.89	59.40	57.55	56.38
9000	86.66	79.43	75.99	70.22	67.98	67.38	66.83	64.75	63.43
10000	96.29	88.26	84.43	78.02	75.54	74.86	74.25	71.94	70.48
15000	144.44	132.39	126.64	117.02	113.30	112.29	111.38	107.91	105.71
20000	192.58	176.51	168.85	156.03	151.07	149.72	148.50	143.88	140.95
25000	240.73	220.64	211.06	195.03	188.84	187.15	185.63	179.84	176.18
30000	288.87	264.77	253.28	234.04	226.60	224.58	222.75	215.81	211.42
35000	337.01	308.89	295.49	273.05	264.37	262.01	259.88	251.78	246.65
36000	346.64	317.72	303.93	280.85	271.92	269.50	267.30	258.97	253.70
37000	356.27	326.54	312.37	288.65	279.48	276.99	274.73	266.17	260.75
38000	365.90	335.37	320.81	296.45	287.03	284.47	282.15	273.36	267.79
39000	375.53	344.20	329.26	304.25	294.58	291.96	289.58	280.55	274.84
40000	385.16	353.02	337.70	312.05	302.14	299.44	297.00	287.75	281.89
41000	394.79	361.85	346.14	319.85	309.69	306.93	304.43	294.94	288.94
42000	404.42	370.67	354.58	327.65	317.24	314.42	311.85	302.14	295.98
43000	414.04	379.50	363.03	335.45	324.80	321.90	319.28	309.33	303.03
44000	423.67	388.32	371.47	343.26	332.35	329.39	326.70	316.52	310.08
45000	433.30	397.15	379.91	351.06	339.90	336.87	334.13	323.72	317.12
46000	442.93	405.97	388.35	358.86	347.46	344.36	341.55	330.91	324.17
47000	452.56	414.80	396.80	366.66	355.01	351.85	348.98	338.10	331.22
48000	462.19	423.62	405.24	374.46	362.56	359.33	356.40	345.30	338.27
49000	471.82	432.45	413.68	382.26	370.11	366.82	363.83	352.49	345.31
50000	481.45	441.27	422.12	390.06	377.67	374.30	371.25	359.68	352.36
51000	491.07	450.10	430.57	397.86	385.22	381.79	378.68	366.88	359.41
52000	500.70	458.93	439.01	405.66	392.77	389.28	386.10	374.07	366.45
53000	510.33	467.75	447.45	413.47	400.33	396.76	393.53	381.26	373.50
54000	519.96	476.58	455.89	421.27	407.88	404.25	400.95	388.46	380.55
55000	529.59	485.40	464.33	429.07	415.43	411.73	408.38	395.65	387.59
56000	539.22	494.23	472.78	436.87	422.99	419.22	415.80	402.85	394.64
57000	548.85	503.05	481.22	444.67	430.54	426.71	423.23	410.04	401.69
58000	558.48	511.88	489.66	452.47	438.09	434.19	430.65	417.23	408.74
59000	568.11	520.70	498.10	460.27	445.65	441.68	438.08	424.43	415.78
60000	577.73	529.53	506.55	468.07	453.20	449.16	445.50	431.62	422.83
61000	587.36	538.35	514.99	475.88	460.75	456.65	452.93	438.81	429.88
62000	596.99	547.18	523.43	483.68	468.31	464.14	460.35	446.01	436.92
63000	606.62	556.00	531.87	491.48	475.86	471.62	467.78	453.20	443.97
64000	616.25	564.83	540.32	499.28	483.41	479.11	475.20	460.39	451.02
65000	625.88	573.66	548.76	507.08	490.97	486.59	482.63	467.59	458.07
66000	635.51	582.48	557.20	514.88	498.52	494.08	490.05	474.78	465.11
67000	645.14	591.31	565.64	522.68	506.07	501.57	497.48	481.98	472.16
68000	654.76	600.13	574.09	530.48	513.63	509.05	504.90	489.17	479.21
69000	664.39	608.96	582.53	538.28	521.18	516.54	512.33	496.36	486.25
70000	674.02	617.78	590.97	546.09	528.73	524.02	519.75	503.56	493.30
75000	722.17	661.91	633.18	585.09	566.50	561.45	556.88	539.52	528.54
80000	770.31	706.04	675.39	624.10	604.27	598.88	594.00	575.49	563.77
100000	962.89	882.54	844.24	780.12	755.33	748.60	742.50	719.36	704.71

8¼% MONTHLY PAYMENT
NECESSARY TO AMORTIZE A LOAN

TERM / AMOUNT	1 YEAR	2 YEARS	3 YEARS	4 YEARS	5 YEARS	7 YEARS	8 YEARS	10 YEARS	12 YEARS
$ 25	2.18	1.14	.79	.62	.51	.40	.36	.31	.28
50	4.36	2.27	1.58	1.23	1.02	.79	.72	.62	.55
75	6.54	3.41	2.36	1.84	1.53	1.18	1.07	.92	.83
100	8.72	4.54	3.15	2.46	2.04	1.58	1.43	1.23	1.10
200	17.43	9.07	6.30	4.91	4.08	3.15	2.86	2.46	2.20
300	26.14	13.61	9.44	7.36	6.12	4.72	4.28	3.68	3.29
400	34.85	18.14	12.59	9.82	8.16	6.29	5.71	4.91	4.39
500	43.56	22.68	15.73	12.27	10.20	7.86	7.14	6.14	5.49
600	52.27	27.21	18.88	14.72	12.24	9.43	8.56	7.36	6.58
700	60.98	31.74	22.02	17.18	14.28	11.00	9.99	8.59	7.68
800	69.69	36.28	25.17	19.63	16.32	12.57	11.42	9.82	8.77
900	78.40	40.81	28.31	22.08	18.36	14.14	12.84	11.04	9.87
1000	87.11	45.35	31.46	24.54	20.40	15.72	14.27	12.27	10.97
2000	174.21	90.69	62.91	49.07	40.80	31.43	28.53	24.54	21.93
3000	261.32	136.03	94.36	73.60	61.19	47.14	42.80	36.80	32.89
4000	348.42	181.37	125.81	98.13	81.59	62.85	57.06	49.07	43.85
5000	435.53	226.71	157.26	122.66	101.99	78.56	71.33	61.33	54.82
6000	522.63	272.05	188.72	147.19	122.38	94.27	85.59	73.60	65.78
7000	609.73	317.39	220.17	171.72	142.78	109.98	99.85	85.86	76.74
8000	696.84	362.74	251.62	196.25	163.18	125.69	114.12	98.13	87.70
9000	783.94	408.08	283.07	220.78	183.57	141.40	128.38	110.39	98.66
10000	871.05	453.42	314.52	245.31	203.97	157.12	142.65	122.66	109.63
15000	1306.57	680.13	471.78	367.96	305.95	235.67	213.97	183.98	164.44
20000	1742.09	906.83	629.04	490.61	407.93	314.23	285.29	245.31	219.25
25000	2177.61	1133.54	786.30	613.27	509.91	392.78	356.61	306.64	274.06
30000	2613.13	1360.25	943.56	735.92	611.89	471.34	427.93	367.96	328.87
35000	3048.65	1586.95	1100.82	858.57	713.87	549.89	499.25	429.29	383.68
36000	3135.75	1632.30	1132.27	883.10	734.27	565.60	513.51	441.55	394.64
37000	3222.86	1677.64	1163.72	907.63	754.67	581.31	527.78	453.82	405.60
38000	3309.96	1722.98	1195.17	932.16	775.06	597.03	542.04	466.08	416.56
39000	3397.06	1768.32	1226.63	956.69	795.46	612.74	556.30	478.35	427.53
40000	3484.17	1813.66	1258.08	981.22	815.86	628.45	570.57	490.62	438.49
41000	3571.27	1859.00	1289.53	1005.75	836.25	644.16	584.83	502.88	449.45
42000	3658.38	1904.34	1320.98	1030.28	856.65	659.87	599.10	515.15	460.41
43000	3745.48	1949.69	1352.43	1054.81	877.04	675.58	613.36	527.41	471.37
44000	3832.58	1995.03	1383.89	1079.34	897.44	691.29	627.62	539.68	482.34
45000	3919.69	2040.37	1415.34	1103.87	917.84	707.00	641.89	551.94	493.30
46000	4006.79	2085.71	1446.79	1128.41	938.23	722.71	656.15	564.21	504.26
47000	4093.90	2131.05	1478.24	1152.94	958.63	738.42	670.42	576.47	515.22
48000	4181.00	2176.39	1509.69	1177.47	979.03	754.14	684.68	588.74	526.18
49000	4268.10	2221.73	1541.14	1202.00	999.42	769.85	698.94	601.00	537.15
50000	4355.21	2267.07	1572.60	1226.53	1019.82	785.56	713.21	613.27	548.11
51000	4442.31	2312.42	1604.05	1251.06	1040.21	801.27	727.47	625.53	559.07
52000	4529.42	2357.76	1635.50	1275.59	1060.61	816.98	741.74	637.80	570.03
53000	4616.52	2403.10	1666.95	1300.12	1081.01	832.69	756.00	650.06	580.99
54000	4703.62	2448.44	1698.40	1324.65	1101.40	848.40	770.27	662.33	591.96
55000	4790.73	2493.78	1729.86	1349.18	1121.80	864.11	784.53	674.59	602.92
56000	4877.83	2539.12	1761.31	1373.71	1142.20	879.82	798.79	686.86	613.88
57000	4964.94	2584.46	1792.76	1398.24	1162.59	895.54	813.06	699.12	624.84
58000	5052.04	2629.81	1824.21	1422.77	1182.99	911.25	827.32	711.39	635.81
59000	5139.14	2675.15	1855.66	1447.30	1203.38	926.96	841.59	723.66	646.77
60000	5226.25	2720.49	1887.11	1471.83	1223.78	942.67	855.85	735.92	657.73
61000	5313.35	2765.83	1918.57	1496.36	1244.18	958.38	870.11	748.19	668.69
62000	5400.46	2811.17	1950.02	1520.89	1264.57	974.09	884.38	760.45	679.65
63000	5487.56	2856.51	1981.47	1545.42	1284.97	989.80	898.64	772.72	690.62
64000	5574.67	2901.85	2012.92	1569.95	1305.37	1005.51	912.91	784.98	701.58
65000	5661.77	2947.20	2044.37	1594.48	1325.76	1021.22	927.17	797.25	712.54
66000	5748.87	2992.54	2075.83	1619.01	1346.16	1036.93	941.43	809.51	723.50
67000	5835.98	3037.88	2107.28	1643.54	1366.55	1052.65	955.70	821.78	734.46
68000	5923.08	3083.22	2138.73	1668.08	1386.95	1068.36	969.96	834.04	745.43
69000	6010.19	3128.56	2170.18	1692.61	1407.35	1084.07	984.23	846.31	756.39
70000	6097.29	3173.90	2201.63	1717.14	1427.74	1099.78	998.49	858.57	767.35
75000	6532.81	3400.61	2358.89	1839.79	1529.72	1178.33	1069.81	919.90	822.16
80000	6968.33	3627.32	2516.15	1962.44	1631.71	1256.89	1141.13	981.23	876.97
100000	8710.41	4534.14	3145.19	2453.05	2039.63	1571.11	1426.41	1226.53	1096.21

MONTHLY PAYMENT 8¼%

NECESSARY TO AMORTIZE A LOAN

TERM / AMOUNT	15 YEARS	18 YEARS	20 YEARS	25 YEARS	28 YEARS	29 YEARS	30 YEARS	35 YEARS	40 YEARS
$ 25	.25	.23	.22	.20	.20	.19	.19	.19	.18
50	.49	.45	.43	.40	.39	.38	.38	.37	.36
75	.73	.67	.64	.60	.58	.57	.57	.55	.54
100	.98	.90	.86	.79	.77	.76	.76	.73	.72
200	1.95	1.79	1.71	1.58	1.53	1.52	1.51	1.46	1.43
300	2.92	2.68	2.56	2.37	2.30	2.28	2.26	2.19	2.15
400	3.89	3.57	3.41	3.16	3.06	3.03	3.01	2.92	2.86
500	4.86	4.46	4.27	3.95	3.82	3.79	3.76	3.65	3.58
600	5.83	5.35	5.12	4.74	4.59	4.55	4.51	4.38	4.29
700	6.80	6.24	5.97	5.52	5.35	5.31	5.26	5.10	5.00
800	7.77	7.13	6.82	6.31	6.12	6.06	6.02	5.83	5.72
900	8.74	8.02	7.67	7.10	6.88	6.82	6.77	6.56	6.43
1000	9.71	8.91	8.53	7.89	7.64	7.58	7.52	7.29	7.15
2000	19.41	17.81	17.05	15.77	15.28	15.15	15.03	14.57	14.29
3000	29.11	26.71	25.57	23.66	22.92	22.72	22.54	21.86	21.43
4000	38.81	35.61	34.09	31.54	30.56	30.30	30.06	29.14	28.57
5000	48.51	44.51	42.61	39.43	38.20	37.87	37.57	36.43	35.71
6000	58.21	53.41	51.13	47.31	45.84	45.44	45.08	43.71	42.85
7000	67.91	62.32	59.65	55.20	53.48	53.01	52.59	51.00	49.99
8000	77.62	71.22	68.17	63.08	61.12	60.59	60.11	58.28	57.14
9000	87.32	80.12	76.69	70.97	68.76	68.16	67.62	65.57	64.28
10000	97.02	89.02	85.21	78.85	76.40	75.73	75.13	72.85	71.42
15000	145.53	133.53	127.81	118.27	114.59	113.60	112.69	109.28	107.13
20000	194.03	178.03	170.42	157.70	152.79	151.46	150.26	145.70	142.83
25000	242.54	222.54	213.02	197.12	190.99	189.33	187.82	182.13	178.54
30000	291.05	267.05	255.62	236.54	229.18	227.19	225.38	218.55	214.25
35000	339.55	311.56	298.23	275.96	267.38	265.05	262.95	254.98	249.95
36000	349.26	320.46	306.75	283.85	275.02	272.63	270.46	262.26	257.09
37000	358.96	329.36	315.27	291.73	282.66	280.20	277.97	269.55	264.24
38000	368.66	338.26	323.79	299.62	290.30	287.77	285.49	276.83	271.38
39000	378.36	347.16	332.31	307.50	297.94	295.35	293.00	284.12	278.52
40000	388.06	356.06	340.83	315.39	305.58	302.92	300.51	291.40	285.66
41000	397.76	364.97	349.35	323.27	313.22	310.49	308.02	298.69	292.80
42000	407.46	373.87	357.87	331.15	320.86	318.06	315.54	305.97	299.94
43000	417.17	382.77	366.39	339.04	328.50	325.64	323.05	313.26	307.08
44000	426.87	391.67	374.91	346.92	336.13	333.21	330.56	320.54	314.23
45000	436.57	400.57	383.43	354.81	343.77	340.78	338.07	327.83	321.37
46000	446.27	409.47	391.96	362.69	351.41	348.36	345.59	335.11	328.51
47000	455.97	418.37	400.48	370.58	359.05	355.93	353.10	342.40	335.65
48000	465.67	427.28	409.00	378.46	366.69	363.50	360.61	349.68	342.79
49000	475.37	436.18	417.52	386.35	374.33	371.07	368.13	356.97	349.93
50000	485.08	445.08	426.04	394.23	381.97	378.65	375.64	364.25	357.07
51000	494.78	453.98	434.56	402.11	389.61	386.22	383.15	371.54	364.22
52000	504.48	462.88	443.08	410.00	397.25	393.79	390.66	378.82	371.36
53000	514.18	471.78	451.60	417.88	404.89	401.37	398.18	386.11	378.50
54000	523.88	480.68	460.12	425.77	412.53	408.94	405.69	393.39	385.64
55000	533.58	489.59	468.64	433.65	420.17	416.51	413.20	400.68	392.78
56000	543.28	498.49	477.16	441.54	427.81	424.08	420.71	407.96	399.92
57000	552.99	507.39	485.68	449.42	435.45	431.66	428.23	415.24	407.06
58000	562.69	516.29	494.20	457.31	443.08	439.23	435.74	422.53	414.21
59000	572.39	525.19	502.72	465.19	450.72	446.80	443.25	429.81	421.35
60000	582.09	534.09	511.24	473.08	458.36	454.38	450.76	437.10	428.49
61000	591.79	543.00	519.77	480.96	466.00	461.95	458.28	444.38	435.63
62000	601.49	551.90	528.29	488.84	473.64	469.52	465.79	451.67	442.77
63000	611.19	560.80	536.81	496.73	481.28	477.09	473.30	458.95	449.91
64000	620.89	569.70	545.33	504.61	488.92	484.67	480.82	466.24	457.05
65000	630.60	578.60	553.85	512.50	496.56	492.24	488.33	473.52	464.20
66000	640.30	587.50	562.37	520.38	504.20	499.81	495.84	480.81	471.34
67000	650.00	596.40	570.89	528.27	511.84	507.39	503.35	488.09	478.48
68000	659.70	605.31	579.41	536.15	519.48	514.96	510.87	495.38	485.62
69000	669.40	614.21	587.93	544.04	527.12	522.53	518.38	502.66	492.76
70000	679.10	623.11	596.45	551.92	534.76	530.10	525.89	509.95	499.90
75000	727.61	667.62	639.05	591.34	572.95	567.97	563.45	546.37	535.61
80000	776.12	712.12	681.66	630.77	611.15	605.83	601.02	582.80	571.32
100000	970.15	890.15	852.07	788.46	763.94	757.29	751.27	728.50	714.14

8⅜% MONTHLY PAYMENT
NECESSARY TO AMORTIZE A LOAN

TERM / AMOUNT	1 YEAR	2 YEARS	3 YEARS	4 YEARS	5 YEARS	7 YEARS	8 YEARS	10 YEARS	12 YEARS
$ 25	2.18	1.14	.79	.62	.52	.40	.36	.31	.28
50	4.36	2.27	1.58	1.23	1.03	.79	.72	.62	.56
75	6.54	3.41	2.37	1.85	1.54	1.19	1.08	.93	.83
100	8.72	4.54	3.16	2.46	2.05	1.58	1.44	1.24	1.11
200	17.44	9.08	6.31	4.92	4.10	3.16	2.87	2.47	2.21
300	26.15	13.62	9.46	7.38	6.14	4.74	4.30	3.70	3.31
400	34.87	18.16	12.61	9.84	8.19	6.31	5.74	4.94	4.42
500	43.59	22.70	15.76	12.30	10.23	7.89	7.17	6.17	5.52
600	52.30	27.24	18.91	14.76	12.28	9.47	8.60	7.40	6.62
700	61.02	31.78	22.06	17.22	14.32	11.05	10.03	8.64	7.73
800	69.73	36.32	25.21	19.68	16.37	12.62	11.47	9.87	8.83
900	78.45	40.86	28.36	22.14	18.42	14.20	12.90	11.10	9.93
1000	87.17	45.40	31.51	24.59	20.46	15.78	14.33	12.34	11.04
2000	174.33	90.80	63.02	49.18	40.92	31.55	28.66	24.67	22.07
3000	261.49	136.20	94.53	73.77	61.37	47.33	42.99	37.00	33.10
4000	348.65	181.60	126.04	98.36	81.83	63.10	57.32	49.33	44.13
5000	435.81	227.00	157.55	122.95	102.29	78.87	71.65	61.66	55.16
6000	522.98	272.40	189.06	147.54	122.74	94.65	85.97	74.00	66.19
7000	610.14	317.79	220.57	172.13	143.20	110.42	100.30	86.33	77.22
8000	697.30	363.19	252.08	196.72	163.66	126.19	114.63	98.66	88.25
9000	784.46	408.59	283.59	221.31	184.11	141.97	128.96	110.99	99.29
10000	871.62	453.99	315.10	245.90	204.57	157.74	143.29	123.32	110.32
15000	1307.43	680.98	472.65	368.84	306.85	236.61	214.93	184.98	165.47
20000	1743.24	907.98	630.20	491.79	409.13	315.48	286.57	246.64	220.63
25000	2179.05	1134.97	787.75	614.74	511.41	394.35	358.21	308.30	275.78
30000	2614.86	1361.96	945.29	737.68	613.70	473.22	429.85	369.96	330.94
35000	3050.67	1588.95	1102.84	860.63	715.98	552.08	501.49	431.62	386.10
36000	3137.83	1634.35	1134.35	885.22	736.43	567.86	515.81	443.95	397.13
37000	3225.00	1679.75	1165.86	909.81	756.89	583.63	530.14	456.28	408.16
38000	3312.16	1725.15	1197.37	934.40	777.35	599.41	544.47	468.61	419.19
39000	3399.32	1770.55	1228.88	958.99	797.80	615.18	558.80	480.95	430.22
40000	3486.48	1815.95	1260.39	983.58	818.26	630.95	573.13	493.28	441.25
41000	3573.64	1861.34	1291.90	1008.17	838.71	646.73	587.45	505.61	452.28
42000	3660.81	1906.74	1323.41	1032.76	859.17	662.50	601.78	517.94	463.32
43000	3747.97	1952.14	1354.92	1057.35	879.63	678.27	616.11	530.27	474.35
44000	3835.13	1997.54	1386.43	1081.94	900.08	694.05	630.44	542.60	485.38
45000	3922.29	2042.94	1417.94	1106.52	920.54	709.82	644.77	554.94	496.41
46000	4009.45	2088.34	1449.45	1131.11	941.00	725.60	659.09	567.27	507.44
47000	4096.61	2133.74	1480.96	1155.70	961.45	741.37	673.42	579.60	518.47
48000	4183.78	2179.13	1512.47	1180.29	981.91	757.14	687.75	591.93	529.50
49000	4270.94	2224.53	1543.98	1204.88	1002.37	772.92	702.08	604.26	540.53
50000	4358.10	2269.93	1575.49	1229.47	1022.82	788.69	716.41	616.60	551.56
51000	4445.26	2315.33	1607.00	1254.06	1043.28	804.46	730.73	628.93	562.60
52000	4532.42	2360.73	1638.51	1278.65	1063.73	820.24	745.06	641.26	573.63
53000	4619.59	2406.13	1670.02	1303.24	1084.19	836.01	759.39	653.59	584.66
54000	4706.75	2451.52	1701.53	1327.83	1104.65	851.78	773.72	665.92	595.69
55000	4793.91	2496.92	1733.04	1352.42	1125.10	867.56	788.05	678.25	606.72
56000	4881.07	2542.32	1764.55	1377.01	1145.56	883.33	802.37	690.59	617.75
57000	4968.23	2587.72	1796.05	1401.60	1166.02	899.11	816.70	702.92	628.78
58000	5055.40	2633.12	1827.56	1426.19	1186.47	914.88	831.03	715.25	639.81
59000	5142.56	2678.52	1859.07	1450.78	1206.93	930.65	845.36	727.58	650.85
60000	5229.72	2723.92	1890.58	1475.36	1227.39	946.43	859.69	739.91	661.88
61000	5316.88	2769.31	1922.09	1499.95	1247.84	962.20	874.01	752.25	672.91
62000	5404.04	2814.71	1953.60	1524.54	1268.30	977.97	888.34	764.58	683.94
63000	5491.21	2860.11	1985.11	1549.13	1288.75	993.75	902.67	776.91	694.97
64000	5578.37	2905.51	2016.62	1573.72	1309.21	1009.52	917.00	789.24	706.00
65000	5665.53	2950.91	2048.13	1598.31	1329.67	1025.30	931.33	801.57	717.03
66000	5752.69	2996.31	2079.64	1622.90	1350.12	1041.07	945.65	813.90	728.06
67000	5839.85	3041.71	2111.15	1647.49	1370.58	1056.84	959.98	826.24	739.10
68000	5927.02	3087.10	2142.66	1672.08	1391.04	1072.62	974.31	838.57	750.13
69000	6014.18	3132.50	2174.17	1696.67	1411.49	1088.39	988.64	850.90	761.16
70000	6101.34	3177.90	2205.68	1721.26	1431.95	1104.16	1002.97	863.23	772.19
75000	6537.15	3404.89	2363.23	1844.20	1534.23	1183.03	1074.61	924.89	827.34
80000	6972.96	3631.89	2520.78	1967.15	1636.51	1261.90	1146.25	986.55	882.50
100000	8716.20	4539.86	3150.97	2458.94	2045.64	1577.37	1432.81	1233.19	1103.12

MONTHLY PAYMENT 8⅜%

NECESSARY TO AMORTIZE A LOAN

TERM / AMOUNT	15 YEARS	18 YEARS	20 YEARS	25 YEARS	28 YEARS	29 YEARS	30 YEARS	35 YEARS	40 YEARS
$ 25	.25	.23	.22	.20	.20	.20	.20	.19	.19
50	.49	.45	.43	.40	.39	.39	.39	.37	.37
75	.74	.68	.65	.60	.58	.58	.58	.56	.55
100	.98	.90	.86	.80	.78	.77	.77	.74	.73
200	1.96	1.80	1.72	1.60	1.55	1.54	1.53	1.48	1.45
300	2.94	2.70	2.58	2.40	2.32	2.30	2.29	2.22	2.18
400	3.91	3.60	3.44	3.19	3.10	3.07	3.05	2.96	2.90
500	4.89	4.49	4.30	3.99	3.87	3.84	3.81	3.69	3.62
600	5.87	5.39	5.16	4.79	4.64	4.60	4.57	4.43	4.35
700	6.85	6.29	6.02	5.58	5.41	5.37	5.33	5.17	5.07
800	7.82	7.19	6.88	6.38	6.19	6.13	6.09	5.91	5.79
900	8.80	8.09	7.74	7.18	6.96	6.90	6.85	6.64	6.52
1000	9.78	8.98	8.60	7.97	7.73	7.67	7.61	7.38	7.24
2000	19.55	17.96	17.20	15.94	15.46	15.33	15.21	14.76	14.48
3000	29.33	26.94	25.80	23.91	23.18	22.99	22.81	22.13	21.71
4000	39.10	35.92	34.40	31.88	30.91	30.65	30.41	29.51	28.95
5000	48.88	44.89	43.00	39.85	38.63	38.31	38.01	36.89	36.19
6000	58.65	53.87	51.60	47.81	46.36	45.97	45.61	44.26	43.42
7000	68.42	62.85	60.20	55.78	54.08	53.63	53.21	51.64	50.66
8000	78.20	71.83	68.80	63.75	61.81	61.29	60.81	59.02	57.89
9000	87.97	80.81	77.40	71.72	69.54	68.95	68.41	66.39	65.13
10000	97.75	89.78	86.00	79.69	77.26	76.61	76.01	73.77	72.37
15000	146.62	134.67	128.99	119.53	115.89	114.91	114.02	110.65	108.55
20000	195.49	179.56	171.99	159.37	154.52	153.21	152.02	147.54	144.73
25000	244.36	224.45	214.99	199.21	193.15	191.51	190.02	184.42	180.91
30000	293.23	269.34	257.98	239.05	231.78	229.81	228.03	221.30	217.09
35000	342.10	314.23	300.98	278.89	270.40	268.11	266.03	258.19	253.27
36000	351.88	323.21	309.58	286.86	278.13	275.77	273.63	265.56	260.50
37000	361.65	332.19	318.18	294.83	285.86	283.43	281.23	272.94	267.74
38000	371.43	341.16	326.78	302.80	293.58	291.09	288.83	280.32	274.97
39000	381.20	350.14	335.38	310.77	301.31	298.75	296.43	287.69	282.21
40000	390.98	359.12	343.98	318.73	309.03	306.41	304.03	295.07	289.45
41000	400.75	368.10	352.58	326.70	316.76	314.07	311.63	302.45	296.68
42000	410.52	377.08	361.17	334.67	324.48	321.73	319.24	309.82	303.92
43000	420.30	386.05	369.77	342.64	332.21	329.39	326.84	317.20	311.15
44000	430.07	395.03	378.37	350.61	339.94	337.05	334.44	324.57	318.39
45000	439.85	404.01	386.97	358.57	347.66	344.71	342.04	331.95	325.63
46000	449.62	412.99	395.57	366.54	355.39	352.37	349.64	339.33	332.86
47000	459.40	421.96	404.17	374.51	363.11	360.03	357.24	346.70	340.10
48000	469.17	430.94	412.77	382.48	370.84	367.69	364.84	354.08	347.33
49000	478.94	439.92	421.37	390.45	378.56	375.35	372.44	361.46	354.57
50000	488.72	448.90	429.97	398.42	386.29	383.01	380.04	368.83	361.81
51000	498.49	457.88	438.57	406.38	394.02	390.67	387.64	376.21	369.04
52000	508.27	466.85	447.17	414.35	401.74	398.33	395.24	383.59	376.28
53000	518.04	475.83	455.77	422.32	409.47	405.99	402.84	390.96	383.51
54000	527.82	484.81	464.37	430.29	417.19	413.65	410.44	398.34	390.75
55000	537.59	493.79	472.97	438.26	424.92	421.31	418.04	405.72	397.99
56000	547.36	502.77	481.56	446.22	432.64	428.97	425.65	413.09	405.22
57000	557.14	511.74	490.16	454.19	440.37	436.63	433.25	420.47	412.46
58000	566.91	520.72	498.76	462.16	448.10	444.29	440.85	427.85	419.69
59000	576.69	529.70	507.36	470.13	455.82	451.95	448.45	435.22	426.93
60000	586.46	538.68	515.96	478.10	463.55	459.61	456.05	442.60	434.17
61000	596.23	547.66	524.56	486.07	471.27	467.27	463.65	449.98	441.40
62000	606.01	556.63	533.16	494.03	479.00	474.93	471.25	457.35	448.64
63000	615.78	565.61	541.76	502.00	486.72	482.59	478.85	464.73	455.87
64000	625.56	574.59	550.36	509.97	494.45	490.25	486.45	472.11	463.11
65000	635.33	583.57	558.96	517.94	502.18	497.91	494.05	479.48	470.35
66000	645.11	592.54	567.56	525.91	509.90	505.57	501.65	486.86	477.58
67000	654.88	601.52	576.16	533.88	517.63	513.23	509.25	494.24	484.82
68000	664.65	610.50	584.76	541.84	525.35	520.89	516.85	501.61	492.05
69000	674.43	619.48	593.36	549.81	533.08	528.55	524.45	508.99	499.29
70000	684.20	628.46	601.95	557.78	540.80	536.21	532.06	516.37	506.53
75000	733.07	673.35	644.95	597.62	579.43	574.51	570.06	553.25	542.71
80000	781.95	718.23	687.95	637.46	618.06	612.81	608.06	590.13	578.89
100000	977.43	897.79	859.93	796.83	772.58	766.02	760.08	737.66	723.61

8½% MONTHLY PAYMENT
NECESSARY TO AMORTIZE A LOAN

TERM / AMOUNT	1 YEAR	2 YEARS	3 YEARS	4 YEARS	5 YEARS	7 YEARS	8 YEARS	10 YEARS	12 YEARS
$ 25	2.19	1.14	.79	.62	.52	.40	.36	.31	.28
50	4.37	2.28	1.58	1.24	1.03	.80	.72	.62	.56
75	6.55	3.41	2.37	1.85	1.54	1.19	1.08	.93	.84
100	8.73	4.55	3.16	2.47	2.06	1.59	1.44	1.24	1.12
200	17.45	9.10	6.32	4.93	4.11	3.17	2.88	2.48	2.23
300	26.17	13.64	9.48	7.40	6.16	4.76	4.32	3.72	3.34
400	34.89	18.19	12.63	9.86	8.21	6.34	5.76	4.96	4.45
500	43.61	22.73	15.79	12.33	10.26	7.92	7.20	6.20	5.56
600	52.34	27.28	18.95	14.79	12.31	9.51	8.64	7.44	6.67
700	61.06	31.82	22.10	17.26	14.37	11.09	10.08	8.68	7.78
800	69.78	36.37	25.26	19.72	16.42	12.67	11.52	9.92	8.89
900	78.50	40.92	28.42	22.19	18.47	14.26	12.96	11.16	10.00
1000	87.22	45.46	31.57	24.65	20.52	15.84	14.40	12.40	11.11
2000	174.44	90.92	63.14	49.30	41.04	31.68	28.79	24.80	22.21
3000	261.66	136.37	94.71	73.95	61.55	47.51	43.18	37.20	33.31
4000	348.88	181.83	126.28	98.60	82.07	63.35	57.57	49.60	44.41
5000	436.10	227.28	157.84	123.25	102.59	79.19	71.97	62.00	55.51
6000	523.32	272.74	189.41	147.89	123.10	95.02	86.36	74.40	66.61
7000	610.54	318.19	220.98	172.54	143.62	110.86	100.75	86.79	77.71
8000	697.76	363.65	252.55	197.19	164.14	126.70	115.14	99.19	88.81
9000	784.98	409.11	284.11	221.84	184.65	142.53	129.53	111.59	99.91
10000	872.20	454.56	315.68	246.49	205.17	158.37	143.93	123.99	111.01
15000	1308.30	681.84	473.52	369.73	307.75	237.55	215.89	185.98	166.51
20000	1744.40	909.12	631.36	492.97	410.34	316.73	287.85	247.98	222.02
25000	2180.50	1136.40	789.19	616.21	512.92	395.92	359.81	309.97	277.52
30000	2616.60	1363.68	947.03	739.45	615.50	475.10	431.77	371.96	333.02
35000	3052.70	1590.95	1104.87	862.70	718.08	554.28	503.73	433.95	388.52
36000	3139.92	1636.41	1136.44	887.34	738.60	570.12	518.12	446.35	399.63
37000	3227.14	1681.86	1168.00	911.99	759.12	585.95	532.51	458.75	410.73
38000	3314.36	1727.32	1199.57	936.64	779.63	601.79	546.91	471.15	421.83
39000	3401.58	1772.78	1231.14	961.29	800.15	617.63	561.30	483.55	432.93
40000	3488.80	1818.23	1262.71	985.94	820.67	633.46	575.69	495.95	444.03
41000	3576.02	1863.69	1294.27	1010.59	841.18	649.30	590.08	508.35	455.13
42000	3663.24	1909.14	1325.84	1035.23	861.70	665.14	604.47	520.74	466.23
43000	3750.46	1954.60	1357.41	1059.88	882.22	680.97	618.87	533.14	477.33
44000	3837.68	2000.05	1388.98	1084.53	902.73	696.81	633.26	545.54	488.43
45000	3924.90	2045.51	1420.54	1109.18	923.25	712.65	647.65	557.94	499.53
46000	4012.11	2090.97	1452.11	1133.83	943.77	728.48	662.04	570.34	510.63
47000	4099.33	2136.42	1483.68	1158.48	964.28	744.32	676.44	582.74	521.73
48000	4186.55	2181.88	1515.25	1183.12	984.80	760.16	690.83	595.14	532.83
49000	4273.77	2227.33	1546.81	1207.77	1005.32	775.99	705.22	607.53	543.93
50000	4360.99	2272.79	1578.38	1232.42	1025.83	791.83	719.61	619.93	555.03
51000	4448.21	2318.24	1609.95	1257.07	1046.35	807.67	734.00	632.33	566.13
52000	4535.43	2363.70	1641.52	1281.72	1066.86	823.50	748.40	644.73	577.23
53000	4622.65	2409.16	1673.08	1306.37	1087.38	839.34	762.79	657.13	588.33
54000	4709.87	2454.61	1704.65	1331.01	1107.90	855.18	777.18	669.53	599.44
55000	4797.09	2500.07	1736.22	1355.66	1128.41	871.01	791.57	681.93	610.54
56000	4884.31	2545.52	1767.79	1380.31	1148.93	886.85	805.96	694.32	621.64
57000	4971.53	2590.98	1799.35	1404.96	1169.45	902.68	820.36	706.72	632.74
58000	5058.75	2636.43	1830.92	1429.61	1189.96	918.52	834.75	719.12	643.84
59000	5145.97	2681.89	1862.49	1454.25	1210.48	934.36	849.14	731.52	654.94
60000	5233.19	2727.35	1894.06	1478.90	1231.00	950.19	863.53	743.92	666.04
61000	5320.41	2772.80	1925.62	1503.55	1251.51	966.03	877.92	756.32	677.14
62000	5407.63	2818.26	1957.19	1528.20	1272.03	981.87	892.32	768.72	688.24
63000	5494.85	2863.71	1988.76	1552.85	1292.55	997.70	906.71	781.11	699.34
64000	5582.07	2909.17	2020.33	1577.50	1313.06	1013.54	921.10	793.51	710.44
65000	5669.29	2954.62	2051.89	1602.14	1333.58	1029.38	935.49	805.91	721.54
66000	5756.51	3000.08	2083.46	1626.79	1354.10	1045.21	949.89	818.31	732.64
67000	5843.73	3045.54	2115.03	1651.44	1374.61	1061.05	964.28	830.71	743.74
68000	5930.95	3090.99	2146.60	1676.09	1395.13	1076.89	978.67	843.11	754.84
69000	6018.17	3136.45	2178.17	1700.74	1415.65	1092.72	993.06	855.51	765.94
70000	6105.39	3181.90	2209.73	1725.39	1436.16	1108.56	1007.45	867.90	777.04
75000	6541.49	3409.18	2367.57	1848.63	1538.74	1187.74	1079.41	929.90	832.55
80000	6977.59	3636.46	2525.41	1971.87	1641.33	1266.92	1151.38	991.89	888.05
100000	8721.98	4545.57	3156.76	2464.84	2051.66	1583.65	1439.22	1239.86	1110.06

MONTHLY PAYMENT 8½%
NECESSARY TO AMORTIZE A LOAN

TERM / AMOUNT	15 YEARS	18 YEARS	20 YEARS	25 YEARS	28 YEARS	29 YEARS	30 YEARS	35 YEARS	40 YEARS
$ 25	.25	.23	.22	.21	.20	.20	.20	.19	.19
50	.50	.46	.44	.41	.40	.39	.39	.38	.37
75	.74	.68	.66	.61	.59	.59	.58	.57	.55
100	.99	.91	.87	.81	.79	.78	.77	.75	.74
200	1.97	1.82	1.74	1.62	1.57	1.55	1.54	1.50	1.47
300	2.96	2.72	2.61	2.42	2.35	2.33	2.31	2.25	2.20
400	3.94	3.63	3.48	3.23	3.13	3.10	3.08	2.99	2.94
500	4.93	4.53	4.34	4.03	3.91	3.88	3.85	3.74	3.67
600	5.91	5.44	5.21	4.84	4.69	4.65	4.62	4.49	4.40
700	6.90	6.34	6.08	5.64	5.47	5.43	5.39	5.23	5.14
800	7.88	7.25	6.95	6.45	6.25	6.20	6.16	5.98	5.87
900	8.87	8.15	7.82	7.25	7.04	6.98	6.93	6.73	6.60
1000	9.85	9.06	8.68	8.06	7.82	7.75	7.69	7.47	7.34
2000	19.70	18.11	17.36	16.11	15.63	15.50	15.38	14.94	14.67
3000	29.55	27.17	26.04	24.16	23.44	23.25	23.07	22.41	22.00
4000	39.39	36.22	34.72	32.21	31.25	31.00	30.76	29.88	29.33
5000	49.24	45.28	43.40	40.27	39.07	38.74	38.45	37.35	36.66
6000	59.09	54.33	52.07	48.32	46.88	46.49	46.14	44.82	43.99
7000	68.94	63.39	60.75	56.37	54.69	54.24	53.83	52.29	51.32
8000	78.78	72.44	69.43	64.42	62.50	61.99	61.52	59.75	58.65
9000	88.63	81.50	78.11	72.48	70.32	69.73	69.21	67.22	65.98
10000	98.48	90.55	86.79	80.53	78.13	77.48	76.90	74.69	73.31
15000	147.72	135.82	130.18	120.79	117.19	116.22	115.34	112.03	109.97
20000	196.95	181.10	173.57	161.05	156.25	154.96	153.79	149.38	146.62
25000	246.19	226.37	216.96	201.31	195.32	193.70	192.23	186.72	183.28
30000	295.43	271.64	260.35	241.57	234.38	232.44	230.68	224.06	219.93
35000	344.66	316.92	303.74	281.83	273.44	271.17	269.12	261.41	256.59
36000	354.51	325.97	312.42	289.89	281.25	278.92	276.81	268.87	263.92
37000	364.36	335.02	321.10	297.94	289.07	286.67	284.50	276.34	271.25
38000	374.21	344.08	329.78	305.99	296.88	294.42	292.19	283.81	278.58
39000	384.05	353.13	338.46	314.04	304.69	302.17	299.88	291.28	285.91
40000	393.90	362.19	347.13	322.10	312.50	309.91	307.57	298.75	293.24
41000	403.75	371.24	355.81	330.15	320.32	317.66	315.26	306.22	300.57
42000	413.60	380.30	364.49	338.20	328.13	325.41	322.95	313.69	307.90
43000	423.44	389.35	373.17	346.25	335.94	333.16	330.64	321.16	315.24
44000	433.29	398.41	381.85	354.30	343.75	340.90	338.33	328.62	322.57
45000	443.14	407.46	390.53	362.36	351.57	348.65	346.02	336.09	329.90
46000	452.99	416.52	399.20	370.41	359.38	356.40	353.71	343.56	337.23
47000	462.83	425.57	407.88	378.46	367.19	364.15	361.39	351.03	344.56
48000	472.68	434.62	416.56	386.51	375.00	371.89	369.08	358.50	351.89
49000	482.53	443.68	425.24	394.57	382.82	379.64	376.77	365.97	359.22
50000	492.37	452.73	433.92	402.62	390.63	387.39	384.46	373.44	366.55
51000	502.22	461.79	442.59	410.67	398.44	395.14	392.15	380.90	373.88
52000	512.07	470.84	451.27	418.72	406.25	402.89	399.84	388.37	381.21
53000	521.92	479.90	459.95	426.78	414.07	410.63	407.53	395.84	388.54
54000	531.76	488.95	468.63	434.83	421.88	418.38	415.22	403.31	395.88
55000	541.61	498.01	477.31	442.88	429.69	426.13	422.91	410.78	403.21
56000	551.46	507.06	485.99	450.93	437.50	433.88	430.60	418.25	410.54
57000	561.31	516.12	494.66	458.98	445.32	441.62	438.29	425.72	417.87
58000	571.15	525.17	503.34	467.04	453.13	449.37	445.97	433.18	425.20
59000	581.00	534.22	512.02	475.09	460.94	457.12	453.66	440.65	432.53
60000	590.85	543.28	520.70	483.14	468.75	464.87	461.35	448.12	439.86
61000	600.70	552.33	529.38	491.19	476.57	472.61	469.04	455.59	447.19
62000	610.54	561.39	538.06	499.25	484.38	480.36	476.73	463.06	454.52
63000	620.39	570.44	546.73	507.30	492.19	488.11	484.42	470.53	461.85
64000	630.24	579.50	555.41	515.35	500.00	495.86	492.11	478.00	469.19
65000	640.09	588.55	564.09	523.40	507.82	503.61	499.80	485.46	476.52
66000	649.93	597.61	572.77	531.45	515.63	511.35	507.49	492.93	483.85
67000	659.78	606.66	581.45	539.51	523.44	519.10	515.18	500.40	491.18
68000	669.63	615.72	590.12	547.56	531.25	526.85	522.87	507.87	498.51
69000	679.48	624.77	598.80	555.61	539.07	534.60	530.56	515.34	505.84
70000	689.32	633.83	607.48	563.66	546.88	542.34	538.24	522.81	513.17
75000	738.56	679.10	650.87	603.93	585.94	581.08	576.69	560.15	549.83
80000	787.80	724.37	694.26	644.19	625.00	619.82	615.14	597.49	586.48
100000	984.74	905.46	867.83	805.23	781.25	774.78	768.92	746.87	733.10

8⅝%

MONTHLY PAYMENT
NECESSARY TO AMORTIZE A LOAN

TERM / AMOUNT	1 YEAR	2 YEARS	3 YEARS	4 YEARS	5 YEARS	7 YEARS	8 YEARS	10 YEARS	12 YEARS
$ 25	2.19	1.14	.80	.62	.52	.40	.37	.32	.28
50	4.37	2.28	1.59	1.24	1.03	.80	.73	.63	.56
75	6.55	3.42	2.38	1.86	1.55	1.20	1.09	.94	.84
100	8.73	4.56	3.17	2.48	2.06	1.59	1.45	1.25	1.12
200	17.46	9.11	6.33	4.95	4.12	3.18	2.90	2.50	2.24
300	26.19	13.66	9.49	7.42	6.18	4.77	4.34	3.74	3.36
400	34.92	18.21	12.66	9.89	8.24	6.36	5.79	4.99	4.47
500	43.64	22.76	15.82	12.36	10.29	7.95	7.23	6.24	5.59
600	52.37	27.31	18.98	14.83	12.35	9.54	8.68	7.48	6.71
700	61.10	31.86	22.14	17.30	14.41	11.13	10.12	8.73	7.82
800	69.83	36.42	25.31	19.77	16.47	12.72	11.57	9.98	8.94
900	78.55	40.97	28.47	22.24	18.52	14.31	13.02	11.22	10.06
1000	87.28	45.52	31.63	24.71	20.58	15.90	14.46	12.47	11.18
2000	174.56	91.03	63.26	49.42	41.16	31.80	28.92	24.94	22.35
3000	261.84	136.54	94.88	74.13	61.74	47.70	43.37	37.40	33.52
4000	349.12	182.06	126.51	98.83	82.31	63.60	57.83	49.87	44.69
5000	436.39	227.57	158.13	123.54	102.89	79.50	72.29	62.33	55.86
6000	523.67	273.08	189.76	148.25	123.47	95.40	86.74	74.80	67.03
7000	610.95	318.60	221.38	172.96	144.04	111.30	101.20	87.26	78.20
8000	698.23	364.11	253.01	197.66	164.62	127.20	115.66	99.73	89.37
9000	785.50	409.62	284.63	222.37	185.20	143.10	130.11	112.19	100.54
10000	872.78	455.13	316.26	247.08	205.77	159.00	144.57	124.66	111.71
15000	1309.17	682.70	474.39	370.62	308.66	238.50	216.85	186.99	167.56
20000	1745.56	910.26	632.51	494.15	411.54	317.99	289.13	249.32	223.41
25000	2181.95	1137.83	790.64	617.69	514.43	397.49	361.42	311.64	279.26
30000	2618.34	1365.39	948.77	741.23	617.31	476.99	433.70	373.97	335.11
35000	3054.72	1592.96	1106.90	864.76	720.19	556.48	505.98	436.30	390.96
36000	3142.00	1638.47	1138.52	889.47	740.77	572.38	520.44	448.76	402.13
37000	3229.28	1683.98	1170.15	914.18	761.35	588.28	534.89	461.23	413.30
38000	3316.56	1729.49	1201.77	938.88	781.92	604.18	549.35	473.69	424.47
39000	3403.83	1775.01	1233.40	963.59	802.50	620.08	563.80	486.16	435.64
40000	3491.11	1820.52	1265.02	988.30	823.08	635.98	578.26	498.63	446.81
41000	3578.39	1866.03	1296.65	1013.01	843.66	651.88	592.72	511.09	457.98
42000	3665.67	1911.55	1328.28	1037.71	864.23	667.78	607.17	523.56	469.15
43000	3752.94	1957.06	1359.90	1062.42	884.81	683.68	621.63	536.02	480.32
44000	3840.22	2002.57	1391.53	1087.13	905.39	699.58	636.09	548.49	491.49
45000	3927.50	2048.08	1423.15	1111.84	925.96	715.48	650.54	560.95	502.66
46000	4014.78	2093.60	1454.78	1136.54	946.54	731.38	665.00	573.42	513.83
47000	4102.06	2139.11	1486.40	1161.25	967.12	747.28	679.46	585.88	525.00
48000	4189.33	2184.62	1518.03	1185.96	987.69	763.18	693.91	598.35	536.17
49000	4276.61	2230.14	1549.65	1210.67	1008.27	779.08	708.37	610.82	547.34
50000	4363.89	2275.65	1581.28	1235.37	1028.85	794.98	722.83	623.28	558.51
51000	4451.17	2321.16	1612.91	1260.08	1049.42	810.88	737.28	635.75	569.68
52000	4538.44	2366.67	1644.53	1284.79	1070.00	826.77	751.74	648.21	580.85
53000	4625.72	2412.19	1676.16	1309.50	1090.58	842.67	766.19	660.68	592.02
54000	4713.00	2457.70	1707.78	1334.20	1111.15	858.57	780.65	673.14	603.19
55000	4800.28	2503.21	1739.41	1358.91	1131.73	874.47	795.11	685.61	614.36
56000	4887.55	2548.73	1771.03	1383.62	1152.31	890.37	809.56	698.07	625.53
57000	4974.83	2594.24	1802.66	1408.32	1172.88	906.27	824.02	710.54	636.70
58000	5062.11	2639.75	1834.28	1433.03	1193.46	922.17	838.48	723.01	647.87
59000	5149.39	2685.26	1865.91	1457.74	1214.04	938.07	852.93	735.47	659.04
60000	5236.67	2730.78	1897.53	1482.45	1234.61	953.97	867.39	747.94	670.21
61000	5323.94	2776.29	1929.16	1507.15	1255.19	969.87	881.85	760.40	681.38
62000	5411.22	2821.80	1960.79	1531.86	1275.77	985.77	896.30	772.87	692.55
63000	5498.50	2867.32	1992.41	1556.57	1296.35	1001.67	910.76	785.33	703.72
64000	5585.78	2912.83	2024.04	1581.28	1316.92	1017.57	925.21	797.80	714.89
65000	5673.05	2958.34	2055.66	1605.98	1337.50	1033.47	939.67	810.26	726.06
66000	5760.33	3003.85	2087.29	1630.69	1358.08	1049.37	954.13	822.73	737.23
67000	5847.61	3049.37	2118.91	1655.40	1378.65	1065.27	968.58	835.19	748.40
68000	5934.89	3094.88	2150.54	1680.11	1399.23	1081.17	983.04	847.66	759.57
69000	6022.16	3140.39	2182.16	1704.81	1419.81	1097.06	997.50	860.13	770.75
70000	6109.44	3185.91	2213.79	1729.52	1440.38	1112.96	1011.95	872.59	781.92
75000	6545.83	3413.47	2371.92	1853.06	1543.27	1192.46	1084.24	934.92	837.77
80000	6982.22	3641.04	2530.04	1976.59	1646.15	1271.96	1156.52	997.25	893.62
100000	8727.77	4551.29	3162.55	2470.74	2057.69	1589.95	1445.65	1246.56	1117.02

MONTHLY PAYMENT $8\frac{5}{8}\%$

NECESSARY TO AMORTIZE A LOAN

TERM / AMOUNT	15 YEARS	18 YEARS	20 YEARS	25 YEARS	28 YEARS	29 YEARS	30 YEARS	35 YEARS	40 YEARS
$ 25	.25	.23	.22	.21	.20	.20	.20	.19	.19
50	.50	.46	.44	.41	.40	.40	.39	.38	.38
75	.75	.69	.66	.62	.60	.59	.59	.57	.56
100	1.00	.92	.88	.82	.79	.79	.78	.76	.75
200	1.99	1.83	1.76	1.63	1.58	1.57	1.56	1.52	1.49
300	2.98	2.74	2.63	2.45	2.37	2.36	2.34	2.27	2.23
400	3.97	3.66	3.51	3.26	3.16	3.14	3.12	3.03	2.98
500	4.97	4.57	4.38	4.07	3.95	3.92	3.89	3.79	3.72
600	5.96	5.48	5.26	4.89	4.74	4.71	4.67	4.54	4.46
700	6.95	6.40	6.14	5.70	5.53	5.49	5.45	5.30	5.20
800	7.94	7.31	7.01	6.51	6.32	6.27	6.23	6.05	5.95
900	8.93	8.22	7.89	7.33	7.11	7.06	7.01	6.81	6.69
1000	9.93	9.14	8.76	8.14	7.90	7.84	7.78	7.57	7.43
2000	19.85	18.27	17.52	16.28	15.80	15.68	15.56	15.13	14.86
3000	29.77	27.40	26.28	24.42	23.70	23.51	23.34	22.69	22.28
4000	39.69	36.53	35.04	32.55	31.60	31.35	31.12	30.25	29.71
5000	49.61	45.66	43.79	40.69	39.50	39.18	38.89	37.81	37.14
6000	59.53	54.79	52.55	48.83	47.40	47.02	46.67	45.37	44.56
7000	69.45	63.93	61.31	56.96	55.30	54.85	54.45	52.93	51.99
8000	79.37	73.06	70.07	65.10	63.20	62.69	62.23	60.49	59.41
9000	89.29	82.19	78.82	73.24	71.10	70.53	70.01	68.05	66.84
10000	99.21	91.32	87.58	81.37	79.00	78.36	77.78	75.61	74.27
15000	148.82	136.98	131.37	122.06	118.50	117.54	116.67	113.42	111.40
20000	198.42	182.64	175.16	162.74	158.00	156.72	155.56	151.22	148.53
25000	248.03	228.29	218.94	203.42	197.49	195.90	194.45	189.03	185.66
30000	297.63	273.95	262.73	244.11	236.99	235.07	233.34	226.83	222.79
35000	347.23	319.61	306.52	284.79	276.49	274.25	272.23	264.64	259.92
36000	357.15	328.74	315.28	292.93	284.39	282.09	280.01	272.20	267.35
37000	367.07	337.87	324.03	301.06	292.29	289.92	287.79	279.76	274.77
38000	377.00	347.01	332.79	309.20	300.19	297.76	295.57	287.32	282.20
39000	386.92	356.14	341.55	317.34	308.09	305.60	303.34	294.88	289.63
40000	396.84	365.27	350.31	325.47	315.99	313.43	311.12	302.44	297.05
41000	406.76	374.40	359.06	333.61	323.89	321.27	318.90	310.00	304.48
42000	416.68	383.53	367.82	341.75	331.79	329.10	326.68	317.57	311.90
43000	426.60	392.66	376.58	349.88	339.69	336.94	334.45	325.13	319.33
44000	436.52	401.79	385.34	358.02	347.59	344.77	342.23	332.69	326.76
45000	446.44	410.93	394.09	366.16	355.49	352.61	350.01	340.25	334.18
46000	456.36	420.06	402.85	374.29	363.39	360.45	357.79	347.81	341.61
47000	466.28	429.19	411.61	382.43	371.29	368.28	365.57	355.37	349.04
48000	476.20	438.32	420.37	390.57	379.19	376.12	373.34	362.93	356.46
49000	486.12	447.45	429.12	398.70	387.08	383.95	381.12	370.49	363.89
50000	496.05	456.58	437.88	406.84	394.98	391.79	388.90	378.05	371.31
51000	505.97	465.72	446.64	414.98	402.88	399.62	396.68	385.61	378.74
52000	515.89	474.85	455.40	423.11	410.78	407.46	404.46	393.17	386.17
53000	525.81	483.98	464.15	431.25	418.68	415.29	412.23	400.74	393.59
54000	535.73	493.11	472.91	439.39	426.58	423.13	420.01	408.30	401.02
55000	545.65	502.24	481.67	447.52	434.48	430.97	427.79	415.86	408.44
56000	555.57	511.37	490.43	455.66	442.38	438.80	435.57	423.42	415.87
57000	565.49	520.51	499.18	463.80	450.28	446.64	443.35	430.98	423.30
58000	575.41	529.64	507.94	471.93	458.18	454.47	451.12	438.54	430.72
59000	585.33	538.77	516.70	480.07	466.08	462.31	458.90	446.10	438.15
60000	595.25	547.90	525.46	488.21	473.98	470.14	466.68	453.66	445.58
61000	605.17	557.03	534.21	496.34	481.88	477.98	474.46	461.22	453.00
62000	615.09	566.16	542.97	504.48	489.78	485.82	482.23	468.78	460.43
63000	625.02	575.29	551.73	512.62	497.68	493.65	490.01	476.35	467.85
64000	634.94	584.43	560.49	520.75	505.58	501.49	497.79	483.91	475.28
65000	644.86	593.56	569.24	528.89	513.48	509.32	505.57	491.47	482.71
66000	654.78	602.69	578.00	537.03	521.38	517.16	513.35	499.03	490.13
67000	664.70	611.82	586.76	545.16	529.28	524.99	521.12	506.59	497.56
68000	674.62	620.95	595.52	553.30	537.18	532.83	528.90	514.15	504.98
69000	684.54	630.08	604.27	561.44	545.08	540.67	536.68	521.71	512.41
70000	694.46	639.22	613.03	569.57	552.98	548.50	544.46	529.27	519.84
75000	744.07	684.87	656.82	610.26	592.47	587.68	583.35	567.08	556.97
80000	793.67	730.53	700.61	650.94	631.97	626.86	622.24	604.88	594.10
100000	992.09	913.16	875.76	813.67	789.96	783.57	777.79	756.10	742.62

8¾% MONTHLY PAYMENT
NECESSARY TO AMORTIZE A LOAN

TERM / AMOUNT	1 YEAR	2 YEARS	3 YEARS	4 YEARS	5 YEARS	7 YEARS	8 YEARS	10 YEARS	12 YEARS
$ 25	2.19	1.14	.80	.62	.52	.40	.37	.32	.29
50	4.37	2.28	1.59	1.24	1.04	.80	.73	.63	.57
75	6.56	3.42	2.38	1.86	1.55	1.20	1.09	.94	.85
100	8.74	4.56	3.17	2.48	2.07	1.60	1.46	1.26	1.13
200	17.47	9.12	6.34	4.96	4.13	3.20	2.91	2.51	2.25
300	26.21	13.68	9.51	7.43	6.20	4.79	4.36	3.76	3.38
400	34.94	18.23	12.68	9.91	8.26	6.39	5.81	5.02	4.50
500	43.67	22.79	15.85	12.39	10.32	7.99	7.27	6.27	5.62
600	52.41	27.35	19.02	14.86	12.39	9.58	8.72	7.52	6.75
700	61.14	31.90	22.18	17.34	14.45	11.18	10.17	8.78	7.87
800	69.87	36.46	25.35	19.82	16.51	12.77	11.62	10.03	9.00
900	78.61	41.02	28.52	22.29	18.58	14.37	13.07	11.28	10.12
1000	87.34	45.58	31.69	24.77	20.64	15.97	14.53	12.54	11.24
2000	174.68	91.15	63.37	49.54	41.28	31.93	29.05	25.07	22.48
3000	262.01	136.72	95.06	74.30	61.92	47.89	43.57	37.60	33.72
4000	349.35	182.29	126.74	99.07	82.55	63.85	58.09	50.14	44.96
5000	436.68	227.86	158.42	123.84	103.19	79.82	72.61	62.67	56.20
6000	524.02	273.43	190.11	148.60	123.83	95.78	87.13	75.20	67.44
7000	611.35	319.00	221.79	173.37	144.47	111.74	101.65	87.73	78.68
8000	698.69	364.57	253.47	198.14	165.10	127.70	116.17	100.27	89.92
9000	786.03	410.14	285.16	222.90	185.74	143.67	130.69	112.80	101.16
10000	873.36	455.71	316.84	247.67	206.38	159.63	145.21	125.33	112.40
15000	1310.04	683.56	475.26	371.50	309.56	239.44	217.82	188.00	168.60
20000	1746.72	911.41	633.68	495.34	412.75	319.25	290.42	250.66	224.80
25000	2183.39	1139.26	792.09	619.17	515.94	399.07	363.03	313.32	281.00
30000	2620.07	1367.11	950.51	743.00	619.12	478.88	435.63	375.99	337.20
35000	3056.75	1594.96	1108.93	866.83	722.31	558.69	508.23	438.65	393.40
36000	3144.09	1640.53	1140.61	891.60	742.95	574.65	522.76	451.18	404.64
37000	3231.42	1686.10	1172.29	916.37	763.58	590.62	537.28	463.71	415.88
38000	3318.76	1731.67	1203.98	941.13	784.22	606.58	551.80	476.25	427.12
39000	3406.09	1777.24	1235.66	965.90	804.86	622.54	566.32	488.78	438.36
40000	3493.43	1822.81	1267.35	990.67	825.49	638.50	580.84	501.31	449.60
41000	3580.76	1868.38	1299.03	1015.43	846.13	654.47	595.36	513.84	460.84
42000	3668.10	1913.95	1330.71	1040.20	866.77	670.43	609.88	526.38	472.08
43000	3755.44	1959.52	1362.40	1064.96	887.41	686.39	624.40	538.91	483.32
44000	3842.77	2005.09	1394.08	1089.73	908.04	702.35	638.92	551.44	494.56
45000	3930.11	2050.66	1425.76	1114.50	928.68	718.32	653.44	563.98	505.80
46000	4017.44	2096.23	1457.45	1139.26	949.32	734.28	667.96	576.51	517.04
47000	4104.78	2141.80	1489.13	1164.03	969.95	750.24	682.48	589.04	528.28
48000	4192.11	2187.37	1520.81	1188.80	990.59	766.20	697.01	601.57	539.52
49000	4279.45	2232.94	1552.50	1213.56	1011.23	782.17	711.53	614.11	550.76
50000	4366.78	2278.51	1584.18	1238.33	1031.87	798.13	726.05	626.64	562.00
51000	4454.12	2324.08	1615.86	1263.10	1052.50	814.09	740.57	639.17	573.24
52000	4541.46	2369.65	1647.55	1287.86	1073.14	830.05	755.09	651.70	584.48
53000	4628.79	2415.22	1679.23	1312.63	1093.78	846.02	769.61	664.24	595.72
54000	4716.13	2460.79	1710.91	1337.40	1114.42	861.98	784.13	676.77	606.96
55000	4803.46	2506.36	1742.60	1362.16	1135.05	877.94	798.65	689.30	618.20
56000	4890.80	2551.93	1774.28	1386.93	1155.69	893.90	813.17	701.83	629.44
57000	4978.13	2597.50	1805.96	1411.70	1176.33	909.87	827.69	714.37	640.68
58000	5065.47	2643.07	1837.65	1436.46	1196.96	925.83	842.21	726.90	651.92
59000	5152.80	2688.64	1869.33	1461.23	1217.60	941.79	856.73	739.43	663.16
60000	5240.14	2734.21	1901.02	1486.00	1238.24	957.75	871.26	751.97	674.40
61000	5327.48	2779.78	1932.70	1510.76	1258.88	973.72	885.78	764.50	685.64
62000	5414.81	2825.35	1964.38	1535.53	1279.51	989.68	900.30	777.03	696.88
63000	5502.15	2870.92	1996.07	1560.29	1300.15	1005.64	914.82	789.56	708.12
64000	5589.48	2916.49	2027.75	1585.06	1320.79	1021.60	929.34	802.10	719.36
65000	5676.82	2962.06	2059.43	1609.83	1341.43	1037.57	943.86	814.63	730.60
66000	5764.15	3007.63	2091.12	1634.59	1362.06	1053.53	958.38	827.16	741.84
67000	5851.49	3053.20	2122.80	1659.36	1382.70	1069.49	972.90	839.69	753.08
68000	5938.82	3098.77	2154.48	1684.13	1403.34	1085.45	987.42	852.23	764.32
69000	6026.16	3144.34	2186.17	1708.89	1423.97	1101.42	1001.94	864.76	775.56
70000	6113.50	3189.91	2217.85	1733.66	1444.61	1117.38	1016.46	877.29	786.80
75000	6550.17	3417.76	2376.27	1857.49	1547.80	1197.19	1089.07	939.96	843.00
80000	6986.85	3645.61	2534.69	1981.33	1650.98	1277.00	1161.67	1002.62	899.20
100000	8733.56	4557.02	3168.36	2476.66	2063.73	1596.25	1452.09	1253.27	1124.00

MONTHLY PAYMENT 8¾%

NECESSARY TO AMORTIZE A LOAN

TERM / AMOUNT	15 YEARS	18 YEARS	20 YEARS	25 YEARS	28 YEARS	29 YEARS	30 YEARS	35 YEARS	40 YEARS
$ 25	.25	.24	.23	.21	.20	.20	.20	.20	.19
50	.50	.47	.45	.42	.40	.40	.40	.39	.38
75	.75	.70	.67	.62	.60	.60	.60	.58	.57
100	1.00	.93	.89	.83	.80	.80	.79	.77	.76
200	2.00	1.85	1.77	1.65	1.60	1.59	1.58	1.54	1.51
300	3.00	2.77	2.66	2.47	2.40	2.38	2.37	2.30	2.26
400	4.00	3.69	3.54	3.29	3.20	3.17	3.15	3.07	3.01
500	5.00	4.61	4.42	4.12	4.00	3.97	3.94	3.83	3.77
600	6.00	5.53	5.31	4.94	4.80	4.76	4.73	4.60	4.52
700	7.00	6.45	6.19	5.76	5.60	5.55	5.51	5.36	5.27
800	8.00	7.37	7.07	6.58	6.39	6.34	6.30	6.13	6.02
900	9.00	8.29	7.96	7.40	7.19	7.14	7.09	6.89	6.77
1000	10.00	9.21	8.84	8.23	7.99	7.93	7.87	7.66	7.53
2000	19.99	18.42	17.68	16.45	15.98	15.85	15.74	15.31	15.05
3000	29.99	27.63	26.52	24.67	23.97	23.78	23.61	22.97	22.57
4000	39.98	36.84	35.35	32.89	31.95	31.70	31.47	30.62	30.09
5000	49.98	46.05	44.19	41.11	39.94	39.62	39.34	38.27	37.61
6000	59.97	55.26	53.03	49.33	47.93	47.55	47.21	45.93	45.14
7000	69.97	64.47	61.86	57.56	55.91	55.47	55.07	53.58	52.66
8000	79.96	73.68	70.70	65.78	63.90	63.40	62.94	61.23	60.18
9000	89.96	82.89	79.54	74.00	71.89	71.32	70.81	68.89	67.70
10000	99.95	92.09	88.38	82.22	79.88	79.24	78.68	76.54	75.22
15000	149.92	138.14	132.56	123.33	119.81	118.86	118.01	114.81	112.83
20000	199.89	184.18	176.75	164.43	159.75	158.48	157.35	153.08	150.44
25000	249.87	230.23	220.93	205.54	199.68	198.10	196.68	191.35	188.05
30000	299.84	276.27	265.12	246.65	239.62	237.72	236.02	229.61	225.66
35000	349.81	322.32	309.30	287.76	279.55	277.34	275.35	267.88	263.26
36000	359.81	331.53	318.14	295.98	287.54	285.27	283.22	275.54	270.79
37000	369.80	340.73	326.98	304.20	295.53	293.19	291.08	283.19	278.31
38000	379.80	349.94	335.82	312.42	303.51	301.12	298.95	290.84	285.83
39000	389.79	359.15	344.65	320.64	311.50	309.04	306.82	298.50	293.35
40000	399.78	368.36	353.49	328.86	319.49	316.96	314.69	306.15	300.87
41000	409.78	377.57	362.33	337.08	327.47	324.89	322.55	313.80	308.39
42000	419.77	386.78	371.16	345.31	335.46	332.81	330.42	321.46	315.92
43000	429.77	395.99	380.00	353.53	343.45	340.74	338.29	329.11	323.44
44000	439.76	405.20	388.84	361.75	351.44	348.66	346.15	336.76	330.96
45000	449.76	414.41	397.67	369.97	359.42	356.58	354.02	344.42	338.48
46000	459.75	423.61	406.51	378.19	367.41	364.51	361.89	352.07	346.00
47000	469.75	432.82	415.35	386.41	375.40	372.43	369.75	359.73	353.53
48000	479.74	442.03	424.19	394.63	383.38	380.36	377.62	367.38	361.05
49000	489.73	451.24	433.02	402.86	391.37	388.28	385.49	375.03	368.57
50000	499.73	460.45	441.86	411.08	399.36	396.20	393.36	382.69	376.09
51000	509.72	469.66	450.70	419.30	407.34	404.13	401.22	390.34	383.61
52000	519.72	478.87	459.53	427.52	415.33	412.05	409.09	397.99	391.13
53000	529.71	488.08	468.37	435.74	423.32	419.97	416.96	405.65	398.66
54000	539.71	497.29	477.21	443.96	431.31	427.90	424.82	413.30	406.18
55000	549.70	506.49	486.05	452.18	439.29	435.82	432.69	420.95	413.70
56000	559.70	515.70	494.88	460.41	447.28	443.75	440.56	428.61	421.22
57000	569.69	524.91	503.72	468.63	455.27	451.67	448.42	436.26	428.74
58000	579.69	534.12	512.56	476.85	463.25	459.59	456.29	443.92	436.26
59000	589.68	543.33	521.39	485.07	471.24	467.52	464.16	451.57	443.79
60000	599.67	552.54	530.23	493.29	479.23	475.44	472.03	459.22	451.31
61000	609.67	561.75	539.07	501.51	487.22	483.37	479.89	466.88	458.83
62000	619.66	570.96	547.91	509.73	495.20	491.29	487.76	474.53	466.35
63000	629.66	580.17	556.74	517.96	503.19	499.21	495.63	482.18	473.87
64000	639.65	589.37	565.58	526.18	511.18	507.14	503.49	489.84	481.39
65000	649.65	598.58	574.42	534.40	519.16	515.06	511.36	497.49	488.92
66000	659.64	607.79	583.25	542.62	527.15	522.99	519.23	505.14	496.44
67000	669.64	617.00	592.09	550.84	535.14	530.91	527.09	512.80	503.96
68000	679.63	626.21	600.93	559.06	543.12	538.83	534.96	520.45	511.48
69000	689.62	635.42	609.77	567.28	551.11	546.76	542.83	528.11	519.00
70000	699.62	644.63	618.60	575.51	559.10	554.68	550.70	535.76	526.52
75000	749.59	690.67	662.79	616.61	599.03	594.30	590.03	574.03	564.13
80000	799.56	736.72	706.97	657.72	638.97	633.92	629.37	612.30	601.74
100000	999.45	920.90	883.72	822.15	798.71	792.40	786.71	765.37	752.18

8⅞%

MONTHLY PAYMENT
NECESSARY TO AMORTIZE A LOAN

TERM / AMOUNT	1 YEAR	2 YEARS	3 YEARS	4 YEARS	5 YEARS	7 YEARS	8 YEARS	10 YEARS	12 YEARS
$ 25	2.19	1.15	.80	.63	.52	.41	.37	.32	.29
50	4.37	2.29	1.59	1.25	1.04	.81	.73	.64	.57
75	6.56	3.43	2.39	1.87	1.56	1.21	1.10	.95	.85
100	8.74	4.57	3.18	2.49	2.07	1.61	1.46	1.27	1.14
200	17.48	9.13	6.35	4.97	4.14	3.21	2.92	2.53	2.27
300	26.22	13.69	9.53	7.45	6.21	4.81	4.38	3.79	3.40
400	34.96	18.26	12.70	9.94	8.28	6.42	5.84	5.05	4.53
500	43.70	22.82	15.88	12.42	10.35	8.02	7.30	6.31	5.66
600	52.44	27.38	19.05	14.90	12.42	9.62	8.76	7.57	6.79
700	61.18	31.94	22.22	17.38	14.49	11.22	10.21	8.83	7.92
800	69.92	36.51	25.40	19.87	16.56	12.83	11.67	10.09	9.05
900	78.66	41.07	28.57	22.35	18.63	14.43	13.13	11.35	10.18
1000	87.40	45.63	31.75	24.83	20.70	16.03	14.59	12.61	11.32
2000	174.79	91.26	63.49	49.66	41.40	32.06	29.18	25.21	22.63
3000	262.19	136.89	95.23	74.48	62.10	48.08	43.76	37.81	33.94
4000	349.58	182.51	126.97	99.31	82.80	64.11	58.35	50.41	45.25
5000	436.97	228.14	158.71	124.13	103.49	80.13	72.93	63.01	56.56
6000	524.37	273.77	190.45	148.96	124.19	96.16	87.52	75.61	67.87
7000	611.76	319.40	222.20	173.79	144.89	112.18	102.10	88.21	79.18
8000	699.15	365.02	253.94	198.61	165.59	128.21	116.69	100.81	90.49
9000	786.55	410.65	285.68	223.44	186.28	144.24	131.27	113.41	101.80
10000	873.94	456.28	317.42	248.26	206.98	160.26	145.86	126.01	113.11
15000	1310.91	684.42	476.13	372.39	310.47	240.39	218.79	189.01	169.66
20000	1747.88	912.55	634.84	496.52	413.96	320.52	291.71	252.01	226.21
25000	2184.84	1140.69	793.54	620.65	517.45	400.65	364.64	315.01	282.76
30000	2621.81	1368.83	952.25	744.78	620.94	480.78	437.57	378.01	339.31
35000	3058.78	1596.96	1110.96	868.91	724.43	560.90	510.50	441.01	395.86
36000	3146.17	1642.59	1142.70	893.73	745.12	576.93	525.08	453.61	407.17
37000	3233.57	1688.22	1174.44	918.56	765.82	592.96	539.67	466.21	418.48
38000	3320.96	1733.85	1206.19	943.38	786.52	608.98	554.25	478.81	429.79
39000	3408.35	1779.47	1237.93	968.21	807.22	625.01	568.84	491.41	441.10
40000	3495.75	1825.10	1269.67	993.03	827.91	641.03	583.42	504.01	452.41
41000	3583.14	1870.73	1301.41	1017.86	848.61	657.06	598.01	516.61	463.72
42000	3670.53	1916.36	1333.15	1042.69	869.31	673.08	612.59	529.21	475.03
43000	3757.93	1961.98	1364.89	1067.51	890.01	689.11	627.18	541.81	486.34
44000	3845.32	2007.61	1396.63	1092.34	910.71	705.14	641.76	554.41	497.65
45000	3932.71	2053.24	1428.38	1117.16	931.40	721.16	656.35	567.01	508.96
46000	4020.11	2098.87	1460.12	1141.99	952.10	737.19	670.94	579.61	520.27
47000	4107.50	2144.49	1491.86	1166.81	972.80	753.21	685.52	592.21	531.58
48000	4194.89	2190.12	1523.60	1191.64	993.50	769.24	700.11	604.81	542.89
49000	4282.29	2235.75	1555.34	1216.47	1014.19	785.26	714.69	617.41	554.20
50000	4369.68	2281.38	1587.08	1241.29	1034.89	801.29	729.28	630.01	565.51
51000	4457.07	2327.00	1618.83	1266.12	1055.59	817.32	743.86	642.61	576.82
52000	4544.47	2372.63	1650.57	1290.94	1076.29	833.34	758.45	655.21	588.13
53000	4631.86	2418.26	1682.31	1315.77	1096.99	849.37	773.03	667.81	599.44
54000	4719.26	2463.89	1714.05	1340.59	1117.68	865.39	787.62	680.41	610.75
55000	4806.65	2509.51	1745.79	1365.42	1138.38	881.42	802.20	693.01	622.06
56000	4894.04	2555.14	1777.53	1390.25	1159.08	897.44	816.79	705.61	633.37
57000	4981.44	2600.77	1809.28	1415.07	1179.78	913.47	831.38	718.21	644.68
58000	5068.83	2646.39	1841.02	1439.90	1200.47	929.50	845.96	730.81	655.99
59000	5156.22	2692.02	1872.76	1464.72	1221.17	945.52	860.55	743.41	667.30
60000	5243.62	2737.65	1904.50	1489.55	1241.87	961.55	875.13	756.01	678.61
61000	5331.01	2783.28	1936.24	1514.37	1262.57	977.57	889.72	768.61	689.92
62000	5418.40	2828.90	1967.98	1539.20	1283.26	993.60	904.30	781.21	701.23
63000	5505.80	2874.53	1999.73	1564.03	1303.96	1009.62	918.89	793.81	712.54
64000	5593.19	2920.16	2031.47	1588.85	1324.66	1025.65	933.47	806.41	723.85
65000	5680.58	2965.79	2063.21	1613.68	1345.36	1041.68	948.06	819.01	735.16
66000	5767.98	3011.41	2094.95	1638.50	1366.06	1057.70	962.64	831.61	746.47
67000	5855.37	3057.04	2126.69	1663.33	1386.75	1073.73	977.23	844.21	757.78
68000	5942.76	3102.67	2158.43	1688.15	1407.45	1089.75	991.81	856.81	769.09
69000	6030.16	3148.30	2190.17	1712.98	1428.15	1105.78	1006.40	869.41	780.40
70000	6117.55	3193.92	2221.92	1737.81	1448.85	1121.80	1020.99	882.01	791.71
75000	6554.52	3422.06	2380.62	1861.93	1552.34	1201.93	1093.91	945.01	848.26
80000	6991.49	3650.20	2539.33	1986.06	1655.82	1282.06	1166.84	1008.01	904.81
100000	8739.36	4562.75	3174.16	2482.58	2069.78	1602.58	1458.55	1260.01	1131.01

MONTHLY PAYMENT 8⅞%

NECESSARY TO AMORTIZE A LOAN

TERM / AMOUNT	15 YEARS	18 YEARS	20 YEARS	25 YEARS	28 YEARS	29 YEARS	30 YEARS	35 YEARS	40 YEARS
$ 25	.26	.24	.23	.21	.21	.21	.20	.20	.20
50	.51	.47	.45	.42	.41	.41	.40	.39	.39
75	.76	.70	.67	.63	.61	.61	.60	.59	.58
100	1.01	.93	.90	.84	.81	.81	.80	.78	.77
200	2.02	1.86	1.79	1.67	1.62	1.61	1.60	1.55	1.53
300	3.03	2.79	2.68	2.50	2.43	2.41	2.39	2.33	2.29
400	4.03	3.72	3.57	3.33	3.23	3.21	3.19	3.10	3.05
500	5.04	4.65	4.46	4.16	4.04	4.01	3.98	3.88	3.81
600	6.05	5.58	5.36	4.99	4.85	4.81	4.78	4.65	4.58
700	7.05	6.51	6.25	5.82	5.66	5.61	5.57	5.43	5.34
800	8.06	7.43	7.14	6.65	6.46	6.42	6.37	6.20	6.10
900	9.07	8.36	8.03	7.48	7.27	7.22	7.17	6.98	6.86
1000	10.07	9.29	8.92	8.31	8.08	8.02	7.96	7.75	7.62
2000	20.14	18.58	17.84	16.62	16.15	16.03	15.92	15.50	15.24
3000	30.21	27.86	26.76	24.92	24.23	24.04	23.87	23.24	22.86
4000	40.28	37.15	35.67	33.23	32.30	32.06	31.83	30.99	30.48
5000	50.35	46.44	44.59	41.54	40.38	40.07	39.79	38.74	38.09
6000	60.42	55.72	53.51	49.84	48.45	48.08	47.74	46.48	45.71
7000	70.48	65.01	62.42	58.15	56.53	56.09	55.70	54.23	53.33
8000	80.55	74.30	71.34	66.46	64.60	64.11	63.66	61.98	60.95
9000	90.62	83.58	80.26	74.76	72.68	72.12	71.61	69.72	68.56
10000	100.69	92.87	89.18	83.07	80.75	80.13	79.57	77.47	76.18
15000	151.03	139.30	133.76	124.60	121.13	120.19	119.35	116.20	114.27
20000	201.37	185.74	178.35	166.14	161.50	160.26	159.13	154.94	152.36
25000	251.72	232.17	222.93	207.67	201.88	200.32	198.92	193.67	190.44
30000	302.06	278.60	267.52	249.20	242.25	240.38	238.70	232.40	228.53
35000	352.40	325.03	312.10	290.73	282.62	280.45	278.48	271.14	266.62
36000	362.47	334.32	321.02	299.04	290.70	288.46	286.44	278.88	274.24
37000	372.54	343.61	329.93	307.35	298.77	296.47	294.39	286.63	281.85
38000	382.61	352.89	338.85	315.65	306.85	304.48	302.35	294.38	289.47
39000	392.67	362.18	347.77	323.96	314.92	312.50	310.31	302.12	297.09
40000	402.74	371.47	356.69	332.27	323.00	320.51	318.26	309.87	304.71
41000	412.81	380.75	365.60	340.57	331.07	328.52	326.22	317.62	312.32
42000	422.88	390.04	374.52	348.88	339.15	336.53	334.18	325.36	319.94
43000	432.95	399.33	383.44	357.19	347.22	344.55	342.13	333.11	327.56
44000	443.02	408.61	392.35	365.49	355.30	352.56	350.09	340.86	335.18
45000	453.08	417.90	401.27	373.80	363.37	360.57	358.05	348.60	342.79
46000	463.15	427.19	410.19	382.11	371.45	368.58	366.00	356.35	350.41
47000	473.22	436.47	419.11	390.41	379.52	376.60	373.96	364.10	358.03
48000	483.29	445.76	428.02	398.72	387.60	384.61	381.91	371.84	365.65
49000	493.36	455.04	436.94	407.03	395.67	392.62	389.87	379.59	373.26
50000	503.43	464.33	445.86	415.33	403.75	400.64	397.83	387.34	380.88
51000	513.50	473.62	454.77	423.64	411.82	408.65	405.78	395.08	388.50
52000	523.56	482.90	463.69	431.94	419.90	416.66	413.74	402.83	396.12
53000	533.63	492.19	472.61	440.25	427.97	424.67	421.70	410.58	403.73
54000	543.70	501.48	481.52	448.56	436.05	432.69	429.65	418.32	411.35
55000	553.77	510.76	490.44	456.86	444.12	440.70	437.61	426.07	418.97
56000	563.84	520.05	499.36	465.17	452.20	448.71	445.57	433.82	426.59
57000	573.91	529.34	508.28	473.48	460.27	456.72	453.52	441.56	434.20
58000	583.97	538.62	517.19	481.78	468.35	464.74	461.48	449.31	441.82
59000	594.04	547.91	526.11	490.09	476.42	472.75	469.44	457.06	449.44
60000	604.11	557.20	535.03	498.40	484.50	480.76	477.39	464.80	457.06
61000	614.18	566.48	543.94	506.70	492.57	488.77	485.35	472.55	464.67
62000	624.25	575.77	552.86	515.01	500.65	496.79	493.30	480.30	472.29
63000	634.32	585.06	561.78	523.32	508.72	504.80	501.26	488.04	479.91
64000	644.39	594.34	570.69	531.62	516.80	512.81	509.22	495.79	487.53
65000	654.45	603.63	579.61	539.93	524.87	520.82	517.17	503.54	495.14
66000	664.52	612.92	588.53	548.24	532.95	528.84	525.13	511.28	502.76
67000	674.59	622.20	597.45	556.54	541.02	536.85	533.09	519.03	510.38
68000	684.66	631.49	606.36	564.85	549.10	544.86	541.04	526.78	518.00
69000	694.73	640.78	615.28	573.16	557.17	552.87	549.00	534.52	525.61
70000	704.80	650.06	624.20	581.46	565.24	560.89	556.96	542.27	533.23
75000	755.14	696.49	668.78	622.99	605.62	600.95	596.74	581.00	571.32
80000	805.48	742.93	713.37	664.53	645.99	641.01	636.52	619.74	609.41
100000	1006.85	928.66	891.71	830.66	807.49	801.27	795.65	774.67	761.76

9% MONTHLY PAYMENT
NECESSARY TO AMORTIZE A LOAN

TERM / AMOUNT	1 YEAR	2 YEARS	3 YEARS	4 YEARS	5 YEARS	7 YEARS	8 YEARS	10 YEARS	12 YEARS
$ 25	2.19	1.15	.80	.63	.52	.41	.37	.32	.29
50	4.38	2.29	1.59	1.25	1.04	.81	.74	.64	.57
75	6.56	3.43	2.39	1.87	1.56	1.21	1.10	.96	.86
100	8.75	4.57	3.18	2.49	2.08	1.61	1.47	1.27	1.14
200	17.50	9.14	6.36	4.98	4.16	3.22	2.94	2.54	2.28
300	26.24	13.71	9.54	7.47	6.23	4.83	4.40	3.81	3.42
400	34.99	18.28	12.72	9.96	8.31	6.44	5.87	5.07	4.56
500	43.73	22.85	15.90	12.45	10.38	8.05	7.33	6.34	5.70
600	52.48	27.42	19.08	14.94	12.46	9.66	8.80	7.61	6.83
700	61.22	31.98	22.26	17.42	14.54	11.27	10.26	8.87	7.97
800	69.97	36.55	25.44	19.91	16.61	12.88	11.73	10.14	9.11
900	78.71	41.12	28.62	22.40	18.69	14.49	13.19	11.41	10.25
1000	87.46	45.69	31.80	24.89	20.76	16.09	14.66	12.67	11.39
2000	174.91	91.37	63.60	49.78	41.52	32.18	29.31	25.34	22.77
3000	262.36	137.06	95.40	74.66	62.28	48.27	43.96	38.01	34.15
4000	349.81	182.74	127.20	99.55	83.04	64.36	58.61	50.68	45.53
5000	437.26	228.43	159.00	124.43	103.80	80.45	73.26	63.34	56.91
6000	524.71	274.11	190.80	149.32	124.56	96.54	87.91	76.01	68.29
7000	612.17	319.80	222.60	174.20	145.31	112.63	102.56	88.68	79.67
8000	699.62	365.48	254.40	199.09	166.07	128.72	117.21	101.35	91.05
9000	787.07	411.17	286.20	223.97	186.83	144.81	131.86	114.01	102.43
10000	874.52	456.85	318.00	248.86	207.59	160.90	146.51	126.68	113.81
15000	1311.78	685.28	477.00	373.28	311.38	241.34	219.76	190.02	170.71
20000	1749.03	913.70	636.00	497.71	415.17	321.79	293.01	253.36	227.61
25000	2186.29	1142.12	795.00	622.13	518.96	402.23	366.26	316.69	284.51
30000	2623.55	1370.55	954.00	746.56	622.76	482.68	439.51	380.03	341.41
35000	3060.81	1598.97	1113.00	870.98	726.55	563.12	512.76	443.37	398.32
36000	3148.26	1644.66	1144.80	895.87	747.31	579.21	527.41	456.04	409.70
37000	3235.71	1690.34	1176.60	920.75	768.06	595.30	542.06	468.71	421.08
38000	3323.16	1736.03	1208.39	945.64	788.82	611.39	556.71	481.37	432.46
39000	3410.61	1781.71	1240.19	970.52	809.58	627.48	571.36	494.04	443.84
40000	3498.06	1827.39	1271.99	995.41	830.34	643.57	586.01	506.71	455.22
41000	3585.52	1873.08	1303.79	1020.29	851.10	659.66	600.66	519.38	466.60
42000	3672.97	1918.76	1335.59	1045.18	871.86	675.75	615.31	532.04	477.98
43000	3760.42	1964.45	1367.39	1070.06	892.61	691.84	629.96	544.71	489.36
44000	3847.87	2010.13	1399.19	1094.95	913.37	707.92	644.61	557.38	500.74
45000	3935.32	2055.82	1430.99	1119.83	934.13	724.01	659.26	570.05	512.12
46000	4022.77	2101.50	1462.79	1144.72	954.89	740.10	673.91	582.71	523.50
47000	4110.22	2147.19	1494.59	1169.60	975.65	756.19	688.56	595.38	534.88
48000	4197.68	2192.87	1526.39	1194.49	996.41	772.28	703.21	608.05	546.26
49000	4285.13	2238.56	1558.19	1219.37	1017.16	788.37	717.86	620.72	557.64
50000	4372.58	2284.24	1589.99	1244.26	1037.92	804.46	732.52	633.38	569.02
51000	4460.03	2329.93	1621.79	1269.14	1058.68	820.55	747.17	646.05	580.40
52000	4547.48	2375.61	1653.59	1294.03	1079.44	836.64	761.82	658.72	591.78
53000	4634.93	2421.30	1685.39	1318.91	1100.20	852.73	776.47	671.39	603.16
54000	4722.38	2466.98	1717.19	1343.80	1120.96	868.82	791.12	684.05	614.54
55000	4809.84	2512.67	1748.99	1368.68	1141.71	884.90	805.77	696.72	625.92
56000	4897.29	2558.35	1780.79	1393.57	1162.47	900.99	820.42	709.39	637.30
57000	4984.74	2604.04	1812.59	1418.45	1183.23	917.08	835.07	722.06	648.68
58000	5072.19	2649.72	1844.39	1443.34	1203.99	933.17	849.72	734.72	660.06
59000	5159.64	2695.40	1876.19	1468.22	1224.75	949.26	864.37	747.39	671.44
60000	5247.09	2741.09	1907.99	1493.11	1245.51	965.35	879.02	760.06	682.82
61000	5334.55	2786.77	1939.79	1517.99	1266.26	981.44	893.67	772.73	694.20
62000	5422.00	2832.46	1971.59	1542.88	1287.02	997.53	908.32	785.39	705.58
63000	5509.45	2878.14	2003.39	1567.76	1307.78	1013.62	922.97	798.06	716.96
64000	5596.90	2923.83	2035.19	1592.65	1328.54	1029.71	937.62	810.73	728.34
65000	5684.35	2969.51	2066.99	1617.53	1349.30	1045.80	952.27	823.40	739.72
66000	5771.80	3015.20	2098.79	1642.42	1370.06	1061.88	966.92	836.07	751.11
67000	5859.25	3060.88	2130.59	1667.30	1390.81	1077.97	981.57	848.73	762.49
68000	5946.71	3106.57	2162.39	1692.19	1411.57	1094.06	996.22	861.40	773.87
69000	6034.16	3152.25	2194.19	1717.07	1432.33	1110.15	1010.87	874.07	785.25
70000	6121.61	3197.94	2225.99	1741.96	1453.09	1126.24	1025.52	886.74	796.63
75000	6558.87	3426.36	2384.98	1866.38	1556.88	1206.69	1098.77	950.07	853.53
80000	6996.12	3654.78	2543.98	1990.81	1660.67	1287.13	1172.02	1013.41	910.43
100000	8745.15	4568.48	3179.98	2488.51	2075.84	1608.91	1465.03	1266.76	1138.04

MONTHLY PAYMENT 9%
NECESSARY TO AMORTIZE A LOAN

TERM / AMOUNT	15 YEARS	18 YEARS	20 YEARS	25 YEARS	28 YEARS	29 YEARS	30 YEARS	35 YEARS	40 YEARS
$ 25	.26	.24	.23	.21	.21	.21	.21	.20	.20
50	.51	.47	.45	.42	.41	.41	.41	.40	.39
75	.77	.71	.68	.63	.62	.61	.61	.59	.58
100	1.02	.94	.90	.84	.82	.82	.81	.79	.78
200	2.03	1.88	1.80	1.68	1.64	1.63	1.61	1.57	1.55
300	3.05	2.81	2.70	2.52	2.45	2.44	2.42	2.36	2.32
400	4.06	3.75	3.60	3.36	3.27	3.25	3.22	3.14	3.09
500	5.08	4.69	4.50	4.20	4.09	4.06	4.03	3.92	3.86
600	6.09	5.62	5.40	5.04	4.90	4.87	4.83	4.71	4.63
700	7.10	6.56	6.30	5.88	5.72	5.68	5.64	5.49	5.40
800	8.12	7.50	7.20	6.72	6.54	6.49	6.44	6.28	6.18
900	9.13	8.43	8.10	7.56	7.35	7.30	7.25	7.06	6.95
1000	10.15	9.37	9.00	8.40	8.17	8.11	8.05	7.84	7.72
2000	20.29	18.73	18.00	16.79	16.33	16.21	16.10	15.68	15.43
3000	30.43	28.10	27.00	25.18	24.49	24.31	24.14	23.52	23.15
4000	40.58	37.46	35.99	33.57	32.66	32.41	32.19	31.36	30.86
5000	50.72	46.83	44.99	41.96	40.82	40.51	40.24	39.20	38.57
6000	60.86	56.19	53.99	50.36	48.98	48.61	48.28	47.04	46.29
7000	71.00	65.56	62.99	58.75	57.15	56.72	56.33	54.88	54.00
8000	81.15	74.92	71.98	67.14	65.31	64.82	64.37	62.72	61.71
9000	91.29	84.29	80.98	75.53	73.47	72.92	72.42	70.56	69.43
10000	101.43	93.65	89.98	83.92	81.63	81.02	80.47	78.40	77.14
15000	152.14	140.47	134.96	125.88	122.45	121.53	120.70	117.60	115.71
20000	202.86	187.29	179.95	167.84	163.26	162.04	160.93	156.80	154.28
25000	253.57	234.12	224.94	209.80	204.08	202.54	201.16	196.00	192.85
30000	304.28	280.94	269.92	251.76	244.89	243.05	241.39	235.20	231.41
35000	355.00	327.76	314.91	293.72	285.71	283.56	281.62	274.40	269.98
36000	365.14	337.13	323.91	302.12	293.87	291.66	289.67	282.24	277.70
37000	375.28	346.49	332.90	310.51	302.04	299.76	297.72	290.08	285.41
38000	385.43	355.85	341.90	318.90	310.20	307.86	305.76	297.92	293.12
39000	395.57	365.22	350.90	327.29	318.36	315.97	313.81	305.76	300.84
40000	405.71	374.58	359.90	335.68	326.52	324.07	321.85	313.60	308.55
41000	415.85	383.95	368.89	344.08	334.69	332.17	329.90	321.44	316.26
42000	426.00	393.31	377.89	352.47	342.85	340.27	337.95	329.28	323.98
43000	436.14	402.68	386.89	360.86	351.01	348.37	345.99	337.12	331.69
44000	446.28	412.04	395.88	369.25	359.18	356.47	354.04	344.96	339.40
45000	456.42	421.41	404.88	377.64	367.34	364.58	362.09	352.80	347.12
46000	466.57	430.77	413.88	386.04	375.50	372.68	370.13	360.64	354.83
47000	476.71	440.13	422.88	394.43	383.67	380.78	378.18	368.48	362.54
48000	486.85	449.50	431.87	402.82	391.83	388.88	386.22	376.32	370.26
49000	497.00	458.86	440.87	411.21	399.99	396.98	394.27	384.16	377.97
50000	507.14	468.23	449.87	419.60	408.15	405.08	402.32	392.00	385.69
51000	517.28	477.59	458.87	428.00	416.32	413.19	410.36	399.84	393.40
52000	527.42	486.96	467.86	436.39	424.48	421.29	418.41	407.68	401.11
53000	537.57	496.32	476.86	444.78	432.64	429.39	426.45	415.52	408.83
54000	547.71	505.69	485.86	453.17	440.81	437.49	434.50	423.36	416.54
55000	557.85	515.05	494.85	461.56	448.97	445.59	442.55	431.20	424.25
56000	567.99	524.41	503.85	469.95	457.13	453.69	450.59	439.04	431.97
57000	578.14	533.78	512.85	478.35	465.30	461.79	458.64	446.88	439.68
58000	588.28	543.14	521.85	486.74	473.46	469.90	466.69	454.72	447.39
59000	598.42	552.51	530.84	495.13	481.62	478.00	474.73	462.56	455.11
60000	608.56	561.87	539.84	503.52	489.78	486.10	482.78	470.40	462.82
61000	618.71	571.24	548.84	511.91	497.95	494.20	490.82	478.24	470.54
62000	628.85	580.60	557.84	520.31	506.11	502.30	498.87	486.08	478.25
63000	638.99	589.97	566.83	528.70	514.27	510.40	506.92	493.92	485.96
64000	649.14	599.33	575.83	537.09	522.44	518.51	514.96	501.76	493.68
65000	659.28	608.69	584.83	545.48	530.60	526.61	523.01	509.60	501.39
66000	669.42	618.06	593.82	553.87	538.76	534.71	531.06	517.44	509.10
67000	679.56	627.42	602.82	562.27	546.93	542.81	539.10	525.28	516.82
68000	689.71	636.79	611.82	570.66	555.09	550.91	547.15	533.12	524.53
69000	699.85	646.15	620.82	579.05	563.25	559.01	555.19	540.96	532.24
70000	709.99	655.52	629.81	587.44	571.41	567.12	563.24	548.80	539.96
75000	760.70	702.34	674.80	629.40	612.23	607.62	603.47	588.00	578.53
80000	811.42	749.16	719.79	671.36	653.04	648.13	643.70	627.20	617.09
100000	1014.27	936.45	899.73	839.20	816.30	810.16	804.63	784.00	771.37

9⅛% MONTHLY PAYMENT

NECESSARY TO AMORTIZE A LOAN

TERM / AMOUNT	1 YEAR	2 YEARS	3 YEARS	4 YEARS	5 YEARS	7 YEARS	8 YEARS	10 YEARS	12 YEARS
$ 25	2.19	1.15	.80	.63	.53	.41	.37	.32	.29
50	4.38	2.29	1.60	1.25	1.05	.81	.74	.64	.58
75	6.57	3.44	2.39	1.88	1.57	1.22	1.11	.96	.86
100	8.76	4.58	3.19	2.50	2.09	1.62	1.48	1.28	1.15
200	17.51	9.15	6.38	4.99	4.17	3.24	2.95	2.55	2.30
300	26.26	13.73	9.56	7.49	6.25	4.85	4.42	3.83	3.44
400	35.01	18.30	12.75	9.98	8.33	6.47	5.89	5.10	4.59
500	43.76	22.88	15.93	12.48	10.41	8.08	7.36	6.37	5.73
600	52.51	27.45	19.12	14.97	12.50	9.70	8.83	7.65	6.88
700	61.26	32.02	22.31	17.47	14.58	11.31	10.31	8.92	8.02
800	70.01	36.60	25.49	19.96	16.66	12.93	11.78	10.19	9.17
900	78.76	41.17	28.68	22.45	18.74	14.54	13.25	11.47	10.31
1000	87.51	45.75	31.86	24.95	20.82	16.16	14.72	12.74	11.46
2000	175.02	91.49	63.72	49.89	41.64	32.31	29.44	25.48	22.91
3000	262.53	137.23	95.58	74.84	62.46	48.46	44.15	38.21	34.36
4000	350.04	182.97	127.44	99.78	83.28	64.62	58.87	50.95	45.81
5000	437.55	228.72	159.29	124.73	104.10	80.77	73.58	63.68	57.26
6000	525.06	274.46	191.15	149.67	124.92	96.92	88.30	76.42	68.71
7000	612.57	320.20	223.01	174.62	145.74	113.07	103.01	89.15	80.16
8000	700.08	365.94	254.87	199.56	166.56	129.23	117.73	101.89	91.61
9000	787.59	411.68	286.73	224.50	187.38	145.38	132.44	114.62	103.06
10000	875.10	457.43	318.58	249.45	208.20	161.53	147.16	127.36	114.51
15000	1312.65	686.14	477.87	374.17	312.29	242.29	220.73	191.03	171.77
20000	1750.19	914.85	637.16	498.89	416.39	323.06	294.31	254.71	229.02
25000	2187.74	1143.56	796.45	623.62	520.48	403.82	367.88	318.39	286.28
30000	2625.29	1372.27	955.74	748.34	624.58	484.58	441.46	382.06	343.53
35000	3062.84	1600.98	1115.03	873.06	728.67	565.35	515.03	445.74	400.78
36000	3150.35	1646.72	1146.89	898.00	749.49	581.50	529.75	458.48	412.23
37000	3237.85	1692.46	1178.75	922.95	770.31	597.65	544.46	471.21	423.69
38000	3325.36	1738.21	1210.61	947.89	791.13	613.80	559.18	483.95	435.14
39000	3412.87	1783.95	1242.46	972.84	811.95	629.96	573.90	496.68	446.59
40000	3500.38	1829.69	1274.32	997.78	832.77	646.11	588.61	509.42	458.04
41000	3587.89	1875.43	1306.18	1022.73	853.59	662.26	603.33	522.15	469.49
42000	3675.40	1921.17	1338.04	1047.67	874.41	678.41	618.04	534.89	480.94
43000	3762.91	1966.92	1369.90	1072.62	895.23	694.57	632.76	547.62	492.39
44000	3850.42	2012.66	1401.75	1097.56	916.04	710.72	647.47	560.36	503.84
45000	3937.93	2058.40	1433.61	1122.50	936.86	726.87	662.19	573.09	515.29
46000	4025.44	2104.14	1465.47	1147.45	957.68	743.02	676.90	585.83	526.74
47000	4112.95	2149.88	1497.33	1172.39	978.50	759.18	691.62	598.57	538.19
48000	4200.46	2195.63	1529.19	1197.34	999.32	775.33	706.33	611.30	549.64
49000	4287.97	2241.37	1561.04	1222.28	1020.14	791.48	721.05	624.04	561.10
50000	4375.48	2287.11	1592.90	1247.23	1040.96	807.63	735.76	636.77	572.55
51000	4462.99	2332.85	1624.76	1272.17	1061.78	823.79	750.48	649.51	584.00
52000	4550.50	2378.60	1656.62	1297.12	1082.60	839.94	765.19	662.24	595.45
53000	4638.01	2424.34	1688.48	1322.06	1103.42	856.09	779.91	674.98	606.90
54000	4725.52	2470.08	1720.33	1347.00	1124.24	872.24	794.62	687.71	618.35
55000	4813.02	2515.82	1752.19	1371.95	1145.05	888.40	809.34	700.45	629.80
56000	4900.53	2561.56	1784.05	1396.89	1165.87	904.55	824.05	713.18	641.25
57000	4988.04	2607.31	1815.91	1421.84	1186.69	920.70	838.77	725.92	652.70
58000	5075.55	2653.05	1847.77	1446.78	1207.51	936.86	853.48	738.65	664.15
59000	5163.06	2698.79	1879.62	1471.73	1228.33	953.01	868.20	751.39	675.60
60000	5250.57	2744.53	1911.48	1496.67	1249.15	969.16	882.91	764.12	687.05
61000	5338.08	2790.27	1943.34	1521.62	1269.97	985.31	897.63	776.86	698.51
62000	5425.59	2836.02	1975.20	1546.56	1290.79	1001.47	912.34	789.60	709.96
63000	5513.10	2881.76	2007.06	1571.50	1311.61	1017.62	927.06	802.33	721.41
64000	5600.61	2927.50	2038.91	1596.45	1332.43	1033.77	941.77	815.07	732.86
65000	5688.12	2973.24	2070.77	1621.39	1353.24	1049.92	956.49	827.80	744.31
66000	5775.63	3018.98	2102.63	1646.34	1374.06	1066.08	971.20	840.54	755.76
67000	5863.14	3064.73	2134.49	1671.28	1394.88	1082.23	985.92	853.27	767.21
68000	5950.65	3110.47	2166.35	1696.23	1415.70	1098.38	1000.63	866.01	778.66
69000	6038.16	3156.21	2198.20	1721.17	1436.52	1114.53	1015.35	878.74	790.11
70000	6125.67	3201.95	2230.06	1746.12	1457.34	1130.69	1030.06	891.48	801.56
75000	6563.21	3430.66	2389.35	1870.84	1561.44	1211.45	1103.64	955.15	858.82
80000	7000.76	3659.37	2548.64	1995.56	1665.53	1292.21	1177.22	1018.83	916.07
100000	8750.95	4574.22	3185.80	2494.45	2081.91	1615.26	1471.52	1273.54	1145.09

MONTHLY PAYMENT 9⅛%
NECESSARY TO AMORTIZE A LOAN

TERM / AMOUNT	15 YEARS	18 YEARS	20 YEARS	25 YEARS	28 YEARS	29 YEARS	30 YEARS	35 YEARS	40 YEARS
$ 25	.26	.24	.23	.22	.21	.21	.21	.20	.20
50	.52	.48	.46	.43	.42	.41	.41	.40	.40
75	.77	.71	.69	.64	.62	.62	.62	.60	.59
100	1.03	.95	.91	.85	.83	.82	.82	.80	.79
200	2.05	1.89	1.82	1.70	1.66	1.64	1.63	1.59	1.57
300	3.07	2.84	2.73	2.55	2.48	2.46	2.45	2.39	2.35
400	4.09	3.78	3.64	3.40	3.31	3.28	3.26	3.18	3.13
500	5.11	4.73	4.54	4.24	4.13	4.10	4.07	3.97	3.91
600	6.14	5.67	5.45	5.09	4.96	4.92	4.89	4.77	4.69
700	7.16	6.61	6.36	5.94	5.78	5.74	5.70	5.56	5.47
800	8.18	7.56	7.27	6.79	6.61	6.56	6.51	6.35	6.25
900	9.20	8.50	8.18	7.63	7.43	7.38	7.33	7.15	7.03
1000	10.22	9.45	9.08	8.48	8.26	8.20	8.14	7.94	7.81
2000	20.44	18.89	18.16	16.96	16.51	16.39	16.28	15.87	15.62
3000	30.66	28.33	27.24	25.44	24.76	24.58	24.41	23.81	23.43
4000	40.87	37.78	36.32	33.92	33.01	32.77	32.55	31.74	31.24
5000	51.09	47.22	45.39	42.39	41.26	40.96	40.69	39.67	39.05
6000	61.31	56.66	54.47	50.87	49.51	49.15	48.82	47.61	46.86
7000	71.53	66.10	63.55	59.35	57.77	57.34	56.96	55.54	54.67
8000	81.74	75.55	72.63	67.83	66.02	65.53	65.10	63.47	62.48
9000	91.96	84.99	81.71	76.30	74.27	73.72	73.23	71.41	70.29
10000	102.18	94.43	90.78	84.78	82.52	81.91	81.37	79.34	78.10
15000	153.26	141.65	136.17	127.17	123.78	122.87	122.05	119.01	117.15
20000	204.35	188.86	181.56	169.56	165.03	163.82	162.73	158.68	156.20
25000	255.43	236.07	226.95	211.95	206.29	204.78	203.41	198.34	195.25
30000	306.52	283.29	272.34	254.34	247.55	245.73	244.09	238.01	234.30
35000	357.61	330.50	317.73	296.73	288.81	286.69	284.78	277.68	273.35
36000	367.82	339.94	326.81	305.20	297.06	294.88	292.91	285.61	281.16
37000	378.04	349.38	335.88	313.68	305.31	303.07	301.05	293.55	288.97
38000	388.26	358.83	344.96	322.16	313.56	311.26	309.19	301.48	296.78
39000	398.47	368.27	354.04	330.64	321.81	319.45	317.32	309.41	304.59
40000	408.69	377.71	363.12	339.11	330.06	327.64	325.46	317.35	312.40
41000	418.91	387.15	372.20	347.59	338.32	335.83	333.59	325.28	320.21
42000	429.13	396.60	381.27	356.07	346.57	344.02	341.73	333.21	328.02
43000	439.34	406.04	390.35	364.55	354.82	352.21	349.87	341.15	335.83
44000	449.56	415.48	399.43	373.02	363.07	360.40	358.00	349.08	343.64
45000	459.78	424.93	408.51	381.50	371.32	368.59	366.14	357.01	351.45
46000	469.99	434.37	417.58	389.98	379.57	376.79	374.28	364.95	359.26
47000	480.21	443.81	426.66	398.46	387.82	384.98	382.41	372.88	367.07
48000	490.43	453.25	435.74	406.94	396.08	393.17	390.55	380.81	374.88
49000	500.65	462.70	444.82	415.41	404.33	401.36	398.69	388.75	382.69
50000	510.86	472.14	453.90	423.89	412.58	409.55	406.82	396.68	390.50
51000	521.08	481.58	462.97	432.37	420.83	417.74	414.96	404.62	398.31
52000	531.30	491.02	472.05	440.85	429.08	425.93	423.09	412.55	406.12
53000	541.51	500.47	481.13	449.32	437.33	434.12	431.23	420.48	413.93
54000	551.73	509.91	490.21	457.80	445.58	442.31	439.37	428.42	421.74
55000	561.95	519.35	499.28	466.28	453.84	450.50	447.50	436.35	429.55
56000	572.17	528.79	508.36	474.76	462.09	458.69	455.64	444.28	437.36
57000	582.38	538.24	517.44	483.24	470.34	466.89	463.78	452.22	445.17
58000	592.60	547.68	526.52	491.71	478.59	475.08	471.91	460.15	452.98
59000	602.82	557.12	535.60	500.19	486.84	483.27	480.05	468.08	460.79
60000	613.03	566.57	544.67	508.67	495.09	491.46	488.18	476.02	468.60
61000	623.25	576.01	553.75	517.15	503.34	499.65	496.32	483.95	476.41
62000	633.47	585.45	562.83	525.62	511.60	507.84	504.46	491.88	484.22
63000	643.69	594.89	571.91	534.10	519.85	516.03	512.59	499.82	492.03
64000	653.90	604.34	580.98	542.58	528.10	524.22	520.73	507.75	499.84
65000	664.12	613.78	590.06	551.06	536.35	532.41	528.87	515.68	507.65
66000	674.34	623.22	599.14	559.53	544.60	540.60	537.00	523.62	515.46
67000	684.55	632.66	608.22	568.01	552.85	548.79	545.14	531.55	523.27
68000	694.77	642.11	617.30	576.49	561.10	556.98	553.28	539.49	531.08
69000	704.99	651.55	626.37	584.97	569.36	565.18	561.41	547.42	538.89
70000	715.21	660.99	635.45	593.45	577.61	573.37	569.55	555.35	546.70
75000	766.29	708.21	680.84	635.83	618.87	614.32	610.23	595.02	585.75
80000	817.38	755.42	726.23	678.22	660.12	655.28	650.91	634.69	624.80
100000	1021.72	944.27	907.79	847.78	825.15	819.09	813.64	793.36	781.00

9¼% MONTHLY PAYMENT
NECESSARY TO AMORTIZE A LOAN

TERM / AMOUNT	1 YEAR	2 YEARS	3 YEARS	4 YEARS	5 YEARS	7 YEARS	8 YEARS	10 YEARS	12 YEARS
$ 25	2.19	1.15	.80	.63	.53	.41	.37	.33	.29
50	4.38	2.29	1.60	1.26	1.05	.82	.74	.65	.58
75	6.57	3.44	2.40	1.88	1.57	1.22	1.11	.97	.87
100	8.76	4.58	3.20	2.51	2.09	1.63	1.48	1.29	1.16
200	17.52	9.16	6.39	5.01	4.18	3.25	2.96	2.57	2.31
300	26.28	13.74	9.58	7.51	6.27	4.87	4.44	3.85	3.46
400	35.03	18.32	12.77	10.01	8.36	6.49	5.92	5.13	4.61
500	43.79	22.90	15.96	12.51	10.44	8.11	7.40	6.41	5.77
600	52.55	27.48	19.15	15.01	12.53	9.73	8.87	7.69	6.92
700	61.30	32.06	22.35	17.51	14.62	11.36	10.35	8.97	8.07
800	70.06	36.64	25.54	20.01	16.71	12.98	11.83	10.25	9.22
900	78.82	41.22	28.73	22.51	18.80	14.60	13.31	11.53	10.37
1000	87.57	45.80	31.92	25.01	20.88	16.22	14.79	12.81	11.53
2000	175.14	91.60	63.84	50.01	41.76	32.44	29.57	25.61	23.05
3000	262.71	137.40	95.75	75.02	62.64	48.65	44.35	38.41	34.57
4000	350.27	183.20	127.67	100.02	83.52	64.87	59.13	51.22	46.09
5000	437.84	229.00	159.59	125.02	104.40	81.09	73.91	64.02	57.61
6000	525.41	274.80	191.50	150.03	125.28	97.30	88.69	76.82	69.13
7000	612.98	320.60	223.42	175.03	146.16	113.52	103.47	89.63	80.66
8000	700.54	366.40	255.33	200.04	167.04	129.73	118.25	102.43	92.18
9000	788.11	412.20	287.25	225.04	187.92	145.95	133.03	115.23	103.70
10000	875.68	458.00	319.17	250.04	208.80	162.17	147.81	128.04	115.22
15000	1313.52	687.00	478.75	375.06	313.20	243.25	221.71	192.05	172.83
20000	1751.35	916.00	638.33	500.08	417.60	324.33	295.61	256.07	230.44
25000	2189.19	1144.99	797.91	625.10	522.00	405.41	369.51	320.09	288.04
30000	2627.03	1373.99	957.49	750.12	626.40	486.49	443.41	384.10	345.65
35000	3064.87	1602.99	1117.07	875.14	730.80	567.57	517.31	448.12	403.26
36000	3152.43	1648.79	1148.99	900.15	751.68	583.79	532.09	460.92	414.78
37000	3240.00	1694.59	1180.90	925.15	772.56	600.01	546.87	473.73	426.30
38000	3327.57	1740.39	1212.82	950.15	793.44	616.22	561.65	486.53	437.82
39000	3415.14	1786.19	1244.74	975.16	814.32	632.44	576.43	499.33	449.35
40000	3502.70	1831.99	1276.65	1000.16	835.20	648.65	591.21	512.14	460.87
41000	3590.27	1877.79	1308.57	1025.17	856.08	664.87	605.99	524.94	472.39
42000	3677.84	1923.59	1340.49	1050.17	876.96	681.09	620.77	537.74	483.91
43000	3765.41	1969.38	1372.40	1075.17	897.84	697.30	635.55	550.55	495.43
44000	3852.97	2015.18	1404.32	1100.18	918.72	713.52	650.33	563.35	506.95
45000	3940.54	2060.98	1436.23	1125.18	939.60	729.74	665.11	576.15	518.48
46000	4028.11	2106.78	1468.15	1150.19	960.48	745.95	679.90	588.96	530.00
47000	4115.68	2152.58	1500.07	1175.19	981.36	762.17	694.68	601.76	541.52
48000	4203.24	2198.38	1531.98	1200.19	1002.24	778.38	709.46	614.56	553.04
49000	4290.81	2244.18	1563.90	1225.20	1023.12	794.60	724.24	627.37	564.56
50000	4378.38	2289.98	1595.82	1250.20	1044.00	810.82	739.02	640.17	576.08
51000	4465.95	2335.78	1627.73	1275.20	1064.88	827.03	753.80	652.97	587.60
52000	4553.51	2381.58	1659.65	1300.21	1085.76	843.25	768.58	665.78	599.13
53000	4641.08	2427.38	1691.56	1325.21	1106.64	859.47	783.36	678.58	610.65
54000	4728.65	2473.18	1723.48	1350.22	1127.52	875.68	798.14	691.38	622.17
55000	4816.21	2518.98	1755.40	1375.22	1148.40	891.90	812.92	704.18	633.69
56000	4903.78	2564.78	1787.31	1400.22	1169.28	908.11	827.70	716.99	645.21
57000	4991.35	2610.58	1819.23	1425.23	1190.16	924.33	842.48	729.79	656.73
58000	5078.92	2656.38	1851.15	1450.23	1211.04	940.55	857.26	742.59	668.26
59000	5166.48	2702.18	1883.06	1475.24	1231.92	956.76	872.04	755.40	679.78
60000	5254.05	2747.98	1914.98	1500.24	1252.80	972.98	886.82	768.20	691.30
61000	5341.62	2793.78	1946.89	1525.24	1273.68	989.20	901.60	781.00	702.82
62000	5429.19	2839.58	1978.81	1550.25	1294.56	1005.41	916.38	793.81	714.34
63000	5516.75	2885.38	2010.73	1575.25	1315.44	1021.63	931.16	806.61	725.86
64000	5604.32	2931.18	2042.64	1600.26	1336.32	1037.84	945.94	819.41	737.39
65000	5691.89	2976.97	2074.56	1625.26	1357.20	1054.06	960.72	832.22	748.91
66000	5779.46	3022.77	2106.48	1650.26	1378.08	1070.28	975.50	845.02	760.43
67000	5867.02	3068.57	2138.39	1675.27	1398.96	1086.49	990.28	857.82	771.95
68000	5954.59	3114.37	2170.31	1700.27	1419.84	1102.71	1005.06	870.63	783.47
69000	6042.16	3160.17	2202.22	1725.28	1440.72	1118.93	1019.84	883.43	794.99
70000	6129.73	3205.97	2234.14	1750.28	1461.60	1135.14	1034.62	896.23	806.51
75000	6567.56	3434.97	2393.72	1875.30	1566.00	1216.22	1108.52	960.25	864.12
80000	7005.40	3663.97	2553.30	2000.32	1670.40	1297.30	1182.42	1024.27	921.73
100000	8756.75	4579.96	3191.63	2500.40	2087.99	1621.63	1478.03	1280.33	1152.16

MONTHLY PAYMENT 9¼%
NECESSARY TO AMORTIZE A LOAN

TERM / AMOUNT	15 YEARS	18 YEARS	20 YEARS	25 YEARS	28 YEARS	29 YEARS	30 YEARS	35 YEARS	40 YEARS
$ 25	.26	.24	.23	.22	.21	.21	.21	.21	.20
50	.52	.48	.46	.43	.42	.42	.42	.41	.40
75	.78	.72	.69	.65	.63	.63	.62	.61	.60
100	1.03	.96	.92	.86	.84	.83	.83	.81	.80
200	2.06	1.91	1.84	1.72	1.67	1.66	1.65	1.61	1.59
300	3.09	2.86	2.75	2.57	2.51	2.49	2.47	2.41	2.38
400	4.12	3.81	3.67	3.43	3.34	3.32	3.30	3.22	3.17
500	5.15	4.77	4.58	4.29	4.18	4.15	4.12	4.02	3.96
600	6.18	5.72	5.50	5.14	5.01	4.97	4.94	4.82	4.75
700	7.21	6.67	6.42	6.00	5.84	5.80	5.76	5.62	5.54
800	8.24	7.62	7.33	6.86	6.68	6.63	6.59	6.43	6.33
900	9.27	8.57	8.25	7.71	7.51	7.46	7.41	7.23	7.12
1000	10.30	9.53	9.16	8.57	8.35	8.29	8.23	8.03	7.91
2000	20.59	19.05	18.32	17.13	16.69	16.57	16.46	16.06	15.82
3000	30.88	28.57	27.48	25.70	25.03	24.85	24.69	24.09	23.72
4000	41.17	38.09	36.64	34.26	33.37	33.13	32.91	32.11	31.63
5000	51.46	47.61	45.80	42.82	41.71	41.41	41.14	40.14	39.54
6000	61.76	57.13	54.96	51.39	50.05	49.69	49.37	48.17	47.44
7000	72.05	66.65	64.12	59.95	58.39	57.97	57.59	56.20	55.35
8000	82.34	76.17	73.27	68.52	66.73	66.25	65.82	64.22	63.26
9000	92.63	85.70	82.43	77.08	75.07	74.53	74.05	72.25	71.16
10000	102.92	95.22	91.59	85.64	83.41	82.81	82.27	80.28	79.07
15000	154.38	142.82	137.39	128.46	125.11	124.21	123.41	120.42	118.60
20000	205.84	190.43	183.18	171.28	166.81	165.62	164.54	160.55	158.14
25000	257.30	238.03	228.97	214.10	208.51	207.02	205.67	200.69	197.67
30000	308.76	285.64	274.77	256.92	250.21	248.42	246.81	240.83	237.20
35000	360.22	333.25	320.56	299.74	291.91	289.82	287.94	280.97	276.74
36000	370.51	342.77	329.72	308.30	300.25	298.10	296.17	288.99	284.64
37000	380.81	352.29	338.88	316.87	308.59	306.38	304.39	297.02	292.55
38000	391.10	361.81	348.03	325.43	316.94	314.66	312.62	305.05	300.46
39000	401.39	371.33	357.19	333.99	325.28	322.94	320.85	313.08	308.36
40000	411.68	380.85	366.35	342.56	333.62	331.23	329.08	321.10	316.27
41000	421.97	390.37	375.51	351.12	341.96	339.51	337.30	329.13	324.18
42000	432.27	399.90	384.67	359.69	350.30	347.79	345.53	337.16	332.08
43000	442.56	409.42	393.83	368.25	358.64	356.07	353.76	345.19	339.99
44000	452.85	418.94	402.99	376.81	366.98	364.35	361.98	353.21	347.90
45000	463.14	428.46	412.15	385.38	375.32	372.63	370.21	361.24	355.80
46000	473.43	437.98	421.30	393.94	383.66	380.91	378.44	369.27	363.71
47000	483.73	447.50	430.46	402.50	392.00	389.19	386.66	377.29	371.62
48000	494.02	457.02	439.62	411.07	400.34	397.47	394.89	385.32	379.52
49000	504.31	466.54	448.78	419.63	408.68	405.75	403.12	393.35	387.43
50000	514.60	476.06	457.94	428.20	417.02	414.03	411.34	401.38	395.34
51000	524.89	485.59	467.10	436.76	425.36	422.31	419.57	409.40	403.24
52000	535.18	495.11	476.26	445.32	433.70	430.59	427.80	417.43	411.15
53000	545.48	504.63	485.41	453.89	442.04	438.87	436.02	425.46	419.06
54000	555.77	514.15	494.57	462.45	450.38	447.15	444.25	433.49	426.96
55000	566.06	523.67	503.73	471.02	458.72	455.43	452.48	441.51	434.87
56000	576.35	533.19	512.89	479.58	467.06	463.71	460.70	449.54	442.77
57000	586.64	542.71	522.05	488.14	475.40	471.99	468.93	457.57	450.68
58000	596.94	552.23	531.21	496.71	483.74	480.27	477.16	465.60	458.59
59000	607.23	561.76	540.37	505.27	492.08	488.56	485.38	473.62	466.49
60000	617.52	571.28	549.53	513.83	500.42	496.84	493.61	481.65	474.40
61000	627.81	580.80	558.68	522.40	508.76	505.12	501.84	489.68	482.31
62000	638.10	590.32	567.84	530.96	517.10	513.40	510.06	497.71	490.21
63000	648.40	599.84	577.00	539.53	525.44	521.68	518.29	505.73	498.12
64000	658.69	609.36	586.16	548.09	533.78	529.96	526.52	513.76	506.03
65000	668.98	618.88	595.32	556.65	542.12	538.24	534.74	521.79	513.93
66000	679.27	628.40	604.48	565.22	550.46	546.52	542.97	529.82	521.84
67000	689.56	637.92	613.64	573.78	558.80	554.80	551.20	537.84	529.75
68000	699.86	647.45	622.79	582.34	567.14	563.08	559.42	545.87	537.65
69000	710.15	656.97	631.95	590.91	575.48	571.36	567.65	553.90	545.56
70000	720.44	666.49	641.11	599.47	583.82	579.64	575.88	561.93	553.47
75000	771.90	714.09	686.91	642.29	625.52	621.04	617.01	602.06	593.00
80000	823.36	761.70	732.70	685.11	667.23	662.45	658.15	642.20	632.53
100000	1029.20	952.12	915.87	856.39	834.03	828.06	822.68	802.75	790.67

9⅜% MONTHLY PAYMENT
NECESSARY TO AMORTIZE A LOAN

TERM / AMOUNT	1 YEAR	2 YEARS	3 YEARS	4 YEARS	5 YEARS	7 YEARS	8 YEARS	10 YEARS	12 YEARS
$ 25	2.20	1.15	.80	.63	.53	.41	.38	.33	.29
50	4.39	2.30	1.60	1.26	1.05	.82	.75	.65	.58
75	6.58	3.44	2.40	1.88	1.58	1.23	1.12	.97	.87
100	8.77	4.59	3.20	2.51	2.10	1.63	1.49	1.29	1.16
200	17.53	9.18	6.40	5.02	4.19	3.26	2.97	2.58	2.32
300	26.29	13.76	9.60	7.52	6.29	4.89	4.46	3.87	3.48
400	35.06	18.35	12.79	10.03	8.38	6.52	5.94	5.15	4.64
500	43.82	22.93	15.99	12.54	10.48	8.15	7.43	6.44	5.80
600	52.58	27.52	19.19	15.04	12.57	9.77	8.91	7.73	6.96
700	61.34	32.10	22.39	17.55	14.66	11.40	10.40	9.01	8.12
800	70.11	36.69	25.58	20.06	16.76	13.03	11.88	10.30	9.28
900	78.87	41.28	28.78	22.56	18.85	14.66	13.37	11.59	10.44
1000	87.63	45.86	31.98	25.07	20.95	16.29	14.85	12.88	11.60
2000	175.26	91.72	63.95	50.13	41.89	32.57	29.70	25.75	23.19
3000	262.88	137.58	95.93	75.20	62.83	48.85	44.54	38.62	34.78
4000	350.51	183.43	127.90	100.26	83.77	65.13	59.39	51.49	46.38
5000	438.13	229.29	159.88	125.32	104.71	81.41	74.23	64.36	57.97
6000	525.76	275.15	191.85	150.39	125.65	97.69	89.08	77.23	69.56
7000	613.38	321.00	223.83	175.45	146.59	113.97	103.92	90.10	81.15
8000	701.01	366.86	255.80	200.51	167.53	130.25	118.77	102.98	92.75
9000	788.63	412.72	287.78	225.58	188.47	146.53	133.61	115.85	104.34
10000	876.26	458.57	319.75	250.64	209.41	162.81	148.46	128.72	115.93
15000	1314.39	687.86	479.62	375.96	314.12	244.21	222.69	193.08	173.89
20000	1752.51	917.14	639.50	501.27	418.82	325.61	296.91	257.43	231.86
25000	2190.64	1146.43	799.37	626.59	523.53	407.01	371.14	321.79	289.82
30000	2628.77	1375.71	959.24	751.91	628.23	488.41	445.37	386.15	347.78
35000	3066.90	1605.00	1119.11	877.23	732.93	569.81	519.60	450.50	405.74
36000	3154.52	1650.86	1151.09	902.29	753.87	586.09	534.44	463.38	417.34
37000	3242.15	1696.71	1183.06	927.35	774.82	602.37	549.29	476.25	428.93
38000	3329.77	1742.57	1215.04	952.42	795.76	618.65	564.13	489.12	440.52
39000	3417.40	1788.43	1247.01	977.48	816.70	634.93	578.98	501.99	452.11
40000	3505.02	1834.28	1278.99	1002.54	837.64	651.21	593.82	514.86	463.71
41000	3592.65	1880.14	1310.96	1027.61	858.58	667.49	608.67	527.73	475.30
42000	3680.27	1926.00	1342.94	1052.67	879.52	683.77	623.51	540.60	486.89
43000	3767.90	1971.86	1374.91	1077.73	900.46	700.05	638.36	553.48	498.48
44000	3855.53	2017.71	1406.89	1102.80	921.40	716.33	653.21	566.35	510.08
45000	3943.15	2063.57	1438.86	1127.86	942.34	732.61	668.05	579.22	521.67
46000	4030.78	2109.43	1470.83	1152.93	963.28	748.89	682.90	592.09	533.26
47000	4118.40	2155.28	1502.81	1177.99	984.22	765.17	697.74	604.96	544.85
48000	4206.03	2201.14	1534.78	1203.05	1005.16	781.45	712.59	617.83	556.45
49000	4293.65	2247.00	1566.76	1228.12	1026.11	797.73	727.43	630.70	568.04
50000	4381.28	2292.85	1598.73	1253.18	1047.05	814.01	742.28	643.58	579.63
51000	4468.90	2338.71	1630.71	1278.24	1067.99	830.29	757.12	656.45	591.22
52000	4556.53	2384.57	1662.68	1303.31	1088.93	846.57	771.97	669.32	602.82
53000	4644.15	2430.43	1694.66	1328.37	1109.87	862.85	786.82	682.19	614.41
54000	4731.78	2476.28	1726.63	1353.43	1130.81	879.13	801.66	695.06	626.00
55000	4819.41	2522.14	1758.61	1378.50	1151.75	895.41	816.51	707.93	637.59
56000	4907.03	2568.00	1790.58	1403.56	1172.69	911.69	831.35	720.80	649.19
57000	4994.66	2613.85	1822.55	1428.62	1193.63	927.97	846.20	733.68	660.78
58000	5082.28	2659.71	1854.53	1453.69	1214.57	944.25	861.04	746.55	672.37
59000	5169.91	2705.57	1886.50	1478.75	1235.51	960.53	875.89	759.42	683.96
60000	5257.53	2751.42	1918.48	1503.81	1256.45	976.81	890.73	772.29	695.56
61000	5345.16	2797.28	1950.45	1528.88	1277.40	993.09	905.58	785.16	707.15
62000	5432.78	2843.14	1982.43	1553.94	1298.34	1009.37	920.42	798.03	718.74
63000	5520.41	2889.00	2014.40	1579.00	1319.28	1025.65	935.27	810.90	730.33
64000	5608.04	2934.85	2046.38	1604.07	1340.22	1041.93	950.12	823.78	741.93
65000	5695.66	2980.71	2078.35	1629.13	1361.16	1058.21	964.96	836.65	753.52
66000	5783.29	3026.57	2110.33	1654.20	1382.10	1074.49	979.81	849.52	765.11
67000	5870.91	3072.42	2142.30	1679.26	1403.04	1090.77	994.65	862.39	776.70
68000	5958.54	3118.28	2174.27	1704.32	1423.98	1107.05	1009.50	875.26	788.30
69000	6046.16	3164.14	2206.25	1729.39	1444.92	1123.33	1024.34	888.13	799.89
70000	6133.79	3209.99	2238.22	1754.45	1465.86	1139.61	1039.19	901.00	811.48
75000	6571.92	3439.28	2398.10	1879.77	1570.57	1221.01	1113.42	965.36	869.45
80000	7010.04	3668.56	2557.97	2005.08	1675.27	1302.41	1187.64	1029.72	927.41
100000	8762.55	4585.70	3197.46	2506.35	2094.09	1628.01	1484.55	1287.15	1159.26

MONTHLY PAYMENT $9\frac{3}{8}\%$

NECESSARY TO AMORTIZE A LOAN

TERM / AMOUNT	15 YEARS	18 YEARS	20 YEARS	25 YEARS	28 YEARS	29 YEARS	30 YEARS	35 YEARS	40 YEARS
$ 25	.26	.25	.24	.22	.22	.21	.21	.21	.21
50	.52	.49	.47	.44	.43	.42	.42	.41	.41
75	.78	.73	.70	.65	.64	.63	.63	.61	.61
100	1.04	.97	.93	.87	.85	.84	.84	.82	.81
200	2.08	1.93	1.85	1.74	1.69	1.68	1.67	1.63	1.61
300	3.12	2.89	2.78	2.60	2.53	2.52	2.50	2.44	2.41
400	4.15	3.85	3.70	3.47	3.38	3.35	3.33	3.25	3.21
500	5.19	4.81	4.62	4.33	4.22	4.19	4.16	4.07	4.01
600	6.23	5.77	5.55	5.20	5.06	5.03	5.00	4.88	4.81
700	7.26	6.73	6.47	6.06	5.91	5.86	5.83	5.69	5.61
800	8.30	7.69	7.40	6.93	6.75	6.70	6.66	6.50	6.41
900	9.34	8.65	8.32	7.79	7.59	7.54	7.49	7.31	7.21
1000	10.37	9.61	9.24	8.66	8.43	8.38	8.32	8.13	8.01
2000	20.74	19.21	18.48	17.31	16.86	16.75	16.64	16.25	16.01
3000	31.11	28.81	27.72	25.96	25.29	25.12	24.96	24.37	24.02
4000	41.47	38.41	36.96	34.61	33.72	33.49	33.27	32.49	32.02
5000	51.84	48.01	46.20	43.26	42.15	41.86	41.59	40.61	40.02
6000	62.21	57.61	55.44	51.91	50.58	50.23	49.91	48.73	48.03
7000	72.57	67.21	64.68	60.56	59.01	58.60	58.23	56.86	56.03
8000	82.94	76.81	73.92	69.21	67.44	66.97	66.54	64.98	64.03
9000	93.31	86.41	83.16	77.86	75.87	75.34	74.86	73.10	72.04
10000	103.67	96.01	92.40	86.51	84.30	83.71	83.18	81.22	80.04
15000	155.51	144.01	138.60	129.76	126.45	125.56	124.77	121.83	120.06
20000	207.34	192.01	184.80	173.01	168.59	167.41	166.35	162.44	160.07
25000	259.18	240.01	231.00	216.26	210.74	209.27	207.94	203.05	200.09
30000	311.01	288.01	277.20	259.51	252.89	251.12	249.53	243.65	240.11
35000	362.85	336.01	323.40	302.76	295.03	292.97	291.12	284.26	280.13
36000	373.22	345.61	332.64	311.41	303.46	301.34	299.43	292.38	288.13
37000	383.58	355.21	341.88	320.06	311.89	309.71	307.75	300.51	296.13
38000	393.95	364.81	351.12	328.71	320.32	318.08	316.07	308.63	304.14
39000	404.32	374.41	360.36	337.36	328.75	326.45	324.39	316.75	312.14
40000	414.68	384.01	369.60	346.01	337.18	334.82	332.70	324.87	320.14
41000	425.05	393.61	378.84	354.66	345.61	343.19	341.02	332.99	328.15
42000	435.42	403.21	388.08	363.31	354.04	351.56	349.34	341.11	336.15
43000	445.78	412.81	397.32	371.97	362.47	359.93	357.66	349.24	344.15
44000	456.15	422.41	406.56	380.62	370.90	368.31	365.97	357.36	352.16
45000	466.52	432.01	415.80	389.27	379.33	376.68	374.29	365.48	360.16
46000	476.88	441.61	425.04	397.92	387.76	385.05	382.61	373.60	368.17
47000	487.25	451.21	434.28	406.57	396.19	393.42	390.93	381.72	376.17
48000	497.62	460.81	443.52	415.22	404.62	401.79	399.24	389.84	384.17
49000	507.99	470.41	452.76	423.87	413.04	410.16	407.56	397.97	392.18
50000	518.35	480.01	462.00	432.52	421.47	418.53	415.88	406.09	400.18
51000	528.72	489.61	471.24	441.17	429.90	426.90	424.20	414.21	408.18
52000	539.09	499.21	480.48	449.82	438.33	435.27	432.51	422.33	416.19
53000	549.45	508.81	489.72	458.47	446.76	443.64	440.83	430.45	424.19
54000	559.82	518.41	498.96	467.12	455.19	452.01	449.15	438.57	432.19
55000	570.19	528.01	508.20	475.77	463.62	460.38	457.47	446.70	440.20
56000	580.55	537.61	517.44	484.42	472.05	468.75	465.78	454.82	448.20
57000	590.92	547.21	526.68	493.07	480.48	477.12	474.10	462.94	456.20
58000	601.29	556.81	535.92	501.72	488.91	485.49	482.42	471.06	464.21
59000	611.66	566.41	545.16	510.37	497.34	493.86	490.74	479.18	472.21
60000	622.02	576.01	554.40	519.02	505.77	502.23	499.05	487.30	480.21
61000	632.39	585.61	563.64	527.67	514.20	510.60	507.37	495.42	488.22
62000	642.76	595.21	572.87	536.32	522.63	518.97	515.69	503.55	496.22
63000	653.12	604.81	582.11	544.97	531.06	527.34	524.01	511.67	504.22
64000	663.49	614.41	591.35	553.62	539.49	535.71	532.32	519.79	512.23
65000	673.86	624.01	600.59	562.27	547.91	544.08	540.64	527.91	520.23
66000	684.22	633.61	609.83	570.92	556.34	552.46	548.96	536.03	528.24
67000	694.59	643.21	619.07	579.57	564.77	560.83	557.28	544.15	536.24
68000	704.96	652.81	628.31	588.22	573.20	569.20	565.59	552.28	544.24
69000	715.32	662.41	637.55	596.87	581.63	577.57	573.91	560.40	552.25
70000	725.69	672.01	646.79	605.52	590.06	585.94	582.23	568.52	560.25
75000	777.53	720.01	692.99	648.77	632.21	627.79	623.82	609.13	600.27
80000	829.36	768.01	739.19	692.02	674.36	669.64	665.40	649.74	640.28
100000	1036.70	960.01	923.99	865.03	842.94	837.05	831.75	812.17	800.35

9½% MONTHLY PAYMENT

NECESSARY TO AMORTIZE A LOAN

TERM / AMOUNT	1 YEAR	2 YEARS	3 YEARS	4 YEARS	5 YEARS	7 YEARS	8 YEARS	10 YEARS	12 YEARS
$ 25	2.20	1.15	.81	.63	.53	.41	.38	.33	.30
50	4.39	2.30	1.61	1.26	1.06	.82	.75	.65	.59
75	6.58	3.45	2.41	1.89	1.58	1.23	1.12	.98	.88
100	8.77	4.60	3.21	2.52	2.11	1.64	1.50	1.30	1.17
200	17.54	9.19	6.41	5.03	4.21	3.27	2.99	2.59	2.34
300	26.31	13.78	9.61	7.54	6.31	4.91	4.48	3.89	3.50
400	35.08	18.37	12.82	10.05	8.41	6.54	5.97	5.18	4.67
500	43.85	22.96	16.02	12.57	10.51	8.18	7.46	6.47	5.84
600	52.62	27.55	19.22	15.08	12.61	9.81	8.95	7.77	7.00
700	61.38	32.15	22.43	17.59	14.71	11.45	10.44	9.06	8.17
800	70.15	36.74	25.63	20.10	16.81	13.08	11.93	10.36	9.34
900	78.92	41.33	28.83	22.62	18.91	14.71	13.42	11.65	10.50
1000	87.69	45.92	32.04	25.13	21.01	16.35	14.92	12.94	11.67
2000	175.37	91.83	64.07	50.25	42.01	32.69	29.83	25.88	23.33
3000	263.06	137.75	96.10	75.37	63.01	49.04	44.74	38.82	35.00
4000	350.74	183.66	128.14	100.50	84.01	65.38	59.65	51.76	46.66
5000	438.42	229.58	160.17	125.62	105.01	81.72	74.56	64.70	58.32
6000	526.11	275.49	192.20	150.74	126.02	98.07	89.47	77.64	69.99
7000	613.79	321.41	224.24	175.87	147.02	114.41	104.38	90.58	81.65
8000	701.47	367.32	256.27	200.99	168.02	130.76	119.29	103.52	93.31
9000	789.16	413.24	288.30	226.11	189.02	147.10	134.20	116.46	104.98
10000	876.84	459.15	320.33	251.24	210.02	163.44	149.11	129.40	116.64
15000	1315.26	688.72	480.50	376.85	315.03	245.16	223.67	194.10	174.96
20000	1753.68	918.29	640.66	502.47	420.04	326.88	298.22	258.80	233.28
25000	2192.09	1147.87	800.83	628.08	525.05	408.60	372.78	323.50	291.60
30000	2630.51	1377.44	960.99	753.70	630.06	490.32	447.33	388.20	349.92
35000	3068.93	1607.01	1121.16	879.31	735.07	572.04	521.89	452.90	408.24
36000	3156.61	1652.93	1153.19	904.44	756.07	588.39	536.80	465.84	419.90
37000	3244.29	1698.84	1185.22	929.56	777.07	604.73	551.71	478.78	431.56
38000	3331.98	1744.76	1217.26	954.68	798.08	621.08	566.62	491.72	443.23
39000	3419.66	1790.67	1249.29	979.81	819.08	637.42	581.53	504.66	454.89
40000	3507.35	1836.58	1281.32	1004.93	840.08	653.76	596.44	517.60	466.55
41000	3595.03	1882.50	1313.36	1030.05	861.08	670.11	611.35	530.53	478.22
42000	3682.71	1928.41	1345.39	1055.18	882.08	686.45	626.26	543.47	489.88
43000	3770.40	1974.33	1377.42	1080.30	903.09	702.80	641.17	556.41	501.55
44000	3858.08	2020.24	1409.45	1105.42	924.09	719.14	656.08	569.35	513.21
45000	3945.76	2066.16	1441.49	1130.55	945.09	735.48	670.99	582.29	524.87
46000	4033.45	2112.07	1473.52	1155.67	966.09	751.83	685.91	595.23	536.54
47000	4121.13	2157.99	1505.55	1180.79	987.09	768.17	700.82	608.17	548.20
48000	4208.81	2203.90	1537.59	1205.92	1008.09	784.52	715.73	621.11	559.86
49000	4296.50	2249.82	1569.62	1231.04	1029.10	800.86	730.64	634.05	571.53
50000	4384.18	2295.73	1601.65	1256.16	1050.10	817.20	745.55	646.99	583.19
51000	4471.86	2341.64	1633.69	1281.28	1071.10	833.55	760.46	659.93	594.86
52000	4559.55	2387.56	1665.72	1306.41	1092.10	849.89	775.37	672.87	606.52
53000	4647.23	2433.47	1697.75	1331.53	1113.10	866.24	790.28	685.81	618.18
54000	4734.91	2479.39	1729.78	1356.65	1134.11	882.58	805.19	698.75	629.85
55000	4822.60	2525.30	1761.82	1381.78	1155.11	898.92	820.10	711.69	641.51
56000	4910.28	2571.22	1793.85	1406.90	1176.11	915.27	835.01	724.63	653.17
57000	4997.97	2617.13	1825.88	1432.02	1197.11	931.61	849.93	737.57	664.84
58000	5085.65	2663.05	1857.92	1457.15	1218.11	947.96	864.84	750.51	676.50
59000	5173.33	2708.96	1889.95	1482.27	1239.11	964.30	879.75	763.45	688.17
60000	5261.02	2754.87	1921.98	1507.39	1260.12	980.64	894.66	776.39	699.83
61000	5348.70	2800.79	1954.01	1532.52	1281.12	996.99	909.57	789.33	711.49
62000	5436.38	2846.70	1986.05	1557.64	1302.12	1013.33	924.48	802.27	723.16
63000	5524.07	2892.62	2018.08	1582.76	1323.12	1029.68	939.39	815.21	734.82
64000	5611.75	2938.53	2050.11	1607.89	1344.12	1046.02	954.30	828.15	746.48
65000	5699.43	2984.45	2082.15	1633.01	1365.13	1062.36	969.21	841.09	758.15
66000	5787.12	3030.36	2114.18	1658.13	1386.13	1078.71	984.12	854.03	769.81
67000	5874.80	3076.28	2146.21	1683.26	1407.13	1095.05	999.03	866.97	781.48
68000	5962.48	3122.19	2178.25	1708.38	1428.13	1111.40	1013.95	879.91	793.14
69000	6050.17	3168.11	2210.28	1733.50	1449.13	1127.74	1028.86	892.85	804.80
70000	6137.85	3214.02	2242.31	1758.62	1470.14	1144.08	1043.77	905.79	816.47
75000	6576.27	3443.59	2402.48	1884.24	1575.14	1225.80	1118.32	970.49	874.78
80000	7014.69	3673.16	2562.64	2009.86	1680.15	1307.52	1192.88	1035.19	933.10
100000	8768.36	4591.45	3203.30	2512.32	2100.19	1634.40	1491.09	1293.98	1166.38

MONTHLY PAYMENT 9½%

NECESSARY TO AMORTIZE A LOAN

TERM / AMOUNT	15 YEARS	18 YEARS	20 YEARS	25 YEARS	28 YEARS	29 YEARS	30 YEARS	35 YEARS	40 YEARS
$ 25	.27	.25	.24	.22	.22	.22	.22	.21	.21
50	.53	.49	.47	.44	.43	.43	.43	.42	.41
75	.79	.73	.70	.66	.64	.64	.64	.62	.61
100	1.05	.97	.94	.88	.86	.85	.85	.83	.82
200	2.09	1.94	1.87	1.75	1.71	1.70	1.69	1.65	1.63
300	3.14	2.91	2.80	2.63	2.56	2.54	2.53	2.47	2.44
400	4.18	3.88	3.73	3.50	3.41	3.39	3.37	3.29	3.25
500	5.23	4.84	4.67	4.37	4.26	4.24	4.21	4.11	4.06
600	6.27	5.81	5.60	5.25	5.12	5.08	5.05	4.93	4.87
700	7.31	6.78	6.53	6.12	5.97	5.93	5.89	5.76	5.68
800	8.36	7.75	7.46	6.99	6.82	6.77	6.73	6.58	6.49
900	9.40	8.72	8.39	7.87	7.67	7.62	7.57	7.40	7.30
1000	10.45	9.68	9.33	8.74	8.52	8.47	8.41	8.22	8.11
2000	20.89	19.36	18.65	17.48	17.04	16.93	16.82	16.44	16.21
3000	31.33	29.04	27.97	26.22	25.56	25.39	25.23	24.65	24.31
4000	41.77	38.72	37.29	34.95	34.08	33.85	33.64	32.87	32.41
5000	52.22	48.40	46.61	43.69	42.60	42.31	42.05	41.09	40.51
6000	62.66	58.08	55.93	52.43	51.12	50.77	50.46	49.30	48.61
7000	73.10	67.76	65.25	61.16	59.64	59.23	58.86	57.52	56.71
8000	83.54	77.44	74.58	69.90	68.16	67.69	67.27	65.73	64.81
9000	93.99	87.12	83.90	78.64	76.67	76.15	75.68	73.95	72.91
10000	104.43	96.80	93.22	87.37	85.19	84.61	84.09	82.17	81.01
15000	156.64	145.19	139.82	131.06	127.79	126.92	126.13	123.25	121.51
20000	208.85	193.59	186.43	174.74	170.38	169.22	168.18	164.33	162.02
25000	261.06	241.98	233.04	218.43	212.98	211.52	210.22	205.41	202.52
30000	313.27	290.38	279.64	262.11	255.57	253.83	252.26	246.49	243.02
35000	365.48	338.77	326.25	305.80	298.16	296.13	294.30	287.57	283.53
36000	375.93	348.45	335.57	314.54	306.68	304.59	302.71	295.79	291.63
37000	386.37	358.13	344.89	323.27	315.20	313.05	311.12	304.00	299.73
38000	396.81	367.81	354.21	332.01	323.72	321.51	319.53	312.22	307.83
39000	407.25	377.49	363.54	340.75	332.24	329.97	327.94	320.43	315.93
40000	417.69	387.17	372.86	349.48	340.76	338.43	336.35	328.65	324.03
41000	428.14	396.85	382.18	358.22	349.28	346.89	344.76	336.87	332.13
42000	438.58	406.53	391.50	366.96	357.80	355.36	353.16	345.08	340.23
43000	449.02	416.21	400.82	375.69	366.31	363.82	361.57	353.30	348.33
44000	459.46	425.89	410.14	384.43	374.83	372.28	369.98	361.51	356.43
45000	469.91	435.57	419.46	393.17	383.35	380.74	378.39	369.73	364.53
46000	480.35	445.24	428.79	401.91	391.87	389.20	386.80	377.95	372.63
47000	490.79	454.92	438.11	410.64	400.39	397.66	395.21	386.16	380.73
48000	501.23	464.60	447.43	419.38	408.91	406.12	403.62	394.38	388.83
49000	511.68	474.28	456.75	428.12	417.43	414.58	412.02	402.59	396.94
50000	522.12	483.96	466.07	436.85	425.95	423.04	420.43	410.81	405.04
51000	532.56	493.64	475.39	445.59	434.46	431.50	428.84	419.03	413.14
52000	543.00	503.32	484.71	454.33	442.98	439.96	437.25	427.24	421.24
53000	553.44	513.00	494.03	463.06	451.50	448.42	445.66	435.46	429.34
54000	563.89	522.68	503.36	471.80	460.02	456.88	454.07	443.68	437.44
55000	574.33	532.36	512.68	480.54	468.54	465.34	462.47	451.89	445.54
56000	584.77	542.04	522.00	489.28	477.06	473.81	470.88	460.11	453.64
57000	595.21	551.71	531.32	498.01	485.58	482.27	479.29	468.32	461.74
58000	605.66	561.39	540.64	506.75	494.10	490.73	487.70	476.54	469.84
59000	616.10	571.07	549.96	515.49	502.62	499.19	496.11	484.76	477.94
60000	626.54	580.75	559.28	524.22	511.13	507.65	504.52	492.97	486.04
61000	636.98	590.43	568.61	532.96	519.65	516.11	512.93	501.19	494.14
62000	647.42	600.11	577.93	541.70	528.17	524.57	521.33	509.40	502.24
63000	657.87	609.79	587.25	550.43	536.69	533.03	529.74	517.62	510.34
64000	668.31	619.47	596.57	559.17	545.21	541.49	538.15	525.84	518.44
65000	678.75	629.15	605.89	567.91	553.73	549.95	546.56	534.05	526.55
66000	689.19	638.83	615.21	576.64	562.25	558.41	554.97	542.27	534.65
67000	699.64	648.51	624.53	585.38	570.77	566.87	563.38	550.48	542.75
68000	710.08	658.18	633.85	594.12	579.28	575.33	571.79	558.70	550.85
69000	720.52	667.86	643.18	602.86	587.80	583.79	580.19	566.92	558.95
70000	730.96	677.54	652.50	611.59	596.32	592.26	588.60	575.13	567.05
75000	783.17	725.94	699.10	655.28	638.92	634.56	630.65	616.21	607.55
80000	835.38	774.33	745.71	698.96	681.51	676.86	672.69	657.29	648.05
100000	1044.23	967.92	932.14	873.70	851.89	846.08	840.86	821.62	810.07

9⅝% MONTHLY PAYMENT

NECESSARY TO AMORTIZE A LOAN

TERM / AMOUNT	1 YEAR	2 YEARS	3 YEARS	4 YEARS	5 YEARS	7 YEARS	8 YEARS	10 YEARS	12 YEARS
$ 25	2.20	1.15	.81	.63	.53	.42	.38	.33	.30
50	4.39	2.30	1.61	1.26	1.06	.83	.75	.66	.59
75	6.59	3.45	2.41	1.89	1.58	1.24	1.13	.98	.89
100	8.78	4.60	3.21	2.52	2.11	1.65	1.50	1.31	1.18
200	17.55	9.20	6.42	5.04	4.22	3.29	3.00	2.61	2.35
300	26.33	13.80	9.63	7.56	6.32	4.93	4.50	3.91	3.53
400	35.10	18.39	12.84	10.08	8.43	6.57	6.00	5.21	4.70
500	43.88	22.99	16.05	12.60	10.54	8.21	7.49	6.51	5.87
600	52.65	27.59	19.26	15.11	12.64	9.85	8.99	7.81	7.05
700	61.42	32.19	22.47	17.63	14.75	11.49	10.49	9.11	8.22
800	70.20	36.78	25.68	20.15	16.86	13.13	11.99	10.41	9.39
900	78.97	41.38	28.89	22.67	18.96	14.77	13.48	11.71	10.57
1000	87.75	45.98	32.10	25.19	21.07	16.41	14.98	13.01	11.74
2000	175.49	91.95	64.19	50.37	42.13	32.82	29.96	26.02	23.48
3000	263.23	137.92	96.28	75.55	63.19	49.23	44.93	39.03	35.21
4000	350.97	183.89	128.37	100.74	84.26	65.64	59.91	52.04	46.95
5000	438.71	229.87	160.46	125.92	105.32	82.05	74.89	65.05	58.68
6000	526.45	275.84	192.55	151.10	126.38	98.45	89.86	78.05	70.42
7000	614.20	321.81	224.64	176.29	147.45	114.86	104.84	91.06	82.15
8000	701.94	367.78	256.74	201.47	168.51	131.27	119.82	104.07	93.89
9000	789.68	413.75	288.83	226.65	189.57	147.68	134.79	117.08	105.62
10000	877.42	459.73	320.92	251.83	210.64	164.09	149.77	130.09	117.36
15000	1316.13	689.59	481.38	377.75	315.95	246.13	224.65	195.13	176.03
20000	1754.84	919.45	641.83	503.66	421.27	328.17	299.53	260.17	234.71
25000	2193.54	1149.31	802.29	629.58	526.58	410.21	374.42	325.21	293.38
30000	2632.25	1379.17	962.75	755.49	631.90	492.25	449.30	390.25	352.06
35000	3070.96	1609.03	1123.20	881.41	737.21	574.29	524.18	455.30	410.74
36000	3158.70	1655.00	1155.30	906.59	758.27	590.70	539.16	468.30	422.47
37000	3246.44	1700.97	1187.39	931.77	779.34	607.10	554.13	481.31	434.21
38000	3334.18	1746.94	1219.48	956.95	800.40	623.51	569.11	494.32	445.94
39000	3421.93	1792.91	1251.57	982.14	821.46	639.92	584.09	507.33	457.68
40000	3509.67	1838.89	1283.66	1007.32	842.53	656.33	599.06	520.34	469.41
41000	3597.41	1884.86	1315.75	1032.50	863.59	672.74	614.04	533.34	481.15
42000	3685.15	1930.83	1347.84	1057.69	884.65	689.14	629.02	546.35	492.88
43000	3772.89	1976.80	1379.94	1082.87	905.71	705.55	643.99	559.36	504.62
44000	3860.63	2022.77	1412.03	1108.05	926.78	721.96	658.97	572.37	516.35
45000	3948.38	2068.75	1444.12	1133.23	947.84	738.37	673.95	585.38	528.09
46000	4036.12	2114.72	1476.21	1158.42	968.90	754.78	688.92	598.39	539.82
47000	4123.86	2160.69	1508.30	1183.60	989.97	771.18	703.90	611.39	551.56
48000	4211.60	2206.66	1540.39	1208.78	1011.03	787.59	718.88	624.40	563.29
49000	4299.34	2252.63	1572.48	1233.97	1032.09	804.00	733.85	637.41	575.03
50000	4387.08	2298.61	1604.58	1259.15	1053.16	820.41	748.83	650.42	586.76
51000	4474.83	2344.58	1636.67	1284.33	1074.22	836.82	763.80	663.43	598.50
52000	4562.57	2390.55	1668.76	1309.51	1095.28	853.22	778.78	676.44	610.23
53000	4650.31	2436.52	1700.85	1334.70	1116.34	869.63	793.76	689.44	621.97
54000	4738.05	2482.50	1732.94	1359.88	1137.41	886.04	808.73	702.45	633.70
55000	4825.79	2528.47	1765.03	1385.06	1158.47	902.45	823.71	715.46	645.44
56000	4913.53	2574.44	1797.12	1410.25	1179.53	918.86	838.69	728.47	657.17
57000	5001.27	2620.41	1829.22	1435.43	1200.60	935.26	853.66	741.48	668.91
58000	5089.02	2666.38	1861.31	1460.61	1221.66	951.67	868.64	754.49	680.64
59000	5176.76	2712.36	1893.40	1485.79	1242.72	968.08	883.62	767.49	692.38
60000	5264.50	2758.33	1925.49	1510.98	1263.79	984.49	898.59	780.50	704.11
61000	5352.24	2804.30	1957.58	1536.16	1284.85	1000.90	913.57	793.51	715.85
62000	5439.98	2850.27	1989.67	1561.34	1305.91	1017.31	928.55	806.52	727.58
63000	5527.72	2896.24	2021.76	1586.53	1326.97	1033.71	943.52	819.53	739.32
64000	5615.47	2942.22	2053.86	1611.71	1348.04	1050.12	958.50	832.54	751.06
65000	5703.21	2988.19	2085.95	1636.89	1369.10	1066.53	973.48	845.54	762.79
66000	5790.95	3034.16	2118.04	1662.07	1390.16	1082.94	988.45	858.55	774.53
67000	5878.69	3080.13	2150.13	1687.26	1411.23	1099.35	1003.43	871.56	786.26
68000	5966.43	3126.10	2182.22	1712.44	1432.29	1115.75	1018.40	884.57	798.00
69000	6054.17	3172.08	2214.31	1737.62	1453.35	1132.16	1033.38	897.58	809.73
70000	6141.92	3218.05	2246.40	1762.81	1474.42	1148.57	1048.36	910.59	821.47
75000	6580.62	3447.91	2406.86	1888.72	1579.73	1230.61	1123.24	975.63	880.14
80000	7019.33	3677.77	2567.32	2014.63	1685.05	1312.65	1198.12	1040.67	938.82
100000	8774.16	4597.21	3209.15	2518.29	2106.31	1640.81	1497.65	1300.83	1173.52

MONTHLY PAYMENT $9\frac{5}{8}\%$

NECESSARY TO AMORTIZE A LOAN

TERM / AMOUNT	15 YEARS	18 YEARS	20 YEARS	25 YEARS	28 YEARS	29 YEARS	30 YEARS	35 YEARS	40 YEARS
$ 25	.27	.25	.24	.23	.22	.22	.22	.21	.21
50	.53	.49	.48	.45	.44	.43	.43	.42	.41
75	.79	.74	.71	.67	.65	.65	.64	.63	.62
100	1.06	.98	.95	.89	.87	.86	.85	.84	.82
200	2.11	1.96	1.89	1.77	1.73	1.72	1.70	1.67	1.64
300	3.16	2.93	2.83	2.65	2.59	2.57	2.55	2.50	2.46
400	4.21	3.91	3.77	3.53	3.45	3.43	3.40	3.33	3.28
500	5.26	4.88	4.71	4.42	4.31	4.28	4.25	4.16	4.10
600	6.32	5.86	5.65	5.30	5.17	5.14	5.10	4.99	4.92
700	7.37	6.84	6.59	6.18	6.03	5.99	5.95	5.82	5.74
800	8.42	7.81	7.53	7.06	6.89	6.85	6.80	6.65	6.56
900	9.47	8.79	8.47	7.95	7.75	7.70	7.65	7.48	7.38
1000	10.52	9.76	9.41	8.83	8.61	8.56	8.50	8.32	8.20
2000	21.04	19.52	18.81	17.65	17.22	17.11	17.00	16.63	16.40
3000	31.56	29.28	28.21	26.48	25.83	25.66	25.50	24.94	24.60
4000	42.08	39.04	37.62	35.30	34.44	34.21	34.00	33.25	32.80
5000	52.59	48.80	47.02	44.13	43.05	42.76	42.50	41.56	40.99
6000	63.11	58.56	56.42	52.95	51.66	51.31	51.00	49.87	49.19
7000	73.63	68.31	65.83	61.77	60.26	59.86	59.50	58.18	57.39
8000	84.15	78.07	75.23	70.60	68.87	68.42	68.00	66.49	65.59
9000	94.67	87.83	84.63	79.42	77.48	76.97	76.50	74.80	73.79
10000	105.18	97.59	94.04	88.25	86.09	85.52	85.00	83.11	81.98
15000	157.77	146.38	141.05	132.37	129.13	128.27	127.50	124.67	122.97
20000	210.36	195.18	188.07	176.49	172.18	171.03	170.00	166.22	163.96
25000	262.95	243.97	235.08	220.61	215.22	213.79	212.50	207.78	204.95
30000	315.54	292.76	282.10	264.73	258.26	256.54	255.00	249.33	245.94
35000	368.13	341.55	329.11	308.85	301.30	299.30	297.50	290.89	286.93
36000	378.65	351.31	338.52	317.67	309.91	307.85	306.00	299.20	295.13
37000	389.16	361.07	347.92	326.49	318.52	316.40	314.50	307.51	303.33
38000	399.68	370.83	357.32	335.32	327.13	324.95	323.00	315.82	311.53
39000	410.20	380.59	366.73	344.14	335.74	333.50	331.50	324.13	319.73
40000	420.72	390.35	376.13	352.97	344.35	342.06	340.00	332.44	327.92
41000	431.24	400.10	385.53	361.79	352.96	350.61	348.50	340.75	336.12
42000	441.75	409.86	394.93	370.61	361.56	359.16	357.00	349.06	344.32
43000	452.27	419.62	404.34	379.44	370.17	367.71	365.50	357.37	352.52
44000	462.79	429.38	413.74	388.26	378.78	376.26	374.00	365.68	360.72
45000	473.31	439.14	423.14	397.09	387.39	384.81	382.50	373.99	368.91
46000	483.82	448.90	432.55	405.91	396.00	393.36	391.00	382.31	377.11
47000	494.34	458.66	441.95	414.73	404.61	401.92	399.50	390.62	385.31
48000	504.86	468.41	451.35	423.56	413.22	410.47	408.00	398.93	393.51
49000	515.38	478.17	460.76	432.38	421.82	419.02	416.50	407.24	401.71
50000	525.90	487.93	470.16	441.21	430.43	427.57	425.00	415.55	409.90
51000	536.41	497.69	479.56	450.03	439.04	436.12	433.50	423.86	418.10
52000	546.93	507.45	488.97	458.85	447.65	444.67	442.00	432.17	426.30
53000	557.45	517.21	498.37	467.68	456.26	453.22	450.50	440.48	434.50
54000	567.97	526.96	507.77	476.50	464.87	461.77	459.00	448.79	442.70
55000	578.48	536.72	517.17	485.33	473.48	470.33	467.50	457.10	450.89
56000	589.00	546.48	526.58	494.15	482.08	478.88	476.00	465.41	459.09
57000	599.52	556.24	535.98	502.97	490.69	487.43	484.50	473.72	467.29
58000	610.04	566.00	545.38	511.80	499.30	495.98	493.00	482.04	475.49
59000	620.56	575.76	554.79	520.62	507.91	504.53	501.50	490.35	483.69
60000	631.07	585.52	564.19	529.45	516.52	513.08	510.00	498.66	491.88
61000	641.59	595.27	573.59	538.27	525.13	521.63	518.50	506.97	500.08
62000	652.11	605.03	583.00	547.09	533.74	530.18	527.00	515.28	508.28
63000	662.63	614.79	592.40	555.92	542.34	538.74	535.50	523.59	516.48
64000	673.14	624.55	601.80	564.74	550.95	547.29	544.00	531.90	524.68
65000	683.66	634.31	611.21	573.57	559.56	555.84	552.50	540.21	532.87
66000	694.18	644.07	620.61	582.39	568.17	564.39	561.00	548.52	541.07
67000	704.70	653.83	630.01	591.21	576.78	572.94	569.50	556.83	549.27
68000	715.22	663.58	639.42	600.04	585.39	581.49	578.00	565.14	557.47
69000	725.73	673.34	648.82	608.86	594.00	590.04	586.50	573.46	565.67
70000	736.25	683.10	658.22	617.69	602.60	598.59	595.00	581.77	573.86
75000	788.84	731.89	705.24	661.81	645.65	641.35	637.50	623.32	614.85
80000	841.43	780.69	752.25	705.93	688.69	684.11	680.00	664.87	655.84
100000	1051.79	975.86	940.31	882.41	860.86	855.13	849.99	831.09	819.80

9¾% MONTHLY PAYMENT
NECESSARY TO AMORTIZE A LOAN

TERM / AMOUNT	1 YEAR	2 YEARS	3 YEARS	4 YEARS	5 YEARS	7 YEARS	8 YEARS	10 YEARS	12 YEARS
$ 25	2.20	1.16	.81	.64	.53	.42	.38	.33	.30
50	4.39	2.31	1.61	1.27	1.06	.83	.76	.66	.60
75	6.59	3.46	2.42	1.90	1.59	1.24	1.13	.99	.89
100	8.78	4.61	3.22	2.53	2.12	1.65	1.51	1.31	1.19
200	17.56	9.21	6.43	5.05	4.23	3.30	3.01	2.62	2.37
300	26.34	13.81	9.65	7.58	6.34	4.95	4.52	3.93	3.55
400	35.12	18.42	12.86	10.10	8.45	6.59	6.02	5.24	4.73
500	43.90	23.02	16.08	12.63	10.57	8.24	7.53	6.54	5.91
600	52.68	27.62	19.29	15.15	12.68	9.89	9.03	7.85	7.09
700	61.46	32.23	22.51	17.67	14.79	11.54	10.53	9.16	8.27
800	70.24	36.83	25.72	20.20	16.90	13.18	12.04	10.47	9.45
900	79.02	41.43	28.94	22.72	19.02	14.83	13.54	11.77	10.63
1000	87.80	46.03	32.15	25.25	21.13	16.48	15.05	13.08	11.81
2000	175.60	92.06	64.30	50.49	42.25	32.95	30.09	26.16	23.62
3000	263.40	138.09	96.45	75.73	63.38	49.42	45.13	39.24	35.43
4000	351.20	184.12	128.60	100.98	84.50	65.89	60.17	52.31	47.23
5000	439.00	230.15	160.75	126.22	105.63	82.37	75.22	65.39	59.04
6000	526.80	276.18	192.90	151.46	126.75	98.84	90.26	78.47	70.85
7000	614.60	322.21	225.05	176.70	147.87	115.31	105.30	91.54	82.65
8000	702.40	368.24	257.20	201.95	169.00	131.78	120.34	104.62	94.46
9000	790.20	414.27	289.35	227.19	190.12	148.26	135.38	117.70	106.27
10000	878.00	460.30	321.50	252.43	211.25	164.73	150.43	130.78	118.07
15000	1317.00	690.45	482.25	378.65	316.87	247.09	225.64	196.16	177.11
20000	1756.00	920.60	643.00	504.86	422.49	329.45	300.85	261.55	236.14
25000	2195.00	1150.75	803.75	631.07	528.11	411.81	376.06	326.93	295.18
30000	2633.99	1380.89	964.50	757.29	633.73	494.17	451.27	392.32	354.21
35000	3072.99	1611.04	1125.25	883.50	739.35	576.54	526.48	457.70	413.24
36000	3160.79	1657.07	1157.40	908.74	760.48	593.01	541.52	470.78	425.05
37000	3248.59	1703.10	1189.55	933.98	781.60	609.48	556.57	483.85	436.86
38000	3336.39	1749.13	1221.70	959.23	802.73	625.95	571.61	496.93	448.66
39000	3424.19	1795.16	1253.85	984.47	823.85	642.42	586.65	510.01	460.47
40000	3511.99	1841.19	1286.00	1009.71	844.97	658.90	601.69	523.09	472.28
41000	3599.79	1887.22	1318.15	1034.96	866.10	675.37	616.74	536.16	484.08
42000	3687.59	1933.25	1350.30	1060.20	887.22	691.84	631.78	549.24	495.89
43000	3775.39	1979.28	1382.45	1085.44	908.35	708.31	646.82	562.32	507.70
44000	3863.19	2025.31	1414.60	1110.68	929.47	724.79	661.86	575.39	519.50
45000	3950.99	2071.34	1446.75	1135.93	950.60	741.26	676.90	588.47	531.31
46000	4038.79	2117.37	1478.90	1161.17	971.72	757.73	691.95	601.55	543.12
47000	4126.59	2163.40	1511.05	1186.41	992.84	774.20	706.99	614.63	554.92
48000	4214.39	2209.43	1543.20	1211.65	1013.97	790.68	722.03	627.70	566.73
49000	4302.19	2255.46	1575.35	1236.90	1035.09	807.15	737.07	640.78	578.54
50000	4389.99	2301.49	1607.50	1262.14	1056.22	823.62	752.12	653.86	590.35
51000	4477.79	2347.52	1639.65	1287.38	1077.34	840.09	767.16	666.93	602.15
52000	4565.59	2393.55	1671.80	1312.62	1098.47	856.56	782.20	680.01	613.96
53000	4653.39	2439.58	1703.95	1337.87	1119.59	873.04	797.24	693.09	625.77
54000	4741.19	2485.60	1736.10	1363.11	1140.71	889.51	812.28	706.16	637.57
55000	4828.99	2531.63	1768.25	1388.35	1161.84	905.98	827.33	719.24	649.38
56000	4916.79	2577.66	1800.40	1413.60	1182.96	922.45	842.37	732.32	661.19
57000	5004.59	2623.69	1832.55	1438.84	1204.09	938.93	857.41	745.40	672.99
58000	5092.39	2669.72	1864.70	1464.08	1225.21	955.40	872.45	758.47	684.80
59000	5180.18	2715.75	1896.85	1489.32	1246.34	971.87	887.49	771.55	696.61
60000	5267.98	2761.78	1929.00	1514.57	1267.46	988.34	902.54	784.63	708.41
61000	5355.78	2807.81	1961.15	1539.81	1288.58	1004.82	917.58	797.70	720.22
62000	5443.58	2853.84	1993.30	1565.05	1309.71	1021.29	932.62	810.78	732.03
63000	5531.38	2899.87	2025.45	1590.29	1330.83	1037.76	947.66	823.86	743.83
64000	5619.18	2945.90	2057.60	1615.54	1351.96	1054.23	962.71	836.93	755.64
65000	5706.98	2991.93	2089.75	1640.78	1373.08	1070.70	977.75	850.01	767.45
66000	5794.78	3037.96	2121.90	1666.02	1394.21	1087.18	992.79	863.09	779.25
67000	5882.58	3083.99	2154.05	1691.27	1415.33	1103.65	1007.83	876.17	791.06
68000	5970.38	3130.02	2186.20	1716.51	1436.45	1120.12	1022.87	889.24	802.87
69000	6058.18	3176.05	2218.35	1741.75	1457.58	1136.59	1037.92	902.32	814.67
70000	6145.98	3222.08	2250.50	1766.99	1478.70	1153.07	1052.96	915.40	826.48
75000	6584.98	3452.23	2411.25	1893.21	1584.32	1235.43	1128.17	980.78	885.52
80000	7023.98	3682.37	2572.00	2019.42	1689.94	1317.79	1203.38	1046.17	944.55
100000	8779.97	4602.97	3215.00	2524.27	2112.43	1647.23	1504.23	1307.71	1180.69

MONTHLY PAYMENT 9¾%
NECESSARY TO AMORTIZE A LOAN

TERM / AMOUNT	15 YEARS	18 YEARS	20 YEARS	25 YEARS	28 YEARS	29 YEARS	30 YEARS	35 YEARS	40 YEARS
$ 25	.27	.25	.24	.23	.22	.22	.22	.22	.21
50	.53	.50	.48	.45	.44	.44	.43	.43	.42
75	.80	.74	.72	.67	.66	.65	.65	.64	.63
100	1.06	.99	.95	.90	.87	.87	.86	.85	.83
200	2.12	1.97	1.90	1.79	1.74	1.73	1.72	1.69	1.66
300	3.18	2.96	2.85	2.68	2.61	2.60	2.58	2.53	2.49
400	4.24	3.94	3.80	3.57	3.48	3.46	3.44	3.37	3.32
500	5.30	4.92	4.75	4.46	4.35	4.33	4.30	4.21	4.15
600	6.36	5.91	5.70	5.35	5.22	5.19	5.16	5.05	4.98
700	7.42	6.89	6.64	6.24	6.09	6.05	6.02	5.89	5.81
800	8.48	7.88	7.59	7.13	6.96	6.92	6.88	6.73	6.64
900	9.54	8.86	8.54	8.03	7.83	7.78	7.74	7.57	7.47
1000	10.60	9.84	9.49	8.92	8.70	8.65	8.60	8.41	8.30
2000	21.19	19.68	18.98	17.83	17.40	17.29	17.19	16.82	16.60
3000	31.79	29.52	28.46	26.74	26.10	25.93	25.78	25.22	24.89
4000	42.38	39.36	37.95	35.65	34.80	34.57	34.37	33.63	33.19
5000	52.97	49.20	47.43	44.56	43.50	43.22	42.96	42.03	41.48
6000	63.57	59.03	56.92	53.47	52.20	51.86	51.55	50.44	49.78
7000	74.16	68.87	66.40	62.38	60.90	60.50	60.15	58.85	58.07
8000	84.75	78.71	75.89	71.30	69.59	69.14	68.74	67.25	66.37
9000	95.35	88.55	85.37	80.21	78.29	77.78	77.33	75.66	74.67
10000	105.94	98.39	94.86	89.12	86.99	86.43	85.92	84.06	82.96
15000	158.91	147.58	142.28	133.68	130.48	129.64	128.88	126.09	124.44
20000	211.88	196.77	189.71	178.23	173.98	172.85	171.84	168.12	165.92
25000	264.85	245.96	237.13	222.79	217.47	216.06	214.79	210.15	207.39
30000	317.81	295.15	284.56	267.35	260.96	259.27	257.75	252.18	248.87
35000	370.78	344.34	331.99	311.90	304.46	302.48	300.71	294.21	290.35
36000	381.38	354.18	341.47	320.81	313.15	311.12	309.30	302.62	298.65
37000	391.97	364.02	350.96	329.73	321.85	319.76	317.89	311.02	306.94
38000	402.56	373.86	360.44	338.64	330.55	328.41	326.48	319.43	315.24
39000	413.16	383.69	369.93	347.55	339.25	337.05	335.08	327.83	323.53
40000	423.75	393.53	379.41	356.46	347.95	345.69	343.67	336.24	331.83
41000	434.34	403.37	388.90	365.37	356.65	354.33	352.26	344.65	340.12
42000	444.94	413.21	398.38	374.28	365.35	362.98	360.85	353.05	348.42
43000	455.53	423.05	407.87	383.19	374.05	371.62	369.44	361.46	356.72
44000	466.12	432.89	417.35	392.11	382.74	380.26	378.03	369.86	365.01
45000	476.72	442.72	426.84	401.02	391.44	388.90	386.62	378.27	373.31
46000	487.31	452.56	436.32	409.93	400.14	397.54	395.22	386.68	381.60
47000	497.91	462.40	445.81	418.84	408.84	406.19	403.81	395.08	389.90
48000	508.50	472.24	455.29	427.75	417.54	414.83	412.40	403.49	398.19
49000	519.09	482.08	464.78	436.66	426.24	423.47	420.99	411.89	406.49
50000	529.69	491.92	474.26	445.57	434.94	432.11	429.58	420.30	414.78
51000	540.28	501.75	483.75	454.49	443.63	440.75	438.17	428.71	423.08
52000	550.87	511.59	493.23	463.40	452.33	449.40	446.77	437.11	431.38
53000	561.47	521.43	502.72	472.31	461.03	458.04	455.36	445.52	439.67
54000	572.06	531.27	512.20	481.22	469.73	466.68	463.95	453.92	447.97
55000	582.65	541.11	521.69	490.13	478.43	475.32	472.54	462.33	456.26
56000	593.25	550.94	531.17	499.04	487.13	483.97	481.13	470.74	464.56
57000	603.84	560.78	540.66	507.95	495.83	492.61	489.72	479.14	472.85
58000	614.44	570.62	550.14	516.86	504.52	501.25	498.31	487.55	481.15
59000	625.03	580.46	559.63	525.78	513.22	509.89	506.91	495.95	489.44
60000	635.62	590.30	569.12	534.69	521.92	518.53	515.50	504.36	497.74
61000	646.22	600.14	578.60	543.60	530.62	527.18	524.09	512.76	506.04
62000	656.81	609.97	588.09	552.51	539.32	535.82	532.68	521.17	514.33
63000	667.40	619.81	597.57	561.42	548.02	544.46	541.27	529.58	522.63
64000	678.00	629.65	607.06	570.33	556.72	553.10	549.86	537.98	530.92
65000	688.59	639.49	616.54	579.24	565.41	561.74	558.46	546.39	539.22
66000	699.18	649.33	626.03	588.16	574.11	570.39	567.05	554.79	547.51
67000	709.78	659.16	635.51	597.07	582.81	579.03	575.64	563.20	555.81
68000	720.37	669.00	645.00	605.98	591.51	587.67	584.23	571.61	564.10
69000	730.97	678.84	654.48	614.89	600.21	596.31	592.82	580.01	572.40
70000	741.56	688.68	663.97	623.80	608.91	604.96	601.41	588.42	580.70
75000	794.53	737.87	711.39	668.36	652.40	648.17	644.37	630.45	622.17
80000	847.50	787.06	758.82	712.91	695.89	691.38	687.33	672.48	663.65
100000	1059.37	983.83	948.52	891.14	869.87	864.22	859.16	840.59	829.56

9⅞% MONTHLY PAYMENT

NECESSARY TO AMORTIZE A LOAN

TERM / AMOUNT	1 YEAR	2 YEARS	3 YEARS	4 YEARS	5 YEARS	7 YEARS	8 YEARS	10 YEARS	12 YEARS
$ 25	2.20	1.16	.81	.64	.53	.42	.38	.33	.30
50	4.40	2.31	1.62	1.27	1.06	.83	.76	.66	.60
75	6.59	3.46	2.42	1.90	1.59	1.25	1.14	.99	.90
100	8.79	4.61	3.23	2.54	2.12	1.66	1.52	1.32	1.19
200	17.58	9.22	6.45	5.07	4.24	3.31	3.03	2.63	2.38
300	26.36	13.83	9.67	7.60	6.36	4.97	4.54	3.95	3.57
400	35.15	18.44	12.89	10.13	8.48	6.62	6.05	5.26	4.76
500	43.93	23.05	16.11	12.66	10.60	8.27	7.56	6.58	5.94
600	52.72	27.66	19.33	15.19	12.72	9.93	9.07	7.89	7.13
700	61.51	32.27	22.55	17.72	14.83	11.58	10.58	9.21	8.32
800	70.29	36.87	25.77	20.25	16.95	13.23	12.09	10.52	9.51
900	79.08	41.48	28.99	22.78	19.07	14.89	13.60	11.84	10.70
1000	87.86	46.09	32.21	25.31	21.19	16.54	15.11	13.15	11.88
2000	175.72	92.18	64.42	50.61	42.38	33.08	30.22	26.30	23.76
3000	263.58	138.27	96.63	75.91	63.56	49.62	45.33	39.44	35.64
4000	351.44	184.35	128.84	101.22	84.75	66.15	60.44	52.59	47.52
5000	439.29	230.44	161.05	126.52	105.93	82.69	75.55	65.73	59.40
6000	527.15	276.53	193.26	151.82	127.12	99.23	90.65	78.88	71.28
7000	615.01	322.62	225.46	177.12	148.30	115.76	105.76	92.03	83.16
8000	702.87	368.70	257.67	202.43	169.49	132.30	120.87	105.17	95.03
9000	790.72	414.79	289.88	227.73	190.68	148.84	135.98	118.32	106.91
10000	878.58	460.88	322.09	253.03	211.86	165.37	151.09	131.46	118.79
15000	1317.87	691.31	483.13	379.54	317.79	248.06	226.63	197.19	178.19
20000	1757.16	921.75	644.18	506.06	423.72	330.74	302.17	262.92	237.58
25000	2196.45	1152.19	805.22	632.57	529.64	413.42	377.71	328.65	296.97
30000	2635.74	1382.62	966.26	759.08	635.57	496.11	453.25	394.38	356.37
35000	3075.03	1613.06	1127.30	885.60	741.50	578.79	528.79	460.11	415.76
36000	3162.88	1659.15	1159.51	910.90	762.69	595.33	543.90	473.26	427.64
37000	3250.74	1705.23	1191.72	936.20	783.87	611.86	559.00	486.41	439.52
38000	3338.60	1751.32	1223.93	961.50	805.06	628.40	574.11	499.55	451.39
39000	3426.46	1797.41	1256.14	986.81	826.24	644.94	589.22	512.70	463.27
40000	3514.32	1843.50	1288.35	1012.11	847.43	661.47	604.33	525.84	475.15
41000	3602.17	1889.58	1320.55	1037.41	868.61	678.01	619.44	538.99	487.03
42000	3690.03	1935.67	1352.76	1062.71	889.80	694.55	634.55	552.13	498.91
43000	3777.89	1981.76	1384.97	1088.02	910.99	711.08	649.65	565.28	510.79
44000	3865.75	2027.84	1417.18	1113.32	932.17	727.62	664.76	578.43	522.67
45000	3953.60	2073.93	1449.39	1138.62	953.36	744.16	679.87	591.57	534.55
46000	4041.46	2120.02	1481.60	1163.92	974.54	760.69	694.98	604.72	546.42
47000	4129.32	2166.11	1513.81	1189.23	995.73	777.23	710.09	617.86	558.30
48000	4217.18	2212.19	1546.01	1214.53	1016.91	793.77	725.19	631.01	570.18
49000	4305.04	2258.28	1578.22	1239.83	1038.10	810.30	740.30	644.16	582.06
50000	4392.89	2304.37	1610.43	1265.13	1059.28	826.84	755.41	657.30	593.94
51000	4480.75	2350.45	1642.64	1290.44	1080.47	843.38	770.52	670.45	605.82
52000	4568.61	2396.54	1674.85	1315.74	1101.66	859.91	785.63	683.59	617.70
53000	4656.47	2442.63	1707.06	1341.04	1122.84	876.45	800.73	696.74	629.58
54000	4744.32	2488.72	1739.27	1366.35	1144.03	892.99	815.84	709.89	641.45
55000	4832.18	2534.80	1771.47	1391.65	1165.21	909.52	830.95	723.03	653.33
56000	4920.04	2580.89	1803.68	1416.95	1186.40	926.06	846.06	736.18	665.21
57000	5007.90	2626.98	1835.89	1442.25	1207.58	942.60	861.17	749.32	677.09
58000	5095.76	2673.07	1868.10	1467.56	1228.77	959.13	876.27	762.47	688.97
59000	5183.61	2719.15	1900.31	1492.86	1249.95	975.67	891.38	775.62	700.85
60000	5271.47	2765.24	1932.52	1518.16	1271.14	992.21	906.49	788.76	712.73
61000	5359.33	2811.33	1964.73	1543.46	1292.33	1008.74	921.60	801.91	724.60
62000	5447.19	2857.41	1996.93	1568.77	1313.51	1025.28	936.71	815.05	736.48
63000	5535.04	2903.50	2029.14	1594.07	1334.70	1041.82	951.82	828.20	748.36
64000	5622.90	2949.59	2061.35	1619.37	1355.88	1058.35	966.92	841.35	760.24
65000	5710.76	2995.68	2093.56	1644.67	1377.07	1074.89	982.03	854.49	772.12
66000	5798.62	3041.76	2125.77	1669.98	1398.25	1091.43	997.14	867.64	784.00
67000	5886.48	3087.85	2157.98	1695.28	1419.44	1107.96	1012.25	880.78	795.88
68000	5974.33	3133.94	2190.19	1720.58	1440.63	1124.50	1027.36	893.93	807.76
69000	6062.19	3180.03	2222.39	1745.88	1461.81	1141.04	1042.46	907.08	819.63
70000	6150.05	3226.11	2254.60	1771.19	1483.00	1157.57	1057.57	920.22	831.51
75000	6589.34	3456.55	2415.64	1897.70	1588.92	1240.26	1133.11	985.95	890.91
80000	7028.63	3686.99	2576.69	2024.21	1694.85	1322.94	1208.65	1051.68	950.30
100000	8785.78	4608.73	3220.86	2530.26	2118.56	1653.67	1510.82	1314.60	1187.87

MONTHLY PAYMENT 9⅞%
NECESSARY TO AMORTIZE A LOAN

TERM / AMOUNT	15 YEARS	18 YEARS	20 YEARS	25 YEARS	28 YEARS	29 YEARS	30 YEARS	35 YEARS	40 YEARS
$ 25	.27	.25	.24	.23	.22	.22	.22	.22	.21
50	.54	.50	.48	.45	.44	.44	.44	.43	.42
75	.81	.75	.72	.68	.66	.66	.66	.64	.63
100	1.07	1.00	.96	.90	.88	.88	.87	.86	.84
200	2.14	1.99	1.92	1.80	1.76	1.75	1.74	1.71	1.68
300	3.21	2.98	2.88	2.70	2.64	2.62	2.61	2.56	2.52
400	4.27	3.97	3.83	3.60	3.52	3.50	3.48	3.41	3.36
500	5.34	4.96	4.79	4.50	4.40	4.37	4.35	4.26	4.20
600	6.41	5.96	5.75	5.40	5.28	5.24	5.22	5.11	5.04
700	7.47	6.95	6.70	6.30	6.16	6.12	6.08	5.96	5.88
800	8.54	7.94	7.66	7.20	7.04	6.99	6.95	6.81	6.72
900	9.61	8.93	8.62	8.10	7.92	7.86	7.82	7.66	7.56
1000	10.67	9.92	9.57	9.00	8.79	8.74	8.69	8.51	8.40
2000	21.34	19.84	19.14	18.00	17.58	17.47	17.37	17.01	16.79
3000	32.01	29.76	28.71	27.00	26.37	26.20	26.06	25.51	25.19
4000	42.68	39.68	38.28	36.00	35.16	34.94	34.74	34.01	33.58
5000	53.35	49.60	47.84	45.00	43.95	43.67	43.42	42.51	41.97
6000	64.02	59.51	57.41	54.00	52.74	52.40	52.11	51.01	50.37
7000	74.69	69.43	66.98	63.00	61.53	61.14	60.79	59.51	58.76
8000	85.36	79.35	76.55	72.00	70.32	69.87	69.47	68.01	67.15
9000	96.03	89.27	86.11	81.00	79.11	78.60	78.16	76.52	75.55
10000	106.70	99.19	95.68	90.00	87.89	87.34	86.84	85.02	83.94
15000	160.05	148.78	143.52	134.99	131.84	131.00	130.26	127.52	125.91
20000	213.40	198.37	191.36	179.99	175.78	174.67	173.67	170.03	167.87
25000	266.75	247.96	239.19	224.98	219.73	218.34	217.09	212.53	209.84
30000	320.10	297.55	287.03	269.98	263.67	262.00	260.51	255.04	251.81
35000	373.44	347.14	334.87	314.97	307.62	305.67	303.93	297.55	293.77
36000	384.11	357.06	344.44	323.97	316.41	314.40	312.61	306.05	302.17
37000	394.78	366.98	354.00	332.97	325.20	323.14	321.29	314.55	310.56
38000	405.45	376.90	363.57	341.97	333.99	331.87	329.98	323.05	318.95
39000	416.12	386.81	373.14	350.97	342.77	340.60	338.66	331.55	327.35
40000	426.79	396.73	382.71	359.97	351.56	349.34	347.34	340.05	335.74
41000	437.46	406.65	392.27	368.97	360.35	358.07	356.03	348.55	344.13
42000	448.13	416.57	401.84	377.96	369.14	366.80	364.71	357.05	352.53
43000	458.80	426.49	411.41	386.96	377.93	375.54	373.39	365.56	360.92
44000	469.47	436.40	420.98	395.96	386.72	384.27	382.08	374.06	369.32
45000	480.14	446.32	430.54	404.96	395.51	393.00	390.76	382.56	377.71
46000	490.81	456.24	440.11	413.96	404.30	401.74	399.45	391.06	386.10
47000	501.48	466.16	449.68	422.96	413.09	410.47	408.13	399.56	394.50
48000	512.15	476.08	459.25	431.96	421.88	419.20	416.81	408.06	402.89
49000	522.82	486.00	468.81	440.96	430.66	427.94	425.50	416.56	411.28
50000	533.49	495.91	478.38	449.96	439.45	436.67	434.18	425.06	419.68
51000	544.16	505.83	487.95	458.96	448.24	445.40	442.86	433.57	428.07
52000	554.83	515.75	497.52	467.96	457.03	454.14	451.55	442.07	436.46
53000	565.50	525.67	507.08	476.95	465.82	462.87	460.23	450.57	444.86
54000	576.17	535.59	516.65	485.95	474.61	471.60	468.91	459.07	453.25
55000	586.84	545.50	526.22	494.95	483.40	480.34	477.60	467.57	461.64
56000	597.51	555.42	535.79	503.95	492.19	489.07	486.28	476.07	470.04
57000	608.18	565.34	545.36	512.95	500.98	497.80	494.96	484.57	478.43
58000	618.85	575.26	554.92	521.95	509.76	506.54	503.65	493.07	486.82
59000	629.52	585.18	564.49	530.95	518.55	515.27	512.33	501.57	495.22
60000	640.19	595.10	574.06	539.95	527.34	524.00	521.01	510.08	503.61
61000	650.86	605.01	583.63	548.95	536.13	532.74	529.70	518.58	512.00
62000	661.53	614.93	593.19	557.95	544.92	541.47	538.38	527.08	520.40
63000	672.20	624.85	602.76	566.94	553.71	550.20	547.06	535.58	528.79
64000	682.87	634.77	612.33	575.94	562.50	558.94	555.75	544.08	537.18
65000	693.54	644.69	621.90	584.94	571.29	567.67	564.43	552.58	545.58
66000	704.21	654.60	631.46	593.94	580.08	576.40	573.12	561.08	553.97
67000	714.88	664.52	641.03	602.94	588.87	585.14	581.80	569.58	562.36
68000	725.55	674.44	650.60	611.94	597.65	593.87	590.48	578.09	570.76
69000	736.21	684.36	660.17	620.94	606.44	602.60	599.17	586.59	579.15
70000	746.88	694.28	669.73	629.94	615.23	611.34	607.85	595.09	587.54
75000	800.23	743.87	717.57	674.93	659.18	655.00	651.27	637.59	629.51
80000	853.58	793.46	765.41	719.93	703.12	698.67	694.68	680.10	671.48
100000	1066.98	991.82	956.76	899.91	878.90	873.34	868.35	850.12	839.35

10% MONTHLY PAYMENT

NECESSARY TO AMORTIZE A LOAN

TERM / AMOUNT	1 YEAR	2 YEARS	3 YEARS	4 YEARS	5 YEARS	7 YEARS	8 YEARS	10 YEARS	12 YEARS
$ 25	2.20	1.16	.81	.64	.54	.42	.38	.34	.30
50	4.40	2.31	1.62	1.27	1.07	.84	.76	.67	.60
75	6.60	3.47	2.43	1.91	1.60	1.25	1.14	1.00	.90
100	8.80	4.62	3.23	2.54	2.13	1.67	1.52	1.33	1.20
200	17.59	9.23	6.46	5.08	4.25	3.33	3.04	2.65	2.40
300	26.38	13.85	9.69	7.61	6.38	4.99	4.56	3.97	3.59
400	35.17	18.46	12.91	10.15	8.50	6.65	6.07	5.29	4.79
500	43.96	23.08	16.14	12.69	10.63	8.31	7.59	6.61	5.98
600	52.75	27.69	19.37	15.22	12.75	9.97	9.11	7.93	7.18
700	61.55	32.31	22.59	17.76	14.88	11.63	10.63	9.26	8.37
800	70.34	36.92	25.82	20.30	17.00	13.29	12.14	10.58	9.57
900	79.13	41.54	29.05	22.83	19.13	14.95	13.66	11.90	10.76
1000	87.92	46.15	32.27	25.37	21.25	16.61	15.18	13.22	11.96
2000	175.84	92.29	64.54	50.73	42.50	33.21	30.35	26.44	23.91
3000	263.75	138.44	96.81	76.09	63.75	49.81	45.53	39.65	35.86
4000	351.67	184.58	129.07	101.46	84.99	66.41	60.70	52.87	47.81
5000	439.58	230.73	161.34	126.82	106.24	83.01	75.88	66.08	59.76
6000	527.50	276.87	193.61	152.18	127.49	99.61	91.05	79.30	71.71
7000	615.42	323.02	225.88	177.54	148.73	116.21	106.22	92.51	83.66
8000	703.33	369.16	258.14	202.91	169.98	132.81	121.40	105.73	95.61
9000	791.25	415.31	290.41	228.27	191.23	149.42	136.57	118.94	107.56
10000	879.16	461.45	322.68	253.63	212.48	166.02	151.75	132.16	119.51
15000	1318.74	692.18	484.01	380.44	318.71	249.02	227.62	198.23	179.27
20000	1758.32	922.90	645.35	507.26	424.95	332.03	303.49	264.31	239.02
25000	2197.90	1153.63	806.68	634.07	531.18	415.03	379.36	330.38	298.77
30000	2637.48	1384.35	968.02	760.88	637.42	498.04	455.23	396.46	358.53
35000	3077.06	1615.08	1129.36	887.70	743.65	581.05	531.10	462.53	418.28
36000	3164.98	1661.22	1161.62	913.06	764.90	597.65	546.27	475.75	430.23
37000	3252.89	1707.37	1193.89	938.42	786.15	614.25	561.45	488.96	442.18
38000	3340.81	1753.51	1226.16	963.78	807.39	630.85	576.62	502.18	454.13
39000	3428.72	1799.66	1258.43	989.15	828.64	647.45	591.80	515.39	466.09
40000	3516.64	1845.80	1290.69	1014.51	849.89	664.05	606.97	528.61	478.04
41000	3604.56	1891.95	1322.96	1039.87	871.13	680.65	622.15	541.82	489.99
42000	3692.47	1938.09	1355.23	1065.23	892.38	697.25	637.32	555.04	501.94
43000	3780.39	1984.24	1387.49	1090.60	913.63	713.86	652.49	568.25	513.89
44000	3868.30	2030.38	1419.76	1115.96	934.87	730.46	667.67	581.47	525.84
45000	3956.22	2076.53	1452.03	1141.32	956.12	747.06	682.84	594.68	537.79
46000	4044.14	2122.67	1484.30	1166.68	977.37	763.66	698.02	607.90	549.74
47000	4132.05	2168.82	1516.56	1192.05	998.62	780.26	713.19	621.11	561.69
48000	4219.97	2214.96	1548.83	1217.41	1019.86	796.86	728.36	634.33	573.64
49000	4307.88	2261.11	1581.10	1242.77	1041.11	813.46	743.54	647.54	585.59
50000	4395.80	2307.25	1613.36	1268.13	1062.36	830.06	758.71	660.76	597.54
51000	4483.72	2353.40	1645.63	1293.50	1083.60	846.67	773.89	673.97	609.49
52000	4571.63	2399.54	1677.90	1318.86	1104.85	863.27	789.06	687.19	621.45
53000	4659.55	2445.69	1710.17	1344.22	1126.10	879.87	804.24	700.40	633.40
54000	4747.46	2491.83	1742.43	1369.58	1147.35	896.47	819.41	713.62	645.35
55000	4835.38	2537.98	1774.70	1394.95	1168.59	913.07	834.58	726.83	657.30
56000	4923.29	2584.12	1806.97	1420.31	1189.84	929.67	849.76	740.05	669.25
57000	5011.21	2630.27	1839.23	1445.67	1211.09	946.27	864.93	753.26	681.20
58000	5099.13	2676.41	1871.50	1471.03	1232.33	962.87	880.11	766.48	693.15
59000	5187.04	2722.56	1903.77	1496.40	1253.58	979.47	895.28	779.69	705.10
60000	5274.96	2768.70	1936.04	1521.76	1274.83	996.08	910.45	792.91	717.05
61000	5362.87	2814.85	1968.30	1547.12	1296.07	1012.68	925.63	806.12	729.00
62000	5450.79	2860.99	2000.57	1572.49	1317.32	1029.28	940.80	819.34	740.95
63000	5538.71	2907.14	2032.84	1597.85	1338.57	1045.88	955.98	832.55	752.90
64000	5626.62	2953.28	2065.10	1623.21	1359.82	1062.48	971.15	845.77	764.86
65000	5714.54	2999.43	2097.37	1648.57	1381.06	1079.08	986.33	858.98	776.81
66000	5802.45	3045.57	2129.64	1673.94	1402.31	1095.68	1001.50	872.20	788.76
67000	5890.37	3091.72	2161.91	1699.30	1423.56	1112.28	1016.67	885.41	800.71
68000	5978.29	3137.86	2194.17	1724.66	1444.80	1128.89	1031.85	898.63	812.66
69000	6066.20	3184.00	2226.44	1750.02	1466.05	1145.49	1047.02	911.85	824.61
70000	6154.12	3230.15	2258.71	1775.39	1487.30	1162.09	1062.20	925.06	836.56
75000	6593.70	3460.87	2420.04	1902.20	1593.53	1245.09	1138.07	991.14	896.31
80000	7033.28	3691.60	2581.38	2029.01	1699.77	1328.10	1213.94	1057.21	956.07
100000	8791.59	4614.50	3226.72	2536.26	2124.71	1660.12	1517.42	1321.51	1195.08

MONTHLY PAYMENT 10%

NECESSARY TO AMORTIZE A LOAN

TERM / AMOUNT	15 YEARS	18 YEARS	20 YEARS	25 YEARS	28 YEARS	29 YEARS	30 YEARS	35 YEARS	40 YEARS
$ 25	.27	.25	.25	.23	.23	.23	.22	.22	.22
50	.54	.50	.49	.46	.45	.45	.44	.43	.43
75	.81	.75	.73	.69	.67	.67	.66	.65	.64
100	1.08	1.00	.97	.91	.89	.89	.88	.86	.85
200	2.15	2.00	1.94	1.82	1.78	1.77	1.76	1.72	1.70
300	3.23	3.00	2.90	2.73	2.67	2.65	2.64	2.58	2.55
400	4.30	4.00	3.87	3.64	3.56	3.53	3.52	3.44	3.40
500	5.38	5.00	4.83	4.55	4.44	4.42	4.39	4.30	4.25
600	6.45	6.00	5.80	5.46	5.33	5.30	5.27	5.16	5.10
700	7.53	7.00	6.76	6.37	6.22	6.18	6.15	6.02	5.95
800	8.60	8.00	7.73	7.27	7.11	7.06	7.03	6.88	6.80
900	9.68	9.00	8.69	8.18	8.00	7.95	7.90	7.74	7.65
1000	10.75	10.00	9.66	9.09	8.88	8.83	8.78	8.60	8.50
2000	21.50	20.00	19.31	18.18	17.76	17.65	17.56	17.20	16.99
3000	32.24	30.00	28.96	27.27	26.64	26.48	26.33	25.80	25.48
4000	42.99	40.00	38.61	36.35	35.52	35.30	35.11	34.39	33.97
5000	53.74	50.00	48.26	45.44	44.40	44.13	43.88	42.99	42.46
6000	64.48	60.00	57.91	54.53	53.28	52.95	52.66	51.59	50.95
7000	75.23	69.99	67.56	63.61	62.16	61.78	61.44	60.18	59.45
8000	85.97	79.99	77.21	72.70	71.04	70.60	70.21	68.78	67.94
9000	96.72	89.99	86.86	81.79	79.92	79.43	78.99	77.38	76.43
10000	107.47	99.99	96.51	90.88	88.80	88.25	87.76	85.97	84.92
15000	161.20	149.98	144.76	136.31	133.20	132.38	131.64	128.96	127.38
20000	214.93	199.97	193.01	181.75	177.60	176.50	175.52	171.94	169.83
25000	268.66	249.97	241.26	227.18	222.00	220.62	219.40	214.92	212.29
30000	322.39	299.96	289.51	272.62	266.39	264.75	263.28	257.91	254.75
35000	376.12	349.95	337.76	318.05	310.79	308.87	307.16	300.89	297.21
36000	386.86	359.95	347.41	327.14	319.67	317.70	315.93	309.49	305.70
37000	397.61	369.95	357.06	336.22	328.55	326.52	324.71	318.08	314.19
38000	408.35	379.95	366.71	345.31	337.43	335.35	333.48	326.68	322.68
39000	419.10	389.94	376.36	354.40	346.31	344.17	342.26	335.28	331.17
40000	429.85	399.94	386.01	363.49	355.19	353.00	351.03	343.87	339.66
41000	440.59	409.94	395.66	372.57	364.07	361.82	359.81	352.47	348.15
42000	451.34	419.94	405.31	381.66	372.95	370.65	368.59	361.07	356.65
43000	462.09	429.94	414.96	390.75	381.83	379.47	377.36	369.66	365.14
44000	472.83	439.94	424.61	399.83	390.71	388.29	386.14	378.26	373.63
45000	483.58	449.93	434.26	408.92	399.59	397.12	394.91	386.86	382.12
46000	494.32	459.93	443.91	418.01	408.47	405.94	403.69	395.45	390.61
47000	505.07	469.93	453.57	427.09	417.35	414.77	412.46	404.05	399.10
48000	515.82	479.93	463.22	436.18	426.23	423.59	421.24	412.65	407.60
49000	526.56	489.93	472.87	445.27	435.11	432.42	430.02	421.24	416.09
50000	537.31	499.93	482.52	454.36	443.99	441.24	438.79	429.84	424.58
51000	548.05	509.93	492.17	463.44	452.86	450.07	447.57	438.44	433.07
52000	558.80	519.92	501.82	472.53	461.74	458.89	456.34	447.03	441.56
53000	569.55	529.92	511.47	481.62	470.62	467.72	465.12	455.63	450.05
54000	580.29	539.92	521.12	490.70	479.50	476.54	473.89	464.23	458.54
55000	591.04	549.92	530.77	499.79	488.38	485.37	482.67	472.82	467.04
56000	601.78	559.92	540.42	508.88	497.26	494.19	491.45	481.42	475.53
57000	612.53	569.92	550.07	517.96	506.14	503.02	500.22	490.02	484.02
58000	623.28	579.91	559.72	527.05	515.02	511.84	509.00	498.62	492.51
59000	634.02	589.91	569.37	536.14	523.90	520.67	517.77	507.21	501.00
60000	644.77	599.91	579.02	545.23	532.78	529.49	526.55	515.81	509.49
61000	655.51	609.91	588.67	554.31	541.66	538.32	535.32	524.41	517.98
62000	666.26	619.91	598.32	563.40	550.54	547.14	544.10	533.00	526.48
63000	677.01	629.91	607.97	572.49	559.42	555.97	552.88	541.60	534.97
64000	687.75	639.90	617.62	581.57	568.30	564.79	561.65	550.20	543.46
65000	698.50	649.90	627.27	590.66	577.18	573.62	570.43	558.79	551.95
66000	709.24	659.90	636.92	599.75	586.06	582.44	579.20	567.39	560.44
67000	719.99	669.90	646.57	608.83	594.94	591.26	587.98	575.99	568.93
68000	730.74	679.90	656.22	617.92	603.82	600.09	596.75	584.58	577.42
69000	741.48	689.90	665.87	627.01	612.70	608.91	605.53	593.18	585.92
70000	752.23	699.90	675.52	636.10	621.58	617.74	614.31	601.78	594.41
75000	805.96	749.89	723.77	681.53	665.98	661.86	658.18	644.76	636.86
80000	859.69	799.88	772.02	726.97	710.37	705.99	702.06	687.74	679.32
100000	1074.61	999.85	965.03	908.71	887.97	882.48	877.58	859.68	849.15

10⅛% MONTHLY PAYMENT
NECESSARY TO AMORTIZE A LOAN

TERM / AMOUNT	1 YEAR	2 YEARS	3 YEARS	4 YEARS	5 YEARS	7 YEARS	8 YEARS	10 YEARS	12 YEARS
$ 25	2.20	1.16	.81	.64	.54	.42	.39	.34	.31
50	4.40	2.32	1.62	1.28	1.07	.84	.77	.67	.61
75	6.60	3.47	2.43	1.91	1.60	1.25	1.15	1.00	.91
100	8.80	4.63	3.24	2.55	2.14	1.67	1.53	1.33	1.21
200	17.60	9.25	6.47	5.09	4.27	3.34	3.05	2.66	2.41
300	26.40	13.87	9.70	7.63	6.40	5.00	4.58	3.99	3.61
400	35.19	18.49	12.94	10.17	8.53	6.67	6.10	5.32	4.81
500	43.99	23.11	16.17	12.72	10.66	8.34	7.63	6.65	6.02
600	52.79	27.73	19.40	15.26	12.79	10.00	9.15	7.98	7.22
700	61.59	32.35	22.63	17.80	14.92	11.67	10.67	9.30	8.42
800	70.38	36.97	25.87	20.34	17.05	13.34	12.20	10.63	9.62
900	79.18	41.59	29.10	22.89	19.18	15.00	13.72	11.96	10.83
1000	87.98	46.21	32.33	25.43	21.31	16.67	15.25	13.29	12.03
2000	175.95	92.41	64.66	50.85	42.62	33.34	30.49	26.57	24.05
3000	263.93	138.61	96.98	76.27	63.93	50.00	45.73	39.86	36.07
4000	351.90	184.82	129.31	101.70	85.24	66.67	60.97	53.14	48.10
5000	439.88	231.02	161.63	127.12	106.55	83.33	76.21	66.43	60.12
6000	527.85	277.22	193.96	152.54	127.86	100.00	91.45	79.71	72.14
7000	615.82	323.42	226.29	177.96	149.17	116.67	106.69	93.00	84.17
8000	703.80	369.63	258.61	203.39	170.47	133.33	121.93	106.28	96.19
9000	791.77	415.83	290.94	228.81	191.78	150.00	137.17	119.56	108.21
10000	879.75	462.03	323.26	254.23	213.09	166.66	152.41	132.85	120.24
15000	1319.62	693.04	484.89	381.34	319.63	249.99	228.61	199.27	180.35
20000	1759.49	924.06	646.52	508.46	426.18	333.32	304.81	265.69	240.47
25000	2199.36	1155.07	808.15	635.57	532.72	416.65	381.01	332.11	300.58
30000	2639.23	1386.08	969.78	762.68	639.26	499.98	457.22	398.54	360.70
35000	3079.10	1617.10	1131.41	889.80	745.81	583.31	533.42	464.96	420.81
36000	3167.07	1663.30	1163.74	915.22	767.11	599.98	548.66	478.24	432.84
37000	3255.04	1709.50	1196.06	940.64	788.42	616.64	563.90	491.53	444.86
38000	3343.02	1755.71	1228.39	966.07	809.73	633.31	579.14	504.81	456.88
39000	3430.99	1801.91	1260.72	991.49	831.04	649.97	594.38	518.10	468.91
40000	3518.97	1848.11	1293.04	1016.91	852.35	666.64	609.62	531.38	480.93
41000	3606.94	1894.31	1325.37	1042.33	873.66	683.30	624.86	544.66	492.95
42000	3694.91	1940.52	1357.69	1067.76	894.97	699.97	640.10	557.95	504.98
43000	3782.89	1986.72	1390.02	1093.18	916.27	716.64	655.34	571.23	517.00
44000	3870.86	2032.92	1422.34	1118.60	937.58	733.30	670.58	584.52	529.02
45000	3958.84	2079.12	1454.67	1144.02	958.89	749.97	685.82	597.80	541.04
46000	4046.81	2125.33	1487.00	1169.45	980.20	766.63	701.06	611.09	553.07
47000	4134.78	2171.53	1519.32	1194.87	1001.51	783.30	716.30	624.37	565.09
48000	4222.76	2217.73	1551.65	1220.29	1022.82	799.97	731.54	637.66	577.11
49000	4310.73	2263.93	1583.97	1245.72	1044.13	816.63	746.78	650.94	589.14
50000	4398.71	2310.14	1616.30	1271.14	1065.44	833.30	762.02	664.22	601.16
51000	4486.68	2356.34	1648.63	1296.56	1086.74	849.96	777.26	677.51	613.18
52000	4574.65	2402.54	1680.95	1321.98	1108.05	866.63	792.51	690.79	625.21
53000	4662.63	2448.74	1713.28	1347.41	1129.36	883.29	807.75	704.08	637.23
54000	4750.60	2494.95	1745.60	1372.83	1150.67	899.96	822.99	717.36	649.25
55000	4838.58	2541.15	1777.93	1398.25	1171.98	916.63	838.23	730.65	661.28
56000	4926.55	2587.35	1810.26	1423.67	1193.29	933.29	853.47	743.93	673.30
57000	5014.52	2633.56	1842.58	1449.10	1214.60	949.96	868.71	757.22	685.32
58000	5102.50	2679.76	1874.91	1474.52	1235.90	966.62	883.95	770.50	697.35
59000	5190.47	2725.96	1907.23	1499.94	1257.21	983.29	899.19	783.78	709.37
60000	5278.45	2772.16	1939.56	1525.36	1278.52	999.96	914.43	797.07	721.39
61000	5366.42	2818.37	1971.89	1550.79	1299.83	1016.62	929.67	810.35	733.41
62000	5454.40	2864.57	2004.21	1576.21	1321.14	1033.29	944.91	823.64	745.44
63000	5542.37	2910.77	2036.54	1601.63	1342.45	1049.95	960.15	836.92	757.46
64000	5630.34	2956.97	2068.86	1627.05	1363.76	1066.62	975.39	850.21	769.48
65000	5718.32	3003.18	2101.19	1652.48	1385.06	1083.28	990.63	863.49	781.51
66000	5806.29	3049.38	2133.51	1677.90	1406.37	1099.95	1005.87	876.77	793.53
67000	5894.27	3095.58	2165.84	1703.32	1427.68	1116.62	1021.11	890.06	805.55
68000	5982.24	3141.78	2198.17	1728.75	1448.99	1133.28	1036.35	903.34	817.58
69000	6070.21	3187.99	2230.49	1754.17	1470.30	1149.95	1051.59	916.63	829.60
70000	6158.19	3234.19	2262.82	1779.59	1491.61	1166.61	1066.83	929.91	841.62
75000	6598.06	3465.20	2424.45	1906.70	1598.15	1249.94	1143.03	996.33	901.74
80000	7037.93	3696.22	2586.08	2033.82	1704.69	1333.27	1219.24	1062.76	961.85
100000	8797.41	4620.27	3232.60	2542.27	2130.87	1666.59	1524.04	1328.44	1202.32

MONTHLY PAYMENT 10⅛%

NECESSARY TO AMORTIZE A LOAN

TERM / AMOUNT	15 YEARS	18 YEARS	20 YEARS	25 YEARS	28 YEARS	29 YEARS	30 YEARS	35 YEARS	40 YEARS
$ 25	.28	.26	.25	.23	.23	.23	.23	.22	.22
50	.55	.51	.49	.46	.45	.45	.45	.44	.43
75	.82	.76	.73	.69	.68	.67	.67	.66	.65
100	1.09	1.01	.98	.92	.90	.90	.89	.87	.86
200	2.17	2.02	1.95	1.84	1.80	1.79	1.78	1.74	1.72
300	3.25	3.03	2.92	2.76	2.70	2.68	2.67	2.61	2.58
400	4.33	4.04	3.90	3.68	3.59	3.57	3.55	3.48	3.44
500	5.42	5.04	4.87	4.59	4.49	4.46	4.44	4.35	4.30
600	6.50	6.05	5.84	5.51	5.39	5.35	5.33	5.22	5.16
700	7.58	7.06	6.82	6.43	6.28	6.25	6.21	6.09	6.02
800	8.66	8.07	7.79	7.35	7.18	7.14	7.10	6.96	6.88
900	9.75	9.08	8.76	8.26	8.08	8.03	7.99	7.83	7.74
1000	10.83	10.08	9.74	9.18	8.98	8.92	8.87	8.70	8.59
2000	21.65	20.16	19.47	18.36	17.95	17.84	17.74	17.39	17.18
3000	32.47	30.24	29.20	27.53	26.92	26.75	26.61	26.08	25.77
4000	43.30	40.32	38.94	36.71	35.89	35.67	35.48	34.78	34.36
5000	54.12	50.40	48.67	45.88	44.86	44.59	44.35	43.47	42.95
6000	64.94	60.48	58.40	55.06	53.83	53.50	53.21	52.16	51.54
7000	75.76	70.56	68.14	64.23	62.80	62.42	62.08	60.85	60.13
8000	86.59	80.64	77.87	73.41	71.77	71.34	70.95	69.55	68.72
9000	97.41	90.72	87.60	82.58	80.74	80.25	79.82	78.24	77.31
10000	108.23	100.79	97.34	91.76	89.71	89.17	88.69	86.93	85.90
15000	162.34	151.19	146.00	137.63	134.56	133.75	133.03	130.39	128.85
20000	216.46	201.58	194.67	183.51	179.42	178.34	177.37	173.86	171.80
25000	270.57	251.98	243.33	229.39	224.27	222.92	221.71	217.32	214.75
30000	324.68	302.37	292.00	275.26	269.12	267.50	266.05	260.78	257.70
35000	378.80	352.77	340.67	321.14	313.97	312.08	310.39	304.24	300.65
36000	389.62	362.85	350.40	330.31	322.94	321.00	319.26	312.94	309.23
37000	400.44	372.93	360.13	339.49	331.91	329.92	328.13	321.63	317.82
38000	411.27	383.01	369.87	348.67	340.89	338.83	337.00	330.32	326.41
39000	422.09	393.09	379.60	357.84	349.86	347.75	345.87	339.01	335.00
40000	432.91	403.16	389.33	367.02	358.83	356.67	354.73	347.71	343.59
41000	443.73	413.24	399.07	376.19	367.80	365.58	363.60	356.40	352.18
42000	454.56	423.32	408.80	385.37	376.77	374.50	372.47	365.09	360.77
43000	465.38	433.40	418.53	394.54	385.74	383.42	381.34	373.78	369.36
44000	476.20	443.48	428.26	403.72	394.71	392.33	390.21	382.48	377.95
45000	487.02	453.56	438.00	412.89	403.68	401.25	399.08	391.17	386.54
46000	497.85	463.64	447.73	422.07	412.65	410.16	407.94	399.86	395.13
47000	508.67	473.72	457.46	431.24	421.62	419.08	416.81	408.55	403.72
48000	519.49	483.80	467.20	440.42	430.59	428.00	425.68	417.25	412.31
49000	530.31	493.87	476.93	449.59	439.56	436.91	434.55	425.94	420.90
50000	541.14	503.95	486.66	458.77	448.53	445.83	443.42	434.63	429.49
51000	551.96	514.03	496.40	467.94	457.50	454.75	452.28	443.32	438.08
52000	562.78	524.11	506.13	477.12	466.47	463.66	461.15	452.02	446.67
53000	573.61	534.19	515.86	486.29	475.44	472.58	470.02	460.71	455.26
54000	584.43	544.27	525.60	495.47	484.41	481.50	478.89	469.40	463.85
55000	595.25	554.35	535.33	504.65	493.38	490.41	487.76	478.09	472.44
56000	606.07	564.43	545.06	513.82	502.36	499.33	496.63	486.79	481.03
57000	616.90	574.51	554.80	523.00	511.33	508.25	505.49	495.48	489.62
58000	627.72	584.59	564.53	532.17	520.30	517.16	514.36	504.17	498.21
59000	638.54	594.66	574.26	541.35	529.27	526.08	523.23	512.86	506.80
60000	649.36	604.74	584.00	550.52	538.24	535.00	532.10	521.56	515.39
61000	660.19	614.82	593.73	559.70	547.21	543.91	540.97	530.25	523.98
62000	671.01	624.90	603.46	568.87	556.18	552.83	549.84	538.94	532.57
63000	681.83	634.98	613.20	578.05	565.15	561.75	558.70	547.63	541.16
64000	692.65	645.06	622.93	587.22	574.12	570.66	567.57	556.33	549.75
65000	703.48	655.14	632.66	596.40	583.09	579.58	576.44	565.02	558.34
66000	714.30	665.22	642.39	605.57	592.06	588.49	585.31	573.71	566.93
67000	725.12	675.30	652.13	614.75	601.03	597.41	594.18	582.40	575.52
68000	735.95	685.38	661.86	623.92	610.00	606.33	603.04	591.10	584.11
69000	746.77	695.45	671.59	633.10	618.97	615.24	611.91	599.79	592.70
70000	757.59	705.53	681.33	642.27	627.94	624.16	620.78	608.48	601.29
75000	811.70	755.93	729.99	688.15	672.80	668.74	665.12	651.94	644.23
80000	865.82	806.32	778.66	734.03	717.65	713.33	709.46	695.41	687.18
100000	1082.27	1007.90	973.32	917.53	897.06	891.66	886.83	869.26	858.98

10¼% MONTHLY PAYMENT
NECESSARY TO AMORTIZE A LOAN

TERM / AMOUNT	1 YEAR	2 YEARS	3 YEARS	4 YEARS	5 YEARS	7 YEARS	8 YEARS	10 YEARS	12 YEARS
$ 25	2.21	1.16	.81	.64	.54	.42	.39	.34	.31
50	4.41	2.32	1.62	1.28	1.07	.84	.77	.67	.61
75	6.61	3.47	2.43	1.92	1.61	1.26	1.15	1.01	.91
100	8.81	4.63	3.24	2.55	2.14	1.68	1.54	1.34	1.21
200	17.61	9.26	6.48	5.10	4.28	3.35	3.07	2.68	2.42
300	26.41	13.88	9.72	7.65	6.42	5.02	4.60	4.01	3.63
400	35.22	18.51	12.96	10.20	8.55	6.70	6.13	5.35	4.84
500	44.02	23.14	16.20	12.75	10.69	8.37	7.66	6.68	6.05
600	52.82	27.76	19.44	15.29	12.83	10.04	9.19	8.02	7.26
700	61.63	32.39	22.67	17.84	14.96	11.72	10.72	9.35	8.47
800	70.43	37.01	25.91	20.39	17.10	13.39	12.25	10.69	9.68
900	79.23	41.64	29.15	22.94	19.24	15.06	13.78	12.02	10.89
1000	88.04	46.27	32.39	25.49	21.38	16.74	15.31	13.36	12.10
2000	176.07	92.53	64.77	50.97	42.75	33.47	30.62	26.71	24.20
3000	264.10	138.79	97.16	76.45	64.12	50.20	45.93	40.07	36.29
4000	352.13	185.05	129.54	101.94	85.49	66.93	61.23	53.42	48.39
5000	440.17	231.31	161.93	127.42	106.86	83.66	76.54	66.77	60.48
6000	528.20	277.57	194.31	152.90	128.23	100.39	91.85	80.13	72.58
7000	616.23	323.83	226.70	178.38	149.60	117.12	107.15	93.48	84.67
8000	704.26	370.09	259.08	203.87	170.97	133.85	122.46	106.84	96.77
9000	792.29	416.35	291.47	229.35	192.34	150.58	137.77	120.19	108.87
10000	880.33	462.61	323.85	254.83	213.71	167.31	153.07	133.54	120.96
15000	1320.49	693.91	485.78	382.25	320.56	250.96	229.61	200.31	181.44
20000	1760.65	925.21	647.70	509.66	427.41	334.62	306.14	267.08	241.92
25000	2200.81	1156.51	809.62	637.08	534.26	418.27	382.67	333.85	302.40
30000	2640.97	1387.82	971.55	764.49	641.11	501.92	459.21	400.62	362.87
35000	3081.13	1619.12	1133.47	891.90	747.96	585.58	535.74	467.39	423.35
36000	3169.16	1665.38	1165.85	917.39	769.33	602.31	551.05	480.75	435.45
37000	3257.20	1711.64	1198.24	942.87	790.70	619.04	566.36	494.10	447.54
38000	3345.23	1757.90	1230.62	968.35	812.08	635.77	581.66	507.45	459.64
39000	3433.26	1804.16	1263.01	993.83	833.45	652.50	596.97	520.81	471.74
40000	3521.29	1850.42	1295.39	1019.32	854.82	669.23	612.28	534.16	483.83
41000	3609.33	1896.68	1327.78	1044.80	876.19	685.96	627.58	547.51	495.93
42000	3697.36	1942.94	1360.16	1070.28	897.56	702.69	642.89	560.87	508.02
43000	3785.39	1989.20	1392.55	1095.77	918.93	719.42	658.20	574.22	520.12
44000	3873.42	2035.46	1424.93	1121.25	940.30	736.15	673.50	587.58	532.21
45000	3961.45	2081.72	1457.32	1146.73	961.67	752.88	688.81	600.93	544.31
46000	4049.49	2127.98	1489.70	1172.21	983.04	769.61	704.12	614.28	556.40
47000	4137.52	2174.24	1522.09	1197.70	1004.41	786.35	719.42	627.64	568.50
48000	4225.55	2220.50	1554.47	1223.18	1025.78	803.08	734.73	640.99	580.60
49000	4313.58	2266.76	1586.85	1248.66	1047.15	819.81	750.04	654.35	592.69
50000	4401.62	2313.02	1619.24	1274.15	1068.52	836.54	765.34	667.70	604.79
51000	4489.65	2359.29	1651.62	1299.63	1089.89	853.27	780.65	681.05	616.88
52000	4577.68	2405.55	1684.01	1325.11	1111.26	870.00	795.96	694.41	628.98
53000	4665.71	2451.81	1716.39	1350.59	1132.63	886.73	811.26	707.76	641.07
54000	4753.74	2498.07	1748.78	1376.08	1154.00	903.46	826.57	721.12	653.17
55000	4841.78	2544.33	1781.16	1401.56	1175.37	920.19	841.88	734.47	665.27
56000	4929.81	2590.59	1813.55	1427.04	1196.74	936.92	857.18	747.82	677.36
57000	5017.84	2636.85	1845.93	1452.53	1218.11	953.65	872.49	761.18	689.46
58000	5105.87	2683.11	1878.32	1478.01	1239.48	970.38	887.80	774.53	701.55
59000	5193.90	2729.37	1910.70	1503.49	1260.85	987.11	903.10	787.89	713.65
60000	5281.94	2775.63	1943.09	1528.97	1282.22	1003.84	918.41	801.24	725.74
61000	5369.97	2821.89	1975.47	1554.46	1303.59	1020.57	933.72	814.59	737.84
62000	5458.00	2868.15	2007.86	1579.94	1324.96	1037.30	949.02	827.95	749.94
63000	5546.03	2914.41	2040.24	1605.42	1346.33	1054.04	964.33	841.30	762.03
64000	5634.07	2960.67	2072.63	1630.91	1367.70	1070.77	979.64	854.65	774.13
65000	5722.10	3006.93	2105.01	1656.39	1389.07	1087.50	994.95	868.01	786.22
66000	5810.13	3053.19	2137.39	1681.87	1410.44	1104.23	1010.25	881.36	798.32
67000	5898.16	3099.45	2169.78	1707.35	1431.81	1120.96	1025.56	894.72	810.41
68000	5986.19	3145.71	2202.16	1732.84	1453.18	1137.69	1040.87	908.07	822.51
69000	6074.23	3191.97	2234.55	1758.32	1474.55	1154.42	1056.17	921.42	834.60
70000	6162.26	3238.23	2266.93	1783.80	1495.92	1171.15	1071.48	934.78	846.70
75000	6602.42	3469.53	2428.86	1911.22	1602.77	1254.80	1148.01	1001.55	907.18
80000	7042.58	3700.84	2590.78	2038.63	1709.63	1338.46	1224.55	1068.32	967.66
100000	8803.23	4626.04	3238.47	2548.29	2137.03	1673.07	1530.68	1335.40	1209.57

MONTHLY PAYMENT 10¼%

NECESSARY TO AMORTIZE A LOAN

TERM / AMOUNT	15 YEARS	18 YEARS	20 YEARS	25 YEARS	28 YEARS	29 YEARS	30 YEARS	35 YEARS	40 YEARS
$ 25	.28	.26	.25	.24	.23	.23	.23	.22	.22
50	.55	.51	.50	.47	.46	.46	.45	.44	.44
75	.82	.77	.74	.70	.68	.68	.68	.66	.66
100	1.09	1.02	.99	.93	.91	.91	.90	.88	.87
200	2.18	2.04	1.97	1.86	1.82	1.81	1.80	1.76	1.74
300	3.27	3.05	2.95	2.78	2.72	2.71	2.69	2.64	2.61
400	4.36	4.07	3.93	3.71	3.63	3.61	3.59	3.52	3.48
500	5.45	5.08	4.91	4.64	4.54	4.51	4.49	4.40	4.35
600	6.54	6.10	5.89	5.56	5.44	5.41	5.38	5.28	5.22
700	7.63	7.12	6.88	6.49	6.35	6.31	6.28	6.16	6.09
800	8.72	8.13	7.86	7.42	7.25	7.21	7.17	7.04	6.96
900	9.81	9.15	8.84	8.34	8.16	8.11	8.07	7.91	7.82
1000	10.90	10.16	9.82	9.27	9.07	9.01	8.97	8.79	8.69
2000	21.80	20.32	19.64	18.53	18.13	18.02	17.93	17.58	17.38
3000	32.70	30.48	29.45	27.80	27.19	27.03	26.89	26.37	26.07
4000	43.60	40.64	39.27	37.06	36.25	36.04	35.85	35.16	34.76
5000	54.50	50.80	49.09	46.32	45.31	45.05	44.81	43.95	43.45
6000	65.40	60.96	58.90	55.59	54.38	54.06	53.77	52.74	52.13
7000	76.30	71.12	68.72	64.85	63.44	63.06	62.73	61.52	60.82
8000	87.20	81.28	78.54	74.12	72.50	72.07	71.69	70.31	69.51
9000	98.10	91.44	88.35	83.38	81.56	81.08	80.65	79.10	78.20
10000	109.00	101.60	98.17	92.64	90.62	90.09	89.62	87.89	86.89
15000	163.50	152.40	147.25	138.96	135.93	135.13	134.42	131.83	130.33
20000	218.00	203.20	196.33	185.28	181.24	180.18	179.23	175.78	173.77
25000	272.49	254.00	245.42	231.60	226.55	225.22	224.03	219.72	217.21
30000	326.99	304.80	294.50	277.92	271.86	270.26	268.84	263.66	260.65
35000	381.49	355.60	343.58	324.24	317.17	315.30	313.64	307.60	304.09
36000	392.39	365.76	353.40	333.50	326.23	324.31	322.60	316.39	312.78
37000	403.29	375.92	363.21	342.77	335.29	333.32	331.56	325.18	321.47
38000	414.19	386.08	373.03	352.03	344.35	342.33	340.52	333.97	330.16
39000	425.09	396.24	382.85	361.29	353.41	351.34	349.48	342.76	338.84
40000	435.99	406.40	392.66	370.56	362.48	360.35	358.45	351.55	347.53
41000	446.88	416.56	402.48	379.82	371.54	369.36	367.41	360.34	356.22
42000	457.78	426.72	412.30	389.09	380.60	378.36	376.37	369.12	364.91
43000	468.68	436.88	422.11	398.35	389.66	387.37	385.33	377.91	373.60
44000	479.58	447.04	431.93	407.61	398.72	396.38	394.29	386.70	382.29
45000	490.48	457.20	441.74	416.88	407.78	405.39	403.25	395.49	390.97
46000	501.38	467.36	451.56	426.14	416.85	414.40	412.21	404.28	399.66
47000	512.28	477.52	461.38	435.41	425.91	423.41	421.17	413.07	408.35
48000	523.18	487.68	471.19	444.67	434.97	432.41	430.13	421.86	417.04
49000	534.08	497.84	481.01	453.93	444.03	441.42	439.09	430.64	425.73
50000	544.98	508.00	490.83	463.20	453.09	450.43	448.06	439.43	434.41
51000	555.88	518.15	500.64	472.46	462.15	459.44	457.02	448.22	443.10
52000	566.78	528.31	510.46	481.72	471.22	468.45	465.98	457.01	451.79
53000	577.68	538.47	520.28	490.99	480.28	477.46	474.94	465.80	460.48
54000	588.58	548.63	530.09	500.25	489.34	486.47	483.90	474.59	469.17
55000	599.48	558.79	539.91	509.52	498.40	495.47	492.86	483.38	477.86
56000	610.38	568.95	549.73	518.78	507.46	504.48	501.82	492.16	486.54
57000	621.28	579.11	559.54	528.04	516.53	513.49	510.78	500.95	495.23
58000	632.18	589.27	569.36	537.31	525.59	522.50	519.74	509.74	503.92
59000	643.08	599.43	579.17	546.57	534.65	531.51	528.70	518.53	512.61
60000	653.98	609.59	588.99	555.83	543.71	540.52	537.67	527.32	521.30
61000	664.88	619.75	598.81	565.10	552.77	549.53	546.63	536.11	529.98
62000	675.77	629.91	608.62	574.36	561.83	558.53	555.59	544.90	538.67
63000	686.67	640.07	618.44	583.63	570.90	567.54	564.55	553.68	547.36
64000	697.57	650.23	628.26	592.89	579.96	576.55	573.51	562.47	556.05
65000	708.47	660.39	638.07	602.15	589.02	585.56	582.47	571.26	564.74
66000	719.37	670.55	647.89	611.42	598.08	594.57	591.43	580.05	573.43
67000	730.27	680.71	657.71	620.68	607.14	603.58	600.39	588.84	582.11
68000	741.17	690.87	667.52	629.95	616.20	612.59	609.35	597.63	590.80
69000	752.07	701.03	677.34	639.21	625.27	621.59	618.31	606.42	599.49
70000	762.97	711.19	687.16	648.47	634.33	630.60	627.28	615.20	608.18
75000	817.47	761.99	736.24	694.79	679.64	675.65	672.08	659.15	651.62
80000	871.97	812.79	785.32	741.11	724.95	720.69	716.89	703.09	695.06
100000	1089.96	1015.99	981.65	926.39	906.18	900.86	896.11	878.86	868.82

10⅜% MONTHLY PAYMENT
NECESSARY TO AMORTIZE A LOAN

TERM / AMOUNT	1 YEAR	2 YEARS	3 YEARS	4 YEARS	5 YEARS	7 YEARS	8 YEARS	10 YEARS	12 YEARS
$ 25	2.21	1.16	.82	.64	.54	.42	.39	.34	.31
50	4.41	2.32	1.63	1.28	1.08	.84	.77	.68	.61
75	6.61	3.48	2.44	1.92	1.61	1.26	1.16	1.01	.92
100	8.81	4.64	3.25	2.56	2.15	1.68	1.54	1.35	1.22
200	17.62	9.27	6.49	5.11	4.29	3.36	3.08	2.69	2.44
300	26.43	13.90	9.74	7.67	6.43	5.04	4.62	4.03	3.66
400	35.24	18.53	12.98	10.22	8.58	6.72	6.15	5.37	4.87
500	44.05	23.16	16.23	12.78	10.72	8.40	7.69	6.72	6.09
600	52.86	27.80	19.47	15.33	12.86	10.08	9.23	8.06	7.31
700	61.67	32.43	22.72	17.89	15.01	11.76	10.77	9.40	8.52
800	70.48	37.06	25.96	20.44	17.15	13.44	12.30	10.74	9.74
900	79.29	41.69	29.20	22.99	19.29	15.12	13.84	12.09	10.96
1000	88.10	46.32	32.45	25.55	21.44	16.80	15.38	13.43	12.17
2000	176.19	92.64	64.89	51.09	42.87	33.60	30.75	26.85	24.34
3000	264.28	138.96	97.34	76.63	64.30	50.39	46.12	40.28	36.51
4000	352.37	185.28	129.78	102.18	85.73	67.19	61.50	53.70	48.68
5000	440.46	231.60	162.22	127.72	107.17	83.98	76.87	67.12	60.85
6000	528.55	277.91	194.67	153.26	128.60	100.78	92.24	80.55	73.02
7000	616.64	324.23	227.11	178.81	150.03	117.57	107.62	93.97	85.18
8000	704.73	370.55	259.55	204.35	171.46	134.37	122.99	107.39	97.35
9000	792.82	416.87	292.00	229.89	192.89	151.17	138.36	120.82	109.52
10000	880.91	463.19	324.44	255.44	214.33	167.96	153.74	134.24	121.69
15000	1321.36	694.78	486.66	383.15	321.49	251.94	230.60	201.36	182.53
20000	1761.81	926.37	648.88	510.87	428.65	335.92	307.47	268.48	243.37
25000	2202.26	1157.96	811.09	638.58	535.81	419.89	384.34	335.60	304.22
30000	2642.72	1389.55	973.31	766.30	642.97	503.87	461.20	402.71	365.06
35000	3083.17	1621.14	1135.53	894.01	750.13	587.85	538.07	469.83	425.90
36000	3171.26	1667.46	1167.97	919.55	771.56	604.65	553.44	483.25	438.07
37000	3259.35	1713.78	1200.42	945.10	792.99	621.44	568.82	496.68	450.24
38000	3347.44	1760.10	1232.86	970.64	814.42	638.24	584.19	510.10	462.40
39000	3435.53	1806.41	1265.30	996.18	835.85	655.03	599.56	523.53	474.57
40000	3523.62	1852.73	1297.75	1021.73	857.29	671.83	614.94	536.95	486.74
41000	3611.71	1899.05	1330.19	1047.27	878.72	688.62	630.31	550.37	498.91
42000	3699.80	1945.37	1362.63	1072.81	900.15	705.42	645.68	563.80	511.08
43000	3787.89	1991.69	1395.08	1098.36	921.58	722.22	661.06	577.22	523.25
44000	3875.98	2038.01	1427.52	1123.90	943.01	739.01	676.43	590.64	535.42
45000	3964.07	2084.32	1459.96	1149.44	964.45	755.81	691.80	604.07	547.58
46000	4052.16	2130.64	1492.41	1174.99	985.88	772.60	707.18	617.49	559.75
47000	4140.25	2176.96	1524.85	1200.53	1007.31	789.40	722.55	630.91	571.92
48000	4228.34	2223.28	1557.29	1226.07	1028.74	806.19	737.92	644.34	584.09
49000	4316.43	2269.60	1589.74	1251.61	1050.17	822.99	753.30	657.76	596.26
50000	4404.52	2315.91	1622.18	1277.16	1071.61	839.78	768.67	671.19	608.43
51000	4492.61	2362.23	1654.63	1302.70	1093.04	856.58	784.04	684.61	620.59
52000	4580.71	2408.55	1687.07	1328.24	1114.47	873.38	799.42	698.03	632.76
53000	4668.80	2454.87	1719.51	1353.79	1135.90	890.17	814.79	711.46	644.93
54000	4756.89	2501.19	1751.96	1379.33	1157.33	906.97	830.16	724.88	657.10
55000	4844.98	2547.51	1784.40	1404.87	1178.77	923.76	845.54	738.30	669.27
56000	4933.07	2593.82	1816.84	1430.42	1200.20	940.56	860.91	751.73	681.44
57000	5021.16	2640.14	1849.29	1455.96	1221.63	957.35	876.28	765.15	693.60
58000	5109.25	2686.46	1881.73	1481.50	1243.06	974.15	891.66	778.57	705.77
59000	5197.34	2732.78	1914.17	1507.05	1264.49	990.94	907.03	792.00	717.94
60000	5285.43	2779.10	1946.62	1532.59	1285.93	1007.74	922.40	805.42	730.11
61000	5373.52	2825.42	1979.06	1558.13	1307.36	1024.54	937.78	818.84	742.28
62000	5461.61	2871.73	2011.50	1583.67	1328.79	1041.33	953.15	832.27	754.45
63000	5549.70	2918.05	2043.95	1609.22	1350.22	1058.13	968.52	845.69	766.62
64000	5637.79	2964.37	2076.39	1634.76	1371.65	1074.92	983.90	859.12	778.78
65000	5725.88	3010.69	2108.83	1660.30	1393.09	1091.72	999.27	872.54	790.95
66000	5813.97	3057.01	2141.28	1685.85	1414.52	1108.51	1014.64	885.96	803.12
67000	5902.06	3103.32	2173.72	1711.39	1435.95	1125.31	1030.02	899.39	815.29
68000	5990.15	3149.64	2206.17	1736.93	1457.38	1142.10	1045.39	912.81	827.46
69000	6078.24	3195.96	2238.61	1762.48	1478.82	1158.90	1060.76	926.23	839.63
70000	6166.33	3242.28	2271.05	1788.02	1500.25	1175.70	1076.14	939.66	851.79
75000	6606.78	3473.87	2433.27	1915.73	1607.41	1259.67	1153.00	1006.78	912.64
80000	7047.24	3705.46	2595.49	2043.45	1714.57	1343.65	1229.87	1073.89	973.48
100000	8809.04	4631.82	3244.36	2554.31	2143.21	1679.56	1537.34	1342.37	1216.85

MONTHLY PAYMENT 10⅜%

NECESSARY TO AMORTIZE A LOAN

TERM / AMOUNT	15 YEARS	18 YEARS	20 YEARS	25 YEARS	28 YEARS	29 YEARS	30 YEARS	35 YEARS	40 YEARS
$ 25	.28	.26	.25	.24	.23	.23	.23	.23	.22
50	.55	.52	.50	.47	.46	.46	.46	.45	.44
75	.83	.77	.75	.71	.69	.69	.68	.67	.66
100	1.10	1.03	.99	.94	.92	.92	.91	.89	.88
200	2.20	2.05	1.98	1.88	1.84	1.83	1.82	1.78	1.76
300	3.30	3.08	2.97	2.81	2.75	2.74	2.72	2.67	2.64
400	4.40	4.10	3.96	3.75	3.67	3.65	3.63	3.56	3.52
500	5.49	5.13	4.95	4.68	4.58	4.56	4.53	4.45	4.40
600	6.59	6.15	5.94	5.62	5.50	5.47	5.44	5.34	5.28
700	7.69	7.17	6.93	6.55	6.41	6.38	6.34	6.22	6.16
800	8.79	8.20	7.92	7.49	7.33	7.29	7.25	7.11	7.03
900	9.88	9.22	8.91	8.42	8.24	8.20	8.15	8.00	7.91
1000	10.98	10.25	9.90	9.36	9.16	9.11	9.06	8.89	8.79
2000	21.96	20.49	19.80	18.71	18.31	18.21	18.11	17.77	17.58
3000	32.93	30.73	29.70	28.06	27.46	27.31	27.17	26.66	26.37
4000	43.91	40.97	39.60	37.42	36.62	36.41	36.22	35.54	35.15
5000	54.89	51.21	49.50	46.77	45.77	45.51	45.28	44.43	43.94
6000	65.86	61.45	59.40	56.12	54.92	54.61	54.33	53.31	52.73
7000	76.84	71.69	69.30	65.47	64.08	63.71	63.38	62.20	61.51
8000	87.82	81.93	79.20	74.83	73.23	72.81	72.44	71.08	70.30
9000	98.79	92.17	89.10	84.18	82.38	81.91	81.49	79.97	79.09
10000	109.77	102.41	99.00	93.53	91.54	91.01	90.55	88.85	87.87
15000	164.65	153.62	148.50	140.30	137.30	136.52	135.82	133.28	131.81
20000	219.54	204.82	198.00	187.06	183.07	182.02	181.09	177.70	175.74
25000	274.42	256.03	247.50	233.82	228.84	227.53	226.36	222.13	219.68
30000	329.30	307.23	297.00	280.59	274.60	273.03	271.63	266.55	263.61
35000	384.19	358.44	346.50	327.35	320.37	318.53	316.90	310.97	307.54
36000	395.16	368.68	356.40	336.70	329.52	327.64	325.95	319.86	316.33
37000	406.14	378.92	366.30	346.05	338.68	336.74	335.01	328.74	325.12
38000	417.12	389.16	376.20	355.41	347.83	345.84	344.06	337.63	333.91
39000	428.09	399.40	386.10	364.76	356.98	354.94	353.11	346.51	342.69
40000	439.07	409.64	396.00	374.11	366.14	364.04	362.17	355.40	351.48
41000	450.05	419.88	405.90	383.46	375.29	373.14	371.22	364.28	360.27
42000	461.02	430.12	415.80	392.82	384.44	382.24	380.28	373.17	369.05
43000	472.00	440.36	425.70	402.17	393.60	391.34	389.33	382.05	377.84
44000	482.98	450.60	435.60	411.52	402.75	400.44	398.38	390.94	386.63
45000	493.95	460.85	445.50	420.88	411.90	409.54	407.44	399.82	395.41
46000	504.93	471.09	455.40	430.23	421.05	418.64	416.49	408.71	404.20
47000	515.91	481.33	465.30	439.58	430.21	427.74	425.55	417.59	412.99
48000	526.88	491.57	475.20	448.93	439.36	436.85	434.60	426.48	421.77
49000	537.86	501.81	485.10	458.29	448.51	445.95	443.65	435.36	430.56
50000	548.84	512.05	495.00	467.64	457.67	455.05	452.71	444.25	439.35
51000	559.81	522.29	504.90	476.99	466.82	464.15	461.76	453.13	448.13
52000	570.79	532.53	514.80	486.34	475.97	473.25	470.82	462.02	456.92
53000	581.77	542.77	524.70	495.70	485.13	482.35	479.87	470.90	465.71
54000	592.74	553.01	534.60	505.05	494.28	491.45	488.92	479.79	474.49
55000	603.72	563.25	544.50	514.40	503.43	500.55	497.98	488.67	483.28
56000	614.70	573.50	554.40	523.76	512.59	509.65	507.03	497.56	492.07
57000	625.67	583.74	564.30	533.11	521.74	518.75	516.09	506.44	500.86
58000	636.65	593.98	574.20	542.46	530.89	527.85	525.14	515.33	509.64
59000	647.63	604.22	584.10	551.81	540.05	536.95	534.20	524.21	518.43
60000	658.60	614.46	594.00	561.17	549.20	546.06	543.25	533.09	527.22
61000	669.58	624.70	603.90	570.52	558.35	555.16	552.30	541.98	536.00
62000	680.56	634.94	613.80	579.87	567.51	564.26	561.36	550.86	544.79
63000	691.53	645.18	623.70	589.22	576.66	573.36	570.41	559.75	553.58
64000	702.51	655.42	633.60	598.58	585.81	582.46	579.47	568.63	562.36
65000	713.49	665.66	643.50	607.93	594.97	591.56	588.52	577.52	571.15
66000	724.46	675.90	653.40	617.28	604.12	600.66	597.57	586.40	579.94
67000	735.44	686.15	663.30	626.63	613.27	609.76	606.63	595.29	588.72
68000	746.42	696.39	673.20	635.99	622.43	618.86	615.68	604.17	597.51
69000	757.39	706.63	683.10	645.34	631.58	627.96	624.74	613.06	606.30
70000	768.37	716.87	693.00	654.69	640.73	637.06	633.79	621.94	615.08
75000	823.25	768.07	742.50	701.46	686.50	682.57	679.06	666.37	659.02
80000	878.13	819.28	792.00	748.22	732.27	728.07	724.33	710.79	702.95
100000	1097.67	1024.10	990.00	935.27	915.33	910.09	905.41	888.49	878.69

10½% MONTHLY PAYMENT
NECESSARY TO AMORTIZE A LOAN

TERM / AMOUNT	1 YEAR	2 YEARS	3 YEARS	4 YEARS	5 YEARS	7 YEARS	8 YEARS	10 YEARS	12 YEARS
$ 25	2.21	1.16	.82	.65	.54	.43	.39	.34	.31
50	4.41	2.32	1.63	1.29	1.08	.85	.78	.68	.62
75	6.62	3.48	2.44	1.93	1.62	1.27	1.16	1.02	.92
100	8.82	4.64	3.26	2.57	2.15	1.69	1.55	1.35	1.23
200	17.63	9.28	6.51	5.13	4.30	3.38	3.09	2.70	2.45
300	26.45	13.92	9.76	7.69	6.45	5.06	4.64	4.05	3.68
400	35.26	18.56	13.01	10.25	8.60	6.75	6.18	5.40	4.90
500	44.08	23.19	16.26	12.81	10.75	8.44	7.73	6.75	6.13
600	52.89	27.83	19.51	15.37	12.90	10.12	9.27	8.10	7.35
700	61.71	32.47	22.76	17.93	15.05	11.81	10.81	9.45	8.57
800	70.52	37.11	26.01	20.49	17.20	13.49	12.36	10.80	9.80
900	79.34	41.74	29.26	23.05	19.35	15.18	13.90	12.15	11.02
1000	88.15	46.38	32.51	25.61	21.50	16.87	15.45	13.50	12.25
2000	176.30	92.76	65.01	51.21	42.99	33.73	30.89	26.99	24.49
3000	264.45	139.13	97.51	76.82	64.49	50.59	46.33	40.49	36.73
4000	352.60	185.51	130.01	102.42	85.98	67.45	61.77	53.98	48.97
5000	440.75	231.89	162.52	128.02	107.47	84.31	77.21	67.47	61.21
6000	528.90	278.26	195.02	153.63	128.97	101.17	92.65	80.97	73.45
7000	617.05	324.64	227.52	179.23	150.46	118.03	108.09	94.46	85.69
8000	705.19	371.01	260.02	204.83	171.96	134.89	123.53	107.95	97.94
9000	793.34	417.39	292.53	230.44	193.45	151.75	138.97	121.45	110.18
10000	881.49	463.77	325.03	256.04	214.94	168.61	154.41	134.94	122.42
15000	1322.23	695.65	487.54	384.06	322.41	252.92	231.61	202.41	183.63
20000	1762.98	927.53	650.05	512.07	429.88	337.22	308.81	269.87	244.83
25000	2203.72	1159.41	812.57	640.09	537.35	421.52	386.01	337.34	306.04
30000	2644.46	1391.29	975.08	768.11	644.82	505.83	463.21	404.81	367.25
35000	3085.21	1623.17	1137.59	896.12	752.29	590.13	540.41	472.28	428.45
36000	3173.35	1669.54	1170.09	921.73	773.79	606.99	555.85	485.77	440.70
37000	3261.50	1715.92	1202.60	947.33	795.28	623.85	571.29	499.26	452.94
38000	3349.65	1762.29	1235.10	972.93	816.77	640.71	586.73	512.76	465.18
39000	3437.80	1808.67	1267.60	998.54	838.27	657.57	602.17	526.25	477.42
40000	3525.95	1855.05	1300.10	1024.14	859.76	674.43	617.61	539.74	489.66
41000	3614.10	1901.42	1332.61	1049.74	881.25	691.29	633.05	553.24	501.90
42000	3702.25	1947.80	1365.11	1075.35	902.75	708.15	648.49	566.73	514.14
43000	3790.39	1994.17	1397.61	1100.95	924.24	725.01	663.93	580.23	526.39
44000	3878.54	2040.55	1430.11	1126.55	945.74	741.87	679.37	593.72	538.63
45000	3966.69	2086.93	1462.61	1152.16	967.23	758.74	694.81	607.21	550.87
46000	4054.84	2133.30	1495.12	1177.76	988.72	775.60	710.25	620.71	563.11
47000	4142.99	2179.68	1527.62	1203.36	1010.22	792.46	725.69	634.20	575.35
48000	4231.14	2226.05	1560.12	1228.97	1031.71	809.32	741.13	647.69	587.59
49000	4319.29	2272.43	1592.62	1254.57	1053.21	826.18	756.57	661.19	599.83
50000	4407.44	2318.81	1625.13	1280.17	1074.70	843.04	772.01	674.68	612.08
51000	4495.58	2365.18	1657.63	1305.78	1096.19	859.90	787.45	688.17	624.32
52000	4583.73	2411.56	1690.13	1331.38	1117.69	876.76	802.89	701.67	636.56
53000	4671.88	2457.94	1722.63	1356.98	1139.18	893.62	818.33	715.16	648.80
54000	4760.03	2504.31	1755.14	1382.59	1160.68	910.48	833.77	728.65	661.04
55000	4848.18	2550.69	1787.64	1408.19	1182.17	927.34	849.21	742.15	673.28
56000	4936.33	2597.06	1820.14	1433.79	1203.66	944.20	864.65	755.64	685.52
57000	5024.48	2643.44	1852.64	1459.40	1225.16	961.06	880.09	769.13	697.77
58000	5112.62	2689.82	1885.15	1485.00	1246.65	977.92	895.53	782.63	710.01
59000	5200.77	2736.19	1917.65	1510.60	1268.15	994.78	910.97	796.12	722.25
60000	5288.92	2782.57	1950.15	1536.21	1289.64	1011.65	926.41	809.61	734.49
61000	5377.07	2828.94	1982.65	1561.81	1311.13	1028.51	941.85	823.11	746.73
62000	5465.22	2875.32	2015.16	1587.41	1332.63	1045.37	957.29	836.60	758.97
63000	5553.37	2921.70	2047.66	1613.02	1354.12	1062.23	972.73	850.10	771.21
64000	5641.52	2968.07	2080.16	1638.62	1375.61	1079.09	988.17	863.59	783.46
65000	5729.66	3014.45	2112.66	1664.22	1397.11	1095.95	1003.61	877.08	795.70
66000	5817.81	3060.82	2145.17	1689.83	1418.60	1112.81	1019.05	890.58	807.94
67000	5905.96	3107.20	2177.67	1715.43	1440.10	1129.67	1034.49	904.07	820.18
68000	5994.11	3153.58	2210.17	1741.03	1461.59	1146.53	1049.93	917.56	832.42
69000	6082.26	3199.95	2242.67	1766.64	1483.08	1163.39	1065.37	931.06	844.66
70000	6170.41	3246.33	2275.18	1792.24	1504.58	1180.25	1080.81	944.55	856.90
75000	6611.15	3478.21	2437.69	1920.26	1612.05	1264.56	1158.01	1012.02	918.11
80000	7051.89	3710.09	2600.20	2048.28	1719.52	1348.86	1235.21	1079.48	979.32
100000	8814.87	4637.61	3250.25	2560.34	2149.40	1686.07	1544.01	1349.35	1224.15

MONTHLY PAYMENT 10½%

NECESSARY TO AMORTIZE A LOAN

TERM / AMOUNT	15 YEARS	18 YEARS	20 YEARS	25 YEARS	28 YEARS	29 YEARS	30 YEARS	35 YEARS	40 YEARS
$ 25	.28	.26	.25	.24	.24	.23	.23	.23	.23
50	.56	.52	.50	.48	.47	.46	.46	.45	.45
75	.83	.78	.75	.71	.70	.69	.69	.68	.67
100	1.11	1.04	1.00	.95	.93	.92	.92	.90	.89
200	2.22	2.07	2.00	1.89	1.85	1.84	1.83	1.80	1.78
300	3.32	3.10	3.00	2.84	2.78	2.76	2.75	2.70	2.67
400	4.43	4.13	4.00	3.78	3.70	3.68	3.66	3.60	3.56
500	5.53	5.17	5.00	4.73	4.63	4.60	4.58	4.50	4.45
600	6.64	6.20	6.00	5.67	5.55	5.52	5.49	5.39	5.34
700	7.74	7.23	6.99	6.61	6.48	6.44	6.41	6.29	6.22
800	8.85	8.26	7.99	7.56	7.40	7.36	7.32	7.19	7.11
900	9.95	9.30	8.99	8.50	8.33	8.28	8.24	8.09	8.00
1000	11.06	10.33	9.99	9.45	9.25	9.20	9.15	8.99	8.89
2000	22.11	20.65	19.97	18.89	18.50	18.39	18.30	17.97	17.78
3000	33.17	30.97	29.96	28.33	27.74	27.59	27.45	26.95	26.66
4000	44.22	41.29	39.94	37.77	36.99	36.78	36.59	35.93	35.55
5000	55.27	51.62	49.92	47.21	46.23	45.97	45.74	44.91	44.43
6000	66.33	61.94	59.91	56.66	55.48	55.17	54.89	53.89	53.32
7000	77.38	72.26	69.89	66.10	64.72	64.36	64.04	62.87	62.20
8000	88.44	82.58	79.88	75.54	73.97	73.55	73.18	71.86	71.09
9000	99.49	92.91	89.86	84.98	83.21	82.75	82.33	80.84	79.98
10000	110.54	103.23	99.84	94.42	92.46	91.94	91.48	89.82	88.86
15000	165.81	154.84	149.76	141.63	138.68	137.91	137.22	134.73	133.29
20000	221.08	206.45	199.68	188.84	184.91	183.87	182.95	179.63	177.72
25000	276.35	258.06	249.60	236.05	231.13	229.84	228.69	224.54	222.15
30000	331.62	309.67	299.52	283.26	277.36	275.81	274.43	269.45	266.58
35000	386.89	361.28	349.44	330.47	323.58	321.77	320.16	314.35	311.00
36000	397.95	371.61	359.42	339.91	332.83	330.97	329.31	323.33	319.89
37000	409.00	381.93	369.41	349.35	342.07	340.16	338.46	332.31	328.78
38000	420.06	392.25	379.39	358.79	351.32	349.35	347.61	341.30	337.66
39000	431.11	402.57	389.37	368.24	360.56	358.55	356.75	350.28	346.55
40000	442.16	412.90	399.36	377.68	369.81	367.74	365.90	359.26	355.43
41000	453.22	423.22	409.34	387.12	379.05	376.93	375.05	368.24	364.32
42000	464.27	433.54	419.32	396.56	388.30	386.13	384.20	377.22	373.20
43000	475.33	443.86	429.31	406.00	397.54	395.32	393.34	386.20	382.09
44000	486.38	454.19	439.29	415.44	406.79	404.51	402.49	395.18	390.98
45000	497.43	464.51	449.28	424.89	416.03	413.71	411.64	404.17	399.86
46000	508.49	474.83	459.26	434.33	425.28	422.90	420.79	413.15	408.75
47000	519.54	485.15	469.24	443.77	434.52	432.10	429.93	422.13	417.63
48000	530.60	495.47	479.23	453.21	443.77	441.29	439.08	431.11	426.52
49000	541.65	505.80	489.21	462.65	453.01	450.48	448.23	440.09	435.40
50000	552.70	516.12	499.19	472.10	462.26	459.68	457.37	449.07	444.29
51000	563.76	526.44	509.18	481.54	471.50	468.87	466.52	458.05	453.18
52000	574.81	536.76	519.16	490.98	480.75	478.06	475.67	467.03	462.06
53000	585.87	547.09	529.15	500.42	489.99	487.26	484.82	476.02	470.95
54000	596.92	557.41	539.13	509.86	499.24	496.45	493.96	485.00	479.83
55000	607.97	567.73	549.11	519.30	508.48	505.64	503.11	493.98	488.72
56000	619.03	578.05	559.10	528.75	517.73	514.84	512.26	502.96	497.60
57000	630.08	588.37	569.08	538.19	526.97	524.03	521.41	511.94	506.49
58000	641.14	598.70	579.07	547.63	536.22	533.22	530.55	520.92	515.38
59000	652.19	609.02	589.05	557.07	545.46	542.42	539.70	529.90	524.26
60000	663.24	619.34	599.03	566.51	554.71	551.61	548.85	538.89	533.15
61000	674.30	629.66	609.02	575.96	563.95	560.80	558.00	547.87	542.03
62000	685.35	639.99	619.00	585.40	573.20	570.00	567.14	556.85	550.92
63000	696.41	650.31	628.98	594.84	582.44	579.19	576.29	565.83	559.80
64000	707.46	660.63	638.97	604.28	591.69	588.38	585.44	574.81	568.69
65000	718.51	670.95	648.95	613.72	600.93	597.58	594.59	583.79	577.58
66000	729.57	681.28	658.94	623.16	610.18	606.77	603.73	592.77	586.46
67000	740.62	691.60	668.92	632.61	619.42	615.96	612.88	601.75	595.35
68000	751.68	701.92	678.90	642.05	628.67	625.16	622.03	610.74	604.23
69000	762.73	712.24	688.89	651.49	637.91	634.35	631.18	619.72	613.12
70000	773.78	722.56	698.87	660.93	647.16	643.54	640.32	628.70	622.00
75000	829.05	774.18	748.79	708.14	693.38	689.51	686.06	673.61	666.43
80000	884.32	825.79	798.71	755.35	739.61	735.48	731.80	718.51	710.86
100000	1105.40	1032.23	998.38	944.19	924.51	919.35	914.74	898.14	888.58

10⅝% MONTHLY PAYMENT
NECESSARY TO AMORTIZE A LOAN

TERM / AMOUNT	1 YEAR	2 YEARS	3 YEARS	4 YEARS	5 YEARS	7 YEARS	8 YEARS	10 YEARS	12 YEARS
$ 25	2.21	1.17	.82	.65	.54	.43	.39	.34	.31
50	4.42	2.33	1.63	1.29	1.08	.85	.78	.68	.62
75	6.62	3.49	2.45	1.93	1.62	1.27	1.17	1.02	.93
100	8.83	4.65	3.26	2.57	2.16	1.70	1.56	1.36	1.24
200	17.65	9.29	6.52	5.14	4.32	3.39	3.11	2.72	2.47
300	26.47	13.94	9.77	7.70	6.47	5.08	4.66	4.07	3.70
400	35.29	18.58	13.03	10.27	8.63	6.78	6.21	5.43	4.93
500	44.11	23.22	16.29	12.84	10.78	8.47	7.76	6.79	6.16
600	52.93	27.87	19.54	15.40	12.94	10.16	9.31	8.14	7.39
700	61.75	32.51	22.80	17.97	15.09	11.85	10.86	9.50	8.63
800	70.57	37.15	26.05	20.54	17.25	13.55	12.41	10.86	9.86
900	79.39	41.80	29.31	23.10	19.41	15.24	13.96	12.21	11.09
1000	88.21	46.44	32.57	25.67	21.56	16.93	15.51	13.57	12.32
2000	176.42	92.87	65.13	51.33	43.12	33.86	31.02	27.13	24.63
3000	264.63	139.31	97.69	77.00	64.67	50.78	46.53	40.70	36.95
4000	352.83	185.74	130.25	102.66	86.23	67.71	62.03	54.26	49.26
5000	441.04	232.17	162.81	128.32	107.78	84.63	77.54	67.82	61.58
6000	529.25	278.61	195.37	153.99	129.34	101.56	93.05	81.39	73.89
7000	617.45	325.04	227.93	179.65	150.90	118.49	108.55	94.95	86.21
8000	705.66	371.48	260.50	205.32	172.45	135.41	124.06	108.51	98.52
9000	793.87	417.91	293.06	230.98	194.01	152.34	139.57	122.08	110.84
10000	882.07	464.34	325.62	256.64	215.56	169.26	155.07	135.64	123.15
15000	1323.11	696.51	488.43	384.96	323.34	253.89	232.61	203.46	184.72
20000	1764.14	928.68	651.23	513.28	431.12	338.52	310.14	271.28	246.30
25000	2205.18	1160.85	814.04	641.60	538.90	423.15	387.68	339.09	307.87
30000	2646.21	1393.02	976.85	769.92	646.68	507.78	465.21	406.91	369.44
35000	3087.24	1625.19	1139.65	898.24	754.46	592.41	542.75	474.73	431.02
36000	3175.45	1671.63	1172.22	923.90	776.02	609.34	558.25	488.29	443.33
37000	3263.66	1718.06	1204.78	949.57	797.57	626.26	573.76	501.86	455.65
38000	3351.86	1764.49	1237.34	975.23	819.13	643.19	589.27	515.42	467.96
39000	3440.07	1810.93	1269.90	1000.89	840.68	660.12	604.77	528.98	480.27
40000	3528.28	1857.36	1302.46	1026.56	862.24	677.04	620.28	542.55	492.59
41000	3616.49	1903.80	1335.02	1052.22	883.80	693.97	635.79	556.11	504.90
42000	3704.69	1950.23	1367.58	1077.88	905.35	710.89	651.29	569.68	517.22
43000	3792.90	1996.66	1400.15	1103.55	926.91	727.82	666.80	583.24	529.53
44000	3881.11	2043.10	1432.71	1129.21	948.46	744.74	682.31	596.80	541.85
45000	3969.31	2089.53	1465.27	1154.88	970.02	761.67	697.81	610.37	554.16
46000	4057.52	2135.97	1497.83	1180.54	991.58	778.60	713.32	623.93	566.48
47000	4145.73	2182.40	1530.39	1206.20	1013.13	795.52	728.83	637.49	578.79
48000	4233.93	2228.83	1562.95	1231.87	1034.69	812.45	744.34	651.06	591.11
49000	4322.14	2275.27	1595.51	1257.53	1056.24	829.37	759.84	664.62	603.42
50000	4410.35	2321.70	1628.08	1283.19	1077.80	846.30	775.35	678.18	615.74
51000	4498.55	2368.14	1660.64	1308.86	1099.35	863.23	790.86	691.75	628.05
52000	4586.76	2414.57	1693.20	1334.52	1120.91	880.15	806.36	705.31	640.36
53000	4674.97	2461.00	1725.76	1360.19	1142.47	897.08	821.87	718.88	652.68
54000	4763.17	2507.44	1758.32	1385.85	1164.02	914.00	837.38	732.44	664.99
55000	4851.38	2553.87	1790.88	1411.51	1185.58	930.93	852.88	746.00	677.31
56000	4939.59	2600.30	1823.44	1437.18	1207.13	947.86	868.39	759.57	689.62
57000	5027.79	2646.74	1856.01	1462.84	1228.69	964.78	883.90	773.13	701.94
58000	5116.00	2693.17	1888.57	1488.50	1250.25	981.71	899.40	786.69	714.25
59000	5204.21	2739.61	1921.13	1514.17	1271.80	998.63	914.91	800.26	726.57
60000	5292.42	2786.04	1953.69	1539.83	1293.36	1015.56	930.42	813.82	738.88
61000	5380.62	2832.47	1986.25	1565.50	1314.91	1032.48	945.92	827.38	751.20
62000	5468.83	2878.91	2018.81	1591.16	1336.47	1049.41	961.43	840.95	763.51
63000	5557.04	2925.34	2051.37	1616.82	1358.03	1066.34	976.94	854.51	775.83
64000	5645.24	2971.78	2083.94	1642.49	1379.58	1083.26	992.45	868.07	788.14
65000	5733.45	3018.21	2116.50	1668.15	1401.14	1100.19	1007.95	881.64	800.45
66000	5821.66	3064.64	2149.06	1693.82	1422.69	1117.11	1023.46	895.20	812.77
67000	5909.86	3111.08	2181.62	1719.48	1444.25	1134.04	1038.97	908.77	825.08
68000	5998.07	3157.51	2214.18	1745.14	1465.80	1150.97	1054.47	922.33	837.40
69000	6086.28	3203.95	2246.74	1770.81	1487.36	1167.89	1069.98	935.89	849.71
70000	6174.48	3250.38	2279.30	1796.47	1508.92	1184.82	1085.49	949.46	862.03
75000	6615.52	3482.55	2442.11	1924.79	1616.70	1269.45	1163.02	1017.27	923.60
80000	7056.55	3714.72	2604.92	2053.11	1724.47	1354.08	1240.56	1085.09	985.17
100000	8820.69	4643.40	3256.15	2566.38	2155.59	1692.60	1550.69	1356.36	1231.47

MONTHLY PAYMENT 10⅝%
NECESSARY TO AMORTIZE A LOAN

TERM / AMOUNT	15 YEARS	18 YEARS	20 YEARS	25 YEARS	28 YEARS	29 YEARS	30 YEARS	35 YEARS	40 YEARS
$ 25	.28	.27	.26	.24	.24	.24	.24	.23	.23
50	.56	.53	.51	.48	.47	.47	.47	.46	.45
75	.84	.79	.76	.72	.71	.70	.70	.69	.68
100	1.12	1.05	1.01	.96	.94	.93	.93	.91	.90
200	2.23	2.09	2.02	1.91	1.87	1.86	1.85	1.82	1.80
300	3.34	3.13	3.03	2.86	2.81	2.79	2.78	2.73	2.70
400	4.46	4.17	4.03	3.82	3.74	3.72	3.70	3.64	3.60
500	5.57	5.21	5.04	4.77	4.67	4.65	4.63	4.54	4.50
600	6.68	6.25	6.05	5.72	5.61	5.58	5.55	5.45	5.40
700	7.80	7.29	7.05	6.68	6.54	6.51	6.47	6.36	6.29
800	8.91	8.33	8.06	7.63	7.47	7.43	7.40	7.27	7.19
900	10.02	9.37	9.07	8.58	8.41	8.36	8.32	8.18	8.09
1000	11.14	10.41	10.07	9.54	9.34	9.29	9.25	9.08	8.99
2000	22.27	20.81	20.14	19.07	18.68	18.58	18.49	18.16	17.97
3000	33.40	31.22	30.21	28.60	28.02	27.86	27.73	27.24	26.96
4000	44.53	41.62	40.28	38.13	37.35	37.15	36.97	36.32	35.94
5000	55.66	52.02	50.34	47.66	46.69	46.44	46.21	45.40	44.93
6000	66.79	62.43	60.41	57.19	56.03	55.72	55.45	54.47	53.91
7000	77.93	72.83	70.48	66.72	65.36	65.01	64.69	63.55	62.90
8000	89.06	83.24	80.55	76.25	74.70	74.29	73.93	72.63	71.88
9000	100.19	93.64	90.62	85.79	84.04	83.58	83.17	81.71	80.87
10000	111.32	104.04	100.68	95.32	93.38	92.87	92.41	90.79	89.85
15000	166.98	156.06	151.02	142.97	140.06	139.30	138.62	136.18	134.78
20000	222.64	208.08	201.36	190.63	186.75	185.73	184.82	181.57	179.70
25000	278.30	260.10	251.70	238.29	233.43	232.16	231.03	226.96	224.62
30000	333.95	312.12	302.04	285.94	280.12	278.59	277.23	272.35	269.55
35000	389.61	364.14	352.38	333.60	326.80	325.02	323.44	317.74	314.47
36000	400.74	374.55	362.45	343.13	336.14	334.31	332.68	326.82	323.46
37000	411.87	384.95	372.52	352.66	345.48	343.60	341.92	335.89	332.44
38000	423.01	395.35	382.59	362.19	354.81	352.88	351.16	344.97	341.43
39000	434.14	405.76	392.65	371.72	364.15	362.17	360.40	354.05	350.41
40000	445.27	416.16	402.72	381.25	373.49	371.45	369.64	363.13	359.39
41000	456.40	426.57	412.79	390.79	382.83	380.74	378.89	372.21	368.38
42000	467.53	436.97	422.86	400.32	392.16	390.03	388.13	381.28	377.36
43000	478.66	447.37	432.92	409.85	401.50	399.31	397.37	390.36	386.35
44000	489.80	457.78	442.99	419.38	410.84	408.60	406.61	399.44	395.33
45000	500.93	468.18	453.06	428.91	420.17	417.89	415.85	408.52	404.32
46000	512.06	478.59	463.13	438.44	429.51	427.17	425.09	417.60	413.30
47000	523.19	488.99	473.20	447.97	438.85	436.46	434.33	426.67	422.29
48000	534.32	499.39	483.26	457.50	448.18	445.74	443.57	435.75	431.27
49000	545.45	509.80	493.33	467.04	457.52	455.03	452.81	444.83	440.26
50000	556.59	520.20	503.40	476.57	466.86	464.32	462.05	453.91	449.24
51000	567.72	530.61	513.47	486.10	476.20	473.60	471.29	462.99	458.23
52000	578.85	541.01	523.54	495.63	485.53	482.89	480.54	472.06	467.21
53000	589.98	551.41	533.60	505.16	494.87	492.18	489.78	481.14	476.20
54000	601.11	561.82	543.67	514.69	504.21	501.46	499.02	490.22	485.18
55000	612.24	572.22	553.74	524.22	513.54	510.75	508.26	499.30	494.17
56000	623.38	582.62	563.81	533.75	522.88	520.03	517.50	508.38	503.15
57000	634.51	593.03	573.88	543.29	532.22	529.32	526.74	517.46	512.14
58000	645.64	603.43	583.94	552.82	541.56	538.61	535.98	526.53	521.12
59000	656.77	613.84	594.01	562.35	550.89	547.89	545.22	535.61	530.11
60000	667.90	624.24	604.08	571.88	560.23	557.18	554.46	544.69	539.09
61000	679.03	634.64	614.15	581.41	569.57	566.47	563.70	553.77	548.07
62000	690.16	645.05	624.22	590.94	578.90	575.75	572.95	562.85	557.06
63000	701.30	655.45	634.28	600.47	588.24	585.04	582.19	571.92	566.04
64000	712.43	665.86	644.35	610.00	597.58	594.32	591.43	581.00	575.03
65000	723.56	676.26	654.42	619.54	606.92	603.61	600.67	590.08	584.01
66000	734.69	686.66	664.49	629.07	616.25	612.90	609.91	599.16	593.00
67000	745.82	697.07	674.55	638.60	625.59	622.18	619.15	608.24	601.98
68000	756.95	707.47	684.62	648.13	634.93	631.47	628.39	617.31	610.97
69000	768.09	717.88	694.69	657.66	644.26	640.76	637.63	626.39	619.95
70000	779.22	728.28	704.76	667.19	653.60	650.04	646.87	635.47	628.94
75000	834.88	780.30	755.10	714.85	700.29	696.47	693.08	680.86	673.86
80000	890.53	832.32	805.44	762.50	746.97	742.90	739.28	726.25	718.78
100000	1113.17	1040.40	1006.80	953.13	933.71	928.63	924.10	907.81	898.48

10¾% MONTHLY PAYMENT
NECESSARY TO AMORTIZE A LOAN

TERM / AMOUNT	1 YEAR	2 YEARS	3 YEARS	4 YEARS	5 YEARS	7 YEARS	8 YEARS	10 YEARS	12 YEARS
$ 25	2.21	1.17	.82	.65	.55	.43	.39	.35	.31
50	4.42	2.33	1.64	1.29	1.09	.85	.78	.69	.62
75	6.62	3.49	2.45	1.93	1.63	1.28	1.17	1.03	.93
100	8.83	4.65	3.27	2.58	2.17	1.70	1.56	1.37	1.24
200	17.66	9.30	6.53	5.15	4.33	3.40	3.12	2.73	2.48
300	26.48	13.95	9.79	7.72	6.49	5.10	4.68	4.10	3.72
400	35.31	18.60	13.05	10.29	8.65	6.80	6.23	5.46	4.96
500	44.14	23.25	16.32	12.87	10.81	8.50	7.79	6.82	6.20
600	52.96	27.90	19.58	15.44	12.98	10.20	9.35	8.19	7.44
700	61.79	32.55	22.84	18.01	15.14	11.90	10.91	9.55	8.68
800	70.62	37.20	26.10	20.58	17.30	13.60	12.46	10.91	9.92
900	79.44	41.85	29.36	23.16	19.46	15.30	14.02	12.28	11.15
1000	88.27	46.50	32.63	25.73	21.62	17.00	15.58	13.64	12.39
2000	176.54	92.99	65.25	51.45	43.24	33.99	31.15	27.27	24.78
3000	264.80	139.48	97.87	77.18	64.86	50.98	46.73	40.91	37.17
4000	353.07	185.97	130.49	102.90	86.48	67.97	62.30	54.54	49.56
5000	441.33	232.46	163.11	128.63	108.09	84.96	77.87	68.17	61.95
6000	529.60	278.96	195.73	154.35	129.71	101.95	93.45	81.81	74.33
7000	617.86	325.45	228.35	180.07	151.33	118.94	109.02	95.44	86.72
8000	706.13	371.94	260.97	205.80	172.95	135.94	124.60	109.08	99.11
9000	794.39	418.43	293.59	231.52	194.57	152.93	140.17	122.71	111.50
10000	882.66	464.92	326.21	257.25	216.18	169.92	155.74	136.34	123.89
15000	1323.98	697.38	489.31	385.87	324.27	254.87	233.61	204.51	185.83
20000	1765.31	929.84	652.41	514.49	432.36	339.83	311.48	272.68	247.77
25000	2206.63	1162.30	815.52	643.11	540.45	424.79	389.35	340.85	309.71
30000	2647.96	1394.76	978.62	771.73	648.54	509.74	467.22	409.02	371.65
35000	3089.28	1627.22	1141.72	900.35	756.63	594.70	545.09	477.19	433.59
36000	3177.55	1673.71	1174.34	926.08	778.25	611.69	560.67	490.82	445.97
37000	3265.81	1720.20	1206.96	951.80	799.87	628.68	576.24	504.46	458.36
38000	3354.08	1766.70	1239.58	977.53	821.49	645.67	591.81	518.09	470.75
39000	3442.34	1813.19	1272.20	1003.25	843.11	662.66	607.39	531.73	483.14
40000	3530.61	1859.68	1304.82	1028.98	864.72	679.66	622.96	545.36	495.53
41000	3618.87	1906.17	1337.44	1054.70	886.34	696.65	638.53	558.99	507.91
42000	3707.14	1952.66	1370.06	1080.42	907.96	713.64	654.11	572.63	520.30
43000	3795.40	1999.15	1402.68	1106.15	929.58	730.63	669.68	586.26	532.69
44000	3883.67	2045.65	1435.30	1131.87	951.19	747.62	685.26	599.90	545.08
45000	3971.93	2092.14	1467.93	1157.60	972.81	764.61	700.83	613.53	557.47
46000	4060.20	2138.63	1500.55	1183.32	994.43	781.60	716.40	627.16	569.85
47000	4148.46	2185.12	1533.17	1209.05	1016.05	798.59	731.98	640.80	582.24
48000	4236.73	2231.61	1565.79	1234.77	1037.67	815.59	747.55	654.43	594.63
49000	4324.99	2278.11	1598.41	1260.49	1059.28	832.58	763.13	668.06	607.02
50000	4413.26	2324.60	1631.03	1286.22	1080.90	849.57	778.70	681.70	619.41
51000	4501.52	2371.09	1663.65	1311.94	1102.52	866.56	794.27	695.33	631.80
52000	4589.79	2417.58	1696.27	1337.67	1124.14	883.55	809.85	708.97	644.18
53000	4678.05	2464.07	1728.89	1363.39	1145.76	900.54	825.42	722.60	656.57
54000	4766.32	2510.57	1761.51	1389.12	1167.37	917.53	841.00	736.23	668.96
55000	4854.58	2557.06	1794.13	1414.84	1188.99	934.52	856.57	749.87	681.35
56000	4942.85	2603.55	1826.75	1440.56	1210.61	951.52	872.14	763.50	693.74
57000	5031.12	2650.04	1859.37	1466.29	1232.23	968.51	887.72	777.14	706.12
58000	5119.38	2696.53	1891.99	1492.01	1253.85	985.50	903.29	790.77	718.51
59000	5207.65	2743.02	1924.61	1517.74	1275.46	1002.49	918.87	804.40	730.90
60000	5295.91	2789.52	1957.23	1543.46	1297.08	1019.48	934.44	818.04	743.29
61000	5384.18	2836.01	1989.85	1569.19	1318.70	1036.47	950.01	831.67	755.68
62000	5472.44	2882.50	2022.47	1594.91	1340.32	1053.46	965.59	845.30	768.06
63000	5560.71	2928.99	2055.09	1620.63	1361.94	1070.46	981.16	858.94	780.45
64000	5648.97	2975.48	2087.71	1646.36	1383.55	1087.45	996.73	872.57	792.84
65000	5737.24	3021.98	2120.33	1672.08	1405.17	1104.44	1012.31	886.21	805.23
66000	5825.50	3068.47	2152.95	1697.81	1426.79	1121.43	1027.88	899.84	817.62
67000	5913.77	3114.96	2185.58	1723.53	1448.41	1138.42	1043.46	913.47	830.00
68000	6002.03	3161.45	2218.20	1749.26	1470.03	1155.41	1059.03	927.11	842.39
69000	6090.30	3207.94	2250.82	1774.98	1491.64	1172.40	1074.60	940.74	854.78
70000	6178.56	3254.43	2283.44	1800.70	1513.26	1189.39	1090.18	954.38	867.17
75000	6619.89	3486.89	2446.54	1929.33	1621.35	1274.35	1168.05	1022.55	929.11
80000	7061.21	3719.35	2609.64	2057.95	1729.44	1359.31	1245.92	1090.71	991.05
100000	8826.51	4649.19	3262.05	2572.43	2161.80	1699.13	1557.40	1363.39	1238.81

MONTHLY PAYMENT 10¾%

NECESSARY TO AMORTIZE A LOAN

TERM / AMOUNT	15 YEARS	18 YEARS	20 YEARS	25 YEARS	28 YEARS	29 YEARS	30 YEARS	35 YEARS	40 YEARS
$ 25	.29	.27	.26	.25	.24	.24	.24	.23	.23
50	.57	.53	.51	.49	.48	.47	.47	.46	.46
75	.85	.79	.77	.73	.71	.71	.71	.69	.69
100	1.13	1.05	1.02	.97	.95	.94	.94	.92	.91
200	2.25	2.10	2.04	1.93	1.89	1.88	1.87	1.84	1.82
300	3.37	3.15	3.05	2.89	2.83	2.82	2.81	2.76	2.73
400	4.49	4.20	4.07	3.85	3.78	3.76	3.74	3.68	3.64
500	5.61	5.25	5.08	4.82	4.72	4.69	4.67	4.59	4.55
600	6.73	6.30	6.10	5.78	5.66	5.63	5.61	5.51	5.46
700	7.85	7.35	7.11	6.74	6.61	6.57	6.54	6.43	6.36
800	8.97	8.39	8.13	7.70	7.55	7.51	7.47	7.35	7.27
900	10.09	9.44	9.14	8.66	8.49	8.45	8.41	8.26	8.18
1000	11.21	10.49	10.16	9.63	9.43	9.38	9.34	9.18	9.09
2000	22.42	20.98	20.31	19.25	18.86	18.76	18.67	18.36	18.17
3000	33.63	31.46	30.46	28.87	28.29	28.14	28.01	27.53	27.26
4000	44.84	41.95	40.61	38.49	37.72	37.52	37.34	36.71	36.34
5000	56.05	52.43	50.77	48.11	47.15	46.90	46.68	45.88	45.42
6000	67.26	62.92	60.92	57.73	56.58	56.28	56.01	55.06	54.51
7000	78.47	73.41	71.07	67.35	66.01	65.66	65.35	64.23	63.59
8000	89.68	83.89	81.22	76.97	75.44	75.04	74.68	73.41	72.68
9000	100.89	94.38	91.38	86.59	84.87	84.42	84.02	82.58	81.76
10000	112.10	104.86	101.53	96.21	94.30	93.80	93.35	91.76	90.84
15000	168.15	157.29	152.29	144.32	141.45	140.70	140.03	137.63	136.26
20000	224.19	209.72	203.05	192.42	188.59	187.59	186.70	183.51	181.68
25000	280.24	262.15	253.81	240.53	235.74	234.49	233.38	229.38	227.10
30000	336.29	314.58	304.57	288.63	282.89	281.39	280.05	275.26	272.52
35000	392.34	367.01	355.34	336.74	330.03	328.28	326.72	321.13	317.94
36000	403.55	377.50	365.49	346.36	339.46	337.66	336.06	330.31	327.03
37000	414.76	387.98	375.64	355.98	348.89	347.04	345.39	339.48	336.11
38000	425.97	398.47	385.79	365.60	358.32	356.42	354.73	348.66	345.20
39000	437.17	408.95	395.94	375.22	367.75	365.80	364.06	357.83	354.28
40000	448.38	419.44	406.10	384.84	377.18	375.18	373.40	367.01	363.36
41000	459.59	429.92	416.25	394.46	386.61	384.56	382.73	376.18	372.45
42000	470.80	440.41	426.40	404.08	396.04	393.94	392.07	385.36	381.53
43000	482.01	450.90	436.55	413.70	405.47	403.32	401.40	394.53	390.62
44000	493.22	461.38	446.71	423.33	414.90	412.70	410.74	403.71	399.70
45000	504.43	471.87	456.86	432.95	424.33	422.08	420.07	412.88	408.78
46000	515.64	482.35	467.01	442.57	433.76	431.45	429.41	422.06	417.87
47000	526.85	492.84	477.16	452.19	443.19	440.83	438.74	431.23	426.95
48000	538.06	503.33	487.31	461.81	452.62	450.21	448.08	440.41	436.04
49000	549.27	513.81	497.47	471.43	462.05	459.59	457.41	449.58	445.12
50000	560.48	524.30	507.62	481.05	471.47	468.97	466.75	458.76	454.20
51000	571.69	534.78	517.77	490.67	480.90	478.35	476.08	467.93	463.29
52000	582.90	545.27	527.92	500.29	490.33	487.73	485.42	477.11	472.37
53000	594.11	555.75	538.08	509.91	499.76	497.11	494.75	486.28	481.46
54000	605.32	566.24	548.23	519.54	509.19	506.49	504.08	495.46	490.54
55000	616.53	576.73	558.38	529.16	518.62	515.87	513.42	504.63	499.62
56000	627.74	587.21	568.53	538.78	528.05	525.25	522.75	513.81	508.71
57000	638.95	597.70	578.69	548.40	537.48	534.63	532.09	522.98	517.79
58000	650.15	608.18	588.84	558.02	546.91	544.01	541.42	532.16	526.88
59000	661.36	618.67	598.99	567.64	556.34	553.39	550.76	541.33	535.96
60000	672.57	629.16	609.14	577.26	565.77	562.77	560.09	550.51	545.04
61000	683.78	639.64	619.29	586.88	575.20	572.14	569.43	559.68	554.13
62000	694.99	650.13	629.45	596.50	584.63	581.52	578.76	568.86	563.21
63000	706.20	660.61	639.60	606.12	594.06	590.90	588.10	578.03	572.30
64000	717.41	671.10	649.75	615.74	603.49	600.28	597.43	587.21	581.38
65000	728.62	681.59	659.90	625.37	612.92	609.66	606.77	596.38	590.46
66000	739.83	692.07	670.06	634.99	622.35	619.04	616.10	605.56	599.55
67000	751.04	702.56	680.21	644.61	631.77	628.42	625.44	614.73	608.63
68000	762.25	713.04	690.36	654.23	641.20	637.80	634.77	623.91	617.72
69000	773.46	723.53	700.51	663.85	650.63	647.18	644.11	633.08	626.80
70000	784.67	734.01	710.67	673.47	660.06	656.56	653.44	642.26	635.88
75000	840.72	786.44	761.43	721.57	707.21	703.46	700.12	688.13	681.30
80000	896.76	838.87	812.19	769.68	754.36	750.35	746.79	734.01	726.72
100000	1120.95	1048.59	1015.23	962.10	942.94	937.94	933.49	917.51	908.40

10⅞% MONTHLY PAYMENT
NECESSARY TO AMORTIZE A LOAN

TERM / AMOUNT	1 YEAR	2 YEARS	3 YEARS	4 YEARS	5 YEARS	7 YEARS	8 YEARS	10 YEARS	12 YEARS
$ 25	2.21	1.17	.82	.65	.55	.43	.40	.35	.32
50	4.42	2.33	1.64	1.29	1.09	.86	.79	.69	.63
75	6.63	3.50	2.46	1.94	1.63	1.28	1.18	1.03	.94
100	8.84	4.66	3.27	2.58	2.17	1.71	1.57	1.38	1.25
200	17.67	9.31	6.54	5.16	4.34	3.42	3.13	2.75	2.50
300	26.50	13.97	9.81	7.74	6.51	5.12	4.70	4.12	3.74
400	35.33	18.62	13.08	10.32	8.68	6.83	6.26	5.49	4.99
500	44.17	23.28	16.34	12.90	10.85	8.53	7.83	6.86	6.24
600	53.00	27.93	19.61	15.48	13.01	10.24	9.39	8.23	7.48
700	61.83	32.59	22.88	18.05	15.18	11.94	10.95	9.60	8.73
800	70.66	37.24	26.15	20.63	17.35	13.65	12.52	10.97	9.97
900	79.50	41.90	29.42	23.21	19.52	15.36	14.08	12.34	11.22
1000	88.33	46.55	32.68	25.79	21.69	17.06	15.65	13.71	12.47
2000	176.65	93.10	65.36	51.57	43.37	34.12	31.29	27.41	24.93
3000	264.98	139.65	98.04	77.36	65.05	51.18	46.93	41.12	37.39
4000	353.30	186.20	130.72	103.14	86.73	68.23	62.57	54.82	49.85
5000	441.62	232.75	163.40	128.93	108.41	85.29	78.21	68.53	62.31
6000	529.95	279.30	196.08	154.71	130.09	102.35	93.85	82.23	74.78
7000	618.27	325.85	228.76	180.50	151.77	119.40	109.49	95.94	87.24
8000	706.59	372.40	261.44	206.28	173.45	136.46	125.13	109.64	99.70
9000	794.92	418.95	294.12	232.07	195.13	153.52	140.77	123.34	112.16
10000	883.24	465.50	326.80	257.85	216.81	170.57	156.42	137.05	124.62
15000	1324.86	698.25	490.20	386.78	325.21	255.86	234.62	205.57	186.93
20000	1766.47	931.00	653.60	515.70	433.61	341.14	312.83	274.09	249.24
25000	2208.09	1163.75	816.99	644.63	542.01	426.42	391.03	342.61	311.55
30000	2649.71	1396.50	980.39	773.55	650.41	511.71	469.24	411.14	373.86
35000	3091.32	1629.25	1143.79	902.48	758.81	596.99	547.44	479.66	436.16
36000	3179.65	1675.80	1176.47	928.26	780.49	614.05	563.08	493.36	448.63
37000	3267.97	1722.35	1209.15	954.04	802.17	631.11	578.73	507.07	461.09
38000	3356.29	1768.90	1241.83	979.83	823.85	648.16	594.37	520.77	473.55
39000	3444.62	1815.45	1274.51	1005.61	845.53	665.22	610.01	534.47	486.01
40000	3532.94	1862.00	1307.19	1031.40	867.21	682.28	625.65	548.18	498.47
41000	3621.26	1908.55	1339.87	1057.18	888.89	699.33	641.29	561.88	510.93
42000	3709.59	1955.10	1372.55	1082.97	910.57	716.39	656.93	575.59	523.40
43000	3797.91	2001.65	1405.23	1108.75	932.25	733.45	672.57	589.29	535.86
44000	3886.23	2048.20	1437.91	1134.54	953.93	750.50	688.21	603.00	548.32
45000	3974.56	2094.75	1470.58	1160.32	975.61	767.56	703.85	616.70	560.78
46000	4062.88	2141.30	1503.26	1186.11	997.29	784.62	719.49	630.40	573.24
47000	4151.20	2187.85	1535.94	1211.89	1018.97	801.67	735.14	644.11	585.70
48000	4239.53	2234.40	1568.62	1237.68	1040.65	818.73	750.78	657.81	598.17
49000	4327.85	2280.95	1601.30	1263.46	1062.33	835.79	766.42	671.52	610.63
50000	4416.17	2327.50	1633.98	1289.25	1084.01	852.84	782.06	685.22	623.09
51000	4504.50	2374.05	1666.66	1315.03	1105.69	869.90	797.70	698.93	635.55
52000	4592.82	2420.60	1699.34	1340.82	1127.37	886.96	813.34	712.63	648.01
53000	4681.14	2467.15	1732.02	1366.60	1149.05	904.01	828.98	726.33	660.47
54000	4769.47	2513.70	1764.70	1392.39	1170.73	921.07	844.62	740.04	672.94
55000	4857.79	2560.25	1797.38	1418.17	1192.41	938.13	860.26	753.74	685.40
56000	4946.11	2606.80	1830.06	1443.96	1214.09	955.18	875.91	767.45	697.86
57000	5034.44	2653.35	1862.74	1469.74	1235.77	972.24	891.55	781.15	710.32
58000	5122.76	2699.89	1895.42	1495.53	1257.45	989.30	907.19	794.86	722.78
59000	5211.08	2746.44	1928.10	1521.31	1279.13	1006.36	922.83	808.56	735.24
60000	5299.41	2792.99	1960.78	1547.10	1300.81	1023.41	938.47	822.27	747.71
61000	5387.73	2839.54	1993.46	1572.88	1322.49	1040.47	954.11	835.97	760.17
62000	5476.05	2886.09	2026.14	1598.67	1344.17	1057.53	969.75	849.67	772.63
63000	5564.38	2932.64	2058.82	1624.45	1365.85	1074.58	985.39	863.38	785.09
64000	5652.70	2979.19	2091.50	1650.24	1387.53	1091.64	1001.03	877.08	797.55
65000	5741.02	3025.74	2124.18	1676.02	1409.21	1108.70	1016.68	890.79	810.01
66000	5829.35	3072.29	2156.86	1701.81	1430.89	1125.75	1032.32	904.49	822.48
67000	5917.67	3118.84	2189.54	1727.59	1452.57	1142.81	1047.96	918.20	834.94
68000	6005.99	3165.39	2222.21	1753.38	1474.25	1159.87	1063.60	931.90	847.40
69000	6094.32	3211.94	2254.89	1779.16	1495.93	1176.92	1079.24	945.60	859.86
70000	6182.64	3258.49	2287.57	1804.95	1517.61	1193.98	1094.88	959.31	872.32
75000	6624.26	3491.24	2450.97	1933.87	1626.02	1279.26	1173.09	1027.83	934.63
80000	7065.87	3723.99	2614.37	2062.79	1734.42	1364.55	1251.29	1096.35	996.94
100000	8832.34	4654.99	3267.96	2578.49	2168.02	1705.68	1564.11	1370.44	1246.17

MONTHLY PAYMENT 10⅞%

NECESSARY TO AMORTIZE A LOAN

TERM / AMOUNT	15 YEARS	18 YEARS	20 YEARS	25 YEARS	28 YEARS	29 YEARS	30 YEARS	35 YEARS	40 YEARS
$ 25	.29	.27	.26	.25	.24	.24	.24	.24	.23
50	.57	.53	.52	.49	.48	.48	.48	.47	.46
75	.85	.80	.77	.73	.72	.72	.71	.70	.69
100	1.13	1.06	1.03	.98	.96	.95	.95	.93	.92
200	2.26	2.12	2.05	1.95	1.91	1.90	1.89	1.86	1.84
300	3.39	3.18	3.08	2.92	2.86	2.85	2.83	2.79	2.76
400	4.52	4.23	4.10	3.89	3.81	3.79	3.78	3.71	3.68
500	5.65	5.29	5.12	4.86	4.77	4.74	4.72	4.64	4.60
600	6.78	6.35	6.15	5.83	5.72	5.69	5.66	5.57	5.52
700	7.91	7.40	7.17	6.80	6.67	6.64	6.61	6.50	6.43
800	9.04	8.46	8.19	7.77	7.62	7.58	7.55	7.42	7.35
900	10.16	9.52	9.22	8.74	8.57	8.53	8.49	8.35	8.27
1000	11.29	10.57	10.24	9.72	9.53	9.48	9.43	9.28	9.19
2000	22.58	21.14	20.48	19.43	19.05	18.95	18.86	18.55	18.37
3000	33.87	31.71	30.72	29.14	28.57	28.42	28.29	27.82	27.56
4000	45.16	42.28	40.95	38.85	38.09	37.90	37.72	37.09	36.74
5000	56.44	52.85	51.19	48.56	47.61	47.37	47.15	46.37	45.92
6000	67.73	63.41	61.43	58.27	57.14	56.84	56.58	55.64	55.11
7000	79.02	73.98	71.66	67.98	66.66	66.31	66.01	64.91	64.29
8000	90.31	84.55	81.90	77.69	76.18	75.79	75.44	74.18	73.47
9000	101.59	95.12	92.14	87.40	85.70	85.26	84.87	83.45	82.66
10000	112.88	105.69	102.37	97.11	95.22	94.73	94.29	92.73	91.84
15000	169.32	158.53	153.56	145.67	142.83	142.10	141.44	139.09	137.76
20000	225.76	211.37	204.74	194.22	190.44	189.46	188.58	185.45	183.67
25000	282.20	264.21	255.93	242.78	238.05	236.82	235.73	231.81	229.59
30000	338.63	317.05	307.11	291.33	285.66	284.19	282.87	278.17	275.51
35000	395.07	369.89	358.30	339.89	333.27	331.55	330.02	324.53	321.42
36000	406.36	380.45	368.54	349.60	342.80	341.02	339.45	333.80	330.61
37000	417.65	391.02	378.77	359.31	352.32	350.49	348.87	343.08	339.79
38000	428.93	401.59	389.01	369.02	361.84	359.97	358.30	352.35	348.97
39000	440.22	412.16	399.25	378.73	371.36	369.44	367.73	361.62	358.16
40000	451.51	422.73	409.48	388.44	380.88	378.91	377.16	370.89	367.34
41000	462.80	433.29	419.72	398.15	390.41	388.39	386.59	380.17	376.52
42000	474.08	443.86	429.96	407.86	399.93	397.86	396.02	389.44	385.71
43000	485.37	454.43	440.19	417.57	409.45	407.33	405.45	398.71	394.89
44000	496.66	465.00	450.43	427.28	418.97	416.80	414.88	407.98	404.07
45000	507.95	475.57	460.67	437.00	428.49	426.28	424.31	417.25	413.26
46000	519.23	486.13	470.90	446.71	438.02	435.75	433.73	426.53	422.44
47000	530.52	496.70	481.14	456.42	447.54	445.22	443.16	435.80	431.62
48000	541.81	507.27	491.38	466.13	457.06	454.69	452.59	445.07	440.81
49000	553.10	517.84	501.62	475.84	466.58	464.17	462.02	454.34	449.99
50000	564.39	528.41	511.85	485.55	476.10	473.64	471.45	463.61	459.17
51000	575.67	538.97	522.09	495.26	485.63	483.11	480.88	472.89	468.36
52000	586.96	549.54	532.33	504.97	495.15	492.58	490.31	482.16	477.54
53000	598.25	560.11	542.56	514.68	504.67	502.06	499.74	491.43	486.72
54000	609.54	570.68	552.80	524.39	514.19	511.53	509.17	500.70	495.91
55000	620.82	581.25	563.04	534.10	523.71	521.00	518.59	509.98	505.09
56000	632.11	591.82	573.27	543.82	533.24	530.48	528.02	519.25	514.27
57000	643.40	602.38	583.51	553.53	542.76	539.95	537.45	528.52	523.46
58000	654.69	612.95	593.75	563.24	552.28	549.42	546.88	537.79	532.64
59000	665.97	623.52	603.99	572.95	561.80	558.89	556.31	547.06	541.82
60000	677.26	634.09	614.22	582.66	571.32	568.37	565.74	556.34	551.01
61000	688.55	644.66	624.46	592.37	580.85	577.84	575.17	565.61	560.19
62000	699.84	655.22	634.70	602.08	590.37	587.31	584.60	574.88	569.37
63000	711.12	665.79	644.93	611.79	599.89	596.78	594.03	584.15	578.56
64000	722.41	676.36	655.17	621.50	609.41	606.26	603.45	593.43	587.74
65000	733.70	686.93	665.41	631.21	618.93	615.73	612.88	602.70	596.92
66000	744.99	697.50	675.64	640.92	628.45	625.20	622.31	611.97	606.11
67000	756.27	708.06	685.88	650.63	637.98	634.68	631.74	621.24	615.29
68000	767.56	718.63	696.12	660.35	647.50	644.15	641.17	630.51	624.47
69000	778.85	729.20	706.35	670.06	657.02	653.62	650.60	639.79	633.66
70000	790.14	739.77	716.59	679.77	666.54	663.09	660.03	649.06	642.84
75000	846.58	792.61	767.78	728.32	714.15	710.46	707.17	695.42	688.76
80000	903.01	845.45	818.96	776.88	761.76	757.82	754.32	741.78	734.67
100000	1128.77	1056.81	1023.70	971.09	952.20	947.27	942.90	927.22	918.34

11% MONTHLY PAYMENT
NECESSARY TO AMORTIZE A LOAN

TERM / AMOUNT	1 YEAR	2 YEARS	3 YEARS	4 YEARS	5 YEARS	7 YEARS	8 YEARS	10 YEARS	12 YEARS
$ 25	2.21	1.17	.82	.65	.55	.43	.40	.35	.32
50	4.42	2.34	1.64	1.30	1.09	.86	.79	.69	.63
75	6.63	3.50	2.46	1.94	1.64	1.29	1.18	1.04	.95
100	8.84	4.67	3.28	2.59	2.18	1.72	1.58	1.38	1.26
200	17.68	9.33	6.55	5.17	4.35	3.43	3.15	2.76	2.51
300	26.52	13.99	9.83	7.76	6.53	5.14	4.72	4.14	3.77
400	35.36	18.65	13.10	10.34	8.70	6.85	6.29	5.52	5.02
500	44.20	23.31	16.37	12.93	10.88	8.57	7.86	6.89	6.27
600	53.03	27.97	19.65	15.51	13.05	10.28	9.43	8.27	7.53
700	61.87	32.63	22.92	18.10	15.22	11.99	11.00	9.65	8.78
800	70.71	37.29	26.20	20.68	17.40	13.70	12.57	11.03	10.03
900	79.55	41.95	29.47	23.27	19.57	15.42	14.14	12.40	11.29
1000	88.39	46.61	32.74	25.85	21.75	17.13	15.71	13.78	12.54
2000	176.77	93.22	65.48	51.70	43.49	34.25	31.42	27.56	25.08
3000	265.15	139.83	98.22	77.54	65.23	51.37	47.13	41.33	37.61
4000	353.53	186.44	130.96	103.39	86.97	68.49	62.84	55.11	50.15
5000	441.91	233.04	163.70	129.23	108.72	85.62	78.55	68.88	62.68
6000	530.29	279.65	196.44	155.08	130.46	102.74	94.26	82.66	75.22
7000	618.68	326.26	229.18	180.92	152.20	119.86	109.96	96.43	87.75
8000	707.06	372.87	261.91	206.77	173.94	136.98	125.67	110.21	100.29
9000	795.44	419.48	294.65	232.61	195.69	154.11	141.38	123.98	112.82
10000	883.82	466.08	327.39	258.46	217.43	171.23	157.09	137.76	125.36
15000	1325.73	699.12	491.09	387.69	326.14	256.84	235.63	206.63	188.04
20000	1767.64	932.16	654.78	516.92	434.85	342.45	314.17	275.51	250.72
25000	2209.55	1165.20	818.47	646.14	543.57	428.07	392.72	344.38	313.39
30000	2651.45	1398.24	982.17	775.37	652.28	513.68	471.26	413.26	376.07
35000	3093.36	1631.28	1145.86	904.60	760.99	599.29	549.80	482.13	438.75
36000	3181.74	1677.89	1178.60	930.44	782.73	616.41	565.51	495.91	451.28
37000	3270.13	1724.50	1211.34	956.29	804.47	633.54	581.22	509.68	463.82
38000	3358.51	1771.10	1244.08	982.13	826.22	650.66	596.93	523.46	476.36
39000	3446.89	1817.71	1276.81	1007.98	847.96	667.78	612.63	537.23	488.89
40000	3535.27	1864.32	1309.55	1033.83	869.70	684.90	628.34	551.01	501.43
41000	3623.65	1910.93	1342.29	1059.67	891.44	702.02	644.05	564.78	513.96
42000	3712.03	1957.53	1375.03	1085.52	913.19	719.15	659.76	578.56	526.50
43000	3800.42	2004.14	1407.77	1111.36	934.93	736.27	675.47	592.33	539.03
44000	3888.80	2050.75	1440.51	1137.21	956.67	753.39	691.18	606.11	551.57
45000	3977.18	2097.36	1473.25	1163.05	978.41	770.51	706.88	619.88	564.10
46000	4065.56	2143.97	1505.99	1188.90	1000.16	787.64	722.59	633.66	576.64
47000	4153.94	2190.57	1538.72	1214.74	1021.90	804.76	738.30	647.43	589.18
48000	4242.32	2237.18	1571.46	1240.59	1043.64	821.88	754.01	661.21	601.71
49000	4330.71	2283.79	1604.20	1266.44	1065.38	839.00	769.72	674.98	614.25
50000	4419.09	2330.40	1636.94	1292.28	1087.13	856.13	785.43	688.76	626.78
51000	4507.47	2377.00	1669.68	1318.13	1108.87	873.25	801.13	702.53	639.32
52000	4595.85	2423.61	1702.42	1343.97	1130.61	890.37	816.84	716.31	651.85
53000	4684.23	2470.22	1735.16	1369.82	1152.35	907.49	832.55	730.08	664.39
54000	4772.61	2516.83	1767.90	1395.66	1174.10	924.62	848.26	743.86	676.92
55000	4861.00	2563.44	1800.63	1421.51	1195.84	941.74	863.97	757.63	689.46
56000	4949.38	2610.04	1833.37	1447.35	1217.58	958.86	879.68	771.41	702.00
57000	5037.76	2656.65	1866.11	1473.20	1239.32	975.98	895.39	785.18	714.53
58000	5126.14	2703.26	1898.85	1499.05	1261.07	993.11	911.09	798.96	727.07
59000	5214.52	2749.87	1931.59	1524.89	1282.81	1010.23	926.80	812.73	739.60
60000	5302.90	2796.48	1964.33	1550.74	1304.55	1027.35	942.51	826.51	752.14
61000	5391.29	2843.08	1997.07	1576.58	1326.29	1044.47	958.22	840.28	764.67
62000	5479.67	2889.69	2029.81	1602.43	1348.04	1061.60	973.93	854.06	777.21
63000	5568.05	2936.30	2062.54	1628.27	1369.78	1078.72	989.64	867.83	789.74
64000	5656.43	2982.91	2095.28	1654.12	1391.52	1095.84	1005.34	881.61	802.28
65000	5744.81	3029.51	2128.02	1679.96	1413.26	1112.96	1021.05	895.38	814.82
66000	5833.19	3076.12	2160.76	1705.81	1435.00	1130.09	1036.76	909.16	827.35
67000	5921.58	3122.73	2193.50	1731.66	1456.75	1147.21	1052.47	922.93	839.89
68000	6009.96	3169.34	2226.24	1757.50	1478.49	1164.33	1068.18	936.71	852.42
69000	6098.34	3215.95	2258.98	1783.35	1500.23	1181.45	1083.89	950.48	864.96
70000	6186.72	3262.55	2291.72	1809.19	1521.97	1198.58	1099.59	964.26	877.49
75000	6628.63	3495.59	2455.41	1938.42	1630.69	1284.19	1178.14	1033.13	940.17
80000	7070.54	3728.63	2619.10	2067.65	1739.40	1369.80	1256.68	1102.01	1002.85
100000	8838.17	4660.79	3273.88	2584.56	2174.25	1712.25	1570.85	1377.51	1253.56

MONTHLY PAYMENT 11%

NECESSARY TO AMORTIZE A LOAN

TERM / AMOUNT	15 YEARS	18 YEARS	20 YEARS	25 YEARS	28 YEARS	29 YEARS	30 YEARS	35 YEARS	40 YEARS
$ 25	.29	.27	.26	.25	.25	.24	.24	.24	.24
50	.57	.54	.52	.50	.49	.48	.48	.47	.47
75	.86	.80	.78	.74	.73	.72	.72	.71	.70
100	1.14	1.07	1.04	.99	.97	.96	.96	.94	.93
200	2.28	2.14	2.07	1.97	1.93	1.92	1.91	1.88	1.86
300	3.41	3.20	3.10	2.95	2.89	2.87	2.86	2.82	2.79
400	4.55	4.27	4.13	3.93	3.85	3.83	3.81	3.75	3.72
500	5.69	5.33	5.17	4.91	4.81	4.79	4.77	4.69	4.65
600	6.82	6.40	6.20	5.89	5.77	5.74	5.72	5.63	5.57
700	7.96	7.46	7.23	6.87	6.74	6.70	6.67	6.56	6.50
800	9.10	8.53	8.26	7.85	7.70	7.66	7.62	7.50	7.43
900	10.23	9.59	9.29	8.83	8.66	8.61	8.58	8.44	8.36
1000	11.37	10.66	10.33	9.81	9.62	9.57	9.53	9.37	9.29
2000	22.74	21.31	20.65	19.61	19.23	19.14	19.05	18.74	18.57
3000	34.10	31.96	30.97	29.41	28.85	28.70	28.57	28.11	27.85
4000	45.47	42.61	41.29	39.21	38.46	38.27	38.10	37.48	37.14
5000	56.83	53.26	51.61	49.01	48.08	47.84	47.62	46.85	46.42
6000	68.20	63.91	61.94	58.81	57.69	57.40	57.14	56.22	55.70
7000	79.57	74.56	72.26	68.61	67.31	66.97	66.67	65.59	64.99
8000	90.93	85.21	82.58	78.41	76.92	76.54	76.19	74.96	74.27
9000	102.30	95.86	92.90	88.22	86.54	86.10	85.71	84.33	83.55
10000	113.66	106.51	103.22	98.02	96.15	95.67	95.24	93.70	92.83
15000	170.49	159.76	154.83	147.02	144.23	143.50	142.85	140.55	139.25
20000	227.32	213.01	206.44	196.03	192.30	191.33	190.47	187.40	185.66
25000	284.15	266.27	258.05	245.03	240.37	239.16	238.09	234.24	232.08
30000	340.98	319.52	309.66	294.04	288.45	286.99	285.70	281.09	278.49
35000	397.81	372.77	361.27	343.04	336.52	334.83	333.32	327.94	324.91
36000	409.18	383.42	371.59	352.85	346.14	344.39	342.84	337.31	334.19
37000	420.55	394.07	381.91	362.65	355.75	353.96	352.36	346.68	343.47
38000	431.91	404.72	392.24	372.45	365.37	363.52	361.89	356.05	352.76
39000	443.28	415.37	402.56	382.25	374.98	373.09	371.41	365.42	362.04
40000	454.64	426.02	412.88	392.05	384.60	382.66	380.93	374.79	371.32
41000	466.01	436.68	423.20	401.85	394.21	392.22	390.46	384.16	380.61
42000	477.38	447.33	433.52	411.65	403.83	401.79	399.98	393.53	389.89
43000	488.74	457.98	443.85	421.45	413.44	411.36	409.50	402.90	399.17
44000	500.11	468.63	454.17	431.25	423.06	420.92	419.03	412.27	408.45
45000	511.47	479.28	464.49	441.06	432.67	430.49	428.55	421.64	417.74
46000	522.84	489.93	474.81	450.86	442.29	440.05	438.07	431.01	427.02
47000	534.21	500.58	485.13	460.66	451.90	449.62	447.60	440.38	436.30
48000	545.57	511.23	495.46	470.46	461.52	459.19	457.12	449.74	445.59
49000	556.94	521.88	505.78	480.26	471.13	468.75	466.64	459.11	454.87
50000	568.30	532.53	516.10	490.06	480.74	478.32	476.17	468.48	464.15
51000	579.67	543.18	526.42	499.86	490.36	487.89	485.69	477.85	473.44
52000	591.04	553.83	536.74	509.66	499.97	497.45	495.21	487.22	482.72
53000	602.40	564.48	547.06	519.46	509.59	507.02	504.74	496.59	492.00
54000	613.77	575.13	557.39	529.27	519.20	516.58	514.26	505.96	501.28
55000	625.13	585.78	567.71	539.07	528.82	526.15	523.78	515.33	510.57
56000	636.50	596.43	578.03	548.87	538.43	535.72	533.31	524.70	519.85
57000	647.87	607.08	588.35	558.67	548.05	545.28	542.83	534.07	529.13
58000	659.23	617.73	598.67	568.47	557.66	554.85	552.35	543.44	538.42
59000	670.60	628.38	609.00	578.27	567.28	564.42	561.88	552.81	547.70
60000	681.96	639.03	619.32	588.07	576.89	573.98	571.40	562.18	556.98
61000	693.33	649.69	629.64	597.87	586.51	583.55	580.92	571.55	566.26
62000	704.70	660.34	639.96	607.68	596.12	593.12	590.45	580.92	575.55
63000	716.06	670.99	650.28	617.48	605.74	602.68	599.97	590.29	584.83
64000	727.43	681.64	660.61	627.28	615.35	612.25	609.49	599.66	594.11
65000	738.79	692.29	670.93	637.08	624.97	621.81	619.02	609.03	603.40
66000	750.16	702.94	681.25	646.88	634.58	631.38	628.54	618.40	612.68
67000	761.52	713.59	691.57	656.68	644.20	640.95	638.06	627.77	621.96
68000	772.89	724.24	701.89	666.48	653.81	650.51	647.58	637.14	631.25
69000	784.26	734.89	712.21	676.28	663.43	660.08	657.11	646.51	640.53
70000	795.62	745.54	722.54	686.08	673.04	669.65	666.63	655.88	649.81
75000	852.45	798.79	774.15	735.09	721.11	717.48	714.25	702.72	696.23
80000	909.28	852.04	825.76	784.10	769.19	765.31	761.86	749.57	742.64
100000	1136.60	1065.05	1032.19	980.12	961.48	956.63	952.33	936.96	928.30

11⅛% MONTHLY PAYMENT
NECESSARY TO AMORTIZE A LOAN

TERM / AMOUNT	1 YEAR	2 YEARS	3 YEARS	4 YEARS	5 YEARS	7 YEARS	8 YEARS	10 YEARS	12 YEARS
$ 25	2.22	1.17	.82	.65	.55	.43	.40	.35	.32
50	4.43	2.34	1.64	1.30	1.10	.86	.79	.70	.64
75	6.64	3.50	2.46	1.95	1.64	1.29	1.19	1.04	.95
100	8.85	4.67	3.28	2.60	2.19	1.72	1.58	1.39	1.27
200	17.69	9.34	6.56	5.19	4.37	3.44	3.16	2.77	2.53
300	26.54	14.00	9.84	7.78	6.55	5.16	4.74	4.16	3.79
400	35.38	18.67	13.12	10.37	8.73	6.88	6.32	5.54	5.05
500	44.22	23.34	16.40	12.96	10.91	8.60	7.89	6.93	6.31
600	53.07	28.00	19.68	15.55	13.09	10.32	9.47	8.31	7.57
700	61.91	32.67	22.96	18.14	15.27	12.04	11.05	9.70	8.83
800	70.76	37.34	26.24	20.73	17.45	13.76	12.63	11.08	10.09
900	79.60	42.00	29.52	23.32	19.63	15.47	14.20	12.47	11.35
1000	88.44	46.67	32.80	25.91	21.81	17.19	15.78	13.85	12.61
2000	176.88	93.34	65.60	51.82	43.61	34.38	31.56	27.70	25.22
3000	265.32	140.00	98.40	77.72	65.42	51.57	47.33	41.54	37.83
4000	353.76	186.67	131.20	103.63	87.22	68.76	63.11	55.39	50.44
5000	442.20	233.33	163.99	129.54	109.03	85.95	78.88	69.23	63.05
6000	530.64	280.00	196.79	155.44	130.83	103.13	94.66	83.08	75.66
7000	619.08	326.67	229.59	181.35	152.64	120.32	110.44	96.93	88.27
8000	707.52	373.33	262.39	207.26	174.44	137.51	126.21	110.77	100.88
9000	795.96	420.00	295.19	233.16	196.25	154.70	141.99	124.62	113.49
10000	884.40	466.66	327.98	259.07	218.05	171.89	157.76	138.46	126.10
15000	1326.60	699.99	491.97	388.60	327.08	257.83	236.64	207.69	189.15
20000	1768.80	933.32	655.96	518.13	436.10	343.77	315.52	276.92	252.20
25000	2211.00	1166.65	819.95	647.66	545.13	429.71	394.40	346.15	315.25
30000	2653.20	1399.98	983.94	777.19	654.15	515.65	473.28	415.38	378.29
35000	3095.40	1633.31	1147.93	906.72	763.17	601.59	552.16	484.61	441.34
36000	3183.84	1679.98	1180.73	932.63	784.98	618.78	567.94	498.46	453.95
37000	3272.28	1726.64	1213.53	958.54	806.78	635.97	583.71	512.30	466.56
38000	3360.72	1773.31	1246.33	984.44	828.59	653.16	599.49	526.15	479.17
39000	3449.16	1819.97	1279.12	1010.35	850.39	670.35	615.27	539.99	491.78
40000	3537.60	1866.64	1311.92	1036.26	872.20	687.53	631.04	553.84	504.39
41000	3626.04	1913.31	1344.72	1062.16	894.00	704.72	646.82	567.68	517.00
42000	3714.48	1959.97	1377.52	1088.07	915.81	721.91	662.59	581.53	529.61
43000	3802.92	2006.64	1410.32	1113.97	937.61	739.10	678.37	595.38	542.22
44000	3891.36	2053.30	1443.11	1139.88	959.42	756.29	694.15	609.22	554.83
45000	3979.80	2099.97	1475.91	1165.79	981.22	773.48	709.92	623.07	567.44
46000	4068.24	2146.64	1508.71	1191.69	1003.03	790.66	725.70	636.91	580.05
47000	4156.68	2193.30	1541.51	1217.60	1024.83	807.85	741.47	650.76	592.66
48000	4245.12	2239.97	1574.31	1243.51	1046.64	825.04	757.25	664.61	605.27
49000	4333.56	2286.63	1607.10	1269.41	1068.44	842.23	773.03	678.45	617.88
50000	4422.00	2333.30	1639.90	1295.32	1090.25	859.42	788.80	692.30	630.49
51000	4510.44	2379.97	1672.70	1321.22	1112.05	876.60	804.58	706.14	643.10
52000	4598.88	2426.63	1705.50	1347.13	1133.86	893.79	820.35	719.99	655.71
53000	4687.32	2473.30	1738.30	1373.04	1155.66	910.98	836.13	733.84	668.32
54000	4775.76	2519.96	1771.09	1398.94	1177.46	928.17	851.90	747.68	680.93
55000	4864.20	2566.63	1803.89	1424.85	1199.27	945.36	867.68	761.53	693.53
56000	4952.64	2613.30	1836.69	1450.76	1221.07	962.55	883.46	775.37	706.14
57000	5041.08	2659.96	1869.49	1476.66	1242.88	979.73	899.23	789.22	718.75
58000	5129.52	2706.63	1902.29	1502.57	1264.68	996.92	915.01	803.06	731.36
59000	5217.96	2753.29	1935.08	1528.47	1286.49	1014.11	930.78	816.91	743.97
60000	5306.40	2799.96	1967.88	1554.38	1308.29	1031.30	946.56	830.76	756.58
61000	5394.84	2846.62	2000.68	1580.29	1330.10	1048.49	962.34	844.60	769.19
62000	5483.28	2893.29	2033.48	1606.19	1351.90	1065.68	978.11	858.45	781.80
63000	5571.72	2939.96	2066.28	1632.10	1373.71	1082.86	993.89	872.29	794.41
64000	5660.16	2986.62	2099.07	1658.01	1395.51	1100.05	1009.66	886.14	807.02
65000	5748.60	3033.29	2131.87	1683.91	1417.32	1117.24	1025.44	899.99	819.63
66000	5837.04	3079.95	2164.67	1709.82	1439.12	1134.43	1041.22	913.83	832.24
67000	5925.48	3126.62	2197.47	1735.72	1460.93	1151.62	1056.99	927.68	844.85
68000	6013.92	3173.29	2230.27	1761.63	1482.73	1168.80	1072.77	941.52	857.46
69000	6102.36	3219.95	2263.06	1787.54	1504.54	1185.99	1088.54	955.37	870.07
70000	6190.80	3266.62	2295.86	1813.44	1526.34	1203.18	1104.32	969.21	882.68
75000	6633.00	3499.95	2459.85	1942.98	1635.37	1289.12	1183.20	1038.44	945.73
80000	7075.20	3733.28	2623.84	2072.51	1744.39	1375.06	1262.08	1107.67	1008.78
100000	8844.00	4666.59	3279.80	2590.63	2180.49	1718.83	1577.60	1384.59	1260.97

MONTHLY PAYMENT 11⅛%
NECESSARY TO AMORTIZE A LOAN

TERM / AMOUNT	15 YEARS	18 YEARS	20 YEARS	25 YEARS	28 YEARS	29 YEARS	30 YEARS	35 YEARS	40 YEARS
$ 25	.29	.27	.27	.25	.25	.25	.25	.24	.24
50	.58	.54	.53	.50	.49	.49	.49	.48	.47
75	.86	.81	.79	.75	.73	.73	.73	.72	.71
100	1.15	1.08	1.05	.99	.98	.97	.97	.95	.94
200	2.29	2.15	2.09	1.98	1.95	1.94	1.93	1.90	1.88
300	3.44	3.22	3.13	2.97	2.92	2.90	2.89	2.85	2.82
400	4.58	4.30	4.17	3.96	3.89	3.87	3.85	3.79	3.76
500	5.73	5.37	5.21	4.95	4.86	4.84	4.81	4.74	4.70
600	6.87	6.44	6.25	5.94	5.83	5.80	5.78	5.69	5.63
700	8.02	7.52	7.29	6.93	6.80	6.77	6.74	6.63	6.57
800	9.16	8.59	8.33	7.92	7.77	7.73	7.70	7.58	7.51
900	10.31	9.66	9.37	8.91	8.74	8.70	8.66	8.53	8.45
1000	11.45	10.74	10.41	9.90	9.71	9.67	9.62	9.47	9.39
2000	22.89	21.47	20.82	19.79	19.42	19.33	19.24	18.94	18.77
3000	34.34	32.20	31.23	29.68	29.13	28.99	28.86	28.41	28.15
4000	45.78	42.94	41.63	39.57	38.84	38.65	38.48	37.87	37.54
5000	57.23	53.67	52.04	49.46	48.54	48.31	48.09	47.34	46.92
6000	68.67	64.40	62.45	59.35	58.25	57.97	57.71	56.81	56.30
7000	80.12	75.14	72.85	69.25	67.96	67.63	67.33	66.28	65.68
8000	91.56	85.87	83.26	79.14	77.67	77.29	76.95	75.74	75.07
9000	103.01	96.60	93.67	89.03	87.38	86.95	86.57	85.21	84.45
10000	114.45	107.34	104.08	98.92	97.08	96.61	96.18	94.68	93.83
15000	171.67	161.00	156.11	148.38	145.62	144.91	144.27	142.01	140.75
20000	228.90	214.67	208.15	197.84	194.16	193.21	192.36	189.35	187.66
25000	286.12	268.34	260.18	247.30	242.70	241.51	240.45	236.68	234.57
30000	343.34	322.00	312.22	296.75	291.24	289.81	288.54	284.02	281.49
35000	400.57	375.67	364.25	346.21	339.78	338.11	336.63	331.36	328.40
36000	412.01	386.40	374.66	356.10	349.49	347.77	346.25	340.82	337.78
37000	423.45	397.13	385.07	366.00	359.20	357.43	355.86	350.29	347.16
38000	434.90	407.87	395.47	375.89	368.90	367.09	365.48	359.76	356.55
39000	446.34	418.60	405.88	385.78	378.61	376.75	375.10	369.22	365.93
40000	457.79	429.33	416.29	395.67	388.32	386.41	384.72	378.69	375.31
41000	469.23	440.07	426.70	405.56	398.03	396.07	394.34	388.16	384.69
42000	480.68	450.80	437.10	415.45	407.74	405.73	403.95	397.63	394.08
43000	492.12	461.53	447.51	425.35	417.44	415.39	413.57	407.09	403.46
44000	503.57	472.27	457.92	435.24	427.15	425.05	423.19	416.56	412.84
45000	515.01	483.00	468.32	445.13	436.86	434.71	432.81	426.03	422.23
46000	526.46	493.73	478.73	455.02	446.57	444.37	442.42	435.49	431.61
47000	537.90	504.47	489.14	464.91	456.28	454.03	452.04	444.96	440.99
48000	549.35	515.20	499.55	474.80	465.98	463.69	461.66	454.43	450.37
49000	560.79	525.93	509.95	484.69	475.69	473.35	471.28	463.90	459.76
50000	572.23	536.67	520.36	494.59	485.40	483.01	480.90	473.36	469.14
51000	583.68	547.40	530.77	504.48	495.11	492.67	490.51	482.83	478.52
52000	595.12	558.13	541.17	514.37	504.81	502.33	500.13	492.30	487.90
53000	606.57	568.87	551.58	524.26	514.52	511.99	509.75	501.76	497.29
54000	618.01	579.60	561.99	534.15	524.23	521.65	519.37	511.23	506.67
55000	629.46	590.33	572.39	544.04	533.94	531.31	528.98	520.70	516.05
56000	640.90	601.07	582.80	553.94	543.65	540.97	538.60	530.17	525.44
57000	652.35	611.80	593.21	563.83	553.35	550.63	548.22	539.63	534.82
58000	663.79	622.53	603.62	573.72	563.06	560.29	557.84	549.10	544.20
59000	675.24	633.26	614.02	583.61	572.77	569.95	567.46	558.57	553.58
60000	686.68	644.00	624.43	593.50	582.48	579.61	577.07	568.03	562.97
61000	698.12	654.73	634.84	603.39	592.19	589.27	586.69	577.50	572.35
62000	709.57	665.46	645.24	613.29	601.89	598.93	596.31	586.97	581.73
63000	721.01	676.20	655.65	623.18	611.60	608.59	605.93	596.44	591.11
64000	732.46	686.93	666.06	633.07	621.31	618.25	615.54	605.90	600.50
65000	743.90	697.66	676.47	642.96	631.02	627.91	625.16	615.37	609.88
66000	755.35	708.40	686.87	652.85	640.73	637.57	634.78	624.84	619.26
67000	766.79	719.13	697.28	662.74	650.43	647.23	644.40	634.30	628.64
68000	778.24	729.86	707.69	672.64	660.14	656.89	654.02	643.77	638.03
69000	789.68	740.60	718.09	682.53	669.85	666.55	663.63	653.24	647.41
70000	801.13	751.33	728.50	692.42	679.56	676.22	673.25	662.71	656.79
75000	858.35	805.00	780.54	741.88	728.10	724.52	721.34	710.04	703.71
80000	915.57	858.66	832.57	791.34	776.64	772.82	769.43	757.38	750.62
100000	1144.46	1073.33	1040.71	989.17	970.79	966.02	961.79	946.72	938.27

11¼% MONTHLY PAYMENT
NECESSARY TO AMORTIZE A LOAN

TERM / AMOUNT	1 YEAR	2 YEARS	3 YEARS	4 YEARS	5 YEARS	7 YEARS	8 YEARS	10 YEARS	12 YEARS
$ 25	2.22	1.17	.83	.65	.55	.44	.40	.35	.32
50	4.43	2.34	1.65	1.30	1.10	.87	.80	.70	.64
75	6.64	3.51	2.47	1.95	1.65	1.30	1.19	1.05	.96
100	8.85	4.68	3.29	2.60	2.19	1.73	1.59	1.40	1.27
200	17.70	9.35	6.58	5.20	4.38	3.46	3.17	2.79	2.54
300	26.55	14.02	9.86	7.80	6.57	5.18	4.76	4.18	3.81
400	35.40	18.69	13.15	10.39	8.75	6.91	6.34	5.57	5.08
500	44.25	23.37	16.43	12.99	10.94	8.63	7.93	6.96	6.35
600	53.10	28.04	19.72	15.59	13.13	10.36	9.51	8.36	7.62
700	61.95	32.71	23.01	18.18	15.31	12.08	11.10	9.75	8.88
800	70.80	37.38	26.29	20.78	17.50	13.81	12.68	11.14	10.15
900	79.65	42.06	29.58	23.38	19.69	15.53	14.26	12.53	11.42
1000	88.50	46.73	32.86	25.97	21.87	17.26	15.85	13.92	12.69
2000	177.00	93.45	65.72	51.94	43.74	34.51	31.69	27.84	25.37
3000	265.50	140.18	98.58	77.91	65.61	51.77	47.54	41.76	38.06
4000	354.00	186.90	131.43	103.87	87.47	69.02	63.38	55.67	50.74
5000	442.50	233.62	164.29	129.84	109.34	86.28	79.22	69.59	63.42
6000	530.99	280.35	197.15	155.81	131.21	103.53	95.07	83.51	76.11
7000	619.49	327.07	230.01	181.77	153.08	120.78	110.91	97.42	88.79
8000	707.99	373.80	262.86	207.74	174.94	138.04	126.75	111.34	101.48
9000	796.49	420.52	295.72	233.71	196.81	155.29	142.60	125.26	114.16
10000	884.99	467.24	328.58	259.68	218.68	172.55	158.44	139.17	126.84
15000	1327.48	700.86	492.86	389.51	328.01	258.82	237.66	208.76	190.26
20000	1769.97	934.48	657.15	519.35	437.35	345.09	316.88	278.34	253.68
25000	2212.46	1168.10	821.44	649.18	546.69	431.36	396.09	347.93	317.10
30000	2654.95	1401.72	985.72	779.02	656.02	517.63	475.31	417.51	380.52
35000	3097.45	1635.34	1150.01	908.85	765.36	603.90	554.53	487.10	443.94
36000	3185.94	1682.07	1182.87	934.82	787.23	621.16	570.37	501.01	456.63
37000	3274.44	1728.79	1215.72	960.79	809.10	638.41	586.22	514.93	469.31
38000	3362.94	1775.52	1248.58	986.75	830.96	655.66	602.06	528.85	481.99
39000	3451.44	1822.24	1281.44	1012.72	852.83	672.92	617.90	542.76	494.68
40000	3539.94	1868.96	1314.29	1038.69	874.70	690.17	633.75	556.68	507.36
41000	3628.44	1915.69	1347.15	1064.66	896.56	707.43	649.59	570.60	520.05
42000	3716.93	1962.41	1380.01	1090.62	918.43	724.68	665.44	584.51	532.73
43000	3805.43	2009.14	1412.87	1116.59	940.30	741.93	681.28	598.43	545.41
44000	3893.93	2055.86	1445.72	1142.56	962.17	759.19	697.12	612.35	558.10
45000	3982.43	2102.58	1478.58	1168.52	984.03	776.44	712.97	626.27	570.78
46000	4070.93	2149.31	1511.44	1194.49	1005.90	793.70	728.81	640.18	583.47
47000	4159.43	2196.03	1544.30	1220.46	1027.77	810.95	744.65	654.10	596.15
48000	4247.92	2242.76	1577.15	1246.43	1049.64	828.21	760.50	668.02	608.83
49000	4336.42	2289.48	1610.01	1272.39	1071.50	845.46	776.34	681.93	621.52
50000	4424.92	2336.20	1642.87	1298.36	1093.37	862.71	792.18	695.85	634.20
51000	4513.42	2382.93	1675.72	1324.33	1115.24	879.97	808.03	709.77	646.89
52000	4601.92	2429.65	1708.58	1350.29	1137.11	897.22	823.87	723.68	659.57
53000	4690.42	2476.38	1741.44	1376.26	1158.97	914.48	839.71	737.60	672.25
54000	4778.91	2523.10	1774.30	1402.23	1180.84	931.73	855.56	751.52	684.94
55000	4867.41	2569.82	1807.15	1428.20	1202.71	948.98	871.40	765.43	697.62
56000	4955.91	2616.55	1840.01	1454.16	1224.57	966.24	887.25	779.35	710.31
57000	5044.41	2663.27	1872.87	1480.13	1246.44	983.49	903.09	793.27	722.99
58000	5132.91	2710.00	1905.72	1506.10	1268.31	1000.75	918.93	807.18	735.67
59000	5221.41	2756.72	1938.58	1532.06	1290.18	1018.00	934.78	821.10	748.36
60000	5309.90	2803.44	1971.44	1558.03	1312.04	1035.26	950.62	835.02	761.04
61000	5398.40	2850.17	2004.30	1584.00	1333.91	1052.51	966.46	848.94	773.72
62000	5486.90	2896.89	2037.15	1609.97	1355.78	1069.76	982.31	862.85	786.41
63000	5575.40	2943.62	2070.01	1635.93	1377.65	1087.02	998.15	876.77	799.09
64000	5663.90	2990.34	2102.87	1661.90	1399.51	1104.27	1013.99	890.69	811.78
65000	5752.40	3037.06	2135.73	1687.87	1421.38	1121.53	1029.84	904.60	824.46
66000	5840.89	3083.79	2168.58	1713.83	1443.25	1138.78	1045.68	918.52	837.14
67000	5929.39	3130.51	2201.44	1739.80	1465.11	1156.03	1061.53	932.44	849.83
68000	6017.89	3177.24	2234.30	1765.77	1486.98	1173.29	1077.37	946.35	862.51
69000	6106.39	3223.96	2267.15	1791.73	1508.85	1190.54	1093.21	960.27	875.20
70000	6194.89	3270.68	2300.01	1817.70	1530.72	1207.80	1109.06	974.19	887.88
75000	6637.38	3504.30	2464.30	1947.54	1640.05	1294.07	1188.27	1043.77	951.30
80000	7079.87	3737.92	2628.58	2077.37	1749.39	1380.34	1267.49	1113.36	1014.72
100000	8849.84	4672.40	3285.73	2596.71	2186.74	1725.42	1584.36	1391.69	1268.40

MONTHLY PAYMENT 11¼%

NECESSARY TO AMORTIZE A LOAN

TERM / AMOUNT	15 YEARS	18 YEARS	20 YEARS	25 YEARS	28 YEARS	29 YEARS	30 YEARS	35 YEARS	40 YEARS
$ 25	.29	.28	.27	.25	.25	.25	.25	.24	.24
50	.58	.55	.53	.50	.50	.49	.49	.48	.48
75	.87	.82	.79	.75	.74	.74	.73	.72	.72
100	1.16	1.09	1.05	1.00	.99	.98	.98	.96	.95
200	2.31	2.17	2.10	2.00	1.97	1.96	1.95	1.92	1.90
300	3.46	3.25	3.15	3.00	2.95	2.93	2.92	2.87	2.85
400	4.61	4.33	4.20	4.00	3.93	3.91	3.89	3.83	3.80
500	5.77	5.41	5.25	5.00	4.91	4.88	4.86	4.79	4.75
600	6.92	6.49	6.30	5.99	5.89	5.86	5.83	5.74	5.69
700	8.07	7.58	7.35	6.99	6.87	6.83	6.80	6.70	6.64
800	9.22	8.66	8.40	7.99	7.85	7.81	7.78	7.66	7.59
900	10.38	9.74	9.45	8.99	8.83	8.78	8.75	8.61	8.54
1000	11.53	10.82	10.50	9.99	9.81	9.76	9.72	9.57	9.49
2000	23.05	21.64	20.99	19.97	19.61	19.51	19.43	19.13	18.97
3000	34.58	32.45	31.48	29.95	29.41	29.27	29.14	28.70	28.45
4000	46.10	43.27	41.98	39.93	39.21	39.02	38.86	38.26	37.94
5000	57.62	54.09	52.47	49.92	49.01	48.78	48.57	47.83	47.42
6000	69.15	64.90	62.96	59.90	58.81	58.53	58.28	57.39	56.90
7000	80.67	75.72	73.45	69.88	68.61	68.28	67.99	66.96	66.38
8000	92.19	86.53	83.95	79.86	78.41	78.04	77.71	76.52	75.87
9000	103.72	97.35	94.44	89.85	88.22	87.79	87.42	86.09	85.35
10000	115.24	108.17	104.93	99.83	98.02	97.55	97.13	95.65	94.83
15000	172.86	162.25	157.39	149.74	147.02	146.32	145.69	143.48	142.24
20000	230.47	216.33	209.86	199.65	196.03	195.09	194.26	191.30	189.66
25000	288.09	270.41	262.32	249.56	245.04	243.86	242.82	239.13	237.07
30000	345.71	324.49	314.78	299.48	294.04	292.63	291.38	286.95	284.48
35000	403.33	378.57	367.24	349.39	343.05	341.40	339.95	334.78	331.90
36000	414.85	389.39	377.74	359.37	352.85	351.16	349.66	344.34	341.38
37000	426.37	400.20	388.23	369.35	362.65	360.91	359.37	353.91	350.86
38000	437.90	411.02	398.72	379.34	372.45	370.67	369.08	363.47	360.34
39000	449.42	421.84	409.21	389.32	382.25	380.42	378.80	373.04	369.83
40000	460.94	432.65	419.71	399.30	392.05	390.17	388.51	382.60	379.31
41000	472.47	443.47	430.20	409.28	401.85	399.93	398.22	392.17	388.79
42000	483.99	454.29	440.69	419.27	411.66	409.68	407.93	401.73	398.27
43000	495.51	465.10	451.19	429.25	421.46	419.44	417.65	411.30	407.76
44000	507.04	475.92	461.68	439.23	431.26	429.19	427.36	420.86	417.24
45000	518.56	486.73	472.17	449.21	441.06	438.95	437.07	430.43	426.72
46000	530.08	497.55	482.66	459.20	450.86	448.70	446.79	439.99	436.20
47000	541.61	508.37	493.16	469.18	460.66	458.45	456.50	449.56	445.69
48000	553.13	519.18	503.65	479.16	470.46	468.21	466.21	459.12	455.17
49000	564.65	530.00	514.14	489.14	480.26	477.96	475.92	468.69	464.65
50000	576.18	540.82	524.63	499.12	490.07	487.72	485.64	478.25	474.13
51000	587.70	551.63	535.13	509.11	499.87	497.47	495.35	487.82	483.62
52000	599.22	562.45	545.62	519.09	509.67	507.23	505.06	497.38	493.10
53000	610.75	573.26	556.11	529.07	519.47	516.98	514.77	506.95	502.58
54000	622.27	584.08	566.60	539.05	529.27	526.73	524.49	516.51	512.06
55000	633.79	594.90	577.10	549.04	539.07	536.49	534.20	526.08	521.55
56000	645.32	605.71	587.59	559.02	548.87	546.24	543.91	535.64	531.03
57000	656.84	616.53	598.08	569.00	558.67	556.00	553.62	545.21	540.51
58000	668.36	627.34	608.57	578.98	568.48	565.75	563.34	554.77	549.99
59000	679.89	638.16	619.07	588.97	578.28	575.50	573.05	564.34	559.48
60000	691.41	648.98	629.56	598.95	588.08	585.26	582.76	573.90	568.96
61000	702.94	659.79	640.05	608.93	597.88	595.01	592.47	583.47	578.44
62000	714.46	670.61	650.54	618.91	607.68	604.77	602.19	593.03	587.92
63000	725.98	681.43	661.04	628.90	617.48	614.52	611.90	602.60	597.41
64000	737.51	692.24	671.53	638.88	627.28	624.28	621.61	612.16	606.89
65000	749.03	703.06	682.02	648.86	637.08	634.03	631.32	621.73	616.37
66000	760.55	713.87	692.51	658.84	646.88	643.78	641.04	631.29	625.85
67000	772.08	724.69	703.01	668.83	656.69	653.54	650.75	640.86	635.34
68000	783.60	735.51	713.50	678.81	666.49	663.29	660.46	650.42	644.82
69000	795.12	746.32	723.99	688.79	676.29	673.05	670.18	659.99	654.30
70000	806.65	757.14	734.48	698.77	686.09	682.80	679.89	669.55	663.79
75000	864.26	811.22	786.95	748.68	735.10	731.57	728.45	717.38	711.20
80000	921.88	865.30	839.41	798.60	784.10	780.34	777.01	765.20	758.61
100000	1152.35	1081.63	1049.26	998.24	980.13	975.43	971.27	956.50	948.26

11⅜% MONTHLY PAYMENT
NECESSARY TO AMORTIZE A LOAN

TERM / AMOUNT	1 YEAR	2 YEARS	3 YEARS	4 YEARS	5 YEARS	7 YEARS	8 YEARS	10 YEARS	12 YEARS
$ 25	2.22	1.17	.83	.66	.55	.44	.40	.35	.32
50	4.43	2.34	1.65	1.31	1.10	.87	.80	.70	.64
75	6.65	3.51	2.47	1.96	1.65	1.30	1.20	1.05	.96
100	8.86	4.68	3.30	2.61	2.20	1.74	1.60	1.40	1.28
200	17.72	9.36	6.59	5.21	4.39	3.47	3.19	2.80	2.56
300	26.57	14.04	9.88	7.81	6.58	5.20	4.78	4.20	3.83
400	35.43	18.72	13.17	10.42	8.78	6.93	6.37	5.60	5.11
500	44.28	23.40	16.46	13.02	10.97	8.67	7.96	7.00	6.38
600	53.14	28.07	19.75	15.62	13.16	10.40	9.55	8.40	7.66
700	61.99	32.75	23.05	18.22	15.36	12.13	11.14	9.80	8.94
800	70.85	37.43	26.34	20.83	17.55	13.86	12.73	11.20	10.21
900	79.71	42.11	29.63	23.43	19.74	15.59	14.33	12.59	11.49
1000	88.56	46.79	32.92	26.03	21.93	17.33	15.92	13.99	12.76
2000	177.12	93.57	65.84	52.06	43.86	34.65	31.83	27.98	25.52
3000	265.68	140.35	98.75	78.09	65.79	51.97	47.74	41.97	38.28
4000	354.23	187.13	131.67	104.12	87.72	69.29	63.65	55.96	51.04
5000	442.79	233.92	164.59	130.15	109.65	86.61	79.56	69.95	63.80
6000	531.35	280.70	197.50	156.17	131.58	103.93	95.47	83.93	76.56
7000	619.90	327.48	230.42	182.20	153.51	121.25	111.38	97.92	89.31
8000	708.46	374.26	263.34	208.23	175.44	138.57	127.30	111.91	102.07
9000	797.02	421.04	296.25	234.26	197.37	155.89	143.21	125.90	114.83
10000	885.57	467.83	329.17	260.29	219.30	173.21	159.12	139.89	127.59
15000	1328.36	701.74	493.75	390.43	328.95	259.81	238.68	209.83	191.38
20000	1771.14	935.65	658.34	520.57	438.60	346.41	318.23	279.77	255.17
25000	2213.92	1169.56	822.92	650.71	548.25	433.01	397.79	349.71	318.97
30000	2656.71	1403.47	987.50	780.85	657.90	519.61	477.35	419.65	382.76
35000	3099.49	1637.38	1152.09	910.99	767.55	606.21	556.90	489.59	446.55
36000	3188.05	1684.16	1185.00	937.01	789.48	623.53	572.82	503.58	459.31
37000	3276.60	1730.94	1217.92	963.04	811.41	640.85	588.73	517.57	472.07
38000	3365.16	1777.73	1250.84	989.07	833.34	658.17	604.64	531.55	484.83
39000	3453.72	1824.51	1283.75	1015.10	855.27	675.49	620.55	545.54	497.58
40000	3542.27	1871.29	1316.67	1041.13	877.20	692.81	636.46	559.53	510.34
41000	3630.83	1918.07	1349.59	1067.15	899.13	710.13	652.37	573.52	523.10
42000	3719.39	1964.85	1382.50	1093.18	921.06	727.46	668.28	587.51	535.86
43000	3807.94	2011.64	1415.42	1119.21	942.99	744.78	684.20	601.49	548.62
44000	3896.50	2058.42	1448.33	1145.24	964.92	762.10	700.11	615.48	561.38
45000	3985.06	2105.20	1481.25	1171.27	986.85	779.42	716.02	629.47	574.13
46000	4073.61	2151.98	1514.17	1197.29	1008.78	796.74	731.93	643.46	586.89
47000	4162.17	2198.77	1547.08	1223.32	1030.71	814.06	747.84	657.45	599.65
48000	4250.73	2245.55	1580.00	1249.35	1052.64	831.38	763.75	671.44	612.41
49000	4339.28	2292.33	1612.92	1275.38	1074.57	848.70	779.66	685.42	625.17
50000	4427.84	2339.11	1645.83	1301.41	1096.50	866.02	795.57	699.41	637.93
51000	4516.40	2385.89	1678.75	1327.43	1118.43	883.34	811.49	713.40	650.69
52000	4604.95	2432.68	1711.67	1353.46	1140.36	900.66	827.40	727.39	663.44
53000	4693.51	2479.46	1744.58	1379.49	1162.29	917.98	843.31	741.38	676.20
54000	4782.07	2526.24	1777.50	1405.52	1184.22	935.30	859.22	755.36	688.96
55000	4870.62	2573.02	1810.42	1431.55	1206.15	952.62	875.13	769.35	701.72
56000	4959.18	2619.80	1843.33	1457.57	1228.08	969.94	891.04	783.34	714.48
57000	5047.74	2666.59	1876.25	1483.60	1250.01	987.26	906.95	797.33	727.24
58000	5136.29	2713.37	1909.17	1509.63	1271.94	1004.58	922.87	811.32	739.99
59000	5224.85	2760.15	1942.08	1535.66	1293.87	1021.90	938.78	825.30	752.75
60000	5313.41	2806.93	1975.00	1561.69	1315.80	1039.22	954.69	839.29	765.51
61000	5401.96	2853.72	2007.92	1587.71	1337.73	1056.54	970.60	853.28	778.27
62000	5490.52	2900.50	2040.83	1613.74	1359.66	1073.86	986.51	867.27	791.03
63000	5579.08	2947.28	2073.75	1639.77	1381.59	1091.18	1002.42	881.26	803.79
64000	5667.63	2994.06	2106.67	1665.80	1403.52	1108.50	1018.33	895.25	816.55
65000	5756.19	3040.84	2139.58	1691.83	1425.45	1125.82	1034.25	909.23	829.30
66000	5844.75	3087.63	2172.50	1717.85	1447.38	1143.14	1050.16	923.22	842.06
67000	5933.30	3134.41	2205.42	1743.88	1469.31	1160.46	1066.07	937.21	854.82
68000	6021.86	3181.19	2238.33	1769.91	1491.24	1177.78	1081.98	951.20	867.58
69000	6110.42	3227.97	2271.25	1795.94	1513.17	1195.10	1097.89	965.19	880.34
70000	6198.97	3274.75	2304.17	1821.97	1535.10	1212.42	1113.80	979.17	893.10
75000	6641.76	3508.66	2468.75	1952.11	1644.75	1299.02	1193.36	1049.11	956.89
80000	7084.54	3742.58	2633.33	2082.25	1754.40	1385.62	1272.92	1119.06	1020.68
100000	8855.67	4678.22	3291.66	2602.81	2193.00	1732.03	1591.14	1398.82	1275.85

MONTHLY PAYMENT 11⅜%
NECESSARY TO AMORTIZE A LOAN

TERM / AMOUNT	15 YEARS	18 YEARS	20 YEARS	25 YEARS	28 YEARS	29 YEARS	30 YEARS	35 YEARS	40 YEARS
$ 25	.30	.28	.27	.26	.25	.25	.25	.25	.24
50	.59	.55	.53	.51	.50	.50	.50	.49	.48
75	.88	.82	.80	.76	.75	.74	.74	.73	.72
100	1.17	1.09	1.06	1.01	.99	.99	.99	.97	.96
200	2.33	2.18	2.12	2.02	1.98	1.97	1.97	1.94	1.92
300	3.49	3.27	3.18	3.03	2.97	2.96	2.95	2.90	2.88
400	4.65	4.36	4.24	4.03	3.96	3.94	3.93	3.87	3.84
500	5.81	5.45	5.29	5.04	4.95	4.93	4.91	4.84	4.80
600	6.97	6.54	6.35	6.05	5.94	5.91	5.89	5.80	5.75
700	8.13	7.63	7.41	7.06	6.93	6.90	6.87	6.77	6.71
800	9.29	8.72	8.47	8.06	7.92	7.88	7.85	7.74	7.67
900	10.45	9.81	9.53	9.07	8.91	8.87	8.83	8.70	8.63
1000	11.61	10.90	10.58	10.08	9.90	9.85	9.81	9.67	9.59
2000	23.21	21.80	21.16	20.15	19.79	19.70	19.62	19.33	19.17
3000	34.81	32.70	31.74	30.23	29.69	29.55	29.43	28.99	28.75
4000	46.42	43.60	42.32	40.30	39.58	39.40	39.24	38.66	38.34
5000	58.02	54.50	52.90	50.37	49.48	49.25	49.04	48.32	47.92
6000	69.62	65.40	63.47	60.45	59.37	59.10	58.85	57.98	57.50
7000	81.22	76.30	74.05	70.52	69.27	68.94	68.66	67.65	67.08
8000	92.83	87.20	84.63	80.59	79.16	78.79	78.47	77.31	76.67
9000	104.43	98.10	95.21	90.67	89.06	88.64	88.27	86.97	86.25
10000	116.03	109.00	105.79	100.74	98.95	98.49	98.08	96.63	95.83
15000	174.04	163.50	158.68	151.11	148.43	147.73	147.12	144.95	143.74
20000	232.06	217.99	211.57	201.47	197.90	196.98	196.16	193.26	191.66
25000	290.07	272.49	264.46	251.84	247.37	246.22	245.20	241.58	239.57
30000	348.08	326.99	317.35	302.21	296.85	295.46	294.23	289.89	287.48
35000	406.09	381.49	370.25	352.57	346.32	344.70	343.27	338.21	335.40
36000	417.70	392.39	380.82	362.65	356.22	354.55	353.08	347.87	344.98
37000	429.30	403.28	391.40	372.72	366.11	364.40	362.89	357.53	354.56
38000	440.90	414.18	401.98	382.79	376.01	374.25	372.70	367.20	364.14
39000	452.50	425.08	412.56	392.87	385.90	384.10	382.50	376.86	373.73
40000	464.11	435.98	423.14	402.94	395.80	393.95	392.31	386.52	383.31
41000	475.71	446.88	433.72	413.02	405.69	403.80	402.12	396.18	392.89
42000	487.31	457.78	444.29	423.09	415.59	413.64	411.93	405.85	402.48
43000	498.91	468.68	454.87	433.16	425.48	423.49	421.73	415.51	412.06
44000	510.52	479.58	465.45	443.24	435.38	433.34	431.54	425.17	421.64
45000	522.12	490.48	476.03	453.31	445.27	443.19	441.35	434.84	431.22
46000	533.72	501.38	486.61	463.38	455.17	453.04	451.16	444.50	440.81
47000	545.32	512.28	497.18	473.46	465.06	462.89	460.96	454.16	450.39
48000	556.93	523.18	507.76	483.53	474.95	472.74	470.77	463.82	459.97
49000	568.53	534.08	518.34	493.60	484.85	482.58	480.58	473.49	469.55
50000	580.13	544.98	528.92	503.68	494.74	492.43	490.39	483.15	479.14
51000	591.74	555.88	539.50	513.75	504.64	502.28	500.20	492.81	488.72
52000	603.34	566.78	550.08	523.82	514.53	512.13	510.00	502.48	498.30
53000	614.94	577.68	560.65	533.90	524.43	521.98	519.81	512.14	507.88
54000	626.54	588.58	571.23	543.97	534.32	531.83	529.62	521.80	517.47
55000	638.15	599.47	581.81	554.04	544.22	541.68	539.43	531.47	527.05
56000	649.75	610.37	592.39	564.12	554.11	551.52	549.23	541.13	536.63
57000	661.35	621.27	602.97	574.19	564.01	561.37	559.04	550.79	546.21
58000	672.95	632.17	613.55	584.26	573.90	571.22	568.85	560.45	555.80
59000	684.56	643.07	624.12	594.34	583.80	581.07	578.66	570.12	565.38
60000	696.16	653.97	634.70	604.41	593.69	590.92	588.46	579.78	574.96
61000	707.76	664.87	645.28	614.48	603.59	600.77	598.27	589.44	584.54
62000	719.36	675.77	655.86	624.56	613.48	610.62	608.08	599.11	594.13
63000	730.97	686.67	666.44	634.63	623.38	620.46	617.89	608.77	603.71
64000	742.57	697.57	677.02	644.70	633.27	630.31	627.69	618.43	613.29
65000	754.17	708.47	687.59	654.78	643.17	640.16	637.50	628.09	622.88
66000	765.77	719.37	698.17	664.85	653.06	650.01	647.31	637.76	632.46
67000	777.38	730.27	708.75	674.92	662.96	659.86	657.12	647.42	642.04
68000	788.98	741.17	719.33	685.00	672.85	669.71	666.93	657.08	651.62
69000	800.58	752.07	729.91	695.07	682.75	679.56	676.73	666.75	661.21
70000	812.18	762.97	740.49	705.14	692.64	689.40	686.54	676.41	670.79
75000	870.20	817.46	793.38	755.51	742.11	738.65	735.58	724.72	718.70
80000	928.21	871.96	846.27	805.88	791.59	787.89	784.62	773.04	766.61
100000	1160.26	1089.95	1057.83	1007.35	989.48	984.86	980.77	966.30	958.27

11½% MONTHLY PAYMENT
NECESSARY TO AMORTIZE A LOAN

TERM / AMOUNT	1 YEAR	2 YEARS	3 YEARS	4 YEARS	5 YEARS	7 YEARS	8 YEARS	10 YEARS	12 YEARS
$ 25	2.22	1.18	.83	.66	.55	.44	.40	.36	.33
50	4.44	2.35	1.65	1.31	1.10	.87	.80	.71	.65
75	6.65	3.52	2.48	1.96	1.65	1.31	1.20	1.06	.97
100	8.87	4.69	3.30	2.61	2.20	1.74	1.60	1.41	1.29
200	17.73	9.37	6.60	5.22	4.40	3.48	3.20	2.82	2.57
300	26.59	14.06	9.90	7.83	6.60	5.22	4.80	4.22	3.85
400	35.45	18.74	13.20	10.44	8.80	6.96	6.40	5.63	5.14
500	44.31	23.43	16.49	13.05	11.00	8.70	7.99	7.03	6.42
600	53.17	28.11	19.79	15.66	13.20	10.44	9.59	8.44	7.70
700	62.04	32.79	23.09	18.27	15.40	12.18	11.19	9.85	8.99
800	70.90	37.48	26.39	20.88	17.60	13.91	12.79	11.25	10.27
900	79.76	42.16	29.68	23.49	19.80	15.65	14.39	12.66	11.55
1000	88.62	46.85	32.98	26.09	22.00	17.39	15.98	14.06	12.84
2000	177.24	93.69	65.96	52.18	43.99	34.78	31.96	28.12	25.67
3000	265.85	140.53	98.93	78.27	65.98	52.16	47.94	42.18	38.50
4000	354.47	187.37	131.91	104.36	87.98	69.55	63.92	56.24	51.34
5000	443.08	234.21	164.89	130.45	109.97	86.94	79.90	70.30	64.17
6000	531.70	281.05	197.86	156.54	131.96	104.32	95.88	84.36	77.00
7000	620.31	327.89	230.84	182.63	153.95	121.71	111.86	98.42	89.84
8000	708.93	374.73	263.81	208.72	175.95	139.10	127.84	112.48	102.67
9000	797.54	421.57	296.79	234.81	197.94	156.48	143.82	126.54	115.50
10000	886.16	468.41	329.77	260.90	219.93	173.87	159.80	140.60	128.34
15000	1329.23	702.61	494.65	391.34	329.89	260.80	239.70	210.90	192.50
20000	1772.31	936.81	659.53	521.79	439.86	347.73	319.59	281.20	256.67
25000	2215.38	1171.01	824.41	652.23	549.82	434.67	399.49	351.49	320.83
30000	2658.46	1405.21	989.29	782.68	659.78	521.60	479.39	421.79	385.00
35000	3101.53	1639.42	1154.17	913.12	769.75	608.53	559.28	492.09	449.17
36000	3190.15	1686.26	1187.14	939.21	791.74	625.92	575.26	506.15	462.00
37000	3278.76	1733.10	1220.12	965.30	813.73	643.30	591.24	520.21	474.83
38000	3367.38	1779.94	1253.09	991.39	835.72	660.69	607.22	534.27	487.67
39000	3455.99	1826.78	1286.07	1017.48	857.72	678.08	623.20	548.33	500.50
40000	3544.61	1873.62	1319.05	1043.57	879.71	695.46	639.18	562.39	513.33
41000	3633.22	1920.46	1352.02	1069.65	901.70	712.85	655.16	576.45	526.16
42000	3721.84	1967.30	1385.00	1095.74	923.69	730.24	671.14	590.51	539.00
43000	3810.45	2014.14	1417.97	1121.83	945.69	747.62	687.12	604.57	551.83
44000	3899.07	2060.98	1450.95	1147.92	967.68	765.01	703.10	618.62	564.66
45000	3987.68	2107.82	1483.93	1174.01	989.67	782.40	719.08	632.68	577.50
46000	4076.30	2154.66	1516.90	1200.10	1011.66	799.78	735.06	646.74	590.33
47000	4164.91	2201.50	1549.88	1226.19	1033.66	817.17	751.04	660.80	603.16
48000	4253.53	2248.34	1582.85	1252.28	1055.65	834.56	767.01	674.86	616.00
49000	4342.14	2295.18	1615.83	1278.37	1077.64	851.94	782.99	688.92	628.83
50000	4430.76	2342.02	1648.81	1304.46	1099.64	869.33	798.97	702.98	641.66
51000	4519.37	2388.86	1681.78	1330.54	1121.63	886.71	814.95	717.04	654.50
52000	4607.99	2435.70	1714.76	1356.63	1143.62	904.10	830.93	731.10	667.33
53000	4696.60	2482.54	1747.73	1382.72	1165.61	921.49	846.91	745.16	680.16
54000	4785.22	2529.38	1780.71	1408.81	1187.61	938.87	862.89	759.22	693.00
55000	4873.83	2576.22	1813.69	1434.90	1209.60	956.26	878.87	773.28	705.83
56000	4962.45	2623.06	1846.66	1460.99	1231.59	973.65	894.85	787.34	718.66
57000	5051.06	2669.90	1879.64	1487.08	1253.58	991.03	910.83	801.40	731.50
58000	5139.68	2716.74	1912.61	1513.17	1275.58	1008.42	926.81	815.46	744.33
59000	5228.29	2763.58	1945.59	1539.26	1297.57	1025.81	942.79	829.52	757.16
60000	5316.91	2810.42	1978.57	1565.35	1319.56	1043.19	958.77	843.58	769.99
61000	5405.52	2857.26	2011.54	1591.43	1341.55	1060.58	974.75	857.64	782.83
62000	5494.14	2904.10	2044.52	1617.52	1363.55	1077.97	990.73	871.70	795.66
63000	5582.75	2950.94	2077.49	1643.61	1385.54	1095.35	1006.71	885.76	808.49
64000	5671.37	2997.79	2110.47	1669.70	1407.53	1112.74	1022.68	899.82	821.33
65000	5759.98	3044.63	2143.45	1695.79	1429.52	1130.12	1038.66	913.88	834.16
66000	5848.60	3091.47	2176.42	1721.88	1451.52	1147.51	1054.64	927.93	846.99
67000	5937.21	3138.31	2209.40	1747.97	1473.51	1164.90	1070.62	941.99	859.83
68000	6025.83	3185.15	2242.37	1774.06	1495.50	1182.28	1086.60	956.05	872.66
69000	6114.44	3231.99	2275.35	1800.15	1517.49	1199.67	1102.58	970.11	885.49
70000	6203.06	3278.83	2308.33	1826.24	1539.49	1217.06	1118.56	984.17	898.33
75000	6646.13	3513.03	2473.21	1956.68	1649.45	1303.99	1198.46	1054.47	962.49
80000	7089.21	3747.23	2638.09	2087.13	1759.41	1390.92	1278.35	1124.77	1026.66
100000	8861.51	4684.04	3297.61	2608.91	2199.27	1738.65	1597.94	1405.96	1283.32

MONTHLY PAYMENT 11½%

NECESSARY TO AMORTIZE A LOAN

TERM / AMOUNT	15 YEARS	18 YEARS	20 YEARS	25 YEARS	28 YEARS	29 YEARS	30 YEARS	35 YEARS	40 YEARS
$ 25	.30	.28	.27	.26	.25	.25	.25	.25	.25
50	.59	.55	.54	.51	.50	.50	.50	.49	.49
75	.88	.83	.80	.77	.75	.75	.75	.74	.73
100	1.17	1.10	1.07	1.02	1.00	1.00	1.00	.98	.97
200	2.34	2.20	2.14	2.04	2.00	1.99	1.99	1.96	1.94
300	3.51	3.30	3.20	3.05	3.00	2.99	2.98	2.93	2.91
400	4.68	4.40	4.27	4.07	4.00	3.98	3.97	3.91	3.88
500	5.85	5.50	5.34	5.09	5.00	4.98	4.96	4.89	4.85
600	7.01	6.59	6.40	6.10	6.00	5.97	5.95	5.86	5.81
700	8.18	7.69	7.47	7.12	7.00	6.97	6.94	6.84	6.78
800	9.35	8.79	8.54	8.14	8.00	7.96	7.93	7.81	7.75
900	10.52	9.89	9.60	9.15	8.99	8.95	8.92	8.79	8.72
1000	11.69	10.99	10.67	10.17	9.99	9.95	9.91	9.77	9.69
2000	23.37	21.97	21.33	20.33	19.98	19.89	19.81	19.53	19.37
3000	35.05	32.95	32.00	30.50	29.97	29.83	29.71	29.29	29.05
4000	46.73	43.94	42.66	40.66	39.96	39.78	39.62	39.05	38.74
5000	58.41	54.92	53.33	50.83	49.95	49.72	49.52	48.81	48.42
6000	70.10	65.90	63.99	60.99	59.94	59.66	59.42	58.57	58.10
7000	81.78	76.89	74.66	71.16	69.93	69.61	69.33	68.33	67.78
8000	93.46	87.87	85.32	81.32	79.91	79.55	79.23	78.09	77.47
9000	105.14	98.85	95.98	91.49	89.90	89.49	89.13	87.85	87.15
10000	116.82	109.83	106.65	101.65	99.89	99.44	99.03	97.62	96.83
15000	175.23	164.75	159.97	152.48	149.83	149.15	148.55	146.42	145.25
20000	233.64	219.66	213.29	203.30	199.78	198.87	198.06	195.23	193.66
25000	292.05	274.58	266.61	254.12	249.72	248.58	247.58	244.03	242.08
30000	350.46	329.49	319.93	304.95	299.66	298.30	297.09	292.84	290.49
35000	408.87	384.41	373.26	355.77	349.61	348.01	346.61	341.64	338.90
36000	420.55	395.39	383.92	365.93	359.59	357.96	356.51	351.40	348.59
37000	432.24	406.37	394.58	376.10	369.58	367.90	366.41	361.16	358.27
38000	443.92	417.36	405.25	386.26	379.57	377.84	376.32	370.93	367.95
39000	455.60	428.34	415.91	396.43	389.56	387.79	386.22	380.69	377.63
40000	467.28	439.32	426.58	406.59	399.55	397.73	396.12	390.45	387.32
41000	478.96	450.31	437.24	416.76	409.54	407.67	406.02	400.21	397.00
42000	490.64	461.29	447.91	426.92	419.53	417.62	415.93	409.97	406.68
43000	502.33	472.27	458.57	437.09	429.51	427.56	425.83	419.73	416.37
44000	514.01	483.25	469.23	447.25	439.50	437.50	435.73	429.49	426.05
45000	525.69	494.24	479.90	457.42	449.49	447.45	445.64	439.25	435.73
46000	537.37	505.22	490.56	467.58	459.48	457.39	455.54	449.01	445.41
47000	549.05	516.20	501.23	477.75	469.47	467.33	465.44	458.78	455.10
48000	560.74	527.19	511.89	487.91	479.46	477.27	475.34	468.54	464.78
49000	572.42	538.17	522.56	498.07	489.45	487.22	485.25	478.30	474.46
50000	584.10	549.15	533.22	508.24	499.43	497.16	495.15	488.06	484.15
51000	595.78	560.14	543.88	518.40	509.42	507.10	505.05	497.82	493.83
52000	607.46	571.12	554.55	528.57	519.41	517.05	514.96	507.58	503.51
53000	619.15	582.10	565.21	538.73	529.40	526.99	524.86	517.34	513.19
54000	630.83	593.08	575.88	548.90	539.39	536.93	534.76	527.10	522.88
55000	642.51	604.07	586.54	559.06	549.38	546.88	544.67	536.86	532.56
56000	654.19	615.05	597.21	569.23	559.37	556.82	554.57	546.63	542.24
57000	665.87	626.03	607.87	579.39	569.35	566.76	564.47	556.39	551.93
58000	677.56	637.02	618.53	589.56	579.34	576.71	574.37	566.15	561.61
59000	689.24	648.00	629.20	599.72	589.33	586.65	584.28	575.91	571.29
60000	700.92	658.98	639.86	609.89	599.32	596.59	594.18	585.67	580.97
61000	712.60	669.97	650.53	620.05	609.31	606.54	604.08	595.43	590.66
62000	724.28	680.95	661.19	630.22	619.30	616.48	613.99	605.19	600.34
63000	735.96	691.93	671.86	640.38	629.29	626.42	623.89	614.95	610.02
64000	747.65	702.91	682.52	650.55	639.28	636.36	633.79	624.71	619.71
65000	759.33	713.90	693.18	660.71	649.26	646.31	643.69	634.47	629.39
66000	771.01	724.88	703.85	670.87	659.25	656.25	653.60	644.24	639.07
67000	782.69	735.86	714.51	681.04	669.24	666.19	663.50	654.00	648.75
68000	794.37	746.85	725.18	691.20	679.23	676.14	673.40	663.76	658.44
69000	806.06	757.83	735.84	701.37	689.22	686.08	683.31	673.52	668.12
70000	817.74	768.81	746.51	711.53	699.21	696.02	693.21	683.28	677.80
75000	876.15	823.73	799.83	762.36	749.15	745.74	742.72	732.09	726.22
80000	934.56	878.64	853.15	813.18	799.09	795.45	792.24	780.89	774.63
100000	1168.19	1098.30	1066.43	1016.47	998.86	994.32	990.30	976.11	968.29

11⅝% MONTHLY PAYMENT
NECESSARY TO AMORTIZE A LOAN

TERM / AMOUNT	1 YEAR	2 YEARS	3 YEARS	4 YEARS	5 YEARS	7 YEARS	8 YEARS	10 YEARS	12 YEARS
$ 25	2.22	1.18	.83	.66	.56	.44	.41	.36	.33
50	4.44	2.35	1.66	1.31	1.11	.88	.81	.71	.65
75	6.66	3.52	2.48	1.97	1.66	1.31	1.21	1.06	.97
100	8.87	4.69	3.31	2.62	2.21	1.75	1.61	1.42	1.30
200	17.74	9.38	6.61	5.24	4.42	3.50	3.21	2.83	2.59
300	26.61	14.07	9.92	7.85	6.62	5.24	4.82	4.24	3.88
400	35.47	18.76	13.22	10.47	8.83	6.99	6.42	5.66	5.17
500	44.34	23.45	16.52	13.08	11.03	8.73	8.03	7.07	6.46
600	53.21	28.14	19.83	15.70	13.24	10.48	9.63	8.48	7.75
700	62.08	32.83	23.13	18.31	15.44	12.22	11.24	9.90	9.04
800	70.94	37.52	26.43	20.93	17.65	13.97	12.84	11.31	10.33
900	79.81	42.21	29.74	23.54	19.85	15.71	14.45	12.72	11.62
1000	88.68	46.90	33.04	26.16	22.06	17.46	16.05	14.14	12.91
2000	177.35	93.80	66.08	52.31	44.12	34.91	32.10	28.27	25.82
3000	266.03	140.70	99.11	78.46	66.17	52.36	48.15	42.40	38.73
4000	354.70	187.60	132.15	104.61	88.23	69.82	64.20	56.53	51.64
5000	443.37	234.50	165.18	130.76	110.28	87.27	80.24	70.66	64.55
6000	532.05	281.40	198.22	156.91	132.34	104.72	96.29	84.79	77.45
7000	620.72	328.29	231.25	183.06	154.39	122.17	112.34	98.92	90.36
8000	709.39	375.19	264.29	209.21	176.45	139.63	128.39	113.05	103.27
9000	798.07	422.09	297.32	235.36	198.50	157.08	144.43	127.19	116.18
10000	886.74	468.99	330.36	261.51	220.56	174.53	160.48	141.32	129.09
15000	1330.11	703.48	495.54	392.26	330.84	261.80	240.72	211.97	193.63
20000	1773.47	937.98	660.71	523.01	441.11	349.06	320.96	282.63	258.17
25000	2216.84	1172.47	825.89	653.76	551.39	436.33	401.19	353.28	322.71
30000	2660.21	1406.96	991.07	784.51	661.67	523.59	481.43	423.94	387.25
35000	3103.58	1641.45	1156.25	915.26	771.94	610.85	561.67	494.60	451.79
36000	3192.25	1688.35	1189.28	941.41	794.00	628.31	577.72	508.73	464.70
37000	3280.92	1735.25	1222.32	967.56	816.06	645.76	593.76	522.86	477.60
38000	3369.60	1782.15	1255.35	993.71	838.11	663.21	609.81	536.99	490.51
39000	3458.27	1829.05	1288.39	1019.86	860.17	680.66	625.86	551.12	503.42
40000	3546.94	1875.95	1321.42	1046.01	882.22	698.12	641.91	565.25	516.33
41000	3635.62	1922.85	1354.46	1072.16	904.28	715.57	657.95	579.38	529.24
42000	3724.29	1969.74	1387.50	1098.31	926.33	733.02	674.00	593.51	542.15
43000	3812.96	2016.64	1420.53	1124.46	948.39	750.48	690.05	607.64	555.05
44000	3901.64	2063.54	1453.57	1150.61	970.44	767.93	706.10	621.78	567.96
45000	3990.31	2110.44	1486.60	1176.76	992.50	785.38	722.14	635.91	580.87
46000	4078.98	2157.34	1519.64	1202.91	1014.55	802.83	738.19	650.04	593.78
47000	4167.66	2204.24	1552.67	1229.06	1036.61	820.29	754.24	664.17	606.69
48000	4256.33	2251.13	1585.71	1255.21	1058.66	837.74	770.29	678.30	619.59
49000	4345.00	2298.03	1618.74	1281.36	1080.72	855.19	786.33	692.43	632.50
50000	4433.68	2344.93	1651.78	1307.51	1102.78	872.65	802.38	706.56	645.41
51000	4522.35	2391.83	1684.81	1333.66	1124.83	890.10	818.43	720.69	658.32
52000	4611.02	2438.73	1717.85	1359.81	1146.89	907.55	834.48	734.82	671.23
53000	4699.70	2485.63	1750.89	1385.96	1168.94	925.00	850.52	748.96	684.13
54000	4788.37	2532.53	1783.92	1412.11	1191.00	942.46	866.57	763.09	697.04
55000	4877.05	2579.42	1816.96	1438.26	1213.05	959.91	882.62	777.22	709.95
56000	4965.72	2626.32	1849.99	1464.41	1235.11	977.36	898.67	791.35	722.86
57000	5054.39	2673.22	1883.03	1490.56	1257.16	994.82	914.71	805.48	735.77
58000	5143.07	2720.12	1916.06	1516.71	1279.22	1012.27	930.76	819.61	748.68
59000	5231.74	2767.02	1949.10	1542.86	1301.27	1029.72	946.81	833.74	761.58
60000	5320.41	2813.92	1982.13	1569.01	1323.33	1047.17	962.86	847.87	774.49
61000	5409.09	2860.82	2015.17	1595.16	1345.39	1064.63	978.90	862.01	787.40
62000	5497.76	2907.71	2048.21	1621.31	1367.44	1082.08	994.95	876.14	800.31
63000	5586.43	2954.61	2081.24	1647.46	1389.50	1099.53	1011.00	890.27	813.22
64000	5675.11	3001.51	2114.28	1673.61	1411.55	1116.99	1027.05	904.40	826.12
65000	5763.78	3048.41	2147.31	1699.76	1433.61	1134.44	1043.09	918.53	839.03
66000	5852.45	3095.31	2180.35	1725.91	1455.66	1151.89	1059.14	932.66	851.94
67000	5941.13	3142.21	2213.38	1752.06	1477.72	1169.34	1075.19	946.79	864.85
68000	6029.80	3189.11	2246.42	1778.21	1499.77	1186.80	1091.24	960.92	877.76
69000	6118.47	3236.00	2279.45	1804.36	1521.83	1204.25	1107.28	975.05	890.66
70000	6207.15	3282.90	2312.49	1830.51	1543.88	1221.70	1123.33	989.19	903.57
75000	6650.51	3517.40	2477.67	1961.26	1654.16	1308.97	1203.57	1059.84	968.11
80000	7093.88	3751.89	2642.84	2092.01	1764.44	1396.23	1283.81	1130.50	1032.65
100000	8867.35	4689.86	3303.55	2615.01	2205.55	1745.29	1604.76	1413.12	1290.82

MONTHLY PAYMENT 11⅝%

NECESSARY TO AMORTIZE A LOAN

TERM / AMOUNT	15 YEARS	18 YEARS	20 YEARS	25 YEARS	28 YEARS	29 YEARS	30 YEARS	35 YEARS	40 YEARS
$ 25	.30	.28	.27	.26	.26	.26	.25	.25	.25
50	.59	.56	.54	.52	.51	.51	.50	.50	.49
75	.89	.84	.81	.77	.76	.76	.75	.74	.74
100	1.18	1.11	1.08	1.03	1.01	1.01	1.00	.99	.98
200	2.36	2.22	2.16	2.06	2.02	2.01	2.00	1.98	1.96
300	3.53	3.33	3.23	3.08	3.03	3.02	3.00	2.96	2.94
400	4.71	4.43	4.31	4.11	4.04	4.02	4.00	3.95	3.92
500	5.89	5.54	5.38	5.13	5.05	5.02	5.00	4.93	4.90
600	7.06	6.65	6.46	6.16	6.05	6.03	6.00	5.92	5.87
700	8.24	7.75	7.53	7.18	7.06	7.03	7.00	6.91	6.85
800	9.41	8.86	8.61	8.21	8.07	8.04	8.00	7.89	7.83
900	10.59	9.97	9.68	9.24	9.08	9.04	9.00	8.88	8.81
1000	11.77	11.07	10.76	10.26	10.09	10.04	10.00	9.86	9.79
2000	23.53	22.14	21.51	20.52	20.17	20.08	20.00	19.72	19.57
3000	35.29	33.21	32.26	30.77	30.25	30.12	30.00	29.58	29.35
4000	47.05	44.27	43.01	41.03	40.34	40.16	40.00	39.44	39.14
5000	58.81	55.34	53.76	51.29	50.42	50.19	50.00	49.30	48.92
6000	70.57	66.41	64.51	61.54	60.50	60.23	60.00	59.16	58.70
7000	82.34	77.47	75.26	71.80	70.58	70.27	69.99	69.02	68.49
8000	94.10	88.54	86.01	82.05	80.67	80.31	79.99	78.88	78.27
9000	105.86	99.61	96.76	92.31	90.75	90.35	89.99	88.74	88.05
10000	117.62	110.67	107.51	102.57	100.83	100.38	99.99	98.60	97.84
15000	176.43	166.01	161.26	153.85	151.24	150.57	149.98	147.90	146.75
20000	235.23	221.34	215.02	205.13	201.66	200.76	199.97	197.19	195.67
25000	294.04	276.67	268.77	256.41	252.07	250.95	249.96	246.49	244.58
30000	352.85	332.01	322.52	307.69	302.48	301.14	299.96	295.79	293.50
35000	411.66	387.34	376.27	358.97	352.90	351.33	349.95	345.08	342.42
36000	423.42	398.41	387.02	369.23	362.98	361.37	359.95	354.94	352.20
37000	435.18	409.47	397.78	379.48	373.06	371.41	369.95	364.80	361.98
38000	446.94	420.54	408.53	389.74	383.15	381.45	379.94	374.66	371.77
39000	458.70	431.61	419.28	400.00	393.23	391.48	389.94	384.52	381.55
40000	470.46	442.67	430.03	410.25	403.31	401.52	399.94	394.38	391.33
41000	482.23	453.74	440.78	420.51	413.39	411.56	409.94	404.24	401.11
42000	493.99	464.81	451.53	430.77	423.48	421.60	419.94	414.10	410.90
43000	505.75	475.87	462.28	441.02	433.56	431.64	429.94	423.96	420.68
44000	517.51	486.94	473.03	451.28	443.64	441.67	439.93	433.82	430.46
45000	529.27	498.01	483.78	461.53	453.72	451.71	449.93	443.68	440.25
46000	541.03	509.07	494.53	471.79	463.81	461.75	459.93	453.54	450.03
47000	552.79	520.14	505.28	482.05	473.89	471.79	469.93	463.40	459.81
48000	564.56	531.21	516.03	492.30	483.97	481.82	479.93	473.26	469.60
49000	576.32	542.27	526.78	502.56	494.05	491.86	489.93	483.12	479.38
50000	588.08	553.34	537.53	512.82	504.14	501.90	499.92	492.98	489.16
51000	599.84	564.41	548.28	523.07	514.22	511.94	509.92	502.84	498.95
52000	611.60	575.47	559.03	533.33	524.30	521.98	519.92	512.69	508.73
53000	623.36	586.54	569.78	543.58	534.38	532.01	529.92	522.55	518.51
54000	635.13	597.61	580.53	553.84	544.47	542.05	539.92	532.41	528.30
55000	646.89	608.67	591.29	564.10	554.55	552.09	549.92	542.27	538.08
56000	658.65	619.74	602.04	574.35	564.63	562.13	559.92	552.13	547.86
57000	670.41	630.81	612.79	584.61	574.72	572.17	569.91	561.99	557.65
58000	682.17	641.87	623.54	594.87	584.80	582.20	579.91	571.85	567.43
59000	693.93	652.94	634.29	605.12	594.88	592.24	589.91	581.71	577.21
60000	705.69	664.01	645.04	615.38	604.96	602.28	599.91	591.57	586.99
61000	717.46	675.07	655.79	625.63	615.05	612.32	609.91	601.43	596.78
62000	729.22	686.14	666.54	635.89	625.13	622.36	619.91	611.29	606.56
63000	740.98	697.21	677.29	646.15	635.21	632.39	629.90	621.15	616.34
64000	752.74	708.27	688.04	656.40	645.29	642.43	639.90	631.01	626.13
65000	764.50	719.34	698.79	666.66	655.38	652.47	649.90	640.87	635.91
66000	776.26	730.41	709.54	676.92	665.46	662.51	659.90	650.73	645.69
67000	788.02	741.47	720.29	687.17	675.54	672.54	669.90	660.59	655.48
68000	799.79	752.54	731.04	697.43	685.62	682.58	679.90	670.45	665.26
69000	811.55	763.61	741.79	707.68	695.71	692.62	689.89	680.30	675.04
70000	823.31	774.67	752.54	717.94	705.79	702.66	699.89	690.16	684.83
75000	882.12	830.01	806.30	769.22	756.20	752.85	749.88	739.46	733.74
80000	940.92	885.34	860.05	820.50	806.62	803.04	799.88	788.76	782.66
100000	1176.15	1106.68	1075.06	1025.63	1008.27	1003.80	999.84	985.95	978.32

11¾% MONTHLY PAYMENT
NECESSARY TO AMORTIZE A LOAN

TERM / AMOUNT	1 YEAR	2 YEARS	3 YEARS	4 YEARS	5 YEARS	7 YEARS	8 YEARS	10 YEARS	12 YEARS
$ 25	2.22	1.18	.83	.66	.56	.44	.41	.36	.33
50	4.44	2.35	1.66	1.32	1.11	.88	.81	.72	.65
75	6.66	3.53	2.49	1.97	1.66	1.32	1.21	1.07	.98
100	8.88	4.70	3.31	2.63	2.22	1.76	1.62	1.43	1.30
200	17.75	9.40	6.62	5.25	4.43	3.51	3.23	2.85	2.60
300	26.62	14.09	9.93	7.87	6.64	5.26	4.84	4.27	3.90
400	35.50	18.79	13.24	10.49	8.85	7.01	6.45	5.69	5.20
500	44.37	23.48	16.55	13.11	11.06	8.76	8.06	7.11	6.50
600	53.24	28.18	19.86	15.73	13.28	10.52	9.67	8.53	7.79
700	62.12	32.87	23.17	18.35	15.49	12.27	11.29	9.95	9.09
800	70.99	37.57	26.48	20.97	17.70	14.02	12.90	11.37	10.39
900	79.86	42.27	29.79	23.60	19.91	15.77	14.51	12.79	11.69
1000	88.74	46.96	33.10	26.22	22.12	17.52	16.12	14.21	12.99
2000	177.47	93.92	66.20	52.43	44.24	35.04	32.24	28.41	25.97
3000	266.20	140.88	99.29	78.64	66.36	52.56	48.35	42.61	38.95
4000	354.93	187.83	132.39	104.85	88.48	70.08	64.47	56.82	51.94
5000	443.66	234.79	165.48	131.06	110.60	87.60	80.58	71.02	64.92
6000	532.40	281.75	198.58	157.27	132.71	105.12	96.70	85.22	77.90
7000	621.13	328.70	231.67	183.48	154.83	122.64	112.82	99.43	90.89
8000	709.86	375.66	264.77	209.70	176.95	140.16	128.93	113.63	103.87
9000	798.59	422.62	297.86	235.91	199.07	157.68	145.05	127.83	116.85
10000	887.32	469.57	330.96	262.12	221.19	175.20	161.16	142.03	129.84
15000	1330.98	704.36	496.43	393.17	331.78	262.79	241.74	213.05	194.75
20000	1774.64	939.14	661.91	524.23	442.37	350.39	322.32	284.06	259.67
25000	2218.30	1173.93	827.38	655.29	552.96	437.99	402.90	355.08	324.59
30000	2661.96	1408.71	992.86	786.34	663.55	525.58	483.48	426.09	389.50
35000	3105.62	1643.49	1158.33	917.40	774.15	613.18	564.06	497.11	454.42
36000	3194.35	1690.45	1191.43	943.61	796.26	630.70	580.17	511.31	467.40
37000	3283.08	1737.41	1224.52	969.82	818.38	648.22	596.29	525.51	480.39
38000	3371.82	1784.36	1257.62	996.03	840.50	665.74	612.41	539.72	493.37
39000	3460.55	1831.32	1290.71	1022.24	862.62	683.26	628.52	553.92	506.35
40000	3549.28	1878.28	1323.81	1048.46	884.74	700.78	644.64	568.12	519.34
41000	3638.01	1925.23	1356.90	1074.67	906.86	718.30	660.75	582.33	532.32
42000	3726.74	1972.19	1390.00	1100.88	928.97	735.82	676.87	596.53	545.30
43000	3815.48	2019.15	1423.09	1127.09	951.09	753.34	692.98	610.73	558.28
44000	3904.21	2066.10	1456.19	1153.30	973.21	770.85	709.10	624.93	571.27
45000	3992.94	2113.06	1489.28	1179.51	995.33	788.37	725.22	639.14	584.25
46000	4081.67	2160.02	1522.38	1205.72	1017.45	805.89	741.33	653.34	597.23
47000	4170.40	2206.98	1555.47	1231.93	1039.57	823.41	757.45	667.54	610.22
48000	4259.14	2253.93	1588.57	1258.15	1061.68	840.93	773.56	681.75	623.20
49000	4347.87	2300.89	1621.66	1284.36	1083.80	858.45	789.68	695.95	636.18
50000	4436.60	2347.85	1654.76	1310.57	1105.92	875.97	805.79	710.15	649.17
51000	4525.33	2394.80	1687.85	1336.78	1128.04	893.49	821.91	724.36	662.15
52000	4614.06	2441.76	1720.95	1362.99	1150.16	911.01	838.03	738.56	675.13
53000	4702.79	2488.72	1754.04	1389.20	1172.28	928.53	854.14	752.76	688.12
54000	4791.53	2535.67	1787.14	1415.41	1194.39	946.05	870.26	766.96	701.10
55000	4880.26	2582.63	1820.23	1441.62	1216.51	963.57	886.37	781.17	714.08
56000	4968.99	2629.59	1853.33	1467.84	1238.63	981.09	902.49	795.37	727.07
57000	5057.72	2676.54	1886.42	1494.05	1260.75	998.61	918.61	809.57	740.05
58000	5146.45	2723.50	1919.52	1520.26	1282.87	1016.13	934.72	823.78	753.03
59000	5235.19	2770.46	1952.61	1546.47	1304.99	1033.64	950.84	837.98	766.02
60000	5323.92	2817.41	1985.71	1572.68	1327.10	1051.16	966.95	852.18	779.00
61000	5412.65	2864.37	2018.80	1598.89	1349.22	1068.68	983.07	866.38	791.98
62000	5501.38	2911.33	2051.90	1625.10	1371.34	1086.20	999.18	880.59	804.97
63000	5590.11	2958.28	2084.99	1651.31	1393.46	1103.72	1015.30	894.79	817.95
64000	5678.85	3005.24	2118.09	1677.53	1415.58	1121.24	1031.42	908.99	830.93
65000	5767.58	3052.20	2151.18	1703.74	1437.70	1138.76	1047.53	923.20	843.92
66000	5856.31	3099.15	2184.28	1729.95	1459.81	1156.28	1063.65	937.40	856.90
67000	5945.04	3146.11	2217.37	1756.16	1481.93	1173.80	1079.76	951.60	869.88
68000	6033.77	3193.07	2250.47	1782.37	1504.05	1191.32	1095.88	965.81	882.87
69000	6122.50	3240.02	2283.56	1808.58	1526.17	1208.84	1111.99	980.01	895.85
70000	6211.24	3286.98	2316.66	1834.79	1548.29	1226.36	1128.11	994.21	908.83
75000	6654.90	3521.77	2482.13	1965.85	1658.88	1313.95	1208.69	1065.23	973.75
80000	7098.56	3756.55	2647.61	2096.91	1769.47	1401.55	1289.27	1136.24	1038.67
100000	8873.19	4695.69	3309.51	2621.13	2211.84	1751.94	1611.58	1420.30	1298.33

MONTHLY PAYMENT 11¾%

NECESSARY TO AMORTIZE A LOAN

TERM / AMOUNT	15 YEARS	18 YEARS	20 YEARS	25 YEARS	28 YEARS	29 YEARS	30 YEARS	35 YEARS	40 YEARS
$ 25	.30	.28	.28	.26	.26	.26	.26	.25	.25
50	.60	.56	.55	.52	.51	.51	.51	.50	.50
75	.89	.84	.82	.78	.77	.76	.76	.75	.75
100	1.19	1.12	1.09	1.04	1.02	1.02	1.01	1.00	.99
200	2.37	2.24	2.17	2.07	2.04	2.03	2.02	2.00	1.98
300	3.56	3.35	3.26	3.11	3.06	3.04	3.03	2.99	2.97
400	4.74	4.47	4.34	4.14	4.08	4.06	4.04	3.99	3.96
500	5.93	5.58	5.42	5.18	5.09	5.07	5.05	4.98	4.95
600	7.11	6.70	6.51	6.21	6.11	6.08	6.06	5.98	5.94
700	8.29	7.81	7.59	7.25	7.13	7.10	7.07	6.98	6.92
800	9.48	8.93	8.67	8.28	8.15	8.11	8.08	7.97	7.91
900	10.66	10.04	9.76	9.32	9.16	9.12	9.09	8.97	8.90
1000	11.85	11.16	10.84	10.35	10.18	10.14	10.10	9.96	9.89
2000	23.69	22.31	21.68	20.70	20.36	20.27	20.19	19.92	19.77
3000	35.53	33.46	32.52	31.05	30.54	30.40	30.29	29.88	29.66
4000	47.37	44.61	43.35	41.40	40.71	40.54	40.38	39.84	39.54
5000	59.21	55.76	54.19	51.74	50.89	50.67	50.48	49.79	49.42
6000	71.05	66.91	65.03	62.09	61.07	60.80	60.57	59.75	59.31
7000	82.89	78.06	75.86	72.44	71.24	70.94	70.66	69.71	69.19
8000	94.74	89.21	86.70	82.79	81.42	81.07	80.76	79.67	79.07
9000	106.58	100.36	97.54	93.14	91.60	91.20	90.85	89.63	88.96
10000	118.42	111.51	108.38	103.48	101.77	101.33	100.95	99.58	98.84
15000	177.62	167.27	162.56	155.22	152.66	152.00	151.42	149.37	148.26
20000	236.83	223.02	216.75	206.96	203.54	202.66	201.89	199.16	197.68
25000	296.04	278.77	270.93	258.70	254.43	253.33	252.36	248.95	247.10
30000	355.24	334.53	325.12	310.44	305.31	303.99	302.83	298.74	296.51
35000	414.45	390.28	379.30	362.18	356.20	354.66	353.30	348.53	345.93
36000	426.29	401.43	390.14	372.53	366.37	364.79	363.39	358.49	355.82
37000	438.13	412.58	400.98	382.88	376.55	374.92	373.49	368.45	365.70
38000	449.97	423.73	411.81	393.23	386.73	385.06	383.58	378.41	375.58
39000	461.82	434.88	422.65	403.58	396.90	395.19	393.67	388.36	385.47
40000	473.66	446.03	433.49	413.92	407.08	405.32	403.77	398.32	395.35
41000	485.50	457.18	444.32	424.27	417.26	415.45	413.86	408.28	405.23
42000	497.34	468.34	455.16	434.62	427.44	425.59	423.96	418.24	415.12
43000	509.18	479.49	466.00	444.97	437.61	435.72	434.05	428.20	425.00
44000	521.02	490.64	476.84	455.32	447.79	445.85	444.15	438.15	434.89
45000	532.86	501.79	487.67	465.66	457.97	455.99	454.24	448.11	444.77
46000	544.71	512.94	498.51	476.01	468.14	466.12	464.33	458.07	454.65
47000	556.55	524.09	509.35	486.36	478.32	476.25	474.43	468.03	464.54
48000	568.39	535.24	520.18	496.71	488.50	486.39	484.52	477.99	474.42
49000	580.23	546.39	531.02	507.06	498.67	496.52	494.62	487.94	484.30
50000	592.07	557.54	541.86	517.40	508.85	506.65	504.71	497.90	494.19
51000	603.91	568.69	552.70	527.75	519.03	516.78	514.80	507.86	504.07
52000	615.75	579.84	563.53	538.10	529.20	526.92	524.90	517.82	513.95
53000	627.59	590.99	574.37	548.45	539.38	537.05	534.99	527.78	523.84
54000	639.44	602.14	585.21	558.80	549.56	547.18	545.09	537.73	533.72
55000	651.28	613.29	596.04	569.14	559.74	557.32	555.18	547.69	543.61
56000	663.12	624.45	606.88	579.49	569.91	567.45	565.27	557.65	553.49
57000	674.96	635.60	617.72	589.84	580.09	577.58	575.37	567.61	563.37
58000	686.80	646.75	628.56	600.19	590.27	587.71	585.46	577.57	573.26
59000	698.64	657.90	639.39	610.54	600.44	597.85	595.56	587.52	583.14
60000	710.48	669.05	650.23	620.88	610.62	607.98	605.65	597.48	593.02
61000	722.33	680.20	661.07	631.23	620.80	618.11	615.74	607.44	602.91
62000	734.17	691.35	671.90	641.58	630.97	628.25	625.84	617.40	612.79
63000	746.01	702.50	682.74	651.93	641.15	638.38	635.93	627.36	622.67
64000	757.85	713.65	693.58	662.28	651.33	648.51	646.03	637.31	632.56
65000	769.69	724.80	704.41	672.62	661.50	658.64	656.12	647.27	642.44
66000	781.53	735.95	715.25	682.97	671.68	668.78	666.22	657.23	652.33
67000	793.37	747.10	726.09	693.32	681.86	678.91	676.31	667.19	662.21
68000	805.21	758.25	736.93	703.67	692.04	689.04	686.40	677.14	672.09
69000	817.06	769.41	747.76	714.02	702.21	699.18	696.50	687.10	681.98
70000	828.90	780.56	758.60	724.36	712.39	709.31	706.59	697.06	691.86
75000	888.10	836.31	812.79	776.10	763.27	759.97	757.06	746.85	741.28
80000	947.31	892.06	866.97	827.84	814.16	810.64	807.53	796.64	790.70
100000	1184.14	1115.08	1083.71	1034.80	1017.70	1013.30	1009.41	995.80	988.37

11⅞% MONTHLY PAYMENT
NECESSARY TO AMORTIZE A LOAN

TERM / AMOUNT	1 YEAR	2 YEARS	3 YEARS	4 YEARS	5 YEARS	7 YEARS	8 YEARS	10 YEARS	12 YEARS
$ 25	2.22	1.18	.83	.66	.56	.44	.41	.36	.33
50	4.44	2.36	1.66	1.32	1.11	.88	.81	.72	.66
75	6.66	3.53	2.49	1.98	1.67	1.32	1.22	1.08	.98
100	8.88	4.71	3.32	2.63	2.22	1.76	1.62	1.43	1.31
200	17.76	9.41	6.64	5.26	4.44	3.52	3.24	2.86	2.62
300	26.64	14.11	9.95	7.89	6.66	5.28	4.86	4.29	3.92
400	35.52	18.81	13.27	10.51	8.88	7.04	6.48	5.71	5.23
500	44.40	23.51	16.58	13.14	11.10	8.80	8.10	7.14	6.53
600	53.28	28.21	19.90	15.77	13.31	10.56	9.72	8.57	7.84
700	62.16	32.92	23.21	18.40	15.53	12.32	11.33	10.00	9.15
800	71.04	37.62	26.53	21.02	17.75	14.07	12.95	11.42	10.45
900	79.92	42.32	29.84	23.65	19.97	15.83	14.57	12.85	11.76
1000	88.80	47.02	33.16	26.28	22.19	17.59	16.19	14.28	13.06
2000	177.59	94.04	66.31	52.55	44.37	35.18	32.37	28.55	26.12
3000	266.38	141.05	99.47	78.82	66.55	52.76	48.56	42.83	39.18
4000	355.17	188.07	132.62	105.10	88.73	70.35	64.74	57.10	52.24
5000	443.96	235.08	165.78	131.37	110.91	87.93	80.93	71.38	65.30
6000	532.75	282.10	198.93	157.64	133.09	105.52	97.11	85.65	78.36
7000	621.54	329.11	232.09	183.91	155.27	123.11	113.29	99.93	91.42
8000	710.33	376.13	265.24	210.19	177.46	140.69	129.48	114.20	104.47
9000	799.12	423.14	298.40	236.46	199.64	158.28	145.66	128.48	117.53
10000	887.91	470.16	331.55	262.73	221.82	175.86	161.85	142.75	130.59
15000	1331.86	705.23	497.32	394.09	332.72	263.79	242.77	214.13	195.88
20000	1775.81	940.31	663.10	525.46	443.63	351.72	323.69	285.50	261.18
25000	2219.76	1175.38	828.87	656.82	554.54	439.65	404.61	356.88	326.47
30000	2663.71	1410.46	994.64	788.18	665.44	527.58	485.53	428.25	391.76
35000	3107.67	1645.53	1160.42	919.54	776.35	615.51	566.45	499.63	457.06
36000	3196.46	1692.55	1193.57	945.82	798.53	633.10	582.64	513.90	470.12
37000	3285.25	1739.56	1226.73	972.09	820.71	650.69	598.82	528.18	483.17
38000	3374.04	1786.58	1259.88	998.36	842.90	668.27	615.01	542.45	496.23
39000	3462.83	1833.59	1293.04	1024.63	865.08	685.86	631.19	556.73	509.29
40000	3551.62	1880.61	1326.19	1050.91	887.26	703.44	647.37	571.00	522.35
41000	3640.41	1927.62	1359.35	1077.18	909.44	721.03	663.56	585.28	535.41
42000	3729.20	1974.64	1392.50	1103.45	931.62	738.62	679.74	599.55	548.47
43000	3817.99	2021.66	1425.65	1129.72	953.80	756.20	695.93	613.83	561.53
44000	3906.78	2068.67	1458.81	1156.00	975.98	773.79	712.11	628.10	574.58
45000	3995.57	2115.69	1491.96	1182.27	998.16	791.37	728.30	642.38	587.64
46000	4084.36	2162.70	1525.12	1208.54	1020.35	808.96	744.48	656.65	600.70
47000	4173.15	2209.72	1558.27	1234.81	1042.53	826.54	760.66	670.93	613.76
48000	4261.94	2256.73	1591.43	1261.09	1064.71	844.13	776.85	685.20	626.82
49000	4350.73	2303.75	1624.58	1287.36	1086.89	861.72	793.03	699.48	639.88
50000	4439.52	2350.76	1657.74	1313.63	1109.07	879.30	809.22	713.75	652.94
51000	4528.31	2397.78	1690.89	1339.90	1131.25	896.89	825.40	728.03	665.99
52000	4617.10	2444.79	1724.05	1366.18	1153.43	914.47	841.59	742.30	679.05
53000	4705.89	2491.81	1757.20	1392.45	1175.62	932.06	857.77	756.58	692.11
54000	4794.68	2538.82	1790.36	1418.72	1197.80	949.65	873.95	770.85	705.17
55000	4883.47	2585.84	1823.51	1444.99	1219.98	967.23	890.14	785.13	718.23
56000	4972.26	2632.85	1856.66	1471.27	1242.16	984.82	906.32	799.40	731.29
57000	5061.05	2679.87	1889.82	1497.54	1264.34	1002.40	922.51	813.68	744.35
58000	5149.84	2726.88	1922.97	1523.81	1286.52	1019.99	938.69	827.95	757.40
59000	5238.63	2773.90	1956.13	1550.08	1308.70	1037.58	954.88	842.23	770.46
60000	5327.42	2820.91	1989.28	1576.36	1330.88	1055.16	971.06	856.50	783.52
61000	5416.21	2867.93	2022.44	1602.63	1353.07	1072.75	987.24	870.78	796.58
62000	5505.01	2914.94	2055.59	1628.90	1375.25	1090.33	1003.43	885.05	809.64
63000	5593.80	2961.96	2088.75	1655.17	1397.43	1107.92	1019.61	899.33	822.70
64000	5682.59	3008.97	2121.90	1681.45	1419.61	1125.51	1035.80	913.60	835.76
65000	5771.38	3055.99	2155.06	1707.72	1441.79	1143.09	1051.98	927.88	848.82
66000	5860.17	3103.00	2188.21	1733.99	1463.97	1160.68	1068.16	942.15	861.87
67000	5948.96	3150.02	2221.37	1760.26	1486.15	1178.26	1084.35	956.43	874.93
68000	6037.75	3197.03	2254.52	1786.54	1508.34	1195.85	1100.53	970.70	887.99
69000	6126.54	3244.05	2287.68	1812.81	1530.52	1213.44	1116.72	984.97	901.05
70000	6215.33	3291.06	2320.83	1839.08	1552.70	1231.02	1132.90	999.25	914.11
75000	6659.28	3526.14	2486.60	1970.44	1663.60	1318.95	1213.82	1070.62	979.40
80000	7103.23	3761.21	2652.38	2101.81	1774.51	1406.88	1294.74	1142.00	1044.69
100000	8879.04	4701.52	3315.47	2627.26	2218.14	1758.60	1618.43	1427.50	1305.87

MONTHLY PAYMENT 11⅞%

NECESSARY TO AMORTIZE A LOAN

TERM / AMOUNT	15 YEARS	18 YEARS	20 YEARS	25 YEARS	28 YEARS	29 YEARS	30 YEARS	35 YEARS	40 YEARS
$ 25	.30	.29	.28	.27	.26	.26	.26	.26	.25
50	.60	.57	.55	.53	.52	.52	.51	.51	.50
75	.90	.85	.82	.79	.78	.77	.77	.76	.75
100	1.20	1.13	1.10	1.05	1.03	1.03	1.02	1.01	1.00
200	2.39	2.25	2.19	2.09	2.06	2.05	2.04	2.02	2.00
300	3.58	3.38	3.28	3.14	3.09	3.07	3.06	3.02	3.00
400	4.77	4.50	4.37	4.18	4.11	4.10	4.08	4.03	4.00
500	5.97	5.62	5.47	5.22	5.14	5.12	5.10	5.03	5.00
600	7.16	6.75	6.56	6.27	6.17	6.14	6.12	6.04	6.00
700	8.35	7.87	7.65	7.31	7.19	7.16	7.14	7.04	6.99
800	9.54	8.99	8.74	8.36	8.22	8.19	8.16	8.05	7.99
900	10.73	10.12	9.84	9.40	9.25	9.21	9.18	9.06	8.99
1000	11.93	11.24	10.93	10.44	10.28	10.23	10.20	10.06	9.99
2000	23.85	22.47	21.85	20.88	20.55	20.46	20.39	20.12	19.97
3000	35.77	33.71	32.78	31.32	30.82	30.69	30.58	30.17	29.96
4000	47.69	44.94	43.70	41.76	41.09	40.92	40.77	40.23	39.94
5000	59.61	56.18	54.62	52.20	51.36	51.15	50.96	50.29	49.93
6000	71.53	67.41	65.55	62.64	61.63	61.37	61.15	60.34	59.91
7000	83.45	78.65	76.47	73.08	71.90	71.60	71.34	70.40	69.89
8000	95.38	89.88	87.40	83.52	82.18	81.83	81.53	80.46	79.88
9000	107.30	101.12	98.32	93.96	92.45	92.06	91.72	90.51	89.86
10000	119.22	112.35	109.24	104.40	102.72	102.29	101.91	100.57	99.85
15000	178.83	168.53	163.86	156.60	154.08	153.43	152.86	150.85	149.77
20000	238.43	224.70	218.48	208.80	205.43	204.57	203.81	201.14	199.69
25000	298.04	280.88	273.10	261.00	256.79	255.71	254.76	251.42	249.61
30000	357.65	337.05	327.72	313.20	308.15	306.85	305.71	301.70	299.53
35000	417.25	393.23	382.34	365.40	359.50	357.99	356.66	351.99	349.45
36000	429.17	404.46	393.26	375.84	369.78	368.22	366.85	362.04	359.44
37000	441.10	415.70	404.19	386.28	380.05	378.45	377.04	372.10	369.42
38000	453.02	426.93	415.11	396.72	390.32	388.67	387.23	382.16	379.41
39000	464.94	438.17	426.03	407.16	400.59	398.90	397.42	392.21	389.39
40000	476.86	449.40	436.96	417.60	410.86	409.13	407.61	402.27	399.38
41000	488.78	460.64	447.88	428.04	421.13	419.36	417.80	412.33	409.36
42000	500.70	471.87	458.81	438.48	431.40	429.59	427.99	422.38	419.34
43000	512.62	483.11	469.73	448.92	441.68	439.82	438.18	432.44	429.33
44000	524.55	494.34	480.65	459.36	451.95	450.04	448.37	442.50	439.31
45000	536.47	505.58	491.58	469.80	462.22	460.27	458.56	452.55	449.30
46000	548.39	516.81	502.50	480.24	472.49	470.50	468.75	462.61	459.28
47000	560.31	528.05	513.43	490.68	482.76	480.73	478.94	472.67	469.26
48000	572.23	539.28	524.35	501.12	493.03	490.96	489.13	482.72	479.25
49000	584.15	550.52	535.27	511.56	503.30	501.18	499.32	492.78	489.23
50000	596.07	561.75	546.20	522.00	513.58	511.41	509.51	502.84	499.22
51000	608.00	572.99	557.12	532.44	523.85	521.64	519.70	512.89	509.20
52000	619.92	584.22	568.04	542.88	534.12	531.87	529.89	522.95	519.19
53000	631.84	595.46	578.97	553.32	544.39	542.10	540.08	533.01	529.17
54000	643.76	606.69	589.89	563.76	554.66	552.32	550.27	543.06	539.15
55000	655.68	617.93	600.82	574.20	564.93	562.55	560.46	553.12	549.14
56000	667.60	629.16	611.74	584.64	575.20	572.78	570.65	563.18	559.12
57000	679.52	640.40	622.66	595.08	585.48	583.01	580.84	573.23	569.11
58000	691.44	651.63	633.59	605.52	595.75	593.24	591.03	583.29	579.09
59000	703.37	662.87	644.51	615.96	606.02	603.47	601.22	593.35	589.08
60000	715.29	674.10	655.44	626.40	616.29	613.69	611.41	603.40	599.06
61000	727.21	685.34	666.36	636.84	626.56	623.92	621.60	613.46	609.04
62000	739.13	696.57	677.28	647.28	636.83	634.15	631.79	623.52	619.03
63000	751.05	707.81	688.21	657.72	647.10	644.38	641.98	633.57	629.01
64000	762.97	719.04	699.13	668.16	657.38	654.61	652.17	643.63	639.00
65000	774.89	730.28	710.05	678.60	667.65	664.83	662.36	653.69	648.98
66000	786.82	741.51	720.98	689.04	677.92	675.06	672.55	663.74	658.97
67000	798.74	752.75	731.90	699.48	688.19	685.29	682.74	673.80	668.95
68000	810.66	763.98	742.83	709.92	698.46	695.52	692.93	683.86	678.93
69000	822.58	775.22	753.75	720.36	708.73	705.75	703.12	693.91	688.92
70000	834.50	786.45	764.67	730.80	719.00	715.98	713.31	703.97	698.90
75000	894.11	842.63	819.29	783.00	770.36	767.12	764.26	754.25	748.82
80000	953.72	898.80	873.91	835.20	821.72	818.26	815.21	804.54	798.75
100000	1192.14	1123.50	1092.39	1044.00	1027.15	1022.82	1019.01	1005.67	998.43

12% MONTHLY PAYMENT

NECESSARY TO AMORTIZE A LOAN

TERM / AMOUNT	1 YEAR	2 YEARS	3 YEARS	4 YEARS	5 YEARS	7 YEARS	8 YEARS	10 YEARS	12 YEARS
$ 25	2.23	1.18	.84	.66	.56	.45	.41	.36	.33
50	4.45	2.36	1.67	1.32	1.12	.89	.82	.72	.66
75	6.67	3.54	2.50	1.98	1.67	1.33	1.22	1.08	.99
100	8.89	4.71	3.33	2.64	2.23	1.77	1.63	1.44	1.32
200	17.77	9.42	6.65	5.27	4.45	3.54	3.26	2.87	2.63
300	26.66	14.13	9.97	7.91	6.68	5.30	4.88	4.31	3.95
400	35.54	18.83	13.29	10.54	8.90	7.07	6.51	5.74	5.26
500	44.43	23.54	16.61	13.17	11.13	8.83	8.13	7.18	6.57
600	53.31	28.25	19.93	15.81	13.35	10.60	9.76	8.61	7.89
700	62.20	32.96	23.26	18.44	15.58	12.36	11.38	10.05	9.20
800	71.08	37.66	26.58	21.07	17.80	14.13	13.01	11.48	10.51
900	79.97	42.37	29.90	23.71	20.03	15.89	14.63	12.92	11.83
1000	88.85	47.08	33.22	26.34	22.25	17.66	16.26	14.35	13.14
2000	177.70	94.15	66.43	52.67	44.49	35.31	32.51	28.70	26.27
3000	266.55	141.23	99.65	79.01	66.74	52.96	48.76	43.05	39.41
4000	355.40	188.30	132.86	105.34	88.98	70.62	65.02	57.39	52.54
5000	444.25	235.37	166.08	131.67	111.23	88.27	81.27	71.74	65.68
6000	533.10	282.45	199.29	158.01	133.47	105.92	97.52	86.09	78.81
7000	621.95	329.52	232.51	184.34	155.72	123.57	113.77	100.43	91.94
8000	710.80	376.59	265.72	210.68	177.96	141.23	130.03	114.78	105.08
9000	799.64	423.67	298.93	237.01	200.21	158.88	146.28	129.13	118.21
10000	888.49	470.74	332.15	263.34	222.45	176.53	162.53	143.48	131.35
15000	1332.74	706.11	498.22	395.01	333.67	264.80	243.80	215.21	197.02
20000	1776.98	941.47	664.29	526.68	444.89	353.06	325.06	286.95	262.69
25000	2221.22	1176.84	830.36	658.35	556.12	441.32	406.33	358.68	328.36
30000	2665.47	1412.21	996.43	790.02	667.34	529.59	487.59	430.42	394.03
35000	3109.71	1647.58	1162.51	921.69	778.56	617.85	568.85	502.15	459.70
36000	3198.56	1694.65	1195.72	948.02	800.81	635.50	585.11	516.50	472.84
37000	3287.41	1741.72	1228.93	974.36	823.05	653.16	601.36	530.85	485.97
38000	3376.26	1788.80	1262.15	1000.69	845.29	670.81	617.61	545.19	499.10
39000	3465.11	1835.87	1295.36	1027.02	867.54	688.46	633.87	559.54	512.24
40000	3553.96	1882.94	1328.58	1053.36	889.78	706.11	650.12	573.89	525.37
41000	3642.81	1930.02	1361.79	1079.69	912.03	723.77	666.37	588.24	538.51
42000	3731.65	1977.09	1395.01	1106.03	934.27	741.42	682.62	602.58	551.64
43000	3820.50	2024.16	1428.22	1132.36	956.52	759.07	698.88	616.93	564.78
44000	3909.35	2071.24	1461.43	1158.69	978.76	776.73	715.13	631.28	577.91
45000	3998.20	2118.31	1494.65	1185.03	1001.01	794.38	731.38	645.62	591.04
46000	4087.05	2165.38	1527.86	1211.36	1023.25	812.03	747.64	659.97	604.18
47000	4175.90	2212.46	1561.08	1237.70	1045.49	829.68	763.89	674.32	617.31
48000	4264.75	2259.53	1594.29	1264.03	1067.74	847.34	780.14	688.67	630.45
49000	4353.60	2306.61	1627.51	1290.36	1089.98	864.99	796.39	703.01	643.58
50000	4442.44	2353.68	1660.72	1316.70	1112.23	882.64	812.65	717.36	656.71
51000	4531.29	2400.75	1693.93	1343.03	1134.47	900.29	828.90	731.71	669.85
52000	4620.14	2447.83	1727.15	1369.36	1156.72	917.95	845.15	746.05	682.98
53000	4708.99	2494.90	1760.36	1395.70	1178.96	935.60	861.41	760.40	696.12
54000	4797.84	2541.97	1793.58	1422.03	1201.21	953.25	877.66	774.75	709.25
55000	4886.69	2589.05	1826.79	1448.37	1223.45	970.91	893.91	789.10	722.39
56000	4975.54	2636.12	1860.01	1474.70	1245.69	988.56	910.16	803.44	735.52
57000	5064.39	2683.19	1893.22	1501.03	1267.94	1006.21	926.42	817.79	748.65
58000	5153.23	2730.27	1926.43	1527.37	1290.18	1023.86	942.67	832.14	761.79
59000	5242.08	2777.34	1959.65	1553.70	1312.43	1041.52	958.92	846.48	774.92
60000	5330.93	2824.41	1992.86	1580.04	1334.67	1059.17	975.18	860.83	788.06
61000	5419.78	2871.49	2026.08	1606.37	1356.92	1076.82	991.43	875.18	801.19
62000	5508.63	2918.56	2059.29	1632.70	1379.16	1094.47	1007.68	889.52	814.32
63000	5597.48	2965.63	2092.51	1659.04	1401.41	1112.13	1023.93	903.87	827.46
64000	5686.33	3012.71	2125.72	1685.37	1423.65	1129.78	1040.19	918.22	840.59
65000	5775.18	3059.78	2158.94	1711.70	1445.89	1147.43	1056.44	932.57	853.73
66000	5864.03	3106.85	2192.15	1738.04	1468.14	1165.09	1072.69	946.91	866.86
67000	5952.87	3153.93	2225.36	1764.37	1490.38	1182.74	1088.95	961.26	880.00
68000	6041.72	3201.00	2258.58	1790.71	1512.63	1200.39	1105.20	975.61	893.13
69000	6130.57	3248.07	2291.79	1817.04	1534.87	1218.04	1121.45	989.95	906.26
70000	6219.42	3295.15	2325.01	1843.37	1557.12	1235.70	1137.70	1004.30	919.40
75000	6663.66	3530.52	2491.08	1975.04	1668.34	1323.96	1218.97	1076.04	985.07
80000	7107.91	3765.88	2657.15	2106.71	1779.56	1412.22	1300.23	1147.77	1050.74
100000	8884.88	4707.35	3321.44	2633.39	2224.45	1765.28	1625.29	1434.71	1313.42

MONTHLY PAYMENT 12%

NECESSARY TO AMORTIZE A LOAN

TERM / AMOUNT	15 YEARS	18 YEARS	20 YEARS	25 YEARS	28 YEARS	29 YEARS	30 YEARS	35 YEARS	40 YEARS
$ 25	.31	.29	.28	.27	.26	.26	.26	.26	.26
50	.61	.57	.56	.53	.52	.52	.52	.51	.51
75	.91	.85	.83	.79	.78	.78	.78	.77	.76
100	1.21	1.14	1.11	1.06	1.04	1.04	1.03	1.02	1.01
200	2.41	2.27	2.21	2.11	2.08	2.07	2.06	2.04	2.02
300	3.61	3.40	3.31	3.16	3.11	3.10	3.09	3.05	3.03
400	4.81	4.53	4.41	4.22	4.15	4.13	4.12	4.07	4.04
500	6.01	5.66	5.51	5.27	5.19	5.17	5.15	5.08	5.05
600	7.21	6.80	6.61	6.32	6.22	6.20	6.18	6.10	6.06
700	8.41	7.93	7.71	7.38	7.26	7.23	7.21	7.11	7.06
800	9.61	9.06	8.81	8.43	8.30	8.26	8.23	8.13	8.07
900	10.81	10.19	9.91	9.48	9.33	9.30	9.26	9.14	9.08
1000	12.01	11.32	11.02	10.54	10.37	10.33	10.29	10.16	10.09
2000	24.01	22.64	22.03	21.07	20.74	20.65	20.58	20.32	20.17
3000	36.01	33.96	33.04	31.60	31.10	30.98	30.86	30.47	30.26
4000	48.01	45.28	44.05	42.13	41.47	41.30	41.15	40.63	40.34
5000	60.01	56.60	55.06	52.67	51.84	51.62	51.44	50.78	50.43
6000	72.02	67.92	66.07	63.20	62.20	61.95	61.72	60.94	60.51
7000	84.02	79.24	77.08	73.73	72.57	72.27	72.01	71.09	70.60
8000	96.02	90.56	88.09	84.26	82.93	82.59	82.29	81.25	80.68
9000	108.02	101.88	99.10	94.80	93.30	92.92	92.58	91.40	90.77
10000	120.02	113.20	110.11	105.33	103.67	103.24	102.87	101.56	100.85
15000	180.03	169.80	165.17	157.99	155.50	154.86	154.30	152.34	151.28
20000	240.04	226.40	220.22	210.65	207.33	206.48	205.73	203.11	201.70
25000	300.05	282.99	275.28	263.31	259.16	258.09	257.16	253.89	252.13
30000	360.06	339.59	330.33	315.97	310.99	309.71	308.59	304.67	302.55
35000	420.06	396.19	385.39	368.63	362.82	361.33	360.02	355.45	352.98
36000	432.07	407.51	396.40	379.17	373.19	371.65	370.31	365.60	363.06
37000	444.07	418.83	407.41	389.70	383.55	381.98	380.59	375.76	373.15
38000	456.07	430.15	418.42	400.23	393.92	392.30	390.88	385.91	383.23
39000	468.07	441.47	429.43	410.76	404.28	402.62	401.16	396.07	393.32
40000	480.07	452.79	440.44	421.29	414.65	412.95	411.45	406.22	403.40
41000	492.07	464.10	451.45	431.83	425.02	423.27	421.74	416.38	413.49
42000	504.08	475.42	462.46	442.36	435.38	433.60	432.02	426.54	423.57
43000	516.08	486.74	473.47	452.89	445.75	443.92	442.31	436.69	433.66
44000	528.08	498.06	484.48	463.42	456.11	454.24	452.59	446.85	443.74
45000	540.08	509.38	495.49	473.96	466.48	464.57	462.88	457.00	453.83
46000	552.08	520.70	506.50	484.49	476.85	474.89	473.17	467.16	463.91
47000	564.08	532.02	517.52	495.02	487.21	485.21	483.45	477.31	474.00
48000	576.09	543.34	528.53	505.55	497.58	495.54	493.74	487.47	484.08
49000	588.09	554.66	539.54	516.08	507.95	505.86	504.03	497.62	494.17
50000	600.09	565.98	550.55	526.62	518.31	516.18	514.31	507.78	504.25
51000	612.09	577.30	561.56	537.15	528.68	526.51	524.60	517.94	514.34
52000	624.09	588.62	572.57	547.68	539.04	536.83	534.88	528.09	524.42
53000	636.09	599.94	583.58	558.21	549.41	547.16	545.17	538.25	534.51
54000	648.10	611.26	594.59	568.75	559.78	557.48	555.46	548.40	544.59
55000	660.10	622.58	605.60	579.28	570.14	567.80	565.74	558.56	554.68
56000	672.10	633.90	616.61	589.81	580.51	578.13	576.03	568.71	564.76
57000	684.10	645.22	627.62	600.34	590.87	588.45	586.31	578.87	574.85
58000	696.10	656.54	638.63	610.88	601.24	598.77	596.60	589.02	584.93
59000	708.10	667.86	649.65	621.41	611.61	609.10	606.89	599.18	595.02
60000	720.11	679.18	660.66	631.94	621.97	619.42	617.17	609.33	605.10
61000	732.11	690.49	671.67	642.47	632.34	629.74	627.46	619.49	615.19
62000	744.11	701.81	682.68	653.00	642.71	640.07	637.74	629.65	625.27
63000	756.11	713.13	693.69	663.54	653.07	650.39	648.03	639.80	635.36
64000	768.11	724.45	704.70	674.07	663.44	660.71	658.32	649.96	645.44
65000	780.11	735.77	715.71	684.60	673.80	671.04	668.60	660.11	655.53
66000	792.12	747.09	726.72	695.13	684.17	681.36	678.89	670.27	665.61
67000	804.12	758.41	737.73	705.67	694.54	691.69	689.18	680.42	675.70
68000	816.12	769.73	748.74	716.20	704.90	702.01	699.46	690.58	685.78
69000	828.12	781.05	759.75	726.73	715.27	712.33	709.75	700.73	695.87
70000	840.12	792.37	770.77	737.26	725.63	722.66	720.03	710.89	705.95
75000	900.13	848.97	825.82	789.92	777.46	774.27	771.46	761.67	756.38
80000	960.14	905.57	880.87	842.58	829.30	825.89	822.90	812.44	806.80
100000	1200.17	1131.96	1101.09	1053.23	1036.62	1032.36	1028.62	1015.55	1008.50

12⅛% MONTHLY PAYMENT

NECESSARY TO AMORTIZE A LOAN

TERM / AMOUNT	1 YEAR	2 YEARS	3 YEARS	4 YEARS	5 YEARS	7 YEARS	8 YEARS	10 YEARS	12 YEARS
$ 25	2.23	1.18	.84	.66	.56	.45	.41	.37	.34
50	4.45	2.36	1.67	1.32	1.12	.89	.82	.73	.67
75	6.67	3.54	2.50	1.98	1.68	1.33	1.23	1.09	1.00
100	8.90	4.72	3.33	2.64	2.24	1.78	1.64	1.45	1.33
200	17.79	9.43	6.66	5.28	4.47	3.55	3.27	2.89	2.65
300	26.68	14.14	9.99	7.92	6.70	5.32	4.90	4.33	3.97
400	35.57	18.86	13.31	10.56	8.93	7.09	6.53	5.77	5.29
500	44.46	23.57	16.64	13.20	11.16	8.86	8.17	7.21	6.61
600	53.35	28.28	19.97	15.84	13.39	10.64	9.80	8.66	7.93
700	62.24	33.00	23.30	18.48	15.62	12.41	11.43	10.10	9.25
800	71.13	37.71	26.62	21.12	17.85	14.18	13.06	11.54	10.57
900	80.02	42.42	29.95	23.76	20.08	15.95	14.69	12.98	11.89
1000	88.91	47.14	33.28	26.40	22.31	17.72	16.33	14.42	13.21
2000	177.82	94.27	66.55	52.80	44.62	35.44	32.65	28.84	26.42
3000	266.73	141.40	99.83	79.19	66.93	53.16	48.97	43.26	39.63
4000	355.63	188.53	133.10	105.59	89.24	70.88	65.29	57.68	52.84
5000	444.54	235.66	166.38	131.98	111.54	88.60	81.61	72.10	66.05
6000	533.45	282.80	199.65	158.38	133.85	106.32	97.93	86.52	79.26
7000	622.36	329.93	232.92	184.77	156.16	124.04	114.26	100.94	92.47
8000	711.26	377.06	266.20	211.17	178.47	141.76	130.58	115.36	105.68
9000	800.17	424.19	299.47	237.56	200.77	159.48	146.90	129.78	118.89
10000	889.08	471.32	332.75	263.96	223.08	177.20	163.22	144.20	132.10
15000	1333.61	706.98	499.12	395.93	334.62	265.80	244.83	216.30	198.15
20000	1778.15	942.64	665.49	527.91	446.16	354.40	326.44	288.39	264.20
25000	2222.69	1178.30	831.86	659.89	557.70	443.00	408.04	360.49	330.25
30000	2667.22	1413.96	998.23	791.86	669.23	531.59	489.65	432.59	396.30
35000	3111.76	1649.62	1164.60	923.84	780.77	620.19	571.26	504.69	462.35
36000	3200.67	1696.75	1197.87	950.23	803.08	637.91	587.58	519.11	475.56
37000	3289.57	1743.88	1231.14	976.63	825.39	655.63	603.90	533.52	488.77
38000	3378.48	1791.02	1264.42	1003.02	847.70	673.35	620.23	547.94	501.98
39000	3467.39	1838.15	1297.69	1029.42	870.00	691.07	636.55	562.36	515.19
40000	3556.30	1885.28	1330.97	1055.82	892.31	708.79	652.87	576.78	528.40
41000	3645.20	1932.41	1364.24	1082.21	914.62	726.51	669.19	591.20	541.61
42000	3734.11	1979.54	1397.51	1108.61	936.93	744.23	685.51	605.62	554.82
43000	3823.02	2026.68	1430.79	1135.00	959.23	761.95	701.83	620.04	568.03
44000	3911.93	2073.81	1464.06	1161.40	981.54	779.67	718.16	634.46	581.24
45000	4000.83	2120.94	1497.34	1187.79	1003.85	797.39	734.48	648.88	594.45
46000	4089.74	2168.07	1530.61	1214.19	1026.16	815.11	750.80	663.30	607.66
47000	4178.65	2215.20	1563.89	1240.58	1048.47	832.83	767.12	677.72	620.87
48000	4267.55	2262.33	1597.16	1266.98	1070.77	850.55	783.44	692.14	634.08
49000	4356.46	2309.47	1630.43	1293.37	1093.08	868.27	799.76	706.56	647.29
50000	4445.37	2356.60	1663.71	1319.77	1115.39	885.99	816.08	720.98	660.50
51000	4534.28	2403.73	1696.98	1346.16	1137.70	903.71	832.41	735.40	673.71
52000	4623.18	2450.86	1730.26	1372.56	1160.00	921.43	848.73	749.82	686.92
53000	4712.09	2497.99	1763.53	1398.95	1182.31	939.15	865.05	764.24	700.13
54000	4801.00	2545.13	1796.80	1425.35	1204.62	956.87	881.37	778.66	713.34
55000	4889.91	2592.26	1830.08	1451.74	1226.93	974.59	897.69	793.07	726.55
56000	4978.81	2639.39	1863.35	1478.14	1249.23	992.31	914.01	807.49	739.76
57000	5067.72	2686.52	1896.63	1504.53	1271.54	1010.03	930.34	821.91	752.97
58000	5156.63	2733.65	1929.90	1530.93	1293.85	1027.74	946.66	836.33	766.18
59000	5245.53	2780.79	1963.17	1557.32	1316.16	1045.46	962.98	850.75	779.39
60000	5334.44	2827.92	1996.45	1583.72	1338.46	1063.18	979.30	865.17	792.60
61000	5423.35	2875.05	2029.72	1610.12	1360.77	1080.90	995.62	879.59	805.81
62000	5512.26	2922.18	2063.00	1636.51	1383.08	1098.62	1011.94	894.01	819.02
63000	5601.16	2969.31	2096.27	1662.91	1405.39	1116.34	1028.27	908.43	832.23
64000	5690.07	3016.44	2129.54	1689.30	1427.70	1134.06	1044.59	922.85	845.44
65000	5778.98	3063.58	2162.82	1715.70	1450.00	1151.78	1060.91	937.27	858.65
66000	5867.89	3110.71	2196.09	1742.09	1472.31	1169.50	1077.23	951.69	871.86
67000	5956.79	3157.84	2229.37	1768.49	1494.62	1187.22	1093.55	966.11	885.07
68000	6045.70	3204.97	2262.64	1794.88	1516.93	1204.94	1109.87	980.53	898.28
69000	6134.61	3252.10	2295.91	1821.28	1539.23	1222.66	1126.20	994.95	911.49
70000	6223.51	3299.24	2329.19	1847.67	1561.54	1240.38	1142.52	1009.37	924.70
75000	6668.05	3534.90	2495.56	1979.65	1673.08	1328.98	1224.12	1081.46	990.75
80000	7112.59	3770.55	2661.93	2111.63	1784.62	1417.58	1305.73	1153.56	1056.80
100000	8890.73	4713.19	3327.41	2639.53	2230.77	1771.97	1632.16	1441.95	1321.00

MONTHLY PAYMENT 12⅛%

NECESSARY TO AMORTIZE A LOAN

TERM / AMOUNT	15 YEARS	18 YEARS	20 YEARS	25 YEARS	28 YEARS	29 YEARS	30 YEARS	35 YEARS	40 YEARS
$ 25	.31	.29	.28	.27	.27	.27	.26	.26	.26
50	.61	.58	.56	.54	.53	.53	.52	.52	.51
75	.91	.86	.84	.80	.79	.79	.78	.77	.77
100	1.21	1.15	1.11	1.07	1.05	1.05	1.04	1.03	1.02
200	2.42	2.29	2.22	2.13	2.10	2.09	2.08	2.06	2.04
300	3.63	3.43	3.33	3.19	3.14	3.13	3.12	3.08	3.06
400	4.84	4.57	4.44	4.25	4.19	4.17	4.16	4.11	4.08
500	6.05	5.71	5.55	5.32	5.24	5.21	5.20	5.13	5.10
600	7.25	6.85	6.66	6.38	6.28	6.26	6.23	6.16	6.12
700	8.46	7.99	7.77	7.44	7.33	7.30	7.27	7.18	7.14
800	9.67	9.13	8.88	8.50	8.37	8.34	8.31	8.21	8.15
900	10.88	10.27	9.99	9.57	9.42	9.38	9.35	9.23	9.17
1000	12.09	11.41	11.10	10.63	10.47	10.42	10.39	10.26	10.19
2000	24.17	22.81	22.20	21.25	20.93	20.84	20.77	20.51	20.38
3000	36.25	34.22	33.30	31.88	31.39	31.26	31.15	30.77	30.56
4000	48.33	45.62	44.40	42.50	41.85	41.68	41.53	41.02	40.75
5000	60.42	57.03	55.50	53.13	52.31	52.10	51.92	51.28	50.93
6000	72.50	68.43	66.59	63.75	62.77	62.52	62.30	61.53	61.12
7000	84.58	79.83	77.69	74.38	73.23	72.94	72.68	71.79	71.31
8000	96.66	91.24	88.79	85.00	83.69	83.36	83.06	82.04	81.49
9000	108.74	102.64	99.89	95.63	94.15	93.78	93.45	92.30	91.68
10000	120.83	114.05	110.99	106.25	104.62	104.20	103.83	102.55	101.86
15000	181.24	171.07	166.48	159.38	156.92	156.29	155.74	153.82	152.79
20000	241.65	228.09	221.97	212.50	209.23	208.39	207.65	205.10	203.72
25000	302.06	285.11	277.46	265.62	261.53	260.49	259.57	256.37	254.65
30000	362.47	342.13	332.95	318.75	313.84	312.58	311.48	307.64	305.58
35000	422.88	399.15	388.44	371.87	366.14	364.68	363.39	358.91	356.51
36000	434.96	410.56	399.54	382.50	376.60	375.10	373.77	369.17	366.70
37000	447.05	421.96	410.64	393.12	387.06	385.52	384.16	379.42	376.88
38000	459.13	433.37	421.73	403.74	397.53	395.94	394.54	389.68	387.07
39000	471.21	444.77	432.83	414.37	407.99	406.36	404.92	399.93	397.25
40000	483.29	456.18	443.93	424.99	418.45	416.77	415.30	410.19	407.44
41000	495.38	467.58	455.03	435.62	428.91	427.19	425.69	420.44	417.63
42000	507.46	478.98	466.13	446.24	439.37	437.61	436.07	430.70	427.81
43000	519.54	490.39	477.22	456.87	449.83	448.03	446.45	440.95	438.00
44000	531.62	501.79	488.32	467.49	460.29	458.45	456.83	451.20	448.18
45000	543.70	513.20	499.42	478.12	470.75	468.87	467.22	461.46	458.37
46000	555.79	524.60	510.52	488.74	481.21	479.29	477.60	471.71	468.56
47000	567.87	536.01	521.62	499.37	491.68	489.71	487.98	481.97	478.74
48000	579.95	547.41	532.72	509.99	502.14	500.13	498.36	492.22	488.93
49000	592.03	558.81	543.81	520.62	512.60	510.55	508.74	502.48	499.11
50000	604.12	570.22	554.91	531.24	523.06	520.97	519.13	512.73	509.30
51000	616.20	581.62	566.01	541.87	533.52	531.39	529.51	522.99	519.48
52000	628.28	593.03	577.11	552.49	543.98	541.81	539.89	533.24	529.67
53000	640.36	604.43	588.21	563.12	554.44	552.22	550.27	543.49	539.86
54000	652.44	615.84	599.30	573.74	564.90	562.64	560.66	553.75	550.04
55000	664.53	627.24	610.40	584.36	575.36	573.06	571.04	564.00	560.23
56000	676.61	638.64	621.50	594.99	585.82	583.48	581.42	574.26	570.41
57000	688.69	650.05	632.60	605.61	596.29	593.90	591.80	584.51	580.60
58000	700.77	661.45	643.70	616.24	606.75	604.32	602.19	594.77	590.79
59000	712.86	672.86	654.79	626.86	617.21	614.74	612.57	605.02	600.97
60000	724.94	684.26	665.89	637.49	627.67	625.16	622.95	615.28	611.16
61000	737.02	695.67	676.99	648.11	638.13	635.58	633.33	625.53	621.34
62000	749.10	707.07	688.09	658.74	648.59	646.00	643.72	635.79	631.53
63000	761.18	718.47	699.19	669.36	659.05	656.42	654.10	646.04	641.71
64000	773.27	729.88	710.29	679.99	669.51	666.84	664.48	656.29	651.90
65000	785.35	741.28	721.38	690.61	679.97	677.26	674.86	666.55	662.09
66000	797.43	752.69	732.48	701.24	690.44	687.67	685.25	676.80	672.27
67000	809.51	764.09	743.58	711.86	700.90	698.09	695.63	687.06	682.46
68000	821.60	775.50	754.68	722.49	711.36	708.51	706.01	697.31	692.64
69000	833.68	786.90	765.78	733.11	721.82	718.93	716.39	707.57	702.83
70000	845.76	798.30	776.87	743.74	732.28	729.35	726.78	717.82	713.02
75000	906.17	855.32	832.36	796.86	784.58	781.45	778.69	769.09	763.95
80000	966.58	912.35	887.86	849.98	836.89	833.54	830.60	820.37	814.87
100000	1208.23	1140.43	1109.82	1062.48	1046.11	1041.93	1038.25	1025.46	1018.59

12¼% MONTHLY PAYMENT
NECESSARY TO AMORTIZE A LOAN

TERM / AMOUNT	1 YEAR	2 YEARS	3 YEARS	4 YEARS	5 YEARS	7 YEARS	8 YEARS	10 YEARS	12 YEARS
$ 25	2.23	1.18	.84	.67	.56	.45	.41	.37	.34
50	4.45	2.36	1.67	1.33	1.12	.89	.82	.73	.67
75	6.68	3.54	2.51	1.99	1.68	1.34	1.23	1.09	1.00
100	8.90	4.72	3.34	2.65	2.24	1.78	1.64	1.45	1.33
200	17.80	9.44	6.67	5.30	4.48	3.56	3.28	2.90	2.66
300	26.69	14.16	10.01	7.94	6.72	5.34	4.92	4.35	3.99
400	35.59	18.88	13.34	10.59	8.95	7.12	6.56	5.80	5.32
500	44.49	23.60	16.67	13.23	11.19	8.90	8.20	7.25	6.65
600	53.38	28.32	20.01	15.88	13.43	10.68	9.84	8.70	7.98
700	62.28	33.04	23.34	18.52	15.66	12.46	11.48	10.15	9.31
800	71.18	37.76	26.67	21.17	17.90	14.23	13.12	11.60	10.63
900	80.07	42.48	30.01	23.82	20.14	16.01	14.76	13.05	11.96
1000	88.97	47.20	33.34	26.46	22.38	17.79	16.40	14.50	13.29
2000	177.94	94.39	66.67	52.92	44.75	35.58	32.79	28.99	26.58
3000	266.90	141.58	100.01	79.38	67.12	53.37	49.18	43.48	39.86
4000	355.87	188.77	133.34	105.83	89.49	71.15	65.57	57.97	53.15
5000	444.83	235.96	166.67	132.29	111.86	88.94	81.96	72.46	66.43
6000	533.80	283.15	200.01	158.75	134.23	106.73	98.35	86.96	79.72
7000	622.77	330.34	233.34	185.20	156.60	124.51	114.74	101.45	93.01
8000	711.73	377.53	266.68	211.66	178.97	142.30	131.13	115.94	106.29
9000	800.70	424.72	300.01	238.12	201.34	160.09	147.52	130.43	119.58
10000	889.66	471.91	333.34	264.57	223.71	177.87	163.91	144.92	132.86
15000	1334.49	707.86	500.01	396.86	335.57	266.81	245.86	217.38	199.29
20000	1779.32	943.81	666.68	529.14	447.42	355.74	327.82	289.84	265.72
25000	2224.15	1179.76	833.35	661.42	559.28	444.67	409.77	362.30	332.15
30000	2668.98	1415.71	1000.02	793.71	671.13	533.61	491.72	434.76	398.58
35000	3113.81	1651.67	1166.69	925.99	782.99	622.54	573.67	507.22	465.01
36000	3202.77	1698.86	1200.02	952.45	805.36	640.33	590.06	521.72	478.30
37000	3291.74	1746.05	1233.36	978.90	827.73	658.11	606.45	536.21	491.59
38000	3380.70	1793.24	1266.69	1005.36	850.10	675.90	622.84	550.70	504.87
39000	3469.67	1840.43	1300.02	1031.82	872.47	693.69	639.24	565.19	518.16
40000	3558.64	1887.62	1333.36	1058.28	894.84	711.47	655.63	579.68	531.44
41000	3647.60	1934.81	1366.69	1084.73	917.22	729.26	672.02	594.18	544.73
42000	3736.57	1982.00	1400.03	1111.19	939.59	747.05	688.41	608.67	558.02
43000	3825.53	2029.19	1433.36	1137.65	961.96	764.83	704.80	623.16	571.30
44000	3914.50	2076.38	1466.69	1164.10	984.33	782.62	721.19	637.65	584.59
45000	4003.47	2123.57	1500.03	1190.56	1006.70	800.41	737.58	652.14	597.87
46000	4092.43	2170.76	1533.36	1217.02	1029.07	818.19	753.97	666.64	611.16
47000	4181.40	2217.95	1566.70	1243.47	1051.44	835.98	770.36	681.13	624.45
48000	4270.36	2265.14	1600.03	1269.93	1073.81	853.77	786.75	695.62	637.73
49000	4359.33	2312.33	1633.36	1296.39	1096.18	871.55	803.14	710.11	651.02
50000	4448.29	2359.52	1666.70	1322.84	1118.55	889.34	819.53	724.60	664.30
51000	4537.26	2406.71	1700.03	1349.30	1140.93	907.13	835.92	739.10	677.59
52000	4626.23	2453.90	1733.36	1375.76	1163.30	924.91	852.31	753.59	690.88
53000	4715.19	2501.09	1766.70	1402.21	1185.67	942.70	868.70	768.08	704.16
54000	4804.16	2548.28	1800.03	1428.67	1208.04	960.49	885.09	782.57	717.45
55000	4893.12	2595.47	1833.37	1455.13	1230.41	978.27	901.48	797.06	730.73
56000	4982.09	2642.66	1866.70	1481.58	1252.78	996.06	917.87	811.56	744.02
57000	5071.05	2689.85	1900.03	1508.04	1275.15	1013.85	934.26	826.05	757.31
58000	5160.02	2737.04	1933.37	1534.50	1297.52	1031.63	950.65	840.54	770.59
59000	5248.99	2784.23	1966.70	1560.95	1319.89	1049.42	967.05	855.03	783.88
60000	5337.95	2831.42	2000.04	1587.41	1342.26	1067.21	983.44	869.52	797.16
61000	5426.92	2878.61	2033.37	1613.87	1364.64	1084.99	999.83	884.02	810.45
62000	5515.88	2925.80	2066.70	1640.32	1387.01	1102.78	1016.22	898.51	823.73
63000	5604.85	2972.99	2100.04	1666.78	1409.38	1120.57	1032.61	913.00	837.02
64000	5693.82	3020.18	2133.37	1693.24	1431.75	1138.35	1049.00	927.49	850.31
65000	5782.78	3067.37	2166.70	1719.69	1454.12	1156.14	1065.39	941.98	863.59
66000	5871.75	3114.57	2200.04	1746.15	1476.49	1173.93	1081.78	956.48	876.88
67000	5960.71	3161.76	2233.37	1772.61	1498.86	1191.71	1098.17	970.97	890.16
68000	6049.68	3208.95	2266.71	1799.06	1521.23	1209.50	1114.56	985.46	903.45
69000	6138.64	3256.14	2300.04	1825.52	1543.60	1227.29	1130.95	999.95	916.74
70000	6227.61	3303.33	2333.37	1851.98	1565.97	1245.07	1147.34	1014.44	930.02
75000	6672.44	3539.28	2500.04	1984.26	1677.83	1334.01	1229.29	1086.90	996.45
80000	7117.27	3775.23	2666.71	2116.55	1789.68	1422.94	1311.25	1159.36	1062.88
100000	8896.58	4719.04	3333.39	2645.68	2237.10	1778.68	1639.06	1449.20	1328.60

MONTHLY PAYMENT 12¼%

NECESSARY TO AMORTIZE A LOAN

TERM / AMOUNT	15 YEARS	18 YEARS	20 YEARS	25 YEARS	28 YEARS	29 YEARS	30 YEARS	35 YEARS	40 YEARS
$ 25	.31	.29	.28	.27	.27	.27	.27	.26	.26
50	.61	.58	.56	.54	.53	.53	.53	.52	.52
75	.92	.87	.84	.81	.80	.79	.79	.78	.78
100	1.22	1.15	1.12	1.08	1.06	1.06	1.05	1.04	1.03
200	2.44	2.30	2.24	2.15	2.12	2.11	2.10	2.08	2.06
300	3.65	3.45	3.36	3.22	3.17	3.16	3.15	3.11	3.09
400	4.87	4.60	4.48	4.29	4.23	4.21	4.20	4.15	4.12
500	6.09	5.75	5.60	5.36	5.28	5.26	5.24	5.18	5.15
600	7.30	6.90	6.72	6.44	6.34	6.31	6.29	6.22	6.18
700	8.52	8.05	7.83	7.51	7.39	7.37	7.34	7.25	7.21
800	9.74	9.20	8.95	8.58	8.45	8.42	8.39	8.29	8.23
900	10.95	10.35	10.07	9.65	9.51	9.47	9.44	9.32	9.26
1000	12.17	11.49	11.19	10.72	10.56	10.52	10.48	10.36	10.29
2000	24.33	22.98	22.38	21.44	21.12	21.04	20.96	20.71	20.58
3000	36.49	34.47	33.56	32.16	31.67	31.55	31.44	31.07	30.87
4000	48.66	45.96	44.75	42.87	42.23	42.07	41.92	41.42	41.15
5000	60.82	57.45	55.93	53.59	52.79	52.58	52.40	51.77	51.44
6000	72.98	68.94	67.12	64.31	63.34	63.10	62.88	62.13	61.73
7000	85.15	80.43	78.30	75.03	73.90	73.61	73.36	72.48	72.01
8000	97.31	91.92	89.49	85.74	84.45	84.13	83.84	82.83	82.30
9000	109.47	103.41	100.68	96.46	95.01	94.64	94.32	93.19	92.59
10000	121.63	114.90	111.86	107.18	105.57	105.16	104.79	103.54	102.87
15000	182.45	172.34	167.79	160.77	158.35	157.73	157.19	155.31	154.31
20000	243.26	229.79	223.72	214.35	211.13	210.31	209.58	207.08	205.74
25000	304.08	287.24	279.65	267.94	263.91	262.88	261.98	258.85	257.18
30000	364.89	344.68	335.57	321.53	316.69	315.46	314.37	310.62	308.61
35000	425.71	402.13	391.50	375.12	369.47	368.03	366.77	362.38	360.05
36000	437.87	413.62	402.69	385.83	380.03	378.55	377.25	372.74	370.33
37000	450.04	425.11	413.87	396.55	390.58	389.06	387.73	383.09	380.62
38000	462.20	436.60	425.06	407.27	401.14	399.58	398.21	393.45	390.91
39000	474.36	448.09	436.25	417.99	411.70	410.09	408.68	403.80	401.19
40000	486.52	459.58	447.43	428.70	422.25	420.61	419.16	414.15	411.48
41000	498.69	471.07	458.62	439.42	432.81	431.12	429.64	424.51	421.77
42000	510.85	482.55	469.80	450.14	443.37	441.64	440.12	434.86	432.05
43000	523.01	494.04	480.99	460.85	453.92	452.15	450.60	445.21	442.34
44000	535.18	505.53	492.17	471.57	464.48	462.67	461.08	455.57	452.63
45000	547.34	517.02	503.36	482.29	475.03	473.18	471.56	465.92	462.91
46000	559.50	528.51	514.54	493.01	485.59	483.70	482.04	476.28	473.20
47000	571.67	540.00	525.73	503.72	496.15	494.21	492.52	486.63	483.49
48000	583.83	551.49	536.92	514.44	506.70	504.73	503.00	496.98	493.77
49000	595.99	562.98	548.10	525.16	517.26	515.24	513.47	507.34	504.06
50000	608.15	574.47	559.29	535.88	527.82	525.76	523.95	517.69	514.35
51000	620.32	585.96	570.47	546.59	538.37	536.27	534.43	528.04	524.63
52000	632.48	597.45	581.66	557.31	548.93	546.79	544.91	538.40	534.92
53000	644.64	608.94	592.84	568.03	559.48	557.31	555.39	548.75	545.21
54000	656.81	620.43	604.03	578.75	570.04	567.82	565.87	559.11	555.50
55000	668.97	631.91	615.22	589.46	580.60	578.34	576.35	569.46	565.78
56000	681.13	643.40	626.40	600.18	591.15	588.85	586.83	579.81	576.07
57000	693.30	654.89	637.59	610.90	601.71	599.37	597.31	590.17	586.36
58000	705.46	666.38	648.77	621.62	612.27	609.88	607.78	600.52	596.64
59000	717.62	677.87	659.96	632.33	622.82	620.40	618.26	610.87	606.93
60000	729.78	689.36	671.14	643.05	633.38	630.91	628.74	621.23	617.22
61000	741.95	700.85	682.33	653.77	643.93	641.43	639.22	631.58	627.50
62000	754.11	712.34	693.52	664.49	654.49	651.94	649.70	641.94	637.79
63000	766.27	723.83	704.70	675.20	665.05	662.46	660.18	652.29	648.08
64000	778.44	735.32	715.89	685.92	675.60	672.97	670.66	662.64	658.36
65000	790.60	746.81	727.07	696.64	686.16	683.49	681.14	673.00	668.65
66000	802.76	758.30	738.26	707.36	696.72	694.00	691.62	683.35	678.94
67000	814.93	769.79	749.44	718.07	707.27	704.52	702.10	693.70	689.22
68000	827.09	781.28	760.63	728.79	717.83	715.03	712.57	704.06	699.51
69000	839.25	792.76	771.81	739.51	728.38	725.55	723.05	714.41	709.80
70000	851.41	804.25	783.00	750.23	738.94	736.06	733.53	724.76	720.09
75000	912.23	861.70	838.93	803.81	791.72	788.64	785.93	776.53	771.52
80000	973.04	919.15	894.86	857.40	844.50	841.21	838.32	828.30	822.95
100000	1216.30	1148.93	1118.57	1071.75	1055.63	1051.51	1047.90	1035.38	1028.69

12⅜% MONTHLY PAYMENT
NECESSARY TO AMORTIZE A LOAN

TERM / AMOUNT	1 YEAR	2 YEARS	3 YEARS	4 YEARS	5 YEARS	7 YEARS	8 YEARS	10 YEARS	12 YEARS
$ 25	2.23	1.19	.84	.67	.57	.45	.42	.37	.34
50	4.46	2.37	1.67	1.33	1.13	.90	.83	.73	.67
75	6.68	3.55	2.51	1.99	1.69	1.34	1.24	1.10	1.01
100	8.91	4.73	3.34	2.66	2.25	1.79	1.65	1.46	1.34
200	17.81	9.45	6.68	5.31	4.49	3.58	3.30	2.92	2.68
300	26.71	14.18	10.02	7.96	6.74	5.36	4.94	4.37	4.01
400	35.61	18.90	13.36	10.61	8.98	7.15	6.59	5.83	5.35
500	44.52	23.63	16.70	13.26	11.22	8.93	8.23	7.29	6.69
600	53.42	28.35	20.04	15.92	13.47	10.72	9.88	8.74	8.02
700	62.32	33.08	23.38	18.57	15.71	12.50	11.53	10.20	9.36
800	71.22	37.80	26.72	21.22	17.95	14.29	13.17	11.66	10.69
900	80.13	42.53	30.06	23.87	20.20	16.07	14.82	13.11	12.03
1000	89.03	47.25	33.40	26.52	22.44	17.86	16.46	14.57	13.37
2000	178.05	94.50	66.79	53.04	44.87	35.71	32.92	29.13	26.73
3000	267.08	141.75	100.19	79.56	67.31	53.57	49.38	43.70	40.09
4000	356.10	189.00	133.58	106.08	89.74	71.42	65.84	58.26	53.45
5000	445.13	236.25	166.97	132.60	112.18	89.27	82.30	72.83	66.82
6000	534.15	283.50	200.37	159.11	134.61	107.13	98.76	87.39	80.18
7000	623.18	330.75	233.76	185.63	157.05	124.98	115.22	101.96	93.54
8000	712.20	378.00	267.15	212.15	179.48	142.84	131.68	116.52	106.90
9000	801.22	425.24	300.55	238.67	201.91	160.69	148.14	131.09	120.26
10000	890.25	472.49	333.94	265.19	224.35	178.54	164.60	145.65	133.63
15000	1335.37	708.74	500.91	397.78	336.52	267.81	246.90	218.48	200.44
20000	1780.49	944.98	667.88	530.37	448.69	357.08	329.20	291.30	267.25
25000	2225.61	1181.22	834.85	662.96	560.87	446.35	411.49	364.12	334.06
30000	2670.73	1417.47	1001.82	795.55	673.04	535.62	493.79	436.95	400.87
35000	3115.86	1653.71	1168.78	928.15	785.21	624.89	576.09	509.77	467.68
36000	3204.88	1700.96	1202.18	954.66	807.64	642.75	592.55	524.33	481.04
37000	3293.90	1748.21	1235.57	981.18	830.08	660.60	609.01	538.90	494.41
38000	3382.93	1795.46	1268.97	1007.70	852.51	678.45	625.47	553.46	507.77
39000	3471.95	1842.71	1302.36	1034.22	874.95	696.31	641.93	568.03	521.13
40000	3560.98	1889.96	1335.75	1060.74	897.38	714.16	658.39	582.59	534.49
41000	3650.00	1937.21	1369.15	1087.26	919.82	732.02	674.85	597.16	547.85
42000	3739.03	1984.45	1402.54	1113.77	942.25	749.87	691.31	611.72	561.22
43000	3828.05	2031.70	1435.93	1140.29	964.68	767.72	707.77	626.29	574.58
44000	3917.07	2078.95	1469.33	1166.81	987.12	785.58	724.23	640.85	587.94
45000	4006.10	2126.20	1502.72	1193.33	1009.55	803.43	740.69	655.42	601.30
46000	4095.12	2173.45	1536.12	1219.85	1031.99	821.28	757.15	669.98	614.66
47000	4184.15	2220.70	1569.51	1246.37	1054.42	839.14	773.61	684.55	628.03
48000	4273.17	2267.95	1602.90	1272.88	1076.86	856.99	790.07	699.11	641.39
49000	4362.20	2315.20	1636.30	1299.40	1099.29	874.85	806.52	713.68	654.75
50000	4451.22	2362.44	1669.69	1325.92	1121.73	892.70	822.98	728.24	668.11
51000	4540.24	2409.69	1703.08	1352.44	1144.16	910.55	839.44	742.81	681.48
52000	4629.27	2456.94	1736.48	1378.96	1166.59	928.41	855.90	757.37	694.84
53000	4718.29	2504.19	1769.87	1405.48	1189.03	946.26	872.36	771.93	708.20
54000	4807.32	2551.44	1803.26	1431.99	1211.46	964.12	888.82	786.50	721.56
55000	4896.34	2598.69	1836.66	1458.51	1233.90	981.97	905.28	801.06	734.92
56000	4985.37	2645.94	1870.05	1485.03	1256.33	999.82	921.74	815.63	748.29
57000	5074.39	2693.19	1903.45	1511.55	1278.77	1017.68	938.20	830.19	761.65
58000	5163.42	2740.43	1936.84	1538.07	1301.20	1035.53	954.66	844.76	775.01
59000	5252.44	2787.68	1970.23	1564.59	1323.64	1053.39	971.12	859.32	788.37
60000	5341.46	2834.93	2003.63	1591.10	1346.07	1071.24	987.58	873.89	801.73
61000	5430.49	2882.18	2037.02	1617.62	1368.50	1089.09	1004.04	888.45	815.10
62000	5519.51	2929.43	2070.41	1644.14	1390.94	1106.95	1020.50	903.02	828.46
63000	5608.54	2976.68	2103.81	1670.66	1413.37	1124.80	1036.96	917.58	841.82
64000	5697.56	3023.93	2137.20	1697.18	1435.81	1142.65	1053.42	932.15	855.18
65000	5786.59	3071.18	2170.60	1723.70	1458.24	1160.51	1069.88	946.71	868.55
66000	5875.61	3118.42	2203.99	1750.21	1480.68	1178.36	1086.34	961.28	881.91
67000	5964.63	3165.67	2237.38	1776.73	1503.11	1196.22	1102.80	975.84	895.27
68000	6053.66	3212.92	2270.78	1803.25	1525.54	1214.07	1119.26	990.41	908.63
69000	6142.68	3260.17	2304.17	1829.77	1547.98	1231.92	1135.72	1004.97	921.99
70000	6231.71	3307.42	2337.56	1856.29	1570.41	1249.78	1152.18	1019.53	935.36
75000	6676.83	3543.66	2504.53	1988.88	1682.59	1339.05	1234.47	1092.36	1002.17
80000	7121.95	3779.91	2671.50	2121.47	1794.76	1428.32	1316.77	1165.18	1068.98
100000	8902.44	4724.88	3339.38	2651.84	2243.45	1785.40	1645.96	1456.48	1336.22

MONTHLY PAYMENT $12\frac{3}{8}\%$

NECESSARY TO AMORTIZE A LOAN

TERM / AMOUNT	15 YEARS	18 YEARS	20 YEARS	25 YEARS	28 YEARS	29 YEARS	30 YEARS	35 YEARS	40 YEARS
$ 25	.31	.29	.29	.28	.27	.27	.27	.27	.26
50	.62	.58	.57	.55	.54	.54	.53	.53	.52
75	.92	.87	.85	.82	.80	.80	.80	.79	.78
100	1.23	1.16	1.13	1.09	1.07	1.07	1.06	1.05	1.04
200	2.45	2.32	2.26	2.17	2.14	2.13	2.12	2.10	2.08
300	3.68	3.48	3.39	3.25	3.20	3.19	3.18	3.14	3.12
400	4.90	4.63	4.51	4.33	4.27	4.25	4.24	4.19	4.16
500	6.13	5.79	5.64	5.41	5.33	5.31	5.29	5.23	5.20
600	7.35	6.95	6.77	6.49	6.40	6.37	6.35	6.28	6.24
700	8.58	8.11	7.90	7.57	7.46	7.43	7.41	7.32	7.28
800	9.80	9.26	9.02	8.65	8.53	8.49	8.47	8.37	8.32
900	11.02	10.42	10.15	9.73	9.59	9.56	9.52	9.41	9.35
1000	12.25	11.58	11.28	10.82	10.66	10.62	10.58	10.46	10.39
2000	24.49	23.15	22.55	21.63	21.31	21.23	21.16	20.91	20.78
3000	36.74	34.73	33.83	32.44	31.96	31.84	31.73	31.36	31.17
4000	48.98	46.30	45.10	43.25	42.61	42.45	42.31	41.82	41.56
5000	61.22	57.88	56.37	54.06	53.26	53.06	52.88	52.27	51.94
6000	73.47	69.45	67.65	64.87	63.91	63.67	63.46	62.72	62.33
7000	85.71	81.03	78.92	75.68	74.57	74.28	74.03	73.18	72.72
8000	97.96	92.60	90.19	86.49	85.22	84.89	84.61	83.63	83.11
9000	110.20	104.18	101.47	97.30	95.87	95.51	95.19	94.08	93.50
10000	122.44	115.75	112.74	108.11	106.52	106.12	105.76	104.54	103.88
15000	183.66	173.62	169.11	162.16	159.78	159.17	158.64	156.80	155.82
20000	244.88	231.50	225.47	216.21	213.04	212.23	211.52	209.07	207.76
25000	306.10	289.37	281.84	270.26	266.29	265.28	264.40	261.33	259.70
30000	367.32	347.24	338.21	324.32	319.55	318.34	317.28	313.60	311.64
35000	428.54	405.11	394.57	378.37	372.81	371.40	370.15	365.86	363.58
36000	440.79	416.69	405.85	389.18	383.46	382.01	380.73	376.31	373.97
37000	453.03	428.26	417.12	399.99	394.11	392.62	391.31	386.77	384.36
38000	465.28	439.84	428.39	410.80	404.76	403.23	401.88	397.22	394.75
39000	477.52	451.41	439.67	421.61	415.42	413.84	412.46	407.67	405.14
40000	489.76	462.99	450.94	432.42	426.07	424.45	423.03	418.13	415.52
41000	502.01	474.56	462.21	443.23	436.72	435.06	433.61	428.58	425.91
42000	514.25	486.13	473.49	454.04	447.37	445.67	444.18	439.03	436.30
43000	526.50	497.71	484.76	464.85	458.02	456.28	454.76	449.49	446.69
44000	538.74	509.28	496.03	475.66	468.67	466.90	465.33	459.94	457.08
45000	550.98	520.86	507.31	486.47	479.33	477.51	475.91	470.39	467.46
46000	563.23	532.43	518.58	497.28	489.98	488.12	486.49	480.85	477.85
47000	575.47	544.01	529.86	508.09	500.63	498.73	497.06	491.30	488.24
48000	587.72	555.58	541.13	518.90	511.28	509.34	507.64	501.75	498.63
49000	599.96	567.16	552.40	529.71	521.93	519.95	518.21	512.20	509.02
50000	612.20	578.73	563.68	540.52	532.58	530.56	528.79	522.66	519.40
51000	624.45	590.31	574.95	551.33	543.24	541.17	539.36	533.11	529.79
52000	636.69	601.88	586.22	562.14	553.89	551.79	549.94	543.56	540.18
53000	648.94	613.45	597.50	572.96	564.54	562.40	560.52	554.02	550.57
54000	661.18	625.03	608.77	583.77	575.19	573.01	571.09	564.47	560.96
55000	673.42	636.60	620.04	594.58	585.84	583.62	581.67	574.92	571.34
56000	685.67	648.18	631.32	605.39	596.49	594.23	592.24	585.38	581.73
57000	697.91	659.75	642.59	616.20	607.14	604.84	602.82	595.83	592.12
58000	710.16	671.33	653.86	627.01	617.80	615.45	613.39	606.28	602.51
59000	722.40	682.90	665.14	637.82	628.45	626.06	623.97	616.74	612.90
60000	734.64	694.48	676.41	648.63	639.10	636.67	634.55	627.19	623.28
61000	746.89	706.05	687.68	659.44	649.75	647.29	645.12	637.64	633.67
62000	759.13	717.63	698.96	670.25	660.40	657.90	655.70	648.09	644.06
63000	771.38	729.20	710.23	681.06	671.05	668.51	666.27	658.55	654.45
64000	783.62	740.77	721.50	691.87	681.71	679.12	676.85	669.00	664.84
65000	795.86	752.35	732.78	702.68	692.36	689.73	687.42	679.45	675.22
66000	808.11	763.92	744.05	713.49	703.01	700.34	698.00	689.91	685.61
67000	820.35	775.50	755.32	724.30	713.66	710.95	708.58	700.36	696.00
68000	832.60	787.07	766.60	735.11	724.31	721.56	719.15	710.81	706.39
69000	844.84	798.65	777.87	745.92	734.96	732.17	729.73	721.27	716.78
70000	857.08	810.22	789.14	756.73	745.61	742.79	740.30	731.72	727.16
75000	918.30	868.09	845.51	810.78	798.87	795.84	793.18	783.98	779.10
80000	979.52	925.97	901.88	864.84	852.13	848.90	846.06	836.25	831.04
100000	1224.40	1157.46	1127.35	1081.04	1065.16	1061.12	1057.57	1045.31	1038.80

12½% MONTHLY PAYMENT
NECESSARY TO AMORTIZE A LOAN

TERM / AMOUNT	1 YEAR	2 YEARS	3 YEARS	4 YEARS	5 YEARS	7 YEARS	8 YEARS	10 YEARS	12 YEARS
$ 25	2.23	1.19	.84	.67	.57	.45	.42	.37	.34
50	4.46	2.37	1.68	1.33	1.13	.90	.83	.74	.68
75	6.69	3.55	2.51	2.00	1.69	1.35	1.24	1.10	1.01
100	8.91	4.74	3.35	2.66	2.25	1.80	1.66	1.47	1.35
200	17.82	9.47	6.70	5.32	4.50	3.59	3.31	2.93	2.69
300	26.73	14.20	10.04	7.98	6.75	5.38	4.96	4.40	4.04
400	35.64	18.93	13.39	10.64	9.00	7.17	6.62	5.86	5.38
500	44.55	23.66	16.73	13.29	11.25	8.97	8.27	7.32	6.72
600	53.45	28.39	20.08	15.95	13.50	10.76	9.92	8.79	8.07
700	62.36	33.12	23.42	18.61	15.75	12.55	11.58	10.25	9.41
800	71.27	37.85	26.77	21.27	18.00	14.34	13.23	11.72	10.76
900	80.18	42.58	30.11	23.93	20.25	16.13	14.88	13.18	12.10
1000	89.09	47.31	33.46	26.58	22.50	17.93	16.53	14.64	13.44
2000	178.17	94.62	66.91	53.16	45.00	35.85	33.06	29.28	26.88
3000	267.25	141.93	100.37	79.74	67.50	53.77	49.59	43.92	40.32
4000	356.34	189.23	133.82	106.32	90.00	71.69	66.12	58.56	53.76
5000	445.42	236.54	167.27	132.90	112.49	89.61	82.65	73.19	67.20
6000	534.50	283.85	200.73	159.48	134.99	107.53	99.18	87.83	80.64
7000	623.59	331.16	234.18	186.06	157.49	125.45	115.71	102.47	94.08
8000	712.67	378.46	267.63	212.64	179.99	143.37	132.24	117.11	107.51
9000	801.75	425.77	301.09	239.22	202.49	161.30	148.76	131.74	120.95
10000	890.83	473.08	334.54	265.80	224.98	179.22	165.29	146.38	134.39
15000	1336.25	709.61	501.81	398.70	337.47	268.82	247.94	219.57	201.58
20000	1781.66	946.15	669.08	531.60	449.96	358.43	330.58	292.76	268.78
25000	2227.08	1182.69	836.35	664.50	562.45	448.04	413.23	365.95	335.97
30000	2672.49	1419.22	1003.61	797.40	674.94	537.64	495.87	439.13	403.16
35000	3117.91	1655.76	1170.88	930.30	787.43	627.25	578.51	512.32	470.36
36000	3206.99	1703.07	1204.34	956.88	809.93	645.17	595.04	526.96	483.79
37000	3296.07	1750.38	1237.79	983.46	832.43	663.09	611.57	541.60	497.23
38000	3385.15	1797.68	1271.24	1010.04	854.93	681.01	628.10	556.23	510.67
39000	3474.24	1844.99	1304.70	1036.62	877.42	698.93	644.63	570.87	524.11
40000	3563.32	1892.30	1338.15	1063.20	899.92	716.85	661.16	585.51	537.55
41000	3652.40	1939.60	1371.60	1089.78	922.42	734.78	677.69	600.15	550.99
42000	3741.49	1986.91	1405.06	1116.36	944.92	752.70	694.21	614.78	564.43
43000	3830.57	2034.22	1438.51	1142.94	967.42	770.62	710.74	629.42	577.86
44000	3919.65	2081.53	1471.96	1169.52	989.91	788.54	727.27	644.06	591.30
45000	4008.73	2128.83	1505.42	1196.10	1012.41	806.46	743.80	658.70	604.74
46000	4097.82	2176.14	1538.87	1222.68	1034.91	824.38	760.33	673.34	618.18
47000	4186.90	2223.45	1572.33	1249.26	1057.41	842.30	776.86	687.97	631.62
48000	4275.98	2270.76	1605.78	1275.84	1079.91	860.22	793.39	702.61	645.06
49000	4365.07	2318.06	1639.23	1302.42	1102.40	878.15	809.92	717.25	658.50
50000	4454.15	2365.37	1672.69	1329.00	1124.90	896.07	826.45	731.89	671.93
51000	4543.23	2412.68	1706.14	1355.58	1147.40	913.99	842.97	746.52	685.37
52000	4632.31	2459.99	1739.59	1382.16	1169.90	931.91	859.50	761.16	698.81
53000	4721.40	2507.29	1773.05	1408.74	1192.40	949.83	876.03	775.80	712.25
54000	4810.48	2554.60	1806.50	1435.32	1214.89	967.75	892.56	790.44	725.69
55000	4899.56	2601.91	1839.95	1461.90	1237.39	985.67	909.09	805.07	739.13
56000	4988.65	2649.21	1873.41	1488.48	1259.89	1003.59	925.62	819.71	752.57
57000	5077.73	2696.52	1906.86	1515.06	1282.39	1021.52	942.15	834.35	766.00
58000	5166.81	2743.83	1940.32	1541.64	1304.89	1039.44	958.68	848.99	779.44
59000	5255.89	2791.14	1973.77	1568.22	1327.38	1057.36	975.20	863.62	792.88
60000	5344.98	2838.44	2007.22	1594.80	1349.88	1075.28	991.73	878.26	806.32
61000	5434.06	2885.75	2040.68	1621.38	1372.38	1093.20	1008.26	892.90	819.76
62000	5523.14	2933.06	2074.13	1647.96	1394.88	1111.12	1024.79	907.54	833.20
63000	5612.23	2980.37	2107.58	1674.54	1417.38	1129.04	1041.32	922.17	846.64
64000	5701.31	3027.67	2141.04	1701.12	1439.87	1146.96	1057.85	936.81	860.07
65000	5790.39	3074.98	2174.49	1727.70	1462.37	1164.89	1074.38	951.45	873.51
66000	5879.47	3122.29	2207.94	1754.28	1484.87	1182.81	1090.91	966.09	886.95
67000	5968.56	3169.59	2241.40	1780.86	1507.37	1200.73	1107.44	980.73	900.39
68000	6057.64	3216.90	2274.85	1807.44	1529.86	1218.65	1123.96	995.36	913.83
69000	6146.72	3264.21	2308.31	1834.02	1552.36	1236.57	1140.49	1010.00	927.27
70000	6235.81	3311.52	2341.76	1860.60	1574.86	1254.49	1157.02	1024.64	940.71
75000	6681.22	3548.05	2509.03	1993.50	1687.35	1344.10	1239.67	1097.83	1007.90
80000	7126.63	3784.59	2676.30	2126.40	1799.84	1433.70	1322.31	1171.01	1075.09
100000	8908.29	4730.74	3345.37	2658.00	2249.80	1792.13	1652.89	1463.77	1343.86

MONTHLY PAYMENT 12½%

NECESSARY TO AMORTIZE A LOAN

TERM / AMOUNT	15 YEARS	18 YEARS	20 YEARS	25 YEARS	28 YEARS	29 YEARS	30 YEARS	35 YEARS	40 YEARS
$ 25	.31	.30	.29	.28	.27	.27	.27	.27	.27
50	.62	.59	.57	.55	.54	.54	.54	.53	.53
75	.93	.88	.86	.82	.81	.81	.81	.80	.79
100	1.24	1.17	1.14	1.10	1.08	1.08	1.07	1.06	1.05
200	2.47	2.34	2.28	2.19	2.15	2.15	2.14	2.12	2.10
300	3.70	3.50	3.41	3.28	3.23	3.22	3.21	3.17	3.15
400	4.94	4.67	4.55	4.37	4.30	4.29	4.27	4.23	4.20
500	6.17	5.84	5.69	5.46	5.38	5.36	5.34	5.28	5.25
600	7.40	7.00	6.82	6.55	6.45	6.43	6.41	6.34	6.30
700	8.63	8.17	7.96	7.64	7.53	7.50	7.48	7.39	7.35
800	9.87	9.33	9.09	8.73	8.60	8.57	8.54	8.45	8.40
900	11.10	10.50	10.23	9.82	9.68	9.64	9.61	9.50	9.45
1000	12.33	11.67	11.37	10.91	10.75	10.71	10.68	10.56	10.49
2000	24.66	23.33	22.73	21.81	21.50	21.42	21.35	21.11	20.98
3000	36.98	34.99	34.09	32.72	32.25	32.13	32.02	31.66	31.47
4000	49.31	46.65	45.45	43.62	42.99	42.83	42.70	42.22	41.96
5000	61.63	58.31	56.81	54.52	53.74	53.54	53.37	52.77	52.45
6000	73.96	69.97	68.17	65.43	64.49	64.25	64.04	63.32	62.94
7000	86.28	81.63	79.53	76.33	75.23	74.96	74.71	73.87	73.43
8000	98.61	93.29	90.90	87.23	85.98	85.66	85.39	84.43	83.92
9000	110.93	104.95	102.26	98.14	96.73	96.37	96.06	94.98	94.41
10000	123.26	116.61	113.62	109.04	107.48	107.08	106.73	105.53	104.90
15000	184.88	174.91	170.43	163.56	161.21	160.62	160.09	158.29	157.34
20000	246.51	233.21	227.23	218.08	214.95	214.15	213.46	211.06	209.79
25000	308.14	291.51	284.04	272.59	268.68	267.69	266.82	263.82	262.23
30000	369.76	349.81	340.85	327.11	322.42	321.23	320.18	316.58	314.68
35000	431.39	408.11	397.65	381.63	376.15	374.76	373.55	369.34	367.13
36000	443.71	419.77	409.02	392.53	386.90	385.47	384.22	379.90	377.62
37000	456.04	431.43	420.38	403.44	397.65	396.18	394.89	390.45	388.11
38000	468.36	443.09	431.74	414.34	408.40	406.89	405.56	401.00	398.59
39000	480.69	454.75	443.10	425.24	419.14	417.59	416.24	411.55	409.08
40000	493.01	466.41	454.46	436.15	429.89	428.30	426.91	422.11	419.57
41000	505.34	478.07	465.82	447.05	440.64	439.01	437.58	432.66	430.06
42000	517.66	489.73	477.18	457.95	451.38	449.72	448.25	443.21	440.55
43000	529.99	501.39	488.55	468.86	462.13	460.42	458.93	453.76	451.04
44000	542.31	513.05	499.91	479.76	472.88	471.13	469.60	464.32	461.53
45000	554.64	524.71	511.27	490.66	483.63	481.84	480.27	474.87	472.02
46000	566.97	536.37	522.63	501.57	494.37	492.55	490.94	485.42	482.51
47000	579.29	548.03	533.99	512.47	505.12	503.25	501.62	495.97	493.00
48000	591.62	559.69	545.35	523.37	515.87	513.96	512.29	506.53	503.49
49000	603.94	571.35	556.71	534.28	526.61	524.67	522.96	517.08	513.98
50000	616.27	583.01	568.08	545.18	537.36	535.38	533.63	527.63	524.46
51000	628.59	594.67	579.44	556.09	548.11	546.08	544.31	538.18	534.95
52000	640.92	606.33	590.80	566.99	558.86	556.79	554.98	548.74	545.44
53000	653.24	617.99	602.16	577.89	569.60	567.50	565.65	559.29	555.93
54000	665.57	629.65	613.52	588.80	580.35	578.21	576.32	569.84	566.42
55000	677.89	641.31	624.88	599.70	591.10	588.91	587.00	580.39	576.91
56000	690.22	652.97	636.24	610.60	601.84	599.62	597.67	590.95	587.40
57000	702.54	664.63	647.61	621.51	612.59	610.33	608.34	601.50	597.89
58000	714.87	676.29	658.97	632.41	623.34	621.03	619.01	612.05	608.38
59000	727.19	687.95	670.33	643.31	634.09	631.74	629.69	622.61	618.87
60000	739.52	699.61	681.69	654.22	644.83	642.45	640.36	633.16	629.36
61000	751.84	711.27	693.05	665.12	655.58	653.16	651.03	643.71	639.85
62000	764.17	722.93	704.41	676.02	666.33	663.86	661.70	654.26	650.34
63000	776.49	734.59	715.77	686.93	677.07	674.57	672.38	664.82	660.82
64000	788.82	746.25	727.13	697.83	687.82	685.28	683.05	675.37	671.31
65000	801.14	757.91	738.50	708.74	698.57	695.99	693.72	685.92	681.80
66000	813.47	769.57	749.86	719.64	709.32	706.69	704.40	696.47	692.29
67000	825.79	781.23	761.22	730.54	720.06	717.40	715.07	707.03	702.78
68000	838.12	792.89	772.58	741.45	730.81	728.11	725.74	717.58	713.27
69000	850.45	804.55	783.94	752.35	741.56	738.82	736.41	728.13	723.76
70000	862.77	816.21	795.30	763.25	752.30	749.52	747.09	738.68	734.25
75000	924.40	874.51	852.11	817.77	806.04	803.06	800.45	791.45	786.69
80000	986.02	932.81	908.92	872.29	859.78	856.60	853.81	844.21	839.14
100000	1232.53	1166.01	1136.15	1090.36	1074.72	1070.75	1067.26	1055.26	1048.92

12⅝% MONTHLY PAYMENT
NECESSARY TO AMORTIZE A LOAN

TERM / AMOUNT	1 YEAR	2 YEARS	3 YEARS	4 YEARS	5 YEARS	7 YEARS	8 YEARS	10 YEARS	12 YEARS
$ 25	2.23	1.19	.84	.67	.57	.45	.42	.37	.34
50	4.46	2.37	1.68	1.34	1.13	.90	.83	.74	.68
75	6.69	3.56	2.52	2.00	1.70	1.35	1.25	1.11	1.02
100	8.92	4.74	3.36	2.67	2.26	1.80	1.66	1.48	1.36
200	17.83	9.48	6.71	5.33	4.52	3.60	3.32	2.95	2.71
300	26.75	14.21	10.06	8.00	6.77	5.40	4.98	4.42	4.06
400	35.66	18.95	13.41	10.66	9.03	7.20	6.64	5.89	5.41
500	44.58	23.69	16.76	13.33	11.29	9.00	8.30	7.36	6.76
600	53.49	28.42	20.11	15.99	13.54	10.80	9.96	8.83	8.11
700	62.40	33.16	23.46	18.65	15.80	12.60	11.62	10.30	9.47
800	71.32	37.90	26.82	21.32	18.05	14.40	13.28	11.77	10.82
900	80.23	42.63	30.17	23.98	20.31	16.19	14.94	13.24	12.17
1000	89.15	47.37	33.52	26.65	22.57	17.99	16.60	14.72	13.52
2000	178.29	94.74	67.03	53.29	45.13	35.98	33.20	29.43	27.04
3000	267.43	142.10	100.55	79.93	67.69	53.97	49.80	44.14	40.55
4000	356.57	189.47	134.06	106.57	90.25	71.96	66.40	58.85	54.07
5000	445.71	236.83	167.57	133.21	112.81	89.95	83.00	73.56	67.58
6000	534.85	284.20	201.09	159.86	135.37	107.94	99.59	88.27	81.10
7000	624.00	331.57	234.60	186.50	157.94	125.93	116.19	102.98	94.61
8000	713.14	378.93	268.11	213.14	180.50	143.91	132.79	117.69	108.13
9000	802.28	426.30	301.63	239.78	203.06	161.90	149.39	132.40	121.64
10000	891.42	473.66	335.14	266.42	225.62	179.89	165.99	147.11	135.16
15000	1337.13	710.49	502.71	399.63	338.43	269.84	248.98	220.67	202.73
20000	1782.83	947.32	670.28	532.84	451.24	359.78	331.97	294.22	270.31
25000	2228.54	1184.15	837.85	666.05	564.04	449.72	414.96	367.77	337.88
30000	2674.25	1420.98	1005.41	799.26	676.85	539.67	497.95	441.33	405.46
35000	3119.96	1657.81	1172.98	932.47	789.66	629.61	580.94	514.88	473.04
36000	3209.10	1705.18	1206.50	959.11	812.22	647.60	597.54	529.59	486.55
37000	3298.24	1752.54	1240.01	985.75	834.78	665.59	614.14	544.30	500.07
38000	3387.38	1799.91	1273.52	1012.39	857.34	683.58	630.74	559.01	513.58
39000	3476.52	1847.27	1307.04	1039.03	879.91	701.56	647.33	573.72	527.10
40000	3565.66	1894.64	1340.55	1065.67	902.47	719.55	663.93	588.43	540.61
41000	3654.80	1942.01	1374.06	1092.32	925.03	737.54	680.53	603.14	554.13
42000	3743.95	1989.37	1407.58	1118.96	947.59	755.53	697.13	617.85	567.64
43000	3833.09	2036.74	1441.09	1145.60	970.15	773.52	713.73	632.57	581.16
44000	3922.23	2084.10	1474.60	1172.24	992.71	791.51	730.33	647.28	594.67
45000	4011.37	2131.47	1508.12	1198.88	1015.28	809.50	746.92	661.99	608.19
46000	4100.51	2178.84	1541.63	1225.53	1037.84	827.49	763.52	676.70	621.70
47000	4189.65	2226.20	1575.14	1252.17	1060.40	845.47	780.12	691.41	635.22
48000	4278.79	2273.57	1608.66	1278.81	1082.96	863.46	796.72	706.12	648.73
49000	4367.94	2320.93	1642.17	1305.45	1105.52	881.45	813.32	720.83	662.25
50000	4457.08	2368.30	1675.69	1332.09	1128.08	899.44	829.91	735.54	675.76
51000	4546.22	2415.66	1709.20	1358.73	1150.64	917.43	846.51	750.25	689.28
52000	4635.36	2463.03	1742.71	1385.38	1173.21	935.42	863.11	764.96	702.79
53000	4724.50	2510.40	1776.23	1412.02	1195.77	953.41	879.71	779.67	716.31
54000	4813.64	2557.76	1809.74	1438.66	1218.33	971.40	896.31	794.38	729.83
55000	4902.78	2605.13	1843.25	1465.30	1240.89	989.38	912.91	809.09	743.34
56000	4991.93	2652.49	1876.77	1491.94	1263.45	1007.37	929.50	823.80	756.86
57000	5081.07	2699.86	1910.28	1518.58	1286.01	1025.36	946.10	838.52	770.37
58000	5170.21	2747.23	1943.79	1545.23	1308.58	1043.35	962.70	853.23	783.89
59000	5259.35	2794.59	1977.31	1571.87	1331.14	1061.34	979.30	867.94	797.40
60000	5348.49	2841.96	2010.82	1598.51	1353.70	1079.33	995.90	882.65	810.92
61000	5437.63	2889.32	2044.34	1625.15	1376.26	1097.32	1012.49	897.36	824.43
62000	5526.77	2936.69	2077.85	1651.79	1398.82	1115.31	1029.09	912.07	837.95
63000	5615.92	2984.06	2111.36	1678.44	1421.38	1133.29	1045.69	926.78	851.46
64000	5705.06	3031.42	2144.88	1705.08	1443.95	1151.28	1062.29	941.49	864.98
65000	5794.20	3078.79	2178.39	1731.72	1466.51	1169.27	1078.89	956.20	878.49
66000	5883.34	3126.15	2211.90	1758.36	1489.07	1187.26	1095.49	970.91	892.01
67000	5972.48	3173.52	2245.42	1785.00	1511.63	1205.25	1112.08	985.62	905.52
68000	6061.62	3220.88	2278.93	1811.64	1534.19	1223.24	1128.68	1000.33	919.04
69000	6150.76	3268.25	2312.44	1838.29	1556.75	1241.23	1145.28	1015.04	932.55
70000	6239.91	3315.62	2345.96	1864.93	1579.31	1259.21	1161.88	1029.75	946.07
75000	6685.61	3552.45	2513.53	1998.14	1692.12	1349.16	1244.87	1103.31	1013.64
80000	7131.32	3789.27	2681.09	2131.34	1804.93	1439.10	1327.86	1176.86	1081.22
100000	8914.15	4736.59	3351.37	2664.18	2256.16	1798.88	1659.82	1471.08	1351.52

MONTHLY PAYMENT $12\frac{5}{8}\%$
NECESSARY TO AMORTIZE A LOAN

TERM / AMOUNT	15 YEARS	18 YEARS	20 YEARS	25 YEARS	28 YEARS	29 YEARS	30 YEARS	35 YEARS	40 YEARS
$ 25	.32	.30	.29	.28	.28	.28	.27	.27	.27
50	.63	.59	.58	.55	.55	.55	.54	.54	.53
75	.94	.89	.86	.83	.82	.82	.81	.80	.80
100	1.25	1.18	1.15	1.10	1.09	1.09	1.08	1.07	1.06
200	2.49	2.35	2.29	2.20	2.17	2.17	2.16	2.14	2.12
300	3.73	3.53	3.44	3.30	3.26	3.25	3.24	3.20	3.18
400	4.97	4.70	4.58	4.40	4.34	4.33	4.31	4.27	4.24
500	6.21	5.88	5.73	5.50	5.43	5.41	5.39	5.33	5.30
600	7.45	7.05	6.87	6.60	6.51	6.49	6.47	6.40	6.36
700	8.69	8.23	8.02	7.70	7.60	7.57	7.54	7.46	7.42
800	9.93	9.40	9.16	8.80	8.68	8.65	8.62	8.53	8.48
900	11.17	10.58	10.31	9.90	9.76	9.73	9.70	9.59	9.54
1000	12.41	11.75	11.45	11.00	10.85	10.81	10.77	10.66	10.60
2000	24.82	23.50	22.90	22.00	21.69	21.61	21.54	21.31	21.19
3000	37.23	35.24	34.35	33.00	32.53	32.42	32.31	31.96	31.78
4000	49.63	46.99	45.80	43.99	43.38	43.22	43.08	42.61	42.37
5000	62.04	58.73	57.25	54.99	54.22	54.02	53.85	53.27	52.96
6000	74.45	70.48	68.70	65.99	65.06	64.83	64.62	63.92	63.55
7000	86.85	82.23	80.15	76.98	75.91	75.63	75.39	74.57	74.14
8000	99.26	93.97	91.60	87.98	86.75	86.44	86.16	85.22	84.73
9000	111.67	105.72	103.05	98.98	97.59	97.24	96.93	95.87	95.32
10000	124.07	117.46	114.50	109.97	108.43	108.04	107.70	106.53	105.91
15000	186.11	176.19	171.75	164.96	162.65	162.06	161.55	159.79	158.86
20000	248.14	234.92	229.00	219.94	216.86	216.08	215.40	213.05	211.82
25000	310.17	293.65	286.25	274.93	271.08	270.10	269.25	266.31	264.77
30000	372.21	352.38	343.49	329.91	325.29	324.12	323.09	319.57	317.72
35000	434.24	411.11	400.74	384.90	379.51	378.14	376.94	372.83	370.67
36000	446.65	422.85	412.19	395.89	390.35	388.94	387.71	383.48	381.26
37000	459.05	434.60	423.64	406.89	401.19	399.75	398.48	394.14	391.85
38000	471.46	446.34	435.09	417.89	412.03	410.55	409.25	404.79	402.44
39000	483.87	458.09	446.54	428.89	422.88	421.36	420.02	415.44	413.04
40000	496.27	469.83	457.99	439.88	433.72	432.16	430.79	426.09	423.63
41000	508.68	481.58	469.44	450.88	444.56	442.96	441.56	436.74	434.22
42000	521.09	493.33	480.89	461.88	455.41	453.77	452.33	447.40	444.81
43000	533.49	505.07	492.34	472.87	466.25	464.57	463.10	458.05	455.40
44000	545.90	516.82	503.79	483.87	477.09	475.37	473.87	468.70	465.99
45000	558.31	528.56	515.24	494.87	487.94	486.18	484.64	479.35	476.58
46000	570.71	540.31	526.69	505.86	498.78	496.98	495.41	490.01	487.17
47000	583.12	552.05	538.14	516.86	509.62	507.79	506.18	500.66	497.76
48000	595.53	563.80	549.59	527.86	520.46	518.59	516.95	511.31	508.35
49000	607.93	575.55	561.04	538.85	531.31	529.39	527.72	521.96	518.94
50000	620.34	587.29	572.49	549.85	542.15	540.20	538.49	532.61	529.53
51000	632.75	599.04	583.94	560.85	552.99	551.00	549.26	543.27	540.12
52000	645.15	610.78	595.39	571.85	563.84	561.81	560.03	553.92	550.71
53000	657.56	622.53	606.84	582.84	574.68	572.61	570.80	564.57	561.30
54000	669.97	634.27	618.29	593.84	585.52	583.41	581.57	575.22	571.89
55000	682.37	646.02	629.74	604.84	596.36	594.22	592.34	585.87	582.48
56000	694.78	657.77	641.19	615.83	607.21	605.02	603.11	596.53	593.07
57000	707.19	669.51	652.63	626.83	618.05	615.82	613.88	607.18	603.66
58000	719.59	681.26	664.08	637.83	628.89	626.63	624.65	617.83	614.26
59000	732.00	693.00	675.53	648.82	639.74	637.43	635.42	628.48	624.85
60000	744.41	704.75	686.98	659.82	650.58	648.24	646.18	639.14	635.44
61000	756.81	716.49	698.43	670.82	661.42	659.04	656.95	649.79	646.03
62000	769.22	728.24	709.88	681.81	672.26	669.84	667.72	660.44	656.62
63000	781.63	739.99	721.33	692.81	683.11	680.65	678.49	671.09	667.21
64000	794.03	751.73	732.78	703.81	693.95	691.45	689.26	681.74	677.80
65000	806.44	763.48	744.23	714.81	704.79	702.26	700.03	692.40	688.39
66000	818.85	775.22	755.68	725.80	715.64	713.06	710.80	703.05	698.98
67000	831.25	786.97	767.13	736.80	726.48	723.86	721.57	713.70	709.57
68000	843.66	798.72	778.58	747.80	737.32	734.67	732.34	724.35	720.16
69000	856.07	810.46	790.03	758.79	748.16	745.47	743.11	735.01	730.75
70000	868.47	822.21	801.48	769.79	759.01	756.28	753.88	745.66	741.34
75000	930.51	880.94	858.73	824.77	813.22	810.29	807.73	798.92	794.29
80000	992.54	939.66	915.98	879.76	867.44	864.31	861.58	852.18	847.25
100000	1240.67	1174.58	1144.97	1099.70	1084.29	1080.39	1076.97	1065.22	1059.06

12¾% MONTHLY PAYMENT

NECESSARY TO AMORTIZE A LOAN

TERM / AMOUNT	1 YEAR	2 YEARS	3 YEARS	4 YEARS	5 YEARS	7 YEARS	8 YEARS	10 YEARS	12 YEARS
$ 25	2.24	1.19	.84	.67	.57	.46	.42	.37	.34
50	4.47	2.38	1.68	1.34	1.14	.91	.84	.74	.68
75	6.70	3.56	2.52	2.01	1.70	1.36	1.26	1.11	1.02
100	8.93	4.75	3.36	2.68	2.27	1.81	1.67	1.48	1.36
200	17.85	9.49	6.72	5.35	4.53	3.62	3.34	2.96	2.72
300	26.77	14.23	10.08	8.02	6.79	5.42	5.01	4.44	4.08
400	35.69	18.97	13.43	10.69	9.06	7.23	6.67	5.92	5.44
500	44.61	23.72	16.79	13.36	11.32	9.03	8.34	7.40	6.80
600	53.53	28.46	20.15	16.03	13.58	10.84	10.01	8.88	8.16
700	62.45	33.20	23.51	18.70	15.84	12.64	11.67	10.35	9.52
800	71.37	37.94	26.86	21.37	18.11	14.45	13.34	11.83	10.88
900	80.29	42.69	30.22	24.04	20.37	16.26	15.01	13.31	12.24
1000	89.21	47.43	33.58	26.71	22.63	18.06	16.67	14.79	13.60
2000	178.41	94.85	67.15	53.41	45.26	36.12	33.34	29.57	27.19
3000	267.61	142.28	100.73	80.12	67.88	54.17	50.01	44.36	40.78
4000	356.81	189.70	134.30	106.82	90.51	72.23	66.68	59.14	54.37
5000	446.01	237.13	167.87	133.52	113.13	90.29	83.34	73.92	67.97
6000	535.21	284.55	201.45	160.23	135.76	108.34	100.01	88.71	81.56
7000	624.41	331.98	235.02	186.93	158.38	126.40	116.68	103.49	95.15
8000	713.61	379.40	268.59	213.63	181.01	144.46	133.35	118.28	108.74
9000	802.81	426.83	302.17	240.34	203.63	162.51	150.01	133.06	122.33
10000	892.01	474.25	335.74	267.04	226.26	180.57	166.68	147.84	135.93
15000	1338.01	711.37	503.61	400.56	339.38	270.85	250.02	221.76	203.89
20000	1784.01	948.49	671.48	534.08	452.51	361.13	333.36	295.68	271.85
25000	2230.01	1185.62	839.35	667.59	565.64	451.41	416.70	369.60	339.81
30000	2676.01	1422.74	1007.21	801.11	678.76	541.69	500.04	443.52	407.77
35000	3122.01	1659.86	1175.08	934.63	791.89	631.98	583.38	517.44	475.73
36000	3211.21	1707.29	1208.66	961.33	814.52	650.03	600.04	532.23	489.32
37000	3300.41	1754.71	1242.23	988.04	837.14	668.09	616.71	547.01	502.91
38000	3389.61	1802.14	1275.80	1014.74	859.77	686.15	633.38	561.80	516.50
39000	3478.81	1849.56	1309.38	1041.44	882.39	704.20	650.05	576.58	530.09
40000	3568.01	1896.98	1342.95	1068.15	905.02	722.26	666.71	591.36	543.69
41000	3657.21	1944.41	1376.53	1094.85	927.64	740.31	683.38	606.15	557.28
42000	3746.41	1991.83	1410.10	1121.56	950.27	758.37	700.05	620.93	570.87
43000	3835.61	2039.26	1443.67	1148.26	972.89	776.43	716.72	635.72	584.46
44000	3924.81	2086.68	1477.25	1174.96	995.52	794.48	733.38	650.50	598.05
45000	4014.01	2134.11	1510.82	1201.67	1018.14	812.54	750.05	665.28	611.65
46000	4103.21	2181.53	1544.39	1228.37	1040.77	830.60	766.72	680.07	625.24
47000	4192.41	2228.96	1577.97	1255.07	1063.39	848.65	783.39	694.85	638.83
48000	4281.61	2276.38	1611.54	1281.78	1086.02	866.71	800.06	709.64	652.42
49000	4370.81	2323.80	1645.11	1308.48	1108.64	884.76	816.72	724.42	666.01
50000	4460.01	2371.23	1678.69	1335.18	1131.27	902.82	833.39	739.20	679.61
51000	4549.21	2418.65	1712.26	1361.89	1153.90	920.88	850.06	753.99	693.20
52000	4638.41	2466.08	1745.84	1388.59	1176.52	938.93	866.73	768.77	706.79
53000	4727.61	2513.50	1779.41	1415.29	1199.15	956.99	883.39	783.56	720.38
54000	4816.81	2560.93	1812.98	1442.00	1221.77	975.05	900.06	798.34	733.97
55000	4906.01	2608.35	1846.56	1468.70	1244.40	993.10	916.73	813.12	747.57
56000	4995.21	2655.78	1880.13	1495.41	1267.02	1011.16	933.40	827.91	761.16
57000	5084.41	2703.20	1913.70	1522.11	1289.65	1029.22	950.07	842.69	774.75
58000	5173.61	2750.62	1947.28	1548.81	1312.27	1047.27	966.73	857.48	788.34
59000	5262.81	2798.05	1980.85	1575.52	1334.90	1065.33	983.40	872.26	801.93
60000	5352.01	2845.47	2014.42	1602.22	1357.52	1083.38	1000.07	887.04	815.53
61000	5441.21	2892.90	2048.00	1628.92	1380.15	1101.44	1016.74	901.83	829.12
62000	5530.41	2940.32	2081.57	1655.63	1402.77	1119.50	1033.40	916.61	842.71
63000	5619.61	2987.75	2115.15	1682.33	1425.40	1137.55	1050.07	931.40	856.30
64000	5708.81	3035.17	2148.72	1709.03	1448.02	1155.61	1066.74	946.18	869.89
65000	5798.01	3082.60	2182.29	1735.74	1470.65	1173.67	1083.41	960.96	883.49
66000	5887.21	3130.02	2215.87	1762.44	1493.27	1191.72	1100.07	975.75	897.08
67000	5976.41	3177.45	2249.44	1789.14	1515.90	1209.78	1116.74	990.53	910.67
68000	6065.61	3224.87	2283.01	1815.85	1538.53	1227.84	1133.41	1005.32	924.26
69000	6154.81	3272.29	2316.59	1842.55	1561.15	1245.89	1150.08	1020.10	937.85
70000	6244.01	3319.72	2350.16	1869.26	1583.78	1263.95	1166.75	1034.88	951.45
75000	6690.01	3556.84	2518.03	2002.77	1696.90	1354.23	1250.08	1108.80	1019.41
80000	7136.01	3793.96	2685.90	2136.29	1810.03	1444.51	1333.42	1182.72	1087.37
100000	8920.01	4742.45	3357.37	2670.36	2262.54	1805.64	1666.78	1478.40	1359.21

MONTHLY PAYMENT 12¾%

NECESSARY TO AMORTIZE A LOAN

TERM / AMOUNT	15 YEARS	18 YEARS	20 YEARS	25 YEARS	28 YEARS	29 YEARS	30 YEARS	35 YEARS	40 YEARS
$ 25	.32	.30	.29	.28	.28	.28	.28	.27	.27
50	.63	.60	.58	.56	.55	.55	.55	.54	.54
75	.94	.89	.87	.84	.83	.82	.82	.81	.81
100	1.25	1.19	1.16	1.11	1.10	1.10	1.09	1.08	1.07
200	2.50	2.37	2.31	2.22	2.19	2.19	2.18	2.16	2.14
300	3.75	3.55	3.47	3.33	3.29	3.28	3.27	3.23	3.21
400	5.00	4.74	4.62	4.44	4.38	4.37	4.35	4.31	4.28
500	6.25	5.92	5.77	5.55	5.47	5.46	5.44	5.38	5.35
600	7.50	7.10	6.93	6.66	6.57	6.55	6.53	6.46	6.42
700	8.75	8.29	8.08	7.77	7.66	7.64	7.61	7.53	7.49
800	10.00	9.47	9.24	8.88	8.76	8.73	8.70	8.61	8.56
900	11.24	10.65	10.39	9.99	9.85	9.82	9.79	9.68	9.63
1000	12.49	11.84	11.54	11.10	10.94	10.91	10.87	10.76	10.70
2000	24.98	23.67	23.08	22.19	21.88	21.81	21.74	21.51	21.39
3000	37.47	35.50	34.62	33.28	32.82	32.71	32.61	32.26	32.08
4000	49.96	47.33	46.16	44.37	43.76	43.61	43.47	43.01	42.77
5000	62.45	59.16	57.70	55.46	54.70	54.51	54.34	53.76	53.46
6000	74.94	71.00	69.23	66.55	65.64	65.41	65.21	64.52	64.16
7000	87.42	82.83	80.77	77.64	76.58	76.31	76.07	75.27	74.85
8000	99.91	94.66	92.31	88.73	87.52	87.21	86.94	86.02	85.54
9000	112.40	106.49	103.85	99.82	98.45	98.11	97.81	96.77	96.23
10000	124.89	118.32	115.39	110.91	109.39	109.01	108.67	107.52	106.92
15000	187.33	177.48	173.08	166.36	164.09	163.51	163.01	161.28	160.38
20000	249.77	236.64	230.77	221.82	218.78	218.01	217.34	215.04	213.84
25000	312.21	295.80	288.46	277.27	273.48	272.52	271.68	268.80	267.30
30000	374.66	354.96	346.15	332.72	328.17	327.02	326.01	322.56	320.76
35000	437.10	414.11	403.84	388.17	382.86	381.52	380.35	376.32	374.22
36000	449.59	425.95	415.38	399.26	393.80	392.42	391.21	387.08	384.92
37000	462.07	437.78	426.92	410.35	404.74	403.32	402.08	397.83	395.61
38000	474.56	449.61	438.45	421.44	415.68	414.22	412.95	408.58	406.30
39000	487.05	461.44	449.99	432.54	426.62	425.12	423.82	419.33	416.99
40000	499.54	473.27	461.53	443.63	437.56	436.02	434.68	430.08	427.68
41000	512.03	485.10	473.07	454.72	448.50	446.93	445.55	440.84	438.38
42000	524.52	496.94	484.61	465.81	459.44	457.83	456.42	451.59	449.07
43000	537.00	508.77	496.14	476.90	470.38	468.73	467.28	462.34	459.76
44000	549.49	520.60	507.68	487.99	481.31	479.63	478.15	473.09	470.45
45000	561.98	532.43	519.22	499.08	492.25	490.53	489.02	483.84	481.14
46000	574.47	544.26	530.76	510.17	503.19	501.43	499.88	494.60	491.84
47000	586.96	556.09	542.30	521.26	514.13	512.33	510.75	505.35	502.53
48000	599.45	567.93	553.83	532.35	525.07	523.23	521.62	516.10	513.22
49000	611.94	579.76	565.37	543.44	536.01	534.13	532.48	526.85	523.91
50000	624.42	591.59	576.91	554.53	546.95	545.03	543.35	537.60	534.60
51000	636.91	603.42	588.45	565.62	557.89	555.93	554.22	548.36	545.30
52000	649.40	615.25	599.99	576.71	568.83	566.83	565.09	559.11	555.99
53000	661.89	627.09	611.53	587.80	579.76	577.73	575.95	569.86	566.68
54000	674.38	638.92	623.06	598.89	590.70	588.63	586.82	580.61	577.37
55000	686.87	650.75	634.60	609.98	601.64	599.53	597.69	591.36	588.06
56000	699.35	662.58	646.14	621.07	612.58	610.43	608.55	602.11	598.75
57000	711.84	674.41	657.68	632.16	623.52	621.33	619.42	612.87	609.45
58000	724.33	686.24	669.22	643.26	634.46	632.23	630.29	623.62	620.14
59000	736.82	698.08	680.75	654.35	645.40	643.13	641.15	634.37	630.83
60000	749.31	709.91	692.29	665.44	656.34	654.03	652.02	645.12	641.52
61000	761.80	721.74	703.83	676.53	667.27	664.94	662.89	655.87	652.21
62000	774.28	733.57	715.37	687.62	678.21	675.84	673.75	666.63	662.91
63000	786.77	745.40	726.91	698.71	689.15	686.74	684.62	677.38	673.60
64000	799.26	757.23	738.44	709.80	700.09	697.64	695.49	688.13	684.29
65000	811.75	769.07	749.98	720.89	711.03	708.54	706.36	698.88	694.98
66000	824.24	780.90	761.52	731.98	721.97	719.44	717.22	709.63	705.67
67000	836.73	792.73	773.06	743.07	732.91	730.34	728.09	720.39	716.37
68000	849.21	804.56	784.60	754.16	743.85	741.24	738.96	731.14	727.06
69000	861.70	816.39	796.14	765.25	754.79	752.14	749.82	741.89	737.75
70000	874.19	828.22	807.67	776.34	765.72	763.04	760.69	752.64	748.44
75000	936.63	887.38	865.36	831.79	820.42	817.54	815.02	806.40	801.90
80000	999.07	946.54	923.05	887.25	875.11	872.04	869.36	860.16	855.36
100000	1248.84	1183.17	1153.82	1109.06	1093.89	1090.05	1086.70	1075.20	1069.20

12⅞% MONTHLY PAYMENT
NECESSARY TO AMORTIZE A LOAN

TERM / AMOUNT	1 YEAR	2 YEARS	3 YEARS	4 YEARS	5 YEARS	7 YEARS	8 YEARS	10 YEARS	12 YEARS
$ 25	2.24	1.19	.85	.67	.57	.46	.42	.38	.35
50	4.47	2.38	1.69	1.34	1.14	.91	.84	.75	.69
75	6.70	3.57	2.53	2.01	1.71	1.36	1.26	1.12	1.03
100	8.93	4.75	3.37	2.68	2.27	1.82	1.68	1.49	1.37
200	17.86	9.50	6.73	5.36	4.54	3.63	3.35	2.98	2.74
300	26.78	14.25	10.10	8.03	6.81	5.44	5.03	4.46	4.11
400	35.71	19.00	13.46	10.71	9.08	7.25	6.70	5.95	5.47
500	44.63	23.75	16.82	13.39	11.35	9.07	8.37	7.43	6.84
600	53.56	28.49	20.19	16.06	13.62	10.88	10.05	8.92	8.21
700	62.49	33.24	23.55	18.74	15.89	12.69	11.72	10.41	9.57
800	71.41	37.99	26.91	21.42	18.16	14.50	13.39	11.89	10.94
900	80.34	42.74	30.28	24.09	20.43	16.32	15.07	13.38	12.31
1000	89.26	47.49	33.64	26.77	22.69	18.13	16.74	14.86	13.67
2000	178.52	94.97	67.27	53.54	45.38	36.25	33.48	29.72	27.34
3000	267.78	142.45	100.91	80.30	68.07	54.38	50.22	44.58	41.01
4000	357.04	189.94	134.54	107.07	90.76	72.50	66.95	59.43	54.68
5000	446.30	237.42	168.17	133.83	113.45	90.63	83.69	74.29	68.35
6000	535.56	284.90	201.81	160.60	136.14	108.75	100.43	89.15	82.02
7000	624.82	332.39	235.44	187.36	158.83	126.87	117.17	104.01	95.69
8000	714.07	379.87	269.08	214.13	181.52	145.00	133.90	118.86	109.36
9000	803.33	427.35	302.71	240.89	204.21	163.12	150.64	133.72	123.03
10000	892.59	474.84	336.34	267.66	226.90	181.25	167.38	148.58	136.70
15000	1338.88	712.25	504.51	401.49	340.34	271.87	251.07	222.87	205.04
20000	1785.18	949.67	672.68	535.31	453.79	362.49	334.75	297.15	273.39
25000	2231.47	1187.08	840.85	669.14	567.23	453.11	418.44	371.44	341.73
30000	2677.76	1424.50	1009.02	802.97	680.68	543.73	502.13	445.73	410.08
35000	3124.06	1661.91	1177.19	936.80	794.12	634.35	585.81	520.02	478.42
36000	3213.32	1709.40	1210.82	963.56	816.81	652.47	602.55	534.87	492.09
37000	3302.57	1756.88	1244.45	990.33	839.50	670.60	619.29	549.73	505.76
38000	3391.83	1804.36	1278.09	1017.09	862.19	688.72	636.03	564.59	519.43
39000	3481.09	1851.85	1311.72	1043.86	884.88	706.84	652.76	579.45	533.10
40000	3570.35	1899.33	1345.36	1070.62	907.57	724.97	669.50	594.30	546.77
41000	3659.61	1946.81	1378.99	1097.39	930.26	743.09	686.24	609.16	560.44
42000	3748.87	1994.30	1412.62	1124.16	952.95	761.22	702.98	624.02	574.10
43000	3838.13	2041.78	1446.26	1150.92	975.64	779.34	719.71	638.87	587.77
44000	3927.39	2089.26	1479.89	1177.69	998.33	797.46	736.45	653.73	601.44
45000	4016.64	2136.75	1513.52	1204.45	1021.02	815.59	753.19	668.59	615.11
46000	4105.90	2184.23	1547.16	1231.22	1043.71	833.71	769.93	683.45	628.78
47000	4195.16	2231.71	1580.79	1257.98	1066.39	851.84	786.66	698.30	642.45
48000	4284.42	2279.20	1614.43	1284.75	1089.08	869.96	803.40	713.16	656.12
49000	4373.68	2326.68	1648.06	1311.51	1111.77	888.08	820.14	728.02	669.79
50000	4462.94	2374.16	1681.69	1338.28	1134.46	906.21	836.88	742.88	683.46
51000	4552.20	2421.64	1715.33	1365.05	1157.15	924.33	853.61	757.73	697.13
52000	4641.45	2469.13	1748.96	1391.81	1179.84	942.46	870.35	772.59	710.79
53000	4730.71	2516.61	1782.60	1418.58	1202.53	960.58	887.09	787.45	724.46
54000	4819.97	2564.09	1816.23	1445.34	1225.22	978.71	903.83	802.31	738.13
55000	4909.23	2611.58	1849.86	1472.11	1247.91	996.83	920.56	817.16	751.80
56000	4998.49	2659.06	1883.50	1498.87	1270.60	1014.95	937.30	832.02	765.47
57000	5087.75	2706.54	1917.13	1525.64	1293.29	1033.08	954.04	846.88	779.14
58000	5177.01	2754.03	1950.76	1552.40	1315.97	1051.20	970.77	861.74	792.81
59000	5266.26	2801.51	1984.40	1579.17	1338.66	1069.33	987.51	876.59	806.48
60000	5355.52	2848.99	2018.03	1605.93	1361.35	1087.45	1004.25	891.45	820.15
61000	5444.78	2896.48	2051.67	1632.70	1384.04	1105.57	1020.99	906.31	833.82
62000	5534.04	2943.96	2085.30	1659.47	1406.73	1123.70	1037.72	921.17	847.48
63000	5623.30	2991.44	2118.93	1686.23	1429.42	1141.82	1054.46	936.02	861.15
64000	5712.56	3038.93	2152.57	1713.00	1452.11	1159.95	1071.20	950.88	874.82
65000	5801.82	3086.41	2186.20	1739.76	1474.80	1178.07	1087.94	965.74	888.49
66000	5891.08	3133.89	2219.83	1766.53	1497.49	1196.19	1104.67	980.60	902.16
67000	5980.33	3181.37	2253.47	1793.29	1520.18	1214.32	1121.41	995.45	915.83
68000	6069.59	3228.86	2287.10	1820.06	1542.87	1232.44	1138.15	1010.31	929.50
69000	6158.85	3276.34	2320.74	1846.82	1565.56	1250.57	1154.89	1025.17	943.17
70000	6248.11	3323.82	2354.37	1873.59	1588.24	1268.69	1171.62	1040.03	956.84
75000	6694.40	3561.24	2522.54	2007.42	1701.69	1359.31	1255.31	1114.31	1025.18
80000	7140.70	3798.66	2690.71	2141.24	1815.14	1449.93	1339.00	1188.60	1093.53
100000	8925.87	4748.32	3363.38	2676.55	2268.92	1812.41	1673.75	1485.75	1366.91

MONTHLY PAYMENT 12⅞%
NECESSARY TO AMORTIZE A LOAN

TERM / AMOUNT	15 YEARS	18 YEARS	20 YEARS	25 YEARS	28 YEARS	29 YEARS	30 YEARS	35 YEARS	40 YEARS
$ 25	.32	.30	.30	.28	.28	.28	.28	.28	.27
50	.63	.60	.59	.56	.56	.55	.55	.55	.54
75	.95	.90	.88	.84	.83	.83	.83	.82	.81
100	1.26	1.20	1.17	1.12	1.11	1.10	1.10	1.09	1.08
200	2.52	2.39	2.33	2.24	2.21	2.20	2.20	2.18	2.16
300	3.78	3.58	3.49	3.36	3.32	3.30	3.29	3.26	3.24
400	5.03	4.77	4.66	4.48	4.42	4.40	4.39	4.35	4.32
500	6.29	5.96	5.82	5.60	5.52	5.50	5.49	5.43	5.40
600	7.55	7.16	6.98	6.72	6.63	6.60	6.58	6.52	6.48
700	8.80	8.35	8.14	7.83	7.73	7.70	7.68	7.60	7.56
800	10.06	9.54	9.31	8.95	8.83	8.80	8.78	8.69	8.64
900	11.32	10.73	10.47	10.07	9.94	9.90	9.87	9.77	9.72
1000	12.58	11.92	11.63	11.19	11.04	11.00	10.97	10.86	10.80
2000	25.15	23.84	23.26	22.37	22.07	22.00	21.93	21.71	21.59
3000	37.72	35.76	34.89	33.56	33.11	33.00	32.90	32.56	32.39
4000	50.29	47.68	46.51	44.74	44.14	43.99	43.86	43.41	43.18
5000	62.86	59.59	58.14	55.93	55.18	54.99	54.83	54.26	53.97
6000	75.43	71.51	69.77	67.11	66.21	65.99	65.79	65.12	64.77
7000	88.00	83.43	81.39	78.30	77.25	76.99	76.76	75.97	75.56
8000	100.57	95.35	93.02	89.48	88.28	87.98	87.72	86.82	86.35
9000	113.14	107.27	104.65	100.66	99.32	98.98	98.68	97.67	97.15
10000	125.71	119.18	116.27	111.85	110.35	109.98	109.65	108.52	107.94
15000	188.56	178.77	174.41	167.77	165.53	164.96	164.47	162.78	161.91
20000	251.41	238.36	232.54	223.69	220.70	219.95	219.29	217.04	215.88
25000	314.26	297.95	290.68	279.61	275.88	274.94	274.11	271.30	269.84
30000	377.11	357.54	348.81	335.54	331.05	329.92	328.94	325.56	323.81
35000	439.96	417.13	406.94	391.46	386.23	384.91	383.76	379.82	377.78
36000	452.54	429.05	418.57	402.64	397.26	395.91	394.72	390.67	388.57
37000	465.11	440.97	430.20	413.83	408.30	406.91	405.69	401.52	399.36
38000	477.68	452.89	441.82	425.01	419.33	417.90	416.65	412.38	410.16
39000	490.25	464.80	453.45	436.19	430.37	428.90	427.62	423.23	420.95
40000	502.82	476.72	465.08	447.38	441.40	439.90	438.58	434.08	431.75
41000	515.39	488.64	476.70	458.56	452.44	450.89	449.54	444.93	442.54
42000	527.96	500.56	488.33	469.75	463.47	461.89	460.51	455.78	453.33
43000	540.53	512.47	499.96	480.93	474.51	472.89	471.47	466.64	464.13
44000	553.10	524.39	511.59	492.12	485.54	483.89	482.44	477.49	474.92
45000	565.67	536.31	523.21	503.30	496.58	494.88	493.40	488.34	485.71
46000	578.24	548.23	534.84	514.48	507.61	505.88	504.37	499.19	496.51
47000	590.81	560.15	546.47	525.67	518.65	516.88	515.33	510.04	507.30
48000	603.38	572.06	558.09	536.85	529.68	527.88	526.30	520.90	518.09
49000	615.95	583.98	569.72	548.04	540.72	538.87	537.26	531.75	528.89
50000	628.52	595.90	581.35	559.22	551.75	549.87	548.22	542.60	539.68
51000	641.09	607.82	592.97	570.41	562.79	560.87	559.19	553.45	550.47
52000	653.66	619.74	604.60	581.59	573.82	571.87	570.15	564.30	561.27
53000	666.23	631.65	616.23	592.77	584.86	582.86	581.12	575.15	572.06
54000	678.80	643.57	627.85	603.96	595.89	593.86	592.08	586.01	582.85
55000	691.37	655.49	639.48	615.14	606.93	604.86	603.05	596.86	593.65
56000	703.94	667.41	651.11	626.33	617.96	615.85	614.01	607.71	604.44
57000	716.51	679.33	662.73	637.51	629.00	626.85	624.97	618.56	615.23
58000	729.08	691.24	674.36	648.70	640.03	637.85	635.94	629.41	626.03
59000	741.65	703.16	685.99	659.88	651.07	648.85	646.90	640.27	636.82
60000	754.22	715.08	697.61	671.07	662.10	659.84	657.87	651.12	647.62
61000	766.79	727.00	709.24	682.25	673.14	670.84	668.83	661.97	658.41
62000	779.36	738.91	720.87	693.43	684.17	681.84	679.80	672.82	669.20
63000	791.93	750.83	732.49	704.62	695.21	692.84	690.76	683.67	680.00
64000	804.50	762.75	744.12	715.80	706.24	703.83	701.73	694.53	690.79
65000	817.07	774.67	755.75	726.99	717.28	714.83	712.69	705.38	701.58
66000	829.64	786.59	767.38	738.17	728.31	725.83	723.65	716.23	712.38
67000	842.21	798.50	779.00	749.36	739.35	736.83	734.62	727.08	723.17
68000	854.78	810.42	790.63	760.54	750.38	747.82	745.58	737.93	733.96
69000	867.35	822.34	802.26	771.72	761.42	758.82	756.55	748.78	744.76
70000	879.92	834.26	813.88	782.91	772.45	769.82	767.51	759.64	755.55
75000	942.78	893.85	872.02	838.83	827.63	824.80	822.33	813.90	809.52
80000	1005.63	953.44	930.15	894.75	882.80	879.79	877.16	868.16	863.49
100000	1257.03	1191.79	1162.69	1118.44	1103.50	1099.74	1096.44	1085.19	1079.36

13% MONTHLY PAYMENT

NECESSARY TO AMORTIZE A LOAN

TERM / AMOUNT	1 YEAR	2 YEARS	3 YEARS	4 YEARS	5 YEARS	7 YEARS	8 YEARS	10 YEARS	12 YEARS
$ 25	2.24	1.19	.85	.68	.57	.46	.43	.38	.35
50	4.47	2.38	1.69	1.35	1.14	.91	.85	.75	.69
75	6.70	3.57	2.53	2.02	1.71	1.37	1.27	1.12	1.04
100	8.94	4.76	3.37	2.69	2.28	1.82	1.69	1.50	1.38
200	17.87	9.51	6.74	5.37	4.56	3.64	3.37	2.99	2.75
300	26.80	14.27	10.11	8.05	6.83	5.46	5.05	4.48	4.13
400	35.73	19.02	13.48	10.74	9.11	7.28	6.73	5.98	5.50
500	44.66	23.78	16.85	13.42	11.38	9.10	8.41	7.47	6.88
600	53.60	28.53	20.22	16.10	13.66	10.92	10.09	8.96	8.25
700	62.53	33.28	23.59	18.78	15.93	12.74	11.77	10.46	9.63
800	71.46	38.04	26.96	21.47	18.21	14.56	13.45	11.95	11.00
900	80.39	42.79	30.33	24.15	20.48	16.38	15.13	13.44	12.38
1000	89.32	47.55	33.70	26.83	22.76	18.20	16.81	14.94	13.75
2000	178.64	95.09	67.39	53.66	45.51	36.39	33.62	29.87	27.50
3000	267.96	142.63	101.09	80.49	68.26	54.58	50.43	44.80	41.24
4000	357.27	190.17	134.78	107.31	91.02	72.77	67.23	59.73	54.99
5000	446.59	237.71	168.47	134.14	113.77	90.96	84.04	74.66	68.74
6000	535.91	285.26	202.17	160.97	136.52	109.16	100.85	89.59	82.48
7000	625.23	332.80	235.86	187.80	159.28	127.35	117.66	104.52	96.23
8000	714.54	380.34	269.56	214.62	182.03	145.54	134.46	119.45	109.98
9000	803.86	427.88	303.25	241.45	204.78	163.73	151.27	134.38	123.72
10000	893.18	475.42	336.94	268.28	227.54	181.92	168.08	149.32	137.47
15000	1339.76	713.13	505.41	402.42	341.30	272.88	252.11	223.97	206.20
20000	1786.35	950.84	673.88	536.55	455.07	363.84	336.15	298.63	274.93
25000	2232.94	1188.55	842.35	670.69	568.83	454.80	420.19	373.28	343.66
30000	2679.52	1426.26	1010.82	804.83	682.60	545.76	504.22	447.94	412.39
35000	3126.11	1663.97	1179.29	938.97	796.36	636.72	588.26	522.59	481.12
36000	3215.43	1711.51	1212.99	965.79	819.12	654.92	605.07	537.52	494.87
37000	3304.74	1759.05	1246.68	992.62	841.87	673.11	621.87	552.45	508.62
38000	3394.06	1806.59	1280.38	1019.45	864.62	691.30	638.68	567.39	522.36
39000	3483.38	1854.14	1314.07	1046.28	887.37	709.49	655.49	582.32	536.11
40000	3572.70	1901.68	1347.76	1073.10	910.13	727.68	672.30	597.25	549.86
41000	3662.01	1949.22	1381.46	1099.93	932.88	745.88	689.10	612.18	563.60
42000	3751.33	1996.76	1415.15	1126.76	955.63	764.07	705.91	627.11	577.35
43000	3840.65	2044.30	1448.84	1153.59	978.39	782.26	722.72	642.04	591.09
44000	3929.97	2091.85	1482.54	1180.41	1001.14	800.45	739.52	656.97	604.84
45000	4019.28	2139.39	1516.23	1207.24	1023.89	818.64	756.33	671.90	618.59
46000	4108.60	2186.93	1549.93	1234.07	1046.65	836.84	773.14	686.83	632.33
47000	4197.92	2234.47	1583.62	1260.90	1069.40	855.03	789.95	701.77	646.08
48000	4287.23	2282.01	1617.31	1287.72	1092.15	873.22	806.75	716.70	659.83
49000	4376.55	2329.55	1651.01	1314.55	1114.91	891.41	823.56	731.63	673.57
50000	4465.87	2377.10	1684.70	1341.38	1137.66	909.60	840.37	746.56	687.32
51000	4555.19	2424.64	1718.40	1368.21	1160.41	927.80	857.18	761.49	701.06
52000	4644.50	2472.18	1752.09	1395.03	1183.16	945.99	873.98	776.42	714.81
53000	4733.82	2519.72	1785.78	1421.86	1205.92	964.18	890.79	791.35	728.56
54000	4823.14	2567.26	1819.48	1448.69	1228.67	982.37	907.60	806.28	742.30
55000	4912.46	2614.81	1853.17	1475.52	1251.42	1000.56	924.40	821.21	756.05
56000	5001.77	2662.35	1886.87	1502.34	1274.18	1018.75	941.21	836.15	769.80
57000	5091.09	2709.89	1920.56	1529.17	1296.93	1036.95	958.02	851.08	783.54
58000	5180.41	2757.43	1954.25	1556.00	1319.68	1055.14	974.83	866.01	797.29
59000	5269.72	2804.97	1987.95	1582.83	1342.44	1073.33	991.63	880.94	811.03
60000	5359.04	2852.51	2021.64	1609.65	1365.19	1091.52	1008.44	895.87	824.78
61000	5448.36	2900.06	2055.34	1636.48	1387.94	1109.71	1025.25	910.80	838.53
62000	5537.68	2947.60	2089.03	1663.31	1410.70	1127.91	1042.05	925.73	852.27
63000	5626.99	2995.14	2122.72	1690.14	1433.45	1146.10	1058.86	940.66	866.02
64000	5716.31	3042.68	2156.42	1716.96	1456.20	1164.29	1075.67	955.59	879.77
65000	5805.63	3090.22	2190.11	1743.79	1478.95	1182.48	1092.48	970.52	893.51
66000	5894.95	3137.77	2223.81	1770.62	1501.71	1200.67	1109.28	985.46	907.26
67000	5984.26	3185.31	2257.50	1797.45	1524.46	1218.87	1126.09	1000.39	921.00
68000	6073.58	3232.85	2291.19	1824.27	1547.21	1237.06	1142.90	1015.32	934.75
69000	6162.90	3280.39	2324.89	1851.10	1569.97	1255.25	1159.71	1030.25	948.50
70000	6252.21	3327.93	2358.58	1877.93	1592.72	1273.44	1176.51	1045.18	962.24
75000	6698.80	3565.64	2527.05	2012.07	1706.49	1364.40	1260.55	1119.84	1030.97
80000	7145.39	3803.35	2695.52	2146.20	1820.25	1455.36	1344.59	1194.49	1099.71
100000	8931.73	4754.19	3369.40	2682.75	2275.31	1819.20	1680.73	1493.11	1374.63

MONTHLY PAYMENT 13%

NECESSARY TO AMORTIZE A LOAN

TERM / AMOUNT	15 YEARS	18 YEARS	20 YEARS	25 YEARS	28 YEARS	29 YEARS	30 YEARS	35 YEARS	40 YEARS
$ 25	.32	.31	.30	.29	.28	.28	.28	.28	.28
50	.64	.61	.59	.57	.56	.56	.56	.55	.55
75	.95	.91	.88	.85	.84	.84	.83	.83	.82
100	1.27	1.21	1.18	1.13	1.12	1.11	1.11	1.10	1.09
200	2.54	2.41	2.35	2.26	2.23	2.22	2.22	2.20	2.18
300	3.80	3.61	3.52	3.39	3.34	3.33	3.32	3.29	3.27
400	5.07	4.81	4.69	4.52	4.46	4.44	4.43	4.39	4.36
500	6.33	6.01	5.86	5.64	5.57	5.55	5.54	5.48	5.45
600	7.60	7.21	7.03	6.77	6.68	6.66	6.64	6.58	6.54
700	8.86	8.41	8.21	7.90	7.80	7.77	7.75	7.67	7.63
800	10.13	9.61	9.38	9.03	8.91	8.88	8.85	8.77	8.72
900	11.39	10.81	10.55	10.16	10.02	9.99	9.96	9.86	9.81
1000	12.66	12.01	11.72	11.28	11.14	11.10	11.07	10.96	10.90
2000	25.31	24.01	23.44	22.56	22.27	22.19	22.13	21.91	21.80
3000	37.96	36.02	35.15	33.84	33.40	33.29	33.19	32.86	32.69
4000	50.61	48.02	46.87	45.12	44.53	44.38	44.25	43.81	43.59
5000	63.27	60.03	58.58	56.40	55.66	55.48	55.31	54.76	54.48
6000	75.92	72.03	70.30	67.68	66.79	66.57	66.38	65.72	65.38
7000	88.57	84.04	82.02	78.95	77.92	77.67	77.44	76.67	76.27
8000	101.22	96.04	93.73	90.23	89.06	88.76	88.50	87.62	87.17
9000	113.88	108.04	105.45	101.51	100.19	99.85	99.56	98.57	98.06
10000	126.53	120.05	117.16	112.79	111.32	110.95	110.62	109.52	108.96
15000	189.79	180.07	175.74	169.18	166.98	166.42	165.93	164.28	163.43
20000	253.05	240.09	234.32	225.57	222.63	221.89	221.24	219.04	217.91
25000	316.32	300.11	292.90	281.96	278.29	277.36	276.55	273.80	272.38
30000	379.58	360.13	351.48	338.36	333.95	332.83	331.86	328.56	326.86
35000	442.84	420.16	410.06	394.75	389.60	388.31	387.17	383.32	381.33
36000	455.49	432.16	421.77	406.03	400.73	399.40	398.24	394.27	392.23
37000	468.14	444.17	433.49	417.30	411.86	410.49	409.30	405.23	403.13
38000	480.80	456.17	445.20	428.58	423.00	421.59	420.36	416.18	414.02
39000	493.45	468.17	456.92	439.86	434.13	432.68	431.42	427.13	424.92
40000	506.10	480.18	468.64	451.14	445.26	443.78	442.48	438.08	435.81
41000	518.75	492.18	480.35	462.42	456.39	454.87	453.55	449.03	446.71
42000	531.41	504.19	492.07	473.70	467.52	465.97	464.61	459.99	457.60
43000	544.06	516.19	503.78	484.97	478.65	477.06	475.67	470.94	468.50
44000	556.71	528.20	515.50	496.25	489.78	488.16	486.73	481.89	479.39
45000	569.36	540.20	527.21	507.53	500.92	499.25	497.79	492.84	490.29
46000	582.02	552.20	538.93	518.81	512.05	510.34	508.86	503.79	501.18
47000	594.67	564.21	550.65	530.09	523.18	521.44	519.92	514.75	512.08
48000	607.32	576.21	562.36	541.37	534.31	532.53	530.98	525.70	522.97
49000	619.97	588.22	574.08	552.64	545.44	543.63	542.04	536.65	533.87
50000	632.63	600.22	585.79	563.92	556.57	554.72	553.10	547.60	544.76
51000	645.28	612.23	597.51	575.20	567.70	565.82	564.17	558.55	555.66
52000	657.93	624.23	609.22	586.48	578.83	576.91	575.23	569.51	566.55
53000	670.58	636.23	620.94	597.76	589.97	588.00	586.29	580.46	577.45
54000	683.24	648.24	632.66	609.04	601.10	599.10	597.35	591.41	588.34
55000	695.89	660.24	644.37	620.31	612.23	610.19	608.41	602.36	599.24
56000	708.54	672.25	656.09	631.59	623.36	621.29	619.48	613.31	610.13
57000	721.19	684.25	667.80	642.87	634.49	632.38	630.54	624.27	621.03
58000	733.85	696.26	679.52	654.15	645.62	643.48	641.60	635.22	631.92
59000	746.50	708.26	691.23	665.43	656.75	654.57	652.66	646.17	642.82
60000	759.15	720.26	702.95	676.71	667.89	665.66	663.72	657.12	653.71
61000	771.80	732.27	714.67	687.98	679.02	676.76	674.79	668.07	664.61
62000	784.46	744.27	726.38	699.26	690.15	687.85	685.85	679.02	675.50
63000	797.11	756.28	738.10	710.54	701.28	698.95	696.91	689.98	686.40
64000	809.76	768.28	749.81	721.82	712.41	710.04	707.97	700.93	697.29
65000	822.41	780.29	761.53	733.10	723.54	721.14	719.03	711.88	708.19
66000	835.06	792.29	773.24	744.38	734.67	732.23	730.10	722.83	719.08
67000	847.72	804.29	784.96	755.65	745.80	743.32	741.16	733.78	729.98
68000	860.37	816.30	796.68	766.93	756.94	754.42	752.22	744.74	740.87
69000	873.02	828.30	808.39	778.21	768.07	765.51	763.28	755.69	751.77
70000	885.67	840.31	820.11	789.49	779.20	776.61	774.34	766.64	762.66
75000	948.94	900.33	878.69	845.88	834.86	832.08	829.65	821.40	817.14
80000	1012.20	960.35	937.27	902.27	890.51	887.55	884.96	876.16	871.62
100000	1265.25	1200.44	1171.58	1127.84	1113.14	1109.44	1106.20	1095.20	1089.52

13⅛% MONTHLY PAYMENT
NECESSARY TO AMORTIZE A LOAN

TERM / AMOUNT	1 YEAR	2 YEARS	3 YEARS	4 YEARS	5 YEARS	7 YEARS	8 YEARS	10 YEARS	12 YEARS
$ 25	2.24	1.20	.85	.68	.58	.46	.43	.38	.35
50	4.47	2.39	1.69	1.35	1.15	.92	.85	.76	.70
75	6.71	3.58	2.54	2.02	1.72	1.37	1.27	1.13	1.04
100	8.94	4.77	3.38	2.69	2.29	1.83	1.69	1.51	1.39
200	17.88	9.53	6.76	5.38	4.57	3.66	3.38	3.01	2.77
300	26.82	14.29	10.13	8.07	6.85	5.48	5.07	4.51	4.15
400	35.76	19.05	13.51	10.76	9.13	7.31	6.76	6.01	5.53
500	44.69	23.81	16.88	13.45	11.41	9.13	8.44	7.51	6.92
600	53.63	28.57	20.26	16.14	13.70	10.96	10.13	9.01	8.30
700	62.57	33.33	23.63	18.83	15.98	12.79	11.82	10.51	9.68
800	71.51	38.09	27.01	21.52	18.26	14.61	13.51	12.01	11.06
900	80.44	42.85	30.38	24.21	20.54	16.44	15.19	13.51	12.45
1000	89.38	47.61	33.76	26.89	22.82	18.26	16.88	15.01	13.83
2000	178.76	95.21	67.51	53.78	45.64	36.52	33.76	30.01	27.65
3000	268.13	142.81	101.27	80.67	68.46	54.78	50.64	45.02	41.48
4000	357.51	190.41	135.02	107.56	91.27	73.04	67.51	60.02	55.30
5000	446.88	238.01	168.78	134.45	114.09	91.30	84.39	75.03	69.12
6000	536.26	285.61	202.53	161.34	136.91	109.56	101.27	90.03	82.95
7000	625.64	333.21	236.28	188.23	159.72	127.82	118.15	105.04	96.77
8000	715.01	380.81	270.04	215.12	182.54	146.08	135.02	120.04	110.59
9000	804.39	428.41	303.79	242.01	205.36	164.34	151.90	135.05	124.42
10000	893.76	476.01	337.55	268.90	228.18	182.60	168.78	150.05	138.24
15000	1340.64	714.01	506.32	403.35	342.26	273.90	253.16	225.08	207.36
20000	1787.52	952.02	675.09	537.80	456.35	365.20	337.55	300.10	276.48
25000	2234.40	1190.02	843.86	672.24	570.43	456.50	421.94	375.13	345.60
30000	2681.28	1428.02	1012.63	806.69	684.52	547.80	506.32	450.15	414.72
35000	3128.16	1666.02	1181.40	941.14	798.60	639.10	590.71	525.18	483.83
36000	3217.54	1713.63	1215.16	968.03	821.42	657.36	607.59	540.18	497.66
37000	3306.91	1761.23	1248.91	994.92	844.24	675.62	624.46	555.19	511.48
38000	3396.29	1808.83	1282.66	1021.81	867.06	693.88	641.34	570.19	525.30
39000	3485.67	1856.43	1316.42	1048.70	889.87	712.14	658.22	585.20	539.13
40000	3575.04	1904.03	1350.17	1075.59	912.69	730.40	675.10	600.20	552.95
41000	3664.42	1951.63	1383.93	1102.48	935.51	748.66	691.97	615.21	566.78
42000	3753.79	1999.23	1417.68	1129.37	958.32	766.92	708.85	630.21	580.60
43000	3843.17	2046.83	1451.44	1156.26	981.14	785.18	725.73	645.22	594.42
44000	3932.55	2094.43	1485.19	1183.15	1003.96	803.44	742.60	660.22	608.25
45000	4021.92	2142.03	1518.94	1210.04	1026.78	821.70	759.48	675.23	622.07
46000	4111.30	2189.63	1552.70	1236.93	1049.59	839.96	776.36	690.23	635.89
47000	4200.67	2237.23	1586.45	1263.82	1072.41	858.22	793.24	705.23	649.72
48000	4290.05	2284.83	1620.21	1290.70	1095.23	876.48	810.11	720.24	663.54
49000	4379.43	2332.43	1653.96	1317.59	1118.04	894.74	826.99	735.24	677.37
50000	4468.80	2380.03	1687.71	1344.48	1140.86	913.00	843.87	750.25	691.19
51000	4558.18	2427.63	1721.47	1371.37	1163.68	931.26	860.74	765.25	705.01
52000	4647.55	2475.23	1755.22	1398.26	1186.49	949.52	877.62	780.26	718.84
53000	4736.93	2522.83	1788.98	1425.15	1209.31	967.78	894.50	795.26	732.66
54000	4826.31	2570.44	1822.73	1452.04	1232.13	986.04	911.38	810.27	746.48
55000	4915.68	2618.04	1856.49	1478.93	1254.95	1004.30	928.25	825.27	760.31
56000	5005.06	2665.64	1890.24	1505.82	1277.76	1022.56	945.13	840.28	774.13
57000	5094.43	2713.24	1923.99	1532.71	1300.58	1040.82	962.01	855.28	787.95
58000	5183.81	2760.84	1957.75	1559.60	1323.40	1059.08	978.89	870.29	801.78
59000	5273.18	2808.44	1991.50	1586.49	1346.21	1077.34	995.76	885.29	815.60
60000	5362.56	2856.04	2025.26	1613.38	1369.03	1095.60	1012.64	900.30	829.43
61000	5451.94	2903.64	2059.01	1640.27	1391.85	1113.86	1029.52	915.30	843.25
62000	5541.31	2951.24	2092.76	1667.16	1414.67	1132.12	1046.39	930.31	857.07
63000	5630.69	2998.84	2126.52	1694.05	1437.48	1150.38	1063.27	945.31	870.90
64000	5720.06	3046.44	2160.27	1720.94	1460.30	1168.64	1080.15	960.32	884.72
65000	5809.44	3094.04	2194.03	1747.83	1483.12	1186.90	1097.03	975.32	898.54
66000	5898.82	3141.64	2227.78	1774.72	1505.93	1205.16	1113.90	990.33	912.37
67000	5988.19	3189.24	2261.54	1801.61	1528.75	1223.42	1130.78	1005.33	926.19
68000	6077.57	3236.84	2295.29	1828.50	1551.57	1241.68	1147.66	1020.34	940.02
69000	6166.94	3284.44	2329.04	1855.39	1574.39	1259.94	1164.54	1035.34	953.84
70000	6256.32	3332.04	2362.80	1882.28	1597.20	1278.20	1181.41	1050.35	967.66
75000	6703.20	3570.05	2531.57	2016.72	1711.29	1369.50	1265.80	1125.37	1036.78
80000	7150.08	3808.05	2700.34	2151.17	1825.37	1460.80	1350.19	1200.40	1105.90
100000	8937.60	4760.06	3375.42	2688.96	2281.72	1826.00	1687.73	1500.49	1382.37

MONTHLY PAYMENT 13⅛%

NECESSARY TO AMORTIZE A LOAN

TERM / AMOUNT	15 YEARS	18 YEARS	20 YEARS	25 YEARS	28 YEARS	29 YEARS	30 YEARS	35 YEARS	40 YEARS
$ 25	.32	.31	.30	.29	.29	.28	.28	.28	.28
50	.64	.61	.60	.57	.57	.56	.56	.56	.55
75	.96	.91	.89	.86	.85	.84	.84	.83	.83
100	1.28	1.21	1.19	1.14	1.13	1.12	1.12	1.11	1.10
200	2.55	2.42	2.37	2.28	2.25	2.24	2.24	2.22	2.20
300	3.83	3.63	3.55	3.42	3.37	3.36	3.35	3.32	3.30
400	5.10	4.84	4.73	4.55	4.50	4.48	4.47	4.43	4.40
500	6.37	6.05	5.91	5.69	5.62	5.60	5.58	5.53	5.50
600	7.65	7.26	7.09	6.83	6.74	6.72	6.70	6.64	6.60
700	8.92	8.47	8.27	7.97	7.86	7.84	7.82	7.74	7.70
800	10.19	9.68	9.45	9.10	8.99	8.96	8.93	8.85	8.80
900	11.47	10.89	10.63	10.24	10.11	10.08	10.05	9.95	9.90
1000	12.74	12.10	11.81	11.38	11.23	11.20	11.16	11.06	11.00
2000	25.47	24.19	23.61	22.75	22.46	22.39	22.32	22.11	22.00
3000	38.21	36.28	35.42	34.12	33.69	33.58	33.48	33.16	33.00
4000	50.94	48.37	47.22	45.50	44.92	44.77	44.64	44.21	43.99
5000	63.68	60.46	59.03	56.87	56.14	55.96	55.80	55.27	54.99
6000	76.41	72.55	70.83	68.24	67.37	67.15	66.96	66.32	65.99
7000	89.15	84.64	82.64	79.61	78.60	78.35	78.12	77.37	76.98
8000	101.88	96.73	94.44	90.99	89.83	89.54	89.28	88.42	87.98
9000	114.62	108.82	106.25	102.36	101.06	100.73	100.44	99.47	98.98
10000	127.35	120.91	118.05	113.73	112.28	111.92	111.60	110.53	109.97
15000	191.03	181.37	177.08	170.59	168.42	167.88	167.40	165.79	164.96
20000	254.70	241.82	236.10	227.46	224.56	223.83	223.20	221.05	219.94
25000	318.37	302.28	295.13	284.32	280.70	279.79	279.00	276.31	274.93
30000	382.05	362.73	354.15	341.18	336.84	335.75	334.80	331.57	329.91
35000	445.72	423.19	413.18	398.05	392.98	391.71	390.60	386.83	384.90
36000	458.46	435.28	424.98	409.42	404.21	402.90	401.76	397.88	395.89
37000	471.19	447.37	436.79	420.79	415.44	414.09	412.92	408.93	406.89
38000	483.93	459.46	448.59	432.16	426.66	425.28	424.08	419.99	417.89
39000	496.66	471.55	460.40	443.54	437.89	436.47	435.24	431.04	428.88
40000	509.40	483.64	472.20	454.91	449.12	447.66	446.40	442.09	439.88
41000	522.13	495.74	484.01	466.28	460.35	458.86	457.56	453.14	450.88
42000	534.87	507.83	495.81	477.65	471.57	470.05	468.72	464.19	461.87
43000	547.60	519.92	507.62	489.03	482.80	481.24	479.88	475.25	472.87
44000	560.34	532.01	519.42	500.40	494.03	492.43	491.04	486.30	483.87
45000	573.07	544.10	531.23	511.77	505.26	503.62	502.20	497.35	494.86
46000	585.80	556.19	543.03	523.14	516.49	514.81	513.35	508.40	505.86
47000	598.54	568.28	554.84	534.52	527.71	526.01	524.51	519.45	516.86
48000	611.27	580.37	566.64	545.89	538.94	537.20	535.67	530.51	527.85
49000	624.01	592.46	578.45	557.26	550.17	548.39	546.83	541.56	538.85
50000	636.74	604.55	590.25	568.63	561.40	559.58	557.99	552.61	549.85
51000	649.48	616.65	602.06	580.01	572.63	570.77	569.15	563.66	560.85
52000	662.21	628.74	613.86	591.38	583.85	581.96	580.31	574.71	571.84
53000	674.95	640.83	625.67	602.75	595.08	593.15	591.47	585.77	582.84
54000	687.68	652.92	637.47	614.12	606.31	604.35	602.63	596.82	593.84
55000	700.42	665.01	649.28	625.50	617.54	615.54	613.79	607.87	604.83
56000	713.15	677.10	661.08	636.87	628.76	626.73	624.95	618.92	615.83
57000	725.89	689.19	672.89	648.24	639.99	637.92	636.11	629.98	626.83
58000	738.62	701.28	684.69	659.61	651.22	649.11	647.27	641.03	637.82
59000	751.36	713.37	696.50	670.99	662.45	660.30	658.43	652.08	648.82
60000	764.09	725.46	708.30	682.36	673.68	671.49	669.59	663.13	659.82
61000	776.83	737.55	720.11	693.73	684.90	682.69	680.75	674.18	670.81
62000	789.56	749.65	731.91	705.10	696.13	693.88	691.91	685.24	681.81
63000	802.30	761.74	743.71	716.48	707.36	705.07	703.07	696.29	692.81
64000	815.03	773.83	755.52	727.85	718.59	716.26	714.23	707.34	703.80
65000	827.77	785.92	767.32	739.22	729.82	727.45	725.39	718.39	714.80
66000	840.50	798.01	779.13	750.60	741.04	738.64	736.55	729.44	725.80
67000	853.24	810.10	790.93	761.97	752.27	749.84	747.71	740.50	736.80
68000	865.97	822.19	802.74	773.34	763.50	761.03	758.87	751.55	747.79
69000	878.70	834.28	814.54	784.71	774.73	772.22	770.03	762.60	758.79
70000	891.44	846.37	826.35	796.09	785.95	783.41	781.19	773.65	769.79
75000	955.11	906.83	885.37	852.95	842.09	839.37	836.99	828.91	824.77
80000	1018.79	967.28	944.40	909.81	898.23	895.32	892.79	884.17	879.75
100000	1273.48	1209.10	1180.50	1137.26	1122.79	1119.15	1115.98	1105.22	1099.69

13¼% MONTHLY PAYMENT
NECESSARY TO AMORTIZE A LOAN

TERM / AMOUNT	1 YEAR	2 YEARS	3 YEARS	4 YEARS	5 YEARS	7 YEARS	8 YEARS	10 YEARS	12 YEARS
$ 25	2.24	1.20	.85	.68	.58	.46	.43	.38	.35
50	4.48	2.39	1.70	1.35	1.15	.92	.85	.76	.70
75	6.71	3.58	2.54	2.03	1.72	1.38	1.28	1.14	1.05
100	8.95	4.77	3.39	2.70	2.29	1.84	1.70	1.51	1.40
200	17.89	9.54	6.77	5.40	4.58	3.67	3.39	3.02	2.79
300	26.84	14.30	10.15	8.09	6.87	5.50	5.09	4.53	4.18
400	35.78	19.07	13.53	10.79	9.16	7.34	6.78	6.04	5.57
500	44.72	23.83	16.91	13.48	11.45	9.17	8.48	7.54	6.96
600	53.67	28.60	20.29	16.18	13.73	11.00	10.17	9.05	8.35
700	62.61	33.37	23.68	18.87	16.02	12.83	11.87	10.56	9.74
800	71.55	38.13	27.06	21.57	18.31	14.67	13.56	12.07	11.13
900	80.50	42.90	30.44	24.26	20.60	16.50	15.26	13.58	12.52
1000	89.44	47.66	33.82	26.96	22.89	18.33	16.95	15.08	13.91
2000	178.87	95.32	67.63	53.91	45.77	36.66	33.90	30.16	27.81
3000	268.31	142.98	101.45	80.86	68.65	54.99	50.85	45.24	41.71
4000	357.74	190.64	135.26	107.81	91.53	73.32	67.79	60.32	55.61
5000	447.18	238.30	169.08	134.76	114.41	91.65	84.74	75.40	69.51
6000	536.61	285.96	202.89	161.72	137.29	109.97	101.69	90.48	83.41
7000	626.05	333.62	236.71	188.67	160.17	128.30	118.64	105.56	97.31
8000	715.48	381.28	270.52	215.62	183.06	146.63	135.58	120.64	111.22
9000	804.92	428.94	304.34	242.57	205.94	164.96	152.53	135.72	125.12
10000	894.35	476.60	338.15	269.52	228.82	183.29	169.48	150.79	139.02
15000	1341.52	714.90	507.22	404.28	343.22	274.93	254.22	226.19	208.52
20000	1788.70	953.19	676.29	539.04	457.63	366.57	338.95	301.58	278.03
25000	2235.87	1191.49	845.37	673.80	572.04	458.21	423.69	376.98	347.54
30000	2683.04	1429.79	1014.44	808.56	686.44	549.85	508.43	452.37	417.04
35000	3130.22	1668.08	1183.51	943.32	800.85	641.49	593.16	527.77	486.55
36000	3219.65	1715.74	1217.33	970.27	823.73	659.82	610.11	542.85	500.45
37000	3309.09	1763.40	1251.14	997.22	846.61	678.15	627.06	557.92	514.35
38000	3398.52	1811.06	1284.96	1024.17	869.49	696.47	644.01	573.00	528.25
39000	3487.95	1858.72	1318.77	1051.12	892.37	714.80	660.95	588.08	542.16
40000	3577.39	1906.38	1352.58	1078.07	915.26	733.13	677.90	603.16	556.06
41000	3666.82	1954.04	1386.40	1105.03	938.14	751.46	694.85	618.24	569.96
42000	3756.26	2001.70	1420.21	1131.98	961.02	769.79	711.80	633.32	583.86
43000	3845.69	2049.36	1454.03	1158.93	983.90	788.12	728.74	648.40	597.76
44000	3935.13	2097.02	1487.84	1185.88	1006.78	806.44	745.69	663.48	611.66
45000	4024.56	2144.68	1521.66	1212.83	1029.66	824.77	762.64	678.56	625.56
46000	4114.00	2192.33	1555.47	1239.79	1052.54	843.10	779.59	693.63	639.47
47000	4203.43	2239.99	1589.29	1266.74	1075.42	861.43	796.53	708.71	653.37
48000	4292.87	2287.65	1623.10	1293.69	1098.31	879.76	813.48	723.79	667.27
49000	4382.30	2335.31	1656.92	1320.64	1121.19	898.08	830.43	738.87	681.17
50000	4471.74	2382.97	1690.73	1347.59	1144.07	916.41	847.38	753.95	695.07
51000	4561.17	2430.63	1724.54	1374.54	1166.95	934.74	864.32	769.03	708.97
52000	4650.60	2478.29	1758.36	1401.50	1189.83	953.07	881.27	784.11	722.87
53000	4740.04	2525.95	1792.17	1428.45	1212.71	971.40	898.22	799.19	736.77
54000	4829.47	2573.61	1825.99	1455.40	1235.59	989.73	915.16	814.27	750.68
55000	4918.91	2621.27	1859.80	1482.35	1258.47	1008.05	932.11	829.34	764.58
56000	5008.34	2668.93	1893.62	1509.30	1281.36	1026.38	949.06	844.42	778.48
57000	5097.78	2716.59	1927.43	1536.25	1304.24	1044.71	966.01	859.50	792.38
58000	5187.21	2764.25	1961.25	1563.21	1327.12	1063.04	982.95	874.58	806.28
59000	5276.65	2811.91	1995.06	1590.16	1350.00	1081.37	999.90	889.66	820.18
60000	5366.08	2859.57	2028.87	1617.11	1372.88	1099.69	1016.85	904.74	834.08
61000	5455.52	2907.22	2062.69	1644.06	1395.76	1118.02	1033.80	919.82	847.98
62000	5544.95	2954.88	2096.50	1671.01	1418.64	1136.35	1050.74	934.90	861.89
63000	5634.39	3002.54	2130.32	1697.96	1441.52	1154.68	1067.69	949.98	875.79
64000	5723.82	3050.20	2164.13	1724.92	1464.41	1173.01	1084.64	965.05	889.69
65000	5813.25	3097.86	2197.95	1751.87	1487.29	1191.33	1101.59	980.13	903.59
66000	5902.69	3145.52	2231.76	1778.82	1510.17	1209.66	1118.53	995.21	917.49
67000	5992.12	3193.18	2265.58	1805.77	1533.05	1227.99	1135.48	1010.29	931.39
68000	6081.56	3240.84	2299.39	1832.72	1555.93	1246.32	1152.43	1025.37	945.29
69000	6170.99	3288.50	2333.21	1859.68	1578.81	1264.65	1169.38	1040.45	959.20
70000	6260.43	3336.16	2367.02	1886.63	1601.69	1282.98	1186.32	1055.53	973.10
75000	6707.60	3574.46	2536.09	2021.39	1716.10	1374.62	1271.06	1130.92	1042.60
80000	7154.77	3812.75	2705.16	2156.14	1830.51	1466.26	1355.80	1206.32	1112.11
100000	8943.47	4765.94	3381.45	2695.18	2288.13	1832.82	1694.75	1507.89	1390.14

MONTHLY PAYMENT 13¼%

NECESSARY TO AMORTIZE A LOAN

TERM / AMOUNT	15 YEARS	18 YEARS	20 YEARS	25 YEARS	28 YEARS	29 YEARS	30 YEARS	35 YEARS	40 YEARS
$ 25	.33	.31	.30	.29	.29	.29	.29	.28	.28
50	.65	.61	.60	.58	.57	.57	.57	.56	.56
75	.97	.92	.90	.87	.85	.85	.85	.84	.84
100	1.29	1.22	1.19	1.15	1.14	1.13	1.13	1.12	1.11
200	2.57	2.44	2.38	2.30	2.27	2.26	2.26	2.24	2.22
300	3.85	3.66	3.57	3.45	3.40	3.39	3.38	3.35	3.33
400	5.13	4.88	4.76	4.59	4.53	4.52	4.51	4.47	4.44
500	6.41	6.09	5.95	5.74	5.67	5.65	5.63	5.58	5.55
600	7.70	7.31	7.14	6.89	6.80	6.78	6.76	6.70	6.66
700	8.98	8.53	8.33	8.03	7.93	7.91	7.89	7.81	7.77
800	10.26	9.75	9.52	9.18	9.06	9.04	9.01	8.93	8.88
900	11.54	10.97	10.71	10.33	10.20	10.16	10.14	10.04	9.99
1000	12.82	12.18	11.90	11.47	11.33	11.29	11.26	11.16	11.10
2000	25.64	24.36	23.79	22.94	22.65	22.58	22.52	22.31	22.20
3000	38.46	36.54	35.69	34.41	33.98	33.87	33.78	33.46	33.30
4000	51.27	48.72	47.58	45.87	45.30	45.16	45.04	44.61	44.40
5000	64.09	60.89	59.48	57.34	56.63	56.45	56.29	55.77	55.50
6000	76.91	73.07	71.37	68.81	67.95	67.74	67.55	66.92	66.60
7000	89.73	85.25	83.27	80.27	79.28	79.03	78.81	78.07	77.70
8000	102.54	97.43	95.16	91.74	90.60	90.32	90.07	89.22	88.79
9000	115.36	109.61	107.05	103.21	101.93	101.60	101.32	100.38	99.89
10000	128.18	121.78	118.95	114.68	113.25	112.89	112.58	111.53	110.99
15000	192.27	182.67	178.42	172.01	169.87	169.34	168.87	167.29	166.49
20000	256.35	243.56	237.89	229.35	226.50	225.78	225.16	223.05	221.98
25000	320.44	304.45	297.36	286.68	283.12	282.23	281.45	278.82	277.47
30000	384.53	365.34	356.83	344.02	339.74	338.67	337.74	334.58	332.97
35000	448.61	426.23	416.31	401.35	396.36	395.11	394.03	390.34	388.46
36000	461.43	438.41	428.20	412.82	407.69	406.40	405.28	401.49	399.56
37000	474.25	450.59	440.09	424.28	419.01	417.69	416.54	412.64	410.66
38000	487.06	462.76	451.99	435.75	430.34	428.98	427.80	423.80	421.76
39000	499.88	474.94	463.88	447.22	441.66	440.27	439.06	434.95	432.85
40000	512.70	487.12	475.78	458.69	452.99	451.56	450.31	446.10	443.95
41000	525.52	499.30	487.67	470.15	464.31	462.85	461.57	457.25	455.05
42000	538.33	511.48	499.57	481.62	475.64	474.14	472.83	468.41	466.15
43000	551.15	523.65	511.46	493.09	486.96	485.43	484.09	479.56	477.25
44000	563.97	535.83	523.35	504.55	498.29	496.71	495.35	490.71	488.35
45000	576.79	548.01	535.25	516.02	509.61	508.00	506.60	501.86	499.45
46000	589.60	560.19	547.14	527.49	520.93	519.29	517.86	513.02	510.55
47000	602.42	572.36	559.04	538.95	532.26	530.58	529.12	524.17	521.64
48000	615.24	584.54	570.93	550.42	543.58	541.87	540.38	535.32	532.74
49000	628.06	596.72	582.83	561.89	554.91	553.16	551.63	546.47	543.84
50000	640.87	608.90	594.72	573.36	566.23	564.45	562.89	557.63	554.94
51000	653.69	621.08	606.61	584.82	577.56	575.74	574.15	568.78	566.04
52000	666.51	633.25	618.51	596.29	588.88	587.03	585.41	579.93	577.14
53000	679.33	645.43	630.40	607.76	600.21	598.31	596.66	591.08	588.24
54000	692.14	657.61	642.30	619.22	611.53	609.60	607.92	602.24	599.33
55000	704.96	669.79	654.19	630.69	622.86	620.89	619.18	613.39	610.43
56000	717.78	681.97	666.09	642.16	634.18	632.18	630.44	624.54	621.53
57000	730.59	694.14	677.98	653.62	645.50	643.47	641.70	635.69	632.63
58000	743.41	706.32	689.87	665.09	656.83	654.76	652.95	646.85	643.73
59000	756.23	718.50	701.77	676.56	668.15	666.05	664.21	658.00	654.83
60000	769.05	730.68	713.66	688.03	679.48	677.34	675.47	669.15	665.93
61000	781.86	742.86	725.56	699.49	690.80	688.62	686.73	680.30	677.03
62000	794.68	755.03	737.45	710.96	702.13	699.91	697.98	691.46	688.12
63000	807.50	767.21	749.35	722.43	713.45	711.20	709.24	702.61	699.22
64000	820.32	779.39	761.24	733.89	724.78	722.49	720.50	713.76	710.32
65000	833.13	791.57	773.13	745.36	736.10	733.78	731.76	724.91	721.42
66000	845.95	803.74	785.03	756.83	747.43	745.07	743.02	736.06	732.52
67000	858.77	815.92	796.92	768.29	758.75	756.36	754.27	747.22	743.62
68000	871.59	828.10	808.82	779.76	770.07	767.65	765.53	758.37	754.72
69000	884.40	840.28	820.71	791.23	781.40	778.94	776.79	769.52	765.82
70000	897.22	852.46	832.61	802.70	792.72	790.22	788.05	780.67	776.91
75000	961.31	913.35	892.08	860.03	849.35	846.67	844.34	836.44	832.41
80000	1025.39	974.23	951.55	917.37	905.97	903.11	900.62	892.20	887.90
100000	1281.74	1217.79	1189.44	1146.71	1132.46	1128.89	1125.78	1115.25	1109.87

13⅜% MONTHLY PAYMENT
NECESSARY TO AMORTIZE A LOAN

TERM / AMOUNT	1 YEAR	2 YEARS	3 YEARS	4 YEARS	5 YEARS	7 YEARS	8 YEARS	10 YEARS	12 YEARS
$ 25	2.24	1.20	.85	.68	.58	.46	.43	.38	.35
50	4.48	2.39	1.70	1.36	1.15	.92	.86	.76	.70
75	6.72	3.58	2.55	2.03	1.73	1.38	1.28	1.14	1.05
100	8.95	4.78	3.39	2.71	2.30	1.84	1.71	1.52	1.40
200	17.90	9.55	6.78	5.41	4.59	3.68	3.41	3.04	2.80
300	26.85	14.32	10.17	8.11	6.89	5.52	5.11	4.55	4.20
400	35.80	19.09	13.55	10.81	9.18	7.36	6.81	6.07	5.60
500	44.75	23.86	16.94	13.51	11.48	9.20	8.51	7.58	6.99
600	53.70	28.64	20.33	16.21	13.77	11.04	10.22	9.10	8.39
700	62.65	33.41	23.72	18.91	16.07	12.88	11.92	10.61	9.79
800	71.60	38.18	27.10	21.62	18.36	14.72	13.62	12.13	11.19
900	80.55	42.95	30.49	24.32	20.66	16.56	15.32	13.64	12.59
1000	89.50	47.72	33.88	27.02	22.95	18.40	17.02	15.16	13.98
2000	178.99	95.44	67.75	54.03	45.90	36.80	34.04	30.31	27.96
3000	268.48	143.16	101.63	81.05	68.84	55.19	51.06	45.46	41.94
4000	357.98	190.88	135.50	108.06	91.79	73.59	68.08	60.62	55.92
5000	447.47	238.60	169.38	135.07	114.73	91.99	85.09	75.77	69.90
6000	536.96	286.31	203.25	162.09	137.68	110.38	102.11	90.92	83.88
7000	626.46	334.03	237.13	189.10	160.62	128.78	119.13	106.08	97.86
8000	715.95	381.75	271.00	216.12	183.57	147.18	136.15	121.23	111.84
9000	805.44	429.47	304.88	243.13	206.51	165.57	153.16	136.38	125.82
10000	894.94	477.19	338.75	270.14	229.46	183.97	170.18	151.54	139.80
15000	1342.40	715.78	508.13	405.21	344.19	275.95	255.27	227.30	209.69
20000	1789.87	954.37	677.50	540.28	458.91	367.93	340.36	303.07	279.59
25000	2237.34	1192.96	846.88	675.35	573.64	459.92	425.45	378.83	349.48
30000	2684.80	1431.55	1016.25	810.42	688.37	551.90	510.54	454.60	419.38
35000	3132.27	1670.14	1185.63	945.49	803.10	643.88	595.62	530.36	489.27
36000	3221.76	1717.86	1219.50	972.51	826.04	662.28	612.64	545.52	503.25
37000	3311.26	1765.58	1253.37	999.52	848.99	680.67	629.66	560.67	517.23
38000	3400.75	1813.29	1287.25	1026.54	871.93	699.07	646.68	575.82	531.21
39000	3490.24	1861.01	1321.12	1053.55	894.88	717.47	663.70	590.97	545.19
40000	3579.74	1908.73	1355.00	1080.56	917.82	735.86	680.71	606.13	559.17
41000	3669.23	1956.45	1388.87	1107.58	940.77	754.26	697.73	621.28	573.15
42000	3758.72	2004.17	1422.75	1134.59	963.72	772.66	714.75	636.43	587.13
43000	3848.22	2051.89	1456.62	1161.61	986.66	791.05	731.77	651.59	601.11
44000	3937.71	2099.60	1490.50	1188.62	1009.61	809.45	748.78	666.74	615.09
45000	4027.20	2147.32	1524.37	1215.63	1032.55	827.85	765.80	681.89	629.07
46000	4116.70	2195.04	1558.25	1242.65	1055.50	846.24	782.82	697.05	643.05
47000	4206.19	2242.76	1592.12	1269.66	1078.44	864.64	799.84	712.20	657.02
48000	4295.68	2290.48	1626.00	1296.68	1101.39	883.03	816.85	727.35	671.00
49000	4385.18	2338.19	1659.87	1323.69	1124.33	901.43	833.87	742.51	684.98
50000	4474.67	2385.91	1693.75	1350.70	1147.28	919.83	850.89	757.66	698.96
51000	4564.16	2433.63	1727.62	1377.72	1170.23	938.22	867.91	772.81	712.94
52000	4653.66	2481.35	1761.50	1404.73	1193.17	956.62	884.93	787.96	726.92
53000	4743.15	2529.07	1795.37	1431.75	1216.12	975.02	901.94	803.12	740.90
54000	4832.64	2576.79	1829.25	1458.76	1239.06	993.41	918.96	818.27	754.88
55000	4922.14	2624.50	1863.12	1485.77	1262.01	1011.81	935.98	833.42	768.86
56000	5011.63	2672.22	1897.00	1512.79	1284.95	1030.21	953.00	848.58	782.84
57000	5101.12	2719.94	1930.87	1539.80	1307.90	1048.60	970.01	863.73	796.82
58000	5190.62	2767.66	1964.75	1566.82	1330.84	1067.00	987.03	878.88	810.80
59000	5280.11	2815.38	1998.62	1593.83	1353.79	1085.40	1004.05	894.04	824.77
60000	5369.60	2863.09	2032.50	1620.84	1376.73	1103.79	1021.07	909.19	838.75
61000	5459.10	2910.81	2066.37	1647.86	1399.68	1122.19	1038.08	924.34	852.73
62000	5548.59	2958.53	2100.25	1674.87	1422.63	1140.59	1055.10	939.50	866.71
63000	5638.08	3006.25	2134.12	1701.89	1445.57	1158.98	1072.12	954.65	880.69
64000	5727.58	3053.97	2168.00	1728.90	1468.52	1177.38	1089.14	969.80	894.67
65000	5817.07	3101.68	2201.87	1755.91	1491.46	1195.77	1106.16	984.95	908.65
66000	5906.56	3149.40	2235.75	1782.93	1514.41	1214.17	1123.17	1000.11	922.63
67000	5996.06	3197.12	2269.62	1809.94	1537.35	1232.57	1140.19	1015.26	936.61
68000	6085.55	3244.84	2303.50	1836.96	1560.30	1250.96	1157.21	1030.41	950.59
69000	6175.04	3292.56	2337.37	1863.97	1583.24	1269.36	1174.23	1045.57	964.57
70000	6264.54	3340.28	2371.25	1890.98	1606.19	1287.76	1191.24	1060.72	978.54
75000	6712.00	3578.87	2540.62	2026.05	1720.92	1379.74	1276.33	1136.49	1048.44
80000	7159.47	3817.46	2709.99	2161.12	1835.64	1471.72	1361.42	1212.25	1118.34
100000	8949.34	4771.82	3387.49	2701.40	2294.55	1839.65	1701.78	1515.31	1397.92

MONTHLY PAYMENT 13⅜%

NECESSARY TO AMORTIZE A LOAN

TERM / AMOUNT	15 YEARS	18 YEARS	20 YEARS	25 YEARS	28 YEARS	29 YEARS	30 YEARS	35 YEARS	40 YEARS
$ 25	.33	.31	.30	.29	.29	.29	.29	.29	.29
50	.65	.62	.60	.58	.58	.57	.57	.57	.57
75	.97	.92	.90	.87	.86	.86	.86	.85	.85
100	1.30	1.23	1.20	1.16	1.15	1.14	1.14	1.13	1.13
200	2.59	2.46	2.40	2.32	2.29	2.28	2.28	2.26	2.25
300	3.88	3.68	3.60	3.47	3.43	3.42	3.41	3.38	3.37
400	5.17	4.91	4.80	4.63	4.57	4.56	4.55	4.51	4.49
500	6.46	6.14	6.00	5.79	5.72	5.70	5.68	5.63	5.61
600	7.75	7.36	7.20	6.94	6.86	6.84	6.82	6.76	6.73
700	9.04	8.59	8.39	8.10	8.00	7.98	7.95	7.88	7.85
800	10.33	9.82	9.59	9.25	9.14	9.11	9.09	9.01	8.97
900	11.62	11.04	10.79	10.41	10.28	10.25	10.23	10.13	10.09
1000	12.91	12.27	11.99	11.57	11.43	11.39	11.36	11.26	11.21
2000	25.81	24.53	23.97	23.13	22.85	22.78	22.72	22.51	22.41
3000	38.71	36.80	35.96	34.69	34.27	34.16	34.07	33.76	33.61
4000	51.61	49.06	47.94	46.25	45.69	45.55	45.43	45.02	44.81
5000	64.51	61.33	59.92	57.81	57.11	56.94	56.78	56.27	56.01
6000	77.41	73.59	71.91	69.37	68.53	68.32	68.14	67.52	67.21
7000	90.31	85.86	83.89	80.94	79.96	79.71	79.50	78.77	78.41
8000	103.21	98.12	95.88	92.50	91.38	91.10	90.85	90.03	89.61
9000	116.11	110.39	107.86	104.06	102.80	102.48	102.21	101.28	100.81
10000	129.01	122.65	119.84	115.62	114.22	113.87	113.56	112.53	112.01
15000	193.51	183.98	179.76	173.43	171.33	170.80	170.34	168.80	168.01
20000	258.01	245.30	239.68	231.24	228.43	227.73	227.12	225.06	224.02
25000	322.51	306.63	299.60	289.05	285.54	284.66	283.90	281.33	280.02
30000	387.01	367.95	359.52	346.85	342.65	341.60	340.68	337.59	336.02
35000	451.51	429.28	419.44	404.66	399.76	398.53	397.46	393.85	392.03
36000	464.41	441.54	431.43	416.22	411.18	409.91	408.82	405.11	403.23
37000	477.31	453.81	443.41	427.79	422.60	421.30	420.17	416.36	414.43
38000	490.21	466.07	455.39	439.35	434.02	432.69	431.53	427.61	425.63
39000	503.11	478.34	467.38	450.91	445.44	444.07	442.88	438.87	436.83
40000	516.01	490.60	479.36	462.47	456.86	455.46	454.24	450.12	448.03
41000	528.91	502.87	491.35	474.03	468.28	466.85	465.59	461.37	459.23
42000	541.81	515.13	503.33	485.59	479.71	478.23	476.95	472.62	470.43
43000	554.71	527.40	515.31	497.16	491.13	489.62	488.31	483.88	481.63
44000	567.61	539.66	527.30	508.72	502.55	501.01	499.66	495.13	492.83
45000	580.51	551.93	539.28	520.28	513.97	512.39	511.02	506.38	504.03
46000	593.41	564.19	551.27	531.84	525.39	523.78	522.37	517.64	515.23
47000	606.31	576.46	563.25	543.40	536.81	535.16	533.73	528.89	526.43
48000	619.21	588.72	575.23	554.96	548.23	546.55	545.09	540.14	537.63
49000	632.11	600.99	587.22	566.52	559.66	557.94	556.44	551.39	548.84
50000	645.01	613.25	599.20	578.09	571.08	569.32	567.80	562.65	560.04
51000	657.91	625.52	611.18	589.65	582.50	580.71	579.15	573.90	571.24
52000	670.81	637.78	623.17	601.21	593.92	592.10	590.51	585.15	582.44
53000	683.71	650.05	635.15	612.77	605.34	603.48	601.87	596.41	593.64
54000	696.61	662.31	647.14	624.33	616.76	614.87	613.22	607.66	604.84
55000	709.51	674.58	659.12	635.89	628.18	626.26	624.58	618.91	616.04
56000	722.41	686.84	671.10	647.46	639.61	637.64	635.93	630.16	627.24
57000	735.31	699.11	683.09	659.02	651.03	649.03	647.29	641.42	638.44
58000	748.21	711.37	695.07	670.58	662.45	660.41	658.64	652.67	649.64
59000	761.11	723.64	707.06	682.14	673.87	671.80	670.00	663.92	660.84
60000	774.01	735.90	719.04	693.70	685.29	683.19	681.36	675.18	672.04
61000	786.92	748.17	731.02	705.26	696.71	694.57	692.71	686.43	683.24
62000	799.82	760.43	743.01	716.83	708.13	705.96	704.07	697.68	694.44
63000	812.72	772.70	754.99	728.39	719.56	717.35	715.42	708.93	705.64
64000	825.62	784.96	766.98	739.95	730.98	728.73	726.78	720.19	716.84
65000	838.52	797.23	778.96	751.51	742.40	740.12	738.14	731.44	728.04
66000	851.42	809.49	790.94	763.07	753.82	751.51	749.49	742.69	739.25
67000	864.32	821.76	802.93	774.63	765.24	762.89	760.85	753.95	750.45
68000	877.22	834.02	814.91	786.20	776.66	774.28	772.20	765.20	761.65
69000	890.12	846.29	826.90	797.76	788.08	785.66	783.56	776.45	772.85
70000	903.02	858.55	838.88	809.32	799.51	797.05	794.91	787.70	784.05
75000	967.52	919.88	898.80	867.13	856.61	853.98	851.69	843.97	840.05
80000	1032.02	981.20	958.72	924.94	913.72	910.91	908.47	900.23	896.05
100000	1290.02	1226.50	1198.40	1156.17	1142.15	1138.64	1135.59	1125.29	1120.07

13½% MONTHLY PAYMENT
NECESSARY TO AMORTIZE A LOAN

TERM / AMOUNT	1 YEAR	2 YEARS	3 YEARS	4 YEARS	5 YEARS	7 YEARS	8 YEARS	10 YEARS	12 YEARS
$ 25	2.24	1.20	.85	.68	.58	.47	.43	.39	.36
50	4.48	2.39	1.70	1.36	1.16	.93	.86	.77	.71
75	6.72	3.59	2.55	2.04	1.73	1.39	1.29	1.15	1.06
100	8.96	4.78	3.40	2.71	2.31	1.85	1.71	1.53	1.41
200	17.92	9.56	6.79	5.42	4.61	3.70	3.42	3.05	2.82
300	26.87	14.34	10.19	8.13	6.91	5.54	5.13	4.57	4.22
400	35.83	19.12	13.58	10.84	9.21	7.39	6.84	6.10	5.63
500	44.78	23.89	16.97	13.54	11.51	9.24	8.55	7.62	7.03
600	53.74	28.67	20.37	16.25	13.81	11.08	10.26	9.14	8.44
700	62.69	33.45	23.76	18.96	16.11	12.93	11.97	10.66	9.85
800	71.65	38.23	27.15	21.67	18.41	14.78	13.68	12.19	11.25
900	80.60	43.00	30.55	24.37	20.71	16.62	15.38	13.71	12.66
1000	89.56	47.78	33.94	27.08	23.01	18.47	17.09	15.23	14.06
2000	179.11	95.56	67.88	54.16	46.02	36.93	34.18	30.46	28.12
3000	268.66	143.34	101.81	81.23	69.03	55.40	51.27	45.69	42.18
4000	358.21	191.11	135.75	108.31	92.04	73.86	68.36	60.91	56.23
5000	447.77	238.89	169.68	135.39	115.05	92.33	85.45	76.14	70.29
6000	537.32	286.67	203.62	162.46	138.06	110.79	102.53	91.37	84.35
7000	626.87	334.44	237.55	189.54	161.07	129.26	119.62	106.60	98.41
8000	716.42	382.22	271.49	216.62	184.08	147.72	136.71	121.82	112.46
9000	805.97	430.00	305.42	243.69	207.09	166.19	153.80	137.05	126.52
10000	895.53	477.78	339.36	270.77	230.10	184.65	170.89	152.28	140.58
15000	1343.29	716.66	509.03	406.15	345.15	276.98	256.33	228.42	210.86
20000	1791.05	955.55	678.71	541.53	460.20	369.30	341.77	304.55	281.15
25000	2238.81	1194.43	848.39	676.91	575.25	461.63	427.21	380.69	351.43
30000	2686.57	1433.32	1018.06	812.29	690.30	553.95	512.65	456.83	421.72
35000	3134.33	1672.20	1187.74	947.68	805.35	646.28	598.09	532.97	492.01
36000	3223.88	1719.98	1221.68	974.75	828.36	664.74	615.18	548.19	506.06
37000	3313.43	1767.75	1255.61	1001.83	851.37	683.21	632.27	563.42	520.12
38000	3402.98	1815.53	1289.55	1028.91	874.38	701.67	649.36	578.65	534.18
39000	3492.53	1863.31	1323.48	1055.98	897.39	720.14	666.44	593.87	548.23
40000	3582.09	1911.09	1357.42	1083.06	920.40	738.60	683.53	609.10	562.29
41000	3671.64	1958.86	1391.35	1110.13	943.41	757.07	700.62	624.33	576.35
42000	3761.19	2006.64	1425.29	1137.21	966.42	775.53	717.71	639.56	590.41
43000	3850.74	2054.42	1459.22	1164.29	989.43	794.00	734.80	654.78	604.46
44000	3940.29	2102.19	1493.16	1191.36	1012.44	812.46	751.88	670.01	618.52
45000	4029.85	2149.97	1527.09	1218.44	1035.45	830.93	768.97	685.24	632.58
46000	4119.40	2197.75	1561.03	1245.52	1058.46	849.39	786.06	700.47	646.63
47000	4208.95	2245.52	1594.96	1272.59	1081.47	867.85	803.15	715.69	660.69
48000	4298.50	2293.30	1628.90	1299.67	1104.48	886.32	820.24	730.92	674.75
49000	4388.05	2341.08	1662.83	1326.74	1127.49	904.78	837.32	746.15	688.81
50000	4477.61	2388.86	1696.77	1353.82	1150.50	923.25	854.41	761.38	702.86
51000	4567.16	2436.63	1730.70	1380.90	1173.51	941.71	871.50	776.60	716.92
52000	4656.71	2484.41	1764.64	1407.97	1196.52	960.18	888.59	791.83	730.98
53000	4746.26	2532.19	1798.58	1435.05	1219.53	978.64	905.68	807.06	745.04
54000	4835.81	2579.96	1832.51	1462.13	1242.54	997.11	922.77	822.29	759.09
55000	4925.37	2627.74	1866.45	1489.20	1265.55	1015.57	939.85	837.51	773.15
56000	5014.92	2675.52	1900.38	1516.28	1288.56	1034.04	956.94	852.74	787.21
57000	5104.47	2723.29	1934.32	1543.36	1311.57	1052.50	974.03	867.97	801.26
58000	5194.02	2771.07	1968.25	1570.43	1334.58	1070.97	991.12	883.20	815.32
59000	5283.57	2818.85	2002.19	1597.51	1357.59	1089.43	1008.21	898.42	829.38
60000	5373.13	2866.63	2036.12	1624.58	1380.60	1107.90	1025.29	913.65	843.44
61000	5462.68	2914.40	2070.06	1651.66	1403.61	1126.36	1042.38	928.88	857.49
62000	5552.23	2962.18	2103.99	1678.74	1426.62	1144.83	1059.47	944.11	871.55
63000	5641.78	3009.96	2137.93	1705.81	1449.63	1163.29	1076.56	959.33	885.61
64000	5731.33	3057.73	2171.86	1732.89	1472.64	1181.76	1093.65	974.56	899.66
65000	5820.89	3105.51	2205.80	1759.97	1495.64	1200.22	1110.74	989.79	913.72
66000	5910.44	3153.29	2239.73	1787.04	1518.65	1218.69	1127.82	1005.02	927.78
67000	5999.99	3201.06	2273.67	1814.12	1541.66	1237.15	1144.91	1020.24	941.84
68000	6089.54	3248.84	2307.60	1841.19	1564.67	1255.62	1162.00	1035.47	955.89
69000	6179.09	3296.62	2341.54	1868.27	1587.68	1274.08	1179.09	1050.70	969.95
70000	6268.65	3344.40	2375.48	1895.35	1610.69	1292.55	1196.18	1065.93	984.01
75000	6716.41	3583.28	2545.15	2030.73	1725.74	1384.87	1281.62	1142.06	1054.29
80000	7164.17	3822.17	2714.83	2166.11	1840.79	1477.20	1367.06	1218.20	1124.58
100000	8955.21	4777.71	3393.53	2707.64	2300.99	1846.49	1708.82	1522.75	1405.72

MONTHLY PAYMENT 13½%
NECESSARY TO AMORTIZE A LOAN

TERM / AMOUNT	15 YEARS	18 YEARS	20 YEARS	25 YEARS	28 YEARS	29 YEARS	30 YEARS	35 YEARS	40 YEARS
$ 25	.33	.31	.31	.30	.29	.29	.29	.29	.29
50	.65	.62	.61	.59	.58	.58	.58	.57	.57
75	.98	.93	.91	.88	.87	.87	.86	.86	.85
100	1.30	1.24	1.21	1.17	1.16	1.15	1.15	1.14	1.14
200	2.60	2.48	2.42	2.34	2.31	2.30	2.30	2.28	2.27
300	3.90	3.71	3.63	3.50	3.46	3.45	3.44	3.41	3.40
400	5.20	4.95	4.83	4.67	4.61	4.60	4.59	4.55	4.53
500	6.50	6.18	6.04	5.83	5.76	5.75	5.73	5.68	5.66
600	7.79	7.42	7.25	7.00	6.92	6.90	6.88	6.82	6.79
700	9.09	8.65	8.46	8.16	8.07	8.04	8.02	7.95	7.92
800	10.39	9.89	9.66	9.33	9.22	9.19	9.17	9.09	9.05
900	11.69	11.12	10.87	10.50	10.37	10.34	10.31	10.22	10.18
1000	12.99	12.36	12.08	11.66	11.52	11.49	11.46	11.36	11.31
2000	25.97	24.71	24.15	23.32	23.04	22.97	22.91	22.71	22.61
3000	38.95	37.06	36.23	34.97	34.56	34.46	34.37	34.07	33.91
4000	51.94	49.41	48.30	46.63	46.08	45.94	45.82	45.42	45.22
5000	64.92	61.77	60.37	58.29	57.60	57.43	57.28	56.77	56.52
6000	77.90	74.12	72.45	69.94	69.12	68.91	68.73	68.13	67.82
7000	90.89	86.47	84.52	81.60	80.63	80.39	80.18	79.48	79.12
8000	103.87	98.82	96.59	93.26	92.15	91.88	91.64	90.83	90.43
9000	116.85	111.18	108.67	104.91	103.67	103.36	103.09	102.19	101.73
10000	129.84	123.53	120.74	116.57	115.19	114.85	114.55	113.54	113.03
15000	194.75	185.29	181.11	174.85	172.78	172.27	171.82	170.31	169.54
20000	259.67	247.05	241.48	233.13	230.37	229.69	229.09	227.07	226.06
25000	324.58	308.81	301.85	291.42	287.97	287.11	286.36	283.84	282.57
30000	389.50	370.57	362.22	349.70	345.56	344.53	343.63	340.61	339.08
35000	454.42	432.34	422.59	407.98	403.15	401.95	400.90	397.37	395.60
36000	467.40	444.69	434.66	419.64	414.67	413.43	412.35	408.73	406.90
37000	480.38	457.04	446.73	431.29	426.19	424.92	423.81	420.08	418.20
38000	493.37	469.39	458.81	442.95	437.71	436.40	435.26	431.43	429.50
39000	506.35	481.75	470.88	454.61	449.23	447.88	446.72	442.79	440.81
40000	519.33	494.10	482.95	466.26	460.74	459.37	458.17	454.14	452.11
41000	532.32	506.45	495.03	477.92	472.26	470.85	469.62	465.49	463.41
42000	545.30	518.80	507.10	489.58	483.78	482.34	481.08	476.85	474.71
43000	558.28	531.15	519.18	501.23	495.30	493.82	492.53	488.20	486.02
44000	571.27	543.51	531.25	512.89	506.82	505.30	503.99	499.55	497.32
45000	584.25	555.86	543.32	524.55	518.34	516.79	515.44	510.91	508.62
46000	597.23	568.21	555.40	536.20	529.86	528.27	526.89	522.26	519.93
47000	610.21	580.56	567.47	547.86	541.37	539.76	538.35	533.62	531.23
48000	623.20	592.92	579.54	559.51	552.89	551.24	549.80	544.97	542.53
49000	636.18	605.27	591.62	571.17	564.41	562.72	561.26	556.32	553.83
50000	649.16	617.62	603.69	582.83	575.93	574.21	572.71	567.68	565.14
51000	662.15	629.97	615.77	594.48	587.45	585.69	584.17	579.03	576.44
52000	675.13	642.33	627.84	606.14	598.97	597.18	595.62	590.38	587.74
53000	688.11	654.68	639.91	617.80	610.48	608.66	607.07	601.74	599.04
54000	701.10	667.03	651.99	629.45	622.00	620.14	618.53	613.09	610.35
55000	714.08	679.38	664.06	641.11	633.52	631.63	629.98	624.44	621.65
56000	727.06	691.73	676.13	652.77	645.04	643.11	641.44	635.80	632.95
57000	740.05	704.09	688.21	664.42	656.56	654.60	652.89	647.15	644.25
58000	753.03	716.44	700.28	676.08	668.08	666.08	664.34	658.50	655.56
59000	766.01	728.79	712.36	687.74	679.60	677.56	675.80	669.86	666.86
60000	779.00	741.14	724.43	699.39	691.11	689.05	687.25	681.21	678.16
61000	791.98	753.50	736.50	711.05	702.63	700.53	698.71	692.56	689.46
62000	804.96	765.85	748.58	722.70	714.15	712.02	710.16	703.92	700.77
63000	817.95	778.20	760.65	734.36	725.67	723.50	721.61	715.27	712.07
64000	830.93	790.55	772.72	746.02	737.19	734.98	733.07	726.62	723.37
65000	843.91	802.91	784.80	757.67	748.71	746.47	744.52	737.98	734.67
66000	856.90	815.26	796.87	769.33	760.23	757.95	755.98	749.33	745.98
67000	869.88	827.61	808.95	780.99	771.74	769.44	767.43	760.68	757.28
68000	882.86	839.96	821.02	792.64	783.26	780.92	778.89	772.04	768.58
69000	895.84	852.31	833.09	804.30	794.78	792.41	790.34	783.39	779.89
70000	908.83	864.67	845.17	815.96	806.30	803.89	801.79	794.74	791.19
75000	973.74	926.43	905.54	874.24	863.89	861.31	859.06	851.51	847.70
80000	1038.66	988.19	965.90	932.52	921.48	918.73	916.33	908.28	904.21
100000	1298.32	1235.24	1207.38	1165.65	1151.85	1148.41	1145.42	1135.35	1130.27

13⅝% MONTHLY PAYMENT
NECESSARY TO AMORTIZE A LOAN

TERM / AMOUNT	1 YEAR	2 YEARS	3 YEARS	4 YEARS	5 YEARS	7 YEARS	8 YEARS	10 YEARS	12 YEARS
$ 25	2.25	1.20	.85	.68	.58	.47	.43	.39	.36
50	4.49	2.40	1.70	1.36	1.16	.93	.86	.77	.71
75	6.73	3.59	2.55	2.04	1.74	1.40	1.29	1.15	1.07
100	8.97	4.79	3.40	2.72	2.31	1.86	1.72	1.54	1.42
200	17.93	9.57	6.80	5.43	4.62	3.71	3.44	3.07	2.83
300	26.89	14.36	10.20	8.15	6.93	5.57	5.15	4.60	4.25
400	35.85	19.14	13.60	10.86	9.23	7.42	6.87	6.13	5.66
500	44.81	23.92	17.00	13.57	11.54	9.27	8.58	7.66	7.07
600	53.77	28.71	20.40	16.29	13.85	11.13	10.30	9.19	8.49
700	62.73	33.49	23.80	19.00	16.16	12.98	12.02	10.72	9.90
800	71.69	38.27	27.20	21.72	18.46	14.83	13.73	12.25	11.31
900	80.65	43.06	30.60	24.43	20.77	16.69	15.45	13.78	12.73
1000	89.62	47.84	34.00	27.14	23.08	18.54	17.16	15.31	14.14
2000	179.23	95.68	68.00	54.28	46.15	37.07	34.32	30.61	28.28
3000	268.84	143.51	101.99	81.42	69.23	55.61	51.48	45.91	42.41
4000	358.45	191.35	135.99	108.56	92.30	74.14	68.64	61.21	56.55
5000	448.06	239.18	169.98	135.70	115.38	92.67	85.80	76.51	70.68
6000	537.67	287.02	203.98	162.84	138.45	111.21	102.96	91.82	84.82
7000	627.28	334.86	237.98	189.98	161.53	129.74	120.12	107.12	98.95
8000	716.89	382.69	271.97	217.11	184.60	148.27	137.28	122.42	113.09
9000	806.50	430.53	305.97	244.25	207.67	166.81	154.43	137.72	127.22
10000	896.11	478.36	339.96	271.39	230.75	185.34	171.59	153.02	141.36
15000	1344.17	717.54	509.94	407.09	346.12	278.01	257.39	229.53	212.04
20000	1792.22	956.72	679.92	542.78	461.49	370.67	343.18	306.04	282.71
25000	2240.27	1195.90	849.90	678.47	576.86	463.34	428.97	382.55	353.39
30000	2688.33	1435.08	1019.88	814.17	692.23	556.01	514.77	459.06	424.07
35000	3136.38	1674.26	1189.86	949.86	807.61	648.68	600.56	535.57	494.74
36000	3225.99	1722.10	1223.85	977.00	830.68	667.21	617.72	550.88	508.88
37000	3315.60	1769.93	1257.85	1004.14	853.75	685.74	634.88	566.18	523.01
38000	3405.21	1817.77	1291.84	1031.28	876.83	704.28	652.04	581.48	537.15
39000	3494.82	1865.61	1325.84	1058.42	899.90	722.81	669.20	596.78	551.29
40000	3584.44	1913.44	1359.84	1085.55	922.98	741.34	686.36	612.08	565.42
41000	3674.05	1961.28	1393.83	1112.69	946.05	759.88	703.51	627.39	579.56
42000	3763.66	2009.11	1427.83	1139.83	969.13	778.41	720.67	642.69	593.69
43000	3853.27	2056.95	1461.82	1166.97	992.20	796.94	737.83	657.99	607.83
44000	3942.88	2104.79	1495.82	1194.11	1015.27	815.48	754.99	673.29	621.96
45000	4032.49	2152.62	1529.82	1221.25	1038.35	834.01	772.15	688.59	636.10
46000	4122.10	2200.46	1563.81	1248.39	1061.42	852.54	789.31	703.90	650.23
47000	4211.71	2248.29	1597.81	1275.53	1084.50	871.08	806.47	719.20	664.37
48000	4301.32	2296.13	1631.80	1302.66	1107.57	889.61	823.63	734.50	678.50
49000	4390.93	2343.96	1665.80	1329.80	1130.65	908.14	840.78	749.80	692.64
50000	4480.54	2391.80	1699.79	1356.94	1153.72	926.68	857.94	765.10	706.78
51000	4570.15	2439.64	1733.79	1384.08	1176.79	945.21	875.10	780.41	720.91
52000	4659.76	2487.47	1767.79	1411.22	1199.87	963.75	892.26	795.71	735.05
53000	4749.38	2535.31	1801.78	1438.36	1222.94	982.28	909.42	811.01	749.18
54000	4838.99	2583.14	1835.78	1465.50	1246.02	1000.81	926.58	826.31	763.32
55000	4928.60	2630.98	1869.77	1492.64	1269.09	1019.35	943.74	841.61	777.45
56000	5018.21	2678.82	1903.77	1519.77	1292.17	1037.88	960.90	856.92	791.59
57000	5107.82	2726.65	1937.76	1546.91	1315.24	1056.41	978.05	872.22	805.72
58000	5197.43	2774.49	1971.76	1574.05	1338.31	1074.95	995.21	887.52	819.86
59000	5287.04	2822.32	2005.76	1601.19	1361.39	1093.48	1012.37	902.82	833.99
60000	5376.65	2870.16	2039.75	1628.33	1384.46	1112.01	1029.53	918.12	848.13
61000	5466.26	2918.00	2073.75	1655.47	1407.54	1130.55	1046.69	933.42	862.26
62000	5555.87	2965.83	2107.74	1682.61	1430.61	1149.08	1063.85	948.73	876.40
63000	5645.48	3013.67	2141.74	1709.75	1453.69	1167.61	1081.01	964.03	890.54
64000	5735.09	3061.50	2175.73	1736.88	1476.76	1186.15	1098.17	979.33	904.67
65000	5824.70	3109.34	2209.73	1764.02	1499.83	1204.68	1115.32	994.63	918.81
66000	5914.32	3157.18	2243.73	1791.16	1522.91	1223.21	1132.48	1009.93	932.94
67000	6003.93	3205.01	2277.72	1818.30	1545.98	1241.75	1149.64	1025.24	947.08
68000	6093.54	3252.85	2311.72	1845.44	1569.06	1260.28	1166.80	1040.54	961.21
69000	6183.15	3300.68	2345.71	1872.58	1592.13	1278.81	1183.96	1055.84	975.35
70000	6272.76	3348.52	2379.71	1899.72	1615.21	1297.35	1201.12	1071.14	989.48
75000	6720.81	3587.70	2549.69	2035.41	1730.58	1390.02	1286.91	1147.65	1060.16
80000	7168.87	3826.88	2719.67	2171.10	1845.95	1482.68	1372.71	1224.16	1130.84
100000	8961.08	4783.60	3399.58	2713.88	2307.43	1853.35	1715.88	1530.20	1413.55

MONTHLY PAYMENT 13⅝%

NECESSARY TO AMORTIZE A LOAN

TERM / AMOUNT	15 YEARS	18 YEARS	20 YEARS	25 YEARS	28 YEARS	29 YEARS	30 YEARS	35 YEARS	40 YEARS
$ 25	.33	.32	.31	.30	.30	.29	.29	.29	.29
50	.66	.63	.61	.59	.59	.58	.58	.58	.58
75	.98	.94	.92	.89	.88	.87	.87	.86	.86
100	1.31	1.25	1.22	1.18	1.17	1.16	1.16	1.15	1.15
200	2.62	2.49	2.44	2.36	2.33	2.32	2.32	2.30	2.29
300	3.92	3.74	3.65	3.53	3.49	3.48	3.47	3.44	3.43
400	5.23	4.98	4.87	4.71	4.65	4.64	4.63	4.59	4.57
500	6.54	6.22	6.09	5.88	5.81	5.80	5.78	5.73	5.71
600	7.84	7.47	7.30	7.06	6.97	6.95	6.94	6.88	6.85
700	9.15	8.71	8.52	8.23	8.14	8.11	8.09	8.02	7.99
800	10.46	9.96	9.74	9.41	9.30	9.27	9.25	9.17	9.13
900	11.76	11.20	10.95	10.58	10.46	10.43	10.40	10.31	10.27
1000	13.07	12.44	12.17	11.76	11.62	11.59	11.56	11.46	11.41
2000	26.14	24.88	24.33	23.51	23.24	23.17	23.11	22.91	22.81
3000	39.20	37.32	36.50	35.26	34.85	34.75	34.66	34.37	34.22
4000	52.27	49.76	48.66	47.01	46.47	46.33	46.22	45.82	45.62
5000	65.34	62.20	60.82	58.76	58.08	57.91	57.77	57.28	57.03
6000	78.40	74.64	72.99	70.51	69.70	69.50	69.32	68.73	68.43
7000	91.47	87.08	85.15	82.27	81.31	81.08	80.87	80.18	79.84
8000	104.54	99.52	97.32	94.02	92.93	92.66	92.43	91.64	91.24
9000	117.60	111.96	109.48	105.77	104.55	104.24	103.98	103.09	102.65
10000	130.67	124.40	121.64	117.52	116.16	115.82	115.53	114.55	114.05
15000	196.00	186.60	182.46	176.28	174.24	173.73	173.29	171.82	171.08
20000	261.33	248.80	243.28	235.03	232.32	231.64	231.06	229.09	228.10
25000	326.67	311.00	304.10	293.79	290.40	289.55	288.82	286.36	285.12
30000	392.00	373.20	364.92	352.55	348.48	347.46	346.58	343.63	342.15
35000	457.33	435.40	425.74	411.31	406.55	405.37	404.34	400.90	399.17
36000	470.40	447.84	437.90	423.06	418.17	416.95	415.90	412.35	410.57
37000	483.46	460.28	450.07	434.81	429.79	428.54	427.45	423.81	421.98
38000	496.53	472.72	462.23	446.56	441.40	440.12	439.00	435.26	433.38
39000	509.60	485.16	474.39	458.31	453.02	451.70	450.55	446.71	444.79
40000	522.66	497.60	486.56	470.06	464.63	463.28	462.11	458.17	456.19
41000	535.73	510.04	498.72	481.81	476.25	474.86	473.66	469.62	467.60
42000	548.79	522.48	510.88	493.57	487.86	486.45	485.21	481.08	479.00
43000	561.86	534.92	523.05	505.32	499.48	498.03	496.76	492.53	490.41
44000	574.93	547.36	535.21	517.07	511.10	509.61	508.32	503.98	501.81
45000	587.99	559.80	547.38	528.82	522.71	521.19	519.87	515.44	513.22
46000	601.06	572.24	559.54	540.57	534.33	532.77	531.42	526.89	524.62
47000	614.13	584.68	571.70	552.32	545.94	544.35	542.97	538.35	536.03
48000	627.19	597.12	583.87	564.08	557.56	555.94	554.53	549.80	547.43
49000	640.26	609.56	596.03	575.83	569.17	567.52	566.08	561.25	558.83
50000	653.33	622.00	608.19	587.58	580.79	579.10	577.63	572.71	570.24
51000	666.39	634.44	620.36	599.33	592.41	590.68	589.18	584.16	581.64
52000	679.46	646.88	632.52	611.08	604.02	602.26	600.74	595.62	593.05
53000	692.53	659.32	644.69	622.83	615.64	613.85	612.29	607.07	604.45
54000	705.59	671.76	656.85	634.58	627.25	625.43	623.84	618.52	615.86
55000	718.66	684.20	669.01	646.34	638.87	637.01	635.40	629.98	627.26
56000	731.72	696.64	681.18	658.09	650.48	648.59	646.95	641.43	638.67
57000	744.79	709.08	693.34	669.84	662.10	660.17	658.50	652.89	650.07
58000	757.86	721.52	705.51	681.59	673.72	671.76	670.05	664.34	661.48
59000	770.92	733.96	717.67	693.34	685.33	683.34	681.61	675.80	672.88
60000	783.99	746.40	729.83	705.09	696.95	694.92	693.16	687.25	684.29
61000	797.06	758.84	742.00	716.84	708.56	706.50	704.71	698.70	695.69
62000	810.12	771.28	754.16	728.60	720.18	718.08	716.26	710.16	707.10
63000	823.19	783.72	766.32	740.35	731.79	729.67	727.82	721.61	718.50
64000	836.26	796.16	778.49	752.10	743.41	741.25	739.37	733.07	729.91
65000	849.32	808.60	790.65	763.85	755.03	752.83	750.92	744.52	741.31
66000	862.39	821.04	802.82	775.60	766.64	764.41	762.47	755.97	752.71
67000	875.46	833.48	814.98	787.35	778.26	775.99	774.03	767.43	764.12
68000	888.52	845.92	827.14	799.10	789.87	787.57	785.58	778.88	775.52
69000	901.59	858.36	839.31	810.86	801.49	799.16	797.13	790.34	786.93
70000	914.65	870.80	851.47	822.61	813.10	810.74	808.68	801.79	798.33
75000	979.99	932.99	912.29	881.36	871.18	868.65	866.45	859.06	855.36
80000	1045.32	995.19	973.11	940.12	929.26	926.56	924.21	916.33	912.38
100000	1306.65	1243.99	1216.38	1175.15	1161.58	1158.20	1155.26	1145.41	1140.47

13¾% MONTHLY PAYMENT
NECESSARY TO AMORTIZE A LOAN

TERM / AMOUNT	1 YEAR	2 YEARS	3 YEARS	4 YEARS	5 YEARS	7 YEARS	8 YEARS	10 YEARS	12 YEARS
$ 25	2.25	1.20	.86	.69	.58	.47	.44	.39	.36
50	4.49	2.40	1.71	1.37	1.16	.94	.87	.77	.72
75	6.73	3.60	2.56	2.05	1.74	1.40	1.30	1.16	1.07
100	8.97	4.79	3.41	2.73	2.32	1.87	1.73	1.54	1.43
200	17.94	9.58	6.82	5.45	4.63	3.73	3.45	3.08	2.85
300	26.91	14.37	10.22	8.17	6.95	5.59	5.17	4.62	4.27
400	35.87	19.16	13.63	10.89	9.26	7.45	6.90	6.16	5.69
500	44.84	23.95	17.03	13.61	11.57	9.31	8.62	7.69	7.11
600	53.81	28.74	20.44	16.33	13.89	11.17	10.34	9.23	8.53
700	62.77	33.53	23.84	19.05	16.20	13.03	12.07	10.77	9.95
800	71.74	38.32	27.25	21.77	18.52	14.89	13.79	12.31	11.38
900	80.71	43.11	30.66	24.49	20.83	16.75	15.51	13.84	12.80
1000	89.67	47.90	34.06	27.21	23.14	18.61	17.23	15.38	14.22
2000	179.34	95.79	68.12	54.41	46.28	37.21	34.46	30.76	28.43
3000	269.01	143.69	102.17	81.61	69.42	55.81	51.69	46.14	42.65
4000	358.68	191.58	136.23	108.81	92.56	74.41	68.92	61.51	56.86
5000	448.35	239.48	170.29	136.01	115.70	93.02	86.15	76.89	71.07
6000	538.02	287.37	204.34	163.21	138.84	111.62	103.38	92.27	85.29
7000	627.69	335.27	238.40	190.41	161.98	130.22	120.61	107.64	99.50
8000	717.36	383.16	272.46	217.61	185.12	148.82	137.84	123.02	113.72
9000	807.03	431.06	306.51	244.82	208.25	167.42	155.07	138.40	127.93
10000	896.70	478.95	340.57	272.02	231.39	186.03	172.30	153.77	142.14
15000	1345.05	718.43	510.85	408.02	347.09	279.04	258.45	230.66	213.21
20000	1793.40	957.90	681.13	544.03	462.78	372.05	344.60	307.54	284.28
25000	2241.74	1197.38	851.41	680.04	578.48	465.06	430.74	384.42	355.35
30000	2690.09	1436.85	1021.69	816.04	694.17	558.07	516.89	461.31	426.42
35000	3138.44	1676.33	1191.98	952.05	809.86	651.08	603.04	538.19	497.49
36000	3228.11	1724.22	1226.03	979.25	833.00	669.68	620.27	553.57	511.70
37000	3317.78	1772.11	1260.09	1006.45	856.14	688.29	637.50	568.94	525.92
38000	3407.45	1820.01	1294.15	1033.65	879.28	706.89	654.73	584.32	540.13
39000	3497.12	1867.90	1328.20	1060.85	902.42	725.49	671.96	599.70	554.34
40000	3586.79	1915.80	1362.26	1088.05	925.56	744.09	689.19	615.07	568.56
41000	3676.46	1963.69	1396.31	1115.26	948.70	762.69	706.42	630.45	582.77
42000	3766.13	2011.59	1430.37	1142.46	971.84	781.30	723.65	645.83	596.99
43000	3855.79	2059.48	1464.43	1169.66	994.98	799.90	740.87	661.20	611.20
44000	3945.46	2107.38	1498.48	1196.86	1018.11	818.50	758.10	676.58	625.41
45000	4035.13	2155.27	1532.54	1224.06	1041.25	837.10	775.33	691.96	639.63
46000	4124.80	2203.17	1566.60	1251.26	1064.39	855.71	792.56	707.33	653.84
47000	4214.47	2251.06	1600.65	1278.46	1087.53	874.31	809.79	722.71	668.05
48000	4304.14	2298.96	1634.71	1305.66	1110.67	892.91	827.02	738.09	682.27
49000	4393.81	2346.85	1668.77	1332.87	1133.81	911.51	844.25	753.46	696.48
50000	4483.48	2394.75	1702.82	1360.07	1156.95	930.11	861.48	768.84	710.70
51000	4573.15	2442.64	1736.88	1387.27	1180.09	948.72	878.71	784.22	724.91
52000	4662.82	2490.54	1770.93	1414.47	1203.22	967.32	895.94	799.59	739.12
53000	4752.49	2538.43	1804.99	1441.67	1226.36	985.92	913.17	814.97	753.34
54000	4842.16	2586.33	1839.05	1468.87	1249.50	1004.52	930.40	830.35	767.55
55000	4931.83	2634.22	1873.10	1496.07	1272.64	1023.12	947.63	845.72	781.77
56000	5021.50	2682.12	1907.16	1523.27	1295.78	1041.73	964.86	861.10	795.98
57000	5111.17	2730.01	1941.22	1550.48	1318.92	1060.33	982.09	876.48	810.19
58000	5200.84	2777.91	1975.27	1577.68	1342.06	1078.93	999.32	891.85	824.41
59000	5290.51	2825.80	2009.33	1604.88	1365.20	1097.53	1016.55	907.23	838.62
60000	5380.18	2873.70	2043.38	1632.08	1388.34	1116.14	1033.78	922.61	852.83
61000	5469.85	2921.59	2077.44	1659.28	1411.47	1134.74	1051.01	937.98	867.05
62000	5559.52	2969.49	2111.50	1686.48	1434.61	1153.34	1068.24	953.36	881.26
63000	5649.19	3017.38	2145.55	1713.68	1457.75	1171.94	1085.47	968.74	895.48
64000	5738.85	3065.28	2179.61	1740.88	1480.89	1190.54	1102.69	984.11	909.69
65000	5828.52	3113.17	2213.67	1768.09	1504.03	1209.15	1119.92	999.49	923.90
66000	5918.19	3161.07	2247.72	1795.29	1527.17	1227.75	1137.15	1014.87	938.12
67000	6007.86	3208.96	2281.78	1822.49	1550.31	1246.35	1154.38	1030.24	952.33
68000	6097.53	3256.86	2315.84	1849.69	1573.45	1264.95	1171.61	1045.62	966.55
69000	6187.20	3304.75	2349.89	1876.89	1596.59	1283.56	1188.84	1061.00	980.76
70000	6276.87	3352.65	2383.95	1904.09	1619.72	1302.16	1206.07	1076.37	994.97
75000	6725.22	3592.12	2554.23	2040.10	1735.42	1395.17	1292.22	1153.26	1066.04
80000	7173.57	3831.59	2724.51	2176.10	1851.11	1488.18	1378.37	1230.14	1137.11
100000	8966.96	4789.49	3405.64	2720.13	2313.89	1860.22	1722.96	1537.67	1421.39

MONTHLY PAYMENT 13¾%

NECESSARY TO AMORTIZE A LOAN

TERM / AMOUNT	15 YEARS	18 YEARS	20 YEARS	25 YEARS	28 YEARS	29 YEARS	30 YEARS	35 YEARS	40 YEARS
$ 25	.33	.32	.31	.30	.30	.30	.30	.29	.29
50	.66	.63	.62	.60	.59	.59	.59	.58	.58
75	.99	.94	.92	.89	.88	.88	.88	.87	.87
100	1.32	1.26	1.23	1.19	1.18	1.17	1.17	1.16	1.16
200	2.63	2.51	2.46	2.37	2.35	2.34	2.34	2.32	2.31
300	3.95	3.76	3.68	3.56	3.52	3.51	3.50	3.47	3.46
400	5.26	5.02	4.91	4.74	4.69	4.68	4.67	4.63	4.61
500	6.58	6.27	6.13	5.93	5.86	5.84	5.83	5.78	5.76
600	7.89	7.52	7.36	7.11	7.03	7.01	7.00	6.94	6.91
700	9.21	8.77	8.58	8.30	8.20	8.18	8.16	8.09	8.06
800	10.52	10.03	9.81	9.48	9.38	9.35	9.33	9.25	9.21
900	11.84	11.28	11.03	10.67	10.55	10.52	10.49	10.40	10.36
1000	13.15	12.53	12.26	11.85	11.72	11.68	11.66	11.56	11.51
2000	26.30	25.06	24.51	23.70	23.43	23.36	23.31	23.11	23.02
3000	39.45	37.59	36.77	35.54	35.14	35.04	34.96	34.67	34.53
4000	52.60	50.12	49.02	47.39	46.86	46.72	46.61	46.22	46.03
5000	65.75	62.64	61.28	59.24	58.57	58.40	58.26	57.78	57.54
6000	78.90	75.17	73.53	71.08	70.28	70.08	69.91	69.33	69.05
7000	92.05	87.70	85.78	82.93	82.00	81.76	81.56	80.89	80.55
8000	105.20	100.23	98.04	94.78	93.71	93.44	93.21	92.44	92.06
9000	118.35	112.75	110.29	106.62	105.42	105.12	104.87	104.00	103.57
10000	131.50	125.28	122.55	118.47	117.14	116.80	116.52	115.55	115.07
15000	197.25	187.92	183.82	177.70	175.70	175.20	174.77	173.33	172.61
20000	263.00	250.56	245.09	236.94	234.27	233.60	233.03	231.10	230.14
25000	328.75	313.20	306.36	296.17	292.83	292.00	291.28	288.88	287.68
30000	394.50	375.83	367.63	355.40	351.40	350.40	349.54	346.65	345.21
35000	460.25	438.47	428.90	414.64	409.96	408.80	407.79	404.42	402.74
36000	473.40	451.00	441.15	426.48	421.68	420.48	419.45	415.98	414.25
37000	486.55	463.53	453.40	438.33	433.39	432.16	431.10	427.53	425.76
38000	499.70	476.06	465.66	450.18	445.10	443.84	442.75	439.09	437.27
39000	512.85	488.58	477.91	462.02	456.82	455.52	454.40	450.64	448.77
40000	526.00	501.11	490.17	473.87	468.53	467.20	466.05	462.20	460.28
41000	539.15	513.64	502.42	485.72	480.24	478.88	477.70	473.75	471.79
42000	552.30	526.17	514.68	497.56	491.96	490.56	489.35	485.31	483.29
43000	565.45	538.69	526.93	509.41	503.67	502.24	501.00	496.86	494.80
44000	578.60	551.22	539.18	521.26	515.38	513.92	512.65	508.42	506.31
45000	591.75	563.75	551.44	533.10	527.09	525.60	524.31	519.97	517.81
46000	604.90	576.28	563.69	544.95	538.81	537.28	535.96	531.53	529.32
47000	618.05	588.80	575.95	556.80	550.52	548.96	547.61	543.08	540.83
48000	631.20	601.33	588.20	568.64	562.23	560.64	559.26	554.64	552.33
49000	644.35	613.86	600.45	580.49	573.95	572.32	570.91	566.19	563.84
50000	657.50	626.39	612.71	592.34	585.66	584.00	582.56	577.75	575.35
51000	670.65	638.91	624.96	604.18	597.37	595.68	594.21	589.30	586.85
52000	683.80	651.44	637.22	616.03	609.09	607.36	605.86	600.86	598.36
53000	696.95	663.97	649.47	627.88	620.80	619.04	617.51	612.41	609.87
54000	710.10	676.50	661.72	639.72	632.51	630.72	629.17	623.97	621.38
55000	723.25	689.03	673.98	651.57	644.23	642.40	640.82	635.52	632.88
56000	736.40	701.55	686.23	663.42	655.94	654.08	652.47	647.08	644.39
57000	749.55	714.08	698.49	675.26	667.65	665.76	664.12	658.63	655.90
58000	762.70	726.61	710.74	687.11	679.36	677.44	675.77	670.19	667.40
59000	775.85	739.14	722.99	698.96	691.08	689.12	687.42	681.74	678.91
60000	789.00	751.66	735.25	710.80	702.79	700.80	699.07	693.30	690.42
61000	802.15	764.19	747.50	722.65	714.50	712.48	710.72	704.85	701.92
62000	815.30	776.72	759.76	734.50	726.22	724.16	722.37	716.41	713.43
63000	828.45	789.25	772.01	746.34	737.93	735.84	734.03	727.96	724.94
64000	841.60	801.77	784.26	758.19	749.64	747.52	745.68	739.52	736.44
65000	854.75	814.30	796.52	770.04	761.36	759.20	757.33	751.07	747.95
66000	867.90	826.83	808.77	781.88	773.07	770.88	768.98	762.63	759.46
67000	881.05	839.36	821.03	793.73	784.78	782.56	780.63	774.18	770.96
68000	894.20	851.88	833.28	805.58	796.50	794.24	792.28	785.73	782.47
69000	907.35	864.41	845.53	817.42	808.21	805.92	803.93	797.29	793.98
70000	920.50	876.94	857.79	829.27	819.92	817.60	815.58	808.84	805.48
75000	986.25	939.58	919.06	888.50	878.49	876.00	873.84	866.62	863.02
80000	1051.99	1002.22	980.33	947.74	937.05	934.40	932.10	924.39	920.55
100000	1314.99	1252.77	1225.41	1184.67	1171.32	1168.00	1165.12	1155.49	1150.69

13⅞% MONTHLY PAYMENT
NECESSARY TO AMORTIZE A LOAN

TERM / AMOUNT	1 YEAR	2 YEARS	3 YEARS	4 YEARS	5 YEARS	7 YEARS	8 YEARS	10 YEARS	12 YEARS
$ 25	2.25	1.20	.86	.69	.59	.47	.44	.39	.36
50	4.49	2.40	1.71	1.37	1.17	.94	.87	.78	.72
75	6.73	3.60	2.56	2.05	1.75	1.41	1.30	1.16	1.08
100	8.98	4.80	3.42	2.73	2.33	1.87	1.74	1.55	1.43
200	17.95	9.60	6.83	5.46	4.65	3.74	3.47	3.10	2.86
300	26.92	14.39	10.24	8.18	6.97	5.61	5.20	4.64	4.29
400	35.90	19.19	13.65	10.91	9.29	7.47	6.93	6.19	5.72
500	44.87	23.98	17.06	13.64	11.61	9.34	8.66	7.73	7.15
600	53.84	28.78	20.48	16.36	13.93	11.21	10.39	9.28	8.58
700	62.81	33.57	23.89	19.09	16.25	13.07	12.12	10.82	10.01
800	71.79	38.37	27.30	21.82	18.57	14.94	13.85	12.37	11.44
900	80.76	43.16	30.71	24.54	20.89	16.81	15.58	13.91	12.87
1000	89.73	47.96	34.12	27.27	23.21	18.68	17.31	15.46	14.30
2000	179.46	95.91	68.24	54.53	46.41	37.35	34.61	30.91	28.59
3000	269.19	143.87	102.36	81.80	69.62	56.02	51.91	46.36	42.88
4000	358.92	191.82	136.47	109.06	92.82	74.69	69.21	61.81	57.17
5000	448.65	239.77	170.59	136.32	116.02	93.36	86.51	77.26	71.47
6000	538.37	287.73	204.71	163.59	139.23	112.03	103.81	92.71	85.76
7000	628.10	335.68	238.82	190.85	162.43	130.70	121.11	108.17	100.05
8000	717.83	383.64	272.94	218.12	185.63	149.37	138.41	123.62	114.34
9000	807.56	431.59	307.06	245.38	208.84	168.04	155.71	139.07	128.64
10000	897.29	479.54	341.17	272.64	232.04	186.72	173.01	154.52	142.93
15000	1345.93	719.31	511.76	408.96	348.06	280.07	259.51	231.78	214.39
20000	1794.57	959.08	682.34	545.28	464.07	373.43	346.01	309.04	285.85
25000	2243.21	1198.85	852.93	681.60	580.09	466.78	432.52	386.29	357.32
30000	2691.85	1438.62	1023.51	817.92	696.11	560.14	519.02	463.55	428.78
35000	3140.50	1678.39	1194.10	954.24	812.13	653.49	605.52	540.81	500.24
36000	3230.22	1726.34	1228.22	981.50	835.33	672.16	622.82	556.26	514.53
37000	3319.95	1774.30	1262.33	1008.77	858.53	690.83	640.12	571.71	528.83
38000	3409.68	1822.25	1296.45	1036.03	881.74	709.50	657.42	587.16	543.12
39000	3499.41	1870.21	1330.57	1063.29	904.94	728.18	674.72	602.62	557.41
40000	3589.14	1918.16	1364.68	1090.56	928.14	746.85	692.02	618.07	571.70
41000	3678.87	1966.11	1398.80	1117.82	951.35	765.52	709.32	633.52	586.00
42000	3768.59	2014.07	1432.92	1145.09	974.55	784.19	726.62	648.97	600.29
43000	3858.32	2062.02	1467.03	1172.35	997.76	802.86	743.92	664.42	614.58
44000	3948.05	2109.97	1501.15	1199.61	1020.96	821.53	761.22	679.87	628.87
45000	4037.78	2157.93	1535.27	1226.88	1044.16	840.20	778.52	695.33	643.17
46000	4127.51	2205.88	1569.38	1254.14	1067.37	858.87	795.83	710.78	657.46
47000	4217.24	2253.84	1603.50	1281.40	1090.57	877.54	813.13	726.23	671.75
48000	4306.96	2301.79	1637.62	1308.67	1113.77	896.21	830.43	741.68	686.04
49000	4396.69	2349.74	1671.74	1335.93	1136.98	914.89	847.73	757.13	700.34
50000	4486.42	2397.70	1705.85	1363.20	1160.18	933.56	865.03	772.58	714.63
51000	4576.15	2445.65	1739.97	1390.46	1183.38	952.23	882.33	788.04	728.92
52000	4665.88	2493.61	1774.09	1417.72	1206.59	970.90	899.63	803.49	743.21
53000	4755.61	2541.56	1808.20	1444.99	1229.79	989.57	916.93	818.94	757.50
54000	4845.33	2589.51	1842.32	1472.25	1252.99	1008.24	934.23	834.39	771.80
55000	4935.06	2637.47	1876.44	1499.51	1276.20	1026.91	951.53	849.84	786.09
56000	5024.79	2685.42	1910.55	1526.78	1299.40	1045.58	968.83	865.29	800.38
57000	5114.52	2733.37	1944.67	1554.04	1322.60	1064.25	986.13	880.74	814.67
58000	5204.25	2781.33	1978.79	1581.31	1345.81	1082.92	1003.43	896.20	828.97
59000	5293.98	2829.28	2012.91	1608.57	1369.01	1101.60	1020.73	911.65	843.26
60000	5383.70	2877.24	2047.02	1635.83	1392.21	1120.27	1038.03	927.10	857.55
61000	5473.43	2925.19	2081.14	1663.10	1415.42	1138.94	1055.33	942.55	871.84
62000	5563.16	2973.14	2115.26	1690.36	1438.62	1157.61	1072.63	958.00	886.14
63000	5652.89	3021.10	2149.37	1717.63	1461.83	1176.28	1089.93	973.45	900.43
64000	5742.62	3069.05	2183.49	1744.89	1485.03	1194.95	1107.23	988.91	914.72
65000	5832.35	3117.01	2217.61	1772.15	1508.23	1213.62	1124.53	1004.36	929.01
66000	5922.07	3164.96	2251.72	1799.42	1531.44	1232.29	1141.83	1019.81	943.31
67000	6011.80	3212.91	2285.84	1826.68	1554.64	1250.96	1159.13	1035.26	957.60
68000	6101.53	3260.87	2319.96	1853.94	1577.84	1269.63	1176.43	1050.71	971.89
69000	6191.26	3308.82	2354.07	1881.21	1601.05	1288.31	1193.74	1066.16	986.18
70000	6280.99	3356.77	2388.19	1908.47	1624.25	1306.98	1211.04	1081.62	1000.48
75000	6729.63	3596.54	2558.78	2044.79	1740.27	1400.33	1297.54	1158.87	1071.94
80000	7178.27	3836.31	2729.36	2181.11	1856.28	1493.69	1384.04	1236.13	1143.40
100000	8972.84	4795.39	3411.70	2726.39	2320.35	1867.11	1730.05	1545.16	1429.25

MONTHLY PAYMENT 13⅞%

NECESSARY TO AMORTIZE A LOAN

TERM / AMOUNT	15 YEARS	18 YEARS	20 YEARS	25 YEARS	28 YEARS	29 YEARS	30 YEARS	35 YEARS	40 YEARS
$ 25	.34	.32	.31	.30	.30	.30	.30	.30	.30
50	.67	.64	.62	.60	.60	.59	.59	.59	.59
75	1.00	.95	.93	.90	.89	.89	.89	.88	.88
100	1.33	1.27	1.24	1.20	1.19	1.18	1.18	1.17	1.17
200	2.65	2.53	2.47	2.39	2.37	2.36	2.35	2.34	2.33
300	3.98	3.79	3.71	3.59	3.55	3.54	3.53	3.50	3.49
400	5.30	5.05	4.94	4.78	4.73	4.72	4.70	4.67	4.65
500	6.62	6.31	6.18	5.98	5.91	5.89	5.88	5.83	5.81
600	7.95	7.57	7.41	7.17	7.09	7.07	7.05	7.00	6.97
700	9.27	8.84	8.65	8.36	8.27	8.25	8.23	8.16	8.13
800	10.59	10.10	9.88	9.56	9.45	9.43	9.40	9.33	9.29
900	11.92	11.36	11.12	10.75	10.63	10.61	10.58	10.50	10.45
1000	13.24	12.62	12.35	11.95	11.82	11.78	11.75	11.66	11.61
2000	26.47	25.24	24.69	23.89	23.63	23.56	23.50	23.32	23.22
3000	39.71	37.85	37.04	35.83	35.44	35.34	35.25	34.97	34.83
4000	52.94	50.47	49.38	47.77	47.25	47.12	47.00	46.63	46.44
5000	66.17	63.08	61.73	59.72	59.06	58.90	58.75	58.28	58.05
6000	79.41	75.70	74.07	71.66	70.87	70.67	70.50	69.94	69.66
7000	92.64	88.31	86.42	83.60	82.68	82.45	82.25	81.60	81.27
8000	105.87	100.93	98.76	95.54	94.49	94.23	94.00	93.25	92.88
9000	119.11	113.55	111.11	107.48	106.30	106.01	105.75	104.91	104.49
10000	132.34	126.16	123.45	119.43	118.11	117.79	117.50	116.56	116.10
15000	198.51	189.24	185.17	179.14	177.16	176.68	176.25	174.84	174.14
20000	264.68	252.32	246.90	238.85	236.22	235.57	235.00	233.12	232.19
25000	330.84	315.40	308.62	298.56	295.27	294.46	293.75	291.40	290.23
30000	397.01	378.47	370.34	358.27	354.32	353.35	352.50	349.68	348.28
35000	463.18	441.55	432.06	417.98	413.38	412.24	411.25	407.96	406.32
36000	476.41	454.17	444.41	429.92	425.19	424.02	423.00	419.61	417.93
37000	489.65	466.78	456.75	441.86	437.00	435.79	434.75	431.27	429.54
38000	502.88	479.40	469.10	453.80	448.81	447.57	446.50	442.92	441.15
39000	516.11	492.01	481.44	465.74	460.62	459.35	458.25	454.58	452.76
40000	529.35	504.63	493.79	477.69	472.43	471.13	470.00	466.23	464.37
41000	542.58	517.25	506.13	489.63	484.24	482.91	481.75	477.89	475.98
42000	555.81	529.86	518.48	501.57	496.05	494.68	493.50	489.55	487.59
43000	569.05	542.48	530.82	513.51	507.86	506.46	505.25	501.20	499.20
44000	582.28	555.09	543.16	525.45	519.67	518.24	517.00	512.86	510.80
45000	595.51	567.71	555.51	537.40	531.48	530.02	528.75	524.51	522.41
46000	608.75	580.32	567.85	549.34	543.30	541.80	540.50	536.17	534.02
47000	621.98	592.94	580.20	561.28	555.11	553.57	552.25	547.82	545.63
48000	635.21	605.56	592.54	573.22	566.92	565.35	564.00	559.48	557.24
49000	648.45	618.17	604.89	585.17	578.73	577.13	575.75	571.14	568.85
50000	661.68	630.79	617.23	597.11	590.54	588.91	587.50	582.79	580.46
51000	674.92	643.40	629.58	609.05	602.35	600.69	599.25	594.45	592.07
52000	688.15	656.02	641.92	620.99	614.16	612.47	611.00	606.10	603.6[illegible]
53000	701.38	668.63	654.26	632.93	625.97	624.24	622.75	617.76	615.2[illegible]
54000	714.62	681.25	666.61	644.88	637.78	636.02	634.50	629.41	626.9[illegible]
55000	727.85	693.86	678.95	656.82	649.59	647.80	646.25	641.07	638.5[illegible]
56000	741.08	706.48	691.30	668.76	661.40	659.58	658.00	652.73	650.1[illegible]
57000	754.32	719.10	703.64	680.70	673.21	671.36	669.75	664.38	661.7[illegible]
58000	767.55	731.71	715.99	692.64	685.02	683.13	681.50	676.04	673.3[illegible]
59000	780.78	744.33	728.33	704.59	696.83	694.91	693.25	687.69	684.[illegible]
60000	794.02	756.94	740.68	716.53	708.64	706.69	705.00	699.35	696.[illegible]
61000	807.25	769.56	753.02	728.47	720.45	718.47	716.75	711.01	708.[illegible]
62000	820.48	782.17	765.37	740.41	732.27	730.25	728.50	722.66	719.[illegible]
63000	833.72	794.79	777.71	752.35	744.08	742.02	740.25	734.32	731.[illegible]
64000	846.95	807.41	790.05	764.30	755.89	753.80	752.00	745.97	742.[illegible]
65000	860.18	820.02	802.40	776.24	767.70	765.58	763.75	757.63	754.60
66000	873.42	832.64	814.74	788.18	779.51	777.36	775.50	769.28	766.20
67000	886.65	845.25	827.09	800.12	791.32	789.14	787.24	780.94	777.81
68000	899.89	857.87	839.43	812.06	803.13	800.91	798.99	792.60	789.42
69000	913.12	870.48	851.78	824.01	814.94	812.69	810.74	804.25	801.03
70000	926.35	883.10	864.12	835.95	826.75	824.47	822.49	815.91	812.64
75000	992.52	946.18	925.84	895.66	885.80	883.36	881.24	874.19	870.69
80000	1058.69	1009.26	987.57	955.37	944.86	942.25	939.99	932.46	928.73
100000	1323.36	1261.57	1234.46	1194.21	1181.07	1177.81	1174.99	1165.58	1160.91

Section 4—1988 Tax Table

For persons with taxable incomes of less than $50,000

Example: Mr. and Mrs. Green are filing a joint return. Their taxable income on line 19 of Form 1040A is $23,250. First, they find the $23,250–23,300 income line. Next, they find the column for married filing jointly and read down the column. The amount shown where the income line and filing status column meet is $3,491. This is the tax amount they must write on line 20 of Form 1040A.

At least	But less than	Single (and 1040EZ filers)	Married filing jointly *	Married filing sepa-rately	Head of a house-hold
		Your tax is—			
23,200	23,250	4,183	3,484	4,569	3,484
23,250	23,300	4,197	(3,491)	4,583	3,491
23,300	23,350	4,211	3,499	4,597	3,499
23,350	23,400	4,225	3,506	4,611	3,506

If 1040A, line 19, OR 1040EZ, line 7 is—		And you are—			
At least	But less than	Single (and 1040EZ filers)	Married filing jointly *	Married filing sepa-rately	Head of a house-hold
		Your tax is—			
$0	$5	$0	$0	$0	$0
5	15	2	2	2	2
15	25	3	3	3	3
25	50	6	6	6	6
50	75	9	9	9	9
75	100	13	13	13	13
100	125	17	17	17	17
125	150	21	21	21	21
150	175	24	24	24	24
175	200	28	28	28	28
200	225	32	32	32	32
225	250	36	36	36	36
250	275	39	39	39	39
275	300	43	43	43	43
300	325	47	47	47	47
325	350	51	51	51	51
350	375	54	54	54	54
375	400	58	58	58	58
400	425	62	62	62	62
425	450	66	66	66	66
450	475	69	69	69	69
475	500	73	73	73	73
500	525	77	77	77	77
525	550	81	81	81	81
550	575	84	84	84	84
575	600	88	88	88	88
600	625	92	92	92	92
625	650	96	96	96	96
650	675	99	99	99	99
675	700	103	103	103	103
700	725	107	107	107	107
725	750	111	111	111	111
750	775	114	114	114	114
775	800	118	118	118	118
800	825	122	122	122	122
825	850	126	126	126	126
850	875	129	129	129	129
875	900	133	133	133	133
900	925	137	137	137	137
925	950	141	141	141	141
950	975	144	144	144	144
975	1,000	148	148	148	148
1,000					
1,000	1,025	152	152	152	152
1,025	1,050	156	156	156	156
1,050	1,075	159	159	159	159
1,075	1,100	163	163	163	163
1,100	1,125	167	167	167	167
1,125	1,150	171	171	171	171
1,150	1,175	174	174	174	174
1,175	1,200	178	178	178	178
1,200	1,225	182	182	182	182
1,225	1,250	186	186	186	186
1,250	1,275	189	189	189	189
1,275	1,300	193	193	193	193
1,300	1,325	197	197	197	197
1,325	1,350	201	201	201	201
1,350	1,375	204	204	204	204
1,375	1,400	208	208	208	208

If 1040A, line 19, OR 1040EZ, line 7 is—		And you are—			
At least	But less than	Single (and 1040EZ filers)	Married filing jointly *	Married filing sepa-rately	Head of a house-hold
		Your tax is—			
1,400	1,425	212	212	212	212
1,425	1,450	216	216	216	216
1,450	1,475	219	219	219	219
1,475	1,500	223	223	223	223
1,500	1,525	227	227	227	227
1,525	1,550	231	231	231	231
1,550	1,575	234	234	234	234
1,575	1,600	238	238	238	238
1,600	1,625	242	242	242	242
1,625	1,650	246	246	246	246
1,650	1,675	249	249	249	249
1,675	1,700	253	253	253	253
1,700	1,725	257	257	257	257
1,725	1,750	261	261	261	261
1,750	1,775	264	264	264	264
1,775	1,800	268	268	268	268
1,800	1,825	272	272	272	272
1,825	1,850	276	276	276	276
1,850	1,875	279	279	279	279
1,875	1,900	283	283	283	283
1,900	1,925	287	287	287	287
1,925	1,950	291	291	291	291
1,950	1,975	294	294	294	294
1,975	2,000	298	298	298	298
2,000					
2,000	2,025	302	302	302	302
2,025	2,050	306	306	306	306
2,050	2,075	309	309	309	309
2,075	2,100	313	313	313	313
2,100	2,125	317	317	317	317
2,125	2,150	321	321	321	321
2,150	2,175	324	324	324	324
2,175	2,200	328	328	328	328
2,200	2,225	332	332	332	332
2,225	2,250	336	336	336	336
2,250	2,275	339	339	339	339
2,275	2,300	343	343	343	343
2,300	2,325	347	347	347	347
2,325	2,350	351	351	351	351
2,350	2,375	354	354	354	354
2,375	2,400	358	358	358	358
2,400	2,425	362	362	362	362
2,425	2,450	366	366	366	366
2,450	2,475	369	369	369	369
2,475	2,500	373	373	373	373
2,500	2,525	377	377	377	377
2,525	2,550	381	381	381	381
2,550	2,575	384	384	384	384
2,575	2,600	388	388	388	388
2,600	2,625	392	392	392	392
2,625	2,650	396	396	396	396
2,650	2,675	399	399	399	399
2,675	2,700	403	403	403	403

If 1040A, line 19, OR 1040EZ, line 7 is—		And you are—			
At least	But less than	Single (and 1040EZ filers)	Married filing jointly *	Married filing sepa-rately	Head of a house-hold
		Your tax is—			
2,700	2,725	407	407	407	407
2,725	2,750	411	411	411	411
2,750	2,775	414	414	414	414
2,775	2,800	418	418	418	418
2,800	2,825	422	422	422	422
2,825	2,850	426	426	426	426
2,850	2,875	429	429	429	429
2,875	2,900	433	433	433	433
2,900	2,925	437	437	437	437
2,925	2,950	441	441	441	441
2,950	2,975	444	444	444	444
2,975	3,000	448	448	448	448
3,000					
3,000	3,050	454	454	454	454
3,050	3,100	461	461	461	461
3,100	3,150	469	469	469	469
3,150	3,200	476	476	476	476
3,200	3,250	484	484	484	484
3,250	3,300	491	491	491	491
3,300	3,350	499	499	499	499
3,350	3,400	506	506	506	506
3,400	3,450	514	514	514	514
3,450	3,500	521	521	521	521
3,500	3,550	529	529	529	529
3,550	3,600	536	536	536	536
3,600	3,650	544	544	544	544
3,650	3,700	551	551	551	551
3,700	3,750	559	559	559	559
3,750	3,800	566	566	566	566
3,800	3,850	574	574	574	574
3,850	3,900	581	581	581	581
3,900	3,950	589	589	589	589
3,950	4,000	596	596	596	596
4,000					
4,000	4,050	604	604	604	604
4,050	4,100	611	611	611	611
4,100	4,150	619	619	619	619
4,150	4,200	626	626	626	626
4,200	4,250	634	634	634	634
4,250	4,300	641	641	641	641
4,300	4,350	649	649	649	649
4,350	4,400	656	656	656	656
4,400	4,450	664	664	664	664
4,450	4,500	671	671	671	671
4,500	4,550	679	679	679	679
4,550	4,600	686	686	686	686
4,600	4,650	694	694	694	694
4,650	4,700	701	701	701	701
4,700	4,750	709	709	709	709
4,750	4,800	716	716	716	716
4,800	4,850	724	724	724	724
4,850	4,900	731	731	731	731
4,900	4,950	739	739	739	739
4,950	5,000	746	746	746	746

* This column must also be used by a qualifying widow(er).

Continued on next page

1988 Tax Table—*Continued*

If 1040A, line 19, OR 1040EZ, line 7 is—		And you are—			
At least	But less than	Single (and 1040EZ filers)	Married filing jointly *	Married filing separately	Head of a household
		Your tax is—			
5,000					
5,000	5,050	754	754	754	754
5,050	5,100	761	761	761	761
5,100	5,150	769	769	769	769
5,150	5,200	776	776	776	776
5,200	5,250	784	784	784	784
5,250	5,300	791	791	791	791
5,300	5,350	799	799	799	799
5,350	5,400	806	806	806	806
5,400	5,450	814	814	814	814
5,450	5,500	821	821	821	821
5,500	5,550	829	829	829	829
5,550	5,600	836	836	836	836
5,600	5,650	844	844	844	844
5,650	5,700	851	851	851	851
5,700	5,750	859	859	859	859
5,750	5,800	866	866	866	866
5,800	5,850	874	874	874	874
5,850	5,900	881	881	881	881
5,900	5,950	889	889	889	889
5,950	6,000	896	896	896	896
6,000					
6,000	6,050	904	904	904	904
6,050	6,100	911	911	911	911
6,100	6,150	919	919	919	919
6,150	6,200	926	926	926	926
6,200	6,250	934	934	934	934
6,250	6,300	941	941	941	941
6,300	6,350	949	949	949	949
6,350	6,400	956	956	956	956
6,400	6,450	964	964	964	964
6,450	6,500	971	971	971	971
6,500	6,550	979	979	979	979
6,550	6,600	986	986	986	986
6,600	6,650	994	994	994	994
6,650	6,700	1,001	1,001	1,001	1,001
6,700	6,750	1,009	1,009	1,009	1,009
6,750	6,800	1,016	1,016	1,016	1,016
6,800	6,850	1,024	1,024	1,024	1,024
6,850	6,900	1,031	1,031	1,031	1,031
6,900	6,950	1,039	1,039	1,039	1,039
6,950	7,000	1,046	1,046	1,046	1,046
7,000					
7,000	7,050	1,054	1,054	1,054	1,054
7,050	7,100	1,061	1,061	1,061	1,061
7,100	7,150	1,069	1,069	1,069	1,069
7,150	7,200	1,076	1,076	1,076	1,076
7,200	7,250	1,084	1,084	1,084	1,084
7,250	7,300	1,091	1,091	1,091	1,091
7,300	7,350	1,099	1,099	1,099	1,099
7,350	7,400	1,106	1,106	1,106	1,106
7,400	7,450	1,114	1,114	1,114	1,114
7,450	7,500	1,121	1,121	1,121	1,121
7,500	7,550	1,129	1,129	1,129	1,129
7,550	7,600	1,136	1,136	1,136	1,136
7,600	7,650	1,144	1,144	1,144	1,144
7,650	7,700	1,151	1,151	1,151	1,151
7,700	7,750	1,159	1,159	1,159	1,159
7,750	7,800	1,166	1,166	1,166	1,166
7,800	7,850	1,174	1,174	1,174	1,174
7,850	7,900	1,181	1,181	1,181	1,181
7,900	7,950	1,189	1,189	1,189	1,189
7,950	8,000	1,196	1,196	1,196	1,196
8,000					
8,000	8,050	1,204	1,204	1,204	1,204
8,050	8,100	1,211	1,211	1,211	1,211
8,100	8,150	1,219	1,219	1,219	1,219
8,150	8,200	1,226	1,226	1,226	1,226
8,200	8,250	1,234	1,234	1,234	1,234
8,250	8,300	1,241	1,241	1,241	1,241
8,300	8,350	1,249	1,249	1,249	1,249
8,350	8,400	1,256	1,256	1,256	1,256
8,400	8,450	1,264	1,264	1,264	1,264
8,450	8,500	1,271	1,271	1,271	1,271
8,500	8,550	1,279	1,279	1,279	1,279
8,550	8,600	1,286	1,286	1,286	1,286
8,600	8,650	1,294	1,294	1,294	1,294
8,650	8,700	1,301	1,301	1,301	1,301
8,700	8,750	1,309	1,309	1,309	1,309
8,750	8,800	1,316	1,316	1,316	1,316
8,800	8,850	1,324	1,324	1,324	1,324
8,850	8,900	1,331	1,331	1,331	1,331
8,900	8,950	1,339	1,339	1,339	1,339
8,950	9,000	1,346	1,346	1,346	1,346
9,000					
9,000	9,050	1,354	1,354	1,354	1,354
9,050	9,100	1,361	1,361	1,361	1,361
9,100	9,150	1,369	1,369	1,369	1,369
9,150	9,200	1,376	1,376	1,376	1,376
9,200	9,250	1,384	1,384	1,384	1,384
9,250	9,300	1,391	1,391	1,391	1,391
9,300	9,350	1,399	1,399	1,399	1,399
9,350	9,400	1,406	1,406	1,406	1,406
9,400	9,450	1,414	1,414	1,414	1,414
9,450	9,500	1,421	1,421	1,421	1,421
9,500	9,550	1,429	1,429	1,429	1,429
9,550	9,600	1,436	1,436	1,436	1,436
9,600	9,650	1,444	1,444	1,444	1,444
9,650	9,700	1,451	1,451	1,451	1,451
9,700	9,750	1,459	1,459	1,459	1,459
9,750	9,800	1,466	1,466	1,466	1,466
9,800	9,850	1,474	1,474	1,474	1,474
9,850	9,900	1,481	1,481	1,481	1,481
9,900	9,950	1,489	1,489	1,489	1,489
9,950	10,000	1,496	1,496	1,496	1,496
10,000					
10,000	10,050	1,504	1,504	1,504	1,504
10,050	10,100	1,511	1,511	1,511	1,511
10,100	10,150	1,519	1,519	1,519	1,519
10,150	10,200	1,526	1,526	1,526	1,526
10,200	10,250	1,534	1,534	1,534	1,534
10,250	10,300	1,541	1,541	1,541	1,541
10,300	10,350	1,549	1,549	1,549	1,549
10,350	10,400	1,556	1,556	1,556	1,556
10,400	10,450	1,564	1,564	1,564	1,564
10,450	10,500	1,571	1,571	1,571	1,571
10,500	10,550	1,579	1,579	1,579	1,579
10,550	10,600	1,586	1,586	1,586	1,586
10,600	10,650	1,594	1,594	1,594	1,594
10,650	10,700	1,601	1,601	1,601	1,601
10,700	10,750	1,609	1,609	1,609	1,609
10,750	10,800	1,616	1,616	1,616	1,616
10,800	10,850	1,624	1,624	1,624	1,624
10,850	10,900	1,631	1,631	1,631	1,631
10,900	10,950	1,639	1,639	1,639	1,639
10,950	11,000	1,646	1,646	1,646	1,646
11,000					
11,000	11,050	1,654	1,654	1,654	1,654
11,050	11,100	1,661	1,661	1,661	1,661
11,100	11,150	1,669	1,669	1,669	1,669
11,150	11,200	1,676	1,676	1,676	1,676
11,200	11,250	1,684	1,684	1,684	1,684
11,250	11,300	1,691	1,691	1,691	1,691
11,300	11,350	1,699	1,699	1,699	1,699
11,350	11,400	1,706	1,706	1,706	1,706
11,400	11,450	1,714	1,714	1,714	1,714
11,450	11,500	1,721	1,721	1,721	1,721
11,500	11,550	1,729	1,729	1,729	1,729
11,550	11,600	1,736	1,736	1,736	1,736
11,600	11,650	1,744	1,744	1,744	1,744
11,650	11,700	1,751	1,751	1,751	1,751
11,700	11,750	1,759	1,759	1,759	1,759
11,750	11,800	1,766	1,766	1,766	1,766
11,800	11,850	1,774	1,774	1,774	1,774
11,850	11,900	1,781	1,781	1,781	1,781
11,900	11,950	1,789	1,789	1,789	1,789
11,950	12,000	1,796	1,796	1,796	1,796
12,000					
12,000	12,050	1,804	1,804	1,804	1,804
12,050	12,100	1,811	1,811	1,811	1,811
12,100	12,150	1,819	1,819	1,819	1,819
12,150	12,200	1,826	1,826	1,826	1,826
12,200	12,250	1,834	1,834	1,834	1,834
12,250	12,300	1,841	1,841	1,841	1,841
12,300	12,350	1,849	1,849	1,849	1,849
12,350	12,400	1,856	1,856	1,856	1,856
12,400	12,450	1,864	1,864	1,864	1,864
12,450	12,500	1,871	1,871	1,871	1,871
12,500	12,550	1,879	1,879	1,879	1,879
12,550	12,600	1,886	1,886	1,886	1,886
12,600	12,650	1,894	1,894	1,894	1,894
12,650	12,700	1,901	1,901	1,901	1,901
12,700	12,750	1,909	1,909	1,909	1,909
12,750	12,800	1,916	1,916	1,916	1,916
12,800	12,850	1,924	1,924	1,924	1,924
12,850	12,900	1,931	1,931	1,931	1,931
12,900	12,950	1,939	1,939	1,939	1,939
12,950	13,000	1,946	1,946	1,946	1,946
13,000					
13,000	13,050	1,954	1,954	1,954	1,954
13,050	13,100	1,961	1,961	1,961	1,961
13,100	13,150	1,969	1,969	1,969	1,969
13,150	13,200	1,976	1,976	1,976	1,976
13,200	13,250	1,984	1,984	1,984	1,984
13,250	13,300	1,991	1,991	1,991	1,991
13,300	13,350	1,999	1,999	1,999	1,999
13,350	13,400	2,006	2,006	2,006	2,006
13,400	13,450	2,014	2,014	2,014	2,014
13,450	13,500	2,021	2,021	2,021	2,021
13,500	13,550	2,029	2,029	2,029	2,029
13,550	13,600	2,036	2,036	2,036	2,036
13,600	13,650	2,044	2,044	2,044	2,044
13,650	13,700	2,051	2,051	2,051	2,051
13,700	13,750	2,059	2,059	2,059	2,059
13,750	13,800	2,066	2,066	2,066	2,066
13,800	13,850	2,074	2,074	2,074	2,074
13,850	13,900	2,081	2,081	2,081	2,081
13,900	13,950	2,089	2,089	2,089	2,089
13,950	14,000	2,096	2,096	2,096	2,096

* This column must also be used by a qualifying widow(er).

Continued on next page

1988 Tax Table—*Continued*

If 1040A, line 19, OR 1040EZ, line 7 is—		And you are—			
At least	But less than	Single (and 1040EZ filers)	Married filing jointly *	Married filing separately	Head of a household
		Your tax is—			
14,000					
14,000	14,050	2,104	2,104	2,104	2,104
14,050	14,100	2,111	2,111	2,111	2,111
14,100	14,150	2,119	2,119	2,119	2,119
14,150	14,200	2,126	2,126	2,126	2,126
14,200	14,250	2,134	2,134	2,134	2,134
14,250	14,300	2,141	2,141	2,141	2,141
14,300	14,350	2,149	2,149	2,149	2,149
14,350	14,400	2,156	2,156	2,156	2,156
14,400	14,450	2,164	2,164	2,164	2,164
14,450	14,500	2,171	2,171	2,171	2,171
14,500	14,550	2,179	2,179	2,179	2,179
14,550	14,600	2,186	2,186	2,186	2,186
14,600	14,650	2,194	2,194	2,194	2,194
14,650	14,700	2,201	2,201	2,201	2,201
14,700	14,750	2,209	2,209	2,209	2,209
14,750	14,800	2,216	2,216	2,216	2,216
14,800	14,850	2,224	2,224	2,224	2,224
14,850	14,900	2,231	2,231	2,231	2,231
14,900	14,950	2,239	2,239	2,245	2,239
14,950	15,000	2,246	2,246	2,259	2,246
15,000					
15,000	15,050	2,254	2,254	2,273	2,254
15,050	15,100	2,261	2,261	2,287	2,261
15,100	15,150	2,269	2,269	2,301	2,269
15,150	15,200	2,276	2,276	2,315	2,276
15,200	15,250	2,284	2,284	2,329	2,284
15,250	15,300	2,291	2,291	2,343	2,291
15,300	15,350	2,299	2,299	2,357	2,299
15,350	15,400	2,306	2,306	2,371	2,306
15,400	15,450	2,314	2,314	2,385	2,314
15,450	15,500	2,321	2,321	2,399	2,321
15,500	15,550	2,329	2,329	2,413	2,329
15,550	15,600	2,336	2,336	2,427	2,336
15,600	15,650	2,344	2,344	2,441	2,344
15,650	15,700	2,351	2,351	2,455	2,351
15,700	15,750	2,359	2,359	2,469	2,359
15,750	15,800	2,366	2,366	2,483	2,366
15,800	15,850	2,374	2,374	2,497	2,374
15,850	15,900	2,381	2,381	2,511	2,381
15,900	15,950	2,389	2,389	2,525	2,389
15,950	16,000	2,396	2,396	2,539	2,396
16,000					
16,000	16,050	2,404	2,404	2,553	2,404
16,050	16,100	2,411	2,411	2,567	2,411
16,100	16,150	2,419	2,419	2,581	2,419
16,150	16,200	2,426	2,426	2,595	2,426
16,200	16,250	2,434	2,434	2,609	2,434
16,250	16,300	2,441	2,441	2,623	2,441
16,300	16,350	2,449	2,449	2,637	2,449
16,350	16,400	2,456	2,456	2,651	2,456
16,400	16,450	2,464	2,464	2,665	2,464
16,450	16,500	2,471	2,471	2,679	2,471
16,500	16,550	2,479	2,479	2,693	2,479
16,550	16,600	2,486	2,486	2,707	2,486
16,600	16,650	2,494	2,494	2,721	2,494
16,650	16,700	2,501	2,501	2,735	2,501
16,700	16,750	2,509	2,509	2,749	2,509
16,750	16,800	2,516	2,516	2,763	2,516
16,800	16,850	2,524	2,524	2,777	2,524
16,850	16,900	2,531	2,531	2,791	2,531
16,900	16,950	2,539	2,539	2,805	2,539
16,950	17,000	2,546	2,546	2,819	2,546

If 1040A, line 19, OR 1040EZ, line 7 is—		And you are—			
At least	But less than	Single (and 1040EZ filers)	Married filing jointly *	Married filing separately	Head of a household
		Your tax is—			
17,000					
17,000	17,050	2,554	2,554	2,833	2,554
17,050	17,100	2,561	2,561	2,847	2,561
17,100	17,150	2,569	2,569	2,861	2,569
17,150	17,200	2,576	2,576	2,875	2,576
17,200	17,250	2,584	2,584	2,889	2,584
17,250	17,300	2,591	2,591	2,903	2,591
17,300	17,350	2,599	2,599	2,917	2,599
17,350	17,400	2,606	2,606	2,931	2,606
17,400	17,450	2,614	2,614	2,945	2,614
17,450	17,500	2,621	2,621	2,959	2,621
17,500	17,550	2,629	2,629	2,973	2,629
17,550	17,600	2,636	2,636	2,987	2,636
17,600	17,650	2,644	2,644	3,001	2,644
17,650	17,700	2,651	2,651	3,015	2,651
17,700	17,750	2,659	2,659	3,029	2,659
17,750	17,800	2,666	2,666	3,043	2,666
17,800	17,850	2,674	2,674	3,057	2,674
17,850	17,900	2,685	2,681	3,071	2,681
17,900	17,950	2,699	2,689	3,085	2,689
17,950	18,000	2,713	2,696	3,099	2,696
18,000					
18,000	18,050	2,727	2,704	3,113	2,704
18,050	18,100	2,741	2,711	3,127	2,711
18,100	18,150	2,755	2,719	3,141	2,719
18,150	18,200	2,769	2,726	3,155	2,726
18,200	18,250	2,783	2,734	3,169	2,734
18,250	18,300	2,797	2,741	3,183	2,741
18,300	18,350	2,811	2,749	3,197	2,749
18,350	18,400	2,825	2,756	3,211	2,756
18,400	18,450	2,839	2,764	3,225	2,764
18,450	18,500	2,853	2,771	3,239	2,771
18,500	18,550	2,867	2,779	3,253	2,779
18,550	18,600	2,881	2,786	3,267	2,786
18,600	18,650	2,895	2,794	3,281	2,794
18,650	18,700	2,909	2,801	3,295	2,801
18,700	18,750	2,923	2,809	3,309	2,809
18,750	18,800	2,937	2,816	3,323	2,816
18,800	18,850	2,951	2,824	3,337	2,824
18,850	18,900	2,965	2,831	3,351	2,831
18,900	18,950	2,979	2,839	3,365	2,839
18,950	19,000	2,993	2,846	3,379	2,846
19,000					
19,000	19,050	3,007	2,854	3,393	2,854
19,050	19,100	3,021	2,861	3,407	2,861
19,100	19,150	3,035	2,869	3,421	2,869
19,150	19,200	3,049	2,876	3,435	2,876
19,200	19,250	3,063	2,884	3,449	2,884
19,250	19,300	3,077	2,891	3,463	2,891
19,300	19,350	3,091	2,899	3,477	2,899
19,350	19,400	3,105	2,906	3,491	2,906
19,400	19,450	3,119	2,914	3,505	2,914
19,450	19,500	3,133	2,921	3,519	2,921
19,500	19,550	3,147	2,929	3,533	2,929
19,550	19,600	3,161	2,936	3,547	2,936
19,600	19,650	3,175	2,944	3,561	2,944
19,650	19,700	3,189	2,951	3,575	2,951
19,700	19,750	3,203	2,959	3,589	2,959
19,750	19,800	3,217	2,966	3,603	2,966
19,800	19,850	3,231	2,974	3,617	2,974
19,850	19,900	3,245	2,981	3,631	2,981
19,900	19,950	3,259	2,989	3,645	2,989
19,950	20,000	3,273	2,996	3,659	2,996

If 1040A, line 19, OR 1040EZ, line 7 is—		And you are—			
At least	But less than	Single (and 1040EZ filers)	Married filing jointly *	Married filing separately	Head of a household
		Your tax is—			
20,000					
20,000	20,050	3,287	3,004	3,673	3,004
20,050	20,100	3,301	3,011	3,687	3,011
20,100	20,150	3,315	3,019	3,701	3,019
20,150	20,200	3,329	3,026	3,715	3,026
20,200	20,250	3,343	3,034	3,729	3,034
20,250	20,300	3,357	3,041	3,743	3,041
20,300	20,350	3,371	3,049	3,757	3,049
20,350	20,400	3,385	3,056	3,771	3,056
20,400	20,450	3,399	3,064	3,785	3,064
20,450	20,500	3,413	3,071	3,799	3,071
20,500	20,550	3,427	3,079	3,813	3,079
20,550	20,600	3,441	3,086	3,827	3,086
20,600	20,650	3,455	3,094	3,841	3,094
20,650	20,700	3,469	3,101	3,855	3,101
20,700	20,750	3,483	3,109	3,869	3,109
20,750	20,800	3,497	3,116	3,883	3,116
20,800	20,850	3,511	3,124	3,897	3,124
20,850	20,900	3,525	3,131	3,911	3,131
20,900	20,950	3,539	3,139	3,925	3,139
20,950	21,000	3,553	3,146	3,939	3,146
21,000					
21,000	21,050	3,567	3,154	3,953	3,154
21,050	21,100	3,581	3,161	3,967	3,161
21,100	21,150	3,595	3,169	3,981	3,169
21,150	21,200	3,609	3,176	3,995	3,176
21,200	21,250	3,623	3,184	4,009	3,184
21,250	21,300	3,637	3,191	4,023	3,191
21,300	21,350	3,651	3,199	4,037	3,199
21,350	21,400	3,665	3,206	4,051	3,206
21,400	21,450	3,679	3,214	4,065	3,214
21,450	21,500	3,693	3,221	4,079	3,221
21,500	21,550	3,707	3,229	4,093	3,229
21,550	21,600	3,721	3,236	4,107	3,236
21,600	21,650	3,735	3,244	4,121	3,244
21,650	21,700	3,749	3,251	4,135	3,251
21,700	21,750	3,763	3,259	4,149	3,259
21,750	21,800	3,777	3,266	4,163	3,266
21,800	21,850	3,791	3,274	4,177	3,274
21,850	21,900	3,805	3,281	4,191	3,281
21,900	21,950	3,819	3,289	4,205	3,289
21,950	22,000	3,833	3,296	4,219	3,296
22,000					
22,000	22,050	3,847	3,304	4,233	3,304
22,050	22,100	3,861	3,311	4,247	3,311
22,100	22,150	3,875	3,319	4,261	3,319
22,150	22,200	3,889	3,326	4,275	3,326
22,200	22,250	3,903	3,334	4,289	3,334
22,250	22,300	3,917	3,341	4,303	3,341
22,300	22,350	3,931	3,349	4,317	3,349
22,350	22,400	3,945	3,356	4,331	3,356
22,400	22,450	3,959	3,364	4,345	3,364
22,450	22,500	3,973	3,371	4,359	3,371
22,500	22,550	3,987	3,379	4,373	3,379
22,550	22,600	4,001	3,386	4,387	3,386
22,600	22,650	4,015	3,394	4,401	3,394
22,650	22,700	4,029	3,401	4,415	3,401
22,700	22,750	4,043	3,409	4,429	3,409
22,750	22,800	4,057	3,416	4,443	3,416
22,800	22,850	4,071	3,424	4,457	3,424
22,850	22,900	4,085	3,431	4,471	3,431
22,900	22,950	4,099	3,439	4,485	3,439
22,950	23,000	4,113	3,446	4,499	3,446

* This column must also be used by a qualifying widow(er).

Continued on next page

1988 Tax Table—*Continued*

If 1040A, line 19, OR 1040EZ, line 7 is—		And you are—			
At least	But less than	Single (and 1040EZ filers)	Married filing jointly *	Married filing sepa-rately	Head of a house-hold
		Your tax is—			
23,000					
23,000	**23,050**	4,127	3,454	4,513	3,454
23,050	**23,100**	4,141	3,461	4,527	3,461
23,100	**23,150**	4,155	3,469	4,541	3,469
23,150	**23,200**	4,169	3,476	4,555	3,476
23,200	**23,250**	4,183	3,484	4,569	3,484
23,250	**23,300**	4,197	3,491	4,583	3,491
23,300	**23,350**	4,211	3,499	4,597	3,499
23,350	**23,400**	4,225	3,506	4,611	3,506
23,400	**23,450**	4,239	3,514	4,625	3,514
23,450	**23,500**	4,253	3,521	4,639	3,521
23,500	**23,550**	4,267	3,529	4,653	3,529
23,550	**23,600**	4,281	3,536	4,667	3,536
23,600	**23,650**	4,295	3,544	4,681	3,544
23,650	**23,700**	4,309	3,551	4,695	3,551
23,700	**23,750**	4,323	3,559	4,709	3,559
23,750	**23,800**	4,337	3,566	4,723	3,566
23,800	**23,850**	4,351	3,574	4,737	3,574
23,850	**23,900**	4,365	3,581	4,751	3,581
23,900	**23,950**	4,379	3,589	4,765	3,592
23,950	**24,000**	4,393	3,596	4,779	3,606
24,000					
24,000	**24,050**	4,407	3,604	4,793	3,620
24,050	**24,100**	4,421	3,611	4,807	3,634
24,100	**24,150**	4,435	3,619	4,821	3,648
24,150	**24,200**	4,449	3,626	4,835	3,662
24,200	**24,250**	4,463	3,634	4,849	3,676
24,250	**24,300**	4,477	3,641	4,863	3,690
24,300	**24,350**	4,491	3,649	4,877	3,704
24,350	**24,400**	4,505	3,656	4,891	3,718
24,400	**24,450**	4,519	3,664	4,905	3,732
24,450	**24,500**	4,533	3,671	4,919	3,746
24,500	**24,550**	4,547	3,679	4,933	3,760
24,550	**24,600**	4,561	3,686	4,947	3,774
24,600	**24,650**	4,575	3,694	4,961	3,788
24,650	**24,700**	4,589	3,701	4,975	3,802
24,700	**24,750**	4,603	3,709	4,989	3,816
24,750	**24,800**	4,617	3,716	5,003	3,830
24,800	**24,850**	4,631	3,724	5,017	3,844
24,850	**24,900**	4,645	3,731	5,031	3,858
24,900	**24,950**	4,659	3,739	5,045	3,872
24,950	**25,000**	4,673	3,746	5,059	3,886
25,000					
25,000	**25,050**	4,687	3,754	5,073	3,900
25,050	**25,100**	4,701	3,761	5,087	3,914
25,100	**25,150**	4,715	3,769	5,101	3,928
25,150	**25,200**	4,729	3,776	5,115	3,942
25,200	**25,250**	4,743	3,784	5,129	3,956
25,250	**25,300**	4,757	3,791	5,143	3,970
25,300	**25,350**	4,771	3,799	5,157	3,984
25,350	**25,400**	4,785	3,806	5,171	3,998
25,400	**25,450**	4,799	3,814	5,185	4,012
25,450	**25,500**	4,813	3,821	5,199	4,026
25,500	**25,550**	4,827	3,829	5,213	4,040
25,550	**25,600**	4,841	3,836	5,227	4,054
25,600	**25,650**	4,855	3,844	5,241	4,068
25,650	**25,700**	4,869	3,851	5,255	4,082
25,700	**25,750**	4,883	3,859	5,269	4,096
25,750	**25,800**	4,897	3,866	5,283	4,110
25,800	**25,850**	4,911	3,874	5,297	4,124
25,850	**25,900**	4,925	3,881	5,311	4,138
25,900	**25,950**	4,939	3,889	5,325	4,152
25,950	**26,000**	4,953	3,896	5,339	4,166

If 1040A, line 19, OR 1040EZ, line 7 is—		And you are—			
At least	But less than	Single (and 1040EZ filers)	Married filing jointly *	Married filing sepa-rately	Head of a house-hold
		Your tax is—			
26,000					
26,000	**26,050**	4,967	3,904	5,353	4,180
26,050	**26,100**	4,981	3,911	5,367	4,194
26,100	**26,150**	4,995	3,919	5,381	4,208
26,150	**26,200**	5,009	3,926	5,395	4,222
26,200	**26,250**	5,023	3,934	5,409	4,236
26,250	**26,300**	5,037	3,941	5,423	4,250
26,300	**26,350**	5,051	3,949	5,437	4,264
26,350	**26,400**	5,065	3,956	5,451	4,278
26,400	**26,450**	5,079	3,964	5,465	4,292
26,450	**26,500**	5,093	3,971	5,479	4,306
26,500	**26,550**	5,107	3,979	5,493	4,320
26,550	**26,600**	5,121	3,986	5,507	4,334
26,600	**26,650**	5,135	3,994	5,521	4,348
26,650	**26,700**	5,149	4,001	5,535	4,362
26,700	**26,750**	5,163	4,009	5,549	4,376
26,750	**26,800**	5,177	4,016	5,563	4,390
26,800	**26,850**	5,191	4,024	5,577	4,404
26,850	**26,900**	5,205	4,031	5,591	4,418
26,900	**26,950**	5,219	4,039	5,605	4,432
26,950	**27,000**	5,233	4,046	5,619	4,446
27,000					
27,000	**27,050**	5,247	4,054	5,633	4,460
27,050	**27,100**	5,261	4,061	5,647	4,474
27,100	**27,150**	5,275	4,069	5,661	4,488
27,150	**27,200**	5,289	4,076	5,675	4,502
27,200	**27,250**	5,303	4,084	5,689	4,516
27,250	**27,300**	5,317	4,091	5,703	4,530
27,300	**27,350**	5,331	4,099	5,717	4,544
27,350	**27,400**	5,345	4,106	5,731	4,558
27,400	**27,450**	5,359	4,114	5,745	4,572
27,450	**27,500**	5,373	4,121	5,759	4,586
27,500	**27,550**	5,387	4,129	5,773	4,600
27,550	**27,600**	5,401	4,136	5,787	4,614
27,600	**27,650**	5,415	4,144	5,801	4,628
27,650	**27,700**	5,429	4,151	5,815	4,642
27,700	**27,750**	5,443	4,159	5,829	4,656
27,750	**27,800**	5,457	4,166	5,843	4,670
27,800	**27,850**	5,471	4,174	5,857	4,684
27,850	**27,900**	5,485	4,181	5,871	4,698
27,900	**27,950**	5,499	4,189	5,885	4,712
27,950	**28,000**	5,513	4,196	5,899	4,726
28,000					
28,000	**28,050**	5,527	4,204	5,913	4,740
28,050	**28,100**	5,541	4,211	5,927	4,754
28,100	**28,150**	5,555	4,219	5,941	4,768
28,150	**28,200**	5,569	4,226	5,955	4,782
28,200	**28,250**	5,583	4,234	5,969	4,796
28,250	**28,300**	5,597	4,241	5,983	4,810
28,300	**28,350**	5,611	4,249	5,997	4,824
28,350	**28,400**	5,625	4,256	6,011	4,838
28,400	**28,450**	5,639	4,264	6,025	4,852
28,450	**28,500**	5,653	4,271	6,039	4,866
28,500	**28,550**	5,667	4,279	6,053	4,880
28,550	**28,600**	5,681	4,286	6,067	4,894
28,600	**28,650**	5,695	4,294	6,081	4,908
28,650	**28,700**	5,709	4,301	6,095	4,922
28,700	**28,750**	5,723	4,309	6,109	4,936
28,750	**28,800**	5,737	4,316	6,123	4,950
28,800	**28,850**	5,751	4,324	6,137	4,964
28,850	**28,900**	5,765	4,331	6,151	4,978
28,900	**28,950**	5,779	4,339	6,165	4,992
28,950	**29,000**	5,793	4,346	6,179	5,006

If 1040A, line 19, OR 1040EZ, line 7 is—		And you are—			
At least	But less than	Single (and 1040EZ filers)	Married filing jointly *	Married filing sepa-rately	Head of a house-hold
		Your tax is—			
29,000					
29,000	**29,050**	5,807	4,354	6,193	5,020
29,050	**29,100**	5,821	4,361	6,207	5,034
29,100	**29,150**	5,835	4,369	6,221	5,048
29,150	**29,200**	5,849	4,376	6,235	5,062
29,200	**29,250**	5,863	4,384	6,249	5,076
29,250	**29,300**	5,877	4,391	6,263	5,090
29,300	**29,350**	5,891	4,399	6,277	5,104
29,350	**29,400**	5,905	4,406	6,291	5,118
29,400	**29,450**	5,919	4,414	6,305	5,132
29,450	**29,500**	5,933	4,421	6,319	5,146
29,500	**29,550**	5,947	4,429	6,333	5,160
29,550	**29,600**	5,961	4,436	6,347	5,174
29,600	**29,650**	5,975	4,444	6,361	5,188
29,650	**29,700**	5,989	4,451	6,375	5,202
29,700	**29,750**	6,003	4,459	6,389	5,216
29,750	**29,800**	6,017	4,470	6,403	5,230
29,800	**29,850**	6,031	4,484	6,417	5,244
29,850	**29,900**	6,045	4,498	6,431	5,258
29,900	**29,950**	6,059	4,512	6,445	5,272
29,950	**30,000**	6,073	4,526	6,459	5,286
30,000					
30,000	**30,050**	6,087	4,540	6,473	5,300
30,050	**30,100**	6,101	4,554	6,487	5,314
30,100	**30,150**	6,115	4,568	6,501	5,328
30,150	**30,200**	6,129	4,582	6,515	5,342
30,200	**30,250**	6,143	4,596	6,529	5,356
30,250	**30,300**	6,157	4,610	6,543	5,370
30,300	**30,350**	6,171	4,624	6,557	5,384
30,350	**30,400**	6,185	4,638	6,571	5,398
30,400	**30,450**	6,199	4,652	6,585	5,412
30,450	**30,500**	6,213	4,666	6,599	5,426
30,500	**30,550**	6,227	4,680	6,613	5,440
30,550	**30,600**	6,241	4,694	6,627	5,454
30,600	**30,650**	6,255	4,708	6,641	5,468
30,650	**30,700**	6,269	4,722	6,655	5,482
30,700	**30,750**	6,283	4,736	6,669	5,496
30,750	**30,800**	6,297	4,750	6,683	5,510
30,800	**30,850**	6,311	4,764	6,697	5,524
30,850	**30,900**	6,325	4,778	6,711	5,538
30,900	**30,950**	6,339	4,792	6,725	5,552
30,950	**31,000**	6,353	4,806	6,739	5,566
31,000					
31,000	**31,050**	6,367	4,820	6,753	5,580
31,050	**31,100**	6,381	4,834	6,767	5,594
31,100	**31,150**	6,395	4,848	6,781	5,608
31,150	**31,200**	6,409	4,862	6,795	5,622
31,200	**31,250**	6,423	4,876	6,809	5,636
31,250	**31,300**	6,437	4,890	6,823	5,650
31,300	**31,350**	6,451	4,904	6,837	5,664
31,350	**31,400**	6,465	4,918	6,851	5,678
31,400	**31,450**	6,479	4,932	6,865	5,692
31,450	**31,500**	6,493	4,946	6,879	5,706
31,500	**31,550**	6,507	4,960	6,893	5,720
31,550	**31,600**	6,521	4,974	6,907	5,734
31,600	**31,650**	6,535	4,988	6,921	5,748
31,650	**31,700**	6,549	5,002	6,935	5,762
31,700	**31,750**	6,563	5,016	6,949	5,776
31,750	**31,800**	6,577	5,030	6,963	5,790
31,800	**31,850**	6,591	5,044	6,977	5,804
31,850	**31,900**	6,605	5,058	6,991	5,818
31,900	**31,950**	6,619	5,072	7,005	5,832
31,950	**32,000**	6,633	5,086	7,019	5,846

* This column must also be used by a qualifying widow(er).

Continued on next page

1988 Tax Table—*Continued*

If 1040A, line 19, OR 1040EZ, line 7 is—		And you are—			
At least	But less than	Single (and 1040EZ filers)	Married filing jointly *	Married filing separately	Head of a household
		Your tax is—			
32,000					
32,000	32,050	6,647	5,100	7,033	5,860
32,050	32,100	6,661	5,114	7,047	5,874
32,100	32,150	6,675	5,128	7,061	5,888
32,150	32,200	6,689	5,142	7,075	5,902
32,200	32,250	6,703	5,156	7,089	5,916
32,250	32,300	6,717	5,170	7,103	5,930
32,300	32,350	6,731	5,184	7,117	5,944
32,350	32,400	6,745	5,198	7,131	5,958
32,400	32,450	6,759	5,212	7,145	5,972
32,450	32,500	6,773	5,226	7,159	5,986
32,500	32,550	6,787	5,240	7,173	6,000
32,550	32,600	6,801	5,254	7,187	6,014
32,600	32,650	6,815	5,268	7,201	6,028
32,650	32,700	6,829	5,282	7,215	6,042
32,700	32,750	6,843	5,296	7,229	6,056
32,750	32,800	6,857	5,310	7,243	6,070
32,800	32,850	6,871	5,324	7,257	6,084
32,850	32,900	6,885	5,338	7,271	6,098
32,900	32,950	6,899	5,352	7,285	6,112
32,950	33,000	6,913	5,366	7,299	6,126
33,000					
33,000	33,050	6,927	5,380	7,313	6,140
33,050	33,100	6,941	5,394	7,327	6,154
33,100	33,150	6,955	5,408	7,341	6,168
33,150	33,200	6,969	5,422	7,355	6,182
33,200	33,250	6,983	5,436	7,369	6,196
33,250	33,300	6,997	5,450	7,383	6,210
33,300	33,350	7,011	5,464	7,397	6,224
33,350	33,400	7,025	5,478	7,411	6,238
33,400	33,450	7,039	5,492	7,425	6,252
33,450	33,500	7,053	5,506	7,439	6,266
33,500	33,550	7,067	5,520	7,453	6,280
33,550	33,600	7,081	5,534	7,467	6,294
33,600	33,650	7,095	5,548	7,481	6,308
33,650	33,700	7,109	5,562	7,495	6,322
33,700	33,750	7,123	5,576	7,509	6,336
33,750	33,800	7,137	5,590	7,523	6,350
33,800	33,850	7,151	5,604	7,537	6,364
33,850	33,900	7,165	5,618	7,551	6,378
33,900	33,950	7,179	5,632	7,565	6,392
33,950	34,000	7,193	5,646	7,579	6,406
34,000					
34,000	34,050	7,207	5,660	7,593	6,420
34,050	34,100	7,221	5,674	7,607	6,434
34,100	34,150	7,235	5,688	7,621	6,448
34,150	34,200	7,249	5,702	7,635	6,462
34,200	34,250	7,263	5,716	7,649	6,476
34,250	34,300	7,277	5,730	7,663	6,490
34,300	34,350	7,291	5,744	7,677	6,504
34,350	34,400	7,305	5,758	7,691	6,518
34,400	34,450	7,319	5,772	7,705	6,532
34,450	34,500	7,333	5,786	7,719	6,546
34,500	34,550	7,347	5,800	7,733	6,560
34,550	34,600	7,361	5,814	7,747	6,574
34,600	34,650	7,375	5,828	7,761	6,588
34,650	34,700	7,389	5,842	7,775	6,602
34,700	34,750	7,403	5,856	7,789	6,616
34,750	34,800	7,417	5,870	7,803	6,630
34,800	34,850	7,431	5,884	7,817	6,644
34,850	34,900	7,445	5,898	7,831	6,658
34,900	34,950	7,459	5,912	7,845	6,672
34,950	35,000	7,473	5,926	7,859	6,686
35,000					
35,000	35,050	7,487	5,940	7,873	6,700
35,050	35,100	7,501	5,954	7,887	6,714
35,100	35,150	7,515	5,968	7,901	6,728
35,150	35,200	7,529	5,982	7,915	6,742
35,200	35,250	7,543	5,996	7,929	6,756
35,250	35,300	7,557	6,010	7,943	6,770
35,300	35,350	7,571	6,024	7,957	6,784
35,350	35,400	7,585	6,038	7,971	6,798
35,400	35,450	7,599	6,052	7,985	6,812
35,450	35,500	7,613	6,066	7,999	6,826
35,500	35,550	7,627	6,080	8,013	6,840
35,550	35,600	7,641	6,094	8,027	6,854
35,600	35,650	7,655	6,108	8,041	6,868
35,650	35,700	7,669	6,122	8,055	6,882
35,700	35,750	7,683	6,136	8,069	6,896
35,750	35,800	7,697	6,150	8,083	6,910
35,800	35,850	7,711	6,164	8,097	6,924
35,850	35,900	7,725	6,178	8,111	6,938
35,900	35,950	7,739	6,192	8,125	6,952
35,950	36,000	7,753	6,206	8,141	6,966
36,000					
36,000	36,050	7,767	6,220	8,157	6,980
36,050	36,100	7,781	6,234	8,174	6,994
36,100	36,150	7,795	6,248	8,190	7,008
36,150	36,200	7,809	6,262	8,207	7,022
36,200	36,250	7,823	6,276	8,223	7,036
36,250	36,300	7,837	6,290	8,240	7,050
36,300	36,350	7,851	6,304	8,256	7,064
36,350	36,400	7,865	6,318	8,273	7,078
36,400	36,450	7,879	6,332	8,289	7,092
36,450	36,500	7,893	6,346	8,306	7,106
36,500	36,550	7,907	6,360	8,322	7,120
36,550	36,600	7,921	6,374	8,339	7,134
36,600	36,650	7,935	6,388	8,355	7,148
36,650	36,700	7,949	6,402	8,372	7,162
36,700	36,750	7,963	6,416	8,388	7,176
36,750	36,800	7,977	6,430	8,405	7,190
36,800	36,850	7,991	6,444	8,421	7,204
36,850	36,900	8,005	6,458	8,438	7,218
36,900	36,950	8,019	6,472	8,454	7,232
36,950	37,000	8,033	6,486	8,471	7,246
37,000					
37,000	37,050	8,047	6,500	8,487	7,260
37,050	37,100	8,061	6,514	8,504	7,274
37,100	37,150	8,075	6,528	8,520	7,288
37,150	37,200	8,089	6,542	8,537	7,302
37,200	37,250	8,103	6,556	8,553	7,316
37,250	37,300	8,117	6,570	8,570	7,330
37,300	37,350	8,131	6,584	8,586	7,344
37,350	37,400	8,145	6,598	8,603	7,358
37,400	37,450	8,159	6,612	8,619	7,372
37,450	37,500	8,173	6,626	8,636	7,386
37,500	37,550	8,187	6,640	8,652	7,400
37,550	37,600	8,201	6,654	8,669	7,414
37,600	37,650	8,215	6,668	8,685	7,428
37,650	37,700	8,229	6,682	8,702	7,442
37,700	37,750	8,243	6,696	8,718	7,456
37,750	37,800	8,257	6,710	8,735	7,470
37,800	37,850	8,271	6,724	8,751	7,484
37,850	37,900	8,285	6,738	8,768	7,498
37,900	37,950	8,299	6,752	8,784	7,512
37,950	38,000	8,313	6,766	8,801	7,526
38,000					
38,000	38,050	8,327	6,780	8,817	7,540
38,050	38,100	8,341	6,794	8,834	7,554
38,100	38,150	8,355	6,808	8,850	7,568
38,150	38,200	8,369	6,822	8,867	7,582
38,200	38,250	8,383	6,836	8,883	7,596
38,250	38,300	8,397	6,850	8,900	7,610
38,300	38,350	8,411	6,864	8,916	7,624
38,350	38,400	8,425	6,878	8,933	7,638
38,400	38,450	8,439	6,892	8,949	7,652
38,450	38,500	8,453	6,906	8,966	7,666
38,500	38,550	8,467	6,920	8,982	7,680
38,550	38,600	8,481	6,934	8,999	7,694
38,600	38,650	8,495	6,948	9,015	7,708
38,650	38,700	8,509	6,962	9,032	7,722
38,700	38,750	8,523	6,976	9,048	7,736
38,750	38,800	8,537	6,990	9,065	7,750
38,800	38,850	8,551	7,004	9,081	7,764
38,850	38,900	8,565	7,018	9,098	7,778
38,900	38,950	8,579	7,032	9,114	7,792
38,950	39,000	8,593	7,046	9,131	7,806
39,000					
39,000	39,050	8,607	7,060	9,147	7,820
39,050	39,100	8,621	7,074	9,164	7,834
39,100	39,150	8,635	7,088	9,180	7,848
39,150	39,200	8,649	7,102	9,197	7,862
39,200	39,250	8,663	7,116	9,213	7,876
39,250	39,300	8,677	7,130	9,230	7,890
39,300	39,350	8,691	7,144	9,246	7,904
39,350	39,400	8,705	7,158	9,263	7,918
39,400	39,450	8,719	7,172	9,279	7,932
39,450	39,500	8,733	7,186	9,296	7,946
39,500	39,550	8,747	7,200	9,312	7,960
39,550	39,600	8,761	7,214	9,329	7,974
39,600	39,650	8,775	7,228	9,345	7,988
39,650	39,700	8,789	7,242	9,362	8,002
39,700	39,750	8,803	7,256	9,378	8,016
39,750	39,800	8,817	7,270	9,395	8,030
39,800	39,850	8,831	7,284	9,411	8,044
39,850	39,900	8,845	7,298	9,428	8,058
39,900	39,950	8,859	7,312	9,444	8,072
39,950	40,000	8,873	7,326	9,461	8,086
40,000					
40,000	40,050	8,887	7,340	9,477	8,100
40,050	40,100	8,901	7,354	9,494	8,114
40,100	40,150	8,915	7,368	9,510	8,128
40,150	40,200	8,929	7,382	9,527	8,142
40,200	40,250	8,943	7,396	9,543	8,156
40,250	40,300	8,957	7,410	9,560	8,170
40,300	40,350	8,971	7,424	9,576	8,184
40,350	40,400	8,985	7,438	9,593	8,198
40,400	40,450	8,999	7,452	9,609	8,212
40,450	40,500	9,013	7,466	9,626	8,226
40,500	40,550	9,027	7,480	9,642	8,240
40,550	40,600	9,041	7,494	9,659	8,254
40,600	40,650	9,055	7,508	9,675	8,268
40,650	40,700	9,069	7,522	9,692	8,282
40,700	40,750	9,083	7,536	9,708	8,296
40,750	40,800	9,097	7,550	9,725	8,310
40,800	40,850	9,111	7,564	9,741	8,324
40,850	40,900	9,125	7,578	9,758	8,338
40,900	40,950	9,139	7,592	9,774	8,352
40,950	41,000	9,153	7,606	9,791	8,366

* This column must also be used by a qualifying widow(er).

Continued on next page

1988 Tax Table—*Continued*

If 1040A, line 19, OR 1040EZ, line 7 is—		And you are—			
At least	But less than	Single (and 1040EZ filers)	Married filing jointly *	Married filing separately	Head of a household
		Your tax is—			
41,000					
41,000	41,050	9,167	7,620	9,807	8,380
41,050	41,100	9,181	7,634	9,824	8,394
41,100	41,150	9,195	7,648	9,840	8,408
41,150	41,200	9,209	7,662	9,857	8,422
41,200	41,250	9,223	7,676	9,873	8,436
41,250	41,300	9,237	7,690	9,890	8,450
41,300	41,350	9,251	7,704	9,906	8,464
41,350	41,400	9,265	7,718	9,923	8,478
41,400	41,450	9,279	7,732	9,939	8,492
41,450	41,500	9,293	7,746	9,956	8,506
41,500	41,550	9,307	7,760	9,972	8,520
41,550	41,600	9,321	7,774	9,989	8,534
41,600	41,650	9,335	7,788	10,005	8,548
41,650	41,700	9,349	7,802	10,022	8,562
41,700	41,750	9,363	7,816	10,038	8,576
41,750	41,800	9,377	7,830	10,055	8,590
41,800	41,850	9,391	7,844	10,071	8,604
41,850	41,900	9,405	7,858	10,088	8,618
41,900	41,950	9,419	7,872	10,104	8,632
41,950	42,000	9,433	7,886	10,121	8,646
42,000					
42,000	42,050	9,447	7,900	10,137	8,660
42,050	42,100	9,461	7,914	10,154	8,674
42,100	42,150	9,475	7,928	10,170	8,688
42,150	42,200	9,489	7,942	10,187	8,702
42,200	42,250	9,503	7,956	10,203	8,716
42,250	42,300	9,517	7,970	10,220	8,730
42,300	42,350	9,531	7,984	10,236	8,744
42,350	42,400	9,545	7,998	10,253	8,758
42,400	42,450	9,559	8,012	10,269	8,772
42,450	42,500	9,573	8,026	10,286	8,786
42,500	42,550	9,587	8,040	10,302	8,800
42,550	42,600	9,601	8,054	10,319	8,814
42,600	42,650	9,615	8,068	10,335	8,828
42,650	42,700	9,629	8,082	10,352	8,842
42,700	42,750	9,643	8,096	10,368	8,856
42,750	42,800	9,657	8,110	10,385	8,870
42,800	42,850	9,671	8,124	10,401	8,884
42,850	42,900	9,685	8,138	10,418	8,898
42,900	42,950	9,699	8,152	10,434	8,912
42,950	43,000	9,713	8,166	10,451	8,926
43,000					
43,000	43,050	9,727	8,180	10,467	8,940
43,050	43,100	9,741	8,194	10,484	8,954
43,100	43,150	9,755	8,208	10,500	8,968
43,150	43,200	9,770	8,222	10,517	8,982
43,200	43,250	9,786	8,236	10,533	8,996
43,250	43,300	9,803	8,250	10,550	9,010
43,300	43,350	9,819	8,264	10,566	9,024
43,350	43,400	9,836	8,278	10,583	9,038
43,400	43,450	9,852	8,292	10,599	9,052
43,450	43,500	9,869	8,306	10,616	9,066
43,500	43,550	9,885	8,320	10,632	9,080
43,550	43,600	9,902	8,334	10,649	9,094
43,600	43,650	9,918	8,348	10,665	9,108
43,650	43,700	9,935	8,362	10,682	9,122
43,700	43,750	9,951	8,376	10,698	9,136
43,750	43,800	9,968	8,390	10,715	9,150
43,800	43,850	9,984	8,404	10,731	9,164
43,850	43,900	10,001	8,418	10,748	9,178
43,900	43,950	10,017	8,432	10,764	9,192
43,950	44,000	10,034	8,446	10,781	9,206

If 1040A, line 19, OR 1040EZ, line 7 is—		And you are—			
At least	But less than	Single (and 1040EZ filers)	Married filing jointly *	Married filing separately	Head of a household
		Your tax is—			
44,000					
44,000	44,050	10,050	8,460	10,797	9,220
44,050	44,100	10,067	8,474	10,814	9,234
44,100	44,150	10,083	8,488	10,830	9,248
44,150	44,200	10,100	8,502	10,847	9,262
44,200	44,250	10,116	8,516	10,863	9,276
44,250	44,300	10,133	8,530	10,880	9,290
44,300	44,350	10,149	8,544	10,896	9,304
44,350	44,400	10,166	8,558	10,913	9,318
44,400	44,450	10,182	8,572	10,929	9,332
44,450	44,500	10,199	8,586	10,946	9,346
44,500	44,550	10,215	8,600	10,962	9,360
44,550	44,600	10,232	8,614	10,979	9,374
44,600	44,650	10,248	8,628	10,995	9,388
44,650	44,700	10,265	8,642	11,012	9,402
44,700	44,750	10,281	8,656	11,028	9,416
44,750	44,800	10,298	8,670	11,045	9,430
44,800	44,850	10,314	8,684	11,061	9,444
44,850	44,900	10,331	8,698	11,078	9,458
44,900	44,950	10,347	8,712	11,094	9,472
44,950	45,000	10,364	8,726	11,111	9,486
45,000					
45,000	45,050	10,380	8,740	11,127	9,500
45,050	45,100	10,397	8,754	11,144	9,514
45,100	45,150	10,413	8,768	11,160	9,528
45,150	45,200	10,430	8,782	11,177	9,542
45,200	45,250	10,446	8,796	11,193	9,556
45,250	45,300	10,463	8,810	11,210	9,570
45,300	45,350	10,479	8,824	11,226	9,584
45,350	45,400	10,496	8,838	11,243	9,598
45,400	45,450	10,512	8,852	11,259	9,612
45,450	45,500	10,529	8,866	11,276	9,626
45,500	45,550	10,545	8,880	11,292	9,640
45,550	45,600	10,562	8,894	11,309	9,654
45,600	45,650	10,578	8,908	11,325	9,668
45,650	45,700	10,595	8,922	11,342	9,682
45,700	45,750	10,611	8,936	11,358	9,696
45,750	45,800	10,628	8,950	11,375	9,710
45,800	45,850	10,644	8,964	11,391	9,724
45,850	45,900	10,661	8,978	11,408	9,738
45,900	45,950	10,677	8,992	11,424	9,752
45,950	46,000	10,694	9,006	11,441	9,766
46,000					
46,000	46,050	10,710	9,020	11,457	9,780
46,050	46,100	10,727	9,034	11,474	9,794
46,100	46,150	10,743	9,048	11,490	9,808
46,150	46,200	10,760	9,062	11,507	9,822
46,200	46,250	10,776	9,076	11,523	9,836
46,250	46,300	10,793	9,090	11,540	9,850
46,300	46,350	10,809	9,104	11,556	9,864
46,350	46,400	10,826	9,118	11,573	9,878
46,400	46,450	10,842	9,132	11,589	9,892
46,450	46,500	10,859	9,146	11,606	9,906
46,500	46,550	10,875	9,160	11,622	9,920
46,550	46,600	10,892	9,174	11,639	9,934
46,600	46,650	10,908	9,188	11,655	9,948
46,650	46,700	10,925	9,202	11,672	9,962
46,700	46,750	10,941	9,216	11,688	9,976
46,750	46,800	10,958	9,230	11,705	9,990
46,800	46,850	10,974	9,244	11,721	10,004
46,850	46,900	10,991	9,258	11,738	10,018
46,900	46,950	11,007	9,272	11,754	10,032
46,950	47,000	11,024	9,286	11,771	10,046

If 1040A, line 19, OR 1040EZ, line 7 is—		And you are—			
At least	But less than	Single (and 1040EZ filers)	Married filing jointly *	Married filing separately	Head of a household
		Your tax is—			
47,000					
47,000	47,050	11,040	9,300	11,787	10,060
47,050	47,100	11,057	9,314	11,804	10,074
47,100	47,150	11,073	9,328	11,820	10,088
47,150	47,200	11,090	9,342	11,837	10,102
47,200	47,250	11,106	9,356	11,853	10,116
47,250	47,300	11,123	9,370	11,870	10,130
47,300	47,350	11,139	9,384	11,886	10,144
47,350	47,400	11,156	9,398	11,903	10,158
47,400	47,450	11,172	9,412	11,919	10,172
47,450	47,500	11,189	9,426	11,936	10,186
47,500	47,550	11,205	9,440	11,952	10,200
47,550	47,600	11,222	9,454	11,969	10,214
47,600	47,650	11,238	9,468	11,985	10,228
47,650	47,700	11,255	9,482	12,002	10,242
47,700	47,750	11,271	9,496	12,018	10,256
47,750	47,800	11,288	9,510	12,035	10,270
47,800	47,850	11,304	9,524	12,051	10,284
47,850	47,900	11,321	9,538	12,068	10,298
47,900	47,950	11,337	9,552	12,084	10,312
47,950	48,000	11,354	9,566	12,101	10,326
48,000					
48,000	48,050	11,370	9,580	12,117	10,340
48,050	48,100	11,387	9,594	12,134	10,354
48,100	48,150	11,403	9,608	12,150	10,368
48,150	48,200	11,420	9,622	12,167	10,382
48,200	48,250	11,436	9,636	12,183	10,396
48,250	48,300	11,453	9,650	12,200	10,410
48,300	48,350	11,469	9,664	12,216	10,424
48,350	48,400	11,486	9,678	12,233	10,438
48,400	48,450	11,502	9,692	12,249	10,452
48,450	48,500	11,519	9,706	12,266	10,466
48,500	48,550	11,535	9,720	12,282	10,480
48,550	48,600	11,552	9,734	12,299	10,494
48,600	48,650	11,568	9,748	12,315	10,508
48,650	48,700	11,585	9,762	12,332	10,522
48,700	48,750	11,601	9,776	12,348	10,536
48,750	48,800	11,618	9,790	12,365	10,550
48,800	48,850	11,634	9,804	12,381	10,564
48,850	48,900	11,651	9,818	12,398	10,578
48,900	48,950	11,667	9,832	12,414	10,592
48,950	49,000	11,684	9,846	12,431	10,606
49,000					
49,000	49,050	11,700	9,860	12,447	10,620
49,050	49,100	11,717	9,874	12,464	10,634
49,100	49,150	11,733	9,888	12,480	10,648
49,150	49,200	11,750	9,902	12,497	10,662
49,200	49,250	11,766	9,916	12,513	10,676
49,250	49,300	11,783	9,930	12,530	10,690
49,300	49,350	11,799	9,944	12,546	10,704
49,350	49,400	11,816	9,958	12,563	10,718
49,400	49,450	11,832	9,972	12,579	10,732
49,450	49,500	11,849	9,986	12,596	10,746
49,500	49,550	11,865	10,000	12,612	10,760
49,550	49,600	11,882	10,014	12,629	10,774
49,600	49,650	11,898	10,028	12,645	10,788
49,650	49,700	11,915	10,042	12,662	10,802
49,700	49,750	11,931	10,056	12,678	10,816
49,750	49,800	11,948	10,070	12,695	10,830
49,800	49,850	11,964	10,084	12,711	10,844
49,850	49,900	11,981	10,098	12,728	10,858
49,900	49,950	11,997	10,112	12,744	10,872
49,950	50,000	12,014	10,126	12,761	10,886

* This column must also be used by a qualifying widow(er).

50,000 or over—use Form 1040

1989 Tax Rate Schedules

Caution: *Use ONLY if your taxable income (Form 1040, line 37) is $50,000 or more. If less, use the* ***Tax Table.***

Schedule X—Use if your filing status is **Single**

If the amount on Form 1040, line 37, is: *Over—*	*But not over—*	Enter on Form 1040, line 38	*of the amount over—*
$0	$18,550	.......**15%**	**$0**
18,550	44,900	**$2,782.50 + 28%**	**18,550**
44,900	93,130	**10,160.50 + 33%**	**44,900**
93,130	....	Use **Worksheet** below to figure your tax.	

Schedule Z—Use if your filing status is **Head of household**

If the amount on Form 1040, line 37, is: *Over—*	*But not over—*	Enter on Form 1040, line 38	*of the amount over—*
$0	$24,850	.......**15%**	**$0**
24,850	64,200	**$3,727.50 + 28%**	**24,850**
64,200	128,810	**14,745.50 + 33%**	**64,200**
128,810	....	Use **Worksheet** below to figure your tax.	

Schedule Y-1—Use if your filing status is **Married filing jointly or Qualifying widow(er)**

If the amount on Form 1040, line 37, is: *Over—*	*But not over—*	Enter on Form 1040, line 38	*of the amount over—*
$0	$30,950	.......**15%**	**$0**
30,950	74,850	**$4,642.50 + 28%**	**30,950**
74,850	155,320	**16,934.50 + 33%**	**74,850**
155,320	....	Use **Worksheet** below to figure your tax.	

Schedule Y-2—Use if your filing status is **Married filing separately**

If the amount on Form 1040, line 37, is: *Over—*	*But not over—*	Enter on Form 1040, line 38	*of the amount over—*
$0	$15,475	.......**15%**	**$0**
15,475	37,425	**$2,321.25 + 28%**	**15,475**
37,425	117,895	**8,467.25 + 33%**	**37,425**
117,895	....	Use **Worksheet** below to figure your tax.	

Accountants' Calculation: Percentage of Ownership

One Method Accountants Use to Value Percentage of Ownership

An investor wants to purchase a rental condominium for $200,000 with a 25 percent down payment ($50,000). Fair market rent is $950 per month. For a long-term tenant (minimum vacancies, minimum headaches), the investor will rent the unit for $855 per month. Rent increases are calculated at 5 percent per year, and expenses of insurance and condo dues go up 4 percent per year. Taxes go up 1 percent per year. Other maintenance factors could be added in, but for this example no other expenses are calculated.

	Year 1	Year 2	Year 3
Rental Income	$10,260	$10,773	$11,312
Less Expenses:			
Insurance	(300)	(312)	(324)
R.E. Taxes	(2,400)	(2,424)	(2,448)
H.O. Dues	(1,200)	(1,248)	(1,298)
Interest @ 11.5% Fixed	(17,219)	(17,145)	(17,063)
	($21,119)	($21,129)	($21,133)
Negative Cash Flow before Taxes	($10,859)	($10,356)	($ 9,821)

Depreciation is based on 65% building and 35% land. 27.5 year straight line. $200,000 × 65% = $130,000 ÷ 27.5 = $4727/year.

($ 4,727) × 37.3% tax bracket (Fed. & State) = $1763

($10,859) × 37.3% tax bracket (Fed. & State) =

$ 4,050	$ 3,863	$ 3,663

Add writeoff of depreciation of $1,763 to each year's tax writeoff. The below figures represent actual tax savings per year.

$ 5,813	$ 5,626	$ 5,426

Now subtract the actual tax savings from the out-of-pocket negative annual cash flow (i.e. $10,859 − $5,813 = $5,046)

($ 5,046)	($ 4,730)	($ 4,395)

Total of 3 years actual negative cash flow equals ($14,171).

Principal paydown is not calculated.

Present Value of Negative Cash Flow

If you put away $11,249 on close of escrow, and it earned 8%, the entire negative cash flow of $14,171 would be funded over 3 years.

On HP12C: Enter $14,171 FV (Future Value), Enter 3 n (years), Enter 8 i (interest rate), Press PV.

What is value of the owner-occupant's contribution to the non-resident owner?

25% down payment: $40,000 from non-resident and $10,000 from owners-occupant
Negative cash flow paid by owner-occupant is $11,249.

Total cash into property over 3 years is $61,249. ($40,000 + $10,000 + $11,249)

Non-resident owner: $40,000 ÷ $61,249 = 65% ownership
Owner-occupant: $21,249 ÷ $61,249 = 35% ownership

The cash each party contributes is a starting point for negotiating the percentage of ownership. Some other factors to consider are the value of the reduced vacancy factor; the value of the reduced management, maintenance and upkeep of the property; and the lower interest rate you were able to obtain because of the owner-occupied status of the loan.

EQUITY SHARE WORKSHEET

Owner-Occupant: ______________________________

Non-resident Owner: ______________________________

____

Property Address: ______________________________

PURCHASE PRICE $__________

Less Down Payment at _____% Down –__________

AMOUNT TO BE FINANCED $__________

Total Down Payment Required: $__________

Less Cash from Owner-Occupant: –__________

Amount Needed from Non-resident Owner: $__________

Closing Costs (Estimate 3% of Purchase Price) Paid According to % of Ownership $__________

Owner-Occupant: $__________

Non-resident Owner: $__________

PERCENTAGE OF OWNERSHIP:

_____ % Owner-Occupant _____ % Non-resident Owner

LOAN INFORMATION

_____ Years FIXED at _____ %

_____ Years VARIABLE at _____ %

_____ % Annual Cap _____ % Lifetime Cap

_____ % Annual Payment Cap if Negative Am Loan

Monthly PRINICPAL & INTEREST (From Amortization Table) $__________

Monthly Property TAX (Tax divided by 12 months) $__________

Monthly INSURANCE Payment (Premium divided by 12 months) $__________

Monthly PITI (Principal, Interest, Tax, Insurance) $__________

If Condo, add monthly Association Dues $__________

TOTAL MONTHLY EXPENSE PAID BY OWNER-OCCUPANT $__________

EQUITY-SHARE PROJECTIONS WORKSHEET

A. PURCHASE INFORMATION:

(O.O.) ____________ (N.O.) ____________
O.O. Contribution $____________ % Ownership ____________
N.O. Contribution $____________ % Ownership ____________
Purchase Price $____________ Loan Amount $____________

B. VALUE OF PROPERTY OVER TEN-YEAR PERIOD AT FOUR RATES OF APPRECIATION

	___ %	___ %	___ %	Best Guess	
Year 1	____	____	____	____	___ %
Year 2	____	____	____	____	___ %
Year 3	____	____	____	____	___ %
Year 4	____	____	____	____	___ %
Year 5	____	____	____	____	___ %
Year 6	____	____	____		
Year 7	____	____	____		
Year 8	____	____	____		
Year 9	____	____	____		
Year 10	____	____	____		

C. OPTION #1: REFINANCE

1. Market Value $____________
2. Times ___% LTV × ______ %*
3. New Loan $____________
4. Less Old Loan $– ____________
5. Gross Profit $____________
6. Less Refi. Costs $– ______ **
7. Net Profit $____________
8. Less O.O. Contr. $– ____________
9. Less N.O. Contr. $– ____________
10. Net Cash Out $____________
11. Times O.O.% × ______ %
12. O.O. Cash Out $____________
13. #10 × N.O.% × ______ %
14. N.O. Cash Out $____________
15. #8 + #12 = O.O. Total Cash Out $____________
16. #9 + #14 = N.O. Total Cash Out $____________
17. New PITI $____________

D. OPTION #2: SELL

18. Sales Price $____________
19. Less Sale Cost × .93***
20. Gross Profit $____________
21. Less Old Loan $– ____________
22. Net Profit $____________
23. Less O.O. Contr. $– ____________
24. Less N.O. Contr. $– ____________
25. Net Cash Out $____________
26. Times O.O.% × ______ %
27. O.O. Cash Out $____________
28. #26 × N.O.% × ______ %
29. N.O. Cash Out $____________
30. #24 + #28 = O.O Total Cash Out $____________
31. #25 + #30 = N.O. Total Cash Out $____________
32. New PITI $____________

*Figure 75% **Figure 2% of Sales Price ***Figure 7% of Sales Price

RENT CALCULATION WORKSHEET—FOR SINGLE FAMILY HOME

Owner-Occupant(s) (O.O.) ______________________ % Ownership ____

Non-resident Owner(s) (N.O.) ______________________ % Ownership ____

______________________ % Ownership ____

Property Address: ______________________________________

Principal & Interest (Paid by O.O.) $__________

Fair Market Rent: $__________

Less Good-Tenant Discount $–__________

RENT: $__________

Times N.O. % Ownership: × __________ %

RENT PAID TO N.O.: $__________

CHECKS WRITTEN BY OWNER-OCCUPANT, SENT TO NON-RESIDENT OWNER:

A. RENT (Payable to Non-resident Owner) Check A $__________

B. PRINCIPAL & INTEREST PAYMENT,
LESS RENT(Check A) (Payable to Lender) Check B $__________

TOTAL PAID BY OWNER-OCCUPANT: $__________

CHECK WRITTEN BY NON-RESIDENT OWNER FROM RENT RECEIVED, SENT TO LENDER:

C. MORTGAGE PAYMENT in the amount of
the RENT (Check A) (Payable to Lender) Check C $__________

TOTAL PAID BY NON-RESIDENT OWNER (Check C) $__________

LESS TOTAL RENT RECEIVED BY NON-RESIDENT OWNER (Check A) $–__________

0

RENT CALCULATION WORKSHEET—FOR CONDOMINIUM

Owner-Occupant(s) (O.O.) ______________________ % Ownership ______

Non-resident Owner(s) (N.O.) ______________________ % Ownership ______

______________________ % Ownership ______

Property Address: ______________________________________

Principal & Interest (Paid by O.O.) $__________

Condo Association Dues (Paid by O.O.) $__________

TOTAL PAID BY O.O.: $__________

Fair Market Rent: $__________

Less Good-Tenant Discount $–__________

RENT: $__________

Times N.O. % Ownership: × __________ %

RENT PAID TO N.O.: $__________

CHECKS WRITTEN BY OWNER-OCCUPANT, SENT TO NON-RESIDENT OWNER:

A. RENT (Payable to Non-resident Owner) Check A $__________

B. O.O. % OF CONDO DUES (Payable to Assoc.) Check B $__________

C. PRINCIPAL & INTEREST PAYMENT PLUS 100% OF CONDO DUES, LESS RENT (Check A) and LESS O.O. % of CONDO DUES (Check B) (Payable to Lender) Check C $__________

TOTAL PAID BY OWNER-OCCUPANT $__________

CHECKS WRITTEN BY NON-RESIDENT OWNER FROM RENT RECEIVED:

D. N.O. % OF CONDO DUES (Payable to Assoc.) Check D $__________

E. Check payable to Lender in the Amount of the RENT (Check A), less N.O. % of Condo Dues (Check D) Check E $__________

TOTAL RENT PAID BY NON-RESIDENT OWNER (Check D + E) $__________

LESS TOTAL RENT RECEIVED BY NON-RESIDENT OWNER (Check A) $–__________

0

Prepared for: ____________________ Prepared by: ____________________

Property Address: ____________________ Loan Amount: ____________________

____

Date: ____________________ LTV: ____________________

LOAN PROGRAM COMPARISONS

1. Loan type					
2. Initial interest rate					
3. Term (25, 30 years)					
4. Lender fees, points					
5. Prepayment penalty					
6. Co-borrowers allowed?					
7. Max. yearly Negative Am					
8. Assumable?					
9. Which index is used?					
10. When is margin set?					
11. How often do interest rate adjustments occur?					
12. How often do payment adjustments occur?					
13. Interest rate caps					
14. What period covered by caps?					
15. Against what interest rate is cap increased?					
16. Are there payment increase caps?					
17. How much? How long?					
18. Do interest and payment caps apply to up and down interest moves?					
19. Does index look to most recent change or the average?					
20. Initial payment					

Section 1034, U.S. Tax Code

SECTION 1034. Rollover of gain on sale of principal residence

(a) Nonrecognition of Gain.—

If property (in this section called "old residence") used by the taxpayer as his principal residence is sold by him, and, within a period beginning 2 years before the date of such sale and ending 2 years after such date, property (in this section called "new residence") is purchased and used by the taxpayer as his principal residence, gain (if any) from such sale shall be recognized only to the extent that the taxpayer's adjusted sales price (as defined in subsection (b)) of the old residence exceeds the taxpayer's cost of purchasing the new residence.

(b) Adjusted Sales Price Defined.—

(1) In general.—For purposes of this section, the term "adjusted sales price" means the amount realized, reduced by the aggregate of the expenses for work performed on the old residence in order to assist the sale.

(2) Limitations.—The reduction provided in paragraph (1) applies only to expenses—

- (A) for work performed during the 90-day period ending on the day on which the contract to sell the old residence is entered into; and
- (B) which are paid on or before the 30th day after the date of the sale of the old residence; and
- (C) which are—
  - (i) not allowable as deductions in computing taxable income under Section 63 (defining taxable income), and
  - (ii) not taken into account the amount realized from the sale of the old residence.

(c) Rules for Application of Section.—For purposes of this section:

(1) An exchange by the taxpayer of his residence for other property shall be treated as a sale of such residence, and the acquisition of a residence or the exchange of property shall be treated as a purchase of such residence.

(2) A residence any part of which was constructed or reconstructed by the taxpayer shall be treated as purchased by the taxpayer. In determining the taxpayer's cost of purchasing a residence, there shall be included only so much of his cost as is attributable to the acquisition, construction, and improvements made which are properly chargeable to capital account, during the period specified in subsection (a)

(3) If a residence is purchased by the taxpayer before the date of his sale of the old residence, the purchased residence shall not be treated as his new residence if sold or otherwise disposed of by him before the date of the sale of the old residence.

(4) If the taxpayer, during the period described in subsection (a), purchases more than one residence which is used by him as his principal residence at some time within 2 years after the date of the sale of the old residence, only the last of such residences so used by him after the date of such sale shall constitute the new residence. If a principal residence is sold in a sale to which subsection (d)(2) applies within 2 years after the sale of the old residence, for purposes of applying the preceding sentence with respect to the old residence, the principal residence so sold shall be treated as the last residence used during such 2-year period.

(d) Limitation.—

(1) In general.—Subsection (a) shall not apply with respect to the sale of the taxpayer's residence if within 2 years before the date of such sale the taxpayer sold at a gain other property used by him as his principal residence, and any part of such gain was not recognized by reason of subsection (a)

(2) Subsequent sale connected with commencing work at new place.—Paragraph (1) shall not apply with respect to the sale of the taxpayer's residence if—

(A) such sale was in connection with the commencement of work by the taxpayer as an employee or as a self-employed individual a new principal place of work, and

(B) if the residence so sold is treated as the former residence for purposes of Section 217 (relating to moving expenses), if the taxpayer would satisfy the conditions of subsection (c) of Section 217 (as modified by the other subsections of such section).

(e) Basis of New Residence.—

Where the purchase of a new residence results, under subsection (a) or under Section 112 (n) of the Internal Revenue Code of 1939, in the non-recognition of gain on the sale of an old residence, in determining the adjusted basis of the new residence as of anytime following the sale of the old residence, the adjustments to basis shall include a reduction by an amount equal to the amount of the gain not so recognized on the sale of the old residence. For this purpose, the amount of the gain not so recognized on the sale of the old residence includes only so much of such gain as is not recognized by reason of the cost, up to such time, or purchasing the new residence.

(f) Tenant-Stockholder in a Cooperative Housing Corporation.—

For purposes of this section, Section 1016 (relating to adjustments to basis), and Section 1223 (relating to holding period), references to property used by the taxpayer as his principal residence, and references to the residence of a taxpayer, shall include stock held by a tenant-stockholder (as defined in Section 216, relating to deduction for amounts representing taxes and interest paid to a cooperative housing corporation) in a cooperative housing corporation (as defined in such section) if—

(1) in the case of stock sold, the house or apartment which the taxpayer was entitled to occupy as such stockholder was used by him as his principal residence, and

(2) in the case of stock purchased, the taxpayer used as his principal residence the house or apartment which he was entitled to occupy as such stockholder.

(g) Husband and Wife.—

If the taxpayer and his spouse, in accordance with regulations which shall be prescribed by the Secretary pursuant to this subsection, consent to the application of paragraph (2) of this subsection, then—

(1) for purposes of this section—

(A) the taxpayer's adjusted sales price of the old residence is the adjusted sales price (of the taxpayer, or of the taxpayer and his spouse) of the old residence, and

(B) the taxpayer's cost of purchasing the new residence is the cost (to the taxpayer, his spouse, or both) of purchasing the new residence (whether held by the taxpayer, his spouse, or the taxpayer and his spouse), and

(2) so much of the gain on the sale of the old residence as it is not recognized solely by reason of this subsection, and so much of the adjustment under subsection (e) to the basis of the new residence as results solely from this subsection shall be allocated between the taxpayer and his spouse as provided in such regulation.

This subsection shall apply only if the old residence and the new residence are each used by the taxpayer and his spouse as their principal residence. In case the taxpayer and his spouse do not consent to the application of paragraph (2) of this subsection then the recognition of gain on the sale of the old residence shall be determined under this section without regard to the rules provided in this subsection.

Section 1031, U.S. Tax Code

SECTION 1031 Exchange of property held for productive use or investment

(a) Nonrecognition of Gain or Loss From Exchanges Solely in Kind.

(1) In general. No gain or loss shall be recognized on the exchange of property held or productive use in a trade or business or for investment if such property is exchanged solely for property of like kind which is to be held either for productive use in a trade or business or for investment.

(2) Exception. This subsection shall not apply to any exchange of—

(A) stock in trade or other property held primarily for sale,
(B) stocks, bonds, or notes,
(C) other securities or evidences or indebtedness or interest,
(D) interests in a partnership,
(E) certificates of trust or beneficial interests, or
(F) choices in action.

(3) Requirement that property be identified and that exchange be completed not more than 180 days after transfer of exchanged property. For purposes of this sub-section, any property received by the taxpayer shall be treated as property which is not like-kind property if—

(A) such property is not identified as property to be received in the exchange on or before the day which is 45 days after the date on which the taxpayer transfers the property relinquished in the exchange, or
(B) such property is received after the earlier of—

(i) the day which is 180 days after the date on which the taxpayer transfers the property relinquished in the exchange, or

(ii) the due date (determined with regard to extension) for the transferor's return of the tax imposed by this chapter for the taxable year in which the transfer of the relinquished property occurs.

(b) Gain From Exchanges Not Solely in Kind.—If an exchange would be within the provisions of subsection (a), of Section 1035(a), or of Section 1036(a), if it were not for the fact that the property received in exchange consists not only of property permitted by such provisions to be received without the recognition of gain, but also of other property or money, then the gain, if any, to the recipient shall be recognized, but in an amount not in excess of the sum of such money and the fair market value of such other property.

(c) Losses From Exchanges Not Solely in Kind.—If an exchange would be within the provisions of subsection (a), of Section 1035(a), of Section 1036(a), or of Section 1037(a), if it were not for the fact that the property received in exchange consists not only of property permitted by such provisions to be received without the recognition of gain or loss, but also of other property or money, then no loss from the exchange shall be recognized.

(d) Basis.—If property was acquired on an exchange described in this section, Section 1035(a), or Section 1037(a), then the basis shall be the same as that of the property exchanged, decreased in the amount of any money received by the taxpayer and increased in the amount of gain or decreased in the amount of loss to the taxpayer that was recognized on such exchange. If the property so acquired consisted in part of the type of property permitted by this section, Section 1035(a), Section 1036(a), or Section 1037(a), to be received without the recognition of gain or loss, and in part of other property, the basis provided in this subsection shall be allocated between the properties (other than money) received, and for the purpose of the allocation there shall be assigned to such other property an amount equivalent to its fair market value at the date of the exchange. For purposes of this section, Section 1035(a), and Section 1036(a), where as part of the consideration to the taxpayer another party to the exchange assumed a liability of the taxpayer or acquired from the taxpayer property subject to a liability, such assumption or acquisition (in the amount of the liability) shall be considered as money received by the taxpayer on the exchange.

SHARED-EQUITY FINANCING AGREEMENT

THIS AGREEMENT is made and entered into this ________ day of ____________, 19__, by and between ________________ ("Owner-Occupants"), and __________________ ("Non-resident Owners"), as tenants-in-common.

RECITALS

This Agreement is entered into on the basis of the following facts, understandings, and intentions of the parties and is pursuant to IRC Section 280A (Attachment A).

A. Non-resident Owners and Owner-Occupants intend to acquire, as tenants-in-common, that certain real property (the "Property") located and described as:
in the city of:

B. Owner-Occupants intend, upon acquisition of the Property, to occupy the Property as a residence.

C. The parties enter into this Agreement in order to set forth their respective rights and obligations.

D. No promises or representations have been made as to what the value of the Property may be in the future.

In consideration of the mutual covenants and agreements contained herein and other valuable consideration, the parties agree as follows:

1. Acquisition of the Property.

(a) The purchase price of the Property is $__________, in accordance with the terms of the agreement entered into with the seller of the Property.

(b) The parties shall obtain a loan (the "Mortgage Loan") in the amount of $______________. The Mortgage Loan will be held by ____.

(c) The balance of the purchase price shall be paid in cash (the "Initial Cash Contributions"). The Cash Contributions shall be paid by the parties hereto into escrow for the purchase of the Property on or before the date of said purchase (the "Closing Date") as follows:

________________ dollars ($______________)
by the Owner-Occupants

________________ dollars ($______________)
by the Non-resident Owners

(d) Closing costs shall be paid in accordance with each party's

Ownership Percentage; except that association dues, if any, interest, and property tax prorations will be paid by Owner-Occupants. A copy of the Escrow Closing Statement will be attached to this Agreement (Attachment B).

(e) It is agreed that any accounting for federal and/or state income tax purposes generated by payment of closing costs for acquisition of the Property, including loan fees, shall be claimed by Owner-Occupants and Non-resident Owners in accordance with the percentages in which they furnish such funds.

2. Ownership percentages.

Non-resident Owners and Owner-Occupants shall own undivided interests in the Property, as tenants-in-common. The percentages of ownership for Non-resident Owners and Owner-Occupants (the "Ownership Percentages") are:

____________________ (%) to ____________________

____________________ (%) to ____________________

3. Maintenance of the Property.

(a)Owner-Occupants shall, at their sole cost and expense, maintain the Property and every part thereof in good and sanitary condition and repair. Owner-Occupants shall repair any and all damage to or in the Property occurring while the Property is held in co-tenancy hereunder, whether or not such damage is covered by insurance. It is agreed that the cost of repairs which do not arise as a result of any failure by Owner-Occupant to maintain the Property pursuant to the provisions hereof, including but not limited to repairs to appliances, heating and air conditioning equipment, plumbing and electrical systems, shall be shared by the parties in accordance with their Ownership Percentages, after Owner-Occupants have paid the first $__________ of such costs in any one calendar year. Repairs which result from or become necessary as a result of Owner-Occupants' failure to maintain the Property and every part thereof as provided herein shall be performed at Owner-Occupants' sole cost and expense. Owner-Occupants shall be responsible for the full cost of repairs of any damages to the property resulting from the lack of care, negligence, or any wilful act by Owner-Occupants. At the termination of this Agreement, the Owner-Occupants shall restore the Property to its present condition, normal wear and tear excepted.

(b)Owner-Occupants shall pay for all water, gas, heat, light, power, telephone service, and all other services and utilities supplied to the Property during the time the Property is held in co-tenancy hereunder.

4. Improvements and Alterations.

(a) Owner-Occupants shall not make or cause to be made any alterations, additions, or improvements on or to the Property or any part thereof without the prior written consent of the Non-resident Owners, except that any alteration, addition, or improvement costing less than $________________ shall not require Non-resident Owners' written consent or contribution, provided that it would not detract from the value or appearance of the Property and provided further that said expenditure, alteration, addition, or improvement shall not be reimbursed upon sale or refinance. Nothing in this Paragraph shall impair Owner-Occupants' obligation to maintain and repair the Property as previously set forth. Should Non-resident Owners consent, in writing, to any alteration, addition, or improvement costing more than $________________, the parties will agree at that time, in writing, as to the division of cost and return due each party upon sale or refinance of the Property.

(b) If improvements or alterations are deemed necessary by the parties upon acquisition of the Property, Owner-Occupants shall contribute to the Property those certain improvements as set forth in Addendum A, attached to this document. The value of said improvements shall be determined by securing bids from Licensed Contractors. These improvements shall be completed within (__________) months of the Closing Date, and the entire cost of supplies, materials, and labor shall be borne by the Owner-Occupants. Upon Sale or other Termination Event, Owner-Occupants shall be entitled to be paid an amount equal to the value established in Addendum A, after all other obligations set forth under Termination Events have been satisfied, and prior to distribution of any profits. The adjustment described in this Paragraph shall not alter the original Ownership Percentages as described in Paragraph 3 for purposes of distribution of any additional amounts as specified under Termination Events of this Agreement.

5. Liens.

The parties hereto shall not permit liens or encumbrances of any kind to be placed against the Property including, but not limited to, taxes, judgments, construction work, repair or restoration, or materials furnished. In the event of a violation of this Paragraph by either party, a default may be declared pursuant to Paragraph 14(b)(ii) and Paragraph 20, and the amount of the lien shall be deducted from the proceeds due to the defaulting party as a result of a sale, refinance, or condemnation of the Property or as a result of any other disposition of the Property.

6. Transactions Requiring Consent of Both Parties.

After acquisition of the Property, the prior written consent of all parties shall be required before any of the following actions may be taken:

(a) The sale, transfer, exchange, lease, or other disposition of all or any portion of or any interest in the Property, except as made pursuant to Paragraphs 14, 16, and 17;

(b) Any modification, amendment, alteration, or extension of the terms of any existing financing on the Property;

(c) Acquisition of any new financing for the Property, or the placing of any further encumbrance on the Property, except financing specifically agreed upon at the time the parties acquire the Property;

(d) Modification of insurance required by the terms of this Agreement; provided, however, that Owner-Occupants may, at Owner-Occupants' sole cost and expense, increase coverage without prior approval of Non-resident Owners.

7. Use of Property.

(a) Owner-Occupants shall use the Property as their primary residence and for no other purpose unless such purpose is agreed upon in writing by all parties hereto.

(b) Owner-Occupants shall not do or permit anything to be done in or about the Property, nor bring or keep anything thereon, which will increase the existing insurance rate or otherwise adversely affect any policy of fire or other insurance on the Property or any part thereof, or use or allow the Property to be used in any way that may conflict with any law, statute, ordinance, or government regulation now in force or which may be enacted. Owner-Occupants shall not cause, maintain, or permit any nuisance or waste to be committed in, or about the Property. Owner-Occupants shall not use the Property for any commercial or business purpose whatsoever except for a home office.

8. Waiver of Right to Partition.

The parties further acknowledge that their relationship as co-owners is not a partnership, and no party shall have any liability for debts or obligations of the other party. Each of the parties acknowledges that it would be prejudicial to the interests of the parties if any party were to file an action for partition of the Property. Accordingly, each of the parties hereby waives any and all right which he or she may otherwise have to seek a partition of the Property by court action, without the prior written consent of all the other parties.

9. Insurance.

(a) The Owner-Occupants shall maintain on the Property at all times fire and casualty insurance with extended coverage endorsements upon all buildings and improvements located on the Property to not less than one hundred percent of the full replacement cost thereof not covered by policies held by other entities such as but not limited to a Homeowners' Association. Such insurance policy shall contain a provision by which its coverage is automatically increased on an annual basis to cover increases in the value of the Property. The right and authority to adjust and settle any loss with the insurer shall be exercisable only by all parties acting jointly. Subject to the requirements of the lender, the insurance proceeds, with the exception of temporary living expenses, received shall be used to pay for restoration and reconstruction of the Property to be commenced as soon as possible after receipt of the proceeds from the insurance, and Owner-Occupants shall use due diligence to repair or reconstruct the Property within a reasonable period of time. Nothing contained in this Paragraph shall be construed to grant to Non-resident Owners any interest in insurance maintained by Owner-Occupants on personal property owned by Owner-Occupants.

(b) At all times while the Property is held in co-tenancy hereunder, there shall be maintained by each party comprehensive public liability insurance covering the Property, insuring against the risks of bodily injury, property damage, and personal injury liability with respect to the Property, with policy limits of not less than $500,000 per occurrence.

(c) Owner-Occupants shall indemnify, defend, and hold the Non-resident Owners harmless from any and all claims, costs, including, without limitation, attorneys' fees, causes of action or liability for any injury or damage to any person or property whatsoever, occurring on or about the Property, or any part thereof, arising out of the intentional or negligent act or omission of any kind by the Owner-Occupants.

(d) If the Property is a condominium, at all times there shall be maintained, at the sole cost of the Owner-Occupants, a condominium insurance policy covering the contents and insuring (to not less than the full replacement cost) against loss of/or damage to the appliances, fixtures, improvements, and other appurtenances which are co-owned by the parties pursuant to the Agreement to the extent not covered by Homeowners' Association dues and/or policy.

(e) Owner-Occupants shall be responsible for compliance with the terms of the insurance policies required hereunder and shall deliver copies of the policies to Non-resident Owners. All such insurance documents shall name Owner-Occupants and Non-resident Owners as joint insureds. Unless Non-resident Owners object in writing within thirty days of receipt of the policy, the insurance shall be deemed in compliance with the terms of this Agreement. No such policy shall be cancelled or subject to reduction of coverage, or other modifications. The Owner-Occupants shall furnish renewals or binders to the Non-resident Owners, or the Non-resident Owners may order such insurance and charge the costs thereof to the Owner-Occupants, which amount shall be payable by the Owner-Occupants upon demand.

(f) If the Non-resident Owners elect to place a Term Life Insurance Policy upon the life of one of the Owner-Occupants for an amount equal to the Mortgage Loan, the Owner-Occupants will co-operate in the acquisition of said policy. The Non-resident Owners shall bear the entire monthly premium of said policy, and shall be named as sole Beneficiary.

10. Loan Interest Payments and Operating Expenses.

(a) Owner-Occupants shall, personally or through a designated collection agency, from the funds jointly contributed by the parties, make timely payments of the Mortgage Loan installments, real property taxes, insurance, fees to Homeowner or Condominium Associations (if any), and other costs of ownership and operation for the Property.

(b) Non-resident Owners shall be obligated to contribute funds only to the extent of the amount of the rent received by Non-resident Owners for their Ownership Percentage in the Property pursuant to Paragraph 11 below.

(c) Owner-Occupants shall be obligated to contribute funds as follows:

(i) Pay rent as defined in compliance with IRC Section 280A and set forth in Paragraph 11 below.

(ii) Pay any additional amounts necessary to meet the total expenses set forth in this Paragraph including, but not limited to, the

Mortgage Loan payments, any increases in the Mortgage Loan payments, late payment penalties, real property taxes and tax assessments, insurance, and Homeowner or Condominium fees (if any). Owner-Occupants understand that the payments may increase or decrease in amounts due to fluctuations in interest rate, taxes or insurance.

(d) Special assessments by Condominium or Homeowners' Associations for capital improvements shall be shared by the parties in accordance with their Ownership Percentages.

(e) Owner-Occupants and Non-resident Owners shall each report for tax purposes those items pertaining to that party and the payments made by that party. For tax purposes, no relationship other than that of tenants-in-common is created or implied hereby. Owner-Occupants and Non-resident Owners shall not be liable for the debts or obligations of the other except as herein provided.

11. Fair Market Rental.

(a) Pursuant to Internal Revenue Code Section 280A, Owner-Occupants shall make payments to Non-resident Owners for Owner-Occupants' use and occupancy of Non-resident Owners' interest in the Property. The parties hereby agree that the fair market rental for the entirety of the Property is ______________ dollars per month. Subject to the provisions of Paragraph 11(b), Owner-Occupants shall pay to Non-resident Owners on the __________ day of each month throughout the term hereof the amount of ______________ dollars as rent for Owner-Occupants' use, occupancy, and enjoyment of Non-resident Owners' __________ Percent Ownership Percentage in the Property (the "Rent").

(b) The Rent will be reviewed annually on the anniversary of the Closing Date. If Owner-Occupants and Non-resident Owners cannot agree upon fair market rent, they shall, at their joint expense, employ a professional Property Manager to conduct a rental survey. If agreement still cannot be reached, each party shall employ a professional Property Manager. Each party shall pay for the Property Manager which that party selected. Non-resident Owners shall have the right to inspect the Property prior to the rental survey and shall provide to the Property Managers a list of those matters, if any, with respect to which Owner-Occupants have not satisfied their obligation of repair and maintenance. In such event, the Property Managers shall determine the fair market rent of the Property as if all such matters had been properly repaired or maintained. The average of the findings of the three rental surveys shall then be deemed to be fair market rent. The parties agree to cooperate in expediting the foregoing procedure to determine the fair market rental within Forty-Five days after failure to agree upon fair market rental.

12. Occupancy and Entry by Non-resident Owners.

Except as otherwise provided, Owner-Occupants shall have exclusive rights to occupancy and possession of the Property and Non-resident Owners shall have no such rights. While the Property is held in co-tenancy hereunder, Non-resident Owners may enter the Property only in the following cases:

(a) Once every ________ months to inspect the Property;

(b) In case of emergency;

(c) To cure defaults by Owner-Occupants of their obligations under this Agreement;

(d) Pursuant to court order; or

(e) In the event Owner-Occupants abandon or surrender the Property;

(f) Upon invitation or permission of the Owner-Occupants;

(g) Under the circumstances specified elsewhere in this Agreement.

Wherever reasonable and practicable, the Non-resident Owners shall give the Owner-Occupants twenty-four hours prior notice of intention to enter or inspect the property. Any such entry or inspection shall be between the hours of 9:00 A.M. and 5:00 P.M. unless otherwise agreed.

13. Additional Contributions.

(a) Should additional contributions be deemed desirable and/or necessary, Owner-Occupants and Non-resident Owners are responsible for making all contributions promptly and fully. To the extent that either Owner-Occupants or Non-resident Owners shall furnish funds for any authorized purpose in excess of their Ownership Percentages of such costs, the party supplying the funds shall receive reimbursement for the amount of those costs plus ________ percent interest per annum, compounded annually.

(b) If any party has not received full reimbursement for additional contributions prior to a Termination Event or Refinancing, the remaining amount due shall be deducted from the pro-rata repayment of the Initial Cash Contribution of the non-contributing party(ies) and, if necessary, from any additional share of the proceeds due the non-contributing party(ies) as described in Paragraph 14(g).

(c) The adjustments described in this Paragraph shall not alter the Ownership Percentages as described in Paragraph 2 for purposes of distribution of any additional amounts as specified in Paragraph 14(g).

14. Termination Events and Procedures.

(a) The Property will not be sold within the first ________ months after Closing Date unless agreed in writing by Owner-Occupants and Non-resident Owners.

(b) The parties agree to sell or exchange the Property and to liquidate the co-ownership upon the occurrence of any of the following (the "Termination Events"):

(i) The vacating or abandonment of the Property by the Owner-Occupants. Should Owner-Occupants abandon or vacate said Property for a continuous period of fourteen days except for holiday vacations, Non-resident Owners shall have the exclusive right to terminate Owner-Occupants' tenancy and to lease said Property. All rental payments received by Non-resident Owners shall be used for Property expenses, including but not limited to, mortgage payments, insurance, taxes, and maintenance.

(ii) Any party's breach of any covenant, obligation, or provision contained in this Agreement, including obligations to make payments required by this Agreement whereby the breach remains unremedied for the period set forth in Paragraph 20, below. Notice to Terminate must be duly noticed in writing. All provisions of Paragraph 20 shall apply.

(iii) The Non-resident Owners' election to terminate this Agreement if Owner-Occupants fail to make any payment as and when required by this Agreement within fifteen calendar days from the date on which such payment was to be made. Notice to Terminate shall be duly noticed in writing. Time is of the essence.

(iv) The making by the Owner-Occupants of any general assignment for the benefit of creditors; the filing against Owner-Occupants of a petition to have them or any one of them adjudged bankrupt, or a petition for reorganization or arrangement under any law relating to bankruptcy, unless, in the case of a petition filed against them, such petition shall be dismissed within sixty days after its filing; the appointment of a trustee or a receiver to take possession of substantially all of their assets, or of Owner-Occupants' interest in this Agreement or the Property, where such seizure shall not be discharged or released within thirty days.

(v) Occurrence of the events specified above in Paragraph 14(iv) occur in relation to the Non-resident Owners, then, Owner-Occupants may at their exclusive option, Terminate this Agreement by serving upon Non-resident Owners, or their Trustee, a Notice to Terminate.

(vi) After ______________ (__________) years from Closing Date, Owner-Occupants or Non-resident Owners may deliver to the other a written Notice to Terminate.

(c) In the event the Non-resident Owners elect to effect a Section 1031 Exchange of their Ownership Percentage in the Property, at no additional expense to the Owner-Occupants, Owner-Occupants agree to co-operate in said exchange for the benefit of the Non-resident Owners.

(d) Upon the occurrence of a Termination Event, the parties shall cause the Property to be sold or exchanged as soon as practicable thereafter, and in any event within one hundred twenty days of the occurrence of such Termination Event. Until the close of escrow for the sale or exchange of the Property, each party shall remain fully liable for all costs, expenses, and rent as set forth in this Agreement.

(e) Unless unanimously agreed otherwise, the parties shall grant an Exclusive Right to Sell listing on the Property to __________ or assignee for a period of not less than one hundred twenty days. Said Broker/s shall cause the Property to be listed in the ____________ Multiple Listing Service and exercise due diligence in marketing the Property.

(f) Each of the parties pledges its interest to the other as security for the obligations set forth herein, including all expenses, costs, and attorneys' fees expended in enforcing this Agreement.

(g) The proceeds from the sale, refinance, condemnation, or other disposition of the Property, after deduction of the then existing Mortgage Loan balance and the closing costs according to Ownership Percentages, shall be distributed as follows: First, to repayment of each party's Initial Cash Contribution, as described in Paragraph 1(c); second, adjusted for any additional contributions, as specified in Paragraph 13; third, adjusted for any improvements per value established in Addendum A, in accordance with Paragraph 4(b); and fourth, the balance to the parties in accordance with their respective Ownership Percentages. In the event of breach or default of any covenant or condition of this Agreement, the non-breaching or non-defaulting parties shall have first priority upon the proceeds of sale to the full extent of their Initial Cash Contribution, all sale closing costs, and any additional contributions, before any return of funds to the breaching or defaulting parties.

15. Appraisal.

Upon notice of termination, the parties shall have thirty days to agree on the listing price or the fair market value of the Property. If the parties are unable to reach agreement, the fair market value (the "Appraisal Value") of the Property shall be determined by certified appraisal to be made by an independent fee appraiser, selected by the mutual agreement of the Owner-Occupants and the Non-resident Owners. If the parties are still unable to reach agreement, the fair market value of the Property shall be determined by certified appraisal to be made by two independent fee appraisers, one to be selected and paid for by the Owner-Occupants and the other to be selected and paid for by the Non-resident Owners. Non-resident Owners shall have the right to inspect the Property prior to the appraisal and shall provide the appraisers with a list of those matters, if any, with respect to which Owner-Occupants have not satisfied their obligation of repair and maintenance. In such event, the appraisers shall determine the Appraisal Value of the Property as if all such matters had been properly repaired or maintained. The Appraisal Value of the Property shall be deemed to be the average of the three appraisal values determined by the appraisers. The parties agree to cooperate in expediting the foregoing procedure to the end that the Appraisal Value be determined within forty-five days after a Termination Event.

16. Owner-Occupants' Option to Purchase.

Within fifteen days after agreement on a price or receipt from the appraisers of the Appraisal Value, Owner-Occupants shall have the first right and option (the "Owner-Occupants' Option") to elect to purchase the Non-resident Owners' interest in the Property. The Purchase Price shall be paid to the Non-resident Owners in cash, unless otherwise agreed to in the written agreement and duly executed by all parties hereto. This option shall be exercised in writing on a bona-fide offer-to-purchase form. All provisions of Paragraph 14(g) shall apply. However, if Owner-Occupants do not remedy a default pursuant to Paragraph 20, then their first option to purchase the Non-resident Owners' interest shall be automatically forfeited without notice or other action on Non-resident Owners' part.

17. Non-resident Owners' Option to Purchase.
In the event Owner-Occupants

(i) Do not exercise the Owner-Occupants' Option by written notice to Non-resident Owners of such exercise within fifteen days after determination of the Appraisal Value;

(ii) Do not close the purchase of Non-resident Owners' interest within ninety days after the Termination Event; then Non-resident Owners may purchase Owner-Occupants' interest in the property on the same terms as specified in Paragraph 16, less the cost of Owner-Occupants' unfulfilled repair and maintenance obligations, if any. Non-resident Owners' option to purchase shall be exercised in writing on a bona-fide offer-to-purchase form. All provisions of Paragraph 14(g) shall apply.

18. Exercise of Option to Purchase.
Exercise of option to purchase, whether by Owner-Occupants or Non-resident Owners, shall be evidenced by written agreement which shall call for a closing at a title or escrow company selected by the purchaser, located within the same county as the Property, not less than thirty days nor more than ninety days from the date of said Termination Event, and cash deposit shall be made into such escrow, within 10 working days thereafter, in an amount of not less than ______________________ ($______________). The premium for a policy of title insurance, recording, escrow, and other closing costs shall be borne by the parties per their Ownership Percentages as reflected in this Agreement. Sole possession shall be given to the Buyer concurrent with the closing of escrow.

19. Default by Owner-Occupants.
In the event of default in payments by the Owner-Occupants on the encumbrances as herein before described, Owner-Occupants' RIGHT TO OCCUPY SAID PROPERTY MAY BE TERMINATED BY NON-RESIDENT OWNERS ON WRITTEN NOTICE TO OWNER-OCCUPANTS EVEN THOUGH OWNER-OCCUPANTS MAY HAVE SOME EQUITABLE INTEREST IN THE PROPERTY. Further, in the event of any default by Owner-Occupants of any of the terms and conditions of this Agreement, Non-resident Owners may terminate the lease provided for in this Agreement, take possession of the Property, and recover

damages pursuant to California Civil Code 1951.2 in addition to all other remedies available to Non-resident Owners at law or in equity.

20. Notice of Default.

In the event of any default by either party, the other party shall give a written notice specifying the nature of the default, after which the defaulting party shall have fifteen days from receipt of said notice to remedy said default. If said default is not remedied in fifteen days:

(a) And the default is by the Owner-Occupants, Non-resident Owners may pay the cost of remedying said default and charge said cost to Owner-Occupants as Additional Contributions pursuant to Paragraph 13.

(b) Or if the default is by the Non-resident Owners, Owner-Occupants may pay the cost of remedying said default and charge said cost to Non-resident Owners as Additional Contributions pursuant to Paragraph 13.

21. Purchase of Defaulting Party's Interest.

In the event that a default by either party is not remedied pursuant to Paragraph 20, then the defaulting party hereby gives the non-defaulting party the right to purchase the defaulting party's interest in the Property exercisable on the terms and conditions set forth in Paragraphs 15, 16, 17, and 18, above.

22. Distribution of Cash from Refinancing or Insurance.

In the event the Property is refinanced, or in the event of receipt of any casualty insurance proceeds or condemnation award with respect to the Property, any cash arising therefrom not used to reconstruct or replace the Property shall be applied and distributed to the parties pursuant to Paragraph 14(g). Non-resident Owners agree to assign Non-resident Owners' interest in any monies paid by the insurance company for Owner-Occupants' personal property to Owner-Occupants.

23. Eminent Domain.

If all or any part of the Property shall be taken or appropriated by any public or quasi-public authority under the power of Eminent Domain (a "Taking"), any award resulting from such Taking shall be distributed to the parties in accordance with Paragraph 14(g).

24. Indemnification.

Owner-Occupants shall hold Non-resident Owners harmless from, and defend and indemnify Non-resident Owners against, any and all claims, costs, including, without limitation, attorneys' fees, causes of action, or liability for any injury or damage to any person or property in, on, or about the Property when such injury or damage shall be caused in part or in whole by the intentional or negligent act or omission of Owner-Occupants, Owner-Occupants' agents, employees, or invitees. Non-resident Owners shall hold Owner-Occupants harmless from, and defend and indemnify Owner-Occupants against, any and all claims, costs, including, without limitation, attorneys' fees, causes of action, or liability for any injury or damage to any person or property in, on, or about the Property when such injury or damage shall be caused in part or in whole by the intentional or negligent act or omission of Non-resident Owners, Non-resident Owners' agents, employees, or invitees.

25. Notices.

Any notice or other communication required or desired to be served, given, or delivered hereunder shall be in writing and shall be deemed to have been duly served, given, or delivered upon personal delivery or upon deposit (within the continental United States) in the United States mail, registered, or certified, with proper postage or other charges prepaid and addressed to the party to be notified as follows:

To Non-resident Owners:______________________________

____

____

To Owner-Occupants:_________________________________

____

____

or in the manner prescribed herein to such other address or addresses of which any party may notify the other party in writing.

26. Successors and Assigns.

Owner-Occupants and Non-resident Owners may not assign, transfer, sell, mortgage, pledge, hypothecate, or encumber the Property or Agreement or any interest therein. Owner-Occupants shall not permit any person other than Owner-Occupants' immediate family to occupy or use the Property or any portion thereof without the prior written consent of Non-resident Owners. The Owner-Occupants must also occupy the Property as a principal residence. Subject to the foregoing restrictions, this Agreement shall inure to the benefit of and bind the heirs, executors, administrators, successors, and assigns of the respective parties hereto.

27. Entire Agreement.

This Agreement contains the entire agreement of the parties with respect to the matters covered herein, and no other agreement, statement, or promise made by any party which is not contained herein shall be binding or valid. This Agreement may be modified or amended only by a written instrument duly executed by all parties hereto.

28. Attorneys' Fees.

If any party should bring legal action to construe or enforce any of the terms or conditions of this Agreement, the prevailing party in that action shall be entitled to recover reasonable attorneys' fees from the non-prevailing party, together with all costs, expenses, and reasonable attorneys' fees incurred in enforcing any judgment entered therein or in an appeal therefrom.

29. Severability.

The provisions of this Agreement are intended to be severable. If any term or provision of this Agreement is illegal or invalid for any reason whatsoever, such illegality or invalidity shall not affect the validity of the remainder of this Agreement.

30. Time is of the essence in this Agreement.

31. Miscellaneous.

This Agreement shall be governed by the laws of the State of California, and any question arising hereunder shall be construed or determined according to such law. Headings at the beginning of each numbered paragraph of this Agreement are solely for the convenience of the parties and are not a part of this Agreement. The singular or plural shall each be deemed to include the others whenever the context so requires. The waiver of any party or the breach by the other of any term, covenant, or condition herein contained shall not be deemed to be a waiver of any subsequent breach of the same or any other term, covenant, or condition herein contained.

32. Further Assurances.

The parties covenant and agree to take such further actions and to execute, acknowledge, and deliver such additional documents including, without limitation, loan documents, escrow instructions, and other instruments as may be reasonably required to implement the terms and conditions of this Agreement.

IN WITNESS HEREOF, this Agreement is entered into on the date first above written. All parties have been advised to seek tax and legal counsel of their own separate choosing as to the terms and conditions herein and fully understand and agree to this Agreement prior to signing this document.

Non-resident Owners

Dated:________________________, 19____ By:____________________

Dated:________________________, 19____ By:____________________

Owner-Occupants

Dated:________________________, 19____ By:____________________

Dated:________________________, 19____ By:____________________